Al-Qushayri's
Epistle
on
Sufism

The Center for Muslim Contribution to Civilization

AL-QUSHAYRI'S

Epistle

ON

Sufism

*Al-Risala al-qushayriyya
fi ʿilm al-tasawwuf*

Abu ʾl-Qasim al-Qushayri

Translated by Professor Alexander D. Knysh

Reviewed by Dr Muhammad Eissa

Garnet
PUBLISHING

AL-QUSHAYRI'S EPISTLE ON SUFISM

Published by
Garnet Publishing Limited
8 Southern Court
South Street
Reading
RG1 4QS
UK

Copyright © 2007 The Center for Muslim
Contribution to Civilization

All rights reserved.
No part of this book may be reproduced in any form or by
any electronic or mechanical means, including information
storage and retrieval systems, without permission in writing
from the publisher, except by a reviewer who may quote
brief passages in a review.

First Edition

ISBN-13: 978-1-85964-186-6
ISBN-10: 1-85964-186-5

British Library Cataloguing-in-Publication Data
A catalogue record for this book is available from the British Library

Jacket design by Garnet Publishing
Typeset by Samantha Barden

Printed in Lebanon

CONTENTS

Foreword	xi
About this Series	xiii
Center for Muslim Contribution to Civilization: Board of Trustees	xv
Center for Muslim Contribution to Civilization: Board	xvi
Acknowledgements	xvii
The Translator's Note	xix
Translator's Introduction: Al-Qushayri's "Epistle on Sufism": The author and his book	xxi
Author's Introduction	1
A chapter explaining the beliefs of the Sufis concerning the fundamentals of religion	4
Section [on divine oneness]	14
Chapter 1 On the masters of this path and their deeds and sayings that show how they uphold the Divine Law	17
Abu Ishaq Ibrahim b. Adham b. Mansur	18
Abu ʾl-Fayd Dhu ʾl-Nun al-Misri	19
Abu ʿAli al-Fudayl b. ʿIyad	20
Abu Mahfuz Maʿruf b. Fayruz al-Karkhi	21
Abu ʾl-Hasan [al-]Sari b. al-Mughallis al-Saqati	23
Abu Nasr Bishr b. al-Harith al-Hafi (the Barefoot)	25
Abu ʿAbdallah al-Harith al-Muhasibi	27
Abu Sulayman Dawud b. Nusayr al-Taʾi	29
Abu ʿAli Shaqiq b. Ibrahim al-Balkhi	30
Abu Yazid b. Tayfur b. ʿIsa al-Bastami	32
Abu Muhammad Sahl b. ʿAbdallah al-Tustari	33
Abu Sulayman ʿAbd al-Rahman b. ʿAtiyya al-Darani	35
Abu ʿAbd al-Rahman Hatim b. ʿUnwan	36
Abu Zakariya Yahya b. Muʿadh al-Razi, the Preacher	37
Abu Hamid Ahmad b. Khadrawayh (Khidruya) al-Balkhi	38
Abu ʾl-Hasan Ahmad b. Abi ʾl-Hawari	39
Abu Hafs ʿUmar b. Maslama al-Haddad	39
Abu Turab ʿAskar b. Husayn al-Nakhshabi	40
Abu Muhammad ʿAbdallah b. Khubayq	41
Abu ʿAli Ahmad b. ʿAsim al-Antaki	41
Abu ʾl-Sari Mansur b. ʿAmmar	42
Abu Salih Hamdun b. Ahmad b. ʿUmara al-Qassar	42
Abu ʾl-Qasim al-Junayd b. Muhammad	43
Abu ʿUthman Saʿid b. Ismaʿil al-Hiri	45
Abu ʾl-Husayn Ahmad b. Muhammad al-Nuri	46
Abu ʿAbdallah Ahmad b. Yahya al-Jallaʾ	47

Abu Muhammad Ruwaym b. Ahmad	48
Abu ʿAbdallah Muhammad b. al-Fadl al-Balkhi	48
Abu Bakr Ahmad b. Nasr al-Zaqqaq al-Kabir	49
Abu ʿAbdallah ʿAmr b. ʿUthman al-Makki	50
Samnun b. Hamza	50
Abu ʿUbayd al-Busri	51
Abu ʾl-Fawaris Shah b. Shujaʿ al-Kirmani	52
Yusuf b. al-Husayn	52
Abu ʿAbdallah Muhammad b. ʿAli al-Tirmidhi	52
Abu Bakr Muhammad b. ʿUmar al-Warraq al-Tirmidhi	53
Abu Saʿid Ahmad b. ʿIsa al-Kharraz	53
Abu ʿAbdallah Muhammad b. Ismaʿil al-Maghribi	54
Abu ʾl-ʿAbbas Ahmad b. Muhammad Masruq	54
Abu ʾl-Hasan ʿAli b. Sahl al-Isbahani	54
Abu Muhammad Ahmad b. Muhammad b. al-Husayn al-Jurayri	55
Abu ʾl-ʿAbbas Ahmad b. Muhammad b. Sahl b. ʿAtaʾ al-Adami	56
Abu Ishaq Ibrahim b. Ahmad al-Khawwas	56
Abu Muhammad ʿAbdallah b. Muhammad al-Kharraz	57
Abu ʾl-Hasan Bunan b. Muhammad al-Hammal	57
Abu Hamza al-Baghdadi al-Bazzaz	57
Abu Bakr Muhammad b. Musa al-Wasiti	58
Abu ʾl-Hasan b. al-Saʾigh	59
Abu Ishaq Ibrahim b. Dawud al-Raqqi	59
Mimshadh al-Dinawari	59
Khayr al-Nassaj	60
Abu Hamza al-Khurasani	60
Abu Bakr Dulaf b. Jahdar al-Shibli	61
Abu Muhammad ʿAbdallah b. Muhammad al-Murtaʿish	62
Abu ʿAli Ahmad b. Muhammad al-Rudhbari	62
Abu Muhammad ʿAbdallah b. Munazil	63
Abu ʿAli Muhammad b. ʿAbd al-Wahhab al-Thaqafi	63
Abu ʾl-Khayr al-Aqtaʿ	64
Abu Bakr Muhammad b. ʿAli al-Kattani	64
Abu Yaʿqub Ishaq b. Muhammad al-Nahrajuri	64
Abu ʾl-Hasan ʿAli b. Muhammad al-Muzayyin	65
Abu ʿAli b. al-Katib	65
Muzaffar al-Qirmisini	65
Abu Bakr ʿAbdallah b. Tahir al-Abhari	66
Abu ʾl-Husayn b. Bunan	66
Abu Ishaq Ibrahim b. Shayban al-Qirmisini	66
Abu Bakr al-Husayn b. ʿAli b. Yazdanyar	67
Abu Saʿid b. al-Aʿrabi	67
Abu ʿAmr Muhammad b. Ibrahim al-Zajjaji al-Naysaburi	67
Abu Muhammad Jaʿfar b. Muhammad b. Nusayr	68
Abu ʾl-ʿAbbas al-Sayyari	68
Abu Bakr Muhammad b. Dawud al-Dinawari	68
Abu Muhammad ʿAbdallah b. Muhammad al-Razi	69

Abu ʿAmr Ismaʿil b. Nujayd	69
Abu ʾl-Hasan ʿAli b. Ahmad b. Sahl al-Bushanji	69
Abu ʿAbdallah Muhammad b. Khafif al-Shirazi	70
Abu ʾl-Husayn Bundar b. al-Husayn al-Shirazi	71
Abu Bakr al-Tamastani	71
Abu ʾl-ʿAbbas Ahmad b. Muhammad al-Dinawari	71
Abu ʿUthman Saʿid b. Sallam al-Maghribi	72
Abu ʾl-Qasim Ibrahim b. Muhammad al-Nasrabadhi	72
Abu ʾl-Hasan ʿAli b. Ibrahim al-Husri al-Basri	73
Abu ʿAbdallah Ahmad b. ʿAtaʾ al-Rudhbari	73
Conclusion	74

Chapter 2 An explanation of the expressions used by this [Sufi] community and of their difficulties — 75

The [mystical] moment (*waqt*)	75
The [mystical] station (*maqam*)	77
The [mystical] state (*hal*)	78
Contraction (*qabd*) and expansion (*bast*)	79
Awe (*hayba*) and intimacy (*uns*)	81
[The states of] ecstatic behavior (*tawajud*), ecstatic rapture (*wajd*), and ecstatic finding (*wujud*)	83
Unification (*jamʿ*) and separation (*farq*)	87
The unification of unification (*jamʿ al-jamʿ*)	88
Annihilation (*fanaʾ*) and subsistence (*baqaʾ*) [in God]	89
Absence (*ghayba*) and presence (*hudur*)	91
Sobriety (*sahw*) and drunkenness (*sukr*)	93
Tasting (*dhawq*) and drinking (*shurb*)	95
Erasure (*mahw*) and affirmation (*ithbat*)	96
Concealment (*satr*) and [self-]manifestation (*tajalli*)	96
Presence (*muhadara*), unveiling (*mukashafa*) and witnessing (*mushahada*)	97
Glimmers (*lawaʾih*), dawnings (*tawaliʿ*) and flashes (*lawamiʿ*)	99
[Unexpected] raids (*bawadih*) and attacks (*hujum*)	100
Inconstancy (*talwin*) and stability (*tamkin*)	100
Proximity (*qurb*) and distance (*buʿd*)	103
The [Divine] Law (*shariʿa*) and the True Reality (*haqiqa*)	105
Breath (*nafas*)	105
Thoughts (*khawatir*)	106
Certain knowledge (*ʿilm al-yaqin*), the essence of certainty (*ʿayn al-yaqin*) and the truth of certainty (*haqq al-yaqin*)	107
Occurrence (*warid*)	108
Witness (*shahid*)	108
The soul (*nafs*)	109
The spirit (*ruh*)	110
The innermost self (*sirr*)	110

Chapter 3 The [mystical] stations (*maqamat*) — 111

Repentance (*tawba*) — 111
Striving (*mujahada*) — 118
Retreat (*khalwa*) and seclusion (*ʿuzla*) — 122
Fear of God (*taqwa*) — 125
Scrupulousness (*waraʿ*) — 129
Renunciation (*zuhd*) — 134
Silence (*samt*) — 138
Fear (*khawf*) — 142
Hope (*rajaʾ*) — 148
Sadness (*huzn*) — 155
Hunger (*juʿ*) and the abandonment of [carnal] desire (*shahwa*) — 157
Humility (*khushuʿ*) and modesty (*tawaduʿ*) — 161
Opposing the soul (*mukhalafat al-nafs*) and remembering its faults (*dhikr ʿuyubiha*) — 167
Envy (*hasad*) — 170
Backbiting (*ghiba*) — 172
Contentment (*qanaʿa*) — 175
Trust in God (*tawakkul*) — 178
Gratitude (*shukr*) — 188
Certainty (*yaqin*) — 193
Patience (*sabr*) — 196
Awareness [of God] (*muraqaba*) — 202
Satisfaction (*rida*) — 205
Servanthood (*ʿubudiyya*) — 210
Desire (*irada*) — 213
Uprightness (*istiqama*) — 217
Sincerity (*ikhlas*) — 220
Truthfulness (*sidq*) — 222
Shame (*haya*) — 226
Freedom (*hurriyya*) — 229
Remembrance (*dhikr*) — 232
Chivalry (*futuwwa*) — 237
Spiritual insight (*firasa*) — 242
Moral character (*khuluq*) — 252
Munificence (*jud*) and generosity (*sakhaʾ*) — 257
Jealousy (*ghayra*) — 264
Friendship with God (*wilaya*) — 268
Supplicatory prayer (*duʿaʾ*) — 273
Poverty (*faqr*) — 280
Sufism (*tasawwuf*) — 288
Good manners (*adab*) — 292
The rules of travel (*safar*) — 297
Companionship (*suhba*) — 302
The Oneness of God (*tawhid*) — 306
How some Sufis [of old] behaved at the time of their departure from this world (*ahwaluhum ʿinda ʾl-khuruj min al-dunya*) — 312

Divine gnosis (*al-maʿrifa [bi-llah]*)	319
Love (*mahabba*)	325
Passionate longing (*shawq*)	335
On how [God] protects the hearts of Sufi masters and on [the necessity of] not opposing them [in anything they do]	339
Listening to music (*samaʿ*)	342
Miracles of God's friends (*karamat al-awliyaʾ*)	357
The vision of the Sufis (*ruʾyat al-qawm*)	392
Spiritual advice for Sufi novices (*wasaya li ʾl-muridin*)	403
Glossary	417
Bibliography	427
Index of proper names, toponyms, and concepts	429

In the Name of God, the Beneficent, the Merciful

FOREWORD

THE interrelationship and interaction of human cultures and civilizations has made the contributions of each the common heritage of men in all ages and all places. Early Muslim scholars were able to communicate with their Western counterparts through contacts made during the Crusades; at Muslim universities and centres of learning in Muslim Spain (al-Andalus, or Andalusia) and Sicily to which many European students went for education; and at the universities and centres of learning in Europe itself (such as Salerno, Padua, Montpellier, Paris, and Oxford), where Islamic works were taught in Latin translations. Among the Muslim scholars well-known in the centres of learning throughout the world were al-Rāzī (Rhazes), Ibn Sīnā (Avicenna), Ibn Rushd (Averroes), al-Khwārizmī and Ibn Khaldūn. Muslim scholars such as these and others produced original works in many fields. Many of them possessed encyclopaedic knowledge and distinguished themselves in many disparate fields of knowledge.

The Center for Muslim Contribution to Civilization was established in order to acquaint non-Muslims with the contributions Islam has made to human civilization as a whole. The Great Books of Islamic Civilization Project attempts to cover the first 800 years of Islam, or what may be called Islam's Classical Period. This project aims at making available in English and other European languages a wide selection of works representative of Islamic civilization in all its diversity. It is made up of translations of original Arabic works that were produced in the formative centuries of Islam, and is meant to serve the needs of a potentially large readership. Not only the specialist and scholar, but the non-specialist with an interest in Islam and its cultural heritage will be able to benefit from the series. Together, the works should serve as a rich source for the study of the early periods of Islamic thought.

In selecting the books for the series, the Center took into account all major areas of Islamic intellectual pursuit that could be represented. Thus the series includes works not only on better-known subjects such as law, theology, jurisprudence, history and politics, but also on subjects such as literature, medicine, astronomy, optics and geography. The specific criteria used to select individual books were these: that a book should give a faithful and comprehensive account of its field; and that it should be an authoritative source. The reader thus has at his disposal virtually a whole library of informative and enlightening works.

Each book in the series has been translated by a qualified scholar and reviewed by another expert. While the style of one translation will naturally differ from another as do the styles of the authors, the translators have endeavoured, to the extent it was possible, to make the works accessible to the common reader. As a rule, the use of footnotes has been kept to a minimum, though a more extensive use of them was necessitated in some cases.

This series is presented in the hope that it will contribute to a greater understanding in the West of the cultural and intellectual heritage of Islam and will therefore provide an important means towards greater understanding of today's world.

May God Help Us!

Muhammad bin Hamad Al-Thani
Chairman of the Board of Trustees

About this Series

THIS series of Arabic works, made available in English translation, represents an outstanding selection of important Islamic studies in a variety of fields of knowledge. The works selected for inclusion in this series meet specific criteria. They are recognized by Muslim scholars as being early and important in their fields, as works whose importance is broadly recognized by international scholars, and as having had a genuinely significant impact on the development of human culture.

Readers will therefore see that this series includes a variety of works in the purely Islamic sciences, such as Qurʾān, *ḥadīth*, theology, prophetic traditions (*sunna*), and jurisprudence (*fiqh*). Also represented will be books by Muslim scientists on medicine, astronomy, geography, physics, chemistry, horticulture, and other fields.

The work of translating these texts has been entrusted to a group of professors in the Islamic and Western worlds who are recognized authorities in their fields. It has been deemed appropriate, in order to ensure accuracy and fluency, that two persons, one with Arabic as his mother tongue and another with English as his mother tongue, should participate together in the translation and revision of each text.

This series is distinguished from other similar intercultural projects by its distinctive objectives and methodology. These works will fill a genuine gap in the library of human thought. They will prove extremely useful to all those with an interest in Islamic culture, its interaction with Western thought, and its impact on culture throughout the world. They will, it is hoped, fulfil an important rôle in enhancing world understanding at a time when there is such evident and urgent need for the development of peaceful coexistence.

This series is published by the Center for Muslim Contribution to Civilization, which serves as a research centre under the patronage of H.H. Sheikh Muhammad bin Hamad al-Thani, the former Minister of Education of Qatar who also chairs the Board of Trustees. The Board is comprised of a group of prominent scholars. These include His Eminence Sheikh Al-Azhar, Arab Republic of Egypt, and Dr Yousef al-Qaradhawi, Director of the Sira and Sunna Research Center. At its inception the Center was directed by the late Dr Muhammad Ibrahim Kazim, former Rector of Qatar University, who established its initial objectives.

The Center was until recently directed by Dr Kamal Naji, the Foreign Cultural Relations Advisor of the Ministry of Education of Qatar. He was assisted by a Board comprising a number of academicians of Qatar University, in addition to a consultative committee chaired by Dr Ezzeddin Ibrahim, former Rector of the University of the United Arab Emirates. A further committee acting on behalf of the Center has been the prominent university professors who act under the chairmanship of Dr Raji Rammuny, Professor of Arabic at the University of Michigan. This committee is charged with making known, in Europe and in America, the books selected for translation, and in selecting and enlisting properly qualified university professors, orientalists and students of Islamic studies to undertake the work of translation and revision, as well as overseeing the publication process.

CENTER FOR MUSLIM CONTRIBUTION TO CIVILIZATION

Board of Trustees

H.E. Sheikh Muhammad bin Hamad al-Thani
Chairman

Members

1. H.Eminence Sheikh al-Azhar, Cairo, Arab Republic of Egypt.
2. Director-General of the Islamic Educational, Scientific and Cultural Organization (ISESCO).
3. Director-General of the Arab League Educational, Cultural and Scientific Organization (ALECSO).
4. H.E. the Minister of Education, State of Qatar.
5. H.E. the Minister of Education, Kuwait.
6. H.E. the Minister of Education, Oman.
7. H.E. the Secretary-General of the Muslim World Association, Saudi Arabia.
8. H.E. Dr Ezzeddin Ibrahim, Cultural Advisor to H.H. the President of the U.A.E.
9. Professor Yousef al-Qaradhawi, Director, Sira and Sunna Research Centre, University of Qatar.
10. Chairman, Arab Historians Union.
11. Professor Cesar Adib Majul, Professor at the American Universities.

Following are the names of the late prominent Muslim figures who (may Allāh have mercy upon them) passed away after they had taken vital roles in the preliminary discussions of the Center's goals, work plan and activities. They are:

1. Dr Kamal Naji, former General Supervisor, Center for Muslim Contribution to Civilization, Qatar (7 October 1997).
2. Sheikh Jad al-Haq Ali Jad al-Haq, Sheikh al-Azhar, Cairo, Arab Republic of Egypt.
3. Dr Muhammad Ibrahim Kazim, former Rector, University of Qatar.
4. Sheikh Abdullah bin Ibrahim al-Ansari, former Chairman, Department for the Revival of Islamic Cultural Heritage, State of Qatar.
5. Muhammad al-Fasi, former Honorary Chairman, Islamic University Rabat, Kingdom of Morocco.
6. Dr Abul-Wafa al-Taftazani, former Deputy Rector, University of Cairo, Arab Republic of Egypt.
7. Senator Mamimatal Tamano, former member of the Philippino Congress and Muslim leader in the Philippines.

CENTER FOR MUSLIM CONTRIBUTION TO CIVILIZATION

BOARD

H.E. Sheikh Muhammad bin Hamad al-Thani
Chairman of the Board of Trustees

Professor Osman Sid-Ahmad Ismail al-Bili
General Supervisor, Professor of Middle Eastern and Islamic History, University of Qatar

MEMBERS

1. H.E. Shaykha Ahmad Almahmud, Minister of Education, State of Qatar.
2. Professor Ibrahim Saleh al-Nuaimi, former Rector, University of Qatar.
3. Professor Yousef al-Qaradhawi, Director, Sira and Sunna Research Centre, University of Qatar.
4. Professor Husam al-Khateeb, Professor of Arabic, Cultural Expert, National Council for Culture, Arts and Heritage, State of Qatar.
5. Professor Abd al-Hamid Ismail al-Ansari, College of Sharia, Law and Islamic Studies.
6. H.E. Dr Hasan al-Nimi, Ambassador, State of Qatar.
7. Dr Hasan al-Ansari, Amiri Diwan, College of Arts and Science, University of Qatar.
8. Dr Ahmad Muhammad Ubaidan (Treasurer) Observer, Advisory Council and Director-General, Trans-Orient Establishment (Doha, Qatar).

CENTER'S ADVISORS

H.E. Dr Ezzeddin Ibrahim
Cultural Advisor to H.H. the President of the U.A.E.

Professor Raji Mahmoud Rammuny
Director of the Center's Translation Committee in the U.S.A.
Professor of Arabic Studies, Department of Near Eastern Studies,
University of Michigan, U.S.A.

Acknowledgements

I would like to take this opportunity to thank the individuals and institutions who have helped me to realize this translation project. My heartfelt gratitude goes to my colleague Professor Raji Rammuny, who commissioned me to translate al-Qushayri's masterpiece on behalf of the Center for Research on the Muslim Contribution to Civilization located in the city of Doha, Qatar. My translation has benefited significantly from the comments and corrections of the reviewer, Dr. Muhammad Eissa, whose meticulous attention to detail deserves the highest praise. My English text was carefully proof-read and edited by my research assistant Victoria (Vika) Gardner, an expert on Central Asian Sufism. Vika's help was absolutely invaluable in improving my English style and rectifying my thinking about Sufism in general and that of al-Qushayri in particular. Last but not least, I would like to thank my wife Anya Knysh for her help in compiling the index and the glossary. I take full responsibility for any mistakes that may have crept into my translation.

Alexander Knysh
University of Michigan

The Translator's Note

In this translation I followed certain conventions that require a brief explanation. First, I have retained all chains of transmission of the pious dicta quoted by al-Qushayri as well as the traditional formulas that are commonly attached to the names of God and the prophets in pre-modern Islamic texts. I have also reproduced the usual Islamic formulas mentioned after the names of deceased individuals, such as "may God be pleased with him" and "may God have mercy on him".

Second, I have included both the traditional Islamic (or *Hijri*) dates and the dates according to the Common Era calendar – for example, 165/781, 406/1016, 420/1029 and so on. I have retained the Arabic definite article *al-* in all personal names, but omitted it in most Arabic terms cited in parentheses – for example, "contentment" (*rida*), instead of (*al-rida*) and "trust in God" (*tawakkul*), instead of (*al-tawakkul*).

Third, I have left all the pronominal references to God (*Allah*) in the masculine spelled with the upper case. This reflects the usage current in the pre-modern epoch before the rise of gender-inclusive language. Although in principle the frequently used word "servant of God" may apply to both males and females, I have opted for the masculine pronoun that is used consistently in medieval Arabic texts in such cases.

Fourth, quotations from the Qurʾan are placed into the footnotes with the number of the chapter (*sura*) followed by a colon and the number of the verse (*aya*). Since I have used Arthur J. Arberry's *The Koran Interpreted* as my primary source of Qurʾanic quotations, I provide the numbering he adopted in his translation, which occasionally departs from the standard numbering used in the majority of editions and translations of the Qurʾan. Despite its archaic Victorian English, I still prefer Arberry's translation to all later renditions of the Qurʾan into English. Occasionally, I modify Arberry's translation to fit the overall context of al-Qushayri's exposition.

Fifth, square brackets [] serve to indicate my addition of words and phrases to the original Arabic text where I think they are implied, but not explicitly mentioned. Occasionally, brackets (along with footnotes) may be used to clarify obscure passages in the Arabic original. Slash signs // mark the beginning of a new page of the Arabic original – namely, Muhammad ʿAbd al-Rahman al-Marʿashali's edition of al-Qushayri's text (see my *Introduction*).

The system of transliteration of Arabic names and words is based on a simplified version of the transliteration adopted by the editorial board of the *International Journal of Middle Eastern Studies*, as stipulated in the "Guidelines for Translators and Reviewers of Great Books of Islamic Civilization".

"Simplified" means that I do not use macroned letters to convey long Arabic vowels, nor do I use dots under certain letters of the Latin alphabet, which in academic literature represent velarized, or "emphatic", Arabic consonants. In a limited number of cases, when it is absolutely unavoidable, I use letters *á*, *í*, and *ú* to convey the long Arabic vowels. Their significance is explained in the footnotes. I mark the Arabic letter ʽ*ayn* with the inverted ʽ in every position and the *hamza* with ʼ only when it appears in the middle or at the end of a word or name.

Finally, I make use of several abbreviations, namely: *EI*, which stands for *The Encyclopaedia of Islam*, 2nd edition; *IM*, which stands for my book *Islamic Mysticism: A Short History*; and "b.", which stands for the Arabic word "ibn", meaning "son".

The translation is supplied with an Index of proper names, toponyms, and concepts and a Glossary of Sufi technical terms (see pages 417–425). Since al-Qushayri often quotes only an abbreviated name of his source and since many such names are identical, the individual in question is not always easy to identify. In such cases, I refer the reader to two or several possible individuals with similar names in the Index. I apologize for any inconvenience this might cause, but things that were obvious for al-Qushayri and his contemporaries are, unfortunately, no longer obvious for us.

TRANSLATOR'S INTRODUCTION

Al-Qushayri's "Epistle on Sufism": The author and his book

The author of the *Epistle on Sufism*, Abu 'l-Qasim ʿAbd al-Karim b. Hawazin al-Qushayri, was born in 376/986 in the region of Ustuwa (or Ustawa), a district in northern Khurasan that was famous for the fertility of its soil and abundant grain production.[1] His parents were Arab settlers whose ancestors had arrived in Iran with the conquering Arab armies and were allotted substantial tracts of land in compensation for their military service. By the time of al-Qushayri's birth, his family must have been speaking Persian at home, but as a son of a country squire he was educated in the intricacies of Arabic language, poetry and polite letters (*adab*). As was common for young men of his social standing he was also trained in martial arts, horsemanship and archery. As a youth al-Qushayri traveled to Nishapur (Naysabur), the political and administrative center of Khurasan and a major center of Islamic scholarship and culture in the eastern part of the Muslim world up to the Mongol conquest of the seventh/thirteenth century.[2] There he attended the lectures and sermons of the renowned Sufi master (*shaykh*) Abu ʿAli al-Hasan al-Daqqaq (d. around 405/1015 or somewhat later), who headed a popular religious school (*madrasa*).[3] A student of Ibrahim b. Muhammad al-Nasrabadhi (d. 367/977), the foremost Sufi master of Khurasan in his age, al-Daqqaq belonged to the spiritual tradition that stretched back to the celebrated Sufis of the Baghdad school, including [al-]Sari al-Saqati (d. 251/865 or somewhat later),[4] al-Junayd al-Baghdadi (d. 297/910), and Abu Bakr al-Shibli (d. 334/946). Al-Qushayri soon became al-Daqqaq's foremost disciple, married his daughter Fatima and eventually succeeded his father-in-law as the head of his religious school. Al-Qushayri repeatedly acknowledges his debt to, and admiration for, his Sufi master throughout his *Epistle*. Al-Daqqaq was instrumental in introducing al-Qushayri to another outstanding Sufi authority of Khurasan, Abu ʿAbd al-Rahman al-Sulami (412/1021), who is quoted on almost every page of the *Epistle*.

A prolific writer and accomplished religious scholar, al-Sulami is rightly considered to be one of the master architects of the classical Sufi tradition along

---

1 It presently belongs to the district of Quchan (Iran).
2 Some sources say that he was fifteen years old at the time of his arrival in Nishapur, but this information is impossible to verify. It is also related that the object of his trip to Nishapur was to reduce the taxes on a village he owned.
3 While this term presupposes a more-or-less structured institution and a set curriculum, one should rather think of an informal circle of students attending the daily lectures and sermons of a popular teacher (*ustadh*), which usually took place at his house.
4 See Alexander Knysh, *Islamic Mysticism: A Short History* (henceforth abbreviated as *IM*), pp. 48–66.

with Abu Nasr al-Sarraj al-Tusi (d. 378/988),⁵ Abu Bakr al-Kalabadhi (d. ca 380/990), Abu Talib al-Makki (d. 386/996), ʿAli b. ʿUthman al-Jullabi al-Hujwiri (d. between 465/1072 and 469/1077), and ʿAbdallah al-Ansari al-Harawi (d. 481/1089).⁶ Despite his preoccupation with the Sufi lore and literature, al-Qushayri's studies at Nishapur were not limited to Sufism. He studied Shafiʿi jurisprudence under the guidance of Muhammad b. Bakr al-Tusi (d. 420/1029) and speculative theology with some leading Ashʿarite scholars of the age, such as Abu Bakr b. Furak (d. 406/1015) and Abu Ishaq al-Isfaraini (d. 418/1027). Somewhat later he went on a pilgrimage in the company of the famous exegetes and *hadith*-collectors Abu Muhammad al-Juwayni (d. 438/1047) and Ahmad al-Bayhaqi (d. 458/1066). A diligent student of the Prophet's Sunna, al-Qushayri "studied *hadith* with at least seventeen different authorities, and in turn transmitted *hadith* to as many as sixty-six students."⁷ While his master al-Daqqaq was still alive, al-Qushayri did not seem to undertake any travels outside of Khurasan. After the city fell under the control of the powerful Saljuq dynasty in 429/1038 al-Qushayri was embroiled in the struggle between the rival scholarly factions of Hanafites and Shafiʿites which competed with one another for ideological ascendancy. In 436/1045 al-Qushayri asserted his position as the leading spokesman of the Shafiʿi-Ashʿarite party of Nishapur by issuing a manifesto in defense of its orthodoxy. His advocacy of the Ashʿarite theological tenets aroused the ire of its Hanafite opponents. When the powerful Saljuq vizier ʿAmid al-Mulk al-Kunduri threw in his lot with al-Qushayri's Hanafite-Muʿtazilite opponents, he was arrested and spent a week in the citadel of Nishapur only to be released after his followers threatened an all-out rebellion of the city's Shafiʿites in 446/1054. In 448/1056 he accepted the invitation of the caliph al-Qaʾim to hold *hadith* sessions at the caliphal palace in Baghdad. Upon his return to Khurasan al-Qushayri had to settle down in Tus,⁸ since Nishapur was still controlled by his Hanafite adversaries. When, in 455/1063, Nizam al-Mulk, the new Saljuq vizier, reversed al-Kunduri's policies and endeavored to reestablish the balance of power between the Shafiʿite and Hanafite parties, al-Qushayri, by then seventy-nine (lunar) years old, was able to return to his native city where he remained until his death in 465/1072. His six sons by his first wife Fatima became respected scholars in their own right and spread the fame of the al-Qushayri family far and wide.⁹ Despite his great renown and the interest he took in Sufi pedagogy,¹⁰ al-Qushayri left surprisingly few disciples. Of these Abu ʿAli Fadl b. Muhammad al-Farmadhi (d. 477/1084),

---

5 This author is also frequently quoted by al-Qushayri.
6 For these writers and their works see *IM*, pp. 116–135.
7 Hamid Algar, "Introduction," in *Principles of Sufism*, translated from the Arabic by B. R. von Schlegell, Mizan Press, Berkeley, 1990, p. iii.
8 A medieval city near present-day Meshhed/Mashhad (Iran).
9 He also had three sons by his second wife.
10 He maintained a Sufi lodge in Nishapur, where he trained his disciples.

a teacher of the great Muslim thinker Abu Hamid Muhammad al-Ghazali (d. 505/1111), was by far the most famous. This paucity of spiritual successors may be attributed in part to al-Qushayri's persona which was academic and methodical rather than charismatic and inspirational.

Al-Qushayri's written legacy includes a long Qur'anic commentary entitled *Lataʾif al-isharat*, which deserves a special mention.[11] Here, as in the *Epistle*, the author pursues a clear apologetic agenda: the advocacy of the teachings, values and practices of "moderate", "Junayd-style" Sufism with a view to demonstrating its full compliance with the precepts of Ashʿarite theology, which al-Qushayri regarded as the only "orthodox" creed. Written in 410/1019, this work consistently draws a parallel between the gradual exegetical progress from the literal to the subtlest meanings (*lataʾif*) of the Qur'anic revelation and the stages of the Sufi's spiritual and experiential journey to God. The success of the exegetical progress and that of the Sufi journey depends on the wayfarer's ability to combine the performance of pious works and feats of spirit with sound doctrinal premises. Giving preference to one over the other will result in failure. Even when this delicate balance is successfully struck, the exegete is still in need of divine assistance in grasping the subtleties of the divine revelation. The same is true of the Sufi seeker's striving toward God – here too one cannot succeed without God's constant guidance and assistance.

Prominent in al-Qushayri's intellectual universe is the notion of a privileged, intuitive knowledge of both God and his word that God grants only to his most intimate, elect "friends", the *awliyaʾ*. This idea is stated clearly in the introduction to the *Lataʾif al-isharat*: "[God] has honored the elect (*asfiyaʾ*) among His servants by [granting them] the understanding of His subtle secrets (*lataʾif asrarih*) and His lights so that they can see the secret allusions and hidden signs contained therein [in the Qur'an]. He has shown their innermost souls hidden things so that by the emanations of the unseen which He has imparted solely to them they can become aware of that which is concealed from all others. Then they have started to speak according to their degrees [of spiritual attainment] and capabilities and God – praise be to Him – inspired in them things by which He has honored them [to the exclusion of other people]. So, they now speak on behalf of Him, inform about the subtle truths that He has imparted them, and point to Him ..." The exegete's progress toward the innermost meaning of the scripture is described by al-Qushayri as a movement from the intellect to the heart (*al-qalb*), then to the spirit (*al-ruh*), then to the innermost secret (*al-sirr*) and, finally, to the secret of secrets (*sirr al-sirr*) of the Qur'anic revelation. As one may expect of a Sufi master, al-Qushayri showed little interest in the historical and legal aspects of the Qur'anic text. For him, they serve as mere windows onto the all-important spiritual and mystical ideas and values of Sufism. Thus, in discussing the spoils of war mentioned in Q. 8:41 al-Qushayri argues: "*Jihad* can be of two

---

11 Ed. Ibrahim Basyuni, 4 vols., Dar al-kitab al-ʿarabi, Cairo, 1968.

types: the external one [waged] against the infidels and the internal one [waged] against [one's] soul and Satan. In the same way as the lesser *jihad* involves [the seizure of] spoils of war after victory, the greater *jihad* too has the spoils of war of its own, which involves taking possession of his soul by the servant of God after it has been held by his two enemies – [his] passions and Satan." A similar parallel is drawn between ordinary fasting which involves abstention from food, sex, and drink and the spiritual abstention of the Sufi from the allure of this world and from seeking the approval of its inhabitants. Despite its overall "moderate" nature, the *Lataʾif al-isharat* is not devoid of the monistic and visionary elements that characterize what is usually described as the more "bold" and "esoteric" trend in Sufi literature. This aspect of al-Qushayri's exegesis comes to the fore in his interpretation of Q. 7:143, in which Moses comes to God at an appointed time and requests that He appear to him only to be humbled by the sight of a mountain crumbling to dust, when God shows Himself to it. Al-Qushayri comments: "Moses came to God as [only] those passionately longing and madly in love could. Moses came without Moses. Moses came, yet nothing of Moses was left to Moses. Thousands of men have traversed great distances, yet no one remembers them, while that Moses made [only] a few steps and [school]children will be reciting until the Day of Judgment: 'When Moses came…'" Despite such deeply esoteric passages, al-Qushayri's commentary remains a typical sample of "moderate" Sufi literature due to its author's over-riding desire to achieve a delicate balance between the mystical, esoteric aspects of the Scripture and his deep respect for its letter, or, in the Sufi parlance, between the *shariʿa* and the *haqiqa*. One should point out that al-Qushayri is also the author of a conventional historical-philological and legal *tafsir* entitled *al-Taysir fi ʾl-tafsir*, which is said to have been written before 410/1019. This is an eloquent testimony to his dual credentials as both a Sufi and a conventional Sunni scholar (*ʿalim*).

Although in his works al-Qushayri addressed a wide variety of subjects,[12] his fame rests primarily on his *Epistle on Sufism* – probably the most popular Sufi manual ever. Written in 437/1045, it has served as a primary text-book for many generations of Sufis down to the present and is considered to be essential reading for any serious Muslim mystic. Al-Qushayri's *Epistle* carries a clear apologetic message – to portray Sufism as a legitimate and respectable Islamic "science" in complete harmony with the letter and spirit of Islamic Law, the *shariʿa*. The author is careful to differentiate between the genuine Sufis and their imitators, whose irresponsible escapades and statements, in his view, have tainted its image in the eyes of outsiders, especially authoritative Sunni scholars. Throughout his book, al-Qushayri consistently seeks to cleanse Sufism of what he perceives as "unbecoming" beliefs and practices, to expose its unscrupulous imitators, and to

---

12 For a list of al-Qushayri's published works see Richard Gramlich, "Introduction (Einleitung)," in his *Das Sendschreiben al-Qušayri's über das Sufitum*, Franz Steiner Verlag, Wiesbaden, 1989, p. 17.

instruct its followers in the exemplary ways of the movement's founding fathers. At the same time, he does not try to conceal from his readers disagreements among Sufi masters over various doctrinal and practical issues.

The *Epistle* consists of several sections. It opens with a relatively short chapter that describes the doctrines of "this [Sufi] community (*ta'ifa*)". It unequivocally demonstrates al-Qushayri's unshakable allegiance to the Ash'arite creed and seeks to assert Sufism's close links to this influential theological school in Sunni Islam. The second section includes 83 biographies of earlier Sufi masters beginning with the semi-legendary figure of Ibrahim b. Adham (d. 162/778) and ending with Ahmad al-Rudhbari (d. 369/960) who had died some six years before the author was born. The biographies are arranged in a roughly chronological order and correspond closely to those found in al-Sulami's "The Generations of Sufis" (*Tabaqat al-sufiyya*), which contains 103 Sufi biographies. Like al-Sulami, al-Qushayri provides a brief summary of biographical data pertaining to each Sufi master, followed by a selection of their statements on various aspects of "Sufi science". In the introduction to the biographical section al-Qushayri takes pains to present the Sufis as the rightful heirs to the Prophet and his pious Companions. Simultaneously, the author bemoans the decline of the originally high moral and ethical standards of the earlier Sufi movement among the author's contemporaries – a *leitmotif* that reappears repeatedly throughout the subsequent narrative. The biographical section is followed by a detailed essay on Sufi terminology. It provides detailed explanations of twenty-seven Sufi terms (complete with etymology and philological analysis) current among al-Qushayri's generation of Sufis. Here quotations of authoritative statements of Sufi masters (both living and dead) are combined with al-Qushayri's own interpretative interventions as well as frequent references to the Qur'an and the Prophet's custom, or Sunna.

The terminological section leads to the systematic one, which describes the major "stations" (*maqamat*) and "states" (*ahwal*) of the mystical path. This part of the *Epistle* exhibits the author's penchant for a fine psychological analysis and his profound understanding of the experiences of mystical wayfarers, from the novice (*murid*) to the accomplished Sufi master (*shaykh*). The concluding chapters discuss the moral and ethical dilemmas that the Sufis face in the course of their progress along the Sufi path as well as the rules of proper behavior, or "good manners" that they must observe in order to succeed in their spiritual undertaking. In particular, the author examines Sufi attitudes toward "spiritual concerts" (*sama'*), travel, death, saintly miracles, visions and dreams, etc. The book is concluded with the author's advice to Sufi novices, which recapitulates and brings into sharp relief the principal themes and rules of proper behavior elucidated in the previous sections.

Generally speaking, al-Qushayri's *Epistle* can be viewed as falling into two distinct sections: the biographical, which attests to the exemplary piety of Sufism's early heroes and their complete religious orthodoxy, and the didactic, which summarizes their teachings, customs and attitudes. According to the apt observation of a contemporary Western student of al-Qushayri's masterpiece, the former serves as the authoritative "support" (*isnad*) of the latter, which presents the main body (*matn*) of Sufi doctrine and practice, in the same way as the chain of authoritative transmitters validates the content of a prophetic report (*hadith*).[13] To push this parallel even further one can say that the numerous quotations from the Qurʾan and the Sunna that richly punctuate al-Qushayri's narrative fulfill the same "supporting" function by validating Sufi concepts, terminology, life-style, and behavior. The author's extensive knowledge of Sufi lore allows him to put it to a wide variety of different uses. One and the same anecdote reappears in different contexts and is deployed to fulfill different didactic functions. Yet, the author's overall strategy remains the same: to educate his readers by the pious precedent, to instill in them admiration for the exemplary ethos of the Sufi masters of old and to encourage them to implement it in their own lives. The continuing relevance of the *Epistle* to the spiritual aspirations of modern Muslims, Sufis and non-Sufis alike, serves as the best evidence of al-Qushayri's remarkable success in achieving his goals.

Despite its obvious normative and didactic agenda and formulaic presentation, the *Epistle* does give the modern reader an illuminating insight into the everyday lives of Sufi devotees and the moral dilemmas and challenges they faced in trying to strike a delicate balance between their ascetic and mystical values and the exigencies of life in a society governed by rank, wealth, and political power. In al-Qushayri's narrative the indigent, downtrodden but righteous always triumph over the wealthy, powerful but impious. God always comes to the rescue of the former and abandons or humbles the latter. In a sense, the Sufi devotees are the true, if uncrowned, "kings" of this world,[14] not those worldly rulers who may appear to be lording it over the common herd of believers. Yet, whenever God's righteous "friends" (*awliyaʾ Allah*) abandon or compromise their pious convictions in the expectation of mundane benefits or comforts, they are swiftly punished by God for their "perfidy". This theme runs like a red thread across the entire texture of al-Qushayri's momentous work. It is intimately linked to another critical theme, that of salvation, which, according to the author of the *Epistle*, even the most advanced Sufi masters and "friends of God" should not take for granted until they die and face God's judgement in the Hereafter. Only after that may they be allowed by God to appear to their former peers and disciples in dreams to inform them of their condition in the afterlife. Even miracle-working, no matter how spectacular, cannot guarantee one a "favorable outcome" in the afterlife, for it may be nothing but a ruse on the part of God aimed at testing the integrity and faith of His servant. These themes are illustrated over and over throughout the entire text of the *Epistle* by the anecdotes

---

13 Jawid Mojaddedi, *The Biographical Tradition in Sufism*, Curzon Press, Richmond, Surrey, 2001, p. 123.

14 As explicitly stated in an anonymous Sufi treatise from the fourth/tenth century; see *Adab al-muluk: Ein Handbuch zur islamischen Mystik aus dem 4./10. Jahrhundert*, ed. Bernd Radtke, Franz Steiner, Beirut, 1991.

and parables that show al-Qushayri's fellow Sufis in a wide variety of contexts: suffering from hunger and thirst in the desert, performing pilgrimage to Mecca, participating in "spiritual concerts", reciting the Qurʾan, waging war against the "infidel" Christian enemy in the marches of Iberia and Anatolia, earning their livelihood, studying under the guidance of a Sufi master, meditating in a retreat, praying and supplicating, working miracles, interacting with the "people of the market-place", their family members and peers, dreaming, and dying. The reader is invited to explore the fascinating world of Islamic ascetic and mystical piety carefully assembled for us by the author.

* * *

In my translation I have relied on several editions of al-Qushayri's *Epistle*, namely, that by ʿAbd al-Halim Mahmud and Mahmud b. al-Sharaf[15] and that by Muhammad ʿAbd al-Rahman al-Marʿashali.[16] I have also used two uncritical editions of al-Qushayri's text, one from Cairo and another from Damascus.[17] The quality of all these editions, including both "critical" ones, leave much to be desired. Furthermore, these "critical" editions are practically identical and do not complement each other. I have also made use of the comments provided by the German translator of the *Risala*, Richard Gramlich,[18] who had in his possession two manuscript copies of the text. I take this opportunity to acknowledge my indebtedness to Gramlich's translation, which I used extensively throughout my own work on this difficult text. I have also collated my translation with two available English ones – a partial one by Barbara von Schlegell that omits all chains of transmission of the pious logia, the biographical section and the latter chapters pertaining to Sufi etiquette, practices, morals and ethics;[19] and a complete one[20] by Rabia Harris, which relegates the chains of transmission to the appendix. While the former is quite readable and relatively accurate (albeit practically devoid of commentary), the latter is but a free paraphrase of the Arabic text, which is frequently misconstrued and, consequently, mistranslated. Harris's translation, too, has no commentary.

Alexander D. Knysh

---

15 *Al-Risala al-qushayriyya*, Dar al-kutub al-haditha, Cairo, 2 vols., 1966.
16 *Al-Risala al-qushayriyya fi ʿilm al-tasawwuf*, Dar ihyaʾ al-turath al-ʿarabi, Beirut, 1998; I used this later edition to indicate page correspondences between the Arabic text and its English translation.
17 *Al-Risala al-qushayriyya fi ʿilm al-tasawwuf*, with commentaries by Zakariya al-Ansari, Dar al-kutub al-ʿarabiyya al-kubra, Mustafa al-Babi al-Halabi, Cairo, 1276 A.H. (1859 C.E.) and *Al-Risala al-qushayriyya*, with commentaries by Mustafa al-ʿArusi and Zakariya al-Ansari, ʿAbd al-Wakil al-Darubi and Tasin ʿArafa, Jamiʿ al-Darwishiyya, 2 vols., Damascus, no date.
18 *Das Sendschreiben al-Qušayris über das Sufitum*, Franz Steiner Verlag, Wiesbaden, 1989.
19 *Principles of Sufism by al-Qushayri*; translated from the Arabic by B. R. von Schlegell with an introduction by Hamid Algar, Mizan Press, Berkeley, CA, 1990.
20 *The Risalah: Principles of Sufism*, translated by Rabia Harris, edited by Laleh Bakhtiar, Kazi Publications, Chicago, IL, 2002. It has several minor omissions toward the end of the text, but can be considered complete for practical purposes.

Author's Introduction

In the name of God, the Merciful, the Compassionate

Praise be to God Who has no rival in the greatness of His sovereignty, Who is unique in the splendor of His might, Who is dignified in the supremacy of His oneness, Who is made holy by the exaltation of His eternity, to Whose Magnitude of Essence there is no likeness or challenger, and Who is elevated in His attributes above any limitation or deficiency! His are the attributes that pertain to none but Him alone and His are the signs that testify that He is not similar to His creatures. Blessed is He, the possessor of the highest dignity! There is no boundary[1] to encircle him, no device to entrap Him, no time to confine Him! No one can be His helper, there can be no offspring next to Him, no number to count Him, no place to contain Him, no time period to embrace Him, no understanding to measure him, and no imagination to picture Him.

Far removed is He from such questions as "How is He?", "Where is He?", or statements such as "Through His creation He has acquired beauty", or "Through His actions He removed from Himself imperfection and deficiency". For "Nothing is like onto Him, He is the Hearing, the Seeing."[2] No living thing can overcome Him, omniscient is He and omnipotent! I praise Him for what He possesses and what He produces. I thank Him for what He withholds and what He bestows. I place my trust in Him and am satisfied with Him. I am content with what He gives and what He does not give.

I testify that that there is no deity but God and that He has no partners. This is the testimony of the one who has absolute confidence in His uniqueness and the one who seeks to secure His assistance. I also testify that our lord Muhammad is His elected servant and his handpicked trustee and that he is God's messenger to all His creatures. May God bless him and his family, [who shine like] lights in the darkness. May God bless his Companions, [who are] the keys to the True Guidance.[3] And may God greet them all with numerous greetings!//12

This is an epistle that the poor one in need of God Most High, ʿAbd al-Karim b. Hawazin al-Qushayri, has addressed to all the Sufi community in the lands of Islam in the year 437.[4]

---

1 The Arabic word *hadd* used here may also mean "definition".
2 Qurʾan (hereafter Q.) 42:11. Unless stated otherwise, translations of the Qurʾan quoted in the text are from Arthur J. Arberry (trans.), *The Koran Interpreted*, Simon and Schuster, New York, 1996.
3 That is, the religion of Islam.
4 1045 C.E.

And now to the main topic – may God be pleased with you! God has made this community[5] His friends of choice[6] and placed them above the rest of His servants and immediately after His messengers and prophets, may God bless and greet them! He has rendered the hearts of the Sufis repositories of His mysteries and marked them off from the other members of His Community by His resplendent light. They are the saviors of all other creatures, who in each and every state of theirs remain with God and through God. He has cleansed them of the turbidity of human nature and elevated them, through the realities of His oneness that were revealed to them, to the vantages from which they contemplate God. And He has granted them success in acquiring the good manners in serving their God and He has given them insights into the working of the decrees dispensed by their Lord. In this way they have become capable of fulfilling all the obligations imposed upon them by God and realized in the most perfect manner all His dispensations in their regard.

Then they returned to God, may He be glorified and exalted, through the sincerity of their need [of God] and in the state of humility; they refused to rely on the good works they had done or on the pure spiritual states that had been bestowed upon them. For they knew that God, may He be great and elevated, does what He wishes and selects any one of His servants He wants, while His creatures cannot pass judgements on Him, nor can any creature have any right against Him. His award is the beginning of all beneficence, His punishment is the just verdict, and His command is the final judgement.//13

Know – may God show mercy to you! – that the majority of those true Sufis have become extinct and, in our age, nothing is left of them but their traces. As a poet put it,

> As for the tents, they look like their tents
> And yet I see that the women of the tribe are not the ones who used to live in them.

This [Sufi] path[7] has been overcome by weakness, nay the path has in fact completely disappeared. Gone are the [Sufi] elders,[8] in whom one could find guidance; few are the young men, whose [exemplary] deeds and customs deserve

---

5 *Hadhihi 'l-ta'ifa*, i.e., the Sufis.
6 *Awliya'*, sing. *wali*. This term, which in Arabic means "close friend" or "protégé", is usually translated into Western languages as "saints"; in what follows we shall translate this word as "friend(s) of God".
7 *Tariqa* (lit. "way" or "path"); this term denotes both the spiritual method peculiar to a given Sufi master and the Sufi institution founded upon it. In the latter meaning, it is similar to a monastic order in Christianity or Buddhism. See *IM*, pp. 301–303.
8 *Shuyukh*; sing. *shaykh*. In what follows this term will be translated as either "elder" or "[Sufi] master".

to be emulated. Scrupulosity has disappeared from this world and rolled up its prayer rug, whereas greed has gained strength and tightened its stranglehold. Respect for the Divine Law has departed from the hearts of men and they have chosen the neglect of religion as their support and rejected the difference between the permissible and the forbidden. They have made disrespect and shamelessness their religion. They have set no store in the devotional acts and become remiss in fasting and praying; they have galloped around in the field of neglectfulness and leaned toward those who blindly follow their lusts. They have thought little about committing sinful deeds. At the same time, they have availed themselves freely of the things they borrow from the commoners, women and rulers.

However, they are not satisfied with indulging in all these evil deeds. They have begun to refer to the highest [divine] mysteries and [mystical] states and to claim that they have freed themselves from the bondage of servility and attained the realities of divine union. They also claim that they reside in God, Who rules over them with His decrees, and that they have become completely obliterated in Him. Therefore, God cannot condemn or blame them for what they do and what they do not do. They have also claimed that the mysteries of divine oneness are unveiled to them, that their souls are taken away from them completely [unto God] and that they have lost the properties of their human natures. After having been completely annihilated [in God], they have found themselves in the presence of God's eternal light. Therefore, when they speak, it is someone else who speaks on their behalf and when they act, it is someone else who performs their acts for them, or rather, they are caused to act by someone else.14// Although in this age of ours we have suffered a lot from this affliction, some of which I have just shown, I have restrained my tongue from lengthy condemnations. I have done this out of concern for this [Sufi] path, for one should not speak ill of its people.⁹ One should not give their opponents a cause to condemn them, since in this country, the suffering of this path at the hands of its opponents and accusers has been particularly severe. I do hope that the cause of this weakness will be removed and God, glory be to Him, in His graciousness, will warn those who have strayed from the [Prophet's] exemplary custom by abandoning the good manners of this path. Since our age keeps bringing only more and more difficulties and the majority of our compatriots continue to stubbornly adhere to their [corrupt] ways and to blindly persist in their delusions, I have begun to fear that the hearts of men might think that this whole affair¹⁰ from the very beginning rested upon all those [faulty] foundations and that its early adherents followed the same [corrupt] habits. So I have composed this epistle for you, may God generously reward you! In it I have mentioned the lives of the masters of this path, their good manners, their high morals, their relationships with one another, their beliefs that they hold in their hearts as well as their ecstatic states they allude to and the characteristics of their spiritual ascent from the beginning to the

---

9 That is, the Sufis.
10 That is, Sufism.

end. In this way, this epistle would give strength to the followers[11] of this path and make you testify that my presentation is correct. As for me, in spreading these laments[12] I shall have a diversion and from the generous God a favor and reward.

So I seek God's help in what I am about to mention and ask Him to protect and defend me from error in this undertaking. I plea to God for forgiveness and pardon. He alone deserves praise and He alone is capable of everything!//15

A chapter explaining the beliefs of the Sufis concerning the fundamentals of religion

Know, may God have mercy on you, that the elders of this path built the foundations of their affair upon the sound fundamental principles of God's oneness. In this way they protected their beliefs from [reprehensible] innovations and tried to bring themselves closer to the ways of the pious forefathers[13] and the followers of the Prophet's Sunna,[14] namely the doctrine of God's oneness that contained neither likening[15] nor stripping.[16] They knew well the true nature of God's eternity and realized fully how an existent entity emerges from non-existence.//16

It is this issue that the great master of this path al-Junayd,[17] may God have mercy on him, mentioned when he said: "The [true] doctrine of oneness consists in separating the eternal from the originated." Thus, they strengthened the fundamentals of the religious belief by clear proofs and irrefutable evidence. Abu Muhammad al-Jurayri,[18] may God have mercy on him, said: "He who does not learn the science of God's oneness by one of its evidential proofs, will place the foot of deception into the chasm of perdition." By this he meant that he who relies exclusively on blind imitation and is unable to contemplate directly the proofs of God's oneness, will stray from the path of salvation and enter the realm of destruction.

Upon looking into their words and examining their statements one will find out that their entire teachings and the quotations thereof confirm that this folk[19] have not failed to realize their goal, nor have they diverged in their quest through any shortcoming.

---

11 *Muridun*; sing. *murid*. Lit. "seeker" or "aspirant", followers of a Sufi master.
12 That is, the author's complaints about the decline of contemporary Sufism from the originally high standards.
13 That is, the members of the first Muslim community in Medina and their immediate successors.
14 The code of exemplary behavior established by the Prophet and his Companions to be emulated by subsequent generations of the Muslims.
15 That is, ascribing to God the attributes of His creatures.
16 That is, declaring God to be devoid of any attributes.
17 The leader of the Baghdad school of Sufism, who died in 298/910. See *IM*, pp. 52–56.
18 A disciple of al-Junayd who succeeded him as the head of the Baghdad school of Sufism after his death. See *IM*, p. 66.
19 *Al-qawm* – that is, the Sufis.

AUTHOR'S INTRODUCTION

In this section we shall mention a summary of their statements in which they deal with the problems of the fundamentals of religion. Then, God willing, we shall proceed to lay down in proper order a synopsis of necessary doctrines in a concise and brief manner.

I heard Shaykh ʿAbd al-Rahman Muhammad b.[20] al-Husayn al-Sulami[21] say: I heard ʿAbdallah b.//17 Musa al-Salami say: I heard Abu Bakr al-Shibli[22] say: "The One[23] is known before any definition and before any letters".[24] This is an unequivocal statement from al-Shibli that the Essence of the Eternal – praise be to Him – has no definition, nor does His speech consist of letters. I heard that Abu Hatim al-Sufi said: I heard Abu Nasr al-Tusi[25] say: Someone asked Ruwaym[26] about the first duty that God – may He be great and exalted – imposed upon His creatures. Ruwaym answered: "Knowledge, because God – may His name be exalted – said: 'I have not created jinn and mankind except to worship Me.'"[27] Ibn ʿAbbas[28] explained: "[That is,] except to know [God]."

Al-Junayd said: "The first act of wisdom required of the servant of God is that each work of art should know its artisan and that each originated thing should know how it came to be. This allows one to distinguish the Creator from His creatures and the Eternal from the originated thing. As a result, the servant of God submits to His call and acknowledges the necessity of obedience toward Him. If, however, one does not know one's owner, one cannot attribute ownership to whom it rightfully belongs."

Muhammad b. al-Husayn told me: I heard Muhammad b. ʿAbdallah al-Razi say: I heard Abu ʾl-Tayyib al-Maraghi say: "To the intellect belongs argumentative proof, to wisdom allegorical allusion and to mystical gnosis[29] direct witnessing. The intellect demonstrates, wisdom alludes, and gnosis witnesses directly the fact that the purest acts of worship can only be obtained by the purest belief in God's oneness."

Someone asked al-Junayd about God's oneness. He answered: "Rendering God one by realizing fully His uniqueness through the perfection of His

---

20 Here and henceforth the letter "b." stands for the Arabic "ibn" (son).
21 A major exponent of Sufism in Khurasan and a teacher of al-Qushayri, who died in 412/1021. See *IM*, pp. 125–127.
22 A famous Sufi of the Baghdad school who studied Sufism under al-Junayd; he died in 334/946. See *IM*, pp. 64–66.
23 That is, God.
24 *Huruf*, sing. *harf*. In Arabic, this word can mean both "letters" and "sounds".
25 Abu Nasr al-Sarraj al-Tusi (d. 378/988), a Khurasani exponent of Sufism who wrote the famous Sufi manual "The Book of the Essentials of Sufism" (*Kitab al-lumaʿ fi ʾl-tasawwuf*). For details see *IM*, pp. 118–120.
26 A famous Sufi master associated with the circle of al-Junayd. He died in 303/915.
27 Q. 51:56.
28 A cousin of the prophet Muhammad by his uncle al-ʿAbbas, Ibn [al-]ʿAbbas distinguished himself as a collector of stories about the Prophet; he was also one of the first Muslim exegetes. He died around 68/686-7. See *EI*, "ʿAbdallah b. al-ʿAbbas".
29 *Maʿrifa*, a Sufi term for divinely inspired, intuitive knowledge of God and the world.

solitude, that is, that He is one and only, 'Who has not begotten and has not been begotten',[30] who has no opponents, rivals or likes, without likening Him [to created things], without asking 'how [He is]', without representing Him as an image or form, in accordance with [the verse] 'Like Him there is naught; He is the Hearing, the Seeing.'"[31]

Muhammad b. Ahmad b. Yahya the Sufi told me: ʿAbdallah b. ʿAli al-Tamimi the Sufi told me: It was said that [Abu] al-Husayn b. ʿAli al-Damaghani said: Someone asked Abu Bakr al-Zahirabadhi about [divine] gnosis.//18 He answered: "Gnosis is a name. Its meaning consists in elevating [God] in the heart in such a way as to prevent you from either stripping [Him] of [His] attributes or likening [Him] to [His] creatures."

Abu ʾl-Hasan al-Bushanji, may God have mercy on him, said: "God's oneness is to know that He is not similar to created essences, yet [at the same time] not devoid of His attributes."

Shaykh Abu ʿAbd al-Rahman al-Sulami – may God have mercy on Him – told us: I heard Muhammad b. Muhammad b. Ghalib say: I heard Abu Nasr Ahmad b. Saʿid al-Isfanjani say: al-Husayn b. Mansur [al-Hallaj][32] said: "Consider everything to be originated in time (i.e., created), for eternity pertains to Him alone. Everything that has appeared [in this world] as a corporal being is bound with accidents. Everything that is assembled by means of an intermediary[33] is held together by its powers. Everything that is affiliated with a moment of time is [one day] abandoned by it.[34] Everything that is sustained by someone else is by necessity dependent on it. Everything that is subject to the imagination can be represented as an image. Everything that is contained by a place can be confined by a space. And everything that belongs to a certain category can be grasped by a qualifier. As for God – praise be upon Him – He cannot be protected by something above Him nor supported by something below Him.[35] He cannot be defined by something that preceded Him, no togetherness can appear next to Him, no behindness can follow Him, no in-frontness can grasp Him, no beforeness can prevail over Him, no afterness can annihilate Him. No term can comprehensively define Him, no becoming can add existence onto Him, no absence can cause Him to disappear.//19 There is no description of Him whatsoever; His actions have no cause; His existence has no end. He is far removed from the characteristics of His creatures, nor does He mix with them; His actions require no intermediary. He is distinct from His creatures through His eternity, while they are distinct from His through their origination in time.

---

30 Q. 112:3.
31 Q. 42:11.
32 A famous (and highly controversial) mystic of al-Junayd's circle, who was tried and executed as a heretic and troublemaker in Baghdad in 309/922. See *IM*, pp. 72–82.
33 That is, any body that was originated through something other than it and is possessed of various sensory and physical faculties.
34 That is, it dies.
35 That is, He cannot be subject to spatial descriptions.

If you ask "When?", His being preceded all time. If you say *huwa*,[36] the [letters] *ha* and *waw* were created by Him. If you ask "Where?", His existence was there before any place. The letters are but His signs; His existence is the confirmation of Him; His knowledge is the knowledge of His oneness; and the knowledge of His oneness is what makes Him distinct from His creatures. Whatever the imagination might fathom regarding Him, He will be different from it. How can anything that originated from Him dwell in Him? How can anything that He produced try to join Him? The eyes cannot contemplate Him nor can thought grasp Him. Closeness to Him is [a sign of] His beneficence; remoteness from Him is [a sign of] His neglect; His elevation takes place without climbing up;[37] His descent occurs without stepping down.[38] He is "the First and the Last, the Manifest and the Hidden",[39] the Close and the Remote, "like Him there is naught; He is the Hearing, the Seeing".[40]

I heard Abu Hatim al-Sijistani say: I heard Abu Nasr al-Sarraj al-Tusi[41] narrating on the authority of Yusuf b. al-Husayn[42] who said: "A certain man came to Dhu 'l-Nun al-Misri[43] and said://20 'Tell me, what is God's oneness?' He [al-Misri] answered: 'To understand that God's power in all things [exists] without mixing, that He crafted them without any implements, that His act [of creation] is the cause of everything that He has crafted, that His act [of creation] had no cause; that neither in the skies above nor on the Earth below is there any planner but God and that whatever you may imagine by your fantasy, God is different from it.'" Al-Junayd said: "The doctrine of God's oneness is your knowledge and confirmation that God was alone in His pre-eternity, with Whom there was no one, and that nothing can do what He does."

Abu 'Abdallah b. Khafif[44] said: "Faith consists in the heart's acceptance of [the mysteries of] the Unknown that God communicates to it." Abu 'l-'Abbas al-Sayyari[45] said: "God's gifts are of two types: graces and afflictions. What He bestows upon you is a grace, while what He takes away from you is an affliction. Therefore, say: 'I am a believer, God willing.'" Abu 'l-'Abbas was the [greatest Sufi] master of his time. I heard [my] teacher Abu 'Ali al-Daqqaq – may God have mercy on him – say: "A man squeezed the leg of Abu 'l-'Abbas al-Sayyari.

---

36 That is, "He" (God).
37 That is, His elevation does not occur in a physical space.
38 A reference to the tradition according to which God descends to the lower heaven in order to communicate with His creatures.
39 Q. 57:3.
40 Q. 42:11.
41 On him see note 000.
42 Yusuf b. al-Husayn al-Razi (d. 304/916), a renowned Sufi from Rayy, Iran. See al-Sulami, *Tabaqat*, pp. 151–156.
43 A famous Sufi master from Upper Egypt, who died in 245/860. See *IM*, pp. 40–42.
44 A famous Sufi from Shiraz, who died in 371/982. See *IM*, pp. 79, 87, 118, and Schimmel, *Mystical Dimensions of Islam*, "index".
45 For his biography see later (p. 68).

He said: 'You are squeezing a leg that has never made a single step toward disobedience of God – may He be great and exalted!'" Abu Bakr al-Wasiti[46] said: "When someone says: 'I am a believer in God in truth', one should tell him: 'The true faith implies scrutiny, understanding and comprehension. If someone loses this, his claim to true faith is invalidated.'"[47] By this he meant the teaching of the people of the [Prophet's] Sunna, according to which the true believer is destined to enter Paradise. If one has not known directly from the mystery of God's wisdom that he is a believer in truth, then his claim is false.

I heard Shaykh ʿAbd al-Rahman al-Sulami say: I heard that Mansur b. ʿAbdallah said://21 I heard Abu ʾl-Husayn al-ʿAnbari say: I heard Sahl b. ʿAbdallah al-Tustari[48] say: "Believers contemplate God with their eyes without comprehension and without ever reaching the limit of their understanding." Abu ʾl-Husayn al-Nuri[49] said: "The Real[50] looked at the hearts of men and did not find a heart that had more passion for Him than the heart of Muhammad – may God bless and greet him. Therefore He bestowed upon him the Ascension[51] in order to hasten the vision [of God by Muhammad] and [their] conversation."

I heard imam[52] Abu Bakr Muhammad b. al-Hasan Ibn Furak[53] – may God have mercy upon him – say: I heard Muhammad b. al-Mahbub, a servant of Abu ʿUthman al-Maghribi,[54] say: "One day Abu ʿUthman told me: 'If someone said to you: "Muhammad, where is your God", what would you tell him?' [The servant] said: I answered: 'Where He has always been.' [Then Abu ʿUthman] said: 'And if this person asks, where God was in eternity, what would you say?' [The servant] said: I answered: '[He was] where He is now.' That is, as He was in no particular place before, so He is now.' [The servant] said: 'He was satisfied with my response and he took off his shirt and gave it to me.'"

I heard the imam Abu Bakr b. Furak – may God have mercy on him – say: I heard Abu ʿUthman al-Maghribi say: "I used to believe in the teaching [that

---

46 A Sufi of al-Junayd's circle, who emigrated to Central Asia (Marw) following the execution of al-Hallaj. He died around 320/932. See *IM*, pp. 100–101.
47 A mere oral proclamation that is not supported by personal conviction, experience and insight is not sufficient to become a true believer.
48 On this famous Sufi of Basra, who died in 283/896, see *IM*, pp. 83–88 and Böwering, *Mystical Vision*.
49 A famous Sufi of al-Junayd's circle who represents the erotic trend in Baghdad mysticism. He died in 295/907. See *IM*, pp. 60–63.
50 That is, God.
51 On Muhammad's Night Journey (*al-israʾ*) and subsequent Ascension (*al-miʿraj*) to Heaven, see the article "al-Miʿradj" in *EI*.
52 Literally "prayer leader", a term that is often applied to any distinguished religious scholar.
53 This individual, who died in 406/1015 at Nishapur, was known primarily as a Shafiʿi jurist and Ashʿari theologian. He was a teacher of al-Qushayri. For details, see the article "Ibn Furak" in *EI*.
54 On this Sufi master, who died in Nishapur in 373/983, see al-Sulami, *Tabaqat*, pp. 358–362 and the sources cited therein. His biography will be mentioned later (see p. 72).

AUTHOR'S INTRODUCTION

postulated] that God is located in a certain direction.[55] However, when I arrived in Baghdad, this [idea] disappeared from my heart. I then wrote to my companions in Mecca, saying: 'I have become Muslim once again.'"[56]

I heard Muhammad b. al-Husayn al-Sulami say: I heard Abu ʿUthman al-Maghribi say, when he was asked about creatures: "[They are but] carcasses and ghosts who are governed by the rulings of Divine Power." Al-Wasiti said: "When the spirits and the bodies [of men] were brought forth by God, they came into being through Him and not through their own essences. Likewise, their thoughts and movements also appeared through God." He meant that the movements and the thoughts are but the ramifications[57] of the bodies and the spirits.//22 In saying so he explained that the acquisitions of the creatures are created by God Most High;[58] likewise, God Most High is the only one Who creates all essences and their accidents.[59]

I heard Shaykh Abu ʿAbd al-Rahman al-Sulami – may God have mercy on him – say: I heard Muhammad b. ʿAbdallah say: I heard Abu Jaʿfar al-Saydalani say: I heard Abu Saʿid al-Kharraz[60] say: "He who thinks that he can achieve his goal by exerting himself is only wearying himself in vain, while he who thinks that he can attain his goal without effort, is but a wishful thinker." Al-Wasiti said: "The stations [of the Sufi path] are but portions apportioned and attributes predetermined [by God's will]. Therefore, how can one strive to attain [something] through one's own actions and how can one seek to achieve [one's goal] through one's own effort?"[61]

Someone asked al-Wasiti whether unbelief [occurs] through God or belongs to Him. He answered: "Unbelief and faith, this world and the next, are all from God, to God, through God and belong to Him. That is, [they] originate from God, then [they] return to Him; [they] subsist and disappear through God and belong to Him as His domain and His creatures."

Al-Junayd said: Someone asked one of the scholars about the doctrine of oneness [of God]. He [the scholar] replied: "This is certitude." Then the inquirer asked: "Explain to me what it is?" [The scholar] answered: "It is when you know that the movement or immobility of creatures are the work of God alone – may

---

55 That is, that God has spatial characteristics and is seated on a physical throne in a concrete location. This teaching was attributed to some Islamic schools of thought, namely the Karramiyya and the Hanbalites.
56 That is, "I have converted to the true Islam."
57 *Furuʿ*, lit. "branches".
58 That is, they receive their acts and thoughts from God, whereupon they appropriate them.
59 This is a reference to the polemic between the Ashʿarite theologians, whose position is upheld by the author, and their opponents, the Muʿtazilites, who treated the essences of things as being self-sufficient carriers of accidents. For details see Frank, *Beings and Their Attributes*, pp. 10–13 et passim.
60 On this controversial Sufi master of the Baghdad school, who was repeatedly exiled for his bold mystical ideas (he died around 286/899 or earlier), see *IM*, pp. 56–60.
61 That is, the success or failure of one's striving was predetermined by God from eternity.

He be great and exalted – and that He has no partners. If you have done this, you have already declared His oneness."

I heard Muhammad b. al-Husayn – may God have mercy on him – say: I heard ʿAbd al-Wahid b. ʿAli say: I heard Muhammad b. Musa al-Wasiti say: I heard Muhammad b. al-Husayn al-Jawhari say: I heard that Dhu ʾl-Nun al-Misri said that a man had come to him and said: "Pray to God on my behalf!//23 Since you are assisted in your knowledge of the Unseen[62] by your realization of the doctrine of God's oneness, God has answered many of your prayers in the past. However, a cry for help does not necessarily save a drowning man."[63] Al-Wasiti said: "Pharaoh claimed lordship openly,[64] while the Muʿtazilites do so covertly, when they say: 'You do what you will.'"[65] Abu ʾl-Husayn al-Nuri said: "God's oneness is when every thought points to God Most High, without being mixed with the thoughts that imply that God is similar [to His creatures]."

Shaykh Abu ʿAbd al-Rahman al-Sulami – may God have mercy on him – said: I heard ʿAbd al-Wahid b. Bakr say: I heard that Hilal b. Ahmad said that someone asked Abu ʿAli al-Rudhbari[66] about God's oneness. He answered: "God's oneness is to keep the heart upright by avoiding the teaching that strips [God of His attributes][67] and by rejecting His similarity [with His creatures].[68] In one phrase, God's oneness is asserted as follows: Whatever [human] imagination and thoughts might ascribe to God, He is the opposite of it, as stated by the Most High: "Like Him there is naught, He is the Hearing and the Seeing."[69] Abu ʾl-Qasim al-Nasrabadhi[70] said: "Paradise subsists because He allows it to subsist. However, His thought of you, His mercy toward you and His love for you subsist as long as He Himself subsists. How different is that which subsists through His own subsistence from that which subsists because He allows it to subsist." The words of Shaykh Abu ʾl-Qasim al-Nasrabadhi are the utmost goal of realization. The People of the Truth[71] say that the attributes of the Essence of the Eternal – glory be to Him – subsist through His own subsistence. He drew attention to this issue and clarified that the Subsistent//24 subsists through His own subsistence, which is contrary to what is claimed by the opponents of the

---

62 That is, the world of the mystery of divine predestination that ordinary mortals cannot access.
63 That is, despite God's predetermination of man's fate, he is still responsible for his actions.
64 When he said [in the Qurʾan 79:24]: "I am your Lord Most High!"
65 That is, they claim that they are the creators of their own actions.
66 A Sufi associated with al-Junayd's circle. His biography is given later (see pp. 62–63), in the biographical section of the "Epistle".
67 The doctrine of the "stripping" of God of His attributes (taʿtil) was attributed to the Muʿtazilites, who insisted that God's attributes do not have independent existence and are but modes of His eternal essence.
68 The doctrine of the "likening" of God to His creatures (tashbih) was ascribed to a number of Islamic schools of thought, including the Karramiyya and some radical Hanbalites.
69 Q. 42:11.
70 A student of al-Shibli, who sympathized with al-Hallaj's teaching. He died in 367/977.
71 That is, the accomplished Sufi masters.

People of the Truth. Muhammad b. al-Husayn said: I heard that al-Nasrabadhi said: "You vacillate between [God's] attributes of action and attributes of the essence.⁷² Both are His – may He be exalted – attributes in truth. When He throws you into confusion by placing you in the station of separation, He binds you with the attributes of His action. When He delivers you to the station of unity, He binds you with the attributes of His essence."

Abu 'l-Qasim al-Nasrabadhi was the master of his age. I heard imam Abu 'l-Ishaq al-Isfaraini⁷³ – may God have mercy on him – say: "When I arrived from Baghdad [to Nishapur]⁷⁴ I began to teach at the Friday mosque of Nishapur the doctrine of the human spirit, arguing that it was created. Abu 'l-Qasim al-Nasrabadhi used to sit at some distance from us and to listen to my speech. After several days he approached us and said to Muhammad al-Farra': 'I testify that I was converted to Islam anew at the hands of this man!' And he pointed at me."⁷⁵

I heard Muhammad b. al-Husayn al-Sulami say: I heard Abu 'l-Husayn al-Farisi say: I heard Ibrahim b. Fatik say: I heard al-Junayd say: "When would He Who has neither a like nor an equal join the one who has both a like and an equal? Is this at all possible? This strange idea can only come true through the kindness of the [All-]Kind in which there can be no grasping, imagining or comprehension, but only the allusion [springing from] certitude and the realization [that comes with] the genuine faith."⁷⁶ Muhammad b. al-Husayn – may God have mercy on him – informed us: I heard ʿAbd al-Wahid b. Bakr say: Ahmad b. Muhammad b. ʿAli al-Bardaʿi told me: Tahir b. Ismaʿil al-Razi told me: someone asked Yahya b. Muʿadh:⁷⁷ "Tell me about God – may He be great and exalted!" He answered: "[Your God] is one God."⁷⁸ He was then asked: "How is He?"⁷⁹ [Yahya] answered: "[He is] the [All-]Powerful Ruler." He was then asked: "Where is He?" [Yahya] said: "[Thy Lord] is ever watching you."⁸⁰ The inquirer said to him: "I did not ask

---

72 According to Ashʿarite theologians, God's attributes are divided into two categories. The first are the attributes that pertain to the essence and are co-eternal with it – e.g., life, will, knowledge, power and so on. The second category comprises the attributes that describe God's acts in the created world, namely His sustenance of His creatures, His determining the death and birth of human beings, His wrath at human disobedience, and His contentment with mankind's good deeds. In theological works, the borderline between these two categories remained blurred and was disputed by various theological factions. See the article "Sifa" in *EI*.
73 On this famous theologian see article "al-Isfaraʾini" in *EI*.
74 A major cultural and religious center in Khurasan, Iran.
75 That is, he embraced the Ashʿarite doctrine of the created spirit.
76 That is, a cognitive union between man and God can only occur through a pure act of faith and certitude. It cannot be achieved through sense perception, intellectual process or the imagination.
77 A famous mystic from Nishapur, who distinguished himself as an eloquent preacher; he died in 258/872. See *IM*, pp. 92–94.
78 Q. 2:163.
79 That is, what is His mode of existence?
80 Q. 89:14.

you about that!" [Yahya] replied: "All other attributes belong to [His] creatures. As for His [genuine] attribute, it is as I have just told you."

Muhammad b. al-Husayn told us: He said I heard Abu Bakr al-Razi say: I heard Abu ʿAli al-Rudhbari say: "Whatever one imagines [about] God in his ignorance, the intellect shows [Him] to be different from that."//25

Ibn Shahin asked al-Junayd about the meaning of the [word] "with". He responded: "'With' has two meanings: the 'with' of the Prophets, which is [God's] assistance and protection, as in the words of God: 'I shall be with you, hearing and seeing.'[81] The 'with' of the commoners, which is [God's] knowledge and understanding, as in the words of God: 'Three men conspire not secretly with one another, but He is the fourth of them.[82]'" To this Ibn Shahin responded: "People like you should be leading this community to God."

Someone asked Dhu ʾl-Nun al-Misri about God's words: "The All-Compassionate sat Himself (istawa) upon the Throne."[83] He answered: "The All-Compassionate asserted His essence, while denying [His location] in a specific place. He exists through His own essence, whereas all other things exist through His command, as He wished [them to be]."[84] Someone asked al-Shibli about the words of God: "The All-Compassionate sat Himself on the Throne." He answered: "The All-Compassionate has existed forever, while the Throne is an originated thing. Therefore, the Throne was firmly installed (istawa) by the All-Compassionate."[85] Someone asked Jaʿfar b. Nusayr about the words of God: "The All-Compassionate sat Himself upon the Throne." He answered: "His knowledge of all things became equal,[86] in that no one thing is closer to Him than the other."

Jaʿfar al-Sadiq[87] said: "Whoever believes that God is [located] in something, [that originated] from something or [rests] upon something, has become//26 a polytheist. In other words, had He been upon something, He would have been carried by it; had He been in something, He would have been confined [by it]; and had He been from something, He would have been an originated being." Jaʿfar al-Sadiq also said about God's words: "Then [He] drew near and hung suspended."[88]

---

81 Q. 20:46.
82 Q. 58:7.
83 Q. 20:5.
84 Meaning God's creative command "Be!"
85 In some contexts, the verb *istawa* may mean either "to [firmly] install [oneself]" or "to raise". As in the next example, various meanings of this Arabic root are brought into play in the sayings of the Sufi masters.
86 A word play on the meaning of the Arabic verb *istawa*, which may mean either "to sit firmly" or "to be equal".
87 The sixth Shiʿi leader (*imam*), to whom many esoteric teachings are ascribed by later Sufi authors. See Böwering, *Mystical Vision*, pp. 140–142.
88 Q. 53:8. The identity of the being seen by Muhammad in this Qurʾanic episode was disputed by Muslim scholars. While some early authorities believed that the Prophet saw God Himself, later exegesis almost uniformly insisted that he saw the angel of Revelation Gabriel; see Josef van Ess, "Vision and Ascension: *Surat al-Najm* and Its Relationship with Muhammad's *miʿraj*" in *Journal of Qurʾanic Studies*, vol. 1/1 (1999), pp. 47–62.

"Whoever imagines that God Himself drew near [to Muhammad] implies that there was a distance [between them]. In reality, 'drawing near' means only that each time [Muhammad] came closer to God, He removed him further from [conventional] knowledge, until there was neither 'nearness' nor 'distance'."

I found in the handwriting of [my] master Abu ʿAli [al-Daqqaq] that someone asked a Sufi where is God? He answered: "May God banish you [from good]! How can you seek the 'where' of witnessing [the divine Essence]?!" Shaykh Abu ʿAbd al-Rahman al-Sulami told us: I heard Abu ʾl-ʿAbbas al-Khashshab al-Baghdadi say: I heard Abu ʾl-Qasim b. Musa say: I heard Muhammad b. Ahmad say: I heard al-Ansari say: I heard al-Kharraz[89] say: "The true essence of closeness [to God] is when the heart loses the perception of all things and the soul finds rest in God Most High."

I heard Muhammad b. al-Husayn say: I heard Muhammad b. ʿAli al-Hafiz say: I heard Abu Muʿadh al-Qazwini say: I heard Abu ʿAli al-Dallal say: I heard Abu ʿAbdallah b. Qahraman say: I heard Ibrahim al-Khawwas[90] say: "I came to a man who was possessed by Satan. I began to utter the call to prayer in his ear. Then Satan called me from the man's belly, saying: 'Let me kill him, for he says that the Qurʾan is created!'"

Ibn ʿAtaʾ[91] said: "When God Most High created the letters,[92] He made them one of His mysteries. When He created Adam, He infused this mystery[93] into him, without however giving it to His angels. The letters[94] streamed from the tongue of Adam – upon him be peace – in different manners and in different languages, and God made them the [outward] forms." By saying this Ibn ʿAtaʾ clearly affirmed that the letters are created.//27 Sahl b. ʿAbdallah[95] said: "The letters are the tongue of action and not the tongue of the essence,[96] for they themselves are an action in that which is acted upon."[97] This too is a clear statement that the letters are created.

In his "Replies to the Questions of the Syrians" al-Junayd said: "Trust in God is an action of the heart; the oneness of God is a word of the heart." This is the teaching of the people of the fundamental principles [of religion], that is, speech

---

89 Abu Saʿid al-Kharraz. See note 60 on page 9.
90 A Sufi of al-Junayd's circle who died in 291/904. See al-Sulami, *Tabaqat*, pp. 220–222 and the biographical chapter of the "Epistle" on page 56.
91 Ahmad b. ʿAtaʾ al-Rudhbari (d. 369/980).
92 *Huruf*, sing. *harf*. In Arabic this word denotes both letters and sounds. Here al-Qushayri refutes the thesis, upheld by some Hanbali scholars, that the letters or sounds of the Qurʾan are uncreated.
93 That is, the knowledge of God.
94 Or the sounds, see note 92.
95 Sahl b. ʿAbdallah al-Tustari (d. 283/896), an early Sufi theorist and exegete from Basra, who exerted a profound influence on the subsequent development of Sufi thought. See *IM*, "Index" and Böwering, *Mystical Vision*.
96 That is, they express God's actions, but not His hidden essence.
97 That is, they are created and take place in the created – that is, in language.

is the entity that resides in the heart; it comes from command and prohibition, from the [prophetic] tradition and search for this tradition. Al-Junayd also said in his "Replies to the Questions of the Syrians": "Only God possesses the knowledge of the Unseen.[98] He knows what was, what will be, what will not be and how this would be, were it to be." Al-Husayn b. al-Mansur [al-Hallaj] said: "He who has realized fully the truth of God's oneness, sheds [such questions as] 'why?' and 'how?'" Muhammad b. al-Husayn related to us: I heard that Mansur b. ʿAbdallah said: I heard Jaʿfar b. Muhammad say: I heard al-Junayd say: "The most noble and exalted counsel is to allow your thought to roam in the arena of God's oneness."

Al-Wasiti said: "God has brought forth nothing more noble than the human spirit." He thus stated clearly that the spirit is created. The master and imam Zayn al-Islam Abu ʾl-Qasim[99] said: "All these stories prove that the beliefs of Sufi masters agree with the teachings of the People of the Truth,[100] as far as the fundamentals of religion are concerned. We stop here in order to avoid going beyond the concision and brevity, which we have pledged to follow [in this work]."

Section [on divine oneness]

The master, the Adornment of Islam, Abu ʾl-Qasim – may God make his glory eternal – said:

The following sections contain their beliefs concerning God's oneness, which we shall present in proper order. The dispersed and collected sayings of the masters of this path, as well as their books, teach about God's oneness as follows://28 God Most High – praise be to Him – is existent, eternal, one, wise, powerful, knowing, overpowering, compassionate, willing, hearing, glorious, exalted, speaking, seeing, proud, strong, living, one, everlasting, and everlasting refuge.[101]

He knows by [His] knowledge;[102] he is powerful by [His] power; he wills by [His] will; he sees by [His] sight; He speaks by [His] speech; He lives by [His] life; He is everlasting by [His] everlastingness. He has two hands, which are His attributes and with which He creates what He wishes and gives it a specific form. He has a face. The attributes of His essence are unique to it. One must not say that they are He or that they are not He. They are [His] eternal attributes and [His] everlasting properties. He is unique in His essence. He is not similar to any originated thing, nor is any created being similar to Him. He is neither a body,

---

98 That is, the world of divine mystery that contains the true realities of all existing things and the knowledge of things to come until the end of time.
99 That is, al-Qushayri.
100 That is, the Sunnites who adhered to al-Ashʿari's theological doctrine.
101 *Al-Samad*; the exact meaning of this epithet of God mentioned in Q. 112:2 remains a matter of dispute. I follow A. J. Arberry's translation.
102 These statements are directed against the Muʿtazilite theologians who considered God's attributes to be mere modes of His being and who tended to allegorize the anthropomorphic features ascribed to God in the Muslim scripture.

nor a substance, nor an accident. His attributes are not accidents and He can be neither fancied by the imagination nor represented by the intellect. He has neither direction nor place and He is not subject to the flow of time or age. His properties neither increase nor decrease. He has neither shape nor corpus and cannot be limited by an end or a limit. No originated thing can dwell in Him, and no cause can move Him to action. He is subject to neither color nor coming-to-be and is in no need of help or assistance. No essence endowed with power can escape His power nor can any creature disengage itself from//29 His command. No known thing eludes His knowledge and no one can reprimand Him for what and how He does what He does.

About Him one ought not ask "where?", "in what way?" or "how?". His existence has no beginning, therefore, one should not ask: "When did He come to be?" His duration has no end and one cannot say [about Him]: "[His] age and time have ended." One cannot say why He did what He did, since His actions have no cause. Nor can one say: "What is He?", for He belongs to no category [of beings] and therefore cannot have any special mark setting Him aside from the other [similar beings]. He will be seen [on the Judgement Day], but not by positioning Himself in front of the viewers, while He will see others without applying [His] eyesight. He fashions [creatures] without touching them directly or handling.

His are the most beautiful names[103] and the most exalted attributes. He "does whatsoever he desires",[104] and [all] creatures obey His verdict. Nothing can happen in His realm unless He so willed, and no event can take place in His kingdom, unless He has predetermined it. When he knows that something should happen, He wills it and it happens indeed. And when He knows that something should not happen, although [in principle] possible, He wills that it should not happen. He is the creator of men's deeds, both good and bad; He is the originator of all the entities and events in this world, rare or numerous. He sends [His] messengers to mankind, although He is under no obligation to do so.

It is He Who causes men to worship Him by communicating with them through the prophets in such a way that no one can either censure or oppose [Him]. It is He Who helped our prophet Muhammad – may God's prayer and blessing be upon him – by evidential miracles and resplendent signs, depriving [his deniers] of an excuse [not to embrace his message] and making clear through him [the distinction between] certain knowledge[105] and denial. It is He Who, at first, protected the sanctity of Islam after the death of His Prophet – may God's prayer and blessing be upon him – through the Rightly-Guided Caliphs,[106] then proceeded to protect and aid the truth by revealing the irrefutable proofs of the religion through lips of His friends.[107] He has since been safeguarding His

---

103 Q. 7:180 and 17:110.
104 Q. 2:253.
105 That is, true faith.
106 That is, the first four successors of the Prophet.
107 Meaning probably both Sufi masters and religious scholars (ʿulamaʾ).

monotheistic Community from agreeing upon error.[108] He has cut the root of falsehood by presenting irrefutable evidence and fulfilled His promise to support His religion, in accordance with His words: "That he [the prophet Muhammad] may uplift it above every religion, though the unbelievers be averse."[109]

These are the passages that present in brief the principles of the Sufi masters. May God grant us success!//30

---

108 According to a famous *hadith* of the Prophet, his community will never agree on an error.
109 Q. 9:33.

Chapter 1

On the Masters of this Path and their Deeds and Sayings that Show How They Uphold the Divine Law[1]

Know – may God Most High have mercy on you – that after the death of the Messenger of God – may God bless and greet him – the best Muslims of the epoch chose to be named by a word that pointed to their companionship with the Messenger of God, for no virtue was superior to it. So, they were called "Companions [of the Prophet]" (*sahaba*). When the people of the next generation succeeded them, those who kept company with the Companions came to be named "Successors" (*tabi'un*). The Successors considered this name to be the noblest of all characteristics. As for those who came after them, they were called "the Successors of the Successors" (*tabi'u al-tabi'in*). After that the people became more and more diverse, and their ranks became distinct from one another. The elect people, who had strong attachment to the affairs of faith, came to be known as "World-renouncers"[2] and "Worshippers".[3] Then there appeared innovations [in religion] and strife among various factions. [Members] of each group claimed that the [true] World-renouncers were among them. As for those elect adherents of the Prophet's custom[4] who kept every breath they made with God[5] and who protected their hearts from the onslaughts of forgetfulness, they were distinguished from the rest by the name "Sufism".[6] This name became widely applied to the greatest among them before the second century of the Hijra.[7]

In this chapter we shall mention the names of the masters of this [Sufi] path from the first generation up until those who live today. We shall also mention some of their biographies and sayings in order to demonstrate their principles and good manners, if God Most High so wills.

---

1 *Al-shari'a*; in what follows this Arabic term will either be translated as the "Divine Law" or left untranslated.
2 *Zuhhad*, sing. *zahid*; in what follows this term may occasionally also be translated as "ascetics".
3 *'Ubbad*, sing. *'abid*.
4 *Sunna*, the exemplary behavior of the Prophet and his closest Companions to be emulated by every righteous Muslim. Occasionally this term is left untranslated.
5 That is, those who examine their actions carefully in order to determine their compliance with God's will as expressed in the shari'a.
6 The Western equivalent of the Arabic word *tasawwuf*.
7 The prophet Muhammad's emigration from Mecca to Medina in 622, which became the first year of the Muslim sacred calendar.

Abu Ishaq Ibrahim b. Adham b. Mansur[8]

He – may God be pleased with him – came from the region of Balkh.[9] He was a son of a king. Once he set out on a hunting trip. As he stirred up a fox or a rabbit and set out to chase it, he heard a voice//31: "O Ibrahim, were you created for this or commanded to do this?" Then he heard the voice again, from behind the saddle bow, saying: "By God, you were not created for this and you were not commanded to do this!" He dismounted from his horse. He then came across a shepherd of his father's, took his woolen shirt and put it on and gave away all his belongings and the horse to the shepherd. Then he began wandering in the desert until he arrived in Mecca, where he attached himself to Sufyan al-Thawri[10] and al-Fudayl b. ʿIyad.[11] After that he journeyed to Syria and died there. He lived by the toil of his hands, such as harvesting, guarding the orchards and so on. [Once] in the desert he met a man who taught him the greatest name of God.[12] After [the man] left, he called upon God by this name and saw al-Khadir,[13] who told him: "My brother [the prophet] David has just taught you God's greatest name." This story was related to us by Shaykh Abu ʿAbd al-Rahman al-Sulami – may God have mercy on him. He said: Muhammad b. al-Husayn Ibn al-Khashshab said: Abu al-Hasan ʿAli b. Muhammad al-Misri said: Abu Saʿid al-Kharraz said: Ibrahim b. Bashshar said: "I was accompanying Ibrahim b. Adham. Once I told him: 'Tell me about the beginning of your affair.' He then recounted this [story] to me."//32

Ibrahim b. Adham was particularly famous for his pious scrupulosity. It is told that he said: "Watch carefully what you eat,[14] and then there will be no harm for you in not staying awake during the night or fasting during the day!" His most common prayer was: "O God, remove me from the disgrace of disobedience to You to the glory of obedience to You!" Someone said to Ibrahim b. Adham: "Meat has become expensive!" He answered: "Make it cheaper", that is, "Do not buy it." He then recited the following verse:

> When something becomes too expensive for me, I abandon it.
> Therefore the more expensive it becomes, the cheaper it is [for me].

---

8 On him, see *IM*, pp. 18–20.
9 Presently in northern Afghanistan.
10 On this renowned early scholar and jurist see the article "Sufyan al-Thawri" in *EI*. He died in 161/777.
11 A famous early ascetic, whom a pious legend portrays as a repented highway robber. See his biography on pages 20–21 and *IM*, pp. 23–24.
12 According to the Islamic tradition, God has ninety-nine "most beautiful names". His hundredth name is hidden from the common people, but may sometimes be revealed by God to His elect friends (*awliyaʾ*). For details see Daniel Gimaret, *Les noms divins en Islam*.
13 On this legendary person, who is usually identified with the unnamed companion of Moses in Q. 59:81, see the article "al-Khadir" in *EI*. Although some Muslim scholars consider him to be a prophet, he is more commonly seen as a friend of God and paragon of the Sufi gnostic.
14 That is, eat only the food that is properly obtained.

Muhammad b. al-Husayn – may God have mercy on him – said: I heard Mansur b. ʿAbdallah say: I heard Muhammad b. Hamid say: I heard Ahmad b. Khadrawayh (Khidruya) say: Ibrahim b. Adham said to a man who was performing a circumambulation [of the Kaʿba]: "Know that you will not attain the rank of the righteous until you have climbed six mountain peaks. First, you must shut the door of pleasant life and open the door of hardship. Second, you must shut the door of [self-]glorification and open the door of humility. Third, you must shut the door of quiet and open the door of self-exertion. Fourth, you must shut the door of sleep and open the door of vigil. Fifth, you must shut the door of wealth and open the door of poverty. Sixth, you must shut the door of hope and open the door of readiness for death."

[Once] Ibrahim b. Adham was guarding a vineyard. A soldier who was passing by told him: "Give me some of those grapes!" Ibrahim b. Adham replied: "The owner forbade me [to do this]." The soldier began to lash him with his whip. Ibrahim b. Adham lowered his head and said: "Beat this head, for it disobeys God often!" On hearing this the soldier was unable to continue the beating and departed.

Sahl b. Ibrahim said: "I was a companion of Ibrahim b. Adham. When I became ill, he spent all his wages on me. When I felt craving for some food, he sold his donkey and spent all of its cost on me. When I began to recover, I asked him: 'Ibrahim, where is the donkey?' He answered: 'I sold it.' I told him: 'What shall I be riding on?' He said: 'On my neck, my brother!' And he carried me for three way-stations."//33

Abu ʾl-Fayd Dhu ʾl-Nun al-Misri[15]

His name is Thawban b. Ibrahim. He was also called Abu ʾl-Fayd b. Ibrahim. His father was a Nubian.[16] He [Dhu ʾl-Nun] died in 245.[17] He excelled in this affair[18] and was unique in his age in respect of knowledge, pious scrupulosity, [spiritual] state, and good manners. Some people denounced him [as a heretic] to [the caliph] al-Mutawakkil[19] and the latter commanded that he be brought before him from Egypt. When [Dhu ʾl-Nun] appeared before him and admonished him, al-Mutawakkil began to cry and [ordered] that he be taken back to Egypt with honor. [Since then] each time someone mentioned pious people to al-Mutawakkil, he would cry and say: "Whenever one speaks of the pious, let them first mention Dhu ʾl-Nun!" He was a slim man with a light skin, whose beard was not white.

I heard Ahmad b. Muhammad say: I heard Saʿid b. ʿUthman say: I heard that Dhu ʾl-Nun said: "Everything hinges on four things: the love of the Glorious

---
15 On this renowned early mystic, see *IM*, pp. 39–42.
16 That is, he came from Nubia, Upper Egypt.
17 That is in 859 or 860 C.E.
18 That is, in Sufism.
19 A caliph of the ʿAbbasid dynasty from 232/847 to 247/861.

One, the hatred of the insufficient,[20] the observance of the revealed[21] and the fear of changing from one state to another."[22]

I heard Muhammad b. al-Husayn – may God have mercy on him – say: I heard Saʿid b. Ahmad b. Jaʿfar say: I heard Muhammad b. Ahmad b. Sahl say: I heard Saʿid b. ʿUthman say: I heard Dhu ʾl-Nun say: "One of the signs of the lover of God is his following in the footsteps of God's beloved[23] – may God bless and greet him – in his character traits, his deeds, his precepts and his customs."//34

Someone asked Dhu ʾl-Nun about ignoble people. He answered: "Those who neither know the way to God, nor try to know it." I heard Abu ʿAbd al-Rahman al-Sulami – may God have mercy on him – say: I heard Abu Bakr b. Muhammad b. ʿAbdallah b. Shadhan say: I heard Yusuf b. al-Husayn say: "One day I was at Dhu ʾl-Nun's teaching session. There came to him Salim al-Maghribi and asked him: ʿAbu ʾl-Fayd, what was the cause of your repentance?'[24] He answered: 'It was something really wonderful that you cannot imitate.' [Salim] said: 'For the sake of God, tell me about it!' Dhu ʾl-Nun said: 'I wanted to go from [old] Cairo[25] to a village in the countryside. I fell asleep in the desert, and when I opened my eyes I saw a small blind fledgling that fell from its nest onto the ground. [Suddenly] the earth cleft and there appeared [from the crack] two food bowls, one silver and the other gold. In one there were sesame seeds, in the other water. The fledgling ate from one bowl and drank from the other. I cried out: "This is enough for me. I have repented!" And I was waiting at God's door until He [agreed to] receive me.'"

I heard Muhammad b. al-Husayn say: I heard ʿAli b. al-Hafiz say: I heard Ibn Rashiq say: I heard Abu Dujana say: I heard Dhu ʾl-Nun say: "Wisdom does not live in a stomach filled with food." Someone asked Dhu ʾl-Nun about repentance. He answered: "The common people repent from [their] sins, whereas [God's] elect people repent from neglectfulness."//35

Abu ʿAli al-Fudayl b. ʿIyad[26]

He came from Khurasan, from the region of Marw.[27] It is said that he was born in Samarkand and grew up at Abiward. He died in Mecca in the month of Muharram, in the year 187.[28] I heard Muhammad b. al-Husayn say: Abu Bakr

---

20 According to some commentators, the insufficient here refers to "this life and its attractions".
21 That is, the Divine Law.
22 According to commentators, this means change from a virtuous state to a less perfect one.
23 That is, the prophet Muhammad.
24 The Sufi path usually begins with repentance.
25 At that time the city of Cairo did not yet exist. It was founded in 359/970 by the Fatimid ruler al-Muʿizz. In Dhu ʾl-Nun's time the capital of Egypt was located at Fustat (old Cairo).
26 A famous early ascetic. See *IM*, pp. 23–24.
27 In the present day Republic of Turkmenistan.
28 That is, in 803 C.E.

Muhammad b. Ja'far told us: al-Hasan b. 'Abdallah al-'Askari told us: the son of Abu Zur'a's brother told us: Muhammad b. Ishaq b. Rahuya (Rahawayh) told us: Abu 'Ammar told us on the authority of al-Fudayl b. Musa that al-Fudayl [b. 'Iyad] was a dangerous young lad, who robbed caravans between Abiward and Sarakhs.[29] The reason for his repentance was the following. He fell in love with a slave girl and, as he was climbing up the wall in order to meet her, he heard a Qur'an reader reciting "Isn't it time that the hearts of those who believe should be humbled to the remembrance of God?"[30] And he said: "O my Lord, it is indeed the time!" and turned back. The night brought him to some ruins. There was a group of people there. Some of them said: "Let's go." Others said: "Let's wait until dawn, for al-Fudayl is on the road and may rob us." [On hearing this] al-Fudayl repented and took them under his protection. [Later] he settled down in the Holy City[31] and died there.

Al-Fudayl said: "When God loves [His] servant, he bestows on him much grief, and when He hates [His] servant, He grants him abundance in this world." Ibn al-Mubarak[32] said: "When al-Fudayl died, sorrow departed [with him]."//36 Al-Fudayl said: "If this world with all that is in it were offered to me and I were not held responsible for enjoying it, I would still turn away from it in disgust, as you would turn away from a decaying corpse, while passing it by, in order not to smear your clothes with it." Al-Fudayl said: "I would rather swear that I am a hypocrite than that I am not a hypocrite." Al-Fudayl said: "Not to act for the sake of others is hypocrisy, while to act for the sake of others is polytheism."

Abu 'Ali al-Razi said: "I accompanied al-Fudayl for thirty years without ever seeing him laughing or smiling, except for the day when his son 'Ali died. I asked him about this. He said: 'If God loves something, I love it too." Al-Fudayl said: "Whenever I disobey God, I know this from the behavior of my donkey and my servant."[33]

Abu Mahfuz Ma'ruf b. Fayruz al-Karkhi[34]

He was a great master whose prayers were answered [by God] and whose grave was [a source] of healing. The inhabitants of Baghdad say that the grave of Ma'ruf is a proven panacea.//37 He was a client of [the imam] 'Ali b. Musa al-Rida[35] and died in the year 200, though some say that he died in 201.[36] He was

---

29 Cities in Khurasan, Iran.
30 Q. 57:16.
31 That is, Mecca.
32 A famous warrior ascetic from the Arab–Byzantine frontier. He died in 181/797; see *IM*, pp. 21–22.
33 That is, God protects him by sending him a warning through them.
34 An early ascetic of Baghdad who died in 200/815. See *IM*, pp. 48–49.
35 The eighth imam of the Shi'ites who died in 203/818.
36 816 C.E.

a teacher of Sari al-Saqati.[37] One day he told [al-Saqati]: "When you need something from God, call upon Him by my name!"

I heard my teacher Abu 'Ali al-Daqqaq – may God have mercy on him – say that Ma'ruf's parents were Christians. While still a child, they entrusted Ma'ruf to their teacher, who used to tell him: "He [God] is the third of the three", to which Ma'ruf always replied: "No, He is one." One day the teacher gave him a severe beating and Ma'ruf ran away. His parents said: "Should he return to us with any religion he wants, we would then join him in it!" Later, he embraced Islam at the hands of [the imam] 'Ali b. Musa al-Rida[38] and returned to his house. He knocked on the door. [His parents] asked: "Who is at the door?" He answered: "Ma'ruf." They asked him: "What is your religion?" He said: "[This is] a monotheistic (*hanafi*) religion." So his parents became Muslims too.

I heard Muhammad b. al-Husayn say: I heard Abu Bakr al-Razi say: I heard Abu Bakr al-Harbi say: I heard Sari al-Saqati[39] say: "I saw in a dream that Ma'ruf was standing under [God's] throne. God – may He be great and exalted – said to His angels: 'Who is this?' They answered: 'You know best, O Lord!' God then said: "This is Ma'ruf al-Karkhi. He is drunk with the love of Me and will regain his full consciousness only after meeting Me!'"

Ma'ruf said: "One of the companions of Dawud al-Ta'i[40] told me: 'Beware of abandoning [good] works, for they bring you near to your Lord's satisfaction.'" I asked: "What are these works?" Dawud al-Ta'i answered: "Obedience to your Lord, rendering service to the Muslims and advising them." I heard Muhammad b. al-Husayn say: I heard Muhammad b. 'Abdallah al-Razi say//38: I heard 'Ali b. Muhammad al-Dallal say: I heard Muhammad b. al-Husayn say: I heard that my father said: "I saw Ma'ruf in a dream after his death. I asked him: 'What did God do to you?' He answered: 'He pardoned me.' I asked him: 'Was this due to your self-renunciation and fear of God?' He said: 'No, this was due to my following the admonition of Ibn al-Sammak[41]: to practice poverty and to love the poor.'"[42] Regarding the admonition of Ibn al-Sammak, Ma'ruf recounted the following: "Once I came to Kufa.[43] There I met a man by the name Ibn al-Sammak, who was preaching to the people. He said in his speech: 'He who turns away from God completely, God too will turn away from him once and for all. And he who will turn to God with his heart, God will turn to him with His mercy and make the faces of all creatures turn toward him. As for him who at one time turns to God and at another forgets Him, God will still show mercy to him at some point in time.' His words sank deeply into my heart. I turned to God

---

37 A famous Baghdad Sufi and uncle of al-Junayd, who died in 253/867. See *IM*, pp. 50–52.
38 The eighth imam (spiritual leader) of the Twelver Shi'ites; died in 203/818.
39 For him, see the next entry.
40 On him see pages 29–30.
41 A popular ascetic and preacher of Kufa who died around 183/800.
42 That is, ascetics and Sufis.
43 A city in Iraq that was famous as a major center of Islamic learning.

– may He be exalted – and abandoned everything I had been doing, except my service of my master ʿAli b. Musa al-Rida.[44] I mentioned these words[45] to my master. He responded: 'This admonition is sufficient for you, should you decide to preach on your own.'" This story was related to me by Muhammad b. al-Husayn, who said: I heard ʿAbd al-Rahim b. ʿAli al-Hafiz say in Baghdad: I heard Muhammad b. ʿUmar b. al-Fadl say: I heard ʿAli b. ʿIsa say: I heard Sari al-Saqati say: I heard how Maʿruf recounted this [story].

On his death bed Maʿruf was asked for a final piece of advice. He said: 'When I die, give away my shirt as alms, for I want to leave this world naked as I came into it."

One day Maʿruf was passing by a water-carrier, who was saying: "May God have mercy on him who drinks." Although Maʿruf was fasting at that time, he came up to the water-carrier and drank." Someone asked him: "Weren't you fasting?" He answered: "Yes, but I hoped to obtain His blessing."//39

Abu ʾl-Hasan [al-]Sari b. al-Mughallis al-Saqati[46]

He was al-Junayd's maternal uncle and teacher and a disciple of Maʿruf al-Karkhi. He was unique in his age as regards pious scrupulosity and the knowledge of the Prophet's custom and divine oneness. I heard Muhammad b. al-Husayn say: I heard ʿAbdallah b. ʿAli al-Tusi say: I heard Abu ʿAmr b. ʿAlwan say: I heard Abu ʾl-ʿAbbas b. Masruq[47] say: "I heard that Sari al-Saqati was plying his trade at the bazaar, while he was a companion of Maʿruf al-Karkhi. Once Maʿruf came to him with an orphan boy. He said [to Sari]: 'Clothe this orphan!' Sari said: 'I clothed him.' Maʿruf rejoiced at this and said: 'May God make this world hateful to you and relieve you of your trade!' So I left my shop and [since that time] there is nothing more hateful to me than this world and all that I have now comes to me through Maʿruf's blessings." I heard Shaykh Abu ʿAbd al-Rahman al-Sulami – may God have mercy on him – say: I heard Abu Bakr al-Razi say: I heard Abu ʿUmar al-Anmati say: I heard al-Junayd say: "I have never seen anyone more devoted to God than al-Sari. I visited him for ninety-eight years without ever seeing him lying down, except when he was on his death bed." It is told that al-Sari said: "Sufism is a name for three things://40 [The Sufi] is the one in whom the light of knowledge does not extinguish the light of scrupulosity. In his inner self he does not speak of any knowledge contradicting the external meaning of the [Holy] Book or the Prophet's custom. [His] miracles do not cause him to violate the sacredness of the divine prohibitions."

---

44 See note 35.
45 That is, those of Ibn al-Sammak.
46 See *IM*, pp. 50–52.
47 On him see page 54.

Al-Sari died in the year 257.⁴⁸ I heard that the master Abu ʿAli al-Daqqaq recounted the following on the authority of al-Junayd – may God have mercy on him. [Al-Junayd] said: "Once al-Sari asked me about the love of God. I answered: 'Some people say that it is compliance [with God's commands]; others that it is giving preference to others over yourself; still others says that it is so and so …' Al-Sari pinched the skin of his elbow and tried to stretch it, but it would not stretch. He then said: 'By God's greatness, if I say that this skin has dried up on the bone due to [my] love of Him, that would be the truth.' He then swooned and his face became round as if it were a radiant moon, though al-Sari was of a pale complexion."

It is related that al-Sari once said: "For thirty years I have regretted that I once said: 'Praise be to God!' Someone asked him how this could be. He answered: 'Once there was a fire in Baghdad. I came across a man who told me that my shop had survived the fire, to which I said: 'Praise be to God!' For thirty years now I have had regrets about having said this, because I wished for myself a better lot than that which had befallen my fellow Muslims." ʿAbdallah b. Yusuf told me: I heard Abu Bakr al-Razi say: I heard Abu Bakr al-Harbi say: I heard al-Sari say that.

It is related about al-Sari that he said: "I am squinting at my nose so many times during the day, because I am afraid that [my face] has become black – that is, that God has blackened my complexion [as a punishment] for what I have done."

I heard Muhammad b. al-Husayn – may God have mercy on him – say: I heard Muhammad b. al-Hasan b. al-Khashshab say: I heard Jaʿfar b. Muhammad b. Nusayr⁴⁹ say: I heard al-Junayd say: I heard al-Sari say: "I know the shortest path leading to Paradise."//41 I asked him what it was. He answered: "Don't take anything from anyone, don't seek anything from anyone and don't possess anything which you would give to anyone."

I heard ʿAbdallah b. Yusuf al-Isbahani say: I heard Abu Nasr al-Sarraj al-Tusi⁵⁰ say: I heard Jaʿfar b. Muhammad b. Nusayr⁵¹ say: I heard al-Junayd b. Muhammad say: I heard al-Sari say: "I wish I could die in a land other than Baghdad." Someone asked him why. He answered: "I am afraid that my grave would not accept me and I would thus be disgraced." I heard ʿAbdallah b. Yusuf al-Isfahani say: I heard Abu ʾl-Hasan b. ʿAbdallah al-Fuwati al-Tarsusi say: I heard al-Junayd say: I heard al-Sari say: "O my God, punish me with whatever as You wish, but do not punish me with the humiliation of the veil!"⁵²

---

48 His date of death varies from one source to another, but most authors agree that he died between 251/865 and 258/871.
49 That is, Jaʿfar al-Khuldi (348/959), a famous Sufi biographer of the Baghdad school.
50 A famous Sufi writer, who died in 378/988. See *IM*, pp. 118–120.
51 See note 49.
52 According to a popular Sufi *hadith*, God's face is hidden behind numerous veils, which He removes one by one as His mystical lover draws ever near Him. See Chittick, *Self-Disclosure of God*, pp. 104–163 and "Index" under "veil".

I heard ʿAbdallah b. Yusuf al-Isfahani say: I heard Abu Bakr al-Razi say: I heard al-Jurayri say: I heard al-Junayd say: "Once I came to visit al-Sari al-Saqati and found him crying. I asked him: 'What made you cry?' He answered: 'Yesterday, my daughter came to me and said: This is a hot night, therefore I will hang this [water-cooling] pitcher here. Then I closed my eyes and fell asleep. In my dream I saw a most beautiful slave girl who had descended from heaven. I asked to whom she belonged. She said that she would belong to whoever did not drink the water that was cooled in a pitcher. I then grabbed the pitcher and smashed it to pieces against the ground.'"

Al-Junayd said: "I [indeed] saw pieces of broken earthenware that he never picked up or touched, until it was completely covered with dust."//42

Abu Nasr Bishr b. al-Harith al-Hafi (the Barefoot)[53]

He came from [the city of] Marw.[54] He lived in Baghdad, where he died. He was a son of ʿAli b. Khashram's sister. He died in the year 227 [842]. He was a man of great stature. The following [episode] became the reason for his repentance.[55] He found on the road a small piece of paper upon which was written the name of God – may He be great and exalted. This sheet was trampled upon [by passers-by]. He picked it up, purchased a *dirham*-worth of perfume, sprinkled the sheet with it and put it in the crack of a wall. Then he saw in a dream as if someone told him: "O Bishr, you perfumed My name and I will perfume yours in this world and the next one!"

I heard Master Abu ʿAli al-Daqqaq – may God have mercy on him – say: "Bishr was passing by a group of people who said: 'This man does not sleep all night and he breaks his fast only once in three days.' On hearing this, Bishr began to cry. When someone asked him why, he said: 'Verily, I do not remember ever saying that I keep vigil during the whole night. Nor have I said that after fasting during the day I do not break my fast at night. However, God, in His kindness and graciousness, has revealed to the hearts [of the people] more than His servant actually does – may He be blessed!' He then proceeded to describe the beginning of the affair,[56] as we have just mentioned."

I heard Shaykh Abu ʿAbd al-Rahman al-Sulami say: I heard Muhammad b. ʿAbdallah al-Razi say: I heard ʿAbd al-Rahman b. Abi Hatim say: I came to know that Bishr b. al-Harith al-Hafi said: "In a dream I saw the Prophet – may peace and blessings be upon him! He asked me: 'Bishr, do you know why God has raised you above your contemporaries?' I said: 'I do not, Messenger of God.' He said: '[It is due to] your following of my custom, your service to the righteous, your admonition of your brothers [in faith] and your love of my Companions

---

53 On him see *IM*, pp. 49–50.
54 An ancient city in present-day Turkmenistan.
55 The journey on the mystical path usually begins with repentance.
56 That is, his conversion to Sufism.

and my family. This is what brought you to the stations of the most pious men!'"

I heard Muhammad b. al-Husayn – may God have mercy on him – say: I heard Muhammad b. ʿAbdallah al-Razi say: I heard Bilal al-Khawwas say: "As I was traveling across the desert of the Israelites,[57] I suddenly saw a man walking by my side. At first I was surprised, but then I came to realize that that was al-Khadir[58] – peace be upon him. I asked him: 'By God, who are you?' He answered: 'Your brother al-Khadir!' I told him that I had a question for him. He said: 'Ask!' 'What do you say about al-Shafiʿi[59] – may God have mercy on him?' He answered: 'He was a [spiritual] peg.'[60] I then asked him: 'What would you say about Ahmad b. Hanbal?'[61] He answered: 'He was a veracious man.'[62] 'And what would you say about Bishr al-Hafi?' He answered: 'After him there was no one like him.'[63] I asked him: 'Owing to what was I able to see you?' He answered: 'Owing to your pious behavior toward your mother.'"

I heard Master Abu ʿAli al-Daqqaq – may God have mercy on him – say: "Once Bishr al-Hafi came to Muʿafa b. ʿImran[64] and knocked on his door. He was asked who it was and he said: 'Bishr al-Hafi (the Barefoot).' Then a young girl told him from behind the door: 'If you were to buy yourself a pair of sandals for a couple of *daniqs*,[65] you would lose your name.'" Muhammad b. ʿAbdallah al-Shirazi reported this story to me. He said: ʿAbd al-ʿAziz b. al-Fadl told me: Muhammad b. Saʿid told me: Muhammad b. ʿAbdallah told me: He said that he heard ʿAbdallah al-Maghazili say that he heard Bishr al-Hafi mention this story. I heard Muhammad b. al-Husayn say: I heard Abu ʾl-Husayn al-Hajjaji//44 say: I heard al-Mahamili say: I heard al-Hasan al-Masuhi say: I heard Bishr al-Harith telling this story.

I heard Muhammad b. al-Husayn say: I heard Abu ʾl-Fadl al-ʿAttar say: I heard Ahmad b. ʿAli al-Dimashqi say: Abu ʿAbdallah b. al-Jallaʾ[66] told me: "I saw

---

57 Probably the Sinai desert.
58 On this legendary personage (usually identified with Moses' mysterious companion in Q. 18:59–81), whom the Sufis consider their holy patron, see the article "al-Khadir" in *EI*.
59 A great jurist and the founder of one of the four Sunni legal schools. See the article "al-Shafiʿi" in *EI*.
60 That is, a member of the invisible hierarchy of the saints who are the real rulers of the universe. The peg (*watad*) is a high, although not the highest, rank in this saintly hierarchy. His name indicates that his function is to keep the universe stable.
61 Another great Sunni scholar, the founder of the Hanbali school of jurisprudence. On him see the article "Ahmad b. Hanbal" in *EI*.
62 *Siddiq* (lit. "faithful", "truthful" or "just"); in the Sufi tradition this Qurʾanic term (Q. 4:71) denotes an advanced rank of sainthood. Cf. Al-Sarraj, *Al-lumaʿ*, p. 72.
63 That is, no one better than him.
64 Al-Muʿafa b. ʿImran b. Nufayl al-Azdi al-Mawsili (d. between 184 and 186/800–802), a famous ascetic of Baghdad.
65 Also *danaq*, a small copper coin worth one-sixth of a *dirham*.
66 On him see page 47.

Dhu ʾl-Nun,⁶⁷ who was famous for his clear expression.⁶⁸ I saw Sahl,⁶⁹ who was famous for his allegorical allusion. I saw Bishr al-Hafi, who was famous for his scrupulousness.⁷⁰ Someone asked him: 'To whom of them are you more inclined?' He said: 'To my teacher, Bishr b. al-Harith.'" It is said that for many years he craved beans, but he [never permitted himself to] eat them. Someone saw him in a dream after he⁷¹ had died and asked him how God treated him. He [Bishr] answered: "[God] pardoned me and said: 'Eat, O you who have not eaten! Drink, O you who have not drunk!'"

Shaykh Abu ʿAbd al-Rahman al-Sulami – may God have mercy on him – told me: ʿUbaydallah b. ʿUthman b. Yahya told me: Abu ʿAmr b. al-Sammak told me: Muhammad b. al-ʿAbbas told me: Abu Bakr b. Bint Muʿawiyya said: I heard that Abu Bakr b. ʿAffan said: I heard Bishr b. al-Harith say: "For forty years I was craving roasted meat, yet I never could afford its price due to the lack of untainted money."⁷²

Someone asked Bishr what he was eating his bread with. He answered: "I think of salvation⁷³ and make it my seasoning."⁷⁴ I was told about this by Muhammad b. al-Husayn – may God have mercy on him. He said ʿUbaydallah b. ʿUthman told: Abu ʿAmr b. al-Sammak related to us: ʿUmar b. Saʿid said: Ibn Abi al-Dunya related to us that a certain man said that this famous story [is indeed] about Bishr.

Bishr said: "That which is permitted tolerates no wastefulness."⁷⁵

Someone saw Bishr in a dream and asked him: "What did God do to you?" He answered: "He pardoned me and gave me a half of Paradise, then said: 'Bishr, even if you were to perform your [ritual] prostrations before Me on the burning coals, you would still be unable to repay Me for the [exalted] place that I allotted you in the hearts of My servants.'"

Bishr said: "A man who loves to be known to people will not taste the sweetness of the Hereafter."//45

Abu ʿAbdallah al-Harith al-Muhasibi⁷⁶

He was unique in his age in regard to [religious] knowledge, pious scrupulosity, acts of devotion and mystical states. He came from Basra and died in Baghdad in

---

67 A famous Sufi of Egypt; on him see pages 19–20.
68 ʿIbara, a clear, unambiguous expression or speech – as opposed to ishara, a mystical allusion, which is often ambiguous in order to conceal its true meaning from the uninitiated.
69 Sahl al-Tustari (d. 283/896), a famous Sufi of Basra; on him see Böwering, *Mystical Vision*, passim.
70 Waraʿ; a Sufi term denoting scrupulous discernment between what is permitted (under the shariʿa law) and what is prohibited.
71 Meaning Bishr.
72 That is, the money that he would consider to have been earned in a proper way.
73 Literally, "health" (al-ʿafiya), but here it probably means "health in the Hereafter".
74 That is, spices that enhance the taste of food.
75 That is, the permitted is rare and hard to come by.
76 On him see *IM*, pp. 43–48.

243.[77] It is said that he inherited from his father the sum of 70 thousand *dirhams*, but he did not take anything from it. It is said that this was because his father was an adherent of [the doctrine of] human free will[78] and he considered that it would be unscrupulous to take anything from his legacy. A sound report from the Prophet – may God bless and greet him – says: "People of two different religions do not inherit anything from one another."

I heard Muhammad b. al-Husayn say: al-Husayn b. Yahya said: Ja'far b. Muhammad b. Nusayr [al-Khuldi] said: I heard Muhammad b. Masruq say: "When al-Harith b. Asad al-Muhasibi died, he had not a single *dirham*. His father left him land and real estate, but he did not take anything from it." I heard that our master Abu 'Ali al-Daqqaq – may God have mercy on him – said: "Whenever al-Harith al-Muhasibi extended his hand to a suspicious food,[79] a vein in his finger would begin to move and he would abstain from it."

Abu 'Abdallah b. Khafif[80] said: "Follow the example of five of our masters and think well of the rest. They are: al-Harith al-Muhasibi, al-Junayd b. Muhammad, Abu Muhammad Ruwaym, Abu'l-'Abbas b. 'Ata' and 'Amr b. 'Uthman al-Makki. They combined knowledge[81] with [mystical] truths."

I heard Abu 'Abd al-Rahman al-Sulami – may God have mercy on him – say: I heard 'Abdallah b. 'Ali al-Tusi say: I heard Ja'far al-Khuldi say: I heard Abu 'Uthman al-Baladi say: al-Harith al-Muhasibi said: "He who has cleansed his inner self with self-observation and sincerity, God will embellish his external form with pious self-exertion and the following of [the Prophet's] Sunna."

It is related that al-Junayd said: "Once I saw al-Harith al-Muhasibi passing by. I noticed traces of hunger on his face.//46 I told him: 'Uncle, come into the house and have something to eat.' He agreed. I entered the house and searched for something to feed him with. At that time, there was in the house some food that was brought to me from a wedding party. So, I took this food and gave it to him. He took a morsel of the food and rolled it in his mouth [with the tongue] several times, then he stood up, threw it into the corridor, and left. When I saw him a few days later, I inquired about this. He answered: 'I was hungry and wanted to make you happy by eating your food. However, there is between me and God a [special] sign. He does not permit me to eat any suspicious food.[82] Therefore He did not allow me to swallow that food. Where did it come to you from?' I said that it was brought to the house of a relative of mine from a wedding party. I asked him whether he would come in today. He said that he

---

77 857 C.E.

78 That is, he taught that men, and not God, are the creators and performers of their acts. This was a thesis later advocated by the religious group known as the Mu'tazilites. See the article "Mu'tazila" in *EI*.

79 That is, the food that was considered to have been improperly obtained – e.g., provided by an unjust ruler.

80 A famous Sufi of Shiraz, who died in 371/982; on him see *IM*, "Index", under "Ibn Khafif".

81 Of the Divine Law.

82 That is, one that was improperly obtained.

would. I gave him a piece of dry bread that we happened to have. He ate it and said: 'If you want to give something to the poor one,[83] it should be something like this [piece of bread].'"

Abu Sulayman Dawud b. Nusayr al-Taʾi

He was a person of great importance. Shaykh Abu ʿAbd al-Rahman al-Sulami – may God have mercy on him – told me: Abu ʿAmr [b.] Matar told me: Muhammad b. Musayyib told me: Ibn Khubayq told me: Yusuf b. Sibat told me: "Dawud al-Taʾi inherited twenty *dinars* and he ate from them for twenty years." I heard our master Abu ʿAli al-Daqqaq – may God have mercy on him – say: "The cause of Dawud's conversion to asceticism was as follows. He used to wander the streets of Baghdad. Once he was passing through a street, when a group of the bodyguards [of Humayd al-Tusi] pushed him away from Humayd al-Tusi. When Dawud noticed Humayd, he said: 'Fie to the world in which Humayd takes precedence over you!'//47 So, he secluded himself in his house and began to practice ascetic austerities and perform acts of devotion."

Once I heard one of the poor[84] say in Baghdad that the cause of his conversion to asceticism was that he heard a bereft woman whining: "On which of your two cheeks have appeared the traces of decay? And which of your eyes has flowed out?"

It is also said that the reason for his conversion to asceticism was that he attended the circle of Abu Hanifa,[85] who told him once: "Abu Sulayman, we have already prepared the [required] equipment."[86] To which Dawud replied: "So what else is left?" Abu Hanifa answered: "[Only] works in accordance with it." So Dawud said: "My soul prompted me toward seclusion. I told her: 'As long as you sit with them,[87] you should not speak about any issue at all!' So for a whole year I was sitting with them, but I never spoke about any issue." Sometimes issues would dawn upon me and I would be as eager to discuss them as the thirsty man is eager to drink cold water, yet I would not talk." Thus he achieved what he achieved.

[Once] Junayd al-Hajjam (the Cupper) cupped Dawud al-Taʾi. The latter gave him a *dinar*. Someone told him that this was too much. He answered: "He who has no manliness[88] has no devotion [to God]." Also he used to say during his night [vigils]: "O my God, my concern for You has annihilated all other mundane concerns and now stands between me and [my] sleep."

---

83 That is, a Sufi.
84 That is, a Sufi.
85 Abu Hanifa al-Nuʿman (d. 150/767), a renowned scholar of Iraq who founded the Hanafi school of law.
86 That is, theoretical knowledge.
87 That is, Abu Hanifa and his followers.
88 *Muruʾa*; on this rather vague moral virtue see *EI* under "Muruʾa". One of its most important aspects is generosity.

I heard Muhammad b. ʿAbdallah al-Sufi say: Muhammad b. Yusuf told me: Saʿid b. ʿAmr told: ʿAli b. Harb al-Mawsili told me: Ismaʿil b. Ziyad al-Taʾi told me: "Dawud al-Taʾi's wetnurse told him: 'Don't you want to eat some bread?' He answered: 'Between the chewing of bread and eating a mess of crumbled bread lies the reading of fifty verses [from the Qurʾan].'"

On the day Dawud died, one of the righteous[89] saw him in a dream as he was running by. He asked him what happened to him. He answered: "I was just released from prison." When the man woke up from his dream, he heard people crying [in the street]: "Dawud al-Taʾi has died!"

Someone asked him for an admonition. He answered: "A soldier of death[90] awaits you!"//48.

Someone came to visit him in his house and saw a jug of water standing right under the sun. He asked him why he did not want to put it in the shade. He answered: "When I put it there, there was no sun, and [later] I was ashamed to show God that I want to walk for the sake of my soul's satisfaction."

Someone came to visit him in his house and started to stare at him. Dawud told him: "Don't you know that they[91] used to refrain from staring [at one another] as much as they refrained from excessive talk?"

ʿAbdallah b. Yusuf al-Isbahani told me: Abu Ishaq Ibrahim b. Muhammad b. Yahya al-Mazakki told me: Qasim b. Ahmad told me: I heard Maymun al-Ghazzal[92] say: I heard Abu ʾl-Rabiʿ al-Wasiti say: I asked Dawud al-Taʾi to admonish me. He said: "Fast in this world, break your fast on death and flee from people as if you are fleeing from wild beasts!"

Abu ʿAli Shaqiq b. Ibrahim al-Balkhi[93]

He was a Sufi master of Khurasan. He spoke a lot about trust in God (*tawakkul*) and was a teacher of Hatim al-Asamm.[94] It is said that the cause of his repentance was as follows. He was an offspring of a wealthy family. As a young man he set out on a journey to the land of Turks.[95] Once he entered a sanctuary of idols, where he saw a custodian of the idols. His head and beard were shaved and he was dressed in a purple robe. Shaqiq al-Balkhi told him: "You have the Creator who is living, All-Knowing and All-Powerful. Worship Him and not those idols who neither help nor harm you!" The custodian answered: "If this were so, then [the Creator] would be able to provide you with sustenance in your own country. Why then did you take pains to come here for trade?"//49 Shaqiq took heed and embarked on the path of world-renunciation.

---

89 That is, a Sufi.
90 In another reading, "the army of the dead".
91 Meaning the first Muslims.
92 In another reading, al-Ghazzali.
93 On him see *IM*, pp. 32–33.
94 See *IM*, pp. 33–34 and pages 36–37 in this book.
95 Probably Central Asia.

Some said that the cause of his conversion to asceticism was as follows. He saw a slave boy who was playing around and rejoicing during a famine, whereas all other people were afraid of it [famine]. Shaqiq asked him: "Where does your liveliness come from? Don't you see that people are suffering from dearth and hunger?" The slave boy said: "What is this to me? My master has a rich village that produces all that we need." Shaqiq took heed and said: "So, his master has a village, and his master is but a poor creature. And yet he [the slave boy] is not concerned about his livelihood. How then can a Muslim be concerned about his livelihood, when his master is so rich?!"

I heard Shaykh Abu ʿAbd al-Rahman al-Sulami – may God have mercy on him – say: I heard Abu ʾl-Husayn b. Ahmad al-ʿAttar al-Balkhi say: I heard Ahmad b. Muhammad al-Bukhari say: Hatim al-Asamm said: "Shaqiq b. Ibrahim was a wealthy man, who adhered to the ways of urban young men and kept company with them.[96] At that time, ʿAli b. ʿIsa b. Mahan was the ruler of Balkh.[97] He was fond of hunting dogs. One of his dogs got lost and it was reported that it was taken by Shaqiq's neighbor. [The ruler] demanded that the man be brought to him. The neighbor ran away, took refuge with Shaqiq and asked for his protection. Shaqiq came to the ruler and said: 'Let him go! The dog is with me and I will return it to you in three days.' They let the man go and Shaqiq went away worried by what he had done. On the third day, one of Shaqiq's friends who was away from Balkh returned there. On the way home he found a dog with a collar and took it with him. He said [to himself]: 'I shall give it to Shaqiq, because he engages in chivalrous behavior.' So he brought the dog to Shaqiq, who recognized in it the ruler's dog. He rejoiced at this and took the dog to the ruler and thus was freed of his obligation. [As a result,] he came to realize [his sinful condition], repented of it and embarked on the path of asceticism."

It is said that Hatim al-Asamm said: "I was fighting Turks side by side with Shaqiq on a day when one could see nothing but falling heads, broken spears and shattered swords. Shaqiq asked me: 'Hatim, how do you feel yourself on a day like this? Don't you feel as if it were the night on which you brought your newlywed wife to your house?'//50 I said: 'By God, no!' He said: 'And I do feel myself today as I did that night!' He then fell asleep in the middle of the battlefield, putting his shield under his head, and I even could hear him snore.'"

Shaqiq said: "If you want to know a man, consider what God has promised to him and what men have promised to him. Then consider to which of these promises his heart is more attached." Shaqiq also said: "Man's fear of God can be known from three things: from what he accepts, from what he rejects and from what he says."

---

96 Apparently, he belonged to the circle of the sons of the local urban elite, who cultivated a sort of camaraderie and chivalrous behavior, known as *futuwwa*. Sometimes such groups served as local militia.

97 A province in present-day Afghanistan.

Abu Yazid b. Tayfur b. ʿIsa al-Bastami[98]

His grandfather was a Zoroastrian who converted to Islam. He had three sons: Adam, Tayfur and ʿAli. All of them were devotees and ascetics. He [Abu Yazid] died in 261 [875], although some say 234 [848].

I heard Muhammad b. al-Husayn – may God have mercy on him – say: I heard Abu ʾl-Hasan al-Farisi say: I heard al-Hasan b. ʿAli say: Someone asked Abu Yazid how he acquired his knowledge [of God]. He answered: "By a hungry stomach and by a naked body." I heard Muhammad b. al-Husayn – may God have mercy on him – say: I heard Mansur b. ʿAbdallah say: I heard ʿAmmi al-Bastami[99] say: I heard my father[100] say: I heard Abu Yazid say: "I have engaged in spiritual struggle and ascetic exercises for thirty years and found that there is nothing harder for me than the knowledge [of the Divine Law] and adherence to it. And were it not for the disagreement of religious scholars, I would have remained where I was [at the beginning], for the disagreement of scholars is a [divine] blessing, except in one issue – that is, the understanding of God's uniqueness."//51 It is said that Abu Yazid did not depart from this world until he had committed to memory the whole of the Qurʾan.

Abu Hatim al-Sijistani informed me: Abu Nasr al-Sarraj told me: He said: I heard Tayfur al-Bastami say: I heard the person nicknamed ʿAmmi al-Bastami say: I heard my father say: Abu Yazid told me: "Let's go and see a man who is famous for his sainthood." And that person was indeed one who was often visited [on account of his sainthood] and was renowned for his asceticism. So we came to visit him. When that man left his house and entered the mosque, he spat in the direction of the *qibla*.[101] [On seeing this] Abu Yazid turned and went away without even greeting the man. He said: "This man cannot be trusted even as far as [the observance of] the manners of the Messenger of God – may God bless and greet him – are concerned! How can one trust his other claims?"

On the same authority as above it is told that Abu Yazid said: "Once I intended to ask God to save me the trouble of caring about food and women. Then I said [to myself] how can I ask God what the Messenger of God – may God bless and greet him – never [dared] to ask? So, I did not ask God [for that]. Then God – may He be blessed and exalted – protected me from the desire of women in such way that I no longer cared whether there was before me a woman or a wall."

I heard Shaykh Abu ʿAbd al-Rahman al-Sulami – may God have mercy on him – say: I heard al-Hasan b. ʿAli say: I heard ʿAmmi al-Bastami say: I heard my father say: "I asked Abu Yazid about his beginnings [as a Sufi] and about his asceticism. He answered: 'Asceticism has no rank.' I asked him how this could be. He answered: 'Because I was in the state of asceticism for three days and left

---

98 Or "al-Bistami" (both pronunciations are possible). On him see *IM*, pp. 68–72.
99 This is a nickname of a famous ascetic Abu ʿImran Musa b. ʿIsa b. Adam.
100 That is, ʿIsa b. Adam al-Bastami (al-Bistami).
101 That is, in the direction of Mecca, toward which the Muslims face during the prayer.

it on the fourth. On the first day I renounced this world and everything in it. On the second day I renounced the Hereafter and everything in it. On the third day I renounced everything other than God. And on the fourth day there was left nothing for me but God alone. So I fell into an ecstasy and I heard a voice telling me: "[When you are] with me, you have no power [of your own]." I cried: "This is exactly what I want!" Then I heard someone say: "You have found [it], you have found [it]!"'"

Someone asked Abu Yazid: "What is the most difficult thing you have ever encountered on your way to God?" He answered: "It is impossible to describe it." Someone then asked him: "What, then, was the easiest thing that you subjected your soul to?" He said: "As for this, yes. I called upon her [the soul] to obey God and she refused. Then I denied her water for one year."

Abu Yazid said: "For thirty years I have been praying. And each time I prayed I felt in my inner self as if I was a Zoroastrian who sought to cut his girdle."[102] I heard Muhammad b. al-Husayn – may God have mercy on him – say: I heard ʿAbdallah b. ʿAli say: I heard Musa b. ʿIsa say: My father told me that Abu Yazid once said: "When you see a man who is endowed with miracles to such an extent that he can sit on the air, do not be deluded by him until you have tested his [attitude toward] what is permitted and what is prohibited, his observance of the legal rules and of the Divine Law."

ʿAmmi al-Bastami (al-Bistami) said on the authority of his father: "One night, Abu Yazid went to a hospice[103] in order to recollect God's name[104] on one of the walls of that hospice. He stayed there until dawn without uttering a word. I asked him about this and he answered: "[While there], there had passed through my mind a [rude] word that I once uttered in my childhood, and I was ashamed to mention God – may He be blessed and exalted."

Abu Muhammad Sahl b. ʿAbdallah al-Tustari[105]

He was one of the greatest Sufi masters. He had no peers in his age in regard to devotional acts and pious scrupulosity. He performed many miracles. He met Dhu ʾl-Nun [al-Misri] during the year when he came [to Mecca] on a pilgrimage. It is said that he died in the year 283, although some say that it was in 273.[106]

Sahl said: "When I was three years old, I used to stay awake during the night watching my uncle Muhammad b. Sawwar perform his prayers. He kept vigil during the night. He used to tell me: 'Go away, Sahl, and have a sleep. You are distracting me!'"

---

102 Non-Muslims living under Muslim jurisdiction were required to wear "a girdle of unbelief" as sign of their affiliation with a non-Muslim community.
103 *Ribat*. This term may also denote a Sufi retreat.
104 *Dhikr*, literally "remembrance" or "recollection" [of God], a common spiritual practice among the Sufis. See *IM*, pp. 317–322.
105 On him see *IM*, pp. 83–87 and Böwering, *Mystical Vision*.
106 That is, 896 and 886 C.E.

I heard Muhammad b. al-Husayn – may God have mercy on him – say: I heard that Abu ʾl-Fath Yusuf b. ʿUmar the Ascetic said: I heard that ʿAbdallah b. ʿAbd al-Hamid said: I heard that ʿUbaydallah b. Luʾluʾ said: I heard that ʿUmar b. Wasil al-Basri recounted about Sahl b. ʿAbdallah that he told him: "One day my uncle asked me: 'Don't you remember God, Who created you?' I asked him: 'How can I remember Him?' He said: 'Say by your heart as you move around in your clothes, without however moving your tongue: "God is my watcher."' I said this for three nights, then I told him about this and he said to me: 'Say this seven times during the night.' I said this, then told him about this. He said to me: 'Say this eleven times during the night.' I said this and I felt the sweetness of this in my heart.//53 After one year my uncle told me: 'Keep on [doing] what I taught you and continue to do this until you enter your grave, for this will benefit you in this world and in the Hereafter.' I kept doing this for many years and I felt the sweetness of this in my innermost heart. One day my uncle told me: 'Sahl, how can a man with whom God is always present and whom He always watches and observes commit a sin? So, stay away from sin!'

"I used to seclude myself [from people]. Then [my parents] sent me to a Qurʾanic school. I told [them]: 'I fear that my internal concentration [on God] might dissipate. Make arrangements with the teacher so that I would come to him for a short while, study with him, and then come back.' So I began to go to the school. I learned the Qurʾan by heart when I was six or seven years old. I was fasting constantly and ate nothing but barley bread until I turned twelve years of age. When I turned thirteen, I came across a problem and asked my family to send me to Basra, so that I could inquire about it. I arrived in Basra and began to ask local scholars about it. However, none of them was able to satisfy me. Then I left for ʿAbbadan[107] in order to meet a man known as Abu Habib Hamza b. ʿAbdallah al-ʿAbbadani. I asked him about this problem and he answered me. I stayed with him for a while benefiting from his teaching and imitating his good manners. Then I returned to Tustar.[108] There my only meal consisted of a sack of barley that one could buy for one *dirham*, which I ground and from which I made bread for myself. Every night, before dawn, I ate of this just one ounce[109] without salt or seasoning. Thus one *dirham* was enough for me for a whole year. I decided to fast for three nights and to break my fast on the fourth, then on the fifth, then on the seventh, then on the fifteenth. In this way I spent twenty years, whereupon I began to roam the land until I again returned to Tustar. There I used to stay awake all night."

I heard Muhammad b. al-Husayn say: I heard Abu ʾl-ʿAbbas al-Baghdadi say: I heard Ibrahim b. Firas say: I heard Nasr b. Ahmad say: Sahl b. ʿAbdallah [al-Tustari] said: "Every deed that the servant [of God] performs without

---

107 An island in the mouth of Shatt al-ʿArab that was frequented by early Sufis and ascetics. See *IM*, pp. 17–18.
108 That is, his native town in Iran.
109 That is, around 33 grams.

imitation,[110] be it obedience [to God] or disobedience, is done to please his own self, whereas every deed//54 that he performs in imitation [of the Prophet or his companions] is painful to the soul."

Abu Sulayman ʿAbd al-Rahman b. ʿAtiyya al-Darani[111]

Daran is a village near Damascus. He died in the year 215.[112]

I heard Muhammad b. al-Husayn say: I heard ʿAbdallah b. Muhammad al-Razi say: Ishaq b. Ibrahim b. Abi Hassan told me: I heard Ahmad b. Abi ʾl-Hawari say: I heard Abu Sulayman say: "He who is doing good during the day, will be rewarded during the night; and he who is doing good during the night, will be rewarded during the day. He who has relinquished his [carnal] desire, God will remove it from his heart, for God – Most High – is too noble to torment the heart with [carnal] desire after it has relinquished it for His sake." According to the same chain of transmission, he also said: "When [desire for] this life settles down in the heart, [desire for] the Hereafter departs from it."

I heard Shaykh Abu ʿAbd al-Rahman al-Sulami – may God have mercy on him – say: I heard al-Husayn b. Yahya say: I heard Jaʿfar b. Muhammad b. Nusayr [al-Khuldi] say: I heard al-Junayd say: Abu Sulayman al-Darani said: "Whenever a word of spiritual wisdom enters my heart, I would not accept it unless it [is confirmed] by two just witnesses, the [Holy] Book and the [Prophet's] Custom." Abu Sulayman said: "The noblest of all deeds is to oppose the lusts of the soul." He said: "Each thing has its sign; the sign of forgetfulness [of God] is when one stops crying." He said: "Each thing has its own rust; the rust on the heart's light is when one's belly is full."

He said: "Whatever distracts you from God Most High – be it wealth or a child – brings you misfortune."

Abu Sulayman also said: "One cold night I was praying in front of a *mihrab*.[113] Cold began to bother me, and I hid one hand//55 from cold, while leaving the other one exposed. Then sleep overcame me and I heard a voice: ʿAbu Sulayman, we have already bestowed upon this one what it deserves. If only there were the other one, so that we could do the same to it!' I then swore to myself that I would never pray without exposing both hands, whether it is cold or warm."

Abu Sulayman said: "Once I overslept my personal prayer.[114] All of sudden I saw a maiden of paradise who said to me: 'You sleep, while I am being prepared for you in the female chamber for five hundred years!'"

---

110 That is, without imitating the actions of the Prophet or an earlier Muslim authority.
111 On him see *IM*, pp. 36–38.
112 That is, 830 C.E.
113 A recess in the wall of the mosque that points toward Mecca, indicating the direction of the prayer.
114 That is, a private, non-canonical prayer.

ʿAbdallah b. Yusuf al-Isbahani told me: Abu ʿAmr al-Jawlasti told me: Muhammad b. Ismaʿil told me: Ahmad b. Abi ʾl-Hawari told me: "Once I came to visit Abu Sulayman and saw him crying. I asked him why he was crying. He said: 'Ahmad, how can I not cry? When the night comes, and the eyes close [for sleep], and each lover secludes himself with his beloved, and the lovers of God sit on their feet [in prayer?], and their tears begin to run from their cheeks down onto the floor of the mosque, the Glorious One – may He be blessed and exalted – looks down and calls out: "Gabriel, before My eyes are those who take delight in my words[115] and who find consolation in My remembrance. I am watching them in their seclusion, I am hearing their sighs, and I am seeing their tears. Why don't you, Gabriel, call upon them and say: 'What is with all this crying?' Have you ever seen a beloved who torments his lovers? Or would it be proper for me to punish people who are full of humble adoration for me? I swear by Myself, when they come before Me on the Day of Resurrection, I will unveil before them My Noble Face, so that they would look at Me and I at them!"'"

Abu ʿAbd al-Rahman Hatim b. ʿUnwan[116]

Some say that his name was Hatim b. Yusuf al-Asamm.[117] He was a great Sufi master of Khurasan.//56 He was a disciple of Shaqiq [al-Balkhi] and a teacher of Ahmad b. Khadrawayh.[118] People say that he was not deaf and that he only feigned deafness once. Hence this nickname.

I heard that my master Abu ʿAli al-Daqqaq – may God have mercy on him – said that [once] a woman came to Hatim and asked him a question. It so happened that as she was with him there came from her an [indecent] noise. She was ashamed of this. Hatim then told her: "Speak louder!" and put on a show of deafness. The woman was very relieved and said [to herself] that he must have not heard the noise. Since then, he came to be known as "The Deaf".

Shaykh Abu ʿAbd al-Rahman al-Sulami – may God have mercy on him – said: I heard Abu ʿAli Saʿid b. Ahmad say: I heard my father say: I heard my uncle Muhammad b. al-Layth say: I heard Hamid al-Laffaf say: I heard Hatim al-Asamm say: "Not a single morning passes without Satan asking me: 'What will you eat [today]?', 'What will you wear?', and 'Where will you live?' I answer him: 'I shall eat death; I shall wear a shroud; and I shall live in a grave.'"

According to the same chain of transmission, he was once asked: "Don't you desire [anything]?" He answered: "All I desire is that I live from morning to evening in good health." Someone asked him: "[Does this mean] that not all of your days are healthy?" He answered: "My day is healthy, when I do not disobey God during it."

---

115 That is, by reciting the Qurʾan.
116 According to an alternative reading, his father's name was ʿUlwan.
117 His last name means "the Deaf". For him see *IM*, p. 33.
118 Or Khidruya; his biography is mentioned on page 38.

It is told that Hatim al-Asamm said: "When I took part in a military expedition, a Turk seized me, threw me on the ground and was about to slaughter me. However, I had no concern for him. I was lying there and waiting for what God Most High had in store for me. As he was groping for his knife, he was hit by a stray arrow that killed him. I pushed him off and stood up."

I heard 'Abdallah b. Yusuf al-Isbahani say: I heard that Abu Nasr Mansur b. Muhammad b. Ibrahim the Jurist said: I heard Abu Muhammad Ja'far b. Muhammad b. Nusayr say: It is told that Hatim said: "Whoever wants to follow our path must adopt four types of death: a white death, that is hunger; a black death, that is to tolerate torments from people; a red death, that is to oppose the urges of the soul in full sincerity; a green death, that is to put one patch upon the other over and over again."

Abu Zakariya Yahya b. Mu'adh al-Razi, the Preacher[119]

He was unique in his time. He was particularly known for his teaching about hope[120] and his doctrine of [mystical] gnosis. He arrived in Balkh, stayed there for some time, then returned to Nishapur,[121] where he died in 258.[122]

I heard Muhammad b. al-Husayn say: I heard 'Ubaydallah b. Muhammad b. Ahmad b. Hamdan al-'Ukbari say: I heard Ahmad b. Muhammad b. al-Sari say: I heard Ahmad b. 'Isa say: I heard Yahya b. Mu'adh say: "How can one be an ascetic, if one has no scrupulosity? At first you must reject [out of scrupulousness] that which is not yours, then renounce [out of asceticism] what is yours." According to the same chain of transmission, he also said: "The hunger of the penitents is a test; the hunger of the ascetics is [self-]restraint; the hunger of the veracious ones is a gift [from God]."[123]

Yahya said: "Forgetfulness[124] is worse than death, because neglectfulness cuts one off from God, while death cuts one off from creatures." Yahya said: "Asceticism [consists of] three things: need, seclusion, and hunger." Yahya said: "The best thing that you can do to your soul is to keep it busy in every moment by that which is better for her."

It is related that, in Balkh, Yahya b. Mu'adh preached that wealth is better [for man] than poverty. Someone gave him thirty thousand *dirhams*. One of the [Sufi] masters said: "May God bless not this money for him." Then Yahya left for Nishapur. [En route] he was stopped by a thief, who robbed him of all his money.

'Abdallah b. Yusuf al-Isbahani informed me: Abu 'l-Qasim 'Abdallah b. al-Husayn b. Baluya the Sufi related to me: I heard Muhammad b. 'Abdallah

---

119 On him see *IM*, pp. 92–94.
120 On this Sufi concept see the section on Sufi terminology (pp. 148–155).
121 A city in Khurasan, Iran.
122 That is, 872 C.E.
123 That is, it comes to them without effort through God's grace.
124 That is, neglect of God's commands and prescriptions.

al-Razi say: I heard al-Husayn b. ʿAluya say://58 I heard Yahya b. Muʿadh al-Razi say: "When someone betrays God in secret, God will expose his true self to everyone."

I heard that ʿAbdallah b. Yusuf said: I heard that Muhammad b. ʿAbd al-ʿAziz the Muezzin said: I heard that Muhammad b. Muhammad al-Jurjani said: I heard that ʿAli b. Muhammad said: I heard that Yahya b. Muʿadh said: "When the evildoers honor you, this is [in fact] your dishonor; when they love you, this is nothing but shame for you; and whoever is in need of you, deserves your contempt."

Abu Hamid Ahmad b. Khadrawayh (Khidruya) al-Balkhi

He was a great Sufi master of Khurasan who kept the company of Abu Turab al-Nakhshabi.[125] He arrived in Nishapur, where he visited Abu Hafs [al-Haddad].[126] He then set out to Bastam in order to meet Abu Yazid al-Bastami. He was famous for his attachment to *futuwwa*.[127]

Abu Hafs said [about him]: "I have seen no one as strongly concentrated [on God] and as sincere in his spiritual state as Ahmad b. Khadrawayh." Abu Yazid [al-Bastami] said: "Ahmad is our teacher."

I heard Muhammad b. al-Husayn – may God have mercy on him – say: I heard Mansur b. ʿAbdallah say: I heard Muhammad b. Hamid say: "I was with Ahmad b. Khadrawayh during his agony of death. He had just turned ninety-five. One of his disciples asked him a question. His eyes filled with tears and he answered: 'My son, the door at which I have been knocking for ninety-five years is about to open before me and I have no inkling whether it will lead me to felicity or infelicity.[128] Do I have the time to answer [such questions]?'"

He had a debt of seven hundred *dinars*. His lenders gathered around him. He looked at them and said://59 "O my Lord, You have determined that pledges serve as a guaranty for money-lenders, and now You are taking from them their guaranty.[129] So settle my accounts!" Then there was a knock on the door and someone asked: "Where are Ahmad's creditors?" His debts were paid and then his spirit departed. He – may God have mercy on him – died in 240.[130]

Ahmad b. Khadrawayh said: "No sleep is heavier than neglectfulness; no slavery is stronger than your carnal desires. Therefore, were neglectfulness not to weigh heavily upon you, you would never succumb to your desire."

---

125 On him see pages 40–41.
126 A leader of the so-called "path of blame" (*al-malamatiyya*) that flourished in Khurasan in the second half of the third/ninth century; he died between 265/874 and 270/879. See *IM*, pp. 94–99.
127 A code of altruistic and self-denying behavior and selfless generosity that was practiced by some Iranian ascetics and Sufis of the age.
128 That is, to Paradise or Hell.
129 That is, God is about to take his soul, leaving his creditors empty-handed.
130 That is, 855 C.E.

Abu ʾl-Hasan Ahmad b. Abi ʾl-Hawari[131]

He came from Damascus and studied under Abu Sulayman al-Darani and others. He died in the year 230.[132] Al-Junayd used to say: "Ahmad b. Abi ʾl-Hawari is the sweet basil of Syria."

I heard Shaykh Abu ʿAbd al-Rahman al-Sulami say: I heard Abu Ahmad al-Hafiz say: I heard Saʿid b. ʿAbd al-ʿAziz al-Halabi say: I heard Ahmad b. Abi ʾl-Hawari say: "Whoever looks at this world with longing and affection, God will remove the light of certitude and renunciation from his heart." According to the same chain of transmission, he said: "Whoever performs a [good] deed without following the custom of the Prophet – may God bless and greet him – his deed is worthless. On the same chain of authorities Ahmad b. Abi ʾl-Hawari said: "The best weeping is when the servant [of God] weeps over the moments of negligence [of God's commands]." Ahmad also said: "God's greatest temptation for His servant is neglectfulness and the hardness of the heart."//60

Abu Hafs ʿUmar b. Maslama[133] al-Haddad[134]

He came from the village called Kuradabadh, near the gate of the city of Nishapur toward the direction of Bukhara. He was a great [Sufi] master and leader. He died around 260.[135]

Abu Hafs said: "Sins are messengers of unbelief in the same way as fever is a messenger of death." Abu Hafs said: "When you see a disciple who likes [spiritual] concerts,[136] know that there is in him a residue of vanity." He said: "Good manners on the outside is the sign of good manners inside." He said: "Chivalry consists in being fair [to others], while not demanding fairness [from others]."

I heard Muhammad b. al-Husayn say: I heard Muhammad b. Musa say: I heard Abu ʿAli al-Thaqafi say: Abu Hafs used to say: "Whoever does not weigh his spiritual states and deeds at every moment against the Book and the [Prophet's] custom, while at the same time being suspicious of his true motives, should not be counted among the [true] men."[137]

---

131 See *IM*, pp. 37–38.
132 That is, 845 C.E.
133 Also ʿAmr b. Salm or ʿAmr b. Aslam.
134 See note 126.
135 That is, 873 C.E.
136 *Samaʿ*, lit. "hearing" [of music and poetry]; a spiritual concert practiced by many Sufis. See *IM*, pp. 322–325.
137 Abu Hafs may be referring to the adherents of the *malamatiyya* movement of Khurasan, whom he and his followers considered to be superior to any other ascetic or mystical group in the area.

Abu Turab ʿAskar b. Husayn al-Nakhshabi[138]

He was a companion of Hatim al-Asamm and Abu Hatim al-ʿAttar al-Basri. He died in the year 245.[139] They say that he died in the desert torn to pieces by the wild beasts.//61 Ibn al-Jallaʾ said: "I have kept the company of six hundred masters, yet have never met anyone equal to four of them. Of these, the first one was Abu Turab."

Abu Turab said: "The poor man's[140] food is whatever he can find; his clothes are whatever covers him; and his home is wherever he ends up staying." Abu Turab said: "When the servant [of God] is sincere in his deeds, he will taste their sweetness before actually performing them; and if he strives to make them perfect, he will taste their sweetness and pleasantness in the process of performing them."

I heard Shaykh Abu ʿAbd al-Rahman al-Sulami – may God have mercy on him – say: I heard my grandfather Ismaʿil b. Nujayd say: "When Abu Turab al-Nakhshabi saw some of his companions doing something he did not like, he would exert himself even more thoroughly and would make his repentance even more stringent. He would say: 'It is my misfortune that these [unfortunates] were reduced to doing what they do, for God – may He be great and exalted – said: "Verily never will God change the condition of a people until they change it themselves."'[141] He also said to his companions: 'He who wears patched rags, is begging [for alms]; he who sits in the [Sufi] hostel[142] or in the mosque, is begging; and he who reads aloud the Qurʾanic text from the book for people to hear is also a beggar.'"

I also heard [Ismaʿil b. Nujayd] say that Abu Turab used to say: "There is a pact between me and God that whenever I extend my hand to a prohibited thing, it does not reach it." Once Abu Turab saw a Sufi disciple of his extending his hand to a [discarded] melon rind after he had been starving for three days. Abu Turab told him: "You are stretching your hand to a melon rind? Then Sufism is not for you. Stick to the bazaar!"

I heard Muhammad b. al-Husayn say: I heard Abu ʾl-ʿAbbas al-Baghdadi say: I heard Abu ʿAbdallah al-Farisi say: I heard Abu ʾl-Husayn al-Razi say: I heard Yusuf b. al-Husayn say: I heard Abu Turab al-Nakhshabi say: "My [animal] soul was never able to obtain anything from me except once. When I was on a trip, it craved bread and eggs. So I turned away from my path and came to a village. Suddenly a man fell upon me and grabbed me, crying: 'This one was together with the thieves!' [The people of the village] threw me to the ground and beat me with a stick seventy times. [As they were doing this], there came upon us a Sufi who shouted: 'Woe unto you! This is Abu Turab al-Nakhshabi!'

---

138 On him see *IM*, pp. 33–34.
139 859 C.E.
140 That is, the Sufi.
141 Q. 13:11.
142 *Khanqah*; a Sufi hostel or lodge; later on, these institutions became the headquarters of Sufi brotherhoods.

So they set me free//62 and apologized before me. The man [who declared me to be a thief] brought me to his house and put in front of me bread and eggs. So I said [to myself]: 'Eat this after seventy lashes!'"

Ibn al-Jalla' narrated: "Abu Turab arrived in Mecca in good spirits. I asked him: 'Where did you eat, master?' He answered: 'I ate one meal in Basra, another one in Nibaj and one meal here.'"

Abu Muhammad 'Abdallah b. Khubayq

He was one of those Sufis who stressed asceticism. A companion of Yusuf b. Asbat, he hailed from Kufa, although he lived in Antioch.

I heard Muhammad b. al-Husayn say: I heard Abu 'l-Faraj al-Warathani say: I heard Abu 'l-Azhar al-Mayyafariqini say: I heard Fath b. Shakhraf say: When I met 'Abdallah b. Khubayq for the first time, he told me: "Khurasanian, there are only four things, no more and no less. [They are]: your eye, your tongue, your heart, and your desire. Watch your eye so that it would not see that which is not permitted; watch your tongue so that you would not say with it the things that God knows you do not mean in your heart; watch your heart so that it would contain neither malice nor envy toward any Muslim; and watch your desire so that you would not wish any evil. If you do not have these qualities, then cover your head with ashes, for you will be among the evildoers."[143]

Ibn Khubayq said: "Worry only about things that may harm you tomorrow. And be happy only about things that may make you happy tomorrow!" Ibn Khubayq said: "When servants [of God] alienate themselves from God, He will alienate from them the hearts [of people]. And when they open their hearts to God, He will make everyone open his heart to them." He said: "The best kind of fear is one that shields you from [committing] sins, that which fills you with sorrow over [the good works] that you missed and that which makes you think about the rest of your life. The best kind of hope is one that renders good works easy for you." He also said: "Listening to falsehood for a long time dulls the sweetness of obedience to God in your heart."

Abu 'Ali Ahmad b. 'Asim al-Antaki[144]

He was a contemporary of Bishr b. al-Harith, al-Sari al-Saqati and al-Harith al-Muhasibi. Abu Sulayman al-Darani used to call him "The Spy of the Hearts" due to his sharp perspicacity.//63

Ahmad b. 'Asim said: "If you want your heart to be serene, help it by protecting your tongue [from unbecoming statements]." Ahmad b. 'Asim said: "God Most High said: 'Your riches and your children are but a trial'[145] and we want this trial to increase ever more."

---

143 That is, on the Day of Judgement.
144 On him see *IM*, pp. 38–39. He died in 220/853.
145 Q. 64:15.

Abu 'l-Sari Mansur b. ʿAmmar[146]

He came from the region of Marw from a village named Dandanaqan, although some say that he came from Bushanj. He later settled in Basra and became a great preacher. Mansur b. ʿAmmar said: "Whoever falls into despair because of the afflictions of this world, exposes his faith to affliction." Mansur b. ʿAmmar said: "The best dress of the servants [of God] is humility and contrition, while the best dress of the gnostics is righteousness, for God Most High said: 'The dress of righteousness, that is the best.'"[147] They say that the reason for his repentance was that he found on the road a piece of paper on which it was written: "In the name of God, the Merciful, the Compassionate." He picked it up, and when he could not find a place for it, he ate it. Then, in a dream, he heard a voice telling him: "The gate of wisdom has opened for you, because of your respect for this piece of paper."

I heard Shaykh Abu ʿAbd al-Rahman al-Sulami say: I heard Abu Bakr al-Razi//64 say: I heard Abu 'l-ʿAbbas al-Qass say: I heard Abu 'l-Hasan al-Shaʿrani say: I saw Mansur b. ʿAmmar in a dream and asked what God had done to him. He answered: "[God] asked me: 'Are you Mansur b. ʿAmmar?' I answered: 'Yes, my Lord.' He said: 'Are you the one who encouraged people to renounce this world, while at the same time desiring it yourself?' I answered: 'Yes, this was so indeed, but I did not begin any of my preaching sessions without first praising You, then Your Prophet, and only after that did I begin to admonish people.' God said: 'This is true, so bring him a chair so that he sing My glory in heaven among My angels, as he sang My glory on earth among My servants.'"

Abu Salih Hamdun b. Ahmad b. ʿUmara al-Qassar[148]

He came from Nishapur. It is through him that the *malamatiyya* teaching[149] spread [among the people of] Nishapur. He was a companion of Salim[150] al-Barusi and Abu Turab al-Nakhshabi. He died in the year 271.[151]

Someone asked Hamdun: "When can a man speak to people?"//65 He answered: "When it becomes known to him that he should fulfill an obligation imposed on him by God Most High. Or when he knows that someone is destined to perish by [adhering to] a reprehensible innovation[152] and he hopes that God would save that person from it." He said: "Whoever thinks that his soul is better than the soul of Pharaoh has shown pride." He also said: "Since I have learned

---

146 He died in Baghdad in 225/839.
147 Q. 7:26.
148 On this representative of the *malamatiyya* movement in Nishapur, see *IM*, pp. 94–96.
149 On this ascetic-mystical movement see *IM*, pp. 94–99.
150 According to some readings, his name was Salm or Salman. See *IM*, p. 95.
151 880 C.E.
152 *Bidʿa*; that is, something that was not practiced by the Prophet, his Companions and the Muslims of the next two generations.

that the Ruler[153] can see through the evildoers, the fear of the Ruler has never departed from my heart." He said: "Whenever you see a drunk man, stagger like him so that you would not elevate yourself above him, thereby calling upon yourself a similar [affliction]."

ʿAbdallah b. Munazil said: I asked Abu Salih to admonish me: "If you can keep yourself from being angry about anything in this life, then do so!"

[Once] a friend of his was dying, as he kept vigil at his bed. When he died, Hamdun put down the fire in the lamp. They told him: "In such circumstances one adds oil to the lamp!" He answered: "Until this moment the oil has belonged to him, but now it belongs to his heirs."

Hamdun said: "He who looks into the ways of the pious ancestors[154] will realize his shortcomings and his inability to attain the rank of the true men." He also said: "Do not disclose to anyone things that you would like to be hidden from you."

Abu ʾl-Qasim al-Junayd b. Muhammad[155]

He was the leader and master of this [Sufi] community.//66 His family originally came from Nihawand, but he was born and raised in Iraq. His father was a glassware merchant. Because of this he was called "the Bottler".[156] He was a jurist who adhered to the school of Abu Thawr.[157] When he was just twenty years old he was already issuing legal opinions in the sessions [that were presided over] by Abu Thawr. He studied under his uncle al-Sari [al-Saqati], under al-Harith al-Muhasibi and under Muhammad b. ʿAli al-Qassab. He died in the year 297.[158]

I heard Muhammad b. al-Husayn – may God have mercy on him – say: I heard Muhammad b. al-Husayn al-Baghdadi say: I heard [Abu Bakr] al-Farghani say: I heard someone asked al-Junayd about the [Sufi] gnostic. He answered: "He who speaks of your secret, even though you yourself remain silent." I heard Shaykh Abu ʿAbd al-Rahman al-Sulami – may God have mercy on him – say: I heard Muhammad b. ʿAbdallah al-Razi say: I heard Abu Muhammad al-Jurayri say: I heard al-Junayd say: "We learned Sufism not through words but through hunger, the renunciation of this world, and through depriving ourselves from the things which we are accustomed to and in which we take delight."

I heard Muhammad b. al-Husayn – may God have mercy on him – say: I heard Abu Bakr al-Razi say: I heard Muhammad al-Jurayri say: I heard Abu Nasr al-Isbahani say: I heard Abu ʿAli al-Rudhbari say: I heard al-Junayd say to a man who discoursed upon [divine] gnosis and said: "The possessors of gnosis

---

153 According to an alternative reading, Satan (*al-shaytan*).
154 That is, the Prophet and the first Muslims.
155 On him see *IM*, pp. 52–56.
156 *Al-Qawariri*.
157 Abu Thawr al-Kalbi (d. 240/854), a renowned jurisprudent and a founder of a school of law that, however, disappeared shortly after his death. See the article "Abu Thawr" in *EI*.
158 910 C.E.

arrive at the state of abandoning any movements[159] through the gates of their devotion and intimate proximity to God – may He be great and exalted." To this al-Junayd replied: "This is the teaching of those who preach the abandonment of pious works. This, in my view, is nothing but a deadly sin. Even those people who steal and fornicate are better than those who teach this. The gnostics, who know God Most High, took their works from God Most High and through them they will return to Him. Were I to live a thousand years, I would not miss a single minor act of devotion unless I were prevented from it [by forces beyond my control]."

Al-Junayd said: "If it were possible for you to have nothing at your home but a few pottery utensils, so be it!" Al-Junayd said: "All paths are closed for God's creatures except for those who follow in the footsteps of the Prophet – may peace and blessings be upon him."//67

I heard Muhammad b. al-Husayn – may God have mercy on him – say: I heard Mansur b. ʿAbdallah say: I heard Abu ʿUmar al-Anmati say: I heard al-Junayd say: "If a righteous man who has spent thousands of years contemplating God would turn away from Him for just one moment, his loss would be greater than his gain." I heard Muhammad b. al-Husayn say: I heard Abu Nasr al-Isbahani say: I heard Abu ʿAli al-Rudhbari say on the authority of al-Junayd: al-Junayd said: "In this affair [of ours][160] one must not follow anyone who has not learned by heart the Qurʾan and written down the reports of the Prophet, because our knowledge is bound by the [Holy] Book and by the [Prophet's] custom." Al-Junayd said: "This teaching of ours is bound by the foundations of the [Sacred] Book and the custom [of the Prophet]." Al-Junayd also said: "This knowledge of ours is reinforced by the reports of the Messenger of God – may God bless and greet him."

Muhammad b. al-Husayn – may God have mercy on him – informed me: I heard Abu ʾl-Husayn b. Faris say: I heard Abu ʾl-Husayn ʿAli b. Ibrahim al-Haddad say: I attended a lecture of the judge Abu ʾl-ʿAbbas b. Surayj.[161] He discoursed on the subject of the roots and the branches [of jurisprudence], and I liked that. When he saw that I liked that, he asked: "Do you know where all this comes from?" I answered: "[Only] the judge [can] say this." He said: "This [came to me] due to my keeping the company of Abu ʾl-Qasim al-Junayd."

Someone asked al-Junayd: "Where did you obtain your knowledge from?" He answered: "Through sitting before God for thirty years under that staircase." And he pointed to the staircase of his house.

I heard the master Abu ʿAli [al-Daqqaq] recount this story. I also heard him say: "Someone saw a rosary in his [al-Junayd's] hand and said to him: 'In spite of your high [spiritual] rank you still hold a rosary in your hand?' He answered: 'I will not abandon the way which has brought me to my Lord.'"

---

159 That is, the performance of the canonical acts of piety, such as prayer or pilgrimage.
160 That is, Sufism.
161 A famous scholar of Baghdad (d. 308/918), who is sometimes considered to be the real founder of the Shafiʿi school of law.

I heard the master Abu ʿAli al-Daqqaq – may God have mercy on him – say: "Every day al-Junayd came to his store, closed its door and performed four hundred prayer prostrations. He then returned to his house."//68

Abu Bakr al-ʿAtawi said: "I was with al-Junayd, when he died. He read the entire text of the Qurʾan and began to recite it anew from 'The Cow'.[162] He reached the seventieth verse, then died – may God have mercy on him!"

Abu ʿUthman Saʿid b. Ismaʿil al-Hiri[163]

He resided in Nishapur. He originally came from the city of Rayy, where he studied with Shah al-Kirmani[164] and Yahya b. Muʿadh al-Razi. He then arrived in Nishapur together with Shah al-Kirmani and came to Abu Hafs al-Haddad. He stayed with him for a while until he completed his studies with him. Abu Hafs gave him his daughter in marriage. He died in the year 298.[165] He lived more than thirty years after Abu Hafs's death.

I heard Muhammad b. al-Husayn – may God have mercy on him – say: I heard Abu ʿAmr b. Hamdan say: I heard Abu ʿUthman say: "Man's faith is not complete until four things have become equal for him in his heart: denial, giving, glory, and humiliation."

I heard Muhammad b. al-Husayn – may God have mercy on him – say: I heard ʿAbd al-Rahman b. ʿAbdallah say: I heard a companion of Abu ʿUthman say: I heard Abu ʿUthman say: "As a young man I studied with Abu Hafs for a while. Once he drove me away from his assembly and told me not to sit with him any longer. So I stood up, and began to withdraw without turning my back on him, so that my face would be facing his. I proceeded in this manner until I disappeared from his sight. Then I made a vow to dig a hole next to his door and not leave it until he ordered me to do so. When he saw that, he brought me close to himself and made me one of his foremost companions."

They say that there are only three [people] in this world, to whom there is no equal://69 Abu ʿUthman at Nishapur, al-Junayd at Baghdad, and Abu ʿAbdallah b. al-Jallaʾ in Syria.

Abu ʿUthman said: "For forty years God Most High has not put me in a spiritual state that I would not like, nor did He transfer me to a state that I would resent."

I heard Shaykh Abu ʿAbd al-Rahman al-Sulami – may God have mercy on him – say: I heard ʿAbdallah b. Muhammad al-Shaʿrani say: I heard Abu ʿUthman say that.

When Abu ʿUthman fell into unconsciousness [on his death bed], his son Abu Bakr tore up the shirt he was wearing. [Suddenly] Abu ʿUthman opened his

---

162 The name of the second (and the longest) chapter of the Qurʾan.
163 A leader of the *malamatiyya* movement in Khurasan who died in 298/910. See *IM*, "Index", under "Abu ʿUthman al-Hiri".
164 For his biography see page 52.
165 910 C.E.

eyes and said: "My son, breaking the Prophet's custom on the outside is a sign of hypocrisy inside!"

I heard Muhammad b. al-Husayn say: I heard Muhammad b. Ahmad al-Malamati say: I heard Abu ʾl-Husayn al-Warraq say: I heard Abu ʿUthman say: "Companionship with God [requires man] to be courteous, to be constantly in awe [of God] and to exercise self-scrutiny. Companionship with the Messenger of God – may God bless and greet him and his family – [requires man] to follow the custom of the Prophet and to adhere to the explicit knowledge.[166] Companionship with the friends of God Most High [requires man] to exercise reverence and to serve [them]. Companionship with the family [requires] proper conduct. Companionship with the brothers[167] [requires] cheerfulness, as long as there is no sin in it. Companionship with ignoramuses [requires man] to pray for them and be kind to them."

I heard ʿAbdallah b. Yusuf al-Isbahani – may God have mercy on him – say: "I heard that Abu ʿAmr b. Nujayd say: I heard Abu ʿUthman say: 'Whoever has appointed the Prophet's custom, in word and in deed, as his commander, will speak [words of] wisdom; and whoever has appointed his passions, in word and deed, as his commander, will speak about [reprehensible] innovation. For God Most High said: "If you obey him [the Prophet], you shall be on the right guidance."'"[168]//70

Abu ʾl-Husayn Ahmad b. Muhammad al-Nuri[169]

He was born and raised in Baghdad, but his family originally came from Baghshur.[170] He studied with al-Sari al-Saqati and Ibn Abi ʾl-Hawari, and was a contemporary of al-Junayd – may God have mercy on him. He died in the year 295 (907). He was a person of great stature, who was well-spoken and amicable. Al-Nuri – may God have mercy on him – said: "Sufism is the abandonment of everything that pleases the soul." He said: "There are two greatest things in this age of ours: a scholar who acts according to his knowledge, and a [divine] gnostic who speaks according to his [true] reality."

I heard Abu ʿAbdallah al-Sufi – may God have mercy on him – say: I heard Ahmad b. Muhammad al-Bardaʿi say: I heard al-Murtaʿish[171] say: I heard al-Nuri say: "Whenever you see someone boasting that he has achieved a spiritual state that places him outside the limits of the Divine Law, do not come near him!"

I heard Shaykh Abu ʿAbd al-Rahman al-Sulami – may God have mercy on him – say: I heard Abu ʾl-ʿAbbas al-Baghdadi say: I heard al-Farghani say: I heard al-Junayd say: "Since al-Nuri died no one has spoken about the true

---

166 That is, to the letter of the Divine Law (al-shariʿa).
167 That is, fellow Sufis.
168 Q. 24:54.
169 On him see IM, pp. 60–63.
170 A village near the city of Herat, Afghanistan.
171 On him see page 62.

nature of sincerity." Abu Ahmad al-Maghazili said: "I have not seen anyone more devoted to God than al-Nuri." Someone said to him: "Not even al-Junayd?" He answered: "Yes, not even al-Junayd."

Al-Nuri said: "Patched frocks [of the Sufis] used to hide pearls. Today, however, they have become a heap of dung upon corpses."[172] They say that he used to leave his house every day carrying some bread with him. He would give out this bread as alms on the way, then, around noon, he would enter the mosque. He would then leave the mosque, open his store and fast. His family thought that he ate at the bazaar, while the people of the bazaar thought that he ate at home. He maintained this practice for twenty years.//71

Abu ʿAbdallah Ahmad b. Yahya al-Jallaʾ

He came from Baghdad, but lived in Ramla[173] and Damascus. He was a great Sufi master of Syria. He studied with Abu Turab [al-Nakhshabi], Dhu ʾl-Nun al-Misri, Abu ʿUbayd al-Busri and his father Yahya al-Jallaʾ.

I heard Muhammad b. al-Husayn – may God have mercy on him – say: I heard Muhammad b. ʿAbd al-ʿAziz al-Tabari say: I heard Abu ʿUmar al-Dimashqi say: I heard Ibn al-Jallaʾ say: "I told my father and mother: 'I want you to give me to God – may He be great and exalted!' They said: 'Yes, we give you to God – may He be great and exalted.' I then left them for a while. I returned to them on a rainy night and knocked on the door. My father asked who was there. I answered: 'I am your son Ahmad.' He said: 'We had a son, but we gave him to God Most High. We are Arabs and therefore do not take our gifts back.' He did not open the door."

Ibn al-Jallaʾ said: "He for whom blame and praise are equal is an ascetic. He who fulfills religious duties in their proper times is a worshipper. He who sees that all actions and works come from God is a true monotheist. For he sees nothing but the One."

When Ibn al-Jallaʾ died, people looked at him [and saw] that he was laughing. The physician said: "He is alive!" He then felt his pulse and said: "No, he is dead." He removed the cover from his face and said: "I do not know whether he is dead or alive!"

Under his skin was a vein in the shape of [the word] "God". Ibn al-Jallaʾ – may God have mercy on him – said: "Once I was walking alongside my [Sufi] master and saw a handsome youth. I asked: 'Master, do you think that God will punish such a [beautiful] form?' He answered: 'So, you looked at him, didn't you? You will soon suffer the consequence [of it]!'//72. And indeed, twenty years later, I forgot the Qurʾan."

---

172 A hint at the deterioration of the original Sufi values at the hands of al-Nuri's contemporaries.
173 A town in Syria/Palestine.

Abu Muhammad Ruwaym b. Ahmad

He was born in Baghdad. A great Sufi master, he died in the year 303.[174] He was a teacher of the Qur'an and jurist, who adhered to the school of Dawud [al-Zahiri].[175]

Ruwaym said: "The wisdom of the wise man consists of dispensing freely pious admonitions to his [Sufi] brethren, while at the same time imposing them stringently upon himself. His dispensation [of the admonitions] to others means adherence to [religious] knowledge, while his stringent imposition of them upon himself is evidence of pious scrupulosity."

I heard Shaykh Abu 'Abd al-Rahman al-Sulami – may God have mercy on him – say: I heard 'Abd al-Wahid b. Bakr say: I heard Abu 'Abdallah b. Khafif say: "I asked Ruwaym to give me a piece of advice. He answered: 'This affair[176] is achieved only by exerting one's spirit. If you enter it through this, fine. If not, then you should not engage in the follies of the Sufis.'"[177]

Ruwaym said: "When you keep company with any group of people, this is better for you than keeping company with the Sufis. This is because all people study the externals [of religion], whereas this [Sufi] community studies the true realities [of things]. While all people seek to impose upon themselves the outward rulings of the Divine Law, the Sufis impose upon themselves the True Reality of pious scrupulosity and continuous sincerity. Therefore if anyone deviates from them in something that they have achieved, God will remove the light of faith from his heart."

Ruwaym said: "I was walking in a street of Baghdad during a hot afternoon. I was thirsty. I came to a house and asked for water. A girl with a pitcher opened the door. When she saw me, she said: '[This is] a Sufi who drinks during the day!' Since then I have never broken my fast [during the day]." Ruwaym said://73 "God has bestowed upon you word and deed.[178] If He takes away from you the word and leaves you with the deed, this is a blessing. If He takes away from you the deed and leaves you with the word, this is an affliction. However, if He takes away both from you, this is a terrible punishment."

Abu 'Abdallah Muhammad b. al-Fadl al-Balkhi

He was a resident of Samarqand, originally from Balkh. He was expelled from Balkh and settled in Samarqand, where he died. He studied with Ahmad Khadrawayh [Khidruya] and others. Abu 'Uthman al-Hiri liked him a lot. He died in the year 319.[179]

---

174 915 C.E.
175 A school of law founded by Dawud al-Zahiri (d. 270/884), a scholar with a literalist turn of mind. Closely affiliated with the Hanbali legal school, the Zahiri school gradually disappeared.
176 That is, the mystical path to God.
177 This phrase indicates that Ruwaym represented a strand of piety that did not necessarily endorse the practices and values of the Sufi tradition of Iraq. See *IM*, pp. 99–101.
178 That is, the gift of speech and the ability to act.
179 931 C.E.

I heard Shaykh Abu ʿAbd al-Rahman al-Sulami – may God have mercy on him – say: I heard Ahmad b. Muhammad al-Farraʾ say: I heard Abu Bakr b. ʿUthman say: Abu ʿUthman al-Hiri wrote [a letter] to Muhammad b. al-Fadl asking him about the signs of wretchedness [in the Hereafter]. He answered: "Three things. When a man is endowed with knowledge but deprived of deeds; when he is endowed with deeds but deprived of sincerity [in performing them]; when he is endowed with the company of the righteous, yet he has no respect for them." Abu ʿUthman al-Hiri used to say: Muhammad b. al-Fadl is a broker of men.[180]

I heard Muhammad b. al-Husayn say: I heard ʿAbdallah al-Razi say: I heard Muhammad b. al-Fadl say: "Rest in the prison[181] is something that the soul should desire." I heard Muhammad b. al-Husayn say: I heard Abu Bakr al-Razi say: I heard Muhammad b. al-Fadl say: "There are four reasons for Islam's departure: [Muslims] do not act in accordance with what they know; they act in accordance with what they do not know; they do not learn what they do not know; they prevent others from learning." According to the same chain of transmission he said://74 "How strange are those people who cross the deserts in order to arrive at His House[182] and to see the traces of prophecy. Why don't they cross their [lower] souls and their passions in order to arrive at their hearts and to see the signs of their Lord – may He be great and exalted!?"

He said: "When you see a [Sufi] novice, who aspires to good things of this world, this means that he turned his back [on God]." Someone asked him about asceticism. He answered: "When one looks at this world and sees only its imperfection and when one turns away from it with pride, dignity and contempt."

Abu Bakr Ahmad b. Nasr al-Zaqqaq al-Kabir

He was a contemporary of al-Junayd and a great [Sufi] master of Egypt. I heard Muhammad b. al-Husayn – may God have mercy on him – say: I heard al-Husayn b. Ahmad say: I heard al-Kattani say: "When al-Zaqqaq died, the poor[183] no longer had reason to visit Egypt."

Al-Zaqqaq said: "Whosoever does not combine [his] poverty with piety is eating prohibited food."

Shaykh Abu ʿAbd al-Rahman al-Sulami – may God have mercy on him – said: I heard Muhammad b. ʿAbdallah b. ʿAbd al-ʿAziz say: I heard al-Zaqqaq say: "I wandered in the desert of the children of Israel[184] for fifteen days. However, when I had finally found the road, I met a soldier, who gave me some water to drink. Its harshness tormented my heart for the next thirty years."[185]

---

180 That is, he can see their true intentions.
181 That is, in this life.
182 That is, the Kaʿba in Mecca, which is the principal sanctuary of Islam.
183 That is, the Sufis.
184 That is, in the Sinai.
185 Soldiers, like all state officials, were seen by the Sufis as instruments of oppression. Therefore, the water received from a soldier's hands was deemed to be impure.

Abu ʿAbdallah ʿAmr b. ʿUthman al-Makki

He met Abu ʿAbdallah al-Nabaji and studied with Abu Saʿid al-Kharraz[186] and others.//75 He was a [great] master of the Sufis and their leader in the science of the fundamentals [of the Divine Law] and the [mystical] path. He died in Baghdad in 291.[187]

I heard Muhammad b. al-Husayn – may God have mercy on him – say: I heard Muhammad b. ʿAbdallah b. Shadhan say: I heard Abu Bakr Muhammad b. Ahmad say: I heard ʿAmr b. ʿUthman al-Makki say: "Whatever good thing, splendor, intimacy, beauty, radiance, form, light, person or image which your heart may fancy, which may occur to you in your thoughts or which may appear in the passing whims of your heart – God Most High is far removed from all of this. Have not you heard the words of God Most High: 'Like Him there is naught, He is the Hearing, the Seeing.'[188] He [also] said: '[He] has not begotten, and has not been begotten, and equal to Him there is not any one.'"[189]

According to the same chain of transmission, he said: "Knowledge is a guide and fear [of God] is a [caravan] driver. The soul, which is [caught] between them, is obstinate, recalcitrant, deceitful and devious. If you keep warning her by the guidance of knowledge and driving her by the threat of fear, you will achieve your goal." He also said: "No [clear] expression can be applied to ecstasy,[190] because it is God's mystery among the believers."

Samnun b. Hamza[191]

His *kunya*[192] was Abu ʾl-Hasan, though some say it was Abu ʾl-Qasim. He studied with al-Sari [al-Saqati], Abu Ahmad al-Qalanisi, Muhammad b. ʿAli al-Qassab and others. It is said that he recited [the following lines]:

> I find no delight in anyone but You
> So test me as you wish!

As soon as he said that, he was afflicted by urine retention. He then began to go around [religious] schools saying [to the students]:[193] "Pray for your uncle the Liar!"//76. As he was reciting these lines, one of his companions said to the other: "I heard, the other day, when I was in the countryside, the voice of our master Samnun that begged and humbly entreated God to cure him." The other man also said: "I too heard that yesterday, when I was in such-and-such place."

---

186 On him see pages 53–54 of this book and *IM*, pp. 56–60.
187 903 C.E.
188 Q. 42:11.
189 Q. 112:3–4.
190 According to an alternative reading, "to the ecstatic [person]".
191 On him see *IM*, pp.63–64.
192 That is, the name of a man's eldest son (filionymic) that usually precedes the given name.
193 This phrase is missing from some versions of the text.

Others confirmed this also. Samnun was told about this. However, when he was afflicted by urine retention, he tolerated it patiently and never complained. When he heard them saying this, while in fact he never had uttered that prayer or said anything [of this], he realized that God wanted him to show his anguish out of respect for the code of God's servant and in order to conceal his true state.[194] [It was then] that he began to walk around the schools, telling [the school-children]: "Pray for your uncle the Liar!"

I heard Muhammad b. al-Husayn – may God have mercy on him – say: I heard Abu 'l-ʿAbbas Muhammad b. al-Hasan al-Baghdadi say: I heard Jaʿfar al-Khuldi say: Ahmad al-Maghazili told me: "There was a man in Baghdad who distributed forty thousand *dinars* among the poor. Samnun said to me: 'Abu Ahmad, don't you see what this [man] has expended and done, while we have nothing to give as charity? Let's go some place and perform there one ritual bending and prostration for each *dirham* he has donated.' So we came to al-Madaʾin[195] and performed forty thousand bending and prostrations."

Samnun had a pleasant character and most of his sayings are about divine love. He was a person of great stature. They say that he died before al-Junayd.

Abu ʿUbayd al-Busri

He belonged to [the generation of] the old Sufi masters and studied with Abu Turab al-Nakhshabi.

I heard Muhammad b. al-Husayn – may God have mercy on him – say: I heard ʿAbdallah b. ʿAli say: I heard al-Duqqi say: I heard Ibn al-Jallaʾ say: "I have met six hundred Sufi masters. Of them no one was equal to the [following] four://77 Dhu 'l-Nun al-Misri, my father,[196] Abu Turab and Abu ʿUbayd al-Busri."

I heard Shaykh Abu ʿAbd al-Rahman al-Sulami – may God have mercy on him – say: I heard Ahmad b. Muhammad al-Baghawi[197] say: I heard Muhammad b. Muʿammar say: I heard Abu Zurʿa al-Hasani[198] say: "One day Abu ʿUbayd was threshing his wheat on a threshing machine. It was just three days before the Pilgrimage season. Two men came up to him and asked: 'Abu ʿUbayd, do you desire to perform a pilgrimage?' He said: 'No.' He then turned to me and said: 'This master of yours is more capable of doing this than these men!'[199] He meant himself."

---

194 That is, his ability to tolerate God's affliction without complaint.
195 The ruins of Ctesiphon, the ancient capital of Sasanian Iran.
196 Yahya al-Jallaʾ, a famous ascetic and Sufi.
197 In a different reading, "al-Thaghri".
198 In a different reading, "al-Janbi."
199 It is not quite clear what he was referring to, but some later Sufi commentators suggested that Abu ʿUbayd hinted at his ability to traverse great distances within minutes (*tayy al-ard*). This explanation seems far-fetched. It is more likely that he implied that staying at home during the pilgrimage and concentrating one's thoughts on God is better than taking part in the noisy and ostentatious collective pilgrimage.

Abu 'l-Fawaris Shah b. Shuja' al-Kirmani

He came from a family of kings. He studied with Abu Turab al-Nakhshabi, Abu 'Ubayd al-Busri and those who belonged to this generation. He was a man of *futuwwa*[200] and of great importance. He died before the year 300.[201]

Shah said: "Pious scrupulosity is a sign of fear of God and avoidance of suspicious things."[202] He also used to say to his companions: "Avoid lies, treachery and backbiting, then do as you see fit."

I heard Shaykh Abu 'Abd al-Rahman al-Sulami say: I heard my grandfather Ibn Nujayd say: Shah al-Kirmani said: "Whoever turns his sight away from the prohibited, restrains himself from passions, fills //78 his interior with constant self-scrutiny and his exterior with the observance of the Prophet's custom, and forces himself to eat only properly obtained [food], will never be failed in his clairvoyance."

Yusuf b. al-Husayn

He was a [Sufi] master of Rayy and [the province of] Jibal.[203] He was unique in his avoidance of pretension. He was knowledgeable and well educated. He studied with Dhu 'l-Nun al-Misri and Abu Turab al-Nakhshabi and a friend of Abu Sa'id al-Kharraz. He died in the year 304.[204]

Yusuf b. al-Husayn said: "I would rather meet God burdened with all possible sins than with one grain of pretence." Yusuf b. al-Husayn said: "When you see a novice having recourse to dispensations [from an obligatory requirement],[205] you must know that nothing good will come out of him." He wrote to al-Junayd: "May God not allow you to taste the temptation of your soul. For once you have tasted it, you will never taste any good forthwith." Yusuf b. al-Husayn said: "I see afflictions of the Sufis in the following things: seeking friendship with adolescents, keeping company with adversaries, and befriending women."

Abu 'Abdallah Muhammad b. 'Ali al-Tirmidhi

He was a great Sufi master, who wrote many works on Sufi science.//79 He studied with Abu Turab al-Nakhshabi, Ahmad b. Khadrawayh [Khidruya], Ibn al-Jalla' and others. Someone asked Muhammad b. 'Ali about the characteristic feature of mankind. He answered: "Outward weakness, yet unlimited pretensions."

---

200 See note 96.
201 912 C.E.
202 That is, the things that may be improper from the viewpoint of the Divine Law (*al-shari'a*).
203 A province in Iran.
204 916 C.E.
205 On the notion of dispensation in Sufism see *IM*, p. 195. Although legitimate from the viewpoint of the Divine Law, many Sufis considered dispensations to be a sign of one's inability to perform one's duties to the full.

Muhammad b. ʿAli said: "I have not written a single letter about the [Divine] Providence in relation to my own condition. However, whenever my personal circumstances have become strained, I found consolation in it."

Abu Bakr Muhammad b. ʿUmar al-Warraq al-Tirmidhi

He resided in Balkh. He studied with Ahmad b. Khadrawayh [Khidruya] and others, and wrote books on [spiritual] self-discipline.

I heard Shaykh Abu ʿAbd al-Rahman al-Sulami say: I heard Muhammad b. al-Husayn – may God have mercy on him – say: I heard Abu Bakr al-Warraq say: "Whosoever [seeks to] satisfy his members' passions, has planted in his heart the tree of repentance." I heard Shaykh Abu ʿAbd al-Rahman al-Sulami say: I heard Abu Bakr al-Balkhi say: I heard Abu Bakr al-Warraq say: "If someone is to ask greed about its father, it would answer that it is doubt in that which has been predetermined [by God]. And if it is asked about its occupation, it would answer that it is the acquisition of ignominy. And if it is asked about its goal, it would answer that it is the exclusion [from God's favor]."

Abu Bakr al-Warraq used to prohibit his companions from travels and journeys. He said: "The key to blessing is to remain patiently in the location of your volition until your volition has come to fruition. And when it has come to fruition, the first traces of blessing will appear upon you."

Abu Saʿid Ahmad b. ʿIsa al-Kharraz[206]

He came from Baghdad.//80 He studied with Dhu ʾl-Nun al-Misri, al-Nibaji, Abu ʿUbayd al-Busri, al-Sari [al-Saqati], Bishr [al-Hafi] and others. He died in the year 277.[207]

Abu Saʿid al-Kharraz said: "Any interior that is at odds with [its] exterior is mistaken." I heard Muhammad b. al-Husayn say: I heard Abu ʿAbdallah al-Razi say: I heard Abu ʾl-ʿAbbas al-Sayyad say: I heard Abu Saʿid al-Kharraz say: "In a dream I saw the Devil. He kept away from me. I said to him: 'Come closer! What's the matter with you?' He answered: 'What can I do to you [folks]?[208] You have divested yourselves of things by which I beguile people!' I asked: 'What is it?' He answered: 'This worldly life!' As he was about to leave, he turned to me and said: 'And yet I have one subtle [ruse] against you.' I asked him what it was. He answered: 'Keeping the company of adolescent boys!'"[209]

Abu Saʿid al-Kharraz said: "I have kept the company of the Sufis for God knows how long and never had any disagreement with them." Someone asked

---

206 On him see *IM*, pp. 56–60.
207 890 C.E.
208 That is, the Sufis.
209 On the practice of mixing with and gazing at beardless boys and adolescents, see Baldick, *Mystical Islam*, pp. 20, 134, 173. It was condemned by some Sufi masters.

him why. He answered: "Because both they and I are fighting our common enemy, our souls."

Abu ʿAbdallah Muhammad b. Ismaʿil al-Maghribi

He was a teacher of Ibrahim b. Shayban and a disciple of ʿAli b. Razin. He lived one hundred and twenty years and died in 299.[210] He was a unique person. For many years he ate nothing that had been touched by the human hand. Instead he ate the roots of some plants, to which he had grown accustomed.

Abu ʿAbdallah al-Maghribi said: "The best of all [pious] works is when you fill the moments [of your life] with acts of obedience [to God]." He also said: "The most despised of all creatures is the poor man who fawns upon a rich man or abases himself before him. And the greatest of all creatures is the rich man who humbles himself before//81 the poor and holds them in high regard."

Abu ʾl-ʿAbbas Ahmad b. Muhammad Masruq

His came from Tus,[211] but he resided in Baghdad. He studied with al-Harith al-Muhasibi and al-Sari al-Saqati, and died in Baghdad in the year 298 or 299.[212]

Ibn Masruq said: "When one watches God Most High in the movements of his heart, God will protect the movements of his limbs." He said: "Holding in high esteem the sacredness of the believers means holding in high esteem the sacredness of God Most High. Through this the servant [of God] will arrive at the station of the true piety."[213] He said: "The tree of [divine] gnosis is watered by contemplation; the tree of negligence [of God] is watered by ignorance; the tree of repentance is watered by remorse. The tree of love [of God] is watered by the water of agreement and compliance [with God's will]."

He also said: "If you aspire to obtain [divine] knowledge without first establishing yourself firmly in the stages of spiritual striving,[214] you will languish in ignorance forever; and if you try to attain spiritual striving without first realizing fully the station of repentance,[215] you will be unaware of what you are trying to achieve."

Abu ʾl-Hasan ʿAli b. Sahl al-Isbahani

He was a contemporary of al-Junayd. When ʿAmr b. ʿUthman al-Makki came to him about a debt that he had incurred, [ʿAli b. Sahl] settled it for him. It was

---

210 That is, in 911 C.E.; according to other sources, he died in 291/904.
211 A city in Iran that was located near present-day Meshhed.
212 That is, 910 or 911 C.E.
213 That is, one should respect the rights of other people as much as one respects the rights of God.
214 That is, the Sufi path.
215 That is, the first station of the Sufi path.

thirty thousand *dirhams*. He met Abu Turab al-Nakhshabi and [the Sufis of] his generation.

I heard Muhammad b. al-Husayn say: I heard Abu Bakr Muhammad b. ʿAbdallah al-Tabari say://82 I heard ʿAli b. Sahl say: "When you hurry to do acts of piety, this is a sign of Godspeed. When you abstain from acts of disobedience [to God] this is a sign of vigilance. When you keep the secret of your heart of hearts, this is a sign of [spiritual] wakefulness. An ostentatious display of presumptions is [an evidence of] human foolishness. He who does not rest the beginnings of his spiritual striving on a sound foundation, will never achieve sound results."

Abu Muhammad Ahmad b. Muhammad b. al-Husayn al-Jurayri[216]

He was one of the greatest companions of al-Junayd. He studied with Sahl b. ʿAbdallah [al-Tustari] and was appointed as successor to al-Junayd [after his death]. He was knowledgeable in the sciences of this community[217] and possessed an [advanced] spiritual state. He died in 311.[218]

I heard Abu ʿAbdallah al-Shirazi [Ibn Khafif] say: I heard Ahmad b. ʿAtaʾ al-Rudhbari say: "Al-Jurayri died in the year of al-Habir.[219] One year later I was passing by that place and saw him sitting there leaning [on something], his knee to his breast and finger pointing to God."

I heard Muhammad b. al-Husayn – may God have mercy on him – say: I heard Abu ʾl-Husayn al-Farisi say: I heard Abu Muhammad al-Jurayri say: "When the [animal] soul prevails over someone, he will become a captive of his lustful urges, imprisoned in the jail of passions. God will then deprive his heart of spiritual knowledge and he will be able neither to enjoy the words of God Most High nor to find pleasure in them, even though he may repeat them constantly with his tongue. For God Most High said: 'I shall turn away from My signs those who wax proud in the earth unjustly.'"[220]

Al-Jurayri said: "One observes the fundamentals [of the Divine Law][221] by implementing [its] branches[222] and one tests the soundness of the branches by comparing them to the fundamentals. One will never//83 attain to the station of the contemplation of the fundamentals unless one holds in high regard the means

---

216 On him see *IM*, p. 66.
217 That is, the Sufis.
218 924 C.E.
219 A dune region in Arabia that was the site of an attack on the Muslim pilgrims by the Qarmati sect led by a ruthless rebel leader, Abu Tahir al-Jannabi. It resulted in the capture and massacre of hundreds of pilgrims. See Halm, *The Empire of the Mahdi*, pp. 252–253. From the context of the story it appears that al-Jurayri was among those massacred by the Qarmatis in the desert.
220 Q. 7:146. In the Qurʾan the word "signs" may also refer to the verses of the Muslim Holy Book.
221 As laid down in the Qurʾan and the Prophet's custom (*al-sunna*).
222 That is, the particular cases to which the fundamentals are applied in everyday legal practice.

and the branches [of the Divine Law]. For God Himself has elevated the latter to a high position."

Abu 'l-'Abbas Ahmad b. Muhammad b. Sahl b. 'Ata' al-Adami[223]

He was a great Sufi master and scholar. [Abu Sa'id] al-Kharraz used to praise him highly. He belonged to the generation of al-Junayd and was a companion of Ibrahim al-Maristani. He died in the year 309.[224]

I heard Muhammad b. al-Husayn say: I heard Abu Sa'id al-Qurashi say: I heard Ibn 'Ata' say: "He who obeys the rulings of the Divine Law, God will enlighten his heart with the light of [divine] gnosis, and there is no better station than following in the footsteps of the Beloved[225] – may God bless and greet him – in his commands, his deeds and his moral character traits." Ibn 'Ata' said: "The greatest negligence is when the servant [of God] neglects God – may He be great and exalted – His commands and prohibitions as well as the proper manners due to Him."

I heard Abu 'Abdallah al-Shirazi [Ibn Khafif] – may God have mercy on him – say: I heard 'Abd al-Rahman Ahmad al-Sufi say: I heard Ibn 'Ata' say: "Whenever you seek something, you should seek it in the arena of [religious] science. If you do not find it [there], [look for it] in the field of wisdom. If you do not find it [there either] weigh it [on the scale] of God's oneness. And if you do not find it in any of these three places, then strike with it the face of Satan."

Abu Ishaq Ibrahim b. Ahmad al-Khawwas

He was a friend of al-Junayd and al-Nuri. He had vast knowledge of trust in God[226] and spiritual self-discipline. He died at Rayy in the year 291.[227] He suffered from a stomach disease.[228] Therefore each time he had to stand up, he had to perform a major ablution. Once he entered water[229] and died there – may God have mercy on him.

I heard that Muhammad b. al-Husayn – may God have mercy on him – said: I heard that Ahmad b. 'Ali b. Ja'far said: I heard that al-Azdi said: I heard that al-Khawwas said: "Five things serve as a cure for the heart: a thoughtful reading of the Qur'an, an empty stomach, night vigils, supplications in the early morning, and keeping the company of the righteous."

---

223 On this famous Sufi theorist and a close friend of al-Hallaj, see *IM*, 'Index" under "Ibn 'Ata'".
224 922 C.E.
225 That is, the prophet Muhammad.
226 On this concept see *IM*, "Index of terms" under "*tawakkul*".
227 903 C.E.
228 It appears that he had chronic diarrhea.
229 Perhaps it was a shallow pool attached to the mosque.

Abu Muhammad ʿAbdallah b. Muhammad al-Kharraz

He came from [the city of] Rayy and resided in Mecca. He studied with Abu Hafs [al-Haddad] and Abu ʿImran al-Kabir. He was one of those who practiced scrupulous discernment. He died before the year 310.[230]

I heard Shaykh Abu ʿAbd al-Rahman al-Sulami say: I heard Abu Nasr al-Tusi say: I heard al-Duqqi say: "I came to Abdallah al-Kharraz after I had fasted for four days. He said: 'One of you has fasted for four days and hunger has begun to call upon him.' He then said: 'If every living soul were to perish for the sake of what it expects from God, do you think that would be a lot?'" Abu Muhammad ʿAbdallah al-Kharraz said: "Hunger is the food of the ascetics and remembrance of God is the food of the gnostics."//85

Abu ʾl-Hasan Bunan b. Muhammad al-Hammal

He came from Wasit,[231] but lived in Egypt where he died in 318.[232] He was a great man, who [was known for his] miracles.

Someone asked Bunan about the most exalted spiritual state of the Sufis. He answered: "Trust in what is predetermined [by God], the fulfillment of [God's] commands, the protection of the heart [from temptations] and withdrawal from both worlds."

I heard that Muhammad b. al-Husayn said: I heard that al-Husayn b. Ahmad al-Razi said: I heard that Abu ʿAli al-Rudhbari said: Bunan al-Hammal was thrown to a lion.[233] The lion sniffed him, but did him no harm. When he was brought back, someone asked him: "What did you feel when the lion was sniffing you?" He said: "I was thinking about the disagreement of the scholars regarding the saliva of wild animals."[234]

Abu Hamza al-Baghdadi al-Bazzaz

He died before al-Junayd. He was a friend of al-Junayd's and studied with al-Sari [al-Saqati] and al-Hasan al-Musuhi. He was an expert on Qurʾan recitation and a jurist. He was a descendant of ʿIsa b. Aban. Ahmad b. Hanbal used to ask him about various [legal] issues: "What do you say about this, Sufi?"

They say that he was speaking [to students] at his assembly on Friday, when suddenly his condition changed [for the worse] and he fell from his chair. He died on the next Friday. They say that he died in the year 289.[235]//86

---

230 923 C.E.
231 A city in Lower Iraq.
232 928 C.E.
233 This was done on the orders of Egypt's ruler Ahmad b. Tulun (r. 254–270/868–884), who was angered by al-Hammal's criticism of his edicts.
234 That is, whether the saliva of the wild beasts is ritually pure or impure.
235 901 C.E.

Abu Hamza said: "Whosoever knows the path of God Most High will travel on it easily and there is no better guide on the path to God than to follow in the footsteps of the Messenger – may God bless and greet him – as regards his spiritual conditions, actions and words." Abu Hamza also said: "Any man can stay away from evil deeds if [God] has endowed him with three things: an empty stomach with a content heart, continual poverty with constant asceticism, and continual patience with constant recollection [of God]."

Abu Bakr Muhammad b. Musa al-Wasiti[236]

He originally came from Khurasan, from the region of Farghana.[237] He studied with al-Junayd and al-Nuri. He was a great scholar. He resided in Marw, where he died after 320.[238]

Al-Wasiti said: "Fear and hope are two reins that restrain the servant [of God] from behaving improperly." He said: "The quest of compensation for the acts of obedience [to God] springs from the forgetfulness of [God's] beneficence." Al-Wasiti said: "When God wants to disgrace His servant, He throws him into this perversity and rotting corpses." He meant the companionship of the youth.

I heard Muhammad b. al-Husayn – may God have mercy on him – say: I heard Muhammad b. ʿAbd al-ʿAziz al-Marwazi say: I heard al-Wasiti say: "They have presented bad manners as sincerity, the greed of their souls as freedom of action and their lowly aspirations as firmness of character. Through this they have lost the true path and found themselves in a narrow spot. There is no life in their [spiritual] visions, there is no piety in their speeches. Whenever they utter a word, they reveal anger; when they make a public address, they show vanity. The impetuosity of their souls speaks about the perfidy of their inner selves, and their voracious appetite for food testifies to the darkness of their hearts. God assail them! How perverted they are!"[239]

I heard the master Abu ʿAli al-Daqqaq – may God have mercy on him – say: "A man from Marw once heard a pharmacist saying://87 '[One Friday] al-Wasiti was passing by my store on the way to the cathedral mosque. Suddenly a strap of his sandal broke. I told him: "Shaykh, would you allow me to repair your sandal?" He said: "Go ahead, repair!" After I repaired the strap, he asked me: "Do you know why the strap of my sandal was broken?" I said: "[No,] tell me!" He said: "Because I did not wash myself for [the sake of] Friday." I told him: "My lord, here's a bath. Do you want to use it?" He said yes. So I took him to the bath and he washed himself.'"

---

236 On him see *IM*, pp. 100–101.
237 In present-day Uzbekistan.
238 932 C.E.
239 Q. 63:4 and 9:30.

Abu ʾl-Hasan b. al-Saʾigh

His name is ʿAli b. Muhammad b. Sahl al-Dinawari. He resided in Egypt, where he died. He was a great Sufi master. Abu ʿUthman al-Maghribi said: "I have not seen any Sufi master who was more enlightened than Abu Yaʿqub al-Nahrajuri; nor did I see a Sufi master who was so full of awe of God as Abu ʾl-Hasan b. al-Saʾigh." He died in the year 330.[240]

Someone asked Ibn al-Saʾigh about providing a proof of an absent thing by using a thing that is in evidence. He said: "How can one provide proof of Him Who has no semblance or equal by using the attributes of those who have both semblance and equals?!" Someone asked him about the characteristics of the Sufi [novice]. He answered by quoting the words of God: "When the earth became strait for them, for all its breadth, and their souls became strait for them."[241] //88 He also said: "The spiritual states are like lightning. When they last, this is nothing but self-deception and the prompting of one's lower nature."

Abu Ishaq Ibrahim b. Dawud al-Raqqi

He was a great Sufi master of Syria, who was a friend of al-Junayd and Ibn al-Jallaʾ. He lived a long life and died 326.[242] Ibrahim al-Raqqi said: "Divine knowledge is the assertion of God as He is and placing Him beyond whatever one might imagine about Him." He said: "[God's] power is evident and the eyes of men are open, yet the light of spiritual sights has grown dimmer." He said: "The weakest of people is he who cannot repel his passions and the strongest of people is he who is capable of repelling them." He also said: "A sign of love of God is when you choose to obey Him and to follow in the footsteps of His Prophet – may God bless and greet him."

Mimshadh al-Dinawari

He was a great Sufi master. He died in 299.[243] Mimshadh said: "The good manners of the novice consist of obeying the commands of Sufi masters, serving his brethren, abandoning everything except the essentials, and observing the good manners prescribed by the Divine Law." Mimshadh said://89 "I have never entered into the presence of any of my Sufi masters without first divesting myself of everything that is mine in order to partake of the blessings that are imparted to me by seeing them and [listening to] their instructions. When anyone enters into the presence of the master with something that is his own, he will be cut off from the blessings of [the master's] vision, admonition and instruction."

---

240 941 C.E.
241 Q. 9:118.
242 937 C.E.
243 911 C.E.

Khayr al-Nassaj

He studied with Abu Hamza al-Baghdadi, met al-Sari [al-Saqati] and was a friend of Abu 'l-Husayn al-Nuri. He lived a very long life. They say that he lived one hundred and twenty years. Al-Shibli and [Ibrahim] al-Khawwas repented during his preaching[244] and he was the teacher of many others. They say that his name was Muhammad b. Isma'il. He came from Samarra.[245] He was named "Khayr al-Nassaj"[246] after the following episode: He set out on a pilgrimage [to Mecca]. [When he reached] the gate of Kufa, a man seized him and said: "You are my slave! Your name is Khayr!" Khayr had a dark complexion. He did not object to the man and the latter employed him as a weaver of silk. Whenever the man called: "Khayr!", he would respond: "At your service!" After a while, the man told him: "I was mistaken. You are not my slave and your name is not Khayr!" So he went away and left the man. He said: "I will not change the name that was given to me by a Muslim."

He said: "Fear is the whip of God by which he straightens the souls that have grown accustomed to bad manners." I heard Abu 'Abd al-Rahman al-Sulami – may God have mercy on him – say: I heard Abu 'l-Hasan al-Qazwini say: I heard Abu 'l-Husayn al-Maliki say: I asked one of those who were present at Khayr al-Nassaj's deathbed about what happened to him. He answered: "When it was the time for the sunset prayer, he lost consciousness. A few moments later he opened his eyes and pointed toward the door of the house saying:[247]//90 'Wait, may God protect you! Both you and I are servants, who take their orders [from God]. What you are ordered to do will not elude you, whereas I shall miss what I am ordered to do.' So he called for water and performed an ablution for the prayer. He then stretched himself [on the bed], closed his eyes, uttered the *shahada*,[248] and passed away."

Someone saw him in a dream and asked him: "What did God do to you?" He answered: "Don't ask me about this. [All I can say is that] I have finally found rest from this filthy world of yours!"

Abu Hamza al-Khurasani

He was from Nishapur, from the quarter called Mulqabadh. He was a friend of al-Junayd, [Abu Sa'id] al-Kharraz and Abu Turab al-Nakhshabi. He was a scrupulous and righteous man.

Abu Hamza said: "When someone is frightened by the reminder about [approaching] death, he begins to love everything that is permanent and hate everything that is transitory." He said: "The [divine] gnostic strives to maintain

---

244 That is, they embraced the Sufi path.
245 A town on the east bank of the river Tigris in Iraq, approximately 80 miles north of Baghdad.
246 That is, "Khayr the Weaver".
247 The context indicates that he was talking to the angel of death, 'Izra'il.
248 That is, the ritual phrase "There is no deity but God and Muhammad is His messenger".

his life day by day, and he receives his livelihood day by day."²⁴⁹ A man asked him for a piece of advice. [He answered]: "Prepare provisions for the journey that lies before you."²⁵⁰

I heard Muhammad b. al-Husayn – may God have mercy on him – say: I heard Abu 'l-Tayyib al-ʿAkki say: I heard Abu 'l-Hasan al-Misri say: I heard Abu Hamza al-Khurasani say: "I wore a woolen cloak in a consecrated state. Thus, year after year I travel a thousand *farsakhs*,²⁵¹ while the sun was rising and setting on me. As soon as I left my consecrated state, I hurried to re-enter it again."²⁵²

He died in the year 290.²⁵³

Abu Bakr Dulaf b. Jahdar al-Shibli²⁵⁴

He was born and raised in Baghdad, though his ancestors hailed from Usrushana²⁵⁵//91. He studied with al-Junayd and his contemporaries, and was [himself] a great master of his time in his spiritual state, acumen and knowledge. He adhered to the Maliki school of law. He lived eighty-seven years and died in the year 334.²⁵⁶ His grave is located in Baghdad.

After al-Shibli had repented during a teaching assembly of Khayr al-Nassaj, he came to Demavend²⁵⁷ and said: "I have been the ruler of your land. Now discharge me [from my duties]!" At the beginning, his self-exertion [on the path of God] had no limit. I heard the master Abu ʿAli al-Daqqaq – may God have mercy on him – say: "I was told that he rubbed a lot of salt into his eyes to prepare himself for night vigils. Therefore sleep never overtook him. The great respect for the Divine Law that he showed on his death bed, as reported by Bakran al-Dinawari, is an ample example [of his great piety]!"²⁵⁸

I heard Shaykh Abu ʿAbd al-Rahman al-Sulami – may God have mercy on him – say: I heard Abu 'l-ʿAbbas al-Baghdadi say: "At the end of his days al-Shibli – may God have mercy on him – used to say:

---

249 A pun on the dual meaning of the Arabic word ʿaysh, which means both "life" and "livelihood" (or "subsistence"). Many Sufi masters insisted that a Sufi should earn enough for one day only and set nothing aside for tomorrow.
250 That is, get ready for the inevitable death and the last judgement.
251 The distance that is covered by a mounted traveler within an hour of journey at a regular pace (approximately three miles).
252 This saying refers to the practice of consecrating oneself before setting out on a pilgrimage to Mecca (*ihram*). Whereas ordinary pilgrims enter the *ihram* only for the duration of the pilgrimage, Abu Hamza claims to have maintained it continuously.
253 902 C.E.
254 On him see *IM*, pp. 64–66.
255 A province in Transoxiana.
256 946 C.E.
257 A province in Iran.
258 The story in question describes the last minutes of al-Shibli's life. Before he died, he confessed that he had once given as alms a *dirham* that he had found in the market, which was his only sin. When Bakran, who performed the last rites on him, neglected to wash his beard al-Shibli, already in coma, grabbed him by the hand and guided it to the beard. See al-Sarraj, *al-Lumaʿ*, p. 210.

There are so many [dangerous] places [in this life] that were I to perish in any of them,
I would be a stern warning for the rest of the family."²⁵⁹

During the month of Ramadan, al-Shibli used to exert himself more than any of his contemporaries. He said: "My Lord has revered this month and I am the first [of my fellow human beings] to glorify it!"//92 I heard the master Abu ʿAli al-Daqqaq recount this story.

Abu Muhammad ʿAbdallah b. Muhammad al-Murtaʿish

He came from Nishapur, from the quarter called al-Hira, although some say that he came from Mulqabadh. He studied with Abu Hafs [al-Haddad] and Abu ʿUthman [al-Hiri].²⁶⁰ He was a great man. He used to stay at the Shuniziyya mosque.²⁶¹ He died in Baghdad in the year 328.²⁶²

Al-Murtaʿish said: "Desire [of God] is restraining [your] soul from what it desires, turning [your] full attention to the commands of God Most High, and satisfaction with what [God] has predetermined for you." He was told that someone can walk on water. He answered: "For me, the person whom God has enabled to resist his passions is far greater than the one who can walk on air."

Abu ʿAli Ahmad b. Muhammad al-Rudhbari

He was born in Baghdad and lived in Egypt, where he died in 322.²⁶³ He studied with al-Junayd, al-Nuri, Ibn al-Jallaʾ and [the Sufis of that] generation. He was one of the cleverest [Sufi] masters who had profound knowledge of the Sufi path.

I heard Shaykh Abu ʿAbd al-Rahman al-Sulami – may God have mercy on him – say: I heard Abu ʾl-Qasim al-Dimashqi say: Someone asked Abu ʿAli al-Rudhbari about a man who liked listening to music and who used to say://93 "This is permitted for me, because I have attained such a degree [of perfection] that any change in my internal state no longer has any influence on me." [Al-Rudhbari] answered: "Yes, he has attained. But he has attained hellfire!" Someone asked him about Sufism. He answered: "This teaching is serious through and through. Do not mix it up with any amusement!"

I heard Muhammad b. al-Husayn – may God have mercy on him – say: I heard Mansur b. ʿAbdallah say: I heard Abu ʿAli al-Rudhbari say: "One sign of delusion is that God treats you well, although you commit sins. You then begin to forsake repentance and remorse as you fancy that [God] will pardon your transgressions and consider this to be God's lenience toward you." He said: "My

---

259 That is, for the rest of mankind.
260 On them see notes 126 and 163.
261 That is, a mosque located near the al-Shuniziyya cemetery of Baghdad.
262 939 C.E.
263 933 C.E.

teacher of Sufism was al-Junayd; my teacher of jurisprudence was Abu ʾl-ʿAbbas b. Surayj,[264] my teacher of polite literature was Thaʿlab[265] and my teacher of prophetic reports was Ibrahim al-Harbi."[266]

Abu Muhammad ʿAbdallah b. Munazil

He was a master of the *malamatiyya*,[267] who was unique in his age. He studied with Hamdun al-Qassar. He was a [great] scholar, who wrote down many prophetic reports. He died at Nishapur in the year 329 or 330.[268]

I heard Muhammad b. al-Husayn – may God have mercy on him – say: I heard ʿAbdallah al-Muʿallim say: I heard ʿAbdallah b. Munazil say: "He who neglects a religious duty will inevitably be tested by God Most High, who will cause him to neglect the Prophet's custom; and as soon as one has been tested by neglecting the Prophet's custom, he will also be tested by a [reprehensible] innovation."[269]

I heard Shaykh Abu ʿAbd al-Rahman al-Sulami say: I heard Abu Ahmad b. ʿIsa say: I heard ʿAbdallah b. Munazil say: "Your best moments are when you are safe from the promptings of your [lower] soul and when [your] neighbors are safe from your thinking ill [of them]."//94

Abu ʿAli Muhammad b. ʿAbd al-Wahhab al-Thaqafi

He was a great religious leader of his age. He studied with Abu Hafs [al-Haddad] and Hamdun al-Qassar. It was during his lifetime that Sufism appeared in Nishapur. He died in 328.[270]

I heard Muhammad b. al-Husayn say: I heard Mansur b. ʿAbdallah say: I heard Abu ʿAli al-Thaqafi say: "If someone could absorb all the sciences and keep the company of many different people, he would still be unable to attain the rank of the real men[271] unless he engages in [ascetic] exercises under the supervision of a [Sufi] master, a religious leader or a sincere preacher. If someone has not learned his manners from a teacher who has shown him the faults of his works and the flippancy of his soul, you must not follow his example in rectifying [your own] works."

Abu ʿAli – may God have mercy on him – said: "There will come a time when life will not be happy for any man in this community unless he seeks the

---

264 A famous legal scholar of Baghdad, who was the head of the Shafiʿi school of law in his age; he died 306/918. See "Ibn Suraydj" in *EI*.
265 A famous grammarian of Kufa, who died in 291/904.
266 A famous traditionalist and man of letters, who died in 285/898. See "Ibrahim al-Harbi" in *EI*.
267 See above note 126.
268 940 or 941 C.E.
269 Many Muslim scholars saw any innovation that was not attested by the Prophet's custom as a grave sin.
270 939 C.E.
271 That is, educated Sufi masters.

support of a hypocrite." He also said: "Say fie to the good things of this life, when it treats you well and fie to the losses [that you suffer] in it, when it turns its back on you. An intelligent man will never put his trust in something that treats you well one moment and turns its back on you the next."

Abu ʾl-Khayr al-Aqtaʿ

He was of Maghribi background and resided at Taynat.[272] He had many miracles and possessed [the gift of] clairvoyance.//95 He was a man of great stature. He died around the year 340.[273]

Abu ʾl-Khayr said: "No-one can achieve a noble [spiritual] state unless he always complies [with God's will],[274] embraces good manners, fulfills all the religious duties and keeps the company of the righteous."

Abu Bakr Muhammad b. ʿAli al-Kattani

He came from Baghdad and studied with al-Junayd, al-Kharraz and al-Nuri. He resided in Mecca until he died in the year 322.[275]

I heard that Shaykh Abu ʿAbd al-Rahman al-Sulami – may God have mercy on him – said: I heard that Abu Bakr al-Razi said: "Al-Kattani saw an old man with white hair and white beard begging among people. He said: 'This is a man who neglected the rights of God in his youth, therefore God neglected him in his old age.' Al-Kattani said: 'Passion is the rein of Satan. Whosoever takes Satan's rein in his hand, inevitably becomes his slave.'"

Abu Yaʿqub Ishaq b. Muhammad al-Nahrajuri

He studied with ʿAmr al-Makki, Abu Yaʿqub al-Susi, al-Junayd and others.//96 He died in Mecca, where he resided for some time, in the year 300.[276]

I heard Muhammad b. al-Husayn say: I heard Abu ʾl-Husayn Ahmad b. ʿAli say: I heard al-Nahrajuri say: "This world is a sea and the next world is a coast. The ship is fear of God, and all people are a party of seafarers."

I heard that Muhammad b. al-Husayn said: I heard that Abu Bakr al-Razi said: I heard that al-Nahrajuri said: "Once I saw a one-eyed man circumambulating the Kaʿba. He was saying: 'I take refuge from you by you!' I asked him what kind of prayer that was. He answered: 'One day I looked at a [handsome] person and took a liking to him. All of a sudden, there was a blow on my eye and it popped out. I heard a voice saying: 'A blow for each look; if you do it again, I'll do it to you again too!'"

---

272 A village in Syria.
273 951 C.E.
274 As expressed in the Qurʾan and the Prophet's custom.
275 933 C.E.
276 912 C.E.

I heard Muhammad b. al-Husayn say: I heard Ahmad b. ʿAli say: I heard al-Nahrajuri say: "The best of all [spiritual] states is one that agrees with the knowledge [of the Divine Law]."

Abu ʾl-Hasan ʿAli b. Muhammad al-Muzayyin

He came from Baghdad. He studied with Sahl b. ʿAbdallah al-Tustari, al-Junayd and [the Sufis of their] generation. He died in Mecca, where he resided, in the year 328.[277] He was famous for his scrupulous piety.//97

I heard Shaykh Abu ʿAbd al-Rahman al-Sulami say: I heard Abu Bakr al-Razi say: I heard al-Muzayyin say: "A sin that follows an [earlier] sin is the punishment for the previous sin. A good deed that follows an [earlier] good deed is the reward for the previous good deed." Someone asked al-Muzayyin about God's oneness. He answered: "When you know that the attributes of the Most High are distinct from the attributes of His creatures. He is different from them in His attributes due to [His] eternity, whereas they differ from Him in their attributes due to their creaturely nature." He also said: "If someone is not fully satisfied with God, God will make him dependent on His creatures; and if someone is fully satisfied with God, God will make His creatures dependent on him."

Abu ʿAli b. al-Katib

His name is al-Hasan b. Ahmad. He studied with Abu ʿAli al-Rudhbari, Abu Bakr al-Misri and others. He was a person of great stature. He died around the year 340.[278] Ibn al-Katib said: "When fear [of God] settles down in the heart, the tongue begins to utter only things that it really means." Ibn al-Katib said://98 "The Muʿtazilites[279] have stripped God of creaturely attributes with the help of the intellect and erred. The Sufis, on the other hand, have stripped God of creaturely attributes with the help of the knowledge [of the Divine Law] and hit the mark."

Muzaffar al-Qirmisini

He was a [Sufi] master from the mountain.[280] He studied with Abu Saʿid al-Kharraz and others.

Muzaffar al-Qirmisini said: "There are three types of fasting. The fasting of the spirit, which is to curtail one's hope; the fasting of the intellect, which is to resist one's passions; and the fasting of the soul, which is to restrain oneself from food and prohibited things." Muzaffar said: "The worst kind of attachment is

---

277 939 C.E.
278 950 C.E.
279 A school of Islamic theology that stressed a rational approach to the Muslim Revelation. They presented God as an absolutely transcendent entity of which no positive judgement can be made, because that would result in likening Him to His creatures. See "Muʿtazila" in *EI*.
280 According to some commentators, this is Mount Qasyun at the outskirts of Damascus (presently within the city limit).

attachment to women in whatever form!" He said: "When hunger is supported by contentment, it becomes a [fertile] field for [pious] thoughts, a spring of wisdom, the revival of prudence, and the lamp of the heart." He said: "The best of the servants' deeds is when [they] protect their moments – that is, they do not fall short in anything, nor do they go beyond a set limit." He also said: "If someone has not learned his good manners from a wise man, then a novice should not study with him."

Abu Bakr ʿAbdallah b. Tahir al-Abhari

He was a friend of al-Shibli and one of the [Sufi] masters of the mountain.[281] He was learned and pious. He studied with Yusuf b. al-Husayn and others.//99 He died around the year 330.[282]

I heard Shaykh Abu ʿAbd al-Rahman al-Sulami say: I heard Mansur b. ʿAbdallah say: I heard Abu Bakr b. Tahir say: "The poor[283] must have no desire. If, however, it is unavoidable, then his desire should not exceed his [minimal] subsistence" – that is, what he requires to live. According to the same chain of transmission, he also said: "When I love a brother in God, I try to deal with him as little as possible in this world."

Abu ʾl-Husayn b. Bunan

He studied with Abu Saʿid al-Kharraz. He was a great [Sufi] master of Egypt. Ibn Bunan said: "If concern for livelihood has settled down in a Sufi's heart, he should preoccupy himself with [pious] works, for this would bring him closer to God. A sign of his heart's reliance on God is that he is more sure about what is in the hands of God than about what is in his own hands." He also said: "Keep away from base morals as you keep away from the things that are prohibited [by the Divine Law]."

Abu Ishaq Ibrahim b. Shayban al-Qirmisini

He was the greatest [Sufi] master of his age. He studied with Abu ʿAbdallah al-Maghribi, [Ibrahim] al-Khawwas and others. I heard Muhammad b. al-Husayn say: I heard Abu Zayd al-Marwazi al-Faqih say: I heard Ibrahim b. Shayban say: "If someone aspires to laziness and idleness, he should practice dispensations."[284] According to the same chain of transmitters, he said: "The knowledge of self-annihilation [in God] and subsistence [in God][285] turns on the sincere profession

---

281 See the previous note.
282 941 C.E.
283 That is, the Sufi master.
284 That is, dispensations from some of the severer Sufi requirements that were seen as legitimate by some Sufi masters, yet were looked down upon by the more stern Sufi shaykhs. For details see *IM*, pp. 194–195.
285 On these notions see "Baka' wa-fana'" in *EI*.

of [the doctrine of] Divine oneness and a true worship of God. The rest is [Devil's] snares and heresy."

Ibrahim also said: "The lowly rabble are those who disobey God – may He be great and exalted."

Abu Bakr al-Husayn b. ʿAli b. Yazdanyar

He came from Urmiya.[286] He practiced a method of Sufism that was peculiar to him and he was learned and pious. He reproached some gnostics[287] for the pronouncements and statements that they had made.

Ibn Yazdanyar said: "Don't try to achieve intimacy with God if you love intimacy with people. Don't try to love God if you like to concern yourself with things that should not concern you. Don't strive to obtain a [high] rank in the eyes of God if you love a [high] rank in the eyes of people."

Abu Saʿid b. al-Aʿrabi

His name is Ahmad b. Muhammad b. Ziyad b. Bishr. He resided at the Holy Sanctuary,[288] where he died in the year 341.[289] He studied with al-Junayd, ʿAmr b. ʿUthman al-Makki, al-Nuri and others.

Ibn al-Aʿrabi said: "The greatest losers are those who show only their good works to people, for He Who is 'nearer to him [man] than the jugular vein'[290] will expose evil deeds [anyway]."

Abu ʿAmr Muhammad b. Ibrahim al-Zajjaji al-Naysaburi

He resided in Mecca for a long time and died there. He studied with al-Junayd, Abu ʿUthman [al-Hiri], al-Nuri, [Ibrahim] al-Khawwas and Ruwaym [b. Ahmad]. He died in the year 348.[291]

I heard Shaykh Abu ʿAbd al-Rahman al-Sulami – may God have mercy on him – say: I heard my grandfather Abu ʿAmr b. Nujayd say: "Someone asked Abu ʿAmr al-Zajjaji: 'How come that you lose control each time you utter [the phrase] "God is the greatest" at the time of the ritual prayer?' He answered: 'Because I fear that I may open my ritual prayer with something other than sincerity. When someone says: "God is the greatest", whereas in his heart there is something that he considers to be greater than God or when, at some point in time, he held something to be greater than God, then he has declared himself to be a liar by his own tongue.'" He said: "When someone speaks about a [spiritual] state that he has not yet attained, his words are a temptation for those who listen

---

286 According to an alternative reading, he was a native of Armenia.
287 Some manuscripts have "Iraqis" instead of "gnostics".
288 That is, in Mecca.
289 952 C.E.
290 Q. 50:16.
291 939 C.E.

to him and an empty claim. [Furthermore,] God will not allow him to attain this state."

He lived in Mecca for many years, yet he never performed his ritual ablutions in the sanctuary. Rather he would go to some place [outside the sanctuary] and perform his ablutions there.[292]

Abu Muhammad Ja'far b. Muhammad b. Nusayr

He was born and raised in Baghdad. He studied with al-Junayd and associated himself with his circle. He also studied with al-Nuri, Ruwaym, Samnun and other [Sufis] of that generation. He died in Baghdad in the year 348.[293]

Ja'far said: "The servant [of God] cannot mix the pleasure of dealing with God with the pleasure of his animal soul. That is why the men of the true realities cut all mundane ties which cut them from God, before these ties can cut them from God."

I heard Muhammad b. al-Husayn say: I heard Muhammad b. 'Abdallah b. Shadhan say: I heard that Ja'far said: "Before the servant [of God] can attain [the state of] direct encounter with God, the fear of God must install itself in his heart. When the fear of God has installed itself in his heart, the blessing of the knowledge [of the Divine Law] will descend upon it and the desire of this world will disappear from it."

Abu ʾl-ʿAbbas al-Sayyari

His name is al-Qasim b. al-Qasim. He came from Marw. He studied with [Abu Bakr] al-Wasiti and followed [his method] in regard to the sciences of this [Sufi] community. He was a [famous] scholar. He died in the year 342.[294]

Someone asked Abu ʾl-ʿAbbas al-Sayyari how the [Sufi] novice should control himself. He answered: "By patiently fulfilling [God's] commands, avoiding that which [God] prohibited, keeping the company of the righteous and serving the poor." He also said: "The intelligent man finds no pleasure whatsoever in contemplating God, because the contemplation of God leads to [his] self-annihilation[295] [in God], and there is no pleasure in this."

Abu Bakr Muhammad b. Dawud al-Dinawari

He was known as "al-Duqqi". He resided in Syria and he lived more than one hundred years. He died in Damascus after 350.[296] He studied with Ibn al-Jallaʾ and al-Zaqqaq.

---

292 He did so out of reverence for the holiness of the Meccan sanctuary.
293 959 C.E.
294 953 C.E.
295 See note 285.
296 961 C.E.

Abu Bakr al-Duqqi said: "The stomach is where [all kinds of] food are gathered. If you put there a pure food, your members will engage only in pious deeds. If you put there a [food of] uncertain origin, your progress along the path to God will become uncertain. When you put there an unlawfully obtained food, a veil will appear between you and God's command."

Abu Muhammad ʿAbdallah b. Muhammad al-Razi

He was born and raised in Nishapur. He studied with Abu ʿUthman al-Hiri, al-Junayd, Yusuf b. al-Husayn, Ruwaym [b. Ahmad], Samnun [al-Muhibb] and others. He died in the year 353.[297]

I heard Muhammad b. al-Husayn – may God have mercy on him – say: I heard ʿAbdallah al-Razi say: Someone asked [ʿAbdallah al-Razi] why people know their faults, yet do not correct them. He answered: "Because they busy themselves with competing with one another in [the superiority of their] knowledge [of the Divine Law] and yet they do not put their knowledge to use. They busy themselves with the externals, instead of busying themselves with improving their internal natures. Therefore God has made their hearts blind and prevented their limbs from performing the acts of worship."

Abu ʿAmr Ismaʿil b. Nujayd

He studied with Abu ʿUthman [al-Hiri] and met al-Junayd. He was a man of great stature and the last of Abu ʿUthman's disciples to die. He died at Mecca in the year 366.[298]

I heard Shaykh Abu ʿAbd al-Rahman al-Sulami – may God have mercy on him – say: I heard my grandfather Abu ʿAmr b. Nujayd say: "If a spiritual state does not spring from the knowledge [of the Divine Law], it brings harm rather than benefit to its possessor." [Al-Sulami] said: I also heard that he said: "If someone has neglected to perform a religious duty imposed upon him by God, he will be deprived of the pleasure of [performing] this duty at some point."

Someone asked him what Sufism is. He answered: "Patience under [God's] commands and prohibitions." [Al-Sulami] said: [Ibn Nujayd] said: "One of the servant's worst afflictions is his satisfaction with what he has achieved."

Abu ʾl-Hasan ʿAli b. Ahmad b. Sahl al-Bushanji

He was one of those men of Khurasan who practiced chivalry. He met Abu ʿUthman [al-Hiri], Ibn ʿAtaʾ [al-Adami], al-Jurayri and Abu ʿAmr al-Dimashqi. He died in 348.[299]

---

297 964 C.E.
298 976 C.E.
299 959 C.E.

Someone asked al-Bushanji what [true] manliness is.[300] He answered//106: "When you relinquish things that [God] prohibited to you in the presence of the noble writing angels."[301] Someone asked him: "Pray to God on my behalf." He said: "May God protect you from your [own] temptation!" He also said: "The beginning of faith is linked to its end."[302]

Abu ʿAbdallah Muhammad b. Khafif al-Shirazi[303]

He studied with Ruwaym [b. Ahmad], al-Jurayri, Ibn ʿAtaʾ [al-Adami] and others. He died in the year 371.[304] He was a great [Sufi] master who was unique in his epoch.

Ibn Khafif said: "[Spiritual] aspiration [to God][305] is constant toil and the forsaking of rest." He said: "Nothing is more dangerous for the [Sufi] novice than to allow himself to rely on dispensations[306] and to accept allegorical interpretations [of the Scripture]." Someone asked him about nearness to God. He answered: "It is when you are getting near to Him by complying [with His will], whereas He is getting near to you by constantly granting you success [in your undertakings]."

I heard Abu ʿAbdallah al-Sufi say: I heard Abu ʿAbdallah b. Khafif say: "During my early days [as a Sufi] I used to recite the phrase 'He is God, One'[307] ten thousand times [as I was performing] any one part of the ritual prayer. Sometimes I recited the entire Qurʾan during each part of the prayer, and sometimes I performed one thousand prayers between the early morning and the late afternoon."

I heard Abu ʿAbdallah b. Bakuya al-Shirazi – may God have mercy on him – say: I heard Abu Ahmad the Junior (al-Saghir) say: "Once a beggar came up [to us] and said to the master Abu ʿAbdallah b. Khafif: 'I hear [Satan's] whisper!' The master told him: 'I am accustomed to the Sufis making mockery of Satan. However, this time Satan is making mockery of them!'"

I heard Abu ʾl-ʿAbbas al-Karkhi say: I heard that Abu ʿAbdallah b. Khafif said: "When I became too frail to perform my supererogatory prayers standing upright, I began to perform each part of the prayer twice in the sitting position. For a report from the Prophet says: 'The prayer of the sitting one is a half of the prayer of the standing one.'"

---

300 Manliness was part of the chivalry code practiced by some young men in Khurasan.
301 That is, the angels who record all of man's deeds; cf. Q. 82:11 "There are over you watchers noble, writers who know whatever you do."
302 For a longer version of this statement that links it to Q. 98:5, see al-Sulami, *Tabaqat*, p. 484. The idea is to emphasize that a declaration of faith must be subsequently supported by the meticulous fulfillment of the requirements of the Divine Law.
303 On him see *IM*, "Index" under "Ibn Khafif".
304 982 C.E.
305 Ibn Khafif is referring here to the progress of the novice along the Sufi path.
306 See note 205.
307 Q. 112:1.

Abu ʾl-Husayn Bundar b. al-Husayn al-Shirazi

He was an expert on the fundamentals [of jurisprudence] and possessor of a great [spiritual] state. He studied with al-Shibli and died in Arrajan[308] in the year 353.[309]

Bundar b. al-Husayn said: "Do not oppose your soul. Leave it to its [true] Master and He will do with it what He wants!" Bundar said: "Keeping the company of the innovators leads to turning one's back on God." Bundar said://108 "Abandon the dictates of your passions for the sake of your hopes."[310]

Abu Bakr al-Tamastani

He studied with Ibrahim al-Dabbagh and others. He was unique in his age in his knowledge and [spiritual] state. He died in Nishapur after the year 340.[311]

Abu Bakr al-Tamastani said: "The greatest bliss is when you leave behind your soul, for the soul is the thickest veil between you and God." I heard Abu ʿAbdallah al-Shirazi – may God have mercy on him – say: I heard Mansur b. ʿAbdallah al-Isbahani say: I heard Abu Bakr al-Tamastani say: "As soon as the heart has become preoccupied [with something other than God], it is punished." He also said: "The path is clear and the [Holy] Book and the Prophet's custom are among us. The merit of the Companions [of the Prophet] is well known due to the fact that they emigrated [with the Prophet][312] and accompanied him. Those of us who have chosen as their companions the [Holy] Book and the Prophet's custom, and who have emigrated with their hearts from their souls and from the creatures to God's presence, are the veracious ones who have thereby achieved their goals."

Abu ʾl-ʿAbbas Ahmad b. Muhammad al-Dinawari

He studied with Yusuf b. al-Husayn, Ibn ʿAtaʾ and al-Jurayri. He was a great and distinguished scholar. He came to Nishapur and stayed there for a while. He was preaching to its people and spoke to them in the language of [divine] gnosis. Thereupon he left for Samarqand, where he died after the year 340.[313]

Abu ʾl-ʿAbbas al-Dinawari said: "The most simple [type of] recollection [of God] is when you forget everything but Him and the ultimate recollection is when the one who recollects [God] forgets his recollection in the process of recollection."//109 Abu ʾl-ʿAbbas said: "The tongue of one's outward state does not change what is inside [one's heart]."[314] Abu ʾl-ʿAbbas al-Dinawari also said: "They have demolished the pillars of Sufism and destroyed its path. They have

---

308 A town in the province of Fars in Iran.
309 964 C.E.
310 That is, salvation.
311 951 C.E.
312 From Mecca to Medina, where the Prophet established the first Muslim community.
313 951 C.E.
314 That is, one's outward state reflects one's inward state.

changed its meanings by giving them new names. They dub desire 'increase', bad manners 'sincerity', the abandoning of truth 'ecstatic utterance',[315] the enjoyment of what is blameworthy 'bliss', the following of one's passions 'temptation', the embrace of this world 'arrival', amorality 'determination', stinginess 'perseverance', begging 'good works', and idle talk 'incurring blame [upon oneself]'. However, this was not the way of the folk[316] [in the past]."

Abu ʿUthman Saʿid b. Sallam al-Maghribi

He was the only one of his kind in his epoch. No one before him had similar qualities. He studied with Ibn al-Katib, Habib al-Maghribi, Abu ʿAmr al-Zajjaji, Ibn al-Saʾigh and others. He died in Nishapur in the year 373.[317] [Before he died,] he asked that the imam Abu Bakr b. Furak[318] pray over his body.

I heard the teacher Abu Bakr b. Furak say: "I was in Abu ʿUthman al-Maghribi's house before he died. ʿAli al-Qawwal the Junior was reciting something. When his [Abu ʿUthman's] condition changed for the worse, we told ʿAli to keep silence. At this point, Shaykh Abu ʿUthman opened his eyes and asked why ʿAli was not reciting anything. I told one of those who were there, 'Ask him, what does he hear?' For I myself was ashamed of asking him about this while he was in such a state. They asked him and he answered://110 'He hears only what [God] allows him to hear.'"[319]

He distinguished himself as a practitioner of strict self-discipline. Abu ʿUthman said: "Fear of God is when one stops at the limits [set by God] without either falling short [keeping back] or overstepping them." He also said: "If you prefer the company of the rich to the company of the poor, God will punish you by the death of the heart."

Abu ʾl-Qasim Ibrahim b. Muhammad al-Nasrabadhi[320]

He was the [greatest Sufi] master of Khurasan in his age. He studied with al-Shibli, Abu ʿAli al-Rudhbari and al-Murtaʿish. He settled in Mecca in the year 366[321] and died there in 367.[322] He was an expert on *hadith* and transmitted many [of them].

I heard Shaykh Abu ʿAbd al-Rahman al-Sulami – may God have mercy on him – say: I heard al-Nasrabadhi say: "When you catch a glimpse of the Divine Truth, allow neither Paradise nor the hellfire to distract you from it. And when

---

315 For this notion see Ernst, *Words of Ecstasy*.
316 *Al-qawm*; that is, the Sufis.
317 983 C.E.
318 On him see article "Ibn Furak" in *EI*.
319 That is, he hears only what his overall spiritual condition in the eyes of God permits him to hear.
320 On him see *IM*, pp. 130 and 138.
321 976 C.E.
322 977 C.E.

Abu 'l-Husayn Bundar b. al-Husayn al-Shirazi

He was an expert on the fundamentals [of jurisprudence] and possessor of a great [spiritual] state. He studied with al-Shibli and died in Arrajan[308] in the year 353.[309]

Bundar b. al-Husayn said: "Do not oppose your soul. Leave it to its [true] Master and He will do with it what He wants!" Bundar said: "Keeping the company of the innovators leads to turning one's back on God." Bundar said://108 "Abandon the dictates of your passions for the sake of your hopes."[310]

Abu Bakr al-Tamastani

He studied with Ibrahim al-Dabbagh and others. He was unique in his age in his knowledge and [spiritual] state. He died in Nishapur after the year 340.[311]

Abu Bakr al-Tamastani said: "The greatest bliss is when you leave behind your soul, for the soul is the thickest veil between you and God." I heard Abu ʿAbdallah al-Shirazi – may God have mercy on him – say: I heard Mansur b. ʿAbdallah al-Isbahani say: I heard Abu Bakr al-Tamastani say: "As soon as the heart has become preoccupied [with something other than God], it is punished." He also said: "The path is clear and the [Holy] Book and the Prophet's custom are among us. The merit of the Companions [of the Prophet] is well known due to the fact that they emigrated [with the Prophet][312] and accompanied him. Those of us who have chosen as their companions the [Holy] Book and the Prophet's custom, and who have emigrated with their hearts from their souls and from the creatures to God's presence, are the veracious ones who have thereby achieved their goals."

Abu 'l-ʿAbbas Ahmad b. Muhammad al-Dinawari

He studied with Yusuf b. al-Husayn, Ibn ʿAtaʾ and al-Jurayri. He was a great and distinguished scholar. He came to Nishapur and stayed there for a while. He was preaching to its people and spoke to them in the language of [divine] gnosis. Thereupon he left for Samarqand, where he died after the year 340.[313]

Abu 'l-ʿAbbas al-Dinawari said: "The most simple [type of] recollection [of God] is when you forget everything but Him and the ultimate recollection is when the one who recollects [God] forgets his recollection in the process of recollection."//109 Abu 'l-ʿAbbas said: "The tongue of one's outward state does not change what is inside [one's heart]."[314] Abu 'l-ʿAbbas al-Dinawari also said: "They have demolished the pillars of Sufism and destroyed its path. They have

---

308 A town in the province of Fars in Iran.
309 964 C.E.
310 That is, salvation.
311 951 C.E.
312 From Mecca to Medina, where the Prophet established the first Muslim community.
313 951 C.E.
314 That is, one's outward state reflects one's inward state.

changed its meanings by giving them new names. They dub desire 'increase', bad manners 'sincerity', the abandoning of truth 'ecstatic utterance',³¹⁵ the enjoyment of what is blameworthy 'bliss', the following of one's passions 'temptation', the embrace of this world 'arrival', amorality 'determination', stinginess 'perseverance', begging 'good works', and idle talk 'incurring blame [upon oneself]'. However, this was not the way of the folk³¹⁶ [in the past]."

Abu 'Uthman Sa'id b. Sallam al-Maghribi

He was the only one of his kind in his epoch. No one before him had similar qualities. He studied with Ibn al-Katib, Habib al-Maghribi, Abu 'Amr al-Zajjaji, Ibn al-Sa'igh and others. He died in Nishapur in the year 373.³¹⁷ [Before he died,] he asked that the imam Abu Bakr b. Furak³¹⁸ pray over his body.

I heard the teacher Abu Bakr b. Furak say: "I was in Abu 'Uthman al-Maghribi's house before he died. 'Ali al-Qawwal the Junior was reciting something. When his [Abu 'Uthman's] condition changed for the worse, we told 'Ali to keep silence. At this point, Shaykh Abu 'Uthman opened his eyes and asked why 'Ali was not reciting anything. I told one of those who were there, 'Ask him, what does he hear?' For I myself was ashamed of asking him about this while he was in such a state. They asked him and he answered://110 'He hears only what [God] allows him to hear.'"³¹⁹

He distinguished himself as a practitioner of strict self-discipline. Abu 'Uthman said: "Fear of God is when one stops at the limits [set by God] without either falling short [keeping back] or overstepping them." He also said: "If you prefer the company of the rich to the company of the poor, God will punish you by the death of the heart."

Abu 'l-Qasim Ibrahim b. Muhammad al-Nasrabadhi³²⁰

He was the [greatest Sufi] master of Khurasan in his age. He studied with al-Shibli, Abu 'Ali al-Rudhbari and al-Murta'ish. He settled in Mecca in the year 366³²¹ and died there in 367.³²² He was an expert on *hadith* and transmitted many [of them].

I heard Shaykh Abu 'Abd al-Rahman al-Sulami – may God have mercy on him – say: I heard al-Nasrabadhi say: "When you catch a glimpse of the Divine Truth, allow neither Paradise nor the hellfire to distract you from it. And when

---

315 For this notion see Ernst, *Words of Ecstasy*.
316 *Al-qawm*; that is, the Sufis.
317 983 C.E.
318 On him see article "Ibn Furak" in *EI*.
319 That is, he hears only what his overall spiritual condition in the eyes of God permits him to hear.
320 On him see *IM*, pp. 130 and 138.
321 976 C.E.
322 977 C.E.

you have returned from this state, honor that which God has [commanded] to honor!"//111 I heard Muhammad b. al-Husayn say: Someone told al-Nasrabadhi that there was a [certain] man, who keeps company with women, saying: "I am protected by God from sinful thought whenever I watch them." He answered: "As long as there is at least a semblance of the human body, there remains [God's] command and prohibition, and man is told to comply with what was commanded and what was prohibited to him. And he who encourages the ambiguous, will eventually be exposed to the prohibited."

I heard Muhammad b. al-Husayn – may God have mercy on him – say: al-Nasrabadhi said: "The root of Sufism is to hold onto the [Holy] Book and the custom [of the Prophet], to abandon passions and innovations, to show respect for the [Sufi] masters, to seek excuses for [God's] creatures, to constantly repeat prayers, and to avoid dispensations from obligatory requirements and allegorical interpretations."

Abu 'l-Hasan 'Ali b. Ibrahim al-Husri al-Basri[323]

He resided in Baghdad. Renowned for his [exalted] spiritual state and eloquence, he was the Sufi master of his age. He belonged to the circle of al-Shibli. He died in Baghdad in the year 371.[324]

Al-Husri said: "Some people say that al-Husri makes no mention of supererogatory acts. Yet, I have been reciting [supererogatory] litanies since my youth, so that whenever I neglect just one bow during the prayer, I am punished." He also said: "If someone lays false claims to the [mystical] reality, his lie will be exposed when the irrefutable divine proofs are revealed."[325]

Abu 'Abdallah Ahmad b. 'Ata' al-Rudhbari

He was a son of Shaykh Abu 'Ali al-Rudhbari's sister. He was the greatest master of Syria in his age. He died in Tyre[326] in 369.[327]//112

I heard Muhammad b. al-Husayn say: I heard 'Ali b. Sa'id al-Massisi say: I heard Ahmad b. 'Ata' al-Rudhbari say: "As I was riding a camel, its foot sank into the sand. I said: 'God is great!' Then the camel also said: 'God is great!'" Whenever Abu 'Abdallah al-Rudhbari and his companions were invited to a house of the common people or non-Sufi folk, he would not tell the poor[328] about this. He would first host them in his house and feed them. After they had eaten, he would tell them about the invitation and they would go together to that place. By that time they would be so well fed that they would not touch the food

---

323 In some editions of the *Epistle* his name is spelled "al-Baqri".
324 981 C.E.
325 That is, on the Day of Judgement.
326 A city in southern Lebanon.
327 980 C.E.
328 That is, his Sufi companions.

prepared for them except a little. He did this so that the common people would not think ill of this [Sufi] community nor commit sins because of them.

It is said that once Abu ʿAli al-Rudhbari walked behind the poor, because it was his wont to do so. As they were on their way to a dinner at somebody's house, a grocer shouted at them: "Look at these transgressors!" And he started to berate them, saying among other things the following: "One of them borrowed one hundred *dirhams* from me and never returned them to me. Where can I find him now?" When they entered the house to which they were invited Abu ʿAbdallah al-Rudhbari said to the host, who was an admirer of the Sufi folk: "If you want my heart to be at ease, lend me one hundred *dirhams*." The host gave them to him immediately. [Abu ʿAbdallah] then said to one of his companions: "Take this hundred [*dirhams*] to such-and-such grocer and tell him that this is the money that one of us borrowed from him. There was an excuse for his not returning it on time, but he has finally sent it to you, so accept his apology!" The man went away and did [as Abu ʿAbdallah told him]. As they were returning from the dinner, they passed by the grocer's store. On seeing them the grocer began to praise them, saying: "They are trustworthy people who keep their promises, they are the righteous!" and suchlike things.//113

Abu ʿAbdallah once said: "The most repugnant creature is a greedy Sufi."

Conclusion

The imam and master Abu ʾl-Qasim – may God be pleased with him – said: Here I have mentioned some of the masters of this [Sufi] community in order to show that all of them have a great respect for the Divine Law, that they are committed to the paths of spiritual [self-]discipline, that they follow unswervingly the Prophet's custom and that they never neglect a single religious rule. They all agree that whoever is remiss in the rules of proper conduct or in striving for perfection and does not build his life on scrupulous piety and fear of God lies before God in whatever he claims. Such a person is deluded. Not only has he perished himself, but also he has caused to perish those who were deluded by his lies.

Chapter 2
AN EXPLANATION OF THE EXPRESSIONS USED BY THIS [SUFI] COMMUNITY AND OF THEIR DIFFICULTIES

It is well known that each group of scholars has its own terms which it employs within itself. These terms are unique to each group, which has agreed on them for its purposes, namely (1) to bring these terms closer to the understanding of those to whom they are addressed, and (2) by articulating them, to help the people of this art to better comprehend their meaning.

The people of this community[1] use these terms among themselves with the goal of unveiling their meaning to one another, achieving concision and concealing them from those who disagree with their method, so that the meaning of their words would be hidden from outsiders. They have done so to protect their mysteries from being spread among those to whom they do not belong. For their realities cannot be assembled by self-exertion or acquired by any deliberate action. They are nothing but [subtle] meanings that God deposits directly into the hearts of [His] folk,[2] [after He has] prepared their innermost selves for [the reception of] these realities.

By this explanation we intend to facilitate the understanding of the meaning of these terms by those who want to follow their [Sufi] path and their custom.

The [mystical] moment (*waqt*)[3]

According to those who have fully realized the true meaning of things,[4] the moment is an expected event whose occurrence depends on a real event. [In other words,] the real event is a moment for the expected event. When you say: "I shall come at the beginning of the month", [your act of] coming is expected,[5] whereas the beginning of the month is real.[6] Thus, the beginning of the month is the moment for [your] coming.

I heard that the master Abu ʿAli al-Daqqaq – may God have mercy on him – said: "The moment is what you are in [now]. If you are in this world, then your moment is this world. If you are in the Hereafter, then your moment is the Hereafter. If you are in joy, then your moment is joy. If you are in sorrow, then your moment is sorrow." By this he meant that a moment is a state that dominates a person.

---

1 That is, the Sufis.
2 That is, the Sufis.
3 The usual meaning of this word is "time". Our translation of the term is determined by its usage in Sufi discourses.
4 *Ahl al-tahqiq*, lit. "truth-realizers", or "verifiers".
5 Because it exists only in your plans.
6 Because it exists independent of your volition.

Sometimes by the moment one means the time in which one finds oneself. Others say that the moment is something that lies between two times – that is, the past and the future.

The Sufis say: "The Sufi is the son of his moment." They mean that he engages in the worship//115 that is most appropriate for his current situation and performs what is required of him at this moment in time. It is said that the poor man[7] does not care about his past or future. All that matters for him is the moment in which he is now. Therefore, they say: "Anyone who preoccupies himself with the past moment wastes another moment."

Sometimes, by the moment the Sufis mean the fulfillment of God's will with regard to them, when they cannot choose any action for themselves [of their free will]. They say: "Someone is under the command of the moment", meaning that he has surrendered to the workings of the unseen,[8] exercising no free choice of his own. This applies only to those things that are not imposed on believers by God or which He requires of them in accordance with the Divine Law. For when you neglect a divine command, or abandon what is prescribed for you by [God], or pay no attention to your shortcomings [in complying with God's will], then you have simply departed from your religion.

They say: "The moment is a sword", meaning that in the same way as the sword cuts [through things], the moment is the [unavoidable] fulfillment of what God has determined and brought to pass. It is also said that the sword is gentle to the touch, yet its edge cuts. He who treats it gently survives, whereas he who resists it will be destroyed. The same is true of the moment. Whosoever surrenders to its command survives, and whosoever resists it is thrown down and falls on his face. They recite the following verse about this:

> As if it were a sword, when you treat it gently, it is gentle to your touch,
> While its edges are harsh, when you treat it harshly.

If someone is assisted by the moment, then this moment becomes [his] moment, but if one is at odds with the moment, then this moment becomes [his] affliction.

I heard the master Abu ʿAli al-Daqqaq say: "The moment is like a file: it grinds you down, yet it does not erase you completely." He meant the following: If it obliterates and annihilates you, you would be saved at the very moment you have become annihilated [from yourself]. However, it takes just a part of you, without erasing you completely. To this effect he recited the following verse:

> Each passing day takes some part of me
> It bestows regrets upon my heart, then goes away.

He also recited:

---

7 That is, the Sufi.
8 That is, divine predestination.

> As with the inhabitants of Hell: when their skin has been burned completely,
> New skins are given to them [to renew] their torments.//116

And to a similar effect:

> Dead he is not, who, in his death, has found repose.
> But dead is he, who is dead among the living.

Clever is he who has come under the command of his moment. If his moment is sobriety, he follows closely the Divine Law; but if his moment is annihilation [in God], he comes under the command of the True Reality.[9]

The [mystical] station (*maqam*)[10]

The station is the good manners which the servant of God realizes after he has entered it.[11] He can arrive at it by means of his own actions, by fulfilling its requirements through [concerted] effort and self-imposed strictures in worshiping [God]. A person's station is where he stands in terms of all of this as well as in terms of [acts of] self-discipline he is practicing to obtain it.

A precondition of the station is that you cannot advance from one station to the next unless you have fulfilled the requirements of the former. [For instance,] if you have not mastered [the station of] contentment (*qana'a*), you cannot achieve [the station of] true trust in God (*tawakkul*); if you have not mastered trust in God, then you cannot earn [the station of] true submission [to the divine will]. Likewise, he who has not mastered [the station of] repentance (*tawba*) cannot obtain [the station of] turning [to God] in repentance (*inaba*); one who has not mastered [the station of] scrupulous discernment [between the licit and the illicit] (*wara'*) is not ready for [the station of] renunciation [of this world].

As for [the word] *muqam*,[12] it means [the act of] "being placed",[13] in the same way as the word *mudkhal* ("entry") may mean the act of being entered or the word *mukhraj* ("exit") may mean the act of being driven out. For one cannot enter a station unless one witnesses God – Most High – placing him into that station. Then and only then can one build one's affair on a sound foundation.[14]

---

9 That is, he becomes witness to God's sublime mysteries that are hidden from the common believers.
10 On this Sufi concept see *IM*, pp. 303–309.
11 That is, the station.
12 A variant reading of the term "station" (*maqam/muqam*). The latter carries slightly different connotations, especially those of passivity, which the author tries to highlight.
13 That is, being placed by God into a certain station.
14 That is, the progress from station to station implies both the wayfarer's personal effort and God's continual assistance without which the goal cannot be achieved.

I heard the master Abu ʿAli al-Daqqaq – may God have mercy on him – say: "When al-Wasiti[15] arrived in Nishapur, he asked the disciples of Abu ʿUthman [al-Hiri][16]: 'What did your master usually command you to do?' They answered: 'He used to command us to practice acts of obedience [toward God], while keeping in sight our shortcomings [in performing them].' Al-Wasiti responded: 'Then he taught you nothing but pure Zoroastrianism (*al-majusiyya al-mahda*).[17] He should have commanded you to forget about them[18] and contemplate the One Who is their true originator and performer!'"[19] In saying so, al-Wasiti only wanted to warn them against self-conceit, not to push them toward the path//117 of negligence or to give them license to transgress any of the good manners.

The [mystical] state (*hal*)[20]

According to the Sufis, the mystical state is something that descends upon the hearts [of the mystics] regardless of their intentions, their [attempts to] attract it, or their [desire to] earn it. This can be [the states of] joy, grief, expansion, contraction, passionate longing, vexation, awe or need.

States are [divine] gifts, whereas stations are earnings. States come without asking, whereas stations are acquired by the sweat of one's brow. The possessor of a station is firmly established in it, whereas the possessor of a state can be taken up out of his state [at any moment].

Someone asked Dhu 'l-Nun al-Misri[21] about the [divine] gnostic. He answered: "He was here [a moment ago], but left." One Sufi master said: "States are like [flashes of] lightning. If they persist, they are but self-deception." The Sufis say: "States are like their name"[22] – that is, they alight upon the heart only to leave it instantaneously. They recite the following poetic lines:

> If it [the state] were not changing constantly, it would not be named *hal*.
> Everything that changes, passes
> Look at the shadow: as soon as it has reached its full size
> And become long, it begins to wane!

Some Sufis have pointed out that the states can last and endure. They say that the states that do not last and continue are but flashes of light (*lawaʾih*) and

---

15 On Abu Bakr al-Wasiti (d. 320/932) see *IM*, pp. 100–101.
16 On this famous ascetic from Nishapur see *IM*, "Index".
17 Because this approach presupposes that human beings have control over their own acts, whereas, in al-Wasiti's view, the only true actor and doer is God. Therefore, he accused Abu ʿUthman and his disciples of practicing "Zoroastrianism" (namely, dualism).
18 That is, the acts of obedience.
19 This anecdote refers to the debates between the supporters of human free will and those who saw all human acts as being predestined and created by God.
20 See *IM*, pp. 303–309.
21 See Chapter 1, pages 19–20.
22 The Arabic root HWL, from which the word *hal* is derived, connotes inconstancy, transition, and change.

unexpected appearances (*bawadih*). Those who experience them have not yet arrived at true states. Only when this experience lasts can it be called "state".

Abu ʿUthman al-Hiri said: "For forty years God has not placed me in a state that I disliked.//118 He was referring to the permanence of [his] contentment,[23] and contentment is counted among the states. On this issue one must say the following: Those who say that the states perdure are correct. A certain experience may become a man's personal portion in which he will grow. The person who has an enduring state also has other states, [named] the "night visitors". They do not persist in the same way as the states that have become part of his persona. When the "night visitors" perdure with him, as were the previous states, he can advance to new states that are more lofty and subtle than the ones before them. Thus he never ceases to advance further and further.

I heard that the master Abu ʿAli al-Daqqaq – may God have mercy on him – commented on the words of the Prophet – may God bless and greet him: "My heart was covered with a veil until I began to ask God's pardon seventy times a day."[24] He [Abu ʿAli] said: "The Prophet – may God bless and greet him – was constantly advancing in his states. Whenever he had advanced from a lower state to a loftier one, he would take notice of the one he had just left behind and consider that state to be a veil in relation to the one in which he now found himself. His states were thus becoming ever more intense."

The favors that God – may He be blessed – has predetermined [for His creatures] are infinite. Since the True Reality of God – Most High – is [supreme] majesty and therefore one can never truly attain Him, then the servant of God has to be constantly advancing in his states. Whenever he has attained an experience, God – may He be blessed – has already predetermined that there is a higher one and that he is bound to attain it. It is in this sense that one should understand their [Sufi] saying: "The good deeds of the righteous are the evil deeds of the ones who are brought nigh [to God]."[25] When someone asked al-Junayd about this [phrase], he recited the following:

> Flashes of light that shine, when they appear,
> Reveal the secret and announce the unification
> [with the Divine].

Contraction (*qabd*) and expansion (*bast*)

These two states come after the servant has advanced above the state of fear and hope. For the divine gnostic contraction is the same as the state of fear is for the beginner. [Likewise,] for the gnostic expansion is the same as the state of hope is for the beginner.//119 The difference between contraction and fear, on the one hand, and between expansion and hope on the other, is this: fear is when

---

23 That is, his contentment with the portion allotted to him by God.
24 Wensinck, *Concordance*, vol. 5, p. 38b.
25 Q. 56:11.

someone fears something in the future – for instance, the loss of something pleasant or the occurrence of something dangerous. Likewise, hope is when one expects something pleasant [to happen] in the future, or anticipates that something unpleasant will go away or that something undesired will come to an end. As for contraction and expansion, they spring from something that is already there. When someone fears or hopes, his heart in both these states is attached to the future. The moment of the person in the state of contraction or expansion is determined by the experience that dominates him in his immediate present.

The characteristics of [the Sufis] in contraction and expansion differ to the extent they differ in their states. One experience may cause a contraction that leaves room in its possessor for other things since he has not perfected it. At the same time, in another person it may leave no room for anything other than this experience, because it consumes him entirely. One Sufi said [about this experience]: "I am crammed full!" – that is, there is no room at all in me [for anything else].

The same is true of a person in the state of expansion. He may experience an expansion that encompasses [at least] some creatures and does not estrange him from most things. At the same time, one may become expanded so much as not to be affected by anything under any condition. I hear that Shaykh Abu ʿAli al-Daqqaq – may God have mercy on him – said: "One Sufi entered the house of Abu Bakr al-Qahtabi.²⁶ The latter had a son who engaged in [unseemly] pastimes that are common among the youth of his age. It so happened that the visitor chanced upon that son while he and his friends were preoccupied with their follies. The visitor felt a great pity for al-Qahtabi and said: 'O poor master! What a terrible affliction this son must be for him!' When the visitor entered al-Qahtabi's room he saw him behave as if he was not aware of [his son's] unseemly entertainment. He was surprised by this and said: 'May I be the ransom of him who cannot be moved even by the steadfast mountains!' Al-Qahtabi replied: 'We have been liberated from the bondage of the things [of this world] since pre-eternity!'"//120

Contraction is caused by an experience that descends upon one's heart. It may imply censure²⁷ or indicate that one is liable for chastisement. As a result, contraction enters the heart and it contracts. When, however, an experience is caused by closeness²⁸ or by [God's] turning [to the servant] with gentleness and hospitality, then what enters the heart is expansion. In general, one's contraction corresponds to one's expansion and one's expansion to one's contraction.

There may be a contraction whose cause and motive elude the person who experiences it. He feels contraction in his heart, yet he does not know its cause.

---

26 In some variants of the text his name is spelled "al-Qahti".
27 That is, God's dissatisfaction with His servant.
28 Between God and man.

Such a person should surrender [to his state], until its time has come.[29] For if he contrives to expel it or tries to anticipate its attack beforehand on his own accord, his contraction will only become worse. This may be seen [by God] as improper behavior on his part. If, on the other hand, he surrenders himself completely to the rule of time, contraction will soon go away, for God – may He be blessed – said: "[It is] God [who] grasps and outspreads."

Expansion may come suddenly. It strikes a man unexpectedly as he is unaware of its motive; it shakes and startles him. This man should try to remain quiet and to observe the rules of proper behavior, since in such a moment he is exposed to a grave danger. May this man then beware of [God's] hidden ruse![30] One of the Sufis said about this: "The door of expansion was open to me, but I slipped and was veiled from my [mystical] station."[31] Some Sufis have said about this: "Stand on the [outstretched] carpets [of closeness to God], but beware of familiarity!"

The people of true realization consider the states of contraction and expansion to be among the things that one should avoid, because in relation to the states above them, such as the servant's annihilation and dissolution in the True Reality,[32] they are but poverty and need.

I heard Shaykh Abu ʿAbd al-Rahman al-Sulami say: I heard al-Husayn b. Yahya say: I heard Jaʿfar b. Muhammad say: I heard al-Junayd say: "My fear of God contracts me; my hope [for His mercy] expands me; the True Reality makes me one [with Him]; the Divine Truth[33] separates me [from Him]. When He grasps me with fear, He detaches[34] me from myself; when He outstretches me with hope, He returns me to myself; when He makes me one by the True Reality, He places me in His presence; when He separates me from the Divine Truth,[35] He makes me witness other things and veils me from Himself. And in all this God Most High is my sole mover, not my restrainer; He is the one who abandons me, not the one who shows intimacy to me. In His presence I taste the food of my existence. O would that He annihilated me from myself, then endowed me with [a new] existence! O would that He took me from myself, then breathed [a new] life into me!"//121

Awe (*hayba*) and intimacy (*uns*)

Both of these are above contraction and expansion, in the same way as contraction is above fear [of God] and expansion is above the station of hope. [Likewise,] awe

---

29 That is, until it leaves the mystic by itself.
30 That is, God can send expansion, which brings excessive joy and exaltation, to him as a temptation.
31 That is, his prior efforts to achieve an advanced station on the path to God were annulled as a result of his slippage.
32 That is, the Godhead.
33 That is, the Divine Law that lays out the rights of God (*huquq Allah*); hence another possible translation: "the Right of God", instead of "the Divine Truth".
34 Lit. "annihilates".
35 See note 33.

is higher than contraction and intimacy is more perfect than expansion. The True Reality of awe is absence.[36] Each awestricken person is absent [from himself]. The awestricken vary in their awe to the extent that they vary in their absence. Some of them [are higher] than others.

Intimacy requires true sobriety, for each intimate [friend] is sober. They too differ from one another according to their personal share.[37] This is why they say: "The minimal requirement for intimacy is when you throw someone into a blazing fire and this does not perturb his intimacy." Al-Junayd – may God have mercy on him – said: "I used to hear al-Sari[38] say: 'The servant of God reaches a point when he can be struck on the face with the sword without taking notice of it.' [At first], my heart refused to believe in it, but gradually it has become clear to me that this was indeed the case."

It is recounted that Abu Muqatil al-ʿAqqi said: "I came to al-Shibli's place and found him plucking out the hair of his eyebrows with a pair of tweezers. I told him: 'O my master, you do this to yourself, but your pain strikes me right in the heart!' He answered: 'Woe to you! The Truth has shown Itself to me and I cannot bear It. And here it is: I inflict pain upon myself in the hope that when I finally feel it, this[39] will be veiled from me. However, I feel no pain, so it is not veiled from me and I cannot bear it any more.'"

When the states of awe and intimacy appear, the people of the Truth[40] consider it to be a deficiency, because they entail a change in the servant of God.//122 The spiritual states of the people of constancy[41] are above such change. They are completely effaced[42] by their encounter with the [Divine] Essence. Therefore they can experience neither awe nor intimacy and have neither knowledge nor sense.

There is a famous story about Abu Saʿid al-Kharraz.[43] He recounted: "Once I was lost in the desert and began to recite [the following verses]:

> I have lost my way and because of my loss I know not who I am
> Except what people say about me and my ilk.
> I raise myself above the jinn and men of this land
> And when I can no longer find anyone, I raise myself above myself!

Suddenly, I heard a voice addressing me:

---

36 From anything other than God.
37 That is, their individuality.
38 Al-Junayd's uncle, a famous mystic of Baghdad. See *IM*, pp. 51–52.
39 The referent of this pronoun is obscure. It may refer to the Truth, in which case it should be in the feminine, which it is not. The editors suggest "the pain (*alam*; masc.) of the Truth", but this seems far-fetched. We may be dealing with a textual corruption.
40 That is, the accomplished Sufi masters and gnostics.
41 *Ahl al-tamkin* – that is, those advanced mystics who are firmly established in their states.
42 Lit. "erased".
43 A Sufi teacher of Baghdad. See *IM*, pp. 56–60.

O you who see [secondary] causes as the pinnacle of your being
And who delight in a contemptible loss[44] and in intimacy
Were you truly one of the people who have found God[45]
You would become absent from all existent beings as well as from the Divine Throne and the Footstool.
You would stand in the presence of God without any mystical state
And you would be protected [by God] from taking notice of both men and jinn!"

The servant of God rises above this state through [the state of] finding God.

[The states of] ecstatic behavior (*tawajud*), ecstatic rapture (*wajd*), and ecstatic finding (*wujud*)

Ecstatic behavior is [an attempt] to deliberately stimulate ecstatic rapture. The person in this state does not experience a complete ecstasy, for if he did, he would be an ecstatic [in the full meaning of this word]. The verbal form *tafaʿul*[46] usually presupposes a [deliberate] display of a certain feature, which does not belong [to the person displaying it]. A poet said [about this]:

I deliberately tried to narrow my eye (*takharaztu*),[47] although my eye is not narrow by its nature
Then I shut my eye tightly, although I am not a one-eyed man.

Some [Sufis] said that ecstatic behavior is inappropriate for the one who seeks to bring it about, because it involves a deliberate effort and thus distances him from true realization. Others [disagreed], saying that it is appropriate for the poor who have divested themselves of everything and who are watching out for such things to happen. Their argument rests on the report from the Messenger of God – may God bless and greet him – that says: "Cry, and if you do not cry, then [at least] pretend that you are crying!"

In a famous story about Abu Muhammad al-Jurayri[48] – may God have mercy on him – he says: "I was in al-Junayd's house together with Ibn Masruq and other [Sufis]. Among us there was a singer. Ibn Masruq rose [in order to dance] and others followed him. Only al-Junayd remained in his place. I asked him: 'O

---

44 Or "pride". A pun based on the two meanings of the word *tih* – namely, "to be lost" and "to be proud".
45 *Ahl al-wujud*. This term carries several connotations, which makes it rather difficult to render into English. One can translate it both as "people who have found [God]" or "people of divine being".
46 That is, the verbal form upon which the word *tawajud* is patterned.
47 This phrase is supposed to highlight the meaning of the verbal form mentioned in the previous note.
48 A Sufi of al-Junayd's circle, who succeeded him as head of the movement. He died in 312/924. See *IM*, p. 66.

my lord, what do you think about [Sufi] concerts?'⁴⁹//123 He answered: 'Thou shalt see the mountains that thou supposest fixed, passing by like clouds.'⁵⁰ He then said: 'And you, Abu Muhammad, what do you think about the concerts?' I answered: 'My lord, when I come to a place where there is a Sufi concert and [see] there a person for whom I have respect, I restrain myself from ecstasy. But when I am alone, I give free rein to my ecstasy and behave ecstatically.'" In this story al-Jurayri explicitly approved ecstatic behavior, and al-Junayd did not object to him.

I heard Abu ʿAli al-Daqqaq – may God have mercy on him – say: "As long as he [al-Jurayri] observed good manners [in the presence of] respectable people in his state of listening to the concert, God preserved his moment for him, due to the blessings that accrue from observing good manners. He then said: 'I restrain myself from ecstasy, but when I am alone I give free rein to my ecstasy and behave ecstatically.' However, one cannot give free rein to ecstasy, as one pleases, after the ecstatic moment and its overwhelming powers are gone. This means that as long as he was sincere in his concern for the dignity of the Sufi master, God prolonged his ecstatic moment, so that he could give free rein to his ecstasy when he was alone."

Ecstatic behavior, according to the description just presented, is the beginning of ecstasy, which is followed by ecstasy proper. As for ecstasy, it is something that encounters your heart and descends upon you without any intention or effort on your part. This is why Sufi masters say: "Ecstasy is an encounter [with the mystical moment] and ecstatic acts are the fruits of [supererogatory] prayers. The more one engages in acts of worship, the more divine graces come to one from God."

I heard the master Abu ʿAli al-Daqqaq – may God have mercy on him – say: "Divine visitations (*waridat*) come from prayers (*awrad*). If one does not engage in the prayers on the outside, one will have no divine visitation inside. Every ecstasy that retains some part of the one who experiences it, is not [a true] ecstasy.//124 In the same way as outward pious acts bestow upon the servant of God the sweetness of obedience, his inward experiences bestow ecstatic moments upon him. Therefore, sweetness is the fruit of pious acts, and ecstatic moments are the products of internal experiences."

As for the finding [of God] (*wujud*), it comes after one has raised oneself above ecstasy. The finding of the True Reality⁵¹ can happen only after one's human nature is completely extinguished, for there is no place for it in the presence of the Master of Reality. Abu ʾl-Husayn al-Nuri said about this: "For twenty years I have remained between finding and losing. That is, when I found my Lord, I lost my heart, and when I found my heart, I lost my Lord." Al-Junayd's words

---

49 *Samaʿ*, lit. "listening [to music]", a Sufi "concert" at which mystical poetry is recited and listened to to the accompaniment of musical instruments. It may sometimes involve ecstatic dances or frantic bodily movements. See *IM*, pp. 322–325.
50 Q. 27:90.
51 That is, God.

point to the same meaning: "The knowledge of God's oneness is different from finding Him, and finding Him is different from knowing Him." Some Sufis recited the following verse to this effect:

> My finding [of God] is when I am absent from my finding[52]
> Due to the sight that has been revealed to me.

Thus, ecstatic behavior is the beginning; finding is the end, and ecstasy is between the beginning and the end.

I heard the master Abu 'Ali al-Daqqaq say: "Ecstatic behavior engrosses the servant; ecstasy consumes him; and finding annihilates him completely. It is as if one first watches the sea; then plunges into it; then drowns in it. Here is the sequence of this state: aspiration, arrival, witnessing, finding, and extinction. [One's] extinction is commensurate with [one's] finding. The person who experiences finding may have two states: sobriety and annihilation.//125 In the state of sobriety he subsists in God; in the state of annihilation he perishes in God. These two states always follow one upon the other in the mystic's [experience]. When he is overtaken by sobriety in God, he begins to move and speak by and through God.[53] The Prophet – peace be upon him – said: "He [man] hears through Me [God] and sees through Me."[54]

I heard Shaykh Abu 'Abd al-Rahman al-Sulami say: I heard Mansur b. 'Abdallah say: "A man came to the teaching assembly of al-Shibli and asked him: 'Do the signs of true finding appear on those who experience it?' He answered: 'Yes, there is a light that shines through together with the lights of ardent passion [for God]. These lights leave their traces on men's complexions, in accordance with the verses of Ibn al-Mu'tazz[55]:

> Water flowed like rain into the cup from a pitcher
> And pearls sprang up from the golden floor
> All those present sang praise to God, when they saw this wonder:
> The light of water in the fire of grapes
> A vintage wine that [the people of] 'Ad[56] had inherited from
> [the inhabitants of] Iram[57]
> It was a treasure that the Persian kings passed on from father to son.'"

---

52 Or from "my existence".
53 A reference to the *hadith* quoted in Ahmad b. Hanbal, *Al-Musnad*, vol. 1, pp. 150–151.
54 A reference to the famous *hadith qudsi* – that is, a statement transmitted from the Prophet in which God is the speaker: "When I love him [man], I become his hearing through which he hears, his eyesight through which he sees, his hand through which he holds, and his foot through which he walks." For details, see Chittick, *The Sufi Path of Knowledge*, pp. 325–331.
55 A famous poet and literary critic of the 'Abbasid period, who was murdered in 296/908 as a result of a coup at the 'Abbasid court.
56 An ancient Arabian tribe that, according to the Qur'an, was destroyed for its sins and disobedience of God's commands.
57 An ancient Arabian city that is believed to have been destroyed by God as a punishment for the transgressions of its inhabitants.

Someone once said to Abu Bakr al-Duqqi[58] that Jahm al-Raqqi had fallen into a trance during a mystical concert. In his excitement, he seized a tree and pulled it up by its roots. Later, both came to the same party. Al-Duqqi was blind. [During the party] Jahm al-Raqqi rose and began to whirl due to the ecstatic state he experienced. Al-Duqqi said: "When he approaches me, give me a sign!" Al-Duqqi was a weak man. In the meantime, al-Raqqi was passing by him. When he drew near, someone said to al-Duqqi: "Here he is!" At that moment al-Duqqi seized al-Raqqi by the ankle and stopped him, so that the man could not move. Jahm cried: "O master, I repent, I repent!" After that [al-Duqqi] let him go. The master and teacher [al-Qushayri] – may God prolong his goodness – said: "Jahm's excitement was right. However, when al-Duqqi seized him by the ankle, he was right too. When al-Raqqi realized that al-Duqqi's state was higher than his own, he returned to the proper conduct and submitted himself [to his superior]. For him who is right, everything is possible."//126

As for the person in whom the state of annihilation prevails, he has neither intellect, nor understanding, nor sensation. I heard Shaykh Abu ʿAbd al-Rahman al-Sulami – may God have mercy on him – say, on the authority of his transmitters, that Abu ʿIqal al-Maghribi lived in Mecca for four years without eating or drinking anything until he passed away. Once, a poor man[59] came to Abu ʿIqal and said: "Peace be upon you!" He answered: "And upon you be peace!" The man then said: "I am so-and-so." Abu ʿIqal told him: "You are so-and-so. How are you doing? What is happening to you?" And then he fell into unconsciousness. The man related: "I would tell him again: 'Peace be upon you!' and Abu ʿIqal would reply: 'And upon you be peace!' as if he had not just seen me." The man said: "I did this several times, whereupon I realized that this person was unconscious. I then left him alone and departed from his house."

I heard Muhammad b. al-Husayn say: I heard that ʿUmar b. Muhammad b. Ahmad said: I heard the wife of Abu ʿAbdallah al-Tarwaghandi say: "In the days of hunger, when people were dying of starvation, Abu ʿAbdallah al-Tarwaghandi entered his house and saw there two *manns*[60] of wheat. He screamed: 'People are starving, while I have wheat in my house!' As a result, he lost his mind and did not come to his senses except during the times of the prayer. He would pray the obligatory prayer and then return to his [disorderly] mental state. He remained in this state until his death."

This story shows that the requirements of the Divine Law were preserved for this man regardless of his being under the sway of the commands pertaining to the True Reality.[61] This is a sign of the people of the True Reality.[62] The reason for his absence from mental discernment was his compassion for fellow

---

58 A Sufi of Baghdad, who died around 366/977.
59 That is, a Sufi.
60 A measure of weight equal to two pounds.
61 *Al-haqiqa*, that is the Divine Absolute.
62 That is, the accomplished Sufi gnostics.

Muslims, which is the best sign that he had achieved perfection in his mystical state.

Unification (*jamʿ*) and separation (*farq*)

The expressions "unification" and "separation" are often mentioned in their [Sufi] discourses. Our master Abu ʿAli al-Daqqaq used to say: "Separation is something that is attributed to you; unification, on the other hand, is something that is taken from you."//127 He meant that whatever the servant of God acquires by means of fulfilling the requirements of his servitude and by means of his status as a human being is separation. As for unification, it is everything that comes from the Real, such as the bringing forth of new entities and the bestowal of grace and favor [upon humans]. These are the minimal requirements for the states of unity and separation, because they[63] continue to take notice of their deeds. When God – may He be exalted – allows a person to continue to take notice of his acts of obedience and disobedience, this person finds himself in a state of separation. When, on the other hand, God – may He be blessed – allows a person to see His own deeds, this person acquires the attribute of unification. Thus the assertion of the created world belongs to separation, whereas the assertion of the Real is an attribute of unification.

There is no escape for the servant of God from both unification and separation, for he who does not have separation cannot achieve perfect servitude and he who does not have unification has no knowledge [of God]. God's words [in the Qurʾan] "Thee only we serve"[64] point to separation, while His words "To Thee alone we have recourse"[65] point to unification. When the servant of God addresses Him – may He be exalted – in his intimate conversation with Him as a beggar, a supplicant, a lauder, a giver of thanks, a renouncer [of evil deeds], or a humble beseecher, he places himself in the position of separation. And when he listens in his inner self to what his Lord tells him and hears in his heart what God imparts to him by calling upon him, admonishing him, instructing him, or intimating [something] to his heart and willing him to follow [this intimation], he finds himself under the sign of unification.

I heard Abu ʿAli al-Daqqaq – may God have mercy on him – say: "A singer recited the following verses before Master Abu Sahl al-Suʿluki – may God have mercy on him:

I have made my vision of You my [greatest] pleasure!

Abu ʾl-Qasim al-Nasrabadhi – may God have mercy on him – was there at that time. Master Abu Sahl said: ' "Made" should be read in the second person.'[66]

---

63 That is, those who experience these states.
64 Q. 1:4.
65 Q. 1:4.
66 That is, "You [God] have made my vision of You my greatest pleasure."

Al-Nasrabadhi said: 'No, it should be read in the first person!' Master Abu Sahl then asked: 'Isn't the essence of unification more complete?'[67] Al-Nasrabadhi fell silent."

I heard that Shaykh Abu ʿAbd al-Rahman al-Sulami interpreted this story in the same way [as Abu Sahl].//128 The meaning of this is as follows. When someone says "made" in the first person, it means that the speaker speaks about the state of his own self, as if the servant of God implies that this action comes from him. As for the one who says that "made" should be in the second person, he absolves himself from any deliberate action and says to his Lord: "It is You Who have distinguished me with this [quality], and not I by means of my own deliberate action!" The first [interpretation] contains the danger of [an egoistic] claim, whereas the second implies the denial of one's free power [to act] and the assertion of [God's] beneficence and generosity. There is a great difference between the one who says: "I worship You through my own [free] effort" and the one who says: "I witness You through Your beneficence and kindness."

The unification of unification (jamʿ al-jamʿ)

The unification of unification is higher than this. People differ on this issue according to the differences in their spiritual states and in their ranks [of spiritual attainment]. When someone reasserts both himself and the created world, yet sees everything [in this world] as being dependent on God, this is unification. When, on the other hand, through the appearance and under the complete domination of the power of the Divine Reality one is rendered incapable of contemplating the created world, barred from one's own self, and taken in one's entirety from sensing anything else, this is the unification of unification.

Thus, separation is seeing something other than God – may He be great and exalted; unification is seeing everything through [the eyes of] God; and the unification of unification is total self-dissolution [in God] and the loss of perception of anything other than God – may He be great and exalted – as a result of the onslaught of the irresistible powers of the Divine Reality.

After this comes the lofty state that the Sufis call "second separation" (farq thani). In this state, the servant of God returns to sobriety whenever he must perform any of his religious duties so that he can fulfill his religious obligations in their proper times. This is a return to God – the most high – through God, not to the servant through the servant. In this state, the servant sees himself being driven by God's will – may He be exalted. He sees God's power as the ultimate source of his essence and his self; he sees God's knowledge and will as the true performer of his actions and the originator of his spiritual states. By the phrase "unification and separation" some Sufis imply that creatures are subject to the dispositions of the Divine Reality.//129 He has united everything under His

---

67 Abu Sahl's interpretation shows God to be the ultimate agent, whereas al-Nasrabadhi's interpretation leaves room for the human agent to exercise his free will.

power and disposal, since He is the Originator of their essences and the Determiner of their attributes. He has then divided them into several classes. Some of them [are destined] to be among the blessed, others [are destined] to be far removed from Him and to be among the wretched; some of them He will guide aright, others He will lead astray and make blind; some of them He will veil from Himself, others He will draw near; some of them He will make His intimates by allowing them to join Him, others He will make despair of His mercy; some of them He will grant His assistance, others He will frustrate in their aspirations to realize His true essence; some of them He will keep sober, others He will obliterate;[68] some of them He will draw nigh, others He will make absent [from themselves]; some of them He brings into His presence, makes them drink and intoxicates them, others He renders miserable and rejects, then banishes and expels. One cannot count all the varieties of His actions, nor can they be exhausted by any explanation and enumeration. They [Sufis] recite the following verses by al-Junayd – may God have mercy on him – about the meaning of unification and separation:

> I have attained a true realization of You in my innermost
> Heart and I conversed with You with my own tongue.
> We were united in one sense and separated in the other.
> At one moment my awe [of You] makes me absent from
> Seeing You directly,
> Yet at the next moment my ecstasy makes You close to my very core!

They [Sufis] also recite the following:

> When He appears to me, nothing seems greater to me than He
> Then I return to the original state as if I never left it.
> I become unified and dispersed from myself through Him,
> For two numbers can join to become a singular one.

Annihilation (fana³) and subsistence (baqa³) [in God]

By "annihilation" the Sufis refer to the disappearance of blameworthy qualities, whereas by "subsistence" they refer to the persistence of praiseworthy qualities. The servant of God cannot but have one of these two types [of qualities], for it is well known that if he does not have one type, he will inevitably have the other. When his blameworthy qualities are annihilated, he will possess praiseworthy ones. Likewise, when he is dominated by blameworthy characteristics, he will be deprived of praiseworthy ones.

Know that the servant of God is characterized by deeds, morals and spiritual states. Deeds are what he undertakes of his own free will.//130 Morals are his inherent predispositions, which, however, can be changed through continual

---

68 That is, He will deprive them of their self-consciousness by having them contemplate His majesty.

exercises. Spiritual states come to the servant from the outset. However, their subsequent purity is determined only by the cleanness of his actions. In this respect they are similar to morals. God allows the person whose heart preoccupies itself with morals through its own [concerted] effort and banishes from it any reprehensible qualities to improve his morals. Likewise, God will allow the person who strives to purify his deeds of his own accord to purify and protect his spiritual states.

When someone abandons the evil deeds denounced by the Divine Law, it is said that he is annihilated from his passions. And when he is annihilated from his passions, he subsists in the service of God through his determination and sincerity. When someone renounces this world, it is said that he is annihilated from his desire [of it]. And when he is annihilated from his desire of it, he subsists in the sincerity of his repentance. When someone has refined his morals by cleansing his heart of envy, malice, avarice, greed, anger, and pride, as well as any other impurities that adhere to the soul, it is said: "He has been annihilated from the base character traits." And when one is annihilated from bad morals, one subsists in chivalry and truthfulness.

When one observes the workings of divine power in the vicissitudes of divine decrees, it is said that one has been annihilated from seeing events as emanating from creatures. And when one is annihilated from perceiving events as products of secondary causes,[69] one subsists in the attributes of the Real.

When the power of the True Reality takes possession of someone, he no longer notices the essences, effects, traces or vestiges of anything other than God. They say of such a person: "He has been annihilated from [God's] creatures and now subsists in God."

The servant of God is annihilated from his blameworthy deeds and base states when he does not perform them, and he is annihilated from his own self and from all creatures when he ceases to perceive both them and himself. When he is annihilated from deeds, morals, and spiritual states, all this no longer exists for him. One can say that someone has been annihilated from himself and from all creatures, yet [in reality] his self and the creatures continue to exist. However, he has no knowledge, perception or sign of them. His self exists and the creatures continue to exist [objectively]. However, he is oblivious of them and is capable of perceiving neither his self nor the creatures.

Imagine, for example, that a man enters into the presence of a mighty ruler or a highly revered person and becomes so self-effaced in his reverence that he forgets about both himself and the other people//131 in the assembly, including the revered individual himself. When he would emerge from the assembly and be asked about the people there and the behavior of the revered individual and about his own behavior, he would not be able to say anything about that. God said: "And when they saw him [Joseph], they so admired him that they cut their hands."[70]

---

69 That is, one begins to see God as the sole cause of all created things.
70 Q. 12:31.

When they[71] met Joseph – upon him be peace – they took no notice at all of the pain from cutting their hands, although they were more feeble than men. They said: "This is no mortal",[72] while he [in fact] was mortal. They said: "He is none other than a noble angel",[73] while he [in fact] was not an angel. And this is the state of [one group of] creatures meeting another creature. You can only imagine the man to whom the sight of God – glory be to Him – were disclosed! If he were to lose the sense of himself and his fellow human beings, would there be any surprise in that?

When a man is annihilated from his ignorance, he subsists in his knowledge and when he is annihilated from his passions, he subsists in his repentance. When he is annihilated from his desire [of this world], he persists in its renunciation. When he is annihilated from his passionate drive, he subsists in his longing for God. This is true of all human characteristics. After the servant of God is annihilated from his characteristics, as we have just described, he advances from this stage [to the next one] at which he loses sight of his annihilation. This is described by a Sufi poet, who said:

> Some people wander across the land by the desert
> While others wander in the arena of His love
> Annihilate yourselves thrice,
> Then subsist close to the Lord!

The first annihilation is from one's self and one's attributes through subsistence in the attributes of God. Then comes the annihilation from the attributes of God in the contemplation of God. Then one is annihilated from the vision of one's own annihilation by being subsumed in the existence of God Himself.//132

Absence (*ghayba*) and presence (*hudur*)

Absence is when the heart is absent from knowing the circumstances of creatures due to the complete absorption of the senses by what has appeared to it [from God]. One may also become absent from oneself and others through remembering [God's] promise of reward and thinking of [God's] punishment. It is said that Rabiʿ b. Khuthaym[74] used to visit Ibn Masʿud[75] – may God be pleased with him. As he was passing by a blacksmith's shop, he saw a red-hot iron in the oven and fainted, and did not come to until the next morning. When he woke up, he was asked about what had happened. He answered: "I remembered how the people of hellfire will sojourn in the fire!" This was an absence that went beyond its limit and turned into a swoon.

---

71 That is, the female guests of Potiphar's wife.
72 Q. 12:32.
73 Q. 12:32.
74 An early Muslim (d. 61/680 or somewhat later), who belonged to the generation of those who came after the Companions of the Prophet.
75 ʿAbdallah b. Masʿud (d. 32/652), an early convert to Islam who was renowned for his expertise on the Qurʾan, which he was writing down directly from the Prophet. He resided in Kufa.

It is recounted of ʿAli b. al-Husayn[76] that he was performing a ritual prayer when suddenly his house caught fire. However, he did not interrupt his prayer. When asked about that, he said: "The Greatest Fire[77] made me oblivious of that fire." Occasionally, a man can be rendered absent from his [self-]perception by something that God – may He be blessed and exalted – reveals to him.

Those who experience absence differ from one another according to their spiritual states. It is well known that the spiritual state[78] of Abu Hafs al-Nisaburi al-Haddad (The "Blacksmith") began when he gave up his profession. He was in his smithy when he heard someone reciting a verse from the Qurʾan. At that moment, he had an experience that made him oblivious of his senses. He put his hand into the fire and took out a piece of red-hot iron. His apprentice saw this and cried: "What is this, master?!" When Abu Hafs realized what had just happened, he gave up his trade and left his smithy [for good].

Once, as al-Junayd was sitting together with his wife, al-Shibli entered the room.[79] The wife hurried to cover herself, but al-Junayd said to her: "Sit still, for al-Shibli is unaware of you!" Al-Junayd conversed with al-Shibli for a while, until the latter broke into tears. When he began to cry, al-Junayd said to his wife: "Cover yourself now, for al-Shibli has come to!"

I heard Abu Nasr the Muezzin (al-Muʾadhdhin) of Nishapur, who was a pious man, say: "I was reading the Qurʾan at the session of Master Abu ʿAli al-Daqqaq at Nishapur, when he was residing there. He used to talk a lot about the *hajj*, and his words left a deep imprint in my heart. When I went on a *hajj* that year, I abandoned my store//133 and my trade. Master Abu ʿAli al-Daqqaq – may God have mercy on him – also went on a *hajj* that same year. When he was living in Nishapur I used to serve him and to attend study sessions at his house. [As I was on my way to Mecca], I saw him in the desert. After he had performed his ablution, he forgot the bottle he used to carry with him. I picked it up and carried it with me. When he resumed his journey, I gave it to him. He said: 'May God reward you for bringing it!' He looked at me for a while, as if he had not seen me before, then said: 'I have seen you once. Who are you?' I answered: 'May God be my helper! I was your companion for many years. I left my home and my possessions because of you, and journeyed in the barren desert together with you, and now you tell that you have seen me once!'"

As for presence, it is when someone is present with God, for when he is absent from creatures, he enters into the presence of God, in the sense that he is present with Him. This is due to the fact that the recollection of God takes full possession of his heart and he finds his heart to be present with God Most High.

---

76 ʿAli b. al-Husayn b. ʿAli b. Abi Talib (d. around 92/710), nicknamed "Zayn al-ʿAbididn", a grandson of the Prophet through the line of his daughter Fatima and his cousin ʿAli; the fourth *imam* of the Shiʿites.
77 That is, the fire of Hell.
78 That is, conversion to the path of asceticism and mysticism.
79 See above, pp. 61–62.

Someone's presence with God corresponds to the level of his absence from creatures. When he is completely absent [from creatures] his presence is complete. When they say that someone is present, this means that his heart is present with God, without being neglectful or forgetful [of Him], and constantly remembering Him. In his presence, God – may He be blessed and exalted – will unveil to him things that He has prepared for him and for him only.

Sometimes Sufis describe the servant's return to self-awareness and to awareness of other creatures as his "presence", meaning that he has returned from his absence [from creatures] to his presence with creatures, after he was present with God.

Their states in absence may vary. The absence of some does not last, whereas the absence of others may last for a while. It is said that Dhu 'l-Nun al-Misri sent one of his companions to Abu Yazid al-Bistami, so that he [the companion] would give him a description of Abu Yazid. When the companion reached the city of Bistam, he asked about the house of Abu Yazid. When he entered the house, Abu Yazid asked him what he wanted. He answered: "I am looking for Abu Yazid al-Bistami." Abu Yazid answered: "Who is Abu Yazid? Where is Abu Yazid? I myself am in search of Abu Yazid." The companion left [Abu Yazid's house], saying: "This is a madman!" He returned to Dhu 'l-Nun and told him about what he had seen. [On hearing this] Dhu 'l-Nun began to cry and said: "My brother Abu Yazid has joined those who travel to God."//134

Sobriety (*sahw*) and drunkenness (*sukr*)

Sobriety is returning to self-consciousness after absence [in God]. Drunkenness is absence [from one's self] through a strong experience [of God]. In a sense, drunkenness is a complement to absence in that the drunken person may be relaxed as long as he is not fully immersed in his drunken state. On the other hand, in this state, any perception of outward things may completely disappear from his heart. This is the state of one who behaves like a drunk, because his drunkenness has not yet taken full control of him and he is still capable of perceiving outward things. At some point, his drunkenness may become so strong that it surpasses [the state of] absence. When the drunkenness of a drunk becomes really strong, his absence may surpass the absence experienced by someone in the state of absence. At the same time, the absence of someone in the state of absence may be more complete than the absence of a drunk, especially when he behaves like a drunk without actually having achieved the state of drunkenness.

The state of absence may visit devotees whose hearts have become preoccupied by the influence of passionate longing [for God] and awe [before Him] as well as by the dictates of fear [of God] and hope [for His mercy]. On the contrary, drunkenness is experienced only by those wont to experience ecstatic states. When the attributes of [God's] beauty are revealed to someone, he experiences the state of drunkenness: his spirit rejoices and his heart becomes intoxicated. Of this state the following poetic verses are recited:

> Your sobriety from my words is a complete reunion,
> Whereas your drunkenness when you contemplate me permits you to indulge in drinking.
> Neither the cup-bearer nor the drunkard get tired of the wine of contemplation, each cup of which makes your heart drunk.

They [Sufis] also recite the following verse:

> The circling of the cup makes some people drunk,
> While I get drunk from the one who passes it around.

They also recite:

> I have two states of intoxication, while my boon companions have only one.
> This is what makes me different from them.

They also recite:

> There are two kinds of drunkenness: the drunkenness of passion and the drunkenness of wine.
> How can a man who has tasted either of them ever come to his senses

Know that one's sobriety corresponds to one's drunkenness. He who experiences true drunkenness, enjoys true sobriety.//135 And he whose drunkenness is mixed with good fortune, experiences a sobriety that is also mixed with good fortune. He who has been truthful in his state [of sobriety] is protected in his drunkenness. Both drunkenness and sobriety imply distinction.[80] However, when one becomes witness to the Power of the Real, one loses one's personal attributes and becomes fully consumed and overwhelmed by it. Of this state it is said:

> When the morning appears to the star of old wine
> The drunk and the sober will become equal.

God Most High said: "And when his Lord revealed Himself to the mountain, He made it crumble to dust; and Moses fell down swooning."[81] He "fell down swooning" in spite of his prophethood and his great stature [as a messenger of God], while the mountain "crumbled to dust" in spite of its superior firmness and strength.

In his state of drunkenness the servant of God finds himself under the mark of a [mystical] state, whereas in his state of sobriety he is under the mark of knowledge. In his state of drunkenness he is protected by God without applying his own effort, while in his state of sobriety he protects himself [from error] through his own actions.

Sobriety and drunkenness come after tasting and drinking.

---

80 That is, in these states one remains aware of the diversity of the surrounding world.
81 Q. 7:139.

Tasting (*dhawq*) and drinking (*shurb*)

Among the words that they[82] use are "tasting" and "drinking". They use these words to describe the fruits of God's self-manifestation, the results of God's self-unveiling and God's unexpected visitations, which they experience. The first of these is tasting, then comes drinking and, finally, the quenching of thirst (*riyy*).//136

They attain the taste of [true] meanings through the purity of their pious deeds; they attain the drinking [of true meanings] through fulfilling the requirements of their spiritual stations; and they quench their thirst [for true meanings] through their constant search for God's presence. The person in the state of tasting is behaving like a drunk; the person in the state of drinking is drunk; the person who has quenched his thirst is sober.

When someone's love [of God] is strong, his state of drinking becomes permanent. And when it becomes permanent, his drinking does not make him drunk. He then becomes sober in God and oblivious of all his [mundane] concerns; he is neither influenced by anything that comes to him [in the empirical world], nor is he changed from the state in which he is now. When one's innermost heart is pure, one's drinking is safe from any taint; and when one's drinking becomes one's nourishment, one can neither abstain from it, nor survive without it.

They recite:

The cup [of wine] is like the mother's milk to us
If we cannot taste it, we cannot survive.

They also recite:

I am surprised when someone says: "I have remembered God."
How can I forget, so that I have to remember what I have forgotten?
I have drunk love one cup after another
But although wine does not run out, I cannot quench my thirst for it.

It is said that Yahya b. Mu'adh wrote to Abu Yazid al-Bistami: "Here's the one[83] who has drunk from the cup of love and will never feel thirst again." Abu Yazid responded to him: "I am surprised at the weakness of your [spiritual] state! Here's a man who has gulped down all the seas of existence, yet his mouth is agape, wanting more."

Know that the cups of closeness [to God] appear from the Unseen and are bestowed only upon those whose hearts are emancipated and whose spirits are free from attachment to the things [of this world].

---

82 That is, the Sufis.
83 That is, himself.

Erasure (*mahw*) and affirmation (*ithbat*)

Erasure is the removal of habitual attributes and affirmation is the fulfillment of the commands of servanthood.//137 When someone has removed blameworthy qualities from his internal states and replaced them with praiseworthy states and actions, he becomes a man of erasure and affirmation.

I heard that master Abu ʿAli al-Daqqaq – may God have mercy on him – said that one Sufi shaykh asked someone [who was discussing erasure and affirmation]: "What do you erase and what do you assert?" The speaker fell silent. [Abu ʿAli] then said: "Don't you know that the mystical moment is both erasure and affirmation? He who has neither erasure nor affirmation is idle and abandoned." Erasure can be of several types: the erasure of faults from one's externals; the removal of forgetfulness from one's internal self; the removal of deficiency from one's innermost heart. The erasure of faults is the affirmation of good deeds; the erasure of forgetfulness is the affirmation of spiritual stations [with God]; and the erasure of deficiency is the affirmation of joining [God]. This is erasure and affirmation in the meaning of servitude. As regards the true erasure and affirmation, they come from [God's] power – that is, erasure is that which God conceals and denies, whereas affirmation is that which He shows and makes manifest. Erasure and affirmation are determined by the divine will, because God Most High said: "God erases and affirms what He wills."[84] It is said that God erases from the hearts of the gnostics any thought of other than Himself and He affirms the remembrance of Himself on His servants' tongues. God erases and affirms for each one in accordance with his internal state. When God – may He be exalted – erases someone's self-perception, He affirms him through His own True Self. When He erases someone's affirmation [through His True Self], He returns him to the vision of other things and settles him in the plains of differentiation.[85]

Someone asked al-Shibli – may God have mercy on him: "Why do I always see you being restless? Isn't He with you and aren't you with Him?" Al-Shibli answered://138 "When I am with Him, I am. However, I am erased in Him!" Obliteration is above erasure, because erasure leaves a trace, while obliteration leaves no trace whatsoever. The ultimate goal of the folk[86] is when God obliterates their self-perception completely, never to return them to themselves.

Concealment (*satr*) and [self-]manifestation (*tajalli*)

The ordinary folk are covered by concealment, whereas the elect are witnessing the permanent self-manifestation [of God]. A report from the Prophet says: "When God manifests Himself to something, it submits to Him." If someone experiences concealment, his self-perception is determined by it, while a person in the state of manifestation is always characterized by submission. Concealment

---

84 Q. 13:39.
85 That is, things other than God.
86 That is, the Sufis.

is a punishment for the ordinary folk and a blessing for the elect. If He did not protect from them what He unveils to them, they would have been completely annihilated by the power of the True Reality. However, He manifests Himself to them, while at the same time concealing Himself from them. I heard that al-Mansur al-Maghribi said: "A poor man came to the camp of a Bedouin tribe. A youth [of the tribe] invited him to his tent. As the youth was serving him [some food], he suddenly fainted. The poor man asked about that. The Bedouin told him: He has a female cousin, whom he loves. As she was entering her tent, the youth saw the dust stirred by the hem of her robe and fell unconscious. The poor man came to the door of the cousin's tent and said: '[I know] that a stranger among you is under your protection. Thus [as a stranger] I have come to speak to you on behalf of this youth, because I feel pity for him being in such a state on account of you.' She answered: 'Good Lord! What a naïve man you are! He cannot endure the sight of the dust raised by my clothes! How can he endure my company?!'"

The ordinary Sufis experience happiness at [divine] self-manifestation and suffer when they experience [divine] self-concealment. As for the elect ones, they vacillate between recklessness and happiness, because when God appears to them they become reckless. However, when He conceals Himself from them, they come to and feel happy.//139

They say that God Most High told Moses – peace be upon him: "What is that, Moses, that thou hast in thy right hand?",[87] thereby distracting him with something that pleased him [in order to lessen] the impact of [divine] unveiling, when God spoke to him. The Prophet – may God bless and greet him – said: "My heart remains covered by a veil as long as I have asked God's pardon seventy times a day." Asking for God's pardon (*istighfar*) means asking God to veil Himself, because the word *ghafr* also means "veil". This is similar to such expressions as "to cover [oneself] with clothing" (*ghafr al-thawb*) and "protective covering" (*mighfar*).[88] It seems that the Prophet was saying that he sought to cover his heart against the onslaught of the True Reality, because creatures cannot survive in the presence of the Real. According to the prophetic report, "Should God unveil His face, the splendor of His countenance would burn everything within the range of His sight."

Presence (*muhadara*), unveiling (*mukashafa*) and witnessing (*mushahada*)

Presence comes first, then unveiling, then witnessing. Presence is the presence of the heart [with God]. It can be achieved through a continuous manifestation of the [divine] proof, during which a person finds himself in [God's] presence through the power of recollection [of God]. This [state] is followed by unveiling, which is presence through clear evidence. In this state one need not see the

---

87 Q. 20:17.
88 This word may also mean "helmet".

[divine] proof or seek the path. One is neither subject to the promptings of doubt, nor veiled from the realm of the Unseen.[89] This [state] is followed by witnessing. This means to be in the presence of the Absolute Truth,[90] where there is no room for doubt.//140 When the sky of the innermost heart is free from the clouds of veiling, the sun of witnessing begins to shine from the zodiacal sign of nobility. The True Reality of witnessing was captured by al-Junayd – may God have mercy on him – when he said: "God's existence appears when you lose yours."

The person in the state of presence is bound by its signs; the person in the state of unveiling rejoices in its attributes. As for the person in the state of witnessing, his self is erased by his knowledge [of God].

No one has expressed the essence of witnessing better than ʿAmr b. ʿUthman al-Makki – may God have mercy on him – when he said that the lights of God's self-manifestation appear to the heart clearly and without interruption. It is like an uninterrupted sequence of lightning in the middle of a dark night: when it occurs, the lightning turns the night into day. The same happens to the heart, when divine self-manifestation descends upon it continuously: it lives in the light of day with no night. Sufis recite the following poetry:

> My night is lit by your face, whereas its darkness encompasses other people
> Therefore the people wander in the darkness, whereas we bask in the light of day.

Al-Nuri said: "One cannot attain true witnessing as long as a single living[91] vein remains in one's body." He also said: "When dawn breaks, one no longer needs a lamp."

Some Sufis argue that witnessing implies some sort of separation, because the form of the verbal noun upon which it is patterned – that is, *mufaʿala* – implies [an action that involves] two subjects. These people are in error, because when the Creator appears, His creatures cease to exist. Besides, not every verbal noun patterned on *mufaʿala* necessarily implies [the presence of] two subjects – for instance, "he traveled" (*safar*) or "he sewed another sole upon the sole" (*taraqa al-naʿl*), and so on.

Sufis recite the following poetry:

> When the dawn breaks, the light of its glow eliminates the light of the stars above.
> It forces them to swill yet another cup [of wine] the strength of which is such that were it to be swallowed by a raging flame it would disappear momentarily.

---

89 That is, the realm of divine mystery that contains the knowledge of the future.
90 *Al-haqq*. This word often designates God.
91 Lit. "standing".

What a marvelous cup this is! It removes them from their own selves, it annihilates them, it steals them from themselves and makes them disappear without any trace! What a cup! "It spares not, neither leaves alone."[92] It obliterated them completely, leaving in them not a sliver of human nature, as in a poem:

They departed, leaving behind neither a sign nor trace.

Glimmers (*lawaʾih*), dawnings (*tawaliʿ*) and flashes (*lawamiʿ*)

The master[93] – may God be pleased with him – said that these words have a similar meaning. They differ very little from one another. They are characteristic of beginners who strive to ascend by their hearts. For them, these rays of the suns of divine knowledge do not last long. God provides nourishment for their hearts at every moment, according to His words: "They shall have their provision at dawn and evening."[94] Each time the firmament of their hearts is obscured by the clouds of selfishness, the glimmers of unveiling and the flashes of closeness [to God] begin to shine in them; and amidst veiling they suddenly begin to see the glimmers [of divine grace]. A poet said:

O blazing lightning! What quarter of the sky will you shine from?

At first there are glimmers, then dawnings, then flashes. The glimmers are like lightning in that they disappear as soon as they appear. A poet said:

We have not seen each other for a long time, but when
we finally met his greeting was like saying "farewell".

Sufis also recite the following verse:

O you, who have come to visit and yet have not visited,
Like a man seeking to take some fire,
Who passed by the door of the house in a hurry.
What it was that prevented him from coming in?

Flashes are brighter than glimmers and they last longer. Flashes can persist for more than one moment, however, as they say://142

The eye is weeping because seeing cannot satisfy it.

They also say:

The eye is hardly able to reach the water of his face
without first choking on its guardian before its thirst is quenched.

---

92 Q. 74:28.
93 That is, al-Qushayri, whose words were probably recorded by his disciples, who later integrated them into the final version of his book.
94 Q. 19:63.

When it appears to you in a flash, it severs you from yourself and unites you with Him. However, no sooner than the light of its day has shone, it is attacked by the warriors of night. The people [in this state] are [oscillating] between joy and sorrow, because they [find themselves] between veiling and unveiling. They say [about this state]:

> The night has enveloped us with its noblest cloak,
> While the morning clad us with its golden gown.

Dawnings are longer in duration, are stronger [in their effect], and last longer. They are better in lifting darkness and banishing doubts, yet they are also susceptible to the danger of setting, lower in apogee and of shorter duration. They are quick to depart and take longer to reappear after they have set.

The characteristics of all these experiences – that is, glimmers, dawnings, and flashes – vary. Some of them leave no trace after their disappearance, like some bright stars, which eclipse, while the night stays on. Others, on the contrary, leave traces behind them. While their signs may disappear, their pain persists. Their light may be gone, while their traces remain. A person who has experienced their onslaught continues to live in the shade of their blessings. He is living in anticipation of their return, making do with what he has.

[Unexpected] raids (*bawadih*) and attacks (*hujum*)

Raids are things that descend instantaneously upon your heart from [the realm of] the unknown. They may cause either joy or sadness.//143

As for attacks, they are things that enter your heart due to the power of the moment,[95] without any effort on your part. They vary in their nature according to the strength or weakness of the experience [that precipitates it].

There are those who are changed by [their] raids and act according to the dictates of [their] attacks. And there are those whose spiritual state and power put them above anything that may befall to them. Such people are the masters of the moment. Of them it is said:

> The vicissitudes of time cannot find their way to them
> For they are the ones who hold the reins of every great affair.

Inconstancy (*talwin*) and stability (*tamkin*)

Inconstancy is an attribute of those [who have] spiritual states, whereas stability is a characteristic of those who have attained true realities.

As long as a man travels along the [mystical] path, he experiences inconstancy, because he continues to rise from one state to another and move from one attribute to another; he leaves one place for another, but once he has arrived, he becomes stable.

---

95 See Chapter 2, pp. 75–77.

They say:

I have settled down in my love of you at a station
Which bewilders the hearts of those who have not yet attained it.

The person in the state of inconstancy is continually on the increase, while the one in the state of stability has arrived at his goal and become united [with it]. The sign of his becoming united is that his entire self no longer takes account of itself.

One of the Sufi masters said: "The journey of those who have sought to conquer their egos has ended. When they have conquered their egos, they have arrived [at their goal]."

The master[96] – may God have mercy on him – said: "He meant that [they] leave behind [their] human characteristics and enter the realm of the True Reality. If this state persists in someone, he has achieved stability."

The master Abu ʿAli al-Daqqaq – may God have mercy on him – used to say: "Moses – may God bless him – was characterized by inconstancy. When he returned after hearing the words of God, he had to cover his face,//144 because he was so strongly affected by [his] spiritual state. As for our Prophet – may God bless and greet him – he was characterized by stability. When he returned [from his journey],[97] he was the same as when he had left, because he was not affected by anything he had seen during that night. Other evidence of this is the story of Joseph – peace be upon him. The women who saw Joseph – peace be upon him – cut their hands when he came out to them because his appearance was so sudden. As for the wife of al-ʿAziz,[98] she turned out to be more perfect than them when tested by Joseph. On that day not a single hair of hers was unsettled [by his presence], because she had attained stability through her [earlier] encounter with Joseph – peace be upon him.

The master [al-Qushayri] said: "Know that a person undergoes change as a result of an experience that visits him for two different reasons – namely, the strength of the experience or the weakness of the person. [Likewise,] a person's stability is due to two reasons – namely, the person's strength or the weakness of the experience that visits him."

I heard that the master Abu ʿAli al-Daqqaq – may God have mercy on him – said: Sufis take two principal approaches to the possibility of the persistence of stability [in a person]. First, it is absolutely unattainable, because the Prophet – may God bless and greet him – said: "Had you always remained in the same condition in which you were when I was with you, the angels would surely greet you."[99] He

---

96 That is, al-Qushayri.
97 Probably from the Prophet's night journey and ascension to heaven (al-israʾ wa ʾl-miʿraj), during which he contemplated God from the distance of "two bows'-lengths or nearer". See Q. 53:1–12.
98 The name of Biblical Potiphar in the Muslim tradition.
99 Ahmad b. Hanbal, Al-Musnad, vol. 4, p. 346.

– may God greet and bless him – said to the same effect: "I have a moment in which only God finds any room in me." He thus mentioned only a specific point [not a constant condition]. According to the second view, in the people of true realities states can persist for a long while because they have advanced beyond the condition in which they are affected by unexpected experiences. [The Prophet] said in his report, "The angels would surely greet you." He thereby did not predicate [his statement] on an impossible condition, for the greeting of angels is inferior to that which he – peace be upon him – ascribed to beginners in the following report: "Verily, the angels lower//145 their wings for [every] seeker of knowledge out of contentment with what he is doing."[100]

As for his saying "I have a moment", its meaning differs according to the understanding of each listener. For the Prophet maintained the truth in all his states.

It is more appropriate to say that a man is subject to inconstancy as long as he progresses toward his goal; his states may increase or decrease. And when he has finally arrived at the True Reality by leaving behind the properties of humanity, God – may He be exalted – makes him stable and prevents him from retreating to the weakness of his self. He thus becomes stable in his state in accordance with his position and with that which he has deserved. Then God – may He be exalted – begins to bestow upon him gifts incessantly, for His possibilities are unlimited. Thus, a mystic whose states are on the increase, is inconstant, or rather he is rendered inconstant [by God], while at its core his spiritual state remains stable. He is continually becoming stable in a state that is higher than the one he has occupied before. He then rises above it to a new state, for God's possibilities have no limit in all respects.

Finally, there are those who have lost awareness of themselves and whose senses have been taken from them in their entirety, for human nature of necessity has a limit. If such a person has abandoned his body, soul and self-perception, as well as his perception of the created world around him, and if his self-oblivion becomes permanent, he becomes erased – that is, for him, there exists neither stability nor inconstancy, neither a [mystical] stage, nor a [mystical] state. And as long as he remains in this condition, he is exempt from worship and [religious] obligations. O Lord, may he be ascribed the things that seem to be done by him, without him actually doing them. In people's minds, such a person is acting on his own, while in fact he is acted upon [by God].

God – may He be exalted – said: "Thou wouldst have thought them awake, as they lay sleeping, while We turned them now to the right, now to the left."[101] May God grant success!

---

100 Ahmad b. Hanbal, *Al-Musnad*, vol. 4, p. 239.
101 Q. 18:18; 18:17, according to Arberry's translation.

Proximity (*qurb*) and distance (*buʿd*)

The first degree of proximity is the proximity to obedience toward God and the state of being always engaged in His worship. As for distance, this means to be sullied by the violation of His will and to be removed from obeying Him.//146 The first degree of distance is distance from Godspeed, which is followed by the distance from attainment. In other words, distance from Godspeed means distance from attainment. The Prophet – may God bless and greet him – said that God – blessings be upon Him – said: "[My servant] draws near Me through nothing more than that which I have made obligatory for him. My servant never ceases drawing nearer to Me through supererogatory works until he loves Me and I love him. Then, when I love him, I become his sight and hearing through which he hears and sees ..."[102]

The proximity of the servant [to God] begins with [his] proximity to the faith in God and the attestation of His veracity. This is followed by the proximity to good deeds and the realization [of the Divine Truth]. As for God's proximity [to His servant], it is the divine knowledge that God bestows upon him today and the contemplation and witnessing [of Himself] that He will grant him in the world to come. It is also various expressions of kindness and beneficence that God will bestow [upon the servant] between now and then.

The servant's proximity to God is impossible unless he distances himself from His creatures. This applies to the conditions of hearts, not to outward phenomena and [empirical] existence. God's proximity through knowledge and power encompasses the entire human race.[103] God's proximity through kindness and help is limited to the believers. God's proximity through special intimacy is restricted to His friends. God – may He be exalted – said: "We are nearer to him [man] than the jugular vein."[104] God – may He be exalted – said: "We are nigher him than you".[105] God – may He be exalted – also said: "He is with you wherever you are."[106] He also said: "Three men conspire not secretly together, but He is the fourth of them."[107]

He who has fully realized proximity to God, observes every single thing that comes to him from God, because watching over him is the guardian of the fear [of God], over whom is the guardian of reverence, over whom is the guardian of humility. They [Sufis] recite the following poetry:

---

102 For a full version of this "sacred hadith" (*hadith qudsi*) and its implications for Sufi theory and practice, see Chittick, *The Sufi Path of Knowledge*, pp. 325–331; cf. idem., *The Self-Disclosure of God*, pp. 290–291.
103 That is, God's knowledge and power apply to all humans (in the act of creation) regardless of their faith or unbelief.
104 Q. 50:16.
105 Q. 56:85; 56:84, according to Arberry's translation.
106 Q. 57:4.
107 Q. 58:7; 58:8, according to Arberry's translation.

As if a watchmen stands guard over my [innermost] thoughts,
While another one is watching over my sight and my tongue.
Since I saw you [for the first time], whenever my eyes see
something that displeases you, I say [to myself]: "They
[the watchmen] must have spotted me."//147
Not a single word addressed to someone other than you
Has come out of my mouth
Without my saying to myself: "They must have overheard me."
And not a single thought about someone apart from you has occurred to me
Without them restraining me away from [from it].
The speeches of sincere friends have made me sick,
And I have withheld from them my sight and my tongue.[108]
It is not renunciation that turns [me] away from them,
Rather, I see only you wherever I turn.

One Sufi shaykh was showing his preference for one of his disciples by his placing him close to himself. When the other disciples asked him about it, the shaykh gave each disciple a bird and asked him to slaughter it, so that no one would observe him [doing this]. Each disciple withdrew to a deserted place in order to slaughter his bird. Only the [favorite] disciple came back with his bird still alive. The shaykh asked him about that. The disciple said: "You commanded me to slaughter the bird, so that no one would see me. However, there is no place where you are not watched by God – glory to Him!" The shaykh said: "This is why I have given him preference over you. You are still governed by the talk of creatures, whereas he is never negligent of God."

When anyone notices [his] proximity, this becomes a veil that separates him from proximity.[109] Whoever sees any place or any breath as belonging to him, is deceived thereby. They say about this: "May God expel you from His proximity!" This means "[expel you] from your vision of His proximity [to you]". The feeling of intimacy in His proximity is a sign of being governed by His power, because God – glory to Him – is behind all intimacy and the sites of [the manifestation of] the True Reality bring about bewilderment and erasure. They recite the following poetic verses to this effect:

You are an affliction for me, because I do not consider my love
to be worthwhile:
Your proximity is the same as your distance.
Shall I ever find my rest?

The master Abu ʿAli al-Daqqaq – may God have mercy on him – often recited the following verse:

---

108 That is, "I wanted neither to see them, nor to talk to them."
109 That is, he continues to see something else alongside God.

Your longing is departure and your love is hate,
Your proximity is distance and your peace is war.

Abu 'l-Husayn al-Nuri once saw a disciple of Abu Hamza[110] and asked him: "Are you a student of Abu Hamza, who discourses on proximity? When you meet him, tell him: 'Abu 'l-Husayn al-Nuri sends you his greetings and tells you that, from where he stands, the greatest proximity is the greatest distance.'"

As for the proximity to the [divine] Essence, "High exalted be God, the true King"[111] from any such thing. For He is far removed from any boundaries, sites,//148 limit or measure. No creature can unite with Him, no previously engendered entity can become separated from Him, because His eternal nature rejects both unification and separation.

There is thus a proximity that is impossible – namely, a co-existence of [other] essences [alongside God's Essence]. There is, however, a proximity that is possible and necessary – namely, a proximity through knowledge and vision. There is also a proximity that is possible. God bestows it upon any of His creatures, as He pleases. This is the proximity of [divine] grace through His kindness [toward His servants].

The [Divine] Law (*shari'a*) and the True Reality (*haqiqa*)

The Law is [God's] command to always comply with [the requirements of] servitude. The True Reality is the contemplation of [divine] Lordship. Any law that is not supported by the True Reality is not accepted [by God]. Likewise, any True Reality that is not bound by the Law is not accepted either.

The Law brings the creatures' obligations [toward God], while the True Reality brings news of God's disposition [of world affairs]. The Law exists so that you would worship Him, while the True Reality exists so that you would see Him. The Law is the fulfillment of what He has commanded, while the True Reality is that which He has executed and predetermined, hidden and manifested.

I heard the master Abu 'Ali al-Daqqaq – may God have mercy on him – say: "God's phrase 'Thee do we serve' means the observance of the Law, and 'To Thee alone we pray for succor'[112] means the affirmation of the True Reality." Know, that the Law is True Reality, in so far as it has come into being through His command, while the True Reality is Law, in so far as the knowledge of God – glory to Him – has come into being through His command.

Breath (*nafas*)

Breath is the perfuming of hearts by the subtle entities emanating from the Unseen. The person who has experienced breaths is more delicate and pure than

---

110 A Sufi of Baghdad who died in 289/902.
111 Q. 20:114; 20:112, according to Arberry's translation.
112 Q. 1:5.

the one who has experienced mystical states. The possessor of the mystical moment is a beginner, the possessor of breaths is one who has reached the goal, while the possessor of mystical states falls in between these two. States are intermediaries, while breaths are the final destination of advancement [toward God].//149

Mystical moments belong to the possessors of hearts, the mystical states belong to the lords of spirits, whereas breaths pertain to the people of innermost secrets.[113]

They say that the noblest of all acts of worship is to count one's breaths with God – glory and blessings to Him. They also say that God created hearts and made them the repositories of knowledge. He then created the innermost secrets, hid them behind hearts, and made them the repositories of the profession of God's unity. Thus, each breath that has not stepped on the carpet of necessity without the guidance of knowledge and the direction of God's unity is dead, and the person who has breathed it will be held responsible for it.

I heard the master Abu 'Ali al-Daqqaq – may God have mercy on him – say: "The gnostic cannot have a breath, because [God] grants him no concession whatsoever. The lover, on the other hand, cannot do without a breath, because if he does not have one, he will inevitably perish, for he has no capacity [to withstand the pressure]."

Thoughts (*khawatir*)

Thoughts are speeches that enter the soul. They may be dictated by an angel or by Satan; sometimes they are the soul's self-suggestions, at other times they come from God – glory to Him. When a thought comes from an angel, it is an inspiration; when it comes from the soul, it is a prompting; when it comes from Satan, it is a [devilish] whispering; when it comes from God – praise be to Him, Who casts it into the heart – it is a real thought. All these are different types of communication.

When a thought comes from an angel, its authenticity is affirmed by [religious] knowledge.[114] Therefore, they say that any thought whose authenticity is not attested by outward [evidence] is false. When, on the other hand, it comes from Satan, it usually incites to disobedience [of God]. Finally, when it comes from the soul, it usually prompts [man] to follow [his] passions and imbues [him] with a feeling of pride. Sufi shaykhs say that if a man partakes of a forbidden food, he is no longer able to discern between angelic inspiration and devilish whispering.//150
I heard Shaykh Abu 'Ali al-Daqqaq – may God have mercy on him – say: "He whose sustenance is known[115] cannot discern between [divine] inspiration and [devilish] whispering. And the heart of him, who through his sincere self-exertion

---

113 That is, the secret recesses of hearts.
114 That is, the Revelation.
115 That is, guaranteed.

has silenced the prompting of his soul, will speak according to the strength of his endeavor."

Sufi masters have agreed that your soul never speaks truth, while your heart never lies. One master said: "Your soul never speaks truth, while your heart never lies. And when you exert yourself to the utmost degree to force your spirit to speak to you, it will never speak to you."[116]

Al-Junayd differentiated between the prompting of the soul and the whispering of Satan. [He said]: "When the soul wants something from you, it persists and keeps reminding you, time and again, until such moment as she has achieved her goal and obtained what she has wanted. O God, may the sincere struggle [against your passions] never stop! For it will keep inciting you over and over again! As for Satan, he may prompt you to commit a foul act and once you have refused to obey him, he will begin inciting you to another foul act. This is because all acts of disobedience are equal for him; therefore he will always be inciting you to commit some foul act, for he does not care what act this may be."

They say that when somebody's thought comes from an angel, it may either agree or disagree with him. However, when someone receives his thought from God, it cannot disagree with him.

Sufi masters have discoursed on the issue of a second thought – namely, if both thoughts come from God, is the second stronger than the first? Al-Junayd said that the first thought is stronger, because when it stays, one returns to contemplation, as required by knowledge. Therefore the passing of the first thought weakens the one that comes next.

However, Ibn ʿAtaʾ [al-Adami] said that the second is stronger than the first, because its power has been increased by the one before it. Abu ʿAbdallah b. Khafif,[117] one of the recent [Sufi] masters, said that they are equal, because both come from God and thus one cannot be better than the other.

[In any event], the first does not stay once the second has arrived, because the traces [of divine grace] cannot last.//151

Certain knowledge (ʿilm al-yaqin), the essence of certainty (ʿayn al-yaqin) and the truth of certainty (haqq al-yaqin)

These words pertain to high [levels] of knowledge. Certainty, according to the common usage, means a knowledge that raises no doubt at all in the person who has it. This word is not applied to God – glory to Him – because [His knowledge] is not subject to any interpretation. Certain knowledge is certainty; likewise, the essence of certainty is the same as certainty and the truth of certainty is the same as certainty. In their [Sufi] parlance, certain knowledge is possible through a proof; the essence of certainty is possible through clear evidence; the truth of certainty is possible through direct witnessing.

---

116 That is, unlike the soul, the spirit is incapable of being prompted.
117 A famous Sufi master of Shiraz (d. 371/982). See *IM*, "Index" under "Ibn Khafif".

Certainty belongs to the people of intellect; the essence of certainty belongs to the people of knowledge;[118] the truth of certainty belongs to the people of divine gnosis. Speaking about this depends on the level of one's realization; it goes back to what we have already mentioned, therefore we limit ourselves to this measure in order to bring this [notion] to [your] attention.

Occurrence (*warid*)

They [Sufis] frequently speak about occurrences. Occurrence is a praiseworthy thought that enters the servant's heart without his invitation. Even if something does not belong to the category of thoughts, it can still be considered an occurrence. An occurrence may come from God or from knowledge.//152 Occurrences are broader than thoughts, because thoughts are characterized by a speech of sorts or something similar to speech. Occurrences can be of the following types: an occurrence of joy, an occurrence of sadness, an occurrence of contraction, an occurrence of expansion and so on.

Witness (*shahid*)[119]

They [Sufis] frequently mention the word "witness". One may be a witness of knowledge, or a witness of ecstasy, or a witness of a mystical state. By the word "witness" they mean that which is present in the heart of a man – that is, what he constantly recollects to the extent that he continues to see and watch it, even though he is [physically] absent from it. Any recollection that takes possession of a man's heart is his sign. If his heart is dominated by knowledge, then he is a witness of knowledge; if it is ecstasy, then he is a witness of ecstasy.

The meaning of "witness" is presence. That which is present in your heart is your witness. Someone asked al-Shibli[120] about witnessing. He answered: "How can we attribute the witnessing of God to ourselves?! It is He Who is our witness."[121] By saying that "God is our witness" he implied that the recollection of God has taken full possession of his heart, has become predominant over it and is ever present in it. When someone's heart becomes attached to a created thing, they say that this thing is his witness – namely, it is ever present in his heart. For love requires a constant recollection of the beloved and takes full possession of [the lover's] heart.

Some Sufis have contrived to etymologize this word in the following manner. They say that the word "witness" is derived from [the act of] witnessing. This is like contemplating a person who is characterized by [great] beauty. When the contemplator's human nature falls away from him, and when his witnessing of that person does not distract him from the spiritual state he is in, nor does the

---

118 That is, those who have already attained knowledge through the intellect.
119 This term can also be translated as "sign".
120 See pp. 61–62.
121 Or sign.

company of that person have any impact on him, that person becomes a witness of the contemplator being annihilated from his ego.//153 On the contrary, when all these things influence him, they become a witness of the persistence of his ego and the preservation of the characteristics of his human nature. And this may be either to his benefit or to his detriment.

The Prophet's words "On the night of ascension I witnessed my Lord in the most beautiful image" are sometimes interpreted in this sense – namely, "The most beautiful image which I witnessed on that night did not prevent me from seeing God Most High [Himself]. On the contrary, I saw the maker of [all] images in a [certain] image and the fashioner of [all] things in a [certain] fashion." By this he meant the vision pertaining to knowledge, not the vision of the eye.

The soul (*nafs*)

In the Arabic language, a thing's "soul" is its being. However, when the Sufis utter the word "soul" they imply neither being nor a [physical] body. Rather, they imply the deficiencies of one's character traits as well as one's reprehensible morals and deeds. The deficiencies of one's character traits fall into two categories: first, those which one acquires by oneself – namely, one's acts of disobedience and one's sins; second, one's [inherent] base morals. They are blameworthy in and of themselves. However, when a man seeks to treat them and fight them, these bad morals are extinguished in him through a strenuous and uninterrupted effort.

The first group of the soul's characteristics is anything that is absolutely prohibited or declared dubious [by the Divine Law]. The second group is the soul's imperfections and baseness in general. As for concrete characteristics, they are pride, wrath, spite, envy, bad temper, lack of tolerance, and similar character traits. However, the most difficult and objectionable characteristic of the soul is that it imagines there is something good about it and that it deserves respect. Therefore these [features] are sometimes considered to be hidden polytheism.//154 To improve one's moral character one has to abandon the soul and try to break it. The best way to do this is to have recourse to the strictures of hunger, thirst, night vigil and other types of self-exertion that lead to the weakening of [the soul's] power. All these practices are part of the abandonment of the soul.

However, the soul may also mean a subtle substance placed in the [human] body, which is the repository of blameworthy character traits in the same way as the spirit is a subtle substance placed in the [human] body, which is the repository of praiseworthy character traits. All these elements are subjugated to one another and their sum total constitutes a human being. The spirit and the soul are subtle substances residing in a certain form in the same way as the angels and demons are characterized by subtlety. This is also the case with vision being the repository of seeing, the ear being the repository of hearing, the nose being the repository of smelling, and the mouth being the repository of tasting. The entity that hears, sees, smells, or tastes constitutes a whole, which is a human being. Likewise, the heart and the spirit are the repositories of praiseworthy characteristics, whereas the soul is the repository of blameworthy ones. At the same time, the soul is part of the whole, and the heart is part of the same whole. Therefore the name and property go back to this same whole.

The spirit (*ruh*)

Those of the people of the Prophet's Sunna who have attained true realization hold different opinions regarding the spirits. Some of them say that they are nothing other than life, while others argue that they are the essences placed into the [human] bodies. Here is a subtle point: God is wont to create life in a [human] body. As long as the spirit resides in the body, a human being remains alive. The spirits, while they reside in bodies, may rise and depart from them at the time of sleep, whereafter they return to the body.

Man is a combination of the spirit and the body, because God Most High, may He be blessed, subjugated parts of this whole to one another. Resurrection will happen to this whole, and so will reward and punishment. The souls are created and those who insist that they are eternal commit a grave mistake.//155 And the Scriptures confirm that they are subtle essences.

The innermost self (*sirr*)

It seems that, like the spirits, the innermost selves are a subtle entity placed in the [human] body. According to Sufi principles, [the innermost self] serves as a repository of direct vision [of God], in the same way as the spirits are the repository of love and the hearts are the repository of knowledge.

They say that the innermost self is something that allows you to catch a glimpse [of God], while the innermost of the innermost self is that which is known to no one but God alone. According to the terminology and principles of the Sufis, the innermost self is more subtle than the spirit, while the spirit is more noble than the heart. They say that the innermost selves are free from the bondage of all things [other than God], from traces and remains. The words "innermost self" denote the [mystical] states that are kept secret between God – glory to Him – and His servant. This meaning is expressed in their saying: "Our innermost selves are virgins, which cannot be deflowered by anyone's imagination." They also say: "The breasts of noble men are the graveyards of innermost secrets." They also say: "If the bone next to my heart learns the secret of my heart, I will surely cast it away."

This is but a small part of the explanation of their terms and of the clarification of the phrases by which they [Sufis] have distinguished themselves from all others. We shall now mention a number of chapters explaining [the meaning of] way-stations, which are the stages of the [mystical] travelers.

Chapter 3
THE [MYSTICAL] STATIONS (*MAQAMAT*)

Repentance (*tawba*)

God Most High says: "And turn all together to God, O you believers; haply so you will prosper."[1] Abu Bakr Muhammad b. al-Husayn b. Furak[2] – may God have mercy on him – related to us: Ahmad b. Mahmud b. Khurrazadh related to us: Muhammad b. Fadl b. Jabir told us: Saʿid b. ʿAbdallah said: Ahmad b. Zakariya said: my father said: I heard Anas b. Malik say: I heard the Messenger of God – may God bless and greet him – say: "One who repents from sin is like one who has never sinned. When God loves a servant, sin will never afflict him." Then he recited [the following verse]: "Truly, God loves those who repent, and He loves those who cleanse themselves."[3] Someone asked: "Messenger of God, what is the sign of repentance?" He answered: "Remorse".

ʿAli b. Ahmad b. ʿAdnan al-Ahwazi related to us that Abu ʾl-Husayn Ahmad b. ʿUbayd al-Saffar said: Muhammad b. al-Fadl b. Jabir related to us that al-Hakam b. Musa related to us that Ghassan b. ʿUbayd b. Abi ʿAtika Tarif b. Salman told us on the authority of Anas b. Malik that the Prophet – may God bless and greet him and his family – said: "There is nothing dearer to God than a repentant youth."

Repentance is the first stage of the [mystical] wayfarers and the first station of the seekers [of God]. In the Arabic language, the true meaning of repentance is "return"; they say: "*taba* [he repented]" in the sense "He returned". Repentance thus is to return from what is blameworthy, according to the Divine Law, to what is praiseworthy.//157 The Prophet – may God bless and greet him – said: "Remorse is repentance." The scholars of the Prophet's Sunna, who specialize in the fundamentals of religion, have said that the three conditions of repentance are as follows: remorse for acts contradicting the Divine Law, immediate abandonment of the sin, and resolve never to commit similar acts of disobedience. These conditions are essential for repentance to be valid.

The scholars have said that the Prophet's statement that remorse is repentance emphasizes its most important aspect, in the same way as the Prophet's saying that the "Pilgrimage is ʿArafat"[4] points out the cornerstone of [the rite of] pilgrimage – namely, to stand and pray there. However, this does not mean that apart from the standing at ʿArafat there are no other important elements of the pilgrimage. Rather, this means that standing there is the cornerstone of the

---

1 Q. 24:31.
2 See Chapter 1 note 53.
3 Q. 2:222.
4 The standing of the pilgrims on the plain of ʿArafat is considered the culmination and the central element of the Muslim pilgrimage, or *hajj*.

Pilgrimage. Likewise, the Prophet's saying that remorse is repentance means that repentance is the cornerstone of remorse. Some of those who have attained true realization have argued that remorse is sufficient to achieve repentance, because it entails the two other conditions, since it is inconceivable that one persists in doing something one regrets or that one regrets something one has resolved to commit in the future. This is a general and summary definition of the meaning of repentance.

From the perspective of a more detailed elucidation and explanation, repentance has its causes, sequence and divisions. At first, the heart awakens from the slumber of heedlessness and the servant becomes aware of his evil condition. He arrives at this through God's help, as, in his mind, he begins to listen to the exhortations of God – glory to Him – by the hearing of his heart. This is mentioned in a prophetic tradition which says: "God's exhorter resides in the heart of every Muslim man." According to another tradition, "There is a piece of flesh in every [human] body. If it is healthy, the whole body is healthy, and if it is sick, the whole body is sick too. This is nothing but the heart." If the servant considers the evil he has done and sees the ugly deeds he has committed, the desire for repentance will enter his heart along with the wish to abstain from wrongdoing. Then God – glory to Him – will help him to strengthen his resolve, to return [to God] in the best manner possible, and to prepare himself for the demands of repentance.//158

The first of these demands is to part company with sinful friends – that is, those who would try to entice him into rejecting his goal and would seek to undermine his sound resolve. This can only be accomplished through perseverance in contemplation, which will increase his desire for repentance and multiply the motives that impel him to fulfill his resolve by strengthening in him fear [of God] and hope [for His mercy]. Then the knot of his persistence in evildoing around his heart will be loosened, as a result of which he will refrain from prohibited things and rein in his ego from pursuing its passions. At that point, he will abandon his sin once and for all and resolve to commit no sinful deeds ever again. If he has proceeded to live in accordance with his goal and act in accordance with his resolve, this means that he has achieved true success in his undertaking. However, should he violate [the demands] of repentance once or twice, his determination would require renewal. This thing may happen many times. However, one should not despair of repentance of such people, for "To each period is a decree established."[5]

It is related that Abu Sulayman al-Darani[6] said: "I attended the assembly of a preacher. While I was there, his words left a deep impression on my heart. However, when I was about to depart, nothing of it remained in my heart. I returned a second time. This time, the effect of his words stayed in my heart

---

5 Q. 13:38.
6 See *IM*, pp. 36–39.

until I returned to my house. I then broke the means of disobedience and embarked on the [Sufi] path." It is related that [on hearing this story] Yahya b. Muʿadh exclaimed: "A sparrow captured a crane!"[7] By the sparrow he meant that preacher, and by the crane Abu Sulayman al-Darani.

It is related that Abu Hafs al-Haddad[8] said: "I abandoned a certain reprehensible action, then returned to it. Then the action abandoned me, and I did not return to it again after that."

It is related that at the beginning of his affair[9] Abu ʿAmr b. Nujayd attended the sessions of Abu ʿUthman [al-Hiri].[10] His speeches affected his heart so that he repented. Then he experienced a relapse and began to hide from Abu ʿUthman whenever he saw him and stopped attending his sessions. One day, Abu ʿUthman met him [on the street]. Abu ʿAmr turned away and went down another path. Abu ʿUthman followed and pursued him until he caught up with him, and exclaimed://159 "My son, don't keep company with anyone who only loves you when you are sinless. In this situation, Abu ʿUthman can be of help to you!" Abu ʿAmr b. Nujayd repented, returned to his intention [to become a Sufi] and achieved success in it.

I heard the shaykh Abu ʿAli al-Daqqaq – may God have mercy on him – say that one seeker (*murid*) repented, then experienced a relapse. One day, he was wondering whether to return [to his repentance] and what would happen if he did. Suddenly he heard a voice: "O so-and-so! You obeyed Us, and We thanked you; you abandoned Us, and We granted you a respite; if you return to Us, We shall accept you!" The young man returned to his intention and succeeded in it.

When the servant abandons acts of disobedience, when the knot of persistence [in sinful deeds] is loosened from his heart, when he resolves never to commit any of them, while at the same time experiencing pangs of sincere remorse in his heart, he will regret his behavior. He then begins to blame himself for his evil states and ugly deeds. All this makes his repentance complete: his striving is now sincere; he has substituted solitude for the company of evil friends by withdrawing from them and has chosen a solitary retreat on account of them; he spends his days and nights in lamenting [his former evil ways] and is showing sincere regret in all of his states; by the rain of his tears he erases the traces of his stumbling; by the beauty of his repentance he treats the wounds of his failings; he is distinguished from his peers by his emaciated look, which points to the authenticity of his state.

No one can fulfill all this without first satisfying the demands of his adversaries and abandoning acts of injustice he has been guilty of perpetrating. For the first stage of repentance is to satisfy his adversaries to the fullest extent

---

7 These images are apparently taken from the famous Arab proverb according to which "one thousand cranes flying in the air cannot substitute one sparrow that you hold in your hand".
8 See *IM*, "Index" under "Abu Hafs al-Haddad".
9 That is, his entering the Sufi path.
10 See Chapter 1, pp. 45–46.

possible. When he has enough means to meet their claims or when they decide to declare him free from their claims, so be it. If not, then he must firmly resolve in his heart to fulfill their claims, as soon as an opportunity presents itself and to turn to God with sincere prayers and supplications on their behalf.//160

Those who repent have [special] features and states, which characterize them. They are considered to be part and parcel of repentance, insofar as they are characteristic of those who possess them. However, they are not necessarily a precondition for the soundness of one's repentance. Statements of Sufi masters about the meaning of repentance point in this direction. I heard the master Abu ʿAli al-Daqqaq – may God have mercy on him – say: "Repentance consists of three parts. Its beginning is *tawba* [repentance], its middle part is *inaba* [turning to God], and its end is *awba* [return to God]." Thus he placed repentance at the beginning, return [to God] at the end and turning to God in the middle. Whoever repents out of fear of [divine] punishment acquires repentance. Whoever repents out of desire of [divine] reward acquires turning to God. And whoever repents out of compliance with [divine] command not out of desire of reward, nor out of fear of punishment, acquires return to God.

They also say that repentance is the characteristic of the believers, because God Most High said: "And turn all together to God [in repentance], O you believers."[11] As for turning to God, this is the characteristic of [God's] friends and those brought nigh, for God Most High says: "[Whosoever] ... turns with a penitent heart."[12] As for return to God, this is the characteristic of the prophets and messengers, for God Most High said: "How excellent a servant [of God] he [Solomon] was. He was ever returning to God in penitence."[13]

I heard that Shaykh Abu ʿAbd al-Rahman al-Sulami said: I heard that Mansur b. ʿAbdallah said: I heard Jaʿfar b. Nusayr say: I heard al-Junayd say: "Repentance has three meanings. The first is regret; the second is the resolve not to revert to what God has forbidden; the third is the striving to right the wrongs done [to other people]."

Sahl b. ʿAbdallah [al-Tustari] said: "Repentance is to refrain from procrastination."//161

I heard Muhammad b. al-Husayn – may God have mercy on him – say: I heard Abu Bakr al-Razi say: I heard Abu ʿAbdallah al-Qurashi say: I heard al-Junayd say: I heard al-Harith [al-Muhasibi] say: "I have never said: 'My God, I ask You for repentance.' Instead, I have said: 'I ask You for the desire to repent.'"

Abu ʿAbdallah al-Shirazi – may God have mercy on him – reported to us: I heard Abu ʿAbdallah b. Muslih at Ahwaz say: I heard Ibn Ziri[14] say: I heard al-Junayd say: "One day I came to al-Sari [al-Saqati]. When I saw that he was distraught, I asked him what had happened. He said: 'A young man came to me

---

11 Q. 24:31.
12 Q. 50:33; according to Arberry's translation, 50:32.
13 Q. 38:30 (according to Arberry's translation, 38:29) and 38:44.
14 Or "Ibn Zizi".

and asked about repentance. I told him: "Repentance is that you not forget your sins." He contradicted me saying: "On the contrary, repentance is that you do forget your sins!"' I [al-Junayd] told him [al-Sari] that, in my opinion, the young man was right. He asked me why. I said that if I were to find myself in the state of estrangement [from God], then to be transported to the state of proximity [to Him], then my remembrance of estrangement in the state of purity is nothing but estrangement. On hearing this, al-Sari fell silent."

I heard Abu Hatim al-Sijistani – may God have mercy on him – say: I heard Abu Nasr al-Sarraj[15] say: someone asked Sahl b. ꜤAbdallah [al-Tustari] about repentance. He answered: "It is when you don't forget your sins." When al-Junayd was asked about repentance, he answered that this is when you forget your sins. Abu Nasr al-Sarraj said: "Sahl was referring to the state of beginners and novices, which is constantly changing. As for al-Junayd, he referred to the repentance of those who have attained the truth; for they do not remember their sins, because the majesty of God Most High and the remembrance of Him have gained complete mastery over their hearts." He [Abu Nasr] then argued that this was similar to Ruwaym's response to a question about repentance, according to which one should repent from one's repentance.

When someone asked Dhu ꜤI-Nun al-Misri about repentance he answered that the common people repent from sins, whereas the elect repent from forgetfulness. Abu ꜤI-Husayn al-Nuri said that repentance means to repent from everything other than God – may He be exalted and glorified.

I heard Muhammad b. Ahmad b. Muhammad al-Sufi say: I heard ꜤAbdallah b. ꜤAli b. Muhammad al-Tamimi say: "What a great difference is between someone who repents from his sins, someone who repents from his forgetfulness and someone who repents from the awareness of his own good works." Al-Wasiti said://162 "The sincere repentance[16] leaves no trace of disobedience on the penitent, be it hidden or manifest. If someone's repentance is pure he does not care where he spends the night or where he spends the day."

I heard Shaykh Abu ꜤAbd al-Rahman al-Sulami say: I heard Muhammad b. Ibrahim b. al-Fadl al-Hashimi say: I heard Muhammad b. al-Rumi say: I heard Yahya b. MuꜤadh say: "My God, I do not say, 'I have repented and will not go back [on my repentance], because I know my true nature. Nor do I pledge to abandon any and all sins, because I know well how weak I am.' I say: 'Perhaps I will not go back to my old ways, because I might die before that!'" Dhu ꜤI-Nun said: "To ask for [God's] forgiveness without abandoning the sin is the repentance of liars."

I heard Muhammad b. al-Husayn say: I heard al-Nasrabadhi say: I heard Ibn Yazdaniyar say that he was asked: "If God's servant departs to meet God, with what principle should he comply?" He said: "He should not return to that which

---

15 The author of a famous Sufi manual entitled "The Book of the Essentials of Sufism". See *IM*, pp. 118–120.
16 Q. 66:8.

he abandoned; nor should he pay any heed to anything save the One for the sake of Whom he has departed this world.[17] He should then guard his innermost heart from noticing that which he has just left behind him." It was said to him: "This is the property of someone who has departed from existence. What about someone who has departed from non-existence?" He answered: "Sweetness in the future substitutes for the bitterness in the past."

Someone asked al-Bushanji about repentance. He answered: "If you remember a sin without taking delight in its recollection, it is repentance." Dhu 'l-Nun said: "The true essence of repentance is that 'the land for all its breadth [is] narrow for you'[18] so that you find no rest for you in it; then your own self becomes narrow for you, as God Most High has mentioned in His Book: 'When the earth became narrow for them ... and their souls became narrow for them, and they thought there was no shelter from God except in Him, then He turned towards them,[19] so that they might also turn.'"[20]

Ibn 'Ata' [al-Adami] said: "There are two kinds of repentance: the repentance of return and the repentance of obedience. The repentance of return [to God] is that someone repents out of fear of God's punishment, whereas the repentance of obedience is that someone repents out of a feeling of shame for God's generosity [toward him]." Abu Hafs was asked: "Why does a repentant person loathe this world?"//163 He answered: "Because it is the place in which he commits his sins." He was then asked: "Isn't it also the place in which God has honored him with repentance?" He answered: "One can have no doubt about one's sins, whereas one can never be certain that one's repentance has been accepted."

Al-Wasiti said: "David – peace be upon him – rejoiced at first, then the sweetness of his obedience [toward God] caused him to breathe a deep sigh. His second spiritual state was more complete than the time when his [true] condition was hidden from him." A Sufi master said: "The repentance of liars is on the tips of their tongues." He meant that they constantly repeat [the phrase]: "May God forgive me." Someone asked Abu Hafs about repentance. He answered: "The servant has nothing to do with repentance, because it comes to him, not from him."

It is said that God – glory to Him – revealed to Adam the following words: "Adam, you have bequeathed to your progeny hardship and affliction, whereas I have bequeathed to them repentance. Whoever among them calls to Me, as you have done, I will answer his prayer as I have answered yours. Adam, I will resurrect the repentant from their graves delighted and laughing. Their prayers will be answered!"

---

17 That is, God.
18 Q. 9:25.
19 That is, repented on their behalf.
20 Q. 9:118.

A man said to Rabiʿa:²¹ "I have committed many sins and acts of disobedience. If I decide to turn to God, would He turn to me?" She answered: "No. Only if He were to turn to you, then you would be able to turn to Him."

Know that God Most High said: "Truly, God loves those who repent, and He loves those who cleanse themselves."²² A man who has succumbed to an error can be certain of his sin. However, if he decides to repent, he can never be certain that God accepts his repentance, especially if he considers himself to be naturally entitled to God's love. In order for the sinner to reach the stage at which he will discover signs of God's love toward him, he must travel a great distance. Therefore it is incumbent upon everyone who knows that he has committed a sin that requires repentance to embrace humility, to renounce all his faults and to ask for God's forgiveness, as in the saying: "Persevere in the dread [of divine punishment] until the appointed time!"²³ The Greatest of All Speakers²⁴ said: "Say: 'If you love God, follow me, and God will love you.'"²⁵ It was part of the Prophet's custom to ask constantly for God's forgiveness. He – may God bless and greet him – said: "My heart is covered by a cloud. Therefore I ask for God's forgiveness//164 seventy times a day."

I heard Abu ʿAbdallah al-Sufi say: I heard al-Husayn b. ʿAli say: I heard Muhammad b. Ahmad say: I heard ʿAbdallah b. Sahl say: I heard Yahya b. Muʿadh say: "One slip after repentance is uglier than seventy before it." I heard Muhammad b. al-Husayn say: I heard Abu ʿAbdallah al-Razi say: I heard Abu ʿUthman [al-Hiri] say commenting on the words of God Almighty and Glorious: "'Truly, unto Us is their return.'²⁶ It means, 'Unto Us is their return, even though they have persisted in acts of disobedience for a long time.'"

I heard Shaykh Abu ʿAbd al-Rahman al-Sulami say: I heard Abu Bakr al-Razi say: I heard Abu ʿUmar al-Anmati say: "'Ali b. ʿIsa the vizier²⁷ rode in a great procession. Some strangers among the onlookers began to inquire: 'Who is this? Who is this?' A woman standing by the side of the road said: 'How long will you keep asking, "Who is this? Who is this?" This is a servant of God, who has fallen from God's grace, so He has afflicted him with what you see.' When ʿAli b. ʿIsa heard this, he returned to his house and resigned from the vizirate. He then departed for Mecca and never left it again."

---

21 Rabiʿa al-ʿAdawiyya (d. 185/801), a legendary female ascetic from Basra. See *IM*, pp. 26–32.
22 Q. 2:222.
23 That is, the day of your death.
24 That is, God.
25 Q. 3:31; 3:29, according to Arberry's translation.
26 Q. 88:25.
27 A famous ʿAbbasid statesman, who was known for his piety and asceticism. He died in 334/946.

Striving (*mujahada*)

God Most High said: "And those who strive for Our sake, surely We shall guide them in Our ways; God is with the good-doers."[28]

Abu ʾl-Husayn ʿAli b. Ahmad al-Ahwazi related to us: Ahmad b. ʿUbayd al-Saffar related to us: al-ʿAbbas b. al-Fadl al-Isqati related to us: Ibn Kasib related to us: Ibn ʿUyayna related to us from ʿAli b. Zayd from Abu Nadra from Abu Saʿid al-Khudri, who said that the Messenger of God was asked about the most noble kind of spiritual self-exertion (*jihad*).[29] He answered: "A word of justice spoken before a despotic ruler." On hearing this tears started to flow from Abu Saʿid's eyes.

I heard the master Abu ʿAli al-Daqqaq – may God have mercy on him – say: "If someone adorns his externals with striving, God will beautify his internal self with the vision of Him." God Most High said: "And those who strive for Our sake, surely We shall guide them in Our ways."[30] //165

Know that anyone who does not strive [for God's sake] from the beginning, will find no trace of this [Sufi] path. I heard Shaykh Abu ʿAbd al-Rahman al-Sulami say: I heard Abu ʿUthman al-Maghribi say: "Anyone who thinks that anything of the path will be revealed or unveiled for him without him exerting himself constantly is in error." I heard the master Abu ʿAli al-Daqqaq – may God have mercy on him – say: "Whoever does not stand up at the beginning of his journey will not be allowed to sit down at its end." I also heard him say: "When people say, 'Movement is a blessing', they imply that bestirring oneself externally brings blessings internally."

I heard Muhammad b. al-Husayn say: I heard Ahmad b. ʿAli b. Jaʿfar say: I heard al-Husayn b. ʿAlluya say: Abu Yazid said: "For twelve years I was the blacksmith of my soul; then for five years I was the mirror of my heart; then for one year I was looking at that which lay between the two, and lo, around the waist of my external being was an infidel's girdle.[31] I then labored for twelve more years to cut it. I then looked, and lo, I saw an infidel's belt wrapped around my inner self. So I spent five more years trying to cut it. As I was wondering how I could cut it, [the truth] was revealed to me. I looked at God's creatures and saw them to be dead. So I uttered 'God is great' over them four times."[32]

I heard Shaykh Abu ʿAbd al-Rahman al-Sulami say: I heard Abu ʾl-ʿAbbas al-Baghdadi say: I heard Jaʿfar say: I heard al-Junayd say: I heard al-Sari [al-Saqati] say: "O young men! Exert yourselves to the fullest, before you have

---

28 Q. 29:69.
29 The Arabic words "striving" (*mujahada*) and "self-exertion [on the path of God]" (*jihad*) are derived from the Arabic verb *jahada*, which means to "exert oneself", "to take pains", "to strive".
30 Q. 29:69.
31 Protected minorities under Muslim rule were required to wear outward signs of their non-Muslim status, including a girdle.
32 Part of the funeral prayer.

reached my age and become decrepit and incapable, as I have." [He said this], although at that time the young men were nowhere near him in regard to the worship of God. I also heard him say: I heard Abu Bakr al-Razi say: I heard ʿAbd al-ʿAziz al-Najrani say: I heard al-Hasan al-Qazzaz say: "This matter[33] is based on three things://166 that you don't eat unless you are starving; that you don't sleep unless you are overpowered [by slumber]; and that you don't speak unless this is absolutely necessary." I also heard him [al-Sulami] say: I heard Mansur b. ʿAbdallah say: I heard Muhammad b. Hamid say: I heard Ahmad b. Khadrawayh say: I heard Ibrahim b. Adham say: "No one will ever attain the degree of the righteous until he has overcome six obstacles: first, that he shut the door of bounty and open the door of hardship; second, that he shut the door of vainglory and open the door of humility; third, that he shut the door of repose and open the door of earnest striving; fourth, that he shut the door of sleep and open the door of night vigil; fifth, that he shut the door of wealth and open the door of poverty; sixth, that he shut the door of hope [for a better future] and open the door of readiness for death."

Shaykh Abu ʿAbd al-Rahman al-Sulami said: I heard my grandfather Abu ʿAmr b. Nujayd say: "When your soul is honored, your faith is debased." I heard Mansur b. ʿAbdallah say: I heard Abu ʿAli al-Rudhbari say: "If a Sufi says after five days [of fasting] that he is hungry, then send him to the bazaar and tell him to earn his livelihood!"

Know that the root and foundation of striving is to wean one's soul from its habits and to accustom it to resist its passions at all times. The soul has two traits that prevent it from doing good. It is totally engrossed in pursuing its desires and refusal to perform acts of obedience. When the soul tries to break loose [from the rider] in pursuit of its passion, he must curb it with the reins of piety. When it becomes refractory in complying with God's will, he should steer it toward opposing its desires. When it rebels and flies into rage, he must bring it under control, for no struggle has a better outcome than one in which anger is conquered by good moral character and its embers are extinguished by [a display] of gentleness. And when the soul discovers the sweet wine of relaxation and finds comfort only in displaying her fine traits and in preening herself before anyone who cares to look at her and takes notice of her, it is necessary to break her of her habit and to make her stop at the abode of humiliation by reminding her of her small worth, her lowly origins and the turpitude of her deeds.

The common folk strive to protect their actions [from sin], while the elect endeavor to purify their [internal] states. For the strictures of hunger and night vigils are simple and easy, whereas the improvement of a man's morals and cleansing//167 them of evil traits is much more difficult.

One of the soul's most sinister traits is its tendency to take delight in fulsome praise. Anyone who partakes of this cup will carry the weight of heaven and earth

---

33 That is, Sufism.

on his eyelids! A sign of this [condition] is that when this drink [of praise] is withheld from him, his spiritual state reverts to indolence and ineptitude.

For many years a certain Sufi master used to pray in the front row of the mosque which he frequented. One day something prevented him from arriving early at the mosque, so he prayed in the last row. After that he was not seen there for a while. When someone asked him about the reason for that, he answered: "I prayed in the front row for so many years. As I was performing my daily prayers, I thought that I was dedicating them to God only. The day I was late I was overcome with a shame of sorts, because the people in the mosque saw me in the last row. I thus came to realize that all my zeal all these years had derived from my desire to be seen doing my prayers."

It is related that Abu Muhammad al-Murtaʿish once said: "I used to go on the pilgrimage without any provisions or riding animal. I then realized that all of my effort was tarnished by my taking pleasure in doing that. One day my mother asked me to bring a jar of water for her. When I found that request burdensome, I suddenly realized that my eagerness to perform the pilgrimages sprang from my soul's taking pleasure in that and from a blemish that still remained in it. For if my soul had been annihilated [by ascetic rigors], it wouldn't have found it burdensome to do something that is prescribed by the Divine Law."[34]

There was a woman who had reached a very old age. Someone asked her about her condition. She answered: "When I was young, I found in my soul the powers and drives that I regarded as coming from the strength of my [spiritual] state. But when I grew older, they disappeared. It was then that I realized that these powers and drives came from the strength of my youth, not from the strength of my spiritual states, as I had imagined." I heard Shaykh Abu ʿAli al-Daqqaq say: "Every Sufi master who has heard this story, could not help feeling great compassion for this old lady and would say that she was absolutely right."

I heard Muhammad b. al-Husayn say: I heard Muhammad b. ʿAbdallah b. Shadhan say: I heard Yusuf b. al-Husayn say: I heard Dhu ʾl-Nun al-Misri say: "God graces His servant with no greater honor than to show him the depravity of his soul. At the same time, God subjects His servant to no greater humiliation than to conceal from him the depravity of his soul."//168 I also heard him [Muhammad b. al-Husayn] say: I heard Muhammad b. ʿAbdallah say: I heard Ibrahim al-Khawwas say: "There has not been a single frightful thing upon which I would not embark."[35] I also heard him say: I heard ʿAbdallah al-Razi say: I heard Muhammad b. al-Fadl say: "Rest is to be free from the aspirations of one's soul."

I heard Abu ʿAbd al-Rahman [al-Sulami] say: I heard Mansur b. ʿAbdallah say: I heard Abu ʿAli al-Rudhbari say: "Misfortunes come upon mankind from three things: disease in natural disposition, clinging to [evil] habits, and bad

---

34 The Qurʾan enjoins Muslims to treat their parents kindly. See, e.g., 17:24.

35 According to one commentary, al-Khawwas refers here to the rigorous ascetic and self-abnegating practices to which he has subjected himself in his search for God's pleasure.

company." I [Mansur b. ʿAbdallah] asked him about disease of natural disposition. He answered that it was eating forbidden food. I asked him about clinging to [evil] habits. He answered that it was looking at and listening to forbidden things and slander. I asked him about bad company. He answered that it was to follow any passion that arises in your soul.

I also heard him say: I heard al-Nasrabadhi say: "Your soul is your prison. When you have escaped from it, you will find yourself in eternal ease." I also heard him say: I heard Muhammad al-Farraʾ say: I heard Abu ʾl-Husayn al-Warraq say: "In the beginning of this affair of ours[36] at the mosque of Abu ʿUthman al-Hiri, our finest practice was to give away everything that was given to us [as pious donation], to spend the night without knowing what our sustenance would be the next day, and when any of us encountered anything disagreeable we took no revenge [on those responsible for it]. Instead, we excused the offenders and showed humility toward them. And when disdain for someone entered our hearts, we placed ourselves at his service and treated him with kindness until [this feeling] ceased." Abu Hafs [al-Haddad] said: "The soul is nothing but darkness; its secret [heart] is its lamp; and the light of this lamp is Godspeed. Whoever is not accompanied by God's assistance in his secret [heart], lingers in total darkness."

The imam and master al-Qushayri said that the meaning of his words "[the soul's] lamp is its secret [heart]" is the secret that exists between the servant and God Most High. This is the site of his sincerity by means of which the servant becomes aware that everything originates from God and not from him or by him. As a result, he frees himself from pretensions to any power and ability [to act on his own] at any time. He then becomes protected from the evil of his soul through God's assistance, for if this assistance is not extended to him,//169 his knowledge of his self and of God will be of no use to him. Therefore, the Sufi masters have said: "He who has no secret [heart] is doomed to persist [in sin]."

Abu ʿUthman [al-Hiri] said: "A man cannot see the faults of his soul, if he keeps finding anything good in it. Only he who blames his soul at all times will be able to see its faults." Abu Hafs [al-Haddad] said: "How swift is the destruction of one who is unable to recognize his faults, for disobedience is the messenger of unbelief." Abu Sulayman [al-Darani] said: "I do not consider a single action of my soul to be good and do not expect it to be counted in my favor." Al-Sari [al-Saqati] said: "Beware of those who frequent the rich, those who recite the Qurʾan in the marketplace and those learned who serve worldly rulers." Dhu ʾl-Nun al-Misri said: "Corruption afflicts men due to the following six things. First, when their desire to work for the sake of the Hereafter is weak; second, when men's bodies become hostages to their lusts; third, when they hold high hopes for the future, while their life is so short; fourth, when they strive to please creatures instead of pleasing their Creator; fifth, when they pursue their passions, while turning their backs on the Prophet's custom (*sunna*); sixth, when

---

36 That is, the Sufi path.

they justify their failings by mentioning the minor slips committed by the noble forbears,[37] while burying their many virtues.

Retreat (*khalwa*) and seclusion (*ʿuzla*)

Abu ʾl-Hasan ʿAli b. Ahmad b. ʿAbdan related to us: Ahmad b. ʿUbayd al-Basri related to us: ʿAbd al-ʿAziz b. Muʿawiyya told us: al-Qaʿnabi told us: ʿAbd al-ʿAziz b. Abi Hazim related to us on the authority of his father, who related to him on the authority of Baʿja b. ʿAbdallah b. Badr al-Juhani on the authority of Abu Hurayra, who said: "The Messenger of God – may God's peace and blessing be upon him – said: 'The best of all possible ways of living is for a man to take the reins of his horse [to fight] in the way of God; if he hears sounds of alarm and panic, he is on his horse's back seeking death or martyrdom in the right place. Or this[38] is the life of a man who tends his sheep and goats on a mountain peak or at the bottom of a valley; he performs his prayers, gives alms and worships his Lord until "there comes to him the Certainty [of death]".[39] People see nothing but good from him.'"//170

Retreat belongs to the elect, while seclusion is a sign of the people of union [with God]. It is incumbent on the seeker, who embarks on the path [to God], to seclude himself from his own kind. Then, at the end of his path, he should practice seclusion in order to achieve intimacy with God.

When a man chooses seclusion he must be sure that he practices it in order to protect other people from his evil, not in order to be safe from their evil. The former comes from his thinking little of himself, while the latter comes from seeing himself to be better than others. A man who thinks little of himself is humble, whereas a man who considers himself to be more worthy than others is vain.

Someone saw a monk and asked him: "You are a monk, aren't you?" He answered: "No, I am guarding a dog. My soul is a dog that bites people. I therefore have removed it from them, so that they be safe from it."

Once someone passed by a righteous man, who, on seeing him, pulled his garment away from him. The passer-by said: "Why are you pulling your garments away from me? My clothes are not impure!" The righteous man answered: "I assumed that you would think that my clothes were impure, so I removed them from your way lest they soil your clothes, not the other way around!"

One of the rules of seclusion is that the man who goes into seclusion must acquire enough knowledge to solidify his faith in the oneness of God in order not to be seduced by Satan's whisperings. Then he should acquire enough knowledge of the Divine Law to be able to fulfill his religious duties, so that his undertaking would rest on a solid foundation. In essence, seclusion is but separation from

---

37 That is, the members of the first Muslim community.
38 That is, the best possible way to live one's life.
39 Q. 15:99.

reprehensible character traits. Its purpose is to turn [bad] qualities into [good] ones, not to withdraw from familiar places [into the desert]. Thus, when someone asks [Sufis] about the gnostic (ʿarif), they answer, "One who is here and not here", meaning that he is [outwardly] with creatures, while in his heart he is separate from them.

I heard the master Abu ʿAli al-Daqqaq – may God have mercy on him – say: "Wear with people what they wear and eat what they eat, but separate yourself from them in your heart of hearts!" I also heard him say: "A man came to me and said: 'I have come to you from far away.' I told him: 'This matter[40] is obtained neither by crossing great distances nor by subjecting oneself to the strictures of travel. Separate from your soul even by a single step, and you will achieve your goal!'"

It is related that Abu Yazid said: "In a dream, I saw my Lord – may He be glorified and exalted. I asked Him: 'How shall I find You?' He answered: 'Leave your soul behind and come!'" I heard Shaykh Abu ʿAbd al-Rahman al-Sulami say: I heard Abu ʿUthman al-Maghribi say: "Whoever chooses retreat over the company of men must be free from all recollections except the recollection of his Lord; he must be free from all desires except the desire of God's satisfaction; he must also be free from all demands of his soul. If he does not meet this condition, his retreat will plunge him into temptation or calamity." It is said that separation from one's self in retreat is the most perfect way to solace.//171

Yahya b. Muʿadh said: "Consider whether your intimacy is your intimacy with retreat, or with Him in retreat. If your intimacy is with retreat, it will disappear when you abandon your retreat. However, if your intimacy is with Him, it will persist regardless of the place you are in, be it in the desert or in the steppe."

I heard Muhammad b. al-Husayn say: I heard Mansur b. ʿAbdallah say: I heard Muhammad b. Hamid say: "A man came to visit Abu Bakr al-Warraq. As he was about to depart, he asked [al-Warraq] to counsel him. He said: 'I have found the best of this world and the next in retreat and frugality, while I have found the worst of the two worlds in abundance and mixing with people.'" I also heard him say: I heard Mansur b. ʿAbdallah say: I heard al-Jurayri say, when asked about seclusion: "It is when you enter into the crowd, while guarding your innermost self from being crowded by the crowd and secluding it from sins. In this way your innermost self will be bound to God." They also say: "Whoever chooses seclusion, attains seclusion."[41]

Sahl [al-Tustari] said: "[Your] seclusion is not sound unless you eat what is lawful [under the Divine Law]. And your eating of lawful food is not sound unless you render to God His due." Dhu ʾl-Nun said: "I have seen nothing more conducive to sincerity than retreat." Abu ʿAbdallah al-Ramli said: "Let your true companion be solitude, your food be hunger, your speech be intimate prayers.

---

40 That is, the knowledge of the Sufi path.
41 According to another reading, "Whoever chooses seclusion, attains greatness" (al-ʿizzu lahu).

Then and only then, will you join God after you die." Dhu 'l-Nun said: "Someone who hides from mankind in retreat is not like one who hides from mankind in God."

I heard Abu 'Abd al-Rahman al-Sulami say: I heard Abu Bakr al-Razi say: I heard Ja'far b. Nusayr say: I heard al-Junayd say: "The hardship of seclusion is easier to bear than the enticement of [human] company." Mak'hul said: "While there is some good in mixing with people, safety lies in seclusion." Yahya b. Mu'adh said: "Solitude is the companion of the truthful."

I heard Shaykh Abu 'Ali al-Daqqaq say: I heard al-Shibli say: "Ruin, ruin, O people!" Someone asked him: "What is the sign of ruin?" He answered: "One of the signs of ruin is intimacy with people!" Yahya b. Abu Kathir said: "Whoever mixes with people seeks to wheedle them, and whoever wheedles them, behaves hypocritically toward them." Shu'ayb b. Harb said: "I came to see Malik b. Mas'ud in Kufa, when he was alone in his house. I asked him whether he felt lonely. He responded: 'I don't think that one can be alone with God!'"

I heard Abu 'Abd al-Rahman al-Sulami say: I heard Abu Bakr al-Razi say: I heard Abu 'Umar al-Anmati say: I heard al-Junayd say: "Whoever wants his religion to be sound and his body and heart to be relieved should isolate himself from people. This is a desolate time and wise is he who chooses seclusion!" I also heard him [al-Sulami] say: I heard Abu Bakr//172 al-Razi say: Abu Ya'qub al-Susi said: "Only the strong are capable of withdrawing themselves from people. For the likes of us living in a community is more beneficial, because some of us imitate others [in good works]."

I heard Abu 'Uthman Sa'id b. Abu Sa'id say: I heard Abu 'l-'Abbas al-Damaghani say: "Al-Shibli gave me the following advice: 'Stick to solitude, erase your name from [the list of] living people and face the wall[42] until you die!'" A man came to Shu'ayb b. Harb. The latter asked him: "What brings you here?" He answered: "I want to be with you." Shu'ayb replied: "O my brother! Worship of God cannot be achieved in the company [of men]. He who is not intimate with God, cannot be intimate with anything!" Some people asked a Sufi: "What is the most remarkable thing you have encountered in your travels?" He replied: "Once I met al-Khidr.[43] He sought my company, but I declined out of fear that it might interfere with my reliance on God." Another Sufi was asked if there was anyone with whom he would feel intimate. He answered "Yes!", whereupon he stretched his hand toward his copy of the Qur'an and pressed it to his heart saying, "This!" They had this meaning in mind when they recited the following verse:

Your books[44] are always with me; they do not leave my bed for a single moment.
And in them there is a cure for the sickness I conceal.

---

42 That is, the prayer niche.
43 A popular person in Sufi literature and Middle Eastern folklore, who is sometimes identified with the prophet Elijah (Ilyas). Al-Khidr is believed to be immortal; he travels freely across land and sea, helping those in need. Sufis consider him to be the model friend of God (*wali*).
44 Or "letters".

A man asked Dhu ʾl-Nun al-Misri: "When will seclusion become right for me?" He answered: "When you are able to seclude yourself from your own self!" Ibn al-Mubarak⁴⁵ was asked about the cure of the heart. He answered: "[It is] to avoid mixing with people!" It is said that when God wants to take his servant from the ignominy of disobedience to the glory of obedience, He graces him with the intimacy of solitude, enriches him with contentment, and allows him to see his faults. Whoever has been given all this, has been given the best of the two worlds!"

Fear of God (*taqwa*)

God Most High said: "Surely the noblest among you in the sight of God is the most Godfearing of you."⁴⁶ Abu ʾl-Hasan ʿAli b. Ahmad b. ʿAbdan informed us: Ahmad b. ʿUbayd al-Saffar informed us: Muhammad b. al-Fadl b. Jabir informed us: ʿAbd al-Aʿla al-Qurashi⁴⁷ related to us: Yaʿqub al-ʿAmmi told us on the authority of Layth, on the authority of Mujahid, on the authority of Abu Saʿid al-Khudri, who said that a man came to the Prophet – may God bless and greet him – and said: "O Prophet of God, advise me!" He answered: "Hold onto fear of God, for it is the quintessence of all good! Perform *jihad*; it is the monasticism//173 of the Muslim! Practice the remembrance of God, for it is a light for you!"

ʿAli b. Ahmad b. ʿAbdan said: Ahmad b. ʿUbayd said: ʿAbbas b. al-Fadl al-Asqati related to us: Ahmad b. Yunus related to us: Abu Hurmuz Nafiʿ b. Hurmuz related to us: I heard Anas [b. Malik] say that someone asked [the Prophet]: "Prophet of God, who are the family of Muhammad?" He answered: "Everyone who fears God!"

Fear of God is the quintessence of all good things. The True Reality of fear of God consists of protecting oneself from God's punishment through obedience to Him. It is said: "So-and-so protected himself with his shield." The root of fear of God is to protect oneself from associating anything or anyone with God; this is to be followed by protecting oneself from acts of disobedience and offenses; this is followed by protecting oneself from dubious things; this is followed by protecting oneself from unnecessary things.

I heard the master Abu ʿAli al-Daqqaq – may God have mercy on him – say: "For each of these divisions there is a special chapter." Some [scholars] have interpreted the Qurʾanic phrase "[O believers,] fear God as He should be feared"⁴⁸ as meaning that God is to be obeyed and not disobeyed, remembered and not forgotten, thanked and not unrequited.

I heard Shaykh Abu ʿAbd al-Rahman al-Sulami say: I heard Ahmad b. ʿAli b. Jaʿfar say: I heard Ahmad b. ʿAsim say: I heard Sahl b. ʿAbdallah say: "There

---

45 An early Muslim ascetic and fighter for religion, who died in 181/797. See *IM*, pp. 21–22.
46 Q. 49:13.
47 In another reading "al-Narsi".
48 Q. 3:102; 3:97 according to Arberry's translation.

is no helper but God, no guide but the Messenger of God, no provisions but fear of God, no deed but one that is graced by patience [in worship]."

I heard Abu Bakr al-Razi say: I heard al-Kattani say: "This world is apportioned according to affliction and the next according to fear of God." I also heard him [al-Sulami] say: I heard Abu Bakr al-Razi say: I heard al-Jurayri say: "No one who has not appointed fear of God as an arbiter between himself and God will ever attain unveiling and contemplation [of divine mysteries]." Al-Nasrabadhi said: "Fear of God means that the servant of God fears everything except God may He be great and exalted!" Sahl [al-Tustari] said: "Whoever desires to achieve perfection in fear of God must abandon all sins." Al-Nasrabadhi said: "He who practices fear of God aspires to separate himself from this world, because God – glory to Him – said: 'The next world is better for those who are Godfearing. Will you not understand?'"[49] A Sufi said: "When someone's fear of God is perfect, God makes turning away from this world easy for him."

Abu 'Abdallah al-Rudhbari said: "Fear of God is to shun anything that distances you from God."//174 Dhu 'l-Nun said: "The Godfearing person is one who does not defile his exterior with acts of opposition [to God's will] nor his interior with diversions [from God] and occupies the station of complete agreement with God."

I heard Muhammad b. al-Husayn – may God have mercy on him – say: "I heard Abu 'l-Husayn al-Farisi say: I heard Ibn 'Ata' say: "Fear of God has two sides: outward and inward. Its outward side is the observance of [God's] boundaries. Its inward side is [pure] intention and sincerity."

Dhu 'l-Nun [al-Misri] said:

There is no living except with men whose hearts long for fear of God and
Whose repose is in the remembrance [of God's name]
[Their] contentment is in the spirit of certainty and its sweetness
As the nursing infant is content with [its mother's] lap.

They say that a man's fear of God is evident in three things: full trust in God with respect to what has not been granted to him; full satisfaction with what has been granted to him; and full patience with respect to what has eluded him. Talq b. Habib said: "Fear of God is to act in obedience to God, illuminated by His light, and to fear His punishment."

I heard Shaykh Abu 'Abd al-Rahman al-Sulami say: I heard Muhammad al-Farra' relate from Abu Hafs the following saying: "Fear of God can only be achieved by [eating] that which is lawful. There is no other way." I also heard him say; I heard Abu Bakr al-Razi say: I heard Abu 'l-Husayn al-Zanjani say: "He whose capital is fear of God gains a profit that tongues are unable to describe." Al-Wasiti said: "Fear of God is to be wary of one's fear of God", meaning to take no notice of it.

---

49 Q. 6:32.

The one who fears God [should be] like Ibn Sirin.[50] Once he bought forty jars of butter. His servant found a [dead] mouse in one of them. Ibn Sirin asked him: "What jar did you find it in?"[51] The servant said that he did not remember, whereupon Ibn Sirin dumped all of the jars onto the ground. Or one should be like Abu Yazid [al-Bistami], who once purchased a measure of saffron in Hamadan.[52] A little of it was left over and when he returned to Bistam[53] he found two ants in it. He then returned to Hamadan and laid down these two ants.

It is related that Abu Hanifa[54] used to avoid sitting in the shade of his neighbor's tree. He would explain this [behavior] by referring to a report from the Prophet that says: "Any loan that brings interest is usury." It is told that Abu Yazid was washing his robe in the desert [outside the city] with a companion of his. The companion said to him: "Let's hang our robes on the wall of this vineyard." Abu Yazid responded: "No, one cannot drive a nail into other people's wall." The companion said: "Let's hang them on this tree." He answered: "No, for they may break the branches." "Then let's spread them out on the grass!" "No," responded Abu Yazid. "No, the grass is fodder for the animals. We cannot block them off from it!" He turned his back to the sun, with his robe on his back, and waited until one side was dry. He then turned it around and waited until the other side was dry.//175

It is told that once Abu Yazid went to the congregational mosque and drove his staff into the ground. It fell upon the staff of an old man next to it and knocked it down. The old man had to lean over in order to pick up his staff. Abu Yazid followed the old man to his house and asked for his forgiveness. He said: "The reason for your leaning over was my negligence in driving my staff into the ground, for this caused you to do so."

Once ʿUtba al-Ghulam was seen breaking into a sweat in wintertime. When asked why, he responded: "This is the place where I disobeyed my Lord!" On being asked for an explanation, he said: "I scraped off a chunk of clay from this wall and had a guest of mine cleanse his hands with it. However, I neglected to ask the owner of the wall for permission."

Ibrahim b. Adham said: "Once I was spending the night in the desert near Jerusalem. After some time two angels descended. One of them asked the other: "Who is this?" He answered: "Ibrahim b. Adham." "That is the one whom God – glory to Him – lowered by one degree!" "Why?" inquired the other angel. "Because he bought some dates in Basra and one of the dates belonging to the grocer fell in among his dates and he did not return it to its owner." Ibrahim

---

50 An early Muslim scholar who was renowned for his piety and scrupulousness. He died in 110/728.
51 According to the shariʿa, any food that came in contact with a dead animal was considered impure.
52 A city in Iran.
53 His native city.
54 A renowned jurist, who founded a school of law named after him. He died in 150/767.

continued: "I returned to Basra and purchased dates from that man, and [while doing this] dropped one date into his dates. I then returned to Jerusalem and spent the night in the desert [again]. After some time, I saw two angels descend from the sky. One said to the other: "Who is here?" He answered: "Ibrahim b. Adham." He then added: "His rank is raised."

It is said that fear of God has several degrees: the common people shun associating anything with God (*shirk*); the elect shun sins; the prophets shun attributing acts [to anyone other than Him] – in other words, their fear comes to them from Him and is [directed] to Him.

The Commander of the Faithful, 'Ali – may God be pleased with him – said: "The most noble of mankind in this world are the generous and the best of mankind in the Hereafter are those who fear God."

'Ali b. Ahmad al-Ahwazi informed us: Abu ʾl-Husayn al-Basri informed us: Bishr b. Musa informed us: Muhammad b. 'Abdallah b. al-Mubarak related to us on the authority of Yahya b. Ayyub, on the authority of 'Ubaydallah b. Zuhr, on the authority of 'Ali b. Yazid, on the authority of al-Qasim, on the authority of Abu Umama from the Prophet – may God's peace and blessing be upon him – that he said: "If someone has looked at the beauty of a woman and lowered his sight with the first look, God will make for him an act of worship whose sweetness will reside in his heart [forever]."

I heard Muhammad b. al-Husayn say: I heard Abu ʾl-'Abbas Muhammad b. al-Husayn say: I heard Muhammad b. 'Abdallah al-Farghani say: "Once al-Junayd was sitting with Ruwaym [b. Ahmad], al-Jurayri, and Ibn 'Ata' [al-Adami].[55]//176 Al-Junayd said: 'One cannot be saved unless one is sincere in taking refuge with God, for God Most High said: "And to the three who were left behind, until the earth, for all its breadth, became narrow for them." '[56] Ruwaym – may God have mercy upon him – said: 'One cannot be saved unless one is sincere in the fear of God, for God Most High said: "But God shall deliver those who were Godfearing to their security."' Al-Jurayri said: 'One cannot be saved unless one keeps trust, for God Most High said: "Those who fulfill God's covenant and break not the compact."'[57] Ibn 'Ata' said: 'One cannot be saved unless one has become ashamed of oneself in truth, for God Most High said: "Does not he know that God sees [everything]?"'"[58]

The master and imam[59] said: "One can be saved only by divine order and decree, for God Most High said: 'As for those unto whom the ample reward has

---

55 They were members of al-Junayd's inner circle; the last named was also a partisan of al-Hallaj.
56 Q. 9:118; according to most exegetes, this verse refers to three Companions of the Prophet, who refused to participate in his military campaign. Later on they repented and were tormented by the feeling of uncertainty as to their status in the eyes of God – namely, whether He had pardoned them.
57 Q. 13:20.
58 Q. 96:4.
59 That is, al-Qushayri.

gone forth from us, [they shall be kept far from it[60]].'"[61] He also said: "One can be saved only by pre-determined choice [of God], for God Most High said: 'We chose them and guided them to a straight path.'"[62]

Scrupulousness (wara')

Abu 'l-Husayn[63] 'Abd al-Rahman b. Ibrahim b. Muhammad b. Yahya al-Muzakki informed us: Muhammad b. Dawud b. Sulayman al-Zahid informed us: Muhammad b. al-Hasan b. Qutayba informed us: Ahmad b. Abu Tahir al-Khurasani told us: Yahya b. al-'Ayzar said: Muhammad b. Yusuf al-Firyabi told us on the authority of Sufyan on the authority of al-Ajlah on the authority of 'Abdallah b. Burayda on the authority of Abu 'l-Aswad al-Du'ali on the authority of Abu Dharr that the Messenger of God – may God's blessing and peace be upon him – said: "One of the best features of a man's Islam is his giving up that which does not concern him."

The imam and master [al-Qushayri] – may God be pleased with him – said: "Scrupulousness is giving up dubious things." Likewise, Ibrahim b. Adham said: "Scrupulousness is giving up whatever is dubious and whatever does not concern you", which means giving up that which is superfluous.//177

Abu Bakr al-Siddiq[64] – may God be pleased with him – said: "We used to abandon seventy kinds of permitted things out of fear of stepping into only one thing that is forbidden." The Prophet – may God's peace and blessing be upon him – told Abu Hurayra: "Be scrupulous and you will be among God's greatest servants!"

I heard Shaykh Abu 'Abd al-Rahman al-Sulami say: I heard Abu 'l-'Abbas al-Baghdadi say: I heard Ja'far b. Muhammad say: I heard al-Junayd say: I heard al-Sari [al-Saqati] say: "The most scrupulous men of their times were: Hudhayfa b. al-Mar'ashi,[65] Yusuf b. Asbat, Ibrahim b. Adham and Sulayman al-Khawwas. They stuck to scrupulousness under any circumstances, and when acquisition of that which is lawful became difficult to them, they took recourse in the absolute minimum." I also heard him [al-Sulami] say: I heard Abu 'l-Qasim al-Dimashqi say: I heard al-Shibli say: "Scrupulousness is to refrain from everything other than God Most High." I also heard him [al-Sulami] say: Abu Ja'far al-Razi informed us: al-'Abbas b. Hamza told us: Ahmad b. Abi 'l-Hawari told us: Ishaq b. Khalaf told us: "To be scrupulous in speech is harder than being scrupulous in [dealing] with gold and silver. Likewise, to abstain from worldly authority (ri'asa) is harder than to abstain from gold and silver, since one expends them freely in one's quest for worldly authority.

---

60 That is, the hellfire.
61 Q. 21:101.
62 Q. 6:87.
63 An alternative reading has "Abu 'l-Hasan".
64 The first successor of the prophet Muhammad (caliph), who died in 11/634.
65 According to an alternative reading, "al-Murta'ish".

Abu Sulayman al-Darani said: "Scrupulousness is the beginning of abstention, just as contentment is an [essential] part of satisfaction." Abu ʿUthman [al-Hiri] said: "The reward for being scrupulous is the lightness of reckoning [on the Day of Judgement]." Yahya b. Muʿadh said: "Scrupulousness consists of embracing the provisions of [religious] knowledge without [delving into] interpretation of it."

I heard Muhammad b. al-Husayn say: I heard al-Husayn b. Ahmad b. Jaʿfar say: I heard Muhammad b. Dawud al-Dinawari say: I heard ʿAbdallah b. al-Jallaʾ say: "I know someone who lived in Mecca for thirty years. During that time he drank nothing of the water of the Zamzam well[66] except that which he would draw with his own leather pitcher and his own rope. Furthermore, [throughout these years] he would never eat any food imported from Egypt."[67]//178

I also heard him say: I heard Abu Bakr al-Razi say: I heard ʿAli b. Musa al-Taharti say: "Once a small coin belonging to ʿAbdallah b. Marwan fell into a filthy well. He spent thirteen *dinars* in wages to pay for retrieving it. When asked about that, he responded: "The name of God Most High was inscribed on it!" I also heard him say: I heard Abu ʾl-Hasan al-Farisi say: I heard Ibn ʿAlluya say: I heard Yahya b. Muʿadh say: "There are two kinds of scrupulousness: the scrupulousness of the externals, which means that one moves only for the sake of God Most High; and the scrupulousness of the interior, which means that only God and God alone can enter your heart."

Yahya b. Muʿadh also said: "One who is neglectful of the fine points of scrupulousness will not receive a sublime gift [from God]." Likewise, it is said: "He who observes his religion meticulously will see his rank raised in importance at the Resurrection." Ibn al-Jallaʾ also said: "He whose poverty is not accompanied by fear of God consumes that which is manifestly forbidden." Yunus b. ʿUbayd said: "Scrupulousness is to abandon every dubious thing and to call your ego to account with every moment."

Sufyan al-Thawri said: "I have not seen anything easier than scrupulousness. Whenever something leaves a mark on your soul, abandon it!" Maʿruf al-Karkhi said: "Guard your tongue from praise as you guard it from censure." Bishr b. al-Harith said: "The three hardest things are: to be generous in penury; to be scrupulous in seclusion; and to tell the truth to someone whom you fear or expect some benefit from."

It is said that the sister of Bishr al-Hafi came to Ahmad b. Hanbal[68] and said: "We were spinning on the roof of our house, when a group of the Zahiri guard[69]

---

66 The sacred well located in the Meccan sanctuary.
67 That is, the food of which provenance he was not sure.
68 A famous scholar of Baghdad (d.241/855), who founded a school of law named after him. He was famous for his piety.
69 That is, representatives of the state government, who were seen by many of the righteous as corrupt and despotic. The implications of this story in the context of the ambivalent relations between Ibn Hanbal (a model traditionalist scholar) and Bishr (a model ascetic) are discussed in Michael Cooperson, "Ahmad Ibn Hanbal and Bishr al-Hafi", *Studia Islamica*, 86/2 (1997), pp. 71–101.

passed us by with their torches. The light [of their torches] fell upon us. Was it permissible for us to spin by their light?" Ahmad [b. Hanbal] asked her: "Who are you? May God keep you in good health!" She said: "I am Bishr al-Hafi's sister."//179 Ahmad wept and said: "Your house is [the seat] of true scrupulousness. Therefore, do not spin in the light [of their torches]!"

ʿAli al-ʿAttar said: "[One day] I was walking through the streets of Basra. [I saw] a few old men sitting there, while some young boys played nearby. I asked [them]: 'Aren't you ashamed of [playing in the presence of] these elders?' One of the boys answered: 'These elders have very little in the way of scrupulousness, so they command little respect!'"

It is said that Malik b. Dinar resided in Basra for forty years. However, he did not consider it proper to eat the dates of that city, be they fresh or dried. He died without tasting any of them even once. Each time the season for ripe dates had passed he would say: "O people of Basra, this stomach of mine has missed nothing of this,[70] nor has anything been added to you." Someone asked Ibrahim b. Adham: "Why don't you drink water from the Zamzam well?" He answered: "If I had a bucket [of my own], I would drink it!"

I heard the master Abu ʿAli al-Daqqaq say: "Whenever al-Harith al-Muhasibi stretched his hand toward any food of suspicious origin, a vein in his fingertip would begin to throb and he would know that it was not permissible for him. [Likewise,] once Bishr al-Hafi was invited to a meal and some food was placed in front of him. He tried to reach out his hand for the food, but his hand would not stretch. He repeated this three times, until a man who knew him said: 'His hand cannot reach out to touch dubious food. Why did the host bother to invite a man like this to his party?'"

Ahmad b. Muhammad b. Yahya al-Sufi informed us: I heard ʿAbdallah b. ʿAli b. Yahya al-Tamimi say: I heard Ahmad b. Muhammad b. Salim at Basra say: Sahl b. ʿAbdallah [al-Tustari] was asked about that which is absolutely lawful. He answered: "This is something with which one cannot disobey God Most High." Sahl also said: "This is something with which God is not forgotten."

Once al-Hasan al-Basri entered Mecca and saw one of the children of ʿAli b. Abi Talib – may God be pleased with him – resting his back against a wall of the Kaʿba and preaching to people. Al-Hasan rushed to him and said: "What is the foundation of religion?" He answered: "Scrupulousness!" [Al-Hasan] then asked: "What is the ruin of religion?" He answered: "Greed!" Al-Hasan marveled at him. Al-Hasan said: "One tiny measure (*mithqal*) of true scrupulousness is better than a thousand measures of fasting and prayer."//180 God Most High revealed to Moses – peace and blessings be upon him: "The ones nearest to Me have reached their position only through scrupulousness and abstention."

---

70 That is, dates.

Abu Hurayra[71] said: "Those who are scrupulous and abstain [from the delights of this world] today will be God's closest friends tomorrow." Sahl b. ʿAbdallah [al-Tustari] said: "A person who does not adhere to scrupulousness would eat an elephant's head, yet would remain hungry." It is related that someone brought to ʿUmar b. ʿAbd al-ʿAziz[72] some musk that was taken as spoils of war. He held his nose closed, saying: "Its only merit is its scent and I would hate to discover its scent without the rest of the Muslims being able to partake of it." Someone asked Abu ʿUthman al-Hiri about scrupulousness. He responded: "Abu Salih Hamdun [al-Qassar] was attending to his friend at his last moment. When the man died, Abu Salih blew out the oil lamp. Someone asked him about this. He answered: 'Until this moment the oil has belonged to him, but now it belongs to his heirs. Go look for some other oil!'"

Kahmas said: "I committed a sin over which I have wept for forty years. Once a brother of mine came to visit me. I bought a piece of fried fish for him. When he had finished [eating it], I took a piece of clay from my neighbor's wall so that he could wash his hands with it. However, I forgot to ask the neighbor's permission!"

It is related that a certain man wrote a note, while residing in a rented house. He wanted to blot what he had written with some dust from the wall of the house. It occurred to him that the house was rented, but he thought that this was of little importance. So he blotted his writing with dust. He then heard a voice say: "He who thinks little of dust [today] will learn that he has a long accounting to do tomorrow!"

Ahmad b. Hanbal pawned a bucket with a grocer at Mecca – may God Most High protect it. When he wanted to redeem it, the grocer brought out two buckets saying: "Take whichever of the two is yours!" Ahmad said: "I am not sure which bucket is mine. So it is yours and my money is also yours!" The grocer said: "This is your bucket! I just wanted to test you." "No, I will not take it!" said Ibn Hanbal. He then walked away, leaving the bucket with the grocer.

Once Ibn al-Mubarak let his expensive horse roam free, while he was performing his noon prayer. The horse grazed in the field of a village that belonged to a [local] ruler. So Ibn al-Mubarak abandoned the horse and [refused to] ever ride it again.//181 It is related that Ibn al-Mubarak once traveled all the way from Merv[73] to Damascus because of a pen that he borrowed from someone in order to return it to its owner.

Al-Nakhaʿi rented a riding animal. When his whip dropped from his hand, he descended, tied the animal, returned and picked up the whip. Someone told him: "It would have been easier for you if you had directed your mount to the

---

71 A close companion of the Prophet (d. 58/678), who was renowned for his prodigious memory. He is credited with narrating some 3,500 traditions from the Prophet.
72 An Umayyad caliph, who was renowned for his piety; he ruled from 99/717 through 101/720.
73 A city in Central Asia.

place where the whip had fallen to pick it up!" He answered: "No, I hired it to go to that place, not this!"

Abu Bakr al-Zaqqaq said: "I wondered about in the wilderness of the Children of Israel for fifteen days. When I finally found the way, I met a soldier, who gave me a drink of water. Its harshness entered my heart and tormented me for thirty years!" It is said that Rabiʿa al-ʿAdawiyya mended a tear in her shirt in the light cast by a ruler's lamp. She lost her heart for a while until she remembered [that episode]. She then ripped her shirt and rediscovered her heart.

Sufyan al-Thawri was seen in a dream. He had a pair of wings with which he was flying from tree to tree in the garden of Paradise. Someone asked him: "By what means did you obtain them?" He answered: "By scrupulousness!" Hassan b. Abu Sinan once came upon some companions of al-Hasan [al-Basri]. He asked "What is the most thing difficult for you?" They answered: "Scrupulousness." He said: "There is nothing easier for me than that." They asked him how that could be. He responded: "For forty years I have not quenched my thirst by drinking from that stream of yours!" Hassan b. Abu Sinan did not sleep on his side, eat cooked food or drink cold water for sixty years. Someone saw him in a dream after his death and asked him: "How has God treated you?" He answered: "Quite well. However, I am barred from entering Paradise on account of a needle I borrowed and never returned."

ʿAbd al-Wahid b. Zayd[74] had a slave who served him for many years. He spent forty years in worship. Before that he had been a grain-measurer. After he died, someone saw him in a dream and asked him: "How has God treated you?" He answered: "Well. However, I am barred from Paradise, because [God held against me] the dust of the grain measure with which I dispensed forty measures."[75]//182

Jesus, son of Mary – peace be upon both of them – passed by a cemetery. He called upon one of the dead lying there, and God Most High restored him to life. Jesus asked him who he was. He answered: "I was a porter. I carried things about for people. One day, I was carrying firewood for someone. I broke off a splinter from that firewood and I have been accountable for that since I died."

Abu Saʿid al-Kharraz was speaking on scrupulousness, when ʿAbbas b. al-Muhtadi passed by. He said: "Abu Saʿid, aren't you ashamed?! You sit under the roof of Abu ʾl-Dawaniq,[76] drink from Zubayda's[77] pool, do business with false coins, and yet you talk about scrupulousness?!"

---

74 A follower of al-Hasan al-Basri, who died around 133/750. See *IM*, pp. 16–18.
75 According to some commentators, his transgression consisted of not having cleaned the bottom of his measure, resulting in him selling his customers short.
76 "Father of Small Change", a derogatory nickname of the ʿAbbasid caliph Abu Jaʿfar al-Mansur (d. 158/775), who was famous for his stinginess.
77 A granddaughter of the caliph al-Mansur, who was married to the "good caliph" Harun al-Rashid. She died in 216/831.

Renunciation (*zuhd*)

Hamza b. Yusuf al-Sahmi al-Jurjani informed us: Abu 'l-Husayn 'Ubaydallah b. Ahmad b. Ya'qub al-Muqri informed us at Baghdad: Ja'far b. Mujashi' told us: Zayd b. Isma'il said: Kathir b. Hisham told us: al-Hakam b. Hisham told us on the authority of Yahya b. Sa'id, on the authority of Abu Farwa, on the authority of Abu Khallad, who was one of the Prophet's Companions, that the Prophet – may God's blessings and peace be upon him – said: "If you see a man who has been graced with renunciation of this world and an eloquent speech, seek his company, for wisdom has been taught to him."

The master and imam Abu 'l-Qasim [al-Qushayri] – may God have mercy on him – said: "The folk's opinions differ regarding renunciation. Some of them argue that one should only renounce that which is prohibited [by the Divine Law], because that which is lawful has been made permissible by God Most High. If God bestows upon his servant licit property and the servant devotes himself to worshiping God out of gratitude for His generosity, then his abandoning this property is no better than keeping it by God's leave.

Others say that the renunciation of that which is prohibited is an obligation, whereas renouncing that which is lawful is a virtue. They also say that having little property – provided that the servant of God endures his condition patiently, satisfied with whatever God has apportioned for him and content with what God bestows upon him – is better than living comfortably and lavishly in this world, for God Most High urged His creatures to abstain from this world, when He said: "The enjoyment of this world is little; the world to come is better for him who fears God."[78] There are many other verses [in the Qur'an] that disparage this world and enjoin men to renounce it.//183

Others argue that if the servant spends his property in obedience to God, is known for his patience, and does not have recourse to what the Law forbids in times of adversity, then renouncing that which is permitted is better for him.

Still others say that he must not abandon that which is permitted to him [by God] on his own accord, nor must he seek that which exceeds his needs. Instead, he must preserve that which has been apportioned for him by God. If God Most High and Exalted bestows upon him some legal [property], he should be grateful to Him. If God Most High's provision for him is sufficient for his needs, then he should not strive to obtain surplus. Patience is best suited for the poor man, while gratitude is more appropriate for one who has licit property.

They recite [the following verse] concerning the meaning of renunciation:

Each speaks about his own moment
And each refers to his own appointed limit.

I heard Shaykh Abu 'Abd al-Rahman al-Sulami – may God have mercy on him – say: Ahmad b. Isma'il al-Azdi told us: 'Imran b. Musa al-Isfanji told us:

---

[78] Q. 4:77; 4:49, according to Arberry's translation.

al-Dawraqi told us: Wakiʿ [b. al-Jarrah][79] said: "Renunciation of this world means cutting short one's hopes rather than eating coarse food or wearing a woolen cloak."

I also heard him [al-Sulami] say: I heard Saʿid b. Ahmad say: I heard ʿAbbas b. ʿIsam say: I heard al-Junayd say: I heard al-Sari al-Saqati say: "God – praise be upon Him – withdraws this world from His friends and protects it from His elect ones; He removes it from the hearts of those He loves,[80] for He would not be pleased with them [enjoying] it."

They say that renunciation is derived from God's words [in the Qurʾan], "That you may not grieve for what escapes you, nor rejoice in what has come to you",[81] because the renouncer does not delight in anything he has of this world, nor is he sorry about losing something of it. Abu ʿUthman [al-Hiri] said: "Renunciation is that you give up this world, then not care about whoever picks it up."

I heard the master Abu ʿAli al-Daqqaq say: "Renunciation is that you give up this world as it is and not say: 'I will build a [Sufi] lodge (*ribat*) or construct a mosque in it.'" Yahya b. Muʿadh said: "Renunciation instills the habit of being generous with [worldly] possessions, while love instills the habit of being generous with one's [own] spirit." Ibn al-Jallaʾ said: "Renunciation is to look at this world with a view to its transience so as to see its total insignificance. Then turning away from it becomes easy for you."//184

Ibn Khafif said: "The mark of renunciation is to preserve equanimity while losing [your] property." He also said: "Renunciation is keeping your heart oblivious of [secondary] means[82] and your hands free from any [worldly] possessions." They also say that renunciation is to restrain oneself from this world without exerting any effort.

I heard Shaykh Abu ʿAbd al-Rahman al-Sulami – may God have mercy on him – say: I heard al-Nasrabadhi say: "The renouncer is a stranger in this world, while the [divine] gnostic is a stranger in the Hereafter." It is also said that to him whose renunciation is sincere, this world will present itself in utter humility. That's why [a proverb] says: "If a hat were to fall from the sky, it would land on the head of someone who does not want it!"

Al-Junayd said: "Renunciation is to free one's heart of whatever one's hands are [already] free of." Abu Sulayman al-Darani said: "Wool is a mark of renunciation. Therefore, one must never wear a woolen garment that costs three *dirhams*, if one's heart is longing for five *dirhams*."

The Muslims of old have held different opinions regarding renunciation. Sufyan al-Thawri, Ahmad b. Hanbal, ʿIsa b. Yunus and a few others have argued

---

79 A famous transmitter of "ascetic" lore, author of a collection of *hadith* dealing with renunciation, titled *Kitab al-zuhd*; he died in 197/812.
80 Or "those who love Him".
81 Q. 57:23.
82 That is, when a man sees God as the ultimate cause of everything in this world.

that renunciation is cutting short one's hopes [for things of this world]. Their sayings seem to indicate that cutting short hopes is one of the signs of renunciation, one of its causes and a reason that necessitates it.

ʿAbdallah b. al-Mubarak said: "Renunciation is to keep trust in God Most High and to love poverty." This was also the opinion of Shaqiq al-Balkhi and Yusuf b. Asbat. Keeping trust in God is also one of the signs of renunciation, for one is capable of renunciation only when one puts one's trust in God Most High.

ʿAbd al-Wahid b. Zayd said: "Renunciation is to give up both the *dinar* and the *dirham*."[83] Abu Sulayman al-Darani said: "Renunciation is to abandon anything that distracts you from God Most High – may He be praised."

I heard Muhammad b. al-Husayn – may God have mercy on him – say: I heard Ahmad b. ʿAli say: I heard Ibrahim b. Fatik say: I heard al-Junayd say that Ruwaym [b. Ahmad] once asked him about renunciation. Al-Junayd answered://185 "It is thinking little of this world and erasing its traces from your heart." Sari [al-Saqati] said: "The renouncer's way is lacking as long as he is not preoccupied with himself,[84] whereas the gnostic's way is lacking as long as he is preoccupied with himself."[85] Someone asked al-Junayd about renunciation. He answered: "It is keeping your hands free from possessions and your heart from attachment [to this world]." Someone asked al-Shibli about renunciation. He answered: "It is to renounce anything other than God Most High."

Yahya b. Muʿadh said: "One cannot attain true renunciation until one has acquired three qualities: works without [any] attachment,[86] speech without greedy intention,[87] and power without overlordship. Abu Hafs said: "One can only renounce that which is lawful. Since there is nothing in this world that is lawful, there can be no renunciation." Abu ʿUthman [al-Hiri] said: "God Most High gives the renouncer more than he desires; He gives the one who desires less than what he desires; and he gives the upright one exactly what he desires."

Yahya b. Muʿadh said: "The renouncer pours vinegar and mustard into your nose, while the gnostic treats you to the scent of musk and ambergris." Al-Hasan al-Basri said: "Renunciation of this world is that you loathe its inhabitants and everything that it contains." One of the Sufis was asked about renunciation of this world. He responded: "To relinquish whatever is in it to whoever is in it." A man asked Dhu ʾl-Nun al-Misri: "When will I renounce the world?" He answered: "Only when you have renounced your own self."

Muhammad b. al-Fadl said: "The ascetics prefer others to themselves when they themselves have enough, while the gallant ones (*fityan*) prefer others to

---

83 That is, everything that has any value, no matter how small.
84 That is, as long as he is distracted by the trappings of the world.
85 That is, as long as he is not fully focused on God. This saying exhibits a typical Sufi preference for knowing God intimately as opposed to simply serving him, albeit in an exemplary manner.
86 That is, acting for the sake of God alone, not for some mundane end.
87 That is, preaching without expecting a recompense.

themselves, even if they are [themselves] in need." God Most High said: "They prefer others above themselves, even though poverty is their lot."[88]

Al-Kattani said: "There is one thing over which the Kufans, the Medinise, the Iraqis and the Syrians have no disagreement: renunciation of this world, generosity of the soul, and [giving] good advice to people." He meant that no one can say that these things are not laudable.//186

A man asked Yahya b. Muʿadh: "When shall I enter the tavern of trust in God, put on the cloak of renunciation and be seated with renouncers?" He answered: "When, in your secret training of your soul, you attain such a degree that were God to withhold your sustenance for three days you would not become any weaker than you were [before]. As long as you have not attained this degree, your sitting on the same carpet with the [genuine] renouncers is sheer ignorance. For I cannot guarantee to you that you will not find yourself disgraced among them!" Bishr al-Hafi said: "Renunciation is like a king who resides only in a heart that is cleansed [of worldly attachments]."

I heard Muhammad b. al-Husayn say: I heard Abu Bakr al-Razi say: I heard Muhammad b. Muhammad b. al-Ashʿath al-Bikandi say: "If someone discourses on renunciation and preaches it to other people, while longing after what they own, then God Most High will remove the love of the next world from his heart." It is also said that when a servant of God renounces this world, God appoints for him an angel who plants wisdom into his heart." Someone asked a Sufi: "Why have you renounced this world?" He answered: "Because it has renounced me!"

Ahmad b. Hanbal said: "Renunciation can be of three different kinds. First, abandoning that which is prohibited by the Divine Law, which is the renunciation of the commoners; second, abandoning excess in that which is lawful, which is the renunciation of the elect; third, abandoning that which distracts God's servant from God Most High, which is the renunciation of the gnostics." I heard master Abu ʿAli al-Daqqaq say: "Someone asked a Sufi why he had renounced the world. He answered: 'After I have renounced most of it, so I no longer have any desire for what little has remained out of it.'"

Yahya b. Muʿadh said: "This world is like an unveiled bride. The one who seeks her becomes her cosmetician, while the one who renounces her blackens her face, tears out her hair, rends her dress. As for the gnostic, he is preoccupied with God alone and pays no attention to her." I heard Abu ʿAbdallah al-Sufi say: I heard Abu al-Tayyib al-Samarri say: I heard al-Junayd say: I heard al-Sari say://187 "I have tried all manner of renunciation and obtained from it all I wished, except for renunciation of people. I have not attained it, nor am I capable [of ever attaining it]." It is said that renouncers have not departed toward [any destination] except their own selves, for they have given up [this world's] transitory bounty for the sake of one that never ends."

Al-Nasrabadhi said: "Renunciation spares the blood of the ascetics and spills the blood of the gnostics." Hatim al-Asamm said: "The renouncer expends his

---

88 Q. 59:9.

purse before he expends his soul, whereas one who pretends to be a renouncer expends his soul before he expends his purse."

I heard Muhammad b. ʿAbdallah say: I heard ʿAli b. al-Husayn say: Ahmad b. al-Husayn informed us: Muhammad b. al-Hasan told us: Muhammad b. Jaʿfar told us: al-Fudayl b. ʿIyad said: "God placed all evil in one house and made its key love of this world. He placed all good in another house and made its key renunciation."

Silence (*samt*)

ʿAbdallah b. Yusuf al-Isbahani informed us: Abu Bakr Muhammad b. al-Husayn al-Qattan told us: Ahmad b. Yusuf al-Sulami told us: ʿAbd al-Razzaq told us: Maʿmar informed us on the authority of al-Zuhri, on the authority of Abu Salama, on the authority of Abu Hurayra that the Messenger of God – may God bless and greet him – said: "Whoever believes in God and the Last Day, let him do no harm to his neighbor; whoever believes in God and the Last Day, let him be generous to his guest; whoever believes in God and the Last Day, let him speak good or be silent!"

ʿAli b. Ahmad b. ʿAbdan informed us: Ahmad b. ʿUbayd told us: Bishr b. Musa al-Asadi told us: Muhammad b. Saʿid al-Isbahani told us on the authority of Ibn al-Mubarak, on the authority of Yahya b. Ayyub, on the authority of ʿUbaydallah b. Zuhr, on the authority of ʿAli b. Yazid, on the authority of al-Qasim, on the authority of Abu Umama: on the authority of ʿUqba b. ʿAmir, who said that he asked: "Messenger of God, what is salvation?" He answered: "Guard your tongue; may your home be spacious enough for you; and weep over your sins!"

The master [al-Qushayri] said: "Silence is safety; this is the root of the matter; if one has allowed oneself//188 to reprimand [another person], then one must repent; in any event, one should always be respectful of the Divine Law, the Commanding of the Right, and the Forbidding of the Wrong." Silence at the right time is an attribute of true men[89] in the same way as speaking when appropriate is one of the noblest of qualities.

I heard master Abu ʿAli al-Daqqaq say: "Whoever remains silent instead of speaking truth is a mute devil."

Silence belongs to the good manners of [Sufi] gatherings, for God Most High said: "And when the Qurʾan is recited, give your ear to it and be silent that you may receive mercy."[90] God also said regarding a meeting of the Messenger of God – may God bless and greet him – and the jinn: "And when they were present with him they said, 'Be silent!'"[91] God Most High also said: "Voices will be hushed to the All-Merciful, so that you will hear nothing but murmuring."[92]

---

89 That is, the Sufis.
90 Q. 7:204; 7:203, according to Arberry's translation.
91 Q. 46:29; 46:28, according to Arberry's translation.
92 Q. 20:108.

How great a difference there is between a servant who is silent in order to protect himself from lies and backbiting and a servant who is silent because he is overwhelmed by the awe of God! They recite the following verses to that effect:

> When we are apart, I keep thinking what I shall say [to you]
> I perfect doggedly the arguments that I will utter
> And when we meet I [suddenly] forget them
> And when I speak, I speak nothing but absurdities.

They also recite the following lines:

> O Layla, how many an urgent need I have
> Why, then, O Layla, when I come to you I no longer know what they are?!

They also recite the following:

> How many stories I have to tell you; however,
> When I am given a chance to meet you, I forget them all!

They also recite the following:

> I have seen how words may adorn a young man;
> However, silence is better for one who chose to be silent
> How many written words have brought death [upon the writer]
> And how many speakers have wished they had remained silent!

There are two types of silence: outer silence and silence of the heart and mind.//189 The heart of one who puts his trust in God restrains itself from asking God for sustenance. The heart of the gnostic remains silent vis-à-vis God's decree because it is endowed by the attribute of compliance. The former is confident of God's good deeds. The latter is satisfied with whatever God decrees [for him]. It is with this meaning in mind that they say:

> God's decisions rule over you
> But the worries of your innermost heart are allayed.

Sometimes silence is caused by the bewilderment of an insight, for when some idea is suddenly unveiled [to you], words fall silent and you can neither explain nor articulate [what you have realized]. In such a state, all evidence is obliterated and there's neither knowledge nor sensation. God Most High said: "On the day when God shall gather the Messengers, and say: 'What answer are you given?' they say, 'We have no knowledge.'"

Those who are exerting themselves [on the path of God] choose silence, because they are aware of the dangers that are present in speech. They are also aware of the pleasures that their egos take in talking and in praising as well as in using eloquent speech to elevate oneself above their peers and suchlike pitfalls that are common among mankind. That's why the practitioners of ascetic self-discipline choose silence, which is one of the major pillars of self-exertion and a chief prerequisite for perfecting one's character. It is said that when Dawud al-Ta'i resolved to stay in his house, he [first] decided to attend the sessions of Abu Hanifa,[93] since he was one of his disciples, and to sit among his fellow scholars without ever speaking about any legal issue that arose. When his soul grew strong in that trait after an entire year of practice, he confined himself to his house and chose seclusion.

Likewise, [the caliph] 'Umar b. 'Abd al-'Aziz – may God have mercy on him – whenever he would write something and find pleasure in his wording, he would tear up his writing and change it.

I heard Shaykh Abu 'Abd al-Rahman al-Sulami – may God have mercy on him – say: 'Abdallah b. Muhammad al-Razi informed us: Abu 'l-'Abbas b. Ishaq al-Sarraj told us: I heard Ahmad b. al-Fath say: I heard Bishr b. al-Harith say: "If speech gives you pleasure, then remain silent; and if silence pleases you, then talk!"

Sahl b. 'Abdallah [al-Tustari] said: "Nobody's silence is complete until he has accustomed himself to retreat, and nobody's repentance is complete//190 until he has accustomed himself to silence."

Abu Bakr al-Farisi said: "If a man has not made silence his homeland, he is talkative even though he is silent. Silence is not limited to the tongue; it should be applied to the heart and all of the limbs." Someone said that he who does not know the true worth of silence will always speak nonsense.

I heard Muhammad b. al-Husayn say: Muhammad b. 'Abdallah b. Shadhan said: Mimshadh al-Dinawari said: "The wise have acquired their wisdom by silence and contemplation." Someone asked Abu Bakr al-Farisi about silence. He answered: "Silence is to abandon concern with past and future." Abu Bakr al-Farisi also said: "If a man speaks about what concerns him and what is unavoidable, than he remains within the domain of silence." It is said that Mu'adh b. Jabal – may God be pleased with him – once said: "Speak little with people and speak a lot with God; perhaps your heart will see God Most High."

Someone asked Dhu 'l-Nun: "Who among mankind is the best protector of his heart?" He answered: "The one who controls his tongue best." Ibn Mas'ud said: "Nothing is more deserving of a long imprisonment than the tongue." 'Ali b. Bakkar said: "God Most High made two doors for everything. However, he made four doors for the tongue – the two lips and the teeth!"

It is related about Abu Bakr al-Siddiq – may God be pleased with him – that for many years he used to hold a stone in his mouth in order to speak less. It is said that Abu Hamza al-Baghdadi – may God have mercy on him – was an eloquent speaker. Once he heard a voice that said to him: "You spoke and your speech was wonderful. Now it remains to you to fall silent and excel in it!" So he

---

93 The famous Iraqi scholar, who is considered to be the founder of the Hanafi school of law.

did not speak until he died about a week or so later. Sometimes silence befalls someone as a chastisement, because he has infringed good manners in some way.

Al-Shibli used to sit with the circle of his disciples. When they would not question him, he would say: "And the word shall fall upon them because of the evil they committed, while they speak naught."[94] Sometimes silence falls upon a speaker, because there is in the audience someone who is more deserving of speech.//191

I heard Ibn al-Sammak say that Shah al-Kirmani and Yahya b. Mu'adh were friends. Although they lived in the same city, Shah would never attend his [friend's] sessions. When someone asked him about that, he answered: "This is the [only] proper [behavior]!" People kept pursuing him until he decided to attend Yahya's session. He sat so that Yahya b. Mu'adh would not observe him. Yahya was about to begin to speak, when he suddenly fell silent. He then said: "There's someone here who deserves to speak more than me." And he was unable to articulate anything coherent after that. Shah then said: "Did not I tell you that it was not appropriate for me to come to his session?"

Sometimes silence falls upon the speaker for a reason that has something to do with his audience – for instance, when there is among them someone who is not fit to hear his speech and therefore God Most High protects the tongue of the speaker out of jealousy to keep that speech from someone who is not supposed to hear it. It might be that silence falls upon the speaker, when God Most High knows that the spiritual state of someone in the audience is such that should he hear this speech, he may become tempted by it. This person may fancy that it corresponds to his own mystical moment, which it is not, or he may [as a result of this speech] be tempted to undertake something that he cannot endure In both cases, God – may He be great and exalted – decides to prevent him from hearing that speech, either protecting him or guarding him from committing an error.

The masters of this [Sufi] path say that sometimes the reason for the speaker's silence is the presence in the audience of a jinn who is not fit to hear this speech. For the sessions of the Sufi masters are not necessarily free from the presence of hosts of jinn. I heard Abu 'Ali al-Daqqaq – may God have mercy on him – say: "Once I fell ill in Merv and desired to return to Nishapur. In my dream I heard a voice saying: 'You cannot leave this city, because a group of jinn have taken a liking to your speeches and are eager to attend your sessions. For their sake, you will be kept in this place!'"

One wise man said: "Man was created with only one tongue, but with two eyes and two ears so that he may listen and see rather than speak!" Once Ibrahim b. Adham was invited to a banquet. When he sat down, they began to gossip about other people. He told them: "We are used to eating the meat after the bread, whereas you have begun by eating the meat!" He alluded to the words of God Most High: "Would any of you//192 like to eat the flesh of his brother

---

94 Q. 27:85.

dead? You would abominate it."⁹⁵ One Sufi said: "Silence is the tongue of humility." Another said: "Learn silence just as you learn speech. For while speech will guide you, silence will guard you." It is also said that silence is the tongue's virtue. They also say that the tongue is like wild beast: if you do not restrain it, it will fall upon you."

Someone asked Abu Hafs [al-Haddad]: "Which quality is preferable for the friend of God: silence or speech?" He answered: "Were the one who speaks to know of all the dangers inherent in speech, he would keep silent, if he could, as long as Noah's lifespan. However, were the silent one to know of all the dangers inherent in silence he would ask God Most High for a life double that of Noah's, so that he could [learn to] speak." It is said that the common people keep silence with their tongues; the gnostics keep silence with their hearts; and God's lovers keep silence by protecting their innermost selves from any [distracting] thought."

It was said to one of them: "Speak!" He answered: "I do not have a tongue with which to speak!" "Then listen!" He responded: "There is no room in me in which I could listen!" One of them said: "I spent thirty years with my tongue hearing nothing but my heart; then I spent another thirty years with my heart hearing nothing but my tongue." Another Sufi said: "Even though your tongue may be silent, you are still not safe from the words that occur in your heart; even though you may become a pile of decaying bones you are still not delivered from the insinuations of your soul; and even though you may exert yourself to the utmost extent, your spirit will still not speak to you, because it conceals the [divine] mystery." They say: "The tongue of the ignorant is the key to his destruction." They also say: "If the lover keeps silent, he perishes; and if the divine gnostic keeps silent, he rules supreme."

I heard Muhammad b. al-Husayn say: I heard ʿAbdallah b. Muhammad al-Razi say: I heard Muhammad b. Nasr al-Saʾigh say: I heard Mardawayh al-Saʾigh say: I heard al-Fudayl b. ʿIyad say: "He who counts his words among his deeds speaks very little and only about things that concern him."//193

Fear (*khawf*)

God Most High said: "They call on their Lord in fear and hope."⁹⁶ Abu Bakr Muhammad b. Ahmad b. ʿAbdus al-Hiri al-ʿAdl informed us: Abu Bakr Muhammad b. Ahmad b. Dalluya al-Daqqaq informed us: Muhammad b. Yazid said: ʿAmir b. Abi ʾl-Furat told us: al-Masʿudi told us on the authority of Muhammad b. ʿAbd al-Rahman, on the authority of ʿIsa b. Talha, on the authority of Abu Hurayra, who said: "The Messenger of God – may God bless and greet him – said: 'One who weeps out of fear of God Most High will not enter the hellfire as long as milk cannot re-enter the udder. Nor will the dust of [striving]

---

95 Q. 49:12.
96 Q. 32:16.

on the path to God and the smoke of Gehenna ever be mingled in the nostrils of one and the same servant of God.'"

Abu Nuʿaym Ahmad b. Muhammad b. Ibrahim al-Mahrajani informed us: Abu Muhammad ʿAbdallah b. Muhammad b. al-Hasan al-Sharafi told us: ʿAbdallah b. Hashim told us: Yahya b. Saʿid al-Qattan told us: Shuʿba told us: Qatada told us on the authority of Anas, who said: "The Messenger of God – may God bless and greet him – said: 'If only you knew what I know you would laugh little and weep much.'"

Fear is a sentiment that has to do with the future, for a man fears that something undesirable might befall him or that something pleasant might elude him. This can only occur to something or someone in the future. As for something that exists here and now, fear does not pertain to it.

Fear of God Most High means that one fears His punishment either in this life or in the Hereafter. God – may He be praised – decreed that His servant should be afraid of Him. He said: "Fear Me, if you are believers."[97] He also said: "So stand in awe of Me."[98] God praised the believers by attributing fear to them, saying: "They fear their Lord above them."[99]

I heard the master Abu ʿAli al-Daqqaq – may God have mercy on him – say: "Fear has different stages: fear, dread, and awe.//194 Fear is a precondition and demand of [true] faith, for God said: 'Fear Me, if you are believers.'[100] Dread is a precondition of religious knowledge, for God Most High said: 'His servants dread God, if they have knowledge.'[101] As for awe, it is a precondition of divine gnosis, for God Most High said: 'God warns you that you stand in awe of Him [only].'"[102]

I heard Shaykh Abu ʿAbd al-Rahman al-Sulami – may God have mercy on him – say: I heard Muhammad b. ʿAli al-Hiri say: I heard Mahfuz say: I heard Abu Hafs [al-Haddad] say: "Fear is the whip of God with which He straightens up those who try to flee from His threshold."

Abu ʾl-Qasim al-Hakim said: "Fear can be of two kinds: terror and dread. A person in the state of terror (*rahab*) takes refuge in flight (*harab*) when he is afraid, whereas a person in the state of dread takes refuge in his Lord." He also said: "The verbs 'he is terrorized' (*rahib*) and 'he fled' (*harab*) may be said to have the same meaning as the verbs *jadhaba* and *jabadha* ('he drew'), which have the same meaning.[103] The one who flees (*haraba*) is drawn by the dictates of his own passion, in the same way as those monks (*ruhban*)[104] who [slavishly] follow their

---

97 Q. 3:175.
98 Q. 16:51; 16:53, according to Arberry's translation.
99 Q. 16:50; 16:52, according to Arberry's translation.
100 Q. 3:175.
101 Q. 35:28; 35:27, according to Arberry's translation.
102 Q. 3:28.
103 That is in both cases, the root consonants of the words are the same, although they are arranged in different combinations.
104 This word is derived from the same Arabic root (*RHB*) as "terror".

passions. However, if they are restrained by the rein of [religious] knowledge and if they fulfill the commands of the Divine Law, then this is dread [not terror]."

I heard Muhammad b. al-Husayn: I heard ʿAbdallah b. Muhammad al-Razi: I heard Abu ʿUthman [al-Hiri] say: I heard Abu Hafs [al-Haddad] say: "Fear is the lamp of the heart by which God's servant can distinguish good from evil that reside in it."

I heard the master Abu ʿAli al-Daqqaq – may God have mercy on him – say: "Fear is that your soul is no longer capable of finding excuses for itself by [saying] 'if only' (ʿasa) or 'may be' (sawfa)." I heard Muhammad b. al-Husayn say: I heard Abu ʾl-Qasim al-Dimashqi say: I heard Abu ʿUmar al-Dimashqi say: "The fearful one is he who is afraid of his own self more than he is afraid of Satan."

Ibn al-Jallaʾ said: "The one who has fear [of God] is protected from things that frighten [other people]."//195 It is said that the one who has fear [of God] is not he who weeps and wipes his eyes. Rather, he is one who abandons anything that he fears might bring [God's] punishment upon him."

Someone told al-Fudayl [b. Iyad]: "Why is it that we do not see any fearful ones?" He answered: "If you yourselves were to have fear, you would see them, for only he who has fear can see the fearful ones, for only the mother who has lost her child likes to see another bereaved mother."

Yahya b. Muʿadh said: "Poor children of Adam! If only they would fear the hellfire as much as they fear poverty, they would no doubt enter Paradise." Shah al-Kirmani said: "One of the signs of fear is constant sadness." Abu ʾl-Qasim al-Hakim said: "The one who is afraid of something runs away from it, whereas the one who fears God – may He be great and exalted – runs to Him."

Someone asked Dhu ʾl-Nun al-Misri – may God have mercy on him: "When will one enter the path of fear?" He responded: "When he will put himself in the position of a sick man, who guards himself from everything out of fear that his illness may be prolonged." Muʿadh b. Jabal – may God be pleased with him – said: "The believer's heart will not be at peace, nor will his heart rest until he has left the bridge of Gehenna behind him." Bishr al-Hafi said: "Fear of God is a king who can reside only in the pious heart." Abu ʿUthman al-Hiri said: "The fearful one is exposed to one deficiency: his reliance on his fear, for this is something of which one cannot be sure." Al-Wasiti said: "Fear is [like] a veil between God Most High and his servant." This statement is problematic. It implies that the one who fears is looking toward a future moment, whereas the children of the [present] moment[105] have no expectation of the future, for [according to a Sufi saying] "the virtues of the pious are the failings of those brought near [God]".

I heard Muhammad b. al-Husayn – may God have mercy on him – say: I heard Muhammad b. ʿAli al-Nahawandi say: I heard Ibn Fatik say: I heard al-Nuri say: "The fearful one runs from his Lord to his Lord."//196 One of them said: "One of the signs of fear is bewilderment at the gate of the unseen."[106]

---

105 Namely, the Sufis; see above, pp. 75–77.
106 That is, no person, no matter how perfect, can foresee his destiny in the Hereafter.

I heard Abu ʿAbdallah al-Sufi say: I heard ʿAli b. Ibrahim al-ʿUkbari say: I heard al-Junayd say, when asked about fear: "It is when you anticipate [divine] punishment with each passing breath." I heard Shaykh Abu ʿAbd al-Rahman al-Sulami – may God have mercy on him – say: I heard al-Husayn b. Ahmad al-Saffar say: Muhammad b. al-Musayyib said: I heard Hashim b. Khalid say: I heard Sulayman al-Darani say: "Whenever fear leaves the heart, it is ruined."

I also heard him say: I heard ʿAbdallah b. Muhammad b. ʿAbd al-Rahman say: I heard Abu ʿUthman [al-Hiri] say: "The true fear is to abstain from sins inwardly and outwardly." Dhu ʾl-Nun said: "People are on the [right] path as long as fear remains with them. When fear leaves them, they stray from the path." Hatim al-Asamm said: "Everything has its adornment; the adornment of worship is fear; and one of the signs of fear is cutting short one's hope for this world." A man told Bishr al-Hafi: "I see that you are afraid of death." He answered: "Entering into the presence of God is a hard thing!"

I heard the master Abu ʿAli al-Daqqaq say: "I went to visit Abu Bakr b. Furak, when he was ill. When he saw me, tears started to drip from his eyes. I told him: 'God Most High may have wished for your recovery and good health!' He said to me: 'Do you think I am afraid of death? No, I am afraid of what will be after death!'"

ʿAli b. Ahmad al-Ahawzi informed us: Ahmad b. ʿUbayd informed us: Muhammad b. ʿUthman related to us: al-Qasim b. Muhammad told us: Yahya b. Yaman told us on the authority of Malik b. Mighwal, on the authority of ʿAbd al-Rahman b. Saʿid b. Mawhab, on the authority of ʿAʾisha – may God be pleased with her: who said: "I asked: 'Messenger of God, "Those who give what they give, their hearts quaking,"[107] are they capable of stealing, committing adultery and drinking wine?'//197 He answered: 'No. However, a man may fast, pray, give alms, and still be afraid that [his worship] may not be accepted from him [by God].'"

Ibn al-Mubarak – may God have mercy on him – said: "The thing that excites fear so that it settles in the heart is continual self-scrutiny both inwardly and outwardly." I heard Muhammad b. al-Husayn say: I heard Muhammad b. al-Hasan say: I heard Abu ʾl-Qasim b. Abi Musa say: ʿAli al-Razi told us: I heard Ibn al-Mubarak – may God have mercy on him – say that.

I heard Muhammad b. al-Husayn say: I heard Abu Bakr al-Razi say: I heard Ibrahim b. Shayban say: "When fear settles in the heart it burns out of it objects of carnal desires and banishes from it the desire of this world." It is said that fear is "the strength of knowledge of how God's decrees come into effect". It is also said that fear is "the movement and trepidation of the heart before the [overwhelming] majesty of the Lord". Abu Sulayman al-Darani said: "Nothing should dominate your heart except fear, for should hope become predominant over it, it becomes spoiled." He then added: "Ahmad,[108] they [Sufis] rise [to the pinnacle of worship of God] thanks to fear. When they lose it, they fall down."

---

107 Q. 23:60.
108 Ahmad b. Abi ʾl-Hawari (d. 230/845 or 246/860), al-Darani's foremost disciple.

Al-Wasiti said: "Fear and hope are the two reins of the human soul that prevent it from following blindly its foolish drives." He also said: "When the Truth (*al-haqq*)[109] manifests itself to the innermost souls, it leaves there no room for either hope or fear."

The master Abu 'l-Qasim [al-Qushayri] said: "There is a difficulty in this statement. It means that God's signs have totally devastated the innermost souls and taken possession of them, leaving in them no room for any temporal things, whereas fear and hope are but residual traces of one's perception of one's own human condition."

Al-Husayn b. al-Mansur [al-Hallaj] said: "When a man fears something other than God – may He be great and exalted – or pins his hopes on something other than Him, God will close for him the doors of every [good] deed and make fear rule over him. God will veil him with seventy veils, the least of which is doubt." There are several things most conducive to fear, such as the contemplation of the final punishment and the dread of having their states changed [by God]. Thus God Most High said: "Yet there would appear to them from God that which they never reckoned with"[110] and "Say: 'Shall We tell you who will be the greatest losers in their works? Those whose striving goes astray//198 in the present life, while they think that they are working good deeds.'"[111]

How many a man with enviable states has seen his states turned into their opposite and tested by becoming associated with evil deeds. Then their intimacy [with God] is changed to estrangement [from Him] and their presence [with God] is changed to absence [from Him].

I often heard the master Abu 'Ali al-Daqqaq – may God have mercy on him – recite the following verses:

> You used to think well of [your] days when they were good [to you]
> You were not afraid of the evil things that destiny may bring
> The nights used to be friendly with you and you were deceived by them
> For dimness may sometimes creep into the clarity of the night.

I heard Mansur b. Khalaf al-Maghribi say: "Two men were following the [Sufi] path (*irada*) together for some time. Then one of them left and abandoned his friend. A long time passed with no news to be heard from him. In the meantime, his friend joined the Muslim army fighting the Byzantine troops.[112] Once the Muslims were confronted by a man clad in armor who challenged one of them to fight him in a duel. One of the Muslim champions came out to fight him and was killed; another one followed in his stead and was also killed; then the third one, who was also killed. Then that Sufi came out to confront him and they

---

109 In Sufi discourses the word *al-haqq* (the Truth) often denotes God.
110 Q. 39:47; 39:49, according to Arberry's translation.
111 Q. 18:103–104.
112 For the "warrior monks", who volunteered to fight against the Byzantine "infidels", see *IM*, pp. 18–22.

exchanged blows. The Byzantine soldier revealed his face and it turned out that he was the friend of the Sufi, who spent many years with him in following the Sufi path and in worship. The Sufi asked: 'What is your story?' The man replied that he had apostatized and married into this people [Byzantines], and that many children had been born to him and that he had amassed a great fortune. The Sufi said to him: 'But you used to read the Qur'an by many modes of recitation!' He answered that he did not remember a single word of it now. The Sufi told him: 'Do not do this! Return [to Islam]!' He answered: 'No, I will not do this, for I have a high rank and great wealth among them. Go away or I will do to you what I have done to those [three]!' The Sufi responded to him saying: 'You have already killed three Muslims, so there will be no blame on you if you depart and I will give you some time to retreat.' As the man began to retreat turning his back, the Sufi rushed after him and stabbed him to death.//199 Thus after all those acts of self-exertion, strictures and ascetic exercises, that man died a Christian!"

They say that when what happened to Iblis happened, Gabriel and Michael – peace be upon them – started to cry and wept for a long time. God Most High asked then: "Why do you cry so profusely?" They answered: "Our Lord, we do not feel safe from your ruse!" God then said: "Be like this! You indeed are not safe from My ruse."

It is related that Sari al-Saqati once said: "I squint at my nose so-and-so many times a day out of fear that my face may have turned black due to my dread of [divine] punishment!" Abu Hafs [al-Haddad] said: "For forty years I believed that God Most High looks at me with displeasure, and my works demonstrate this!" Hatim al-Asamm said: "Don't be deceived by good places, for there never was a better place than Paradise, yet Adam encountered there what he encountered. Don't be deceived by abundant worship, for Iblis encountered what he encountered despite his long worship. Don't be deceived by abundance of knowledge, for Balaam[113] knew God's greatest name, and yet look what has happened to him! Don't be deceived when you see the righteous, for there is no one more righteous than the Chosen One[114] – may God bless and greet him – yet meeting him did not benefit his friends and relatives."

One day, Ibn al-Mubarak came upon his friends and said: "Yesterday, I behaved recklessly with God – may He be great and exalted – for I asked Him for Paradise." It is related that Jesus went on a journey with a righteous man from among the Children of Israel. A sinner who was notorious among the Jews for his turpitude followed them. He sat at a distance from them full of remorse and called upon God – glory be to Him – saying: "O my God, forgive me!" The righteous [Jew], in his turn, called upon God, saying: "O my God, spare me the company of this man tomorrow!" At that moment God revealed to Jesus – peace

---

113 According to some Sufi authors, the figure of Biblical Balaam serves as the prototype of a righteous man, who was led astray by lust and greed.
114 That is, the prophet Muhammad.

be upon him – the following words: "I have responded to both prayers. I have rejected [the prayer] of the righteous one, but I have pardoned the sinner!"

Dhu 'l-Nun al-Misri said: "I asked 'Ulaym why he was nicknamed 'the mad'.//200 He answered: 'After God had kept me away from Himself for a long time, I went mad out of fear of our separation in the future life!'" With this meaning in mind they recite the following [verses]:

> If [the pain] that resides in me were to be placed on a rock, it would wear it down!
> How, on earth, can a lump of clay[115] tolerate this?!

Someone said: "I have seen no man who had greater hope for this [Muslim] community and no greater fear for himself than Ibn Sirin."[116] It is related that Sufyan al-Thawri became ill. When the symptoms of his illness were described to a doctor, he said: "This man's liver was ruptured by his fear." He then came to [Sufyan], felt his pulse and said: "I did not know that there was the like of him [in this religion]!"

Someone asked al-Shibli why the sun turns pale at the sunset. He answered: "Because it was removed from [its] position of perfection. So it turned pale out of fear of standing [before God]. This is similar to [the condition of] the believer. When the term of his departure from this world draws near, his face becomes pale, because he is afraid of standing before God. And when the sun rises again, it looks radiant. So does the believer: when he is risen from his grave, his face radiates light."

It is related that Ahmad b. Hanbal – may God have mercy on him – said: "I asked God – be He great and exalted – to open the door of fear for me. When he opened it, I began to fear that I might lose my mind. So I said: 'O my Lord, give me as much [fear] as I can withstand!' After that I felt relief."

Hope (raja')

God Most High said: "Whosoever hopes to meet with God, God's term is coming."[117] Abu 'l-Hasan 'Ali b. Ahmad al-Ahwazi informed us: Ahmad b. 'Ubayd al-Saffar told us: 'Amr[118] b. Muslim al-Thaqafi told us: al-Hasan b. Khalid told us: al-'Ala' b. Zayd said: "I entered the house of Malik b. Dinar and found that Shahr b. Hawshab was with him. When we were leaving his [Malik's] house, I told Shahr: 'May God Most High have mercy on you! Give me some [good advice as] provision for the road, so that God, too, would do the same for you!' He answered: 'Yes, my aunt Umm al-Darda' related to me from Abu 'l-Darda',[119]

---

115 That is, a human being whose body is made of clay.
116 On him see note 50 above.
117 Q. 29:5; 29:4, according to Arberry's translation.
118 In another reading, "'Umar".
119 These pious individuals in the entourage of the Prophet are often seen by later Sufi authors as archetypal Sufis. See *IM*, pp. 5–6.

who related from the Prophet – may God bless and greet him – that he related from Gabriel – peace be upon him – that he said: "Your Lord – may He be great and exalted – said: 'My servant, as long as you worship Me, have hope in Me and do not give partners to Me,//201 I will pardon you for whatever you have done. Even if you meet Me with [a load of] sins and transgressions big enough to fill the entire earth I will meet you with that much forgiveness. I will forgive you and not care!'""

ʿAli b. Ahmad informed us: Ahmad b. ʿUbayd informed us: Bishr b. Musa told us: Khalaf b. al-Walid told us: Marwan b. Muʿawiyya al-Fazawi[120] told us: Abu Sufyan Tarif told us on the authority of ʿAbdallah b. al-Harith, on the authority of Anas b. Malik, on the authority of the Messenger of God – may God bless and greet him – who said: "God Most High will say on the Day of Judgement: 'Bring out of the fire anyone in whose heart is the amount of faith equal to a grain of barley.' Then He will declare: 'Bring out of the fire anyone in whose heart is the amount of faith equal to a mustard seed.' Then He will say: 'By My majesty and greatness, I will not treat the one who has believed in Me even one moment, night or day, like someone who has not believed in Me at all.'" Hope is the heart's attachment to something it loves that is expected to take place in the future. Just as fear occurs in regard to something that may take place in the future, so does hope occur in regard to something that is anticipated in the future. Hope, therefore, is but the sustenance and freedom of the heart.

There is a difference between hope and longing for something. Longing produces indolence in the person who experiences it, for he does not follow the path of self-exertion and serious determination. The opposite is true of the person who feels hope. Therefore, hope is commendable, while longing is blameworthy.

Sufis have discoursed extensively about hope. Thus Shah al-Kirmani said: "One of the signs of hope is complete obedience [to God]." Ibn Khubayq said: "There are three types of hope. First, when one does good things and hopes that one's actions will be accepted from one [by God]. Second, when one does evil things, then repents and begins to hope that one will be pardoned. Finally, there is the liar, who engages in sinful acts, while saying: 'I hope for forgiveness.' If someone knows he is doing evil, then his fear must dominate over his hope."

It is said that hope is trust in the bounty of the Generous and Loving One. It is also said: "Hope is the vision of God's majesty (*jalal*) with the eye of God's beauty (*jamal*)."[121] They also say: "Hope is the heart's proximity to its Lord's benevolence."//202 It is also said: "[Hope is] the innermost heart's delight at the thought of returning to God among the blessed."[122] It is also said: "[Hope is] seeing God's All-Embracing mercy."

---

120 Or, in another reading, "al-Fazari".
121 In the Sufi tradition, God is seen as having two aspects: majesty and beauty. The former makes God's servants tremble out of fear of His punishment; the latter allows them to see God as a benevolent and forgiving friend.
122 That is, achieving salvation.

I heard Shaykh Abu ʿAbd al-Rahman al-Sulami – may God have mercy on him – say: I heard Mansur b. ʿAbdallah say: I heard Abu ʿAli al-Rudhbari say: "Fear and hope are like two wings of a bird. When they are balanced, the bird's flight is straight and balanced, whereas if one of them is deficient, the flight becomes deficient, too. And when both are missing, the bird enters the precinct of death."

I also heard him [al-Sulami] say: I heard al-Nasrabadhi say: I heard Abu Hatim say: I heard ʿAli b. Shahmardhan say: I heard Ahmad b. ʿAsim al-Antaki say, when asked about signs of hope in the servant: "When God's beneficence encompasses him, he is inspired to gratitude, as he hopes that God will perfect His munificence toward him and His pardon toward him in the Hereafter." Abu ʿAbdallah b. Khafif said: "Hope means to rejoice in anticipation of God's favor [in the Hereafter]." He also said: "[Hope is] the consolation of the heart in anticipation of seeing the generosity of the Beloved One in Whom hope is placed."

I heard Shaykh Abu ʿAbd al-Rahman al-Sulami – may God have mercy on him – say: I heard Abu ʿUthman al-Maghribi say: "He who incites himself to hope [alone] becomes idle, while he who incites himself to fear becomes despondent. There is a time for each of them."

I heard him [al-Sulami] say: Abu ʾl-ʿAbbas al-Baghdadi said: al-Hasan b. Safwan told us: Ibn Abi ʾl-Dunya told us: someone told me on the authority of Bakr b. Sulaym al-Sawwaf, who said: "I came to visit Malik b. Anas on the evening of the day he died. I asked him: 'Abu ʿAbdallah, how do you feel?' He answered: 'I do not know what to tell you except that you will witness forgiveness from God in a measure that you cannot even fathom.' We stayed with him until [he died] and we closed his eyes."

Yahya b. Muʿadh said: "The hope that I place in You when I sin is almost greater than the hope I place in You when I do good works, for, in my good works, I have to rely on sincerity. However, how can I keep them sincere when I am infamous for my imperfection? On the contrary, in my sins I rely on Your pardon, for how can You not pardon me when beneficence is Your [essential] attribute?"

Some people were conversing with Dhu ʾl-Nun when he was on his death bed. He said: "Do not worry about me, for I am surprised at the vastness of God's loving care toward me!"//203 Yahya b. Muʿadh said: "O my God, the sweetest gift in my heart is hope for You; the best words of my tongue are praise for You; and the moment that I shall love most of all is the moment when I shall meet You [in the Hereafter]."

According to one of the commentaries on the Qurʾan, the Messenger of God – may God bless and greet him – once came upon his Companions [while passing] through the gate of Banu Shayba and saw them laughing. He told them: "Are you laughing? If only you knew what I know, you would laugh little and weep much!" He left, but then returned and said: "Gabriel has just descended to me with the words of God Most High, "I am the All-Forgiving, the All-Compassionate."[123]

Abu 'l-Hasan 'Ali b. Ahmad al-Ahwazi said: Abu 'l-Hasan al-Saffar told us: 'Abbas b. Tamim said: Yahya b. Ayyub told us: Muslim b. Salim told us: Kharija b. Mus'ab told us on the authority of Zayd b. Aslam, on the authority of 'Ata' b. Yasar, on the authority of 'A'isha, who said: "I heard the Messenger of God – may God bless and greet him – say: 'God Most High laughs at the desperation and despondency of His servants, for [divine] mercy is so close to them.' I asked: 'O Messenger of God, by my father and mother, how can our Lord – may He be great and exalted – laugh?' He answered: 'By the One in Whose hand is my soul, of course He laughs!'" ['A'isha] then said: "As long as He laughs, good things will continue to come to us!"

Know that laughter is an attribute that pertains to His action,[124] for it manifests His beneficence in the same way as does the saying "The earth 'laughs' through [its] plants."[125] He laughs at their lack of confidence in manifestations of His grace, which will turn out to be far greater than what they have expected from Him.

It is recounted that a Magian[126] sought the hospitality of Abraham the Friend of God – peace be upon him. Abraham told him: "I'll be your host, only if you embrace Islam!"[127] To which the Magian replied: "If I were to embrace Islam, there would be no benefit for you in [hosting] me."[128] When the Magian went away, God Most High revealed to Abraham: "Abraham, you will not feed him unless he changes his religion, whereas We have fed him for seventy years despite his unbelief?! If you were to be his host for just one night, what would it be to you?" Abraham – peace be upon him – rushed after the Magian and invited him to stay with him. The Magian asked him what caused him to change his mind. Abraham told him what had happened to him. The Magian said: "So that's how He treats me!" He then said: "Present [your] Islam to me!" and became a Muslim.

I heard Shaykh Abu 'Ali al-Daqqaq – may God have mercy on him – say: "The master Abu Sahl al-Su'luki saw Abu Sahl al-Zajjaji in a dream. [During his lifetime] Abu Sahl used to teach the doctrine of eternal punishment. [Al-Su'luki] asked him about his condition. He responded: 'I have discovered that things here are easier than I thought.'"

I heard Abu Bakr b. Ishkib say: "I saw the master Abu Sahl al-Su'luki in a dream. His condition was excellent beyond any description. I asked him: 'O

---

123 Q. 15:49.
124 According to Islamic theology, God is possessed of two types of attributes: those of His essence and those of His acts.
125 That is, it sprouts up vegetation.
126 That is, a follower of the Zoroastrian religion.
127 According to the Qur'an, Abraham's religion was pure Islam. See Q. 37:100–104.
128 Because it would be Abraham's duty to host a fellow believer.

master, how did you manage to attain this?' He answered: 'Because I was thinking well of my Lord.'"

When Malik b. Dinar was seen in a dream, he was asked: "What has God done to you?" He responded: "I came to my Lord – may He be great and exalted – [burdened] by many sins. However, all of them were erased by virtue of my having always thought well of Him Most High!"

It is related that the Prophet – may God bless and greet him – said: "God – may He be great and exalted – said: 'I am with My servant when he thinks of Me. I am with him when he remembers Me. If he remembers Me in himself, I will remember him in Myself. If he remembers Me in company, I will remember him in a company better than his. If he draws nearer to Me by one inch, I will draw nearer to him by one cubit. If he draws nearer to Me by one cubit, I will draw nearer to him by one fathom, and when he comes to Me walking, I come to him running.'"[129] This *hadith* was related to us by Abu Nuʿaym ʿAbd al-Malik b. al-Hasan al-Isfaraini, who related it on the authority of Yaʿqub b. Ishaq, on the authority of ʿAli b. Harb, on the authority of Abu Muʿawiyya, on the authority of Muhammad b. ʿUbayd, on the authority of al-Amʿash, on the authority of Abu Salih, on the authority of Abu Hurayra – may God be pleased with him – who related it from the Prophet – may God bless and greet him.

It is said that once Ibn al-Mubarak was fighting an infidel. When the time of the infidel's prayer came, the latter asked Ibn al-Mubarak for a respite, and he granted his request. When the infidel kneeled to perform his prayer, Ibn al-Mubarak wanted to strike him with his sword, but he heard a voice speak to him in the air: "And keep the promise, for every promise will be scrutinized."[130] So he desisted [from killing him]. When the infidel had finished his prayer, he asked: "What prevented you from doing what you intended to do?" Ibn al-Mubarak told him about what he had heard. On hearing that, the infidel exclaimed: "Blessed be the Lord, who censures His friend for the sake of His enemy!" So he embraced Islam and became a good Muslim.

It is said that God prompted men to commit sin when He named Himself "the Forgiver". "For were He to say: 'I will forgive no sins', no Muslim would ever commit a sin." In the same way, He said: "God will not forgive anyone who associates partners with Him,"[131] and indeed no Muslim can ever give partners to Him. However, when He said "He forgives any lesser sin to whomever He wills",[132] they [His servants] began to long for His forgiveness [in lesser matters].

It is related about Ibrahim b. Adham – may God be pleased with him – that he said: "One night I was waiting for a long time for the court around the Kaʿba to become free of people [so that I could perform] my circumambulations. It was

---

129 A famous sacred *hadith* report (*hadith qudsi*) – that is, one of those in which God is the speaker. It is cited in the major Sunni collections of *hadith*.
130 Q. 17:34; 17:36, according to Arberry's translation.
131 Q. 4:116.
132 Q. 4:116.

a dark and rainy night; [the pilgrims] left the sacred precinct and I began walking around the Kaʿba. As I was doing that,//205 I kept repeating: 'O my God, guard me from sin! O my God, guard me from sin!' Suddenly I heard a voice saying to me: 'O Ibn Adham, you ask Me to guard you from sin, and so do the rest of mankind. But if I were to guard you all from sin, to whom, then, should I show My mercy?'"

It is said that while on his death bed Abu ʾl-ʿAbbas b. Surayj[133] had a dream as if the Day of Judgement had already occurred and the All-Powerful was inquiring: "Where are the learned?" When they came, He asked: "What have you done with what you have learned?" [Abu ʾl-ʿAbbas said:] "We answered: 'O Lord, we have fallen short and committed acts of evil!' He repeated his question, as if He were not satisfied with our answer and wanted another one. So I said: 'As for me, my record includes no sin of giving partners to You, and You have promised that You will pardon anything that is less than that.' God said: 'Go forth, I have pardoned all of you.'" Abu ʾl-ʿAbbas died three nights later.

They say that there once was a drunkard. [One day] he gathered together some of his boon companions and gave a slave of his four *dirhams* so that he could buy some fruit for his party. As the slave passed by the door of Mansur b. ʿAmmar's house, where the latter had his teaching session, he heard him [Mansur] asking people to give something to a certain poor man. He was saying: "Whoever gives this man four *dirhams*, I will pray for him four prayers!" So the slave gave the man four *dirhams*. Mansur asked him: "What do you want me to pray for on your behalf?" The slave answered: "I want to be free from my master." Mansur prayed for that and asked: "What else?" He answered: "I want God Most High to recompense me for my four *dirhams*." Mansur prayed for that and asked: "What else?" He answered: "That God grant repentance to my master." Mansur prayed for that and asked: "What else?" He answered: "[Pray] that God pardon me, my master, you and all this folk [at your session]!" Mansur prayed for that. The slave returned to his master, who asked him: "Why are you so late?" The slave told him the story. The master asked: "So, what did he [Mansur] pray for?" He answered: "I asked to be set free." The master said: "Go, you are free now! And what was the second prayer?" He answered: "That God recompense me for those *dirhams*." The master said: "Here are four thousand *dirhams* for you! And what was the third prayer?" He answered: "That God grant you repentance." The master said: "I have already repented. And what was the fourth prayer?" He answered: "That God pardon you, me, the folk [at the session] and the one who said these prayers." The master exclaimed: "This is the only thing I cannot do!" When the master went to sleep that night, he had a dream in which he heard a voice saying: "You have done what it was in your power to do. Now you will see what is in My power to do. I have pardoned you, the slave, Mansur b. ʿAmmar, and the folk who attended his session!"//206

---

133 A famous jurist and theologian of the Shafiʿi school, who was famous for his moral rectitude and piety; he died in Baghdad in 306/918.

It is related that Riyah [b. ʿAmr] al-Qaysi[134] performed pilgrimages [to Mecca] many times. One day, as he was standing under the rainspout [of the Kaʿba], he said: "My God, give such-and-such a number of my pilgrimages to the Messenger – may God greet and bless him; ten of them to his ten Companions; two of them to my parents, and the remainder to all the Muslims!" He kept not a single one for himself. Suddenly he heard a voice that said: "O you, who shows Us his generosity! We pardon you, your parents, and all those who profess the true faith!"

It is related on the authority of ʿAbd al-Wahhab b. ʿAbd al-Majid al-Thaqafi that he said: "Once I saw a funeral bier [pass by] that was carried by three men and one woman. So I took the place of the woman and we headed toward the cemetery. We prayed over it [the bier] and buried it. Then I asked the woman: 'What relation was he to you?' She answered: 'He was my son.' I asked: 'Don't you have any neighbors [to help you]?' She answered: 'I do have neighbors, but they despised him.' I asked: 'Who was he then?' She answered: 'He was effeminate.'[135] I felt pity for her, so I took her to my house and gave her some money, grain and clothing. I went to sleep that night and, in my dream, I saw a visitor, who shone like a full moon. He was dressed in a white garment. He began to thank me. I asked him: 'Who are you?' He answered: 'I am that effeminate man, whom you buried today. My Lord has bestowed mercy on me because of people's contempt for me.'"

I heard the master Abu ʿAli al-Daqqaq – may God have mercy on him – say: "As Abu ʿAmr[136] al-Bikandi was going down the street one day he saw a group of men who wanted to expel a young man from their neighborhood on account of his dissolute behavior. A woman was there, crying. Al-Bikandi was told that that was the mother. Abu ʿAmr had pity for her and interceded with the men on behalf of the youth. He told them: 'Let him go this time for my sake. If he returns to his evil ways, then do with him as you please!' So they let him go, and Abu ʿAmr departed. A few days later he was passing through that neighborhood. Suddenly he heard the old woman[137] crying behind the door [of the youth's house]. He said to himself: 'Perhaps the young man returned to his evil ways and they expelled him from the neighborhood.' He knocked on the old woman's door and asked her about her son. She came out and said that he had died. He asked her how this happened. She said: 'When the time of his death approached, he said to me: "Do not tell our neighbors about my death. They have suffered a great deal because of me, so they will rejoice at my misfortune and will not attend my funeral. When you bury me, bury with me this ring upon which is engraved the word 'In the name of God'. And when you have buried me, ask for God's intercession on my behalf."' She said: 'I fulfilled his last wish, and as I was about

---

134 An early ascetic from Basra, who died in 195/810.
135 This term may also denote a young male prostitute.
136 Or "ʿUmar".
137 That is, the young man's mother.

to depart from his grave, I heard his voice say: "Go now, mother! I have come before [my] Lord the Generous!"'"

It is said that God Most High revealed to [the prophet] David – peace be upon him – //207 [the following words]: "Tell them[138] that I did not create them to profit by them; on the contrary, I created them so that they could profit by Me!" I heard Muhammad b. al-Husayn say: I heard Muhammad b. ʿAbdallah b. Shadhan say: I heard Abu Bakr al-Harbi say: I heard Ibrahim al-Utrush say: "One day we were sitting with Maʿruf al-Karkhi[139] on the banks of the Tigris. [Suddenly] we saw a group of young men pass by in a boat. They were beating tambourines, drinking [wine] and enjoying themselves frivolously. We said to Maʿruf: 'Do you not see how they flaunt their disobedience of God Most High in public?! Ask God to punish them!' Maʿruf raised up his hand and prayed: 'My God make them as merry in the Hereafter as you make them merry in this world!' [Maʿruf's companions] told him: 'Did we not ask you to pray to God to punish them?!' Maʿruf answered: 'If He makes them merry in the Hereafter, then He will have granted them His pardon!'"

I heard Abu ʾl-Hasan ʿAbd al-Rahman al-Muzakki say: I heard Abu Zakariya Yahya b. Muhammad al-Adib say: al-Fadl b. Sadaqa told us: Abu ʿAbdallah al-Husayn b. ʿAbdallah b. Saʿid said: "Yahya b. Aktham the Judge was a friend of mine. I loved him and he loved me. After he died, I longed to see him in a dream, so that I could ask him how God Most High had treated him. One night I saw him in a dream and asked him: 'How has God Most High treated you?' He answered: 'God has forgiven me. However, He reprimanded me, saying: "Yahya, you confused things regarding Me in your earthly life!" I answered: "Yes, My Lord, but I relied on the *hadith* that was communicated to me by Abu Muʿawiyya on the authority of al-ʿAmash, on the authority of Abu Salih, on the authority of Abu Hurayra, who said: 'The Messenger of God – may God bless and greet him – said that You said: "I am ashamed to punish a person with white hair by the [hell]fire."'" God said: "I have forgiven you, Yahya. My Prophet spoke the truth. However, you still confused things regarding Me in your earthly life!"'"

Sadness (*huzn*)

God Most High said: "They said: 'Praise belongs to God Who has put away all sorrow from us.'"[140] ʿAli b. Ahmad b. ʿAbdan informed us: Ahmad b. ʿUbayd informed us: ʿAli b. Hubaysh informed us: Ahmad b. ʿIsa informed us: Ibn Wahb told us: Usama b. Zayd al-Laythi //208 told us on the authority of Muhammad b. ʿAmr b. ʿAtaʾ, who said: I heard ʿAtaʾ b. Yasar say: I heard Abu Saʿid al-Khudri say: I heard the Messenger of God – may God bless and greet him – say: "Whenever the faithful servant of God is afflicted by an ailment, suffering,

---

138 That is, your people.
139 On him, see *IM*, pp. 48–49.
140 Q. 35:34; 35:31, according to Arberry's translation.

sadness or pain that troubles him, God always pardons him for some of his evil deeds."

Sadness is a state that prevents the heart from roaming in the valleys of forgetfulness [of God]. It is one of the characteristic features of the wayfarers on the Sufi path. I heard the master Abu 'Ali al-Daqqaq – may God have mercy on him – say: "The person in the state of sadness travels along the path of God in just one month a greater distance than one without sadness travels in many years."

One *hadith* says: "God loves every sad heart." In the Torah, it is said: "Whenever God loves someone, He places a mourner into his heart, whereas whenever God hates someone, He places a flute into his heart." It is related that the Messenger of God – may God bless and greet him – was constantly in the state of sadness and endless reflection.

Bishr b. al-Harith said: "Sadness is a king. When he resides in a certain place, he refuses to share it with anyone." It is said that the heart that is empty of sadness dilapidates like a house that is empty of tenants. Abu Sa'id al-Qurashi said: "Tears of sadness make one blind, whereas tears of passionate desire only dim one's sight without blinding it altogether. God Most High said: 'And his eyes[141] turned white because of the sorrow that he choked within him.'"[142] Ibn Khafif said: "Sadness is restraining one's ego from plunging into [frivolous] merriment."

Rabi'a al-'Adawiyya heard a man say: "O sadness!" She said to him: "You [should rather] say: 'O how little sadness!' If you were truly sad, you would be unable to breathe!"//209 Sufyan b. 'Uyayna said: "If a person in this [Muslim] community who is overcome with sadness weeps, God Most High will pardon the entire community because of his tears." Dawud al-Ta'i, who was often overcome with sadness, used to repeat during the night: "My God, my preoccupation with You has annihilated my other preoccupations and has deprived me of any sleep." He also used to repeat: "How can one whose afflictions are renewed with every new moment seek comfort from his sadness?!" It is said that sadness deprives one of food, while fear deprives one of sins. A Sufi was asked about evidence of sadness. He answered: "Much sighing." Al-Sari al-Saqati said: "I wish the sadness of all mankind be placed on my shoulders!"

People have discoursed at length about sadness. All of them say that only the sadness that is inspired by [the thoughts of] the Hereafter deserves praise. As for the sadness in this world, it is to be discouraged. The only person to disagree with this is Abu 'Uthman al-Hiri, who said: "Sadness is a virtue in all respects and an advantage for the believer, as long as it was not caused by a sin. Even if it does not raise one to the status of the elect [people of God], it still causes one to purify oneself." One of the Sufi masters said that whenever one of his companions was about to embark on a journey, he would tell him: "If you see a person overcome with sadness, give him my regards!"

---

141 That is, the eyes of Jacob, father of Joseph.
142 Q. 12:84.

I heard the master Abu ʿAli al-Daqqaq say to the sun when it was about to set: "Did you rise today on someone who is overcome with sadness?" One would never see al-Hasan al-Basri without thinking that he had just been afflicted with a terrible tragedy. Wakiʿ [b. al-Jarrah][143] said: "When al-Fudayl [b. ʿIyad] passed away, sadness departed this world [with him]." One of our [pious ancestors] said: "Most of the things that the faithful will find [on the Day of Judgement] in their ledger of good deeds will be related to sadness and sorrow."

I heard Abu ʿAbdallah al-Shirazi say: I heard ʿAli b. Bakran say: I heard Muhammad b. Marwazi say: I heard Ahmad b. Abi Rawh say: I heard my father say: I heard al-Fudayl b. ʿIyad say: "Our pious ancestors used to say that everything must be taxed and the tax of the mind is constant sadness."

I heard Shaykh Abu ʿAbd al-Rahman al-Sulami – may God have mercy on him – say: I heard Muhammad b. Ahmad al-Farraʾ say: I heard Abu ʾl-Husayn al-Warraq say: "One day I asked Abu ʿUthman al-Hiri about sadness. He answered: 'The sad person has no time for questions about sadness. Seek sadness, then ask questions.'"//210

Hunger (*juʿ*) and the abandonment of [carnal] desire (*shahwa*)

God Most High said: "Surely, We shall try you with something of fear and hunger."[144] He also said, at the end of the same verse, promising to reward generously those who patiently endure the hardship of hunger: "But give good tidings unto the patient."[145] He also said: "And give preference to others above yourselves, even though poverty is your portion."[146]

ʿAli b. Ahmad al-Ahwazi informed us: Ahmad b. ʿUbayd al-Saffar told us: ʿAbdallah b. Ayyub told us: Abu ʾl-Walid al-Tayalisi told us: Abu Hashim Sahib al-Zaʿfarani told us: Muhammad b. ʿAbdallah told us on the authority of Anas b. Malik, who said: "Fatima[147] – may God be pleased with her – brought a small piece of bread to the Messenger of God – may God bless and greet him. He asked her: 'Fatima, what is this?' She answered: 'This is a piece of bread that I baked. My heart would not be at peace until I brought you a slice of it.' He told her: 'This is the first piece of food to enter your father's mouth for three days.'" According to a different version [of this story], Fatima brought him a piece of barley bread.

This is why hunger is one of the characteristics of this tribe [the Sufis] and one of the pillars of their striving. The wayfarers [on the mystic path] differ in the extent of their adherence to hunger and abstention from food. They have found the wellsprings of wisdom in hunger. Many tales are told about this.

---

143 An early ascetic and collector of *hadith*, who died in 197/812. See *IM*, p. 21.
144 Q. 2:155; 2:150 in Arberry's translation.
145 Q. 2:155.
146 Q. 59:9.
147 The Prophet's daughter by his first wife Khadija.

I heard Muhammad b. Ahmad al-Sufi say: I heard ʿAbdallah al-Tamimi say: I heard Ibn Salim say: "The proper rule [of one who practices] hunger is to limit one's [daily] meal to the size of a cat's ear." It is said that Sahl b. ʿAbdallah [al-Tustari] ate only one meal for fifteen days and that during the month of Ramadan[148] he would not eat until he saw the new moon and that every night he would break his fast with nothing but water. Yahya b. Muʿadh said: "If hunger were sold in the marketplace, then the seekers of the Hereafter would not need to buy anything else there."

Muhammad b. ʿAbdallah b. ʿUbaydallah informed us: ʿAli b. al-Husayn al-Arrajani//211 told us: Abu Muhammad ʿAbdallah b. Ahmad al-Istakhri told us in Mecca – may God protect it – that Sahl b. ʿAbdallah [al-Tustari] said: "When God Most High created this world, He placed disobedience and ignorance in satiation and He placed wisdom and knowledge in hunger." Yahya b. Muʿadh said: "Hunger is an exercise for aspirants (*muridun*), a trial for the repentant, a discipline for the world renouncers (*zuhhad*) and a blessing for the gnostics (*ʿarifun*)."

I heard the master Abu ʿAli al-Daqqaq – may God have mercy on him – say: "A disciple came to a Sufi master and found him weeping. He asked him: 'Why are you weeping?' He answered: 'I am hungry.' The other exclaimed: 'How can a man like you cry from hunger?' He answered: 'Be silent! Don't you know that He wants me to weep from my hunger?!'"

I heard Abu ʿAbdallah al-Shirazi – may God have mercy on him – say: Muhammad b. Bishr told us: al-Husayn b. Mansur [al-Hallaj] told us: Dawud b. Muʿadh told us: I heard Makhlad say: "Al-Hajjaj b. Furafisa was with us in Syria. He stayed fifty days without drinking water or taking his fill from anything he ate." I heard him [Makhlad] say: Abu Bakr al-Ghazzal[149] said: I heard Muhammad b. ʿAli say: I heard Abu ʿAbdallah Ahmad b. Yahya al-Jallaʾ say: "When Abu Turab al-Nakhshabi[150] came to Mecca – may God protect it – through the desert of Basra, we asked him about what he had eaten [during his journey]. He answered that since he left Basra he had eaten twice: first at Nibaj, then at Dhat ʿIrq, whereupon he had come to them.[151] Thus he had crossed the desert eating only two times." I also heard him [Makhlad] say: ʿAli b. al-Nahhas al-Misri said: Harun b. Muhammad al-Daqqaq said: Abu ʿAbd al-Rahman al-Dirfash[152] told us: Ahmad b. Abi ʾl-Hawari said: I heard ʿAbd al-ʿAziz ʿUmayr say: "A flock of birds was starving for forty days. When they finally flew off and returned after some days, they emanated the smell of musk."

Sahl b. ʿAbdallah [al-Tustari] grew stronger as he fasted and weaker as soon as he ate something.//212 Abu ʿUthman al-Maghribi said: "Al-Rabbani did not eat for forty days, whereas al-Samadani did not eat for eighty days."

---

148 The month of the Muslim fast.
149 Or "Ghazzali".
150 On him see *IM*, pp. 33–34.
151 That is, to Mecca.
152 Or "al-Dirqash".

I heard Shaykh Abu ʿAbd al-Rahman al-Sulami – may God have mercy on him – say: I heard Muhammad b. ʿAli al-ʿAlawi say: I heard ʿAli b. Ibrahim al-Qadi in Damascus say: Muhammad b. ʿAli b. Khalaf said: I heard Ahmad b. Abi ʾl-Hawari say: I heard Sulayman al-Darani say: "The key to this world is satiation and the key to the next world is hunger."

I heard Muhammad b. ʿAbdallah b. ʿUbaydallah say: I heard ʿAli b. Husayn al-Arrajani say: I heard Abu Muhammad al-Istakhri say: I heard Sahl b. ʿAbdallah [al-Tustari] say that he was asked about someone who eats only one meal during the day. He answered: "This is the meal of the truthful." He was then asked about someone who eats two meals during the day. He answered: "This is the meal of the faithful." Finally, he was asked about someone who eats three meals during the day. He answered: "Tell his family to build a trough for him!" I also heard him [Muhammad b. ʿUbaydallah] say: ʿAbd al-ʿAziz b. al-Fadl told us: Abu Bakr al-Saʾih told us: I heard Yahya b. Muʿadh say: "Hunger is a light, while satiation is a fire. Appetite is like firewood, by which fire is kindled. It won't be extinguished until it consumes the one who has it."

I heard Abu Hatim al-Sijistani say: I heard Abu Nasr al-Sarraj al-Tusi say: "One day a Sufi came to visit a [Sufi] master who gave him some food and asked him: 'How long has it been since you have eaten?' The Sufi answered: 'Five days.' The master told him: 'Your hunger is the hunger of the greedy! You still have your garments on, while you go hungry. This is not the hunger of the poor!'"

I heard Muhammad b. al-Husayn say: I heard Muhammad b. Ahmad b. Saʿid al-Razi say: I heard al-ʿAbbas b. Hamza say: I heard Ahmad b. Abi ʾl-Hawari say: Abu Sulayman al-Darani said: "I love not eating one bite of my supper better than staying awake all night in vigil!"

I heard Abu ʾl-Qasim Jaʿfar b. Ahmad al-Razi say: "Abu ʾl-Khayr craved fish for many years. Then some of it came to him from a lawful source. When he stretched his hand toward it in order to eat it, a spike from its bone pricked his finger. Because of this he lost his hand. He exclaimed: 'O Lord, this is what happens to someone who stretches his hand in his desire for a licit thing! What then happens to someone who stretches his hand desiring that which is prohibited?!'"

I heard the master Abu Bakr b. Furak say://213 "Following one's desire for what is licit results in worries about one's family. Imagine what happens to the one who seeks to satisfy his desire for something illicit!" I heard Rustam al-Shirazi al-Sufi say that [the master] Abu ʿAbdallah b. Khafif was attending a dinner party when one of his companions stretched his hand toward food before the master because of his extreme hunger [and poverty]. One of the master's other companions wanted to reprimand the hungry man for his poor manners – namely, for his stretching his hand to food before the master. So he [the companion] put some food in front of the hungry man. The latter realized that he was being reprimanded for his poor manners, so he resolved to keep a fast for fifteen days to punish and discipline himself [for his transgression] and to demonstrate his repentance for his misdemeanor. And he did this despite the poverty he had suffered before that incident."

I heard Muhammad b. ʿAbdallah al-Sufi say: Abu ʾl-Faraj al-Warathani told us: ʿAbdallah b. Muhammad b. Jaʿfar told us: Ibrahim b. Muhammad b. al-Harith told us: Sulayman b. Dawud told us: Jaʿfar b. Sulayman told us: I heard Malik b. Dinar say: "When someone has conquered his mundane desires, Satan is scared of his shadow!" I also heard him [Muhammad b. ʿAbdallah al-Sufi] say: I heard Abu ʿAli al-Rudhbari say: "If the Sufi says after five days [of fasting] that he is hungry, send him to the marketplace and tell him to earn something!" I heard the master Abu ʿAli al-Daqqaq relate on the authority of a Sufi master who said: "In those who are destined to the hellfire, mundane passions have prevailed over caution. That is why they commit sins." I also heard him say that someone asked a Sufi: "Do you not have desire?" He answered: "Yes, I do, but I guard myself [against it]." He also said that someone asked another Sufi: "Do you not have desire?" He answered: "I have the desire not to desire." And this is more perfect [than the first answer].

I heard Abu ʿAbd al-Rahman al-Sulami say: Ahmad b. Mansur informed us: Ibn Makhlad informed us: Abu ʾl-Husayn b. ʿAmr b. al-Jahm told us: I heard Abu Nasr al-Tammar say: "Bishr [al-Hafi] came to me one night. I told him: 'Praise be to God Who brought you here. We received some cotton from Khurasan. [My] daughter has spun it, sold it and bought us some meat, so that you might eat with us!' [Bishr] said: 'If I were to eat with someone, I would eat with you.' He then added: 'For many years I have craved eggplant,//214 but not had a chance to eat it.' I told him: 'Surely, over all these years there must have been at least one eggplant that was licit for you!' He answered: '[I will only eat it] when my love of eggplant has become pure!'"

I heard ʿAbdallah b. Bakuya al-Sufi – may God have mercy on him – say: I heard Abu Ahmad al-Saghir say: "Abu ʿAbdallah b. Khafif ordered that I bring him ten raisins every evening so that he could break his fast on them. One night I felt pity for him, so I served him fifteen raisins. He looked at me and asked: 'Who told you to do this?' He ate ten raisins and left the rest untouched." I heard Muhammad b. ʿAbdallah b. ʿUbaydallah say: I heard Abu ʾl-ʿAbbas Ahmad b. Muhammad b. ʿAbdallah b. al-Farghani say: I heard Abu ʾl-Husayn al-Razi say: I heard Yusuf b. al-Husayn say: I heard Abu Turab al-Nakhshabi say: "Only once in my life did my soul prevail over me in its craving. When I was on a journey, it desired bread and eggs. I turned to a village nearby. Someone rose up and followed me saying: 'This one was with the thieves!' They beat me seventy lashes until one of them recognized me and exclaimed: 'This is Abu Turab al-Nakhshabi!' They apologized to me and one of them invited me to his house out of respect and compassion for me. He served me bread and eggs. I said to my soul: 'Eat them after seventy lashes!'"

Humility (*khushuʿ*) and modesty (*tawaduʿ*)

God Most High said: "Prosperous are the believers who in their prayers are humble."[153] Abu ʾl-Hasan b. ʿAbd al-Rahim[154] b. Ibrahim b. Muhammad Yahya al-Muzakki informed us: Abu ʾl-Fadl Sufyan b. Muhammad al-Jawhari told us: ʿAli b. al-Husayn told us: Yahya b. Hammad told us: Shuʿba told us on the authority of Aban b. Thaʿlab,[155] on the authority of Fadl b. al-Fuqaymi, on the authority of Ibrahim al-Nakhaʿi, on the authority of ʿAlqama b. Qays, on the authority of ʿAbdallah b. Masʿud, who said: "The Prophet – may God bless and greet him – said: 'No one in whose heart there is a grain of pride will ever enter Paradise; and no one in whose heart there is a grain of faith will ever enter the hellfire.' Someone asked: 'Messenger of God, what of a man who wishes his clothes to be beautiful?' The Messenger responded: 'God Most High is beautiful and He loves beauty. As for pride, it is the opposite of truth and disdain to other people!'"//215

ʿAli b. Ahmad a-Awhazi informed us: Ahmad b. ʿUbayd al-Basri informed us: Muhammad b. Fadl b. Jabir told us: Abu Ibrahim told us: ʿAli b. Mushir told us on the authority of Muslim al-ʿAwar, on the authority of Anas b. Malik: "The Messenger of God used to visit the sick, accompany funeral processions, ride a donkey and accept invitations from slaves. On the day [the Jewish tribes] of Qurayza and al-Nadir were conquered, he rode a donkey bridled with a rope of palm fiber and saddled with a saddle of palm fiber."

Humility means submission to [the will of] God, while submissiveness is surrender to [the will of] God and abandoning resistance to God's decree. Hudhayfa said: "Humility is the first thing you lose of your religion." When someone asked a Sufi about humility, he answered: "Humility is when the heart stands before God – praise be to Him – with total concentration." Sahl b. ʿAbdallah [al-Tustari] said: "Satan cannot come near one whose heart is humble." It is said that one of the signs of humility in the servant of God is that when he is prompted to anger, contradicted or rejected, he accepts all that [with equanimity]. [Another] Sufi said: "Humility of the heart is to restrain [your] eyes from looking." Muhammad b. ʿAli al-Tirmidhi said: "Being humble means that the flames of your passion have been extinguished and the vapors of your breast have subsided, while the light of glorification of God has come to shine in your heart. [At this point,] a man's passion dies, his heart is given [a new] life, and his limbs surrender themselves to humility." Al-Hasan al-Basri said: "Humility is when fear settles in your heart permanently."

Someone asked al-Junayd about humility. He answered: "It is the abasement of your heart before the One Who knows that which is hidden."[156]

---

153 Q. 23:1–2.
154 Or "ʿAbd al-Rahman", according to another reading.
155 Or "Taghlab".
156 That is, the destiny of [His] creation from beginning to end.

God Most High said: "The servants of the All-Merciful are those who walk the earth modestly."[157] I heard the master Abu ʿAli al-Daqqaq – may God have mercy on him – say: "This means '[they walk] in submissiveness and humility'." I also heard him say: "[They are humble] those who do not consider the thongs of their sandals to be beautiful as they walk."

[The Sufis] have agreed that humility resides in the heart.//216 Once, a Sufi saw a man with a downcast appearance, lowered gaze and slumped shoulders. He told him: "O so-and-so, humility is here!" and he pointed to his chest, "Not there!" and he pointed to the [man's slumping] shoulders. It is related that the Messenger of God – may God bless and greet him – saw a man playing with his beard during his prayer. He said: "If his heart were humble, his limbs would be humble too." They say that one of the conditions of humility is that one does not notice who is standing to one's left or right during the prayer. One can say that humility is abasing one's innermost self in the presence of God – may He be blessed and exalted – in accordance with the rules of proper behavior (adab). Or it is said that humility is a feebleness that enters one's heart when one contemplates [one's] Lord. Or it is said that humility is the dissolution and shrinking of the heart before the power of the True Reality (al-haqiqa). Or it is said that humility is a prelude to the onset of the conquering powers of awe [of God]. It is also said that humility is a shudder that suddenly attacks one's heart, when the True Reality unveils itself before one.

Al-Fudayl b. ʿIyad said: "One hates to see in a man's outward appearance more humility than in his heart." Abu Sulayman al-Darani said: "If all mankind would join forces to humiliate me as I humiliate myself they would not be able to do this!" They also say: "He who does not abase himself before himself, cannot abase himself before others." ʿUmar b. ʿAbd al-ʿAziz[158] would only prostrate himself [in prayer] upon the dust of the earth.

ʿAli b. Ahmad al-Ahwazi informed us: Ahmad b. ʿUbaydallah al-Basri told us: Ibrahim b. ʿAbdallah told us: Abu ʾl-Hasan b. ʿAli b. Yazid al-Faraʾidi told us: Muhammad b. Kathir – that is, al-Massisi – told us on the authority of Harun b. Hayyan b. Husayf, on the authority of Saʿid b. Jubayr, on the authority of Ibn ʿAbbas – may God be pleased with both of them,[159] that the Messenger of God – may God bless and greet him – said: "A person who has as much as a mustard seed of pride in his heart will never enter Paradise." Mujahid – may God have mercy on him – said: "When God – may He be exalted – drowned the people of Noah, all mountains loomed up proudly. Only al-Judi[160] abased//217 itself. That is why God – may He be exalted – made it the resting place of Noah's [ark]. ʿUmar b. ʿAbd al-ʿAziz – may God be pleased with him – used to walk at

---

157 Q. 25:63; 25:64, according to Arberry's translation.
158 A pious caliph of the Umayyad dynasty.
159 That is, him and his father.
160 A mountain in ancient Mesopotamia (present-day Iraqi Kurdistan) mentioned in the Qurʾan as the destination and docking place of Noah's ark. See Q. 11:44.

brisk pace. [He explained that] saying: "This brings [me] swiftly to my goal and keeps [me] away from vanity."

ʿUmar b. ʿAbd al-ʿAziz – may God be pleased with him – was writing something one night, when a guest came to visit him. [His] lamp had almost gone out. The guest said: "I will go to the lamp and fix it." [ʿUmar] replied: "No, availing oneself of the guest's help is against [the rules of] hospitality." "Then, I will wake up the slave," suggested the guest. [ʿUmar] answered: "No, he has just fallen asleep." He [ʿUmar] then went to the oil container and put oil into the lamp [himself]. The guest exclaimed: "You went and did it yourself, O Commander of the Faithful?!" ʿUmar answered: "I went [to do it] as ʿUmar and I came back [after doing it] as ʿUmar."

Abu Saʿid al-Khudri – may God be pleased with him – related that the Messenger of God – may God bless and greet him – used to feed [his] camel, sweep [his] house, mend [his] sandals, patch [his] clothes, milk [his] sheep, eat with [his] servant and help him grind, when he [the servant] got tired. He was not embarrassed to carry his goods from the bazaar to his family. He would shake hands with both the rich and the poor; he was the first to greet people; he would not scorn any meal of which he was invited to partake, even if this was unripe and dry dates. He made do with free supplies [of provision], he was gentle of character, generous of nature, pleasant of company; his face was cheerful, he smiled much, without laughing and showed [his] sadness without frowning; he was humble without being self-effacing, generous without being extravagant; his heart was gentle, he was compassionate to every Muslim; he would never eat his fill and he would never stretch his hand to a thing that he desired.

I heard Shaykh Abu ʿAbd al-Rahman al-Sulami – may God have mercy on him – say: I heard ʿAbdallah b. Muhammad al-Razi say: I heard Muhammad b. Nasr al-Saʾigh say: I heard Mardawayah al-Saʾigh say: I heard al-Fudayl b. ʿIyad say: "The Qurʾan-reciters (qurraʾ)[161] of the Merciful are characterized by their humility and modesty, whereas the Qurʾan-reciters//218 of the courts are characterized by their haughtiness and pride." Al-Fudayl b. ʿIyad also said: "Whosoever considers himself to be important has no share of modesty." Someone asked al-Fudayl about modesty. He responded: "You should submit yourself to the Truth, let yourself be guided to it, and accept it from whoever speaks it." Al-Fudayl said: "God – Most High, may He be exalted – revealed to the mountains: 'I will speak to a prophet upon one of you!' The mountains raised themselves high in their pride. Only Mount Sinai remained modest. Therefore God – may He be great and exalted – spoke to Moses – peace be upon him – upon it due to its modesty."

I heard Muhammad b. al-Husayn – may God have mercy on him – say: I heard ʿAli b. Ahmad b. Jaʿfar say: I heard Ibrahim b. Fatik say: "Someone asked

---

161 The internally diverse class of early Islamic religious specialists who fulfilled various functions in the early caliphal state, ranging from public Qurʾan recitation to adjudication. They can be seen as the forerunners of the ʿulamaʾ class.

al-Junayd about modesty. He answered: 'Being compassionate and gentle toward your [fellow] creatures.'" Wahb said: "It is written in one of the books that God has revealed [to mankind]: 'I brought forth the particles[162] from the loins of Adam and did not find among them a heart more modest than that of Moses – peace be upon him. Therefore, I chose him [from among them all] and spoke to him.'" Ibn al-Mubarak said: "Being proud towards the rich and being modest towards the poor are [two essential] parts of modesty." Someone asked Abu Yazid [al-Bistami]: "When can a man attain modesty?" He answered: "When he sees neither a state nor a station for himself [in this world] and when he cannot find among mankind anyone who is worse than himself." They say: "Modesty is a blessing no one envies, while pride is a temptation that has no excuse. Greatness lies in modesty, and whoever seeks it in pride will never find it." I heard Shaykh Abu ʿAbd al-Rahman al-Sulami say: I heard Abu Bakr Muhammad b. ʿAbdallah say: I heard Ibrahim b. Shayban say: "Nobility lies in modesty; greatness lies in fear of God; and freedom lies in contentment." I also heard him say: I heard al-Hasan al-Sawi say: I heard Ibn al-Aʿrabi say: I have heard a report from Sufyan al-Thawri in which he said: "The greatest souls among all creatures are five in number. They are: an ascetic scholar, a Sufi jurist (*faqih sufi*), a modest rich man, a grateful poor man, and a member of the Prophet's house who belongs to the Sunni community."[163]

Yahya b. Muʿadh said: "Modesty is excellent for everyone. However, it is especially good for the rich. As for pride, it is repugnant for everyone, but is particularly repugnant for the poor." Ibn ʿAtaʾ said: "Modesty is to accept the Truth from anyone [who speaks it]." It is said that [once] Zayd b. Thabit[164] was riding his horse. Ibn ʿAbbas[165] approached him in order to take hold of the stirrup of his horse. "Stop it, O son of the uncle of the Messenger of God!" said Zayd. "But that's how we were commanded to treat our learned men!" responded Ibn ʿAbbas. Zayd then took Ibn ʿAbbas's hand and kissed it, saying: "And this is how we were commanded to treat the family of the Messenger of God – may God bless and greet him!" ʿUrwa b. al-Zubayr related: "[Once] I saw ʿUmar b. al-Khattab – may God be pleased with him – carrying a waterskin on his shoulder. I told him: 'O Commander of the Faithful, this is not suitable for you!' He answered: 'When the deputations [of the Arabian tribes] came to me in obedience, arrogance entered my soul and I decided to break it!' He proceeded with his waterskin to the house of a woman from among the Helpers[166] and emptied it into her cistern." I heard Abu Hatim al-Sijistani say: I heard Abu Nasr al-Sarraj

---

162 That is, disembodied human souls. This is a reference to the primordial covenant (*mithaq*) between God and mankind alluded to in the Q. 7:172.
163 Many members of the Prophet's family (*ahl al-bayt*) belonged to the Shiʿite (pro-ʿAlid) party, which advocated their right to lead the community of the faithful.
164 A secretary to the prophet Muhammad, who was entrusted with the task of collecting and editing the text of the Qurʾan after the latter's death.
165 A cousin of the Prophet, who was famous for his piety and proficiency in the Qurʾan.
166 The Prophet's early followers at Medina.

al-Tusi[167] say: "When Abu Hurayra[168] was governor of Medina he was seen carrying a bundle of firewood on his back, saying: 'Make way for the governor!'" ʿAbdallah al-Razi said: "Modesty is to refuse to make distinctions in service."

I heard Muhammad b. al-Husayn – may God have mercy on him – say: I heard Muhammad b. Ahmad b. Harun say: I heard Muhammad b. al-ʿAbbas al-Dimashqi say: I heard Ahmad b. Abi ʾl-Hawari say: I heard Abu Sulayman al-Darani say: "Whoever sees any value in himself will never taste the sweetness of service." Yahya b. Muʿadh said: "Being arrogant toward one who is arrogant to you because of his wealth is [nothing but] modesty." Al-Shibli – may God have mercy on him – said: "My modesty has rendered the modesty of the Jews a mere trifle." A man came to al-Shibli, who asked him: "What are you?"//220 He answered: "My master, I am the dot under the letter baʾ."[169] Al-Shibli told him: "Stay with me as long as you do not give yourself an [independent] station!" Ibn ʿAbbas – may God be pleased with both of them[170] – said: "Modesty is that a man drinks the water left behind by his brother." Bishr [al-Hafi] said: "Greet worldly people by neglecting to greet them!" Shuʿyab b. Harb related: "As I was circling around the Kaʿba, someone shoved me with his elbow. When I turned to him, [I saw that] it was al-Fudayl b. ʿIyad, who said: 'Abu Salih, if you [for a moment] thought that among those who had came here for the [pilgrimage] season was someone worse than you and me, your thought was bad indeed!'"

Someone said: "As I was circumambulating the Kaʿba, I saw a man surrounded by [a crowd of people] who thanked and praised him. Because of him they obstructed other pilgrims from circling the Kaʿba. I saw him again sometime after that on a bridge in Baghdad, begging people for handouts. I was [greatly] surprised [by his condition]. He told me: 'I elevated myself in a place, where other people show modesty, so God – may He be blessed – afflicted me with humiliation in a place where others elevate themselves!'" ʿUmar b. ʿAbd al-ʿAziz[171] learned that one of his sons had bought [a signet ring] with a jewel worth one thousand *dirhams*. He wrote to him saying: "I have learned that you have bought a jewel worth one thousand *dirhams*. When you receive this letter, sell [your] ring and fill one thousand stomachs. Then get yourself a ring worth two *dirhams*, make its signet of Chinese iron, and inscribe on it: 'May God have mercy on a man who knows his true worth!'"

It is related that someone offered a slave to a prince to purchase for a thousand *dirhams*. However, when the money was brought to him, he considered the price excessive and he [ordered] the money returned to his coffer. The slave

---

167 The author of an influential early Sufi manual entitled "Essentials of Sufism"; he died in 378/988.
168 A famous Companion of the Prophet, who transmitted many reports about his sayings and deeds.
169 That is, the dot that serves to distinguish one letter of the Arabic alphabet from another, but has no independent status of its own.
170 See note 165; the blessings refer to him and his father.
171 See note 158.

pleaded with him, saying: "My lord, buy me, for I have, for each of these *dirhams*, a quality [the overall value of which] is worth more than a thousand *dirhams*." [The Prince] asked him what that might be. He answered: "The very least of it is that if you were to buy me and elevate me above all the rest of your slaves, I would still not become rude [toward you] and would know that I am but a slave of yours!" So the prince purchased him.

Someone related on the authority of Raja' b. Haya that he said: "As 'Umar b. 'Abd al-'Aziz was delivering a public speech I estimated his garment to be worth twelve *dirhams*. He had a mantel, a turban, a shirt, a pair of trousers and slippers, and a hood."//221 It is said that 'Abdallah b. Muhammad b. Wasi' strutted along with a gait that called for disapproval.[172] His father told him: "Do you know how much I paid for your mother? Three hundred *dirhams*! As for your father, may God not increase the likes of him among the Muslims! And yet you walk like that?!"

I heard Muhammad b. al-Husayn say: I heard Ahmad b. Muhammad al-Farra' say: I heard 'Abdallah b. Munazil say: I heard Hamdun al-Qassar say: "Modesty is that you consider no one to be in need of you, either in this world or in the Hereafter." Ibrahim b. Adham said: "Since I embraced Islam I have rejoiced only three times. First, when I was on board a ship where there was a man who was fond of joking. He would say: 'In the land of the [infidel] Turks we used to grab [captive] infidels like this', and he would grab me by my hair and shake me back and forth. That pleased me, because there was no one on that ship whom he would consider more contemptible. Another time I rested in a mosque overcome with sickness. The [mosque's] muezzin came in and ordered me to get out. However, I was unable [to leave], so he grabbed me by my foot and dragged me out of the mosque. The third time, I was in Syria. I was wearing a fur. When I took a close look at it I could not distinguish between the hair of that fur and the lice [hiding in it], because there were so many of them. I rejoiced at that." In another tale he reported: "I have never experienced a greater joy than when I was sitting one day and a passer-by approached me and urinated on me."

It is reported that Abu Dharr and Bilal[173] were having an argument during which Abu Dharr reproached Bilal for his black skin. The latter complained about that to the Messenger of God – may God's blessing and peace be upon him – who said: "Abu Dharr, something of the pride of the Age of Ignorance[174] still remains in your heart!" [On hearing that,] Abu Dharr threw himself on the ground and vowed that he would not raise his head until Bilal had stepped on his cheek with his foot. He did not get up until Bilal did so.

---

172 That is, his gait exhibited self-conceit and pride.
173 Two Companions of the Prophet, who were renowned for their piety. Bilal was an Ethiopian slave emancipated by the Prophet. He had a beautiful voice and served as the Muslim community's first muezzin.
174 That is, the period of Arab paganism that preceded Islam.

Al-Hasan b. ʿAli – may God be pleased with him – passed by a group of boys who had a few pieces of bread. They invited him to be their guest. He dismounted and ate with them, whereupon he took them to his house, where he fed and clothed them. He commented: "They are better [than me], because they fed me the only thing that they had, whereas I have more than that!"//222 It is said that ʿUmar b. al-Khattab[175] was distributing some clothing taken as spoils of war among the Companions [of the Prophet]. He sent a [precious] Yemeni garment to Muʿadh. The latter sold it, purchased six slaves, then set them free. ʿUmar learned about this. When he was dividing clothes the next time, he sent Muʿadh a less valuable garment. When Muʿadh reproached him for that, ʿUmar answered: "Don't reproach me, for you sold the first one!" "What's the matter with you?" exclaimed Muʿadh, "Give me my share, for I have vowed to hit you over your head with this!"[176] ʿUmar responded: "Here's my head! Old men should treat each other gently."

Opposing the soul[177] (*mukhalafat al-nafs*) and remembering its faults (*dhikr ʿuyubiha*)

God Most High has said: "But for him who feared standing before His Lord[178] and forbade the soul its caprice, surely Paradise will be the refuge."[179]

ʿAli b. Ahmad b. ʿAbdan informed us: Ahmad b. ʿUbayd told us: Tammam told us: Muhammad b. Muʿawiyya al-Naysaburi told us: ʿAli b. Abi ʿAli b. ʿUtba b. Abi Lahab told us on the authority of Muhammad al-Munkadir, on the authority of Jabir – may God have mercy on him – who said that the Prophet – may God bless and greet him – said: "The things that I fear most for my community are: following [one's] passion and expecting too much [of this world]. Following one's passion turns one away from the Truth, whereas expecting too much [of this world] renders one forgetful of the Hereafter. Know, therefore, that struggling against the soul is the beginning of worship."

When [some] Sufi masters were asked about [the meaning of] Islam, they answered: "[It is] slaughtering the soul by the swords of opposition [to it]." "Know that for someone in whom the vagaries of the soul rise, the splendors of intimacy [with God] become extinct." Dhu ʾl-Nun al-Misri said: "Reflection is the key to worship, while the sign of anyone's attaining his goal is his [ability to] oppose his soul and his passions. Opposing them is the abandonment of the desires [associated with them]." Ibn ʿAtaʾ [al-Adami] said: "The soul is naturally

---

175 The second successor (caliph) of the Prophet after Abu Bakr.
176 There are several possible readings of this passage. According to one, Muʿadh promised to hit ʿUmar over his head with the less valuable garment allocated to him. The other possibility is that he wanted to hit ʿUmar with something ("this") that he was holding in his hand.
177 This word can also be translated as "self". In the text that follows I will use both words interchangeably.
178 On the Day of Judgement.
179 Q. 79:40–41.

predisposed to bad behavior. Yet, the servant of God is commanded to observe [the rules of] proper behavior. By its nature the soul [is prone to] wallow in the field of disobedience, while the servant exerts himself in preventing it from engaging in evil pursuits. Whoever gives his soul free rein becomes an accomplice in its depredations."

I heard Shaykh Abu ʿAbd al-Rahman al-Sulami – may God have mercy on him – say: I heard Abu Bakr al-Razi say://223 I heard Abu ʿUmar al-Anmati say: I heard al-Junayd say: "The soul that commands evil[180] pushes [you] to perdition, assists [your] enemies, follows [your] passions, and is suspected of all manner of evil deeds." Abu Hafs said: "Whoever does not constantly suspect his soul, oppose it under all conditions, and force it to do things that it dislikes throughout his lifetime will be deluded. And when one looks with approval at something it has done, one has caused its ruin." For how can an intelligent person be satisfied with his soul? The noble son of the son of the noble son of the noble Joseph, son of Jacob, son of Isaac, son of Abraham the Friend of God, said: "I claim not that my soul was innocent – surely the soul of man commands evil."[181]

I heard Muhammad b. al-Husayn say: I heard Ibrahim b. Miqsam[182] say in Baghdad: I heard Ibn ʿAtaʾ say: I heard al-Junayd say: "One sleepless night I rose up to recite a supererogatory prayer. However, I did not find the sweetness and delight I usually feel when I converse with my Lord. I was bewildered. I tried to go to sleep, but I couldn't. I tried to sit down, but I couldn't. Then I opened the door and went out. [Outside] I came upon a man wrapped in a cloak who was lying on the road. He felt my presence and raised his head saying: 'At last [you have come] Abu ʾl-Qasim!' 'But, sir, did we have an appointment?' I asked. He answered: 'No, but I had asked the Mover of the Hearts to move your heart in my direction.' 'Indeed, he has done so! What is your need?' I asked him. He inquired: 'When does the soul's disease become its cure?' 'When you deny your soul its drives, its disease becomes its cure,' I answered. He then addressed his own soul, saying: 'Listen, I have given you this same answer seven times, yet you refused to hear it from anyone but al-Junayd! So you now you have heard [it from him]!' Then he departed. I did not know who he was and I never met him again after that."

Abu Bakr al-Tamastani said: "To escape from one's soul is the greatest of all blessings, for the soul is the thickest veil between you and God – may He be great and glorious!" Sahl [al-Tustari] said: "There's no better way of worshiping God than to oppose one's soul and passions. I heard Muhammad b. al-Husayn – may God have mercy on him – say: I heard Mansur b. ʿAbdallah say://224 I heard Abu ʿUmar al-Anmati say: I heard someone ask Ibn ʿAtaʾ: "What is the main cause of God's wrath?" He responded: "Paying attention to one's soul and its

---

180 See the next note.
181 Q. 12:53.
182 Or "al-Muqassim".

conditions. However, expecting [divine] rewards for its actions is even worse than that!" I also heard him [Muhammad b. al-Husayn] say: I heard al-Husayn b. Yahya say: I heard Ja'far b. Nusayr say: I heard Ibrahim al-Khawwas[183] say: "When I was on the mountain al-Lukam[184] I saw some pomegranates and craved them. So I came up [to the tree] and picked one of them. When I split it open, I found it to be sour. I went away and left the pomegranate behind. Suddenly I saw a man lying on the ground with many wasps flying around him. I greeted him and he returned my greetings saying: 'And upon you be peace, Ibrahim!' I asked him: 'How do you know me?' He answered: 'Nothing is hidden from one who knows God Most High.' I asked him: 'I see that you have a special status [in the eyes of] God Most High! Why, then, can't you ask Him to protect and shield you from the torment of these wasps?' He answered: 'I, too, can see that you have a special status [in the eyes of] God Most High! Why, then, can't you ask Him to protect you from craving those pomegranates? For the pain caused by the sting of the pomegranates will afflict you in the afterlife [in the same way as] the pain caused by the sting of the wasps afflicts [me] in this world!' I left him and walked away."

It is related that Ibrahim b. Shayban said: "For forty years I did not sleep under my roof nor in a place that had a lock on it. I occasionally desired to eat my fill of lentils. However, it never happened. Once, when I was in Syria, someone brought me a large bowl full of lentils. So I ate some of it and left. [Suddenly] I saw glass bottles with samples of some liquid, which I assumed to be vinegar. However, someone in the crowd told me: 'What are you looking at? These are samples of wine and those jugs there are [full of] wine!' I said to myself: 'This is my duty!' So I entered the wineseller's store and started to empty those jugs. At first, he thought that I was doing it by order of the Sultan. However, when he realized that [it was not so], he took me to Ibn Tulun[185] who commanded that I be given two hundred stick blows, then threw me into prison. I stayed there for some time, until my teacher Abu 'Abdallah al-Maghribi entered the country and interceded on my behalf. When he saw me, he asked: 'What did you do?' I answered: 'I got my fill of lentils and two hundred stick blows!' He told me: 'Then you got off lightly!'"

I heard Shaykh Abu 'Abd al-Rahman al-Sulami – may God have mercy on him – say: I heard Abu al-'Abbas al-Baghdadi say: I heard Ja'far b. Nusayr say: I heard al-Junayd say: I heard al-Sari al-Saqati say: "For thirty or forty years my soul urged me to dip a carrot into date syrup. However, I did not feed it to it." I also heard him [al-Sulami] say: "My grandfather said: 'The servant's affliction lies in his contentment with his soul as it is.'" I also heard him say: I heard Muhammad b. 'Abdallah al-Razi say: I heard al-Husayn b. 'Ali al-Qirmisini say:

---

183 A famous Sufi. See pages 56–57.
184 A mountain in Syria.
185 A powerful and fearsome governor of Egypt (d. 270/884), who made himself independent of the 'Abbasid caliph in Baghdad.

'Isam b. Yusuf al-Balkhi sent something to Hatim al-Asamm, who accepted it. Someone asked him why he accepted that. He answered: "When I took it I felt my humiliation and his pride. If I were to reject it, I would have felt my pride and his humiliation. Therefore, I chose his pride over my humiliation and my humiliation over his."

Someone told a Sufi [master]: "I want to go on the *hajj* stripped of any provisions." He said: "First you must strip your heart of forgetfulness, your soul of flippancy, your tongue of prattle and then travel however you wish!" Abu Sulayman al-Darani said: "Whoever does good during the night is rewarded during the day and whoever does good during the day is rewarded during the night; whoever is sincere in renouncing his passion will be spared [the trouble of] feeding it. For God is too noble to punish a heart that has abandoned [its] passion for His sake!" God – may He be exalted – revealed the following [words] to [the prophet] David – peace be upon him: "David, caution and warn your companions against [pursuing their] passions, for when hearts are attached to the passions of this world, their intelligence is veiled from Me!" Someone saw a man sitting suspended in the air. He asked how he had achieved this. The man answered: "I renounced my desire (*hawa*) and God made the air (*hawa'*) subservient to me!" It is said that if [the gratification of] one thousand passions were offered to the [true] believer, he would banish them with [his fear] of God. However, if the gratification of just one desire were to be offered to the sinner, it would banish the fear of God from his heart. It is said: "Do not put your reins into the hands of desire, for it will drive you into darkness."//226 Yusuf b. Asbat said: "Nothing eliminates passions from the heart better than a disquieting fear [of God] and a tireless striving [to please Him]." Al-Khawwas said: "Whoever renounces one passion without immediately discovering in it another one is not sincere in his renunciation."

Ja'far b. Nusayr related: "Al-Junayd gave me one *dirham* and asked me to buy him Waziri figs. I bought him some. When he broke his fast, he took one of them, put it into his mouth, then spat it out and broke into tears saying, 'Take them away [from me]!' When I asked him about this, he answered: 'A voice in my heart cried out: "Aren't you ashamed? At first you renounced a desire for My sake, but now you are returning to it once again!"'"

They recite:

The letter *nun* of [the word] *hawan* ("humiliation") is stolen from [the word] *hawa* ("desire")
Therefore he who succumbs to every passion is subject to humiliation!

Know that the soul has many wicked traits. One of them is envy.

Envy (*hasad*)

God Most High said: "Say: 'I take refuge with the Lord of the Daybreak from the evil of what He has created." He also said: "[I take refuge] from the evil of an envier when he envies."¹⁸⁶ Thus God concluded this chapter, which He revealed as a plea for protection [against evil forces] (ʿawdha), with a mention of envy.

Abu ʾl-Husayn al-Ahwazi informed us: Ahmad b. ʿUbayd al-Basri informed us: Ismaʿil b. al-Fadl told us: Yahya b. Makhlad said: Muʿafa b. ʿImran told us on the authority of al-Harith b. Shihab, on the authority of Maʿbad on the authority of Abu Qilaba, on the authority of Ibn Masʿud, who said that the Prophet – may God bless and greet him – said: "Three things are the root of every sin, so shield and protect yourselves from them. Beware of pride, for pride made Iblis¹⁸⁷ refuse to prostrate himself before Adam; beware of greed, for greed made Adam eat from the Tree [of Knowledge];//227 beware of envy, for one of Adam's sons killed his brother because of it." A Sufi said: "The envier is an infidel, because he is not content with the decree of the One and Only." It is also said: "The envier will never prevail." They say about the words of God Most High, "Say, My Lord has only forbidden indecencies, those that are apparent and those that are hidden", that the words "those that are hidden" refer to envy. And in another [holy] book it is said: "The envier is the denier of My beneficence." It is also said: "Envy becomes evident in you before it becomes evident in your enemy." Al-Asmaʿi¹⁸⁸ said: "I saw a Bedouin who was one hundred and twenty years old. I exclaimed: 'Your life has been long indeed!' He told me: 'I renounced envy, so I endured!'"

Ibn al-Mubarak¹⁸⁹ said: "Praise be to God Who has not placed in the heart of my master that which He has placed into the heart of a man who envies me." According to one tradition, there is an angel who resides in the fifth heaven. When the deed of a [deceased] servant passes by him which glows like the glow of the sun, he would say: "Stop! I am the angel of envy. Strike the doer of this deed in the face with this deed, for he has been envious!" Muʿawiyya¹⁹⁰ said: "I am able to please every person, except the envier. Nothing will ever please him, except the cessation of God's beneficence [toward other people]." It is said: "The envier is a violent tyrant, for he never lets go and leaves nothing behind him." ʿUmar b. ʿAbd al-ʿAziz said: "I have not seen an oppressor who would resemble more the oppressed than the envier. [His is] constant grief and incessant panting." It is said: "Among the sins of the envier is that he flatters, when he is present, backbites when he is absent, and rejoices at calamity when it befalls [others]." Muʿawiyya¹⁹¹ said: "No bad character trait is more just than envy, for it kills the envier before the one whom he envies."//228

It is said that God – may He be exalted – revealed to Solomon, son of David, – peace be upon them: "I command that you not do seven things: do not slander

---

186 Q. 113:1, 2 and 5.
187 That is, Satan.
188 A great Arab philologist and collector of Bedouin lore; he died in 213/828.
189 See *IM*, pp. 21–22.
190 The first caliph and founder of the Umayyad dynasty, who ruled from 41/661 to 60/680.
191 See the previous note.

My righteous servants in their absence, do not envy any of My servants ..."
Solomon exclaimed: "O my Lord, this is enough for me!" Moses – peace be upon him – saw a man next to God's throne and grew envious of him. He asked: "Thanks to what [has he acquired that position]?" Someone answered him: "[Thanks to] his not being envious of people on account of the favors bestowed upon them by God!" It is said that the envier feels perplexed whenever he sees [God's] beneficence [towards others] and rejoices when he sees somebody [committing] a fault. It is said: "If you wish to be safe from the envier, conceal your affairs from him." It is said: "The envier is angry at one who has no sin and stingy with what he does not possess." It is also said: "Beware of exerting yourself in trying to win the affection of one who envies you, for he will never accept your good deeds." It is also said: "Whenever God Most High wishes to give power over [His] servant to an enemy without mercy, He gives it to someone who envies him."

They recite [the following verse]:

> What can say more about man's misfortune
> When you see those who used to envy him
> now have pity on him!

They also recite:

> One can hope that every enmity will eventually be terminated
> Except for the enmity of one who is envious of you.

Ibn al-Muʿtazz recited:[192]

> Tell the envier who is about to breathe out a complaint
> O you who have wronged others, [how can] someone complain about the wrongs done to him?!

They also recite:

> When God wants to make public a virtue that has been hidden
> He bestows upon it the tongue of the envier.

Among the other blameworthy character traits of the human soul is the habit of backbiting.//229

Backbiting (ghiba)

God – may He be exalted – said: "Do not backbite one another; would any of you like to eat the flesh of his brother dead?"[193]

---

192 ʿAbdallah b. al-Muʿtazz (assassinated in 296/908), was son of the thirteenth caliph of the ʿAbbasid dynasty. He distinguished himself as an accomplished poet and literary critic. Upon his father's death he was proclaimed caliph and killed on the same day, giving birth to the famous saying "the caliph of one hour".
193 Q. 49:12.

Abu Saʿid Muhammad b. Ibrahim al-Ismaʿili informed us: Abu Bakr Muhammad b. al-Husayn b. al-Hasan b. al-Khalil informed us: ʿAli b. al-Hasan told us: Ishaq b. ʿIsa b. Bint Dawud b. Abi Hind told us: Muhammad b. Abi Humayd told us on the authority of Musa b. Wardan, on the authority of Abu Hurayra, who said that when a man who had been sitting with the Messenger of God – may God bless and greet him – rose [and left], someone in the gathering said: "How feeble this man is!" The Messenger – may God praise and greet him – retorted: "You have eaten your brother [alive], [when] you backbite him!" God revealed to Moses – peace be upon him: "He who dies after having repented of backbiting will be the last one to enter Paradise and he who dies persisting in it will be the first one to enter the hellfire."

ʿAwf said: "I came to Ibn Sirin[194] and began to discuss [the misdeeds of] al-Hajjaj.[195] Ibn Sirin told me: 'God Most High is a just arbiter. He takes against al-Hajjaj as much as He takes for him. As for you, if you were to meet God – may He be glorious and magnificent – tomorrow, the smallest sin you have committed will be much more grievous for you than the greatest sin committed by al-Hajjaj!'" It is said that Ibrahim b. Adham was invited to a dinner. He attended it. They were discussing a man who did not come. Some of them said: "He is boring!" Ibrahim said: "This is what my soul has done to me! I came to a party where people are slandered in their absence." He left and would not eat for three days after that.

It is said: "The backbiter is like a man who has installed a catapult and started to shoot his good deeds in all directions. He backbites one who is in Khurasan, another who is in Syria, one who is in the Hijaz, another who is in the land of the Turks. He thus scatters his good deeds, and when he finally finds himself standing [before God], he has nothing with him." It is said that a certain servant of God will be given his ledger [of deeds] on the Day of Judgement. He will see not a single good deed in it and will ask [God]: "Where are my prayers, my fasting and my acts of obedience?" He will be told: "All your good works were invalidated due to your backbiting!" It is said: "God will cut in half the sins of a man who has suffered from backbiting." Sufyan b. al-Husayn said: "I was sitting with Iyas b. Muʿawiyya and spoke badly of a man who was not there. Sufyan asked me: 'Have you taken part in the [holy] war against the Turks and the Byzantines this year?' I answered: 'No, I have not.' He said: 'So, the Turks and the Byzantines are safe from you, while your Muslim brother is not!'"//230 It is said that [on the Day of Judgement] a certain man will be given his ledger [of deeds] and will find in it the good deeds he never did. He will be told: "This is your reward for people's backbiting against you of which you were not aware!"

---

194 A famous *hadith* collector and interpreter of dreams, who was renowned for his piety. He died in 110/728.
195 The Umayyad general, who was notorious for his "ruthless efficiency" and cruelty. He died in 95/714.

Someone asked Sufyan al-Thawri about the saying of the Prophet – may God bless and greet him – "Verily, God hates the people of the house of flesheaters." Sufyan responded: "That is, the ones who backbite; as if they eat the other people's flesh." Someone mentioned backbiting in the presence of ʿAbdallah b. al-Mubarak. He commented: "If I were ever to slander anyone in his absence, I would slander my parents, for they are more deserving of my good deeds than anybody else." Yahya b. Muʿadh said: "Let each believer benefit from you in the following three ways: if you cannot be of help to him, at least do not harm him; if you cannot make him happy, at least do not make him sad; if you cannot praise him, at least do not blame him." Someone told al-Hasan al-Basri: "So-and-so slandered you behind your back." He sent that man a plateful of sweetmeats, saying: "It has come to my attention that you have lavished your good deeds upon me, so I would like to recompense you."

ʿAli b. Ahmad al-Ahwazi informed me: Ahmad b. ʿUbayd al-Basri informed us: Ahmad b. ʿAmr al-Qatawani informed us: Sahl b. ʿUthman al-ʿAskari told us: al-Rabiʿ b. Badr told us on the authority of Aban, on the authority of Anas b. Malik that the Messenger of God – may God bless and greet him – said: "He who has renounced the veil of shame, cannot be an object of backbiting." I heard Hamza b. Yusuf al-Sahmi say: I heard Abu Tahir Muhammad b. Usayd al-Raqqi say: I heard Jaʿfar b. Muhammad b. Nusayr say: al-Junayd said: "Once I was sitting in the al-Shuniziyya mosque, waiting for the bier of a newly deceased to arrive, so that I could pray over him. The people of Baghdad were sitting there according to their [social] ranks waiting for the funeral bier to arrive. [Suddenly] I saw a poor man who looked like an ascetic begging from people. I thought to myself: 'If this one would work to sustain himself, it would be better for him.' When I returned home after that, I engaged in my usual routine of reciting a night litany, weeping, praying and so on. However, all my litanies weighed heavily on me. So I just sat there sleepless. Then my eyes closed and, in my dream, I saw that poor man spread upon a table [before me] and I heard voices saying: 'Eat his flesh, for you have slandered him!' The real state [of affairs] was revealed to me and I said: 'No, I did not slander him. I only said something to myself.'//231 I was told: 'This sort of thing is not tolerated from the likes of you. Go and ask his forgiveness!' So in the morning I left my house and began to go around until I saw him at a place with running water where he was picking up leaves from vegetables that were being washed there. I greeted him. He responded saying: 'Abu ʾl-Qasim you have returned [to this again]?' I said: 'No!' He said: 'Then may God forgive both of us!' "

I heard Shaykh Abu ʿAbd al-Rahman al-Sulami – may God have mercy on him – say: I heard Abu Tahir al-Isfaraini say: I heard Abu Jaʿfar al-Balkhi say: "There used to be a man from Balkh[196] who exerted himself in worshiping God. However, he constantly slandered people behind their backs, saying, 'So-and-so

---

196 An area in present day Afghanistan.

is like this, So-and-so is like that', and so on. One day I saw him coming out from a place frequented by effeminate washers. I asked him what had happened to him. He responded: 'My speaking ill of other people has brought this upon me. I was attracted to one of them, and now I have to serve them because of him. All of my old [pious] deeds have vanished, so pray God to forgive me!'"

Contentment (qanaʿa)

God Most High said: "And whosoever does a righteous deed, be it male or female, and is a believer, we shall assuredly give him a goodly life to live."[197] Many commentators say: "The goodly life in this world means contentment."

Shaykh Abu ʿAbd al-Rahman al-Sulami informed us: Abu ʿAmr Muhammad b. Jaʿfar b. Matar said: Muhammad b. Musa al-Hulwani told us: ʿAbdallah b. Ibrahim al-Ghifari told us on the authority of al-Munkadir b. Muhammad, on the authority of his father, on the authority of Jabir b. ʿAbdallah, who said: "The Messenger of God – may God bless and greet him – said: 'Contentment is the treasure that cannot be exhausted.'" Abu ʾl-Hasan al-Ahwazi informed us: Ahmad b. ʿUbaydallah al-Basri told us: ʿAbdallah b. Ayyub al-Qirabi said: Abu ʾl-Rabiʿa al-Zahrani told us: Ismaʿil b. Zakariya//232 told us on the authority of Abu ʾl-Rajaʾ, on the authority of Burd b. Sinan, on the authority of Makhul, on the authority of Wathila b. al-Asqaʿ, on the authority of Abu Hurayra – may God be pleased with him – that the Messenger of God – may God bless and greet him – said: "Be scrupulous and you will be the greatest worshiper of [all] people; be content and you will be the most thankful of [all] people; wish for other people what you wish for yourself, and you will be a faithful [servant]; be a good neighbor to those who live near you and you will be a [true] believer. And laugh little, for much laughter murders the heart!" Bishr al-Hafi said: "Contentment is an angel who dwells only in the believing heart."

They say: "The poor are dead except for those whom God Most High has revived with the power of contentment." I heard Muhammad b. al-Husayn say: I heard ʿAbdallah b. Muhammad al-Shaʿrani say: I heard Ishaq b. Ibrahim b. Abi Hassan al-Anmati say: I heard Ahmad b. Abi ʾl-Hawari say: I heard Sulayman al-Darani say: "Contentment relates to satisfaction (rida) in the same way scrupulousness relates to renunciation [of the world] (zuhd) – that is, contentment is the beginning of satisfaction and scrupulousness is the beginning of renunciation." They say that contentment is to keep your calm in the absence of things that you are accustomed to. Abu Bakr al-Maraghi said: "The intelligent person is one who deals with this world with contentment and deferment, while at the same time aspiring and hastening to the Hereafter and exercising his knowledge and striving in what concerns his faith."

Abu ʿAbdallah b. Khafif said: "Contentment is not to seek what you have lost and to be satisfied with what you have." It is said that the meaning of God's

---

197 Q. 16:97; 16:99, according to Arberry's translation.

words: "God shall provide them with a fair provision"[198] is contentment. Muhammad b. ʿAli al-Tirmidhi said: "Contentment is one's satisfaction with what has been allotted to him [by God]." It is also said that contentment is finding sufficiency in what one has and not aspiring to that which one does not have. Wahb said: "Greatness and wealth went out seeking a companion. They met with contentment and decided to settle down [and seek no more]." It is said: "For him whose contentment is copious [fatty] every broth tastes good. And he who turns to God Most High//233 in every situation will be rewarded by God with contentment." It is said that one day Abu Hazim passed by a butcher, who had some fatty meat. The butcher told him: "Abu Hazim, take some of it, for it is fatty!" He answered that he had no money. The butcher told him: "I will give you a postponement [on your payment]!" Abu Hazim answered: "My soul will give me a still better postponement than you!" Someone asked a Sufi: "Who of mankind is most content?" He answered: "He who is the most helpful to others, while being the least burdensome for them." In the Psalms it is said: "He who is content is rich, even when he goes hungry." It is said that God Most High placed five things in five different places: greatness in obedience, humiliation in disobedience, awe [of God] in the night vigil, wisdom into the empty stomach and wealth in contentment.

I heard Shaykh Abu ʿAbd al-Rahman al-Sulami say: I heard Nasr b. Muhammad say: I heard Sulayman b. Abi Sulayman say: I heard Abu ʾl-Qasim b. Abi Nizar say: I heard Ibrahim al-Maristani say: "Avenge yourself on your greed by contentment as you avenge yourself on your enemy." Dhu ʾl-Nun al-Misri said: "One who is content receives respite from other people and rises above his peers." They say: "One who is content finds rest from [his] labors[199] and rises above all." Al-Kattani said: "One who sells desire for contentment gains greatness and manly honor (*muruwa*)." They say: "One whose eyes aspire after what other people have is gripped by constant sadness and distress." They recite [the following verse]:

> It is better for a young man (*fata*) to remain noble, but hungry
> Than to experience a day of disgrace
> that brings him wealth!

It is said that someone saw a wise man eating vegetables discarded at a spring. He remarked: "If you were to be in the service of the Sultan, you wouldn't have to eat this." The wise man replied: "If you were content with this, you wouldn't have to serve the Sultan!"//234 It is said: "As the eagle flies high in the air neither the hunter's sight nor his desire [to catch it] can reach it. Only when it craves a piece of carrion suspended [in the hunter's] snare does it descend from its height and get entangled in the snare's web." When Moses – peace be upon him

---

198 Q. 22:58; 22:57, according to Arberry's translation.
199 Or "his preoccupations".

– breathed out words of greed, saying: "If thou hadst wished, thou couldst have taken a wage for that",[200] al-Khidr told him: "This is the parting of ways between me and thee."[201] They say that when Moses uttered those words, a gazelle appeared before them. They were both hungry. The side [of the gazelle that] faced Moses – peace be upon him – was not roasted, while the one that faced al-Khidr was roasted.

It is said that the words of God Most High – "Surely the pious shall be in bliss"[202] – refer to contentment [with one's portion] in this life, whereas [God's words] "And the wicked are in fire"[203] refer to desire for [the delights of] this life. It is also said that the words of God Most High – "The freeing of a slave"[204] – refer to setting oneself free from the humiliation of greed. It is said that the words of God Most High – "People of the [Prophet's] House, God only desires to put away from you abomination" – mean avarice and greed, whereas [His words] – "and to cleanse you in the most perfect way"[205] – denote [cleansing] by means of generosity and altruism. It is said that the words of God Most High – [quoting Solomon, who said] "Give me a kingdom such as may not befall anyone after me"[206] – mean "Give me a rank of contentment which will be unique to me and no one else, so that I shall always be satisfied with Your decree." And they say regarding God's words – "Assuredly I will chastise him [the hoopoe][207] with a terrible chastisement"[208] – that they mean "I will deprive him of contentment and try him with greed." [Solomon] wanted to say: "I will ask God Most High to do this to him [the hoopoe]."

Someone asked Abu Yazid al-Bistami: "How have you achieved what you have achieved?"//235 He answered: "I gathered all the [good] things of this world, tied them together with the rope of contentment, placed them in the catapult of sincere striving, and cast them into the sea of despair. Then I rested." I heard Muhammad b. ʿAbdallah al-Sufi[209] say: I heard Muhammad b. Farhan at Samarra say: I heard my uncle ʿAbd al-Wahhab say: "During the days of the pilgrimage season I was sitting with al-Junayd. He was surrounded by a large group of Persians and Arabs who were born in foreign lands. A man came with five hundred *dinars* and put them in front of him saying: 'Distribute them among these poor people.' Al-Junayd asked: 'Do you have more?' The man answered: 'Yes, I have plenty of these.' 'Do you want to have more?' asked al-Junayd. He

---

200 Q. 18:77.
201 Q. 18:78.
202 Q. 82:13.
203 Q. 82:14.
204 Q. 90:13.
205 Q. 33:33.
206 Q. 38:35; 38:34 in Arberry's translation.
207 A reference to the hoopoe, who delivered to Solomon a message about the queen of Sheba.
208 Q. 27:21.
209 Or "al-Sadafi".

answered: 'Yes.' Al-Junayd told him: 'Then take them back, for you are more in need of them than we are!' And he did not accept them."

Trust in God (*tawakkul*)

God – may He be great and Exalted – said: "And whosoever puts his trust in God, He shall suffice him."[210] He also said: "And in God let the believers put all their trust."[211] [Finally,] He said: "Put all your trust in God, if you are believers."[212]

The imam Abu Bakr Muhammad b. al-Hasan b. Furak[213] said: ʿAbdallah b. Jaʿfar b. Ahmad al-Isbahani told us: Yunus b. Habib b. ʿAbd al-Qahir told us: Abu Dawud al-Tayalisi told us: Hammad b. Maslama[214] told us on the authority of ʿAsim b. Bahdala, on the authority of Zirr b. Hubaysh, on the authority of ʿAbdallah b. Masʿud – may God be pleased with him – that: "The Messenger of God – may God bless and greet him – said: 'I was shown all the [religious] communities at the time of the pilgrimage. I saw that my community had filled both the valley and the plain [of ʿArafat]. I was pleased with their great number and their appearance. I was asked: "Are you satisfied?" I answered: "Yes."' [A voice] said [to me]: 'Among these there are seventy thousand who will enter Paradise without reckoning. They have never allowed themselves to be treated by cauterization, nor to divine the future by [observing] birds' flight, nor have resorted to [the magician's] charms. They have put their trust in God alone.' [When the Prophet said this] ʿUkkasha b. Muhsin al-Asadi stood up and requested: 'Messenger of God, pray to God that He would make me one of them!' The Messenger of God replied, saying: 'O God, make him one of them!'//236 Another person stood up and asked: 'Pray to God that He would make me one of them!' The Messenger – may God bless and greet him – answered: "ʿUkkasha has preceded you in this!'"

I heard ʿAbdallah b. Yusuf al-Isbahani say: I heard Abu Nasr al-Sarraj say: I heard Abu Bakr al-Wajihi say: I heard Abu ʿAli al-Rudhbari say: I asked ʿAmr b. Sinan to tell me a story about Sahl b. ʿAbdallah [al-Tustari].[215] ʿAmr said that Sahl once said: "One who trusts God is distinguished by three signs: he does not ask, does not refuse [when given], and does not hold on [to what was given to him]." I heard Shaykh Abu ʿAbd al-Rahman al-Sulami – may God have mercy on him – say: I heard Mansur b. ʿAbdallah say: I heard Abu ʿAbdallah al-Shirazi say: "I heard Abu Musa al-Daylubi say that someone asked Abu Yazid al-Bistami about trust in God. He, in turn, asked me what I thought about it. I answered: 'My companions say: "Even if wild beasts and poisonous snakes were all around you,

---

210 Q. 65:3.
211 Q. 14:11; 14:14 in Arberry's translation.
212 Q. 5:23; 5:26 in Arberry's translation.
213 A famous Ashʿari theologian and teacher of al-Qushayri, who resided in Nishapur. He died in 406/1015.
214 Or "b. al-Salama".
215 On him, see *IM*, pp. 83–88 and Böwering, *Mystical Vision*.

your innermost heart would still not be perturbed!'" Abu Yazid answered: 'Yes, this is close. But if you were to [observe] the people of Paradise enjoying themselves in its gardens and the people of Hell being tortured by its fires, and you would give preference to one over the other, you would leave the realm of trust in God altogether.'" Sahl b. ʿAbdallah said: "The beginning of trust in God is when the servant places himself before God as a dead corpse is placed before the washer of the dead, who turns it however he wishes, while the body has no moves nor will of its own." Hamdun al-Qassar said: "Trust in God is taking refuge in God Most High."

I heard Muhammad b. al-Husayn say: I heard Abu Bakr Muhammad b. Ahmad al-Balkhi say: I heard Muhammad b. Hamid say: I heard Ahmad b. Khadrawayh say: "A man asked Hatim al-Asamm: 'From where do you get your provisions?' He answered: 'To God belong the treasures of the heavens and of the earth, but the hypocrites do not understand.'"[216]

Know that the place of trust is in the heart. Outward action does not necessarily contradict trust in the heart. Once the servant has ascertained that determination comes from God Most High, he realizes that any hardship he experiences is pre-determined [by God] and any success he may have is also facilitated by God. ʿAli b. Ahmad b. ʿAbdan informed us: Ahmad b. ʿUbayd al-Basri told us: Ghaylan b. ʿAbd al-Samad told us: Ismaʿil b. Masʿud al-Jahdari told us: Khalid b. Yahya told us: "My uncle al-Mughira b. Abi Qurra recounted on the authority of Anas b. Malik that a certain man came [to the Prophet] riding his she-camel//237 and asked him: 'Messenger of God, should I leave her loose and put my trust in God?' The Prophet responded: 'Tie her up and trust in God!'"

Ibrahim al-Khawwas said: "He who trusts in God when dealing with himself will also trust God when dealing with others." Bishr al-Hafi said: "One Sufi said: 'I have put my trust in God [and failed].' However, he lied to God Most High. If he were indeed to put his trust in God, he would have been content with what God did to him." Someone asked Yahya b. Muʿadh [al-Razi]: "When can a man trust God?" He answered: "When he is content to have God as his trustee."

I heard Shaykh Abu ʿAbd al-Rahman al-Sulami – may God have mercy on him – say: I heard Muhammad b. ʿAli b. al-Husayn say: I heard ʿAbdallah b. Muhammad b. al-Samit say: I heard Ibrahim al-Khawwas say: "As I was journeying in the desert I heard someone speak. I looked around and saw a Bedouin walking along. He told me: 'Ibrahim, trust in God resides with us [people of the desert], so stay with us until your trust has become sound. Don't you see that you are driven to cities by the food that you hope to find there? Therefore, stop pinning your hopes on cities and put your trust in God instead!'" I also heard him [al-Sulami] say: I heard Muhammad b. Ahmad al-Farisi say: I heard Muhammad b. ʿAtaʾ say that someone asked him about the true essence of trust in God. He answered: "It is when anxiety about things of this world does

---

216 Q. 63:7.

not prevail over you despite your dire need of them and when your reliance upon God prevails in you despite your dependence on such things."

I heard Abu Hatim al-Sijistani say: I heard Abu Nasr al-Sarraj say: "The condition for trust in God is what Abu Turab al-Nakhshabi had in mind when he said: 'To prostrate your body in worship, to attach your heart to lordship, and to find solace in sufficiency; when you are given, you are thankful and when you are denied, you persevere.'" Dhu 'l-Nun said: "Trust in God is to give up planning for yourself and to abandon [reliance on your own] power and ability. The servant is capable of trust in God only when he has realized that God – may He be exalted – knows and sees his condition." I heard Muhammad b. al-Husayn say: I heard Abu 'l-Faraj al-Warathani say: I heard Ahmad b. Muhammad al-Qirmisini say: I heard al-Kattani say: I heard Abu Ja'far b. Abi 'l-Faraj say: "Once I saw a villain (*shatir*) nicknamed "A'isha's Camel' being whipped. I asked him: 'When will this lashing be easier for you?' He answered://238 'When the one on whose account I am being whipped will see me.'" I heard 'Abdallah b. Muhammad say: I heard al-Husayn b. Mansur say to Ibrahim al-Khawwas: "What have you achieved throughout all these travels of yours and your wanderings in the deserts?" He answered: "I have persevered in my trust in God, disciplining my soul thereby." Al-Husayn [b. Mansur] asked him: "So you have spent your entire life taking care of your inner self. What about annihilating your inner self through unifying it with God (*tawhid*)?"

I heard Abu Hatim al-Sijistani say: I heard Abu Nasr al-Sarraj say: "Trust in God is what Abu 'Ali al-Daqqaq once said – that is, 'Limiting your livelihood's worth to one day only and giving up concern about what will happen [to you] tomorrow.'" Or, as Sahl b. 'Abdallah said: "Putting yourself in the hands of God, so that he would do with you what He wants." I heard Shaykh Abu 'Abd al-Rahman al-Sulami – may God have mercy on him – say: I heard Muhammad b. Ja'far b. Muhammad say: I heard Abu Bakr al-Bardha'i say: I heard Abu Ya'qub al-Nahrajuri say: "Trust in God in its perfect essence manifested itself in what happened to Abraham. [As he was flying through the air]²¹⁷ he told Gabriel [who had offered him his help]: 'No, not from you!' For his [Abraham's] self had been annihilated in God [to such an extent that] he could see no one else but God alone – may He be great and exalted!"

I also heard him [al-Sulami] say: I heard Sa'id b. Ahmad b. Muhammad say: I heard Muhammad b. Ahmad b. Sahl say: I heard Sa'id b. 'Uthman al-Khayyat say: I heard Dhu 'l-Nun al-Misri say, when asked about trust in God: "Divesting oneself from all masters [other than God] and cutting one's attachment to all causes [other than God]." The inquirer asked him: "Tell me more!" Dhu 'l-Nun responded: "Throwing oneself into worship and ridding oneself of any pretension to lordship." I also heard him say: I heard 'Abdallah b. Munazil say: I heard Hamdun al-Qassar say, when asked about trust in God: "It is as if you had ten

---

217 According to the Biblical and Qur'anic tradition, Abraham was thrown onto a bonfire by his infidel persecutors only to be miraculously rescued by the Archangel Gabriel.

thousand *dirhams* in your possession and one *daniq*²¹⁸ worth of debt, yet you would not be able to rest easy [fearing] that you might die without having this debt settled.//239 Or as if you had a debt of ten thousand *dirhams* and no means to pay it back [after your death], yet you would not despair of God Most High's settling it for you." Someone asked Abu ʿAbdallah al-Qurashi about trust in God. He answered: "Holding on to God in every state." The inquirer asked: "Tell me more!" Al-Qurashi continued: "Giving up reliance on any cause that leads to another cause so as to render God the sole possessor of all causes." Sahl b. ʿAbdallah said: "Trust in God is the [spiritual] state of the Prophet – may God bless and greet him – while earning is his custom (*sunna*). Whoever adheres to his [the Prophet's] state, will never depart from his custom." Abu Saʿid al-Kharraz said: "Trust in God is agitation without rest and rest without agitation." It is also said: "Trust in God is when abundance and scarcity are one and the same to you." Ibn Masruq said: "Trust in God is to surrender oneself to the rule of divine commands and decrees."

I heard Muhammad b. al-Husayn say: I heard ʿAbdallah al-Razi say: I heard Abu ʿUthman al-Hiri say: "Trust in God is to be satisfied with and rely on God Most High." I also heard him [Muhammad b. al-Husayn] say: I heard Muhammad b. Muhammad b. Ghalib relate on the authority of al-Husayn b. Mansur, who said: "The true trust in God is when one does not eat anything in a land where there might be someone more deserving of food than him." I also heard him say: I heard ʿAbdallah b. ʿAli say: I heard Mansur b. Ahmad al-Harbi say: Ibn Abi Shaykh related to us that he heard ʿUmar b. Sinan say: "Once Ibrahim al-Khawwas passed us by. We asked him to tell us about the most wondrous thing he had ever seen during his travels. He answered: "[It is when] I met al-Khidr – peace be on him – and he requested my companionship, yet I was afraid that I might compromise my trust in God by relying on him. So I left him."

Someone asked Sahl b. ʿAbdallah about trust in God. He answered: "It is when a heart lives with God Most High alone without attaching itself to anything else." I heard the master Abu ʿAli al-Daqqaq – may God have mercy on him – say: "The one who puts his trust in God goes through three stages: trust in God, [self-]surrender [to God], and relegating [one's affairs to God]. The one who practices trust in God relies on His promise [of sustenance]; the one who surrenders himself [to God] is content with his knowledge [of God]; and the one who relegates his affairs [to God] is satisfied with His decree."//240 I also heard him [al-Daqqaq] say: "Trust in God is the beginning, [self-]surrender is the middle and relegating [one's affairs to God] is the end." Someone asked al-Daqqaq about trust in God. He answered: "It is eating without appetite." Yahya b. Muʿadh said: "Putting on woolen clothing is [setting up] shop; discoursing about renunciation is a profession; and traveling with caravans [of pilgrims] is ostentation. All these are nothing but attachments [to this world]."

---

218 A coin worth one-sixth of the *dirham*.

A man came to al-Shibli to complain to him about his large family. Al-Shibli retorted: "Go back to your house and expel from it anyone whose sustenance is not obligatory for God Most High!" I heard Shaykh Abu ʿAbd al-Rahman al-Sulami – may God have mercy on him – say: I heard ʿAbdallah b. ʿAli say: I heard Ahmad b. ʿAtaʾ say: I learned from Muhammad b. al-Husayn that Sahl b. ʿAbdallah said: "Whoever condemns stirring oneself [to earn a livelihood] condemns the Prophet's custom; and whoever condemns trust in God [to provide for him] condemns faith." I also heard him [al-Sulami] say: I heard Ahmad b. ʿAli b. Jaʿfar say: I heard Jaʿfar al-Khuldi say: Ibrahim al-Khawwas said: "I was on my way to Mecca, when I met a wild-looking person. I said to myself: 'Is this a man or a jinn?' He answered: 'I am a jinn.' 'Where are you headed?' I asked him. He said that he was going to Mecca. I asked him: 'Do you travel without any provisions?' He said: 'Yes! Among us, too, are those who travel putting their trust in God.' I asked him: 'What, then, is trust in God?' He answered: 'Taking [your provisions] from God Most High.'" I heard him [al-Sulami] say: I heard Abu ʾl-ʿAbbas al-Baghdadi say: I heard al-Farghani say: "Ibrahim al-Khawwas excelled in the art of trust and attained a great sophistication in it. However, he never parted with a needle and thread, a [begging] bowl,[219] and a pair of scissors. Someone asked him: 'Abu Ishaq, why do you carry all these things, while you abstain from all other things?' He answered: 'Things like these do not contradict trust in God, for God – may He be exalted – has made certain rules obligatory for everyone. Thus, a *dervish* has but one piece of clothing, which may be torn. If he does not have a needle and thread, his private parts may be exposed and his prayer becomes invalid;//241 and if he has no bowl, his ablutions may be corrupted. Therefore, if you see a poor man who has neither bowl nor needle and thread, be wary of the perfection of his prayer.'"

I heard the master Abu ʿAli al-Daqqaq – may God have mercy on him – say: "Trust in God is the characteristic of the [ordinary] believers; surrendering oneself to God is the characteristic of the elect; and relegating [one's affairs to God] is the characteristic of those who have achieved unity [with God]. [In other words], trust in God is the characteristic of the common folk; surrendering is the characteristic of the elect; and relegating is the characteristic of the elect of the elect." I also heard him [al-Daqqaq] say: "Trust is the characteristic of the friends of God (*awliyaʾ*); surrendering is the characteristic of Abraham – peace be upon him – and relegating is the characteristic of our prophet Muhammad – may God bless and greet him."

I heard Muhammad b. al-Husayn say: I heard Abu ʾl-ʿAbbas al-Baghdadi say: I heard Muhammad b. ʿAbdallah al-Farghani say: I heard Abu Jaʿfar al-Haddad say: "For more than ten years I lived in the state of trust in God, while working in the bazaar (*suq*). Every day I would receive my wages, but I did not use this money even to pay for a drink of water or for the admission fee to a

---

219 A bowl that could be used for both begging and drinking.

public bath. Instead, I would bring this money to the poor folks who resided at the al-Shuniziyya mosque. In this way I preserved my state [of trust]."

I heard him [Muhammad b. al-Husayn] say: I heard Abu Bakr Muhammad b. ʿAbdallah b. Shadhan say: I heard al-Khawwas say: I heard al-Husayn, brother of Sinan, say: "I made fourteen pilgrimages [to Mecca] in the state of trust, barefoot. Whenever a thorn entered my foot I would remind myself that I had imposed trust in God upon myself, so I would rub it [the thorn] against the ground and walk on." I also heard him say: I heard Muhammad b. ʿAbdallah the Preacher (*waʿiz*) say: I heard Khayr al-Nassaj say: I heard Abu Hamza [al-Baghdadi] say: "When I have a vow to practice trust in God, I'd be ashamed before God Most High to enter the desert with a full stomach lest my journey should rely on my prior satiety with which I had equipped myself in advance."

Someone asked Hamdun al-Qassar about trust in God. He answered: "This is a stage that I have not reached yet. How can one who has not yet perfected his faith speak of trust in God?" They say that the one who trusts God is similar to an infant, who knows nothing but his mother's breast, which he always seeks. Likewise, one who trusts God is always led to his Lord Most High. One of the Sufis related: "I was in the desert walking before a caravan, when I saw someone in front of me. I hurried to catch up with him and saw a woman with a staff in her hand walking slowly. I thought that she was exhausted, so I reached into //242 my pocket and brought out twenty *dirhams*. I told her: 'Take this and wait until the caravan catches up with you. You should then pay your fare with this money and catch up with me in the evening, so that I could arrange everything for you.' She said, as she raised her hand in the air like this and suddenly [I saw] *dinars* in her palm: 'You take *dirhams* out of your pocket (*jayb*) and I take *dinars* out of the unseen (*ghayb*).'"

Once Abu Sulayman al-Darani saw a man in Mecca who would live on nothing but some water from the Zamzam well.[220] Many days elapsed. One day Sulayman asked him: "If the water of Zamzam were to dry up, what would you drink?" The man jumped to his feet, kissed Sulayman's head and said: "May God give you a good reward! You have guided me aright, for I have nearly become a worshiper of Zamzam over the past few days!" Ibrahim al-Khawwas related: "Once on my way to Syria I saw a young man of good manners. He asked me: 'Would you like a companion?' When I told him that I was hungry, he replied: 'Whenever you are hungry, I will be hungry as well!' We had stayed together for four days, until something was given to us and I invited him to partake of it with me. He responded saying: 'I have made a vow not to accept anything from intermediaries.' I told him: 'You are meticulous indeed [in your trust in God]!' He answered: 'None of your idle words! The stern judge is watching [us]. What have you to do with trust in God?' He then added: 'The least [portion of] trust is when you encounter sources of satisfying your needs but your soul aspires toward nothing but Him Who holds all sufficiency!'"

---

220 The sacred well located in the Meccan sanctuary.

They say that trust in God is negating doubts and relegating [all your affairs to] the King of Kings. They say that once a group of men came to al-Junayd – may God have mercy on him – and asked: "Where should we seek our sustenance?" He answered: "If you know where it is, go seek it there!" They asked: "Do we have to ask God for it?" He told them: "If you know that He has forgotten you, remind Him!" They asked: "So should we go home [and sit there] trusting in God?" He answered: "Testing [God's generosity] leads to doubt." "So, what's the trick?" asked they. "The trick is to give up all tricks!" answered al-Junayd. Abu Sulayman al-Darani told Ahmad b. Abi ʾl-Hawari:[221]//243 "Ahmad, the roads to the Hereafter are many. Your master knows many of them except this blessed one [named] trust in God. I have not caught even a whiff of it." It is said that trust in God is to be sure of what is in the hand of God Most High and to despair of what is in the hands of people. It is also said that trust in God is emptying one's innermost heart of any thought of how one can secure one's livelihood.

Someone asked al-Muhasibi – may God have mercy on him – about someone who places his trust in God: "Can he still have any desire?" He answered: "Thoughts and concerns that spring from his [human] nature still occur in him, yet they can do him no harm, for in his abandonment of desire he is reinforced by despairing of what is in the hands of people." It is said that when al-Nuri was starving in the desert, he heard a voice say: "Which thing do you love more: means [of obtaining sustenance] or sufficiency [with what you have]?" He answered: "There's no goal higher than sufficiency!" And he spent seventeen more days without eating anything. Abu ʿAli al-Rudhbari said: "If after five days the poor man[222] says, 'I am hungry', send him to the bazaar and tell him to work and earn [his living]." Abu Turab al-Nakhshabi once saw a Sufi, who after having fasted for three days, stretched his hand to a melon rind. He exclaimed: "Sufism is not for you! Keep to the bazaar!" Abu Yaʿqub al-Aqtaʿ al-Basri said: "Once I went hungry for ten days in the Sacred Precinct [of Mecca]. I felt very weak and my soul began to tempt me. I went to the valley to find something that would abate my weakness. Suddenly, I saw a discarded turnip lying on the ground. I picked it up. I felt that uneasiness entered my heart, as if someone were trying to say to me: 'You have gone hungry for ten days and, in the end, you found your happiness in a rotten turnip!' I threw it away, went to the [Sacred] Mosque and sat there. Suddenly, I saw a non-Arab man who sat in front of me and put before me a satchel, saying: 'This is for you.' 'Why have you chosen me?' I asked him. He responded: 'For ten days we were at sea, and our ship was about to go under. Each of us made a vow that, if God Most High rescued us, he would give something as alms to the first person his eyes fell on among the inhabitants of Mecca. You are the first person I have met.'//244 I asked him to open the satchel. When he opened it [I saw] fine Egyptian cakes, shelled almonds, and cubes of

---

221 On these Syrian Sufis, see *IM*, pp. 36–39.
222 That is, a Sufi.

sugar. I took a handful of each and told him: 'Take the rest to your kids. It is my gift to them. I have taken enough.' Then I said to myself: 'Your provisions were on their way to you for ten days, and you were looking for it in the empty valley!'"

I [al-Qushayri] heard Shaykh Abu ʿAbd al-Rahman al-Sulami say: I heard Abu Bakr al-Razi say: "I was with Mimshadh al-Dinawari, when talk of debts came up. He said: 'Once I had a debt, which weighed heavy on my heart. In my dream I heard a voice say to me: "O miser! You have borrowed such-and-such amount from us. Borrow [more]! The borrowing is on you and the giving is on us!" From then on I never had any financial dealings with either a grocer or a butcher!'"

It is recounted that Bunan the Porter (*al-hammal*) said: "Once I set out on a journey from Egypt to Mecca with some provisions. A woman approached me and said: 'Bunan, you are a porter. You carry [your provisions] on your back, because you do not believe that God will provide for you!' So I threw my provisions away. I continued on my journey without eating anything for three days. Then I found an anklet on the road and said to myself: 'I will carry it until I come upon its owner. Maybe he will give me something when I return it to him.' Then the same woman appeared before me and told me: 'So now you are a merchant! You say: "Maybe I will come upon its owner, so that I could take something from him!"' She then threw a few coins at me, saying: 'Spend them!' They lasted almost until I reached Mecca." It is related that Bunan was in need of a slave girl to serve him. His need came to the attention of his friends, who collected her price for him and told him: "Here's the money. A group [of slaves] will come to you and you will purchase the one who suits you most." When the group arrived, the opinions of all agreed on a certain woman and they told him [Bunan]: "This one is right for you!" They [the friends] asked her owner what her price was. He answered that she was not for sale. When they pleaded with him, he said: "This woman belongs to Bunan the Porter. A woman from Samarqand wants to present her to him." So she was brought to Bunan. She told him [her] story.

I heard Muhammad b. al-Husayn say: I heard Muhammad b. al-Hasan al-Makhzumi say: Ahmad b. Muhammad b. Salih told us: Muhammad b. ʿAbdun told us: al-Hasan al-Khayyat told us: "I was with Bishr al-Hafi, when a group of strangers came to his house and greeted him. He asked them where they were from.//245 They answered: 'We are from Syria. We have come to greet you on our way to the pilgrimage.' He told them: 'May God Most High reward you!' They invited him to go with them. He said: 'On three conditions: we do not carry any [provisions] with us; we do not ask [anyone] for anything; and if someone gives something to us, we shall not accept it.' They answered: 'As for not carrying anything with us, yes; as for not asking for anything, yes; however, as for not accepting anything, we cannot do this.' He told them: 'You should set out with trust in [God's] providing for the pilgrims!' He then told [me]: 'Hasan, there are three types of the poor. First, the poor one who does not ask and, if given anything, would not accept it; this one belongs to those who subsist by [their] spirits. Second, the poor one who does not ask for anything, but, if given anything, would accept it; for such people tables [of food] will be set in the precincts of Paradise. Third, the poor one who asks for something and, if given, accepts only the bare minimum of it; his penance is his benefaction."

Someone said to Habib al-'Ajami: "Why did you give up trade?" He answered: "I found the Guarantor to be trustworthy." It is said that once upon a time one man embarked on a journey carrying a loaf of bread. He made a vow, saying: "When I eat it, I will die!" God dispatched an angel to him, saying: "If he eats it, provide for him; if he does not eat it, do not give anything to him!" So the loaf remained with that man until he died. He did not touch it and it remained intact. It is said that to the one who enters into the arena of relegation [of one's affairs to God], the object of his desire will be brought as a bride is brought to her husband. The difference between negligence and relegation is this: [your] negligence concerns the rights of God Most High,[223] which is blameworthy, whereas relegation concerns your own rights,[224] which is praiseworthy. 'Abdallah b. al-Mubarak said: "Whoever takes a *fils*[225] worth of the forbidden has no trust in God." I heard Muhammad b. 'Abdallah al-Sufi – may God have mercy on him – say: I heard Nasr b. Abi Nasr al-'Attar say: I heard 'Ali b. Muhammad al-Misri say: I heard Abu Sa'id al-Kharraz say: "Once I went into the desert without any provisions. Suddenly I was overcome with need. At some distance I saw a [caravan] station. I rejoiced that I had reached [my destination]. Then I thought to myself: 'I have found respite and put my trust into something other than Him!' So I made a vow not to enter this way-station unless someone carried me there. So I dug a hole for myself in the sand and buried my body in it up to my chest. In the middle of the night [the inhabitants of the way-station] heard a voice saying: 'O people of the way-station, one of the friends of God Most High has buried himself in the sand. Go to him!' So a group of people came to me. They brought me out and carried me to the way-station."//246

I heard Shaykh Abu 'Abd al-Sulami – may God have mercy on him – say: I heard Muhammad b. Hasan al-Makhzumi say: I heard Ibn al-Maliki say: Abu Hamza al-Khurasani said: "One year I went on the pilgrimage. As I was walking along the road, I fell into a well. My soul prompted me to cry for help. However, I said to myself: 'No, by God, I will never cry for help!' Before I could finish with this thought, two men passed by the mouth of the well. One of them said to the other: 'Come on, let's cover the mouth of this well lest someone fall into it.' They brought some reed and mats and blocked off the mouth of the well. I wanted to cry out, then said to myself: 'I will cry to the One Who is nearer to me than they!' So I did not say a word. After a while, something came by, opened the mouth of the well, and lowered its leg into the pit, as if it wanted to tell me in a growl: 'Hold onto me!' When I realized that this [invitation] came from Him, I grabbed hold of it and it pulled me out. And, lo, it turned out to be a lion. Then it went away. Suddenly [I heard] a voice, saying: 'Abu Hamza, isn't this better!? I have

---

223 That is, you neglect your obligations toward Him.
224 That is, you forfeit them in favor of God.
225 A small coin.

saved you from one peril by another one!' As I continued on my way, I recited [the following verses]:

> I am afraid to show You what I try to conceal, while my innermost self
> reveals what my gaze relates to it
> My shame before You forbade me to conceal my passion
> By giving me understanding of Yourself You allowed me
> to be rid of a veil [between You and me]
> You treated me gently by exposing my outer self to
> my hidden one and gentleness was achieved through another
> gentleness
> You showed Yourself to me in the realm of the unseen, as
> If You wanted to intimate to me that You were within my grasp
> When I saw you, my awe of You made me feel lonely
> Then You became my intimate friend by showing me Your kindness
> and affection
> You revived [Your] lover after he had died from love of You
> Thus, life and death rub shoulders: this is indeed a marvelous thing!"

I heard Muhammad b. al-Hasan – may God have mercy on him – say: I heard Mansur b. ʿAbdallah say: I heard Abu Saʿid al-Taharti say: I heard Hudhayfa al-Marʿashi – a servant and companion of Ibrahim b. Adham – say that someone asked him:[226] "What is the most marvelous thing you ever saw from him?" He answered://247 "We were on our way to Mecca without finding anything to eat for many days. Finally, we reached Kufa and took shelter in a ruined mosque. Ibrahim b. Adham looked at me and said: 'Hudhayfa, I see that you are hungry.' I replied: 'Yes, you are right.' He asked me to bring him some paper and writing utensils. When I brought them to him, he wrote: 'In the name of God, the Compassionate, the Merciful. You are the One who is sought after in every state and pointed to by every sign:

> I praise [You], I thank [You], and I remember Your name
> And yet I am hungry, thirsty, and naked
> These are six qualities: I am responsible for half of them,
> So take responsibility for the other half, O Maker
> Should I praise anyone but You, I will be plunged into a raging fire
> Hold back Your servant from entering the fire
> My asking You is like being in the fire for me
> I wonder if You would force me to enter the fire?'

He gave me that piece of paper, saying: 'Go out and do not allow your heart to attach itself to anyone, except God Most High. Give this paper to the first person you meet.' I went out and the first person whom I met was a man on a

---

226 That is, al-Marʿashi.

mule. I gave him the paper. He took it and started to cry. He then asked me: 'Where is the one who wrote this?' I answered that he was in such-and-such mosque. He gave me a purse with six hundred *dinars*. When I met another man I asked him who the man on the mule was. He answered that he was a Christian. I returned to Ibrahim b. Adham and told him the story. He told me: 'Do not touch it [the purse], for he will soon be here.' After a short while the Christian indeed arrived. He prostrated himself in front of Ibrahim b. Adham and became a Muslim."

Gratitude (*shukr*)

God – may He be great and exalted – said: "If you are grateful, surely I will increase you."[227] Abu ʾl-Hasan ʿAli b. Ahmad b. ʿAbdan [al-Ahwazi] told us: Abu ʾl-Hasan//248 al-Saffar informed us: al-Asqati told us: Minjab told us: Yahya b. Yaʿla told us on the authority of Abu Khabab, on the authority of ʿAtaʾ: "I came to see ʿAʾisha – may God be pleased with her – with ʿUbayd b. ʿUmayr. I said: 'Tell us of the most wondrous thing you ever saw of the Messenger of God – may God bless and greet him.' She wept and asked: 'Was there anything he did that was not wondrous? He came to me one night and went to bed with me (or perhaps she said: 'under the bedclothes with me'), so that his skin would touch mine. He then asked: "O daughter of Abu Bakr, let me worship my Lord."' She said: 'I told him that I loved being close to him. Then I let him go. He stood up and went to a water-skin to perform his ablutions. He poured out much water. He then began to pray. [As he was praying] he wept profusely so that his tears began to stream down his chest. He wept as he was bending; he wept as he was prostrating himself; he wept as he raised his head [after finishing a prayer cycle]. He did so, until Bilal[228] came and called him to utter the call to prayer. I asked him: "Messenger of God, what makes you weep after God has forgiven you all your past and future sins?" He asked me: "Am I not a grateful servant? How can I not weep after God has revealed to me this verse: 'Surely in the creation of the heavens and the earth ... [are signs for a people who understand].'"'"[229]

The master [al-Qushayri] said: "The True Reality of gratitude, according to the people of true realization (*ahl al-tahqiq*)[230] is to recognize humbly the beneficence of the Benefactor, for God – praise be to Him – called Himself "The Grateful" (*al-shakur*) in an allegorical sense, not in a real one. This means that He rewards His servants for their gratitude. He thus described His reward for

---

227 Q. 14:7.
228 A black (Abyssinian) Companion of the Prophet, who was famous for his beautiful voice and who therefore was appointed to perform the call to prayer in the first Muslim community at Medina.
229 Q. 2:164; 2:158, according to Arberry's translation.
230 That is, accomplished Sufi masters.

the gratitude of His servants, as [His own] gratitude in the same way as He said [about evildoers]: 'The recompense of evil is evil.'"[231]

It is said that God Most High's gratitude consists of His giving an abundant reward for even a minor [good] deed, as in the [Arabic] phrase, "a grateful beast of burden", [which is said] when it accumulates more fat in comparison to the [small] amount of fodder given to it. One can say that the True Reality of gratitude is to praise the Benefactor by mentioning His beneficence. Likewise, the servant's praise of God Most High consists of his mentioning His beneficence toward him. As for the servant's beneficence, it consists of obeying God Most High. As for God's beneficence, it consists of His bestowal upon the servant//249 of the ability to [express] his gratitude to Him. The gratitude of the servant in its true sense is when he acknowledges his Lord's beneficence by his tongue, while at the same time confirming it by his heart. Thus, gratitude falls into the following categories: the gratitude of the tongue when the servant humbly acknowledges God's beneficence; the gratitude of the body and [its] limbs, which is characterized by fidelity and service; and the gratitude of the heart when [the servant] exerts himself on the carpet of witnessing [God] while preserving His sanctity. It is said that the learned express their gratitude by their words; the worshipers by their deeds; the divine gnostics by their rectitude in all of their states.

Abu Bakr al-Warraq said: "Gratitude for [God's] beneficence is bearing witness to [God's] gift, while preserving [God's] sanctity." Hamdun al-Qassar said: "Gratitude for [God's] beneficence is when you consider yourself to be an uninvited guest at its feast." Al-Junayd said: "There's an air of imperfection about gratitude, for [one who expresses his gratitude] seeks an increase [in divine beneficence], while he should be content with the portion allotted to him by God Most High." Abu ʿUthman [al-Hiri] said: "Gratitude is to realize one's inability to be grateful." It is also said that to be grateful for gratitude is better than simple gratitude, because you see that your gratitude stems from His giving you this ability, and this ability is [God's] greatest beneficence toward you. So you thank Him for giving you [the ability] to be grateful; then you thank Him for the [gift of the] gratitude for gratitude, and so on without end. It is said that gratitude is to give credit humbly for the beneficence to the [true] Benefactor. Al-Junayd said: "Gratitude is to consider yourself to be undeserving of beneficence." Ruwaym b. Ahmad said: "Gratitude is to exhaust your ability [to be grateful]." It is said that the ordinary grateful person is grateful [to God] for what he has, while the truly grateful one is grateful [to God] for what he has lost. Likewise, they say that the ordinary grateful is grateful for a gift, while the truly grateful one is grateful for the denial of the gift.//250 They also say that the ordinary grateful person is grateful for beneficence, while the truly grateful is grateful for adversity. They also say that the ordinary grateful person thanks [God] at a time of abundance, whereas the truly grateful one thanks [God] at a time of deprivation.

---

231 Q. 42:40; 42:37, according to Arberry's translation.

I heard Shaykh Abu ʿAbd al-Rahman al-Sulami – may God have mercy on him – say: I heard the master Abu Sahl al-Suʿluki say: I heard al-Murtaʿish say: I heard al-Junayd say: "Once, as I was playing before al-Sari[232] (I was a seven-year-old boy at that time), his visitors began to discuss gratitude. He asked me: '[My] boy, what is gratitude?' I replied: 'That you do not disobey God with all the beneficence He has bestowed upon you!' He then said: 'Soon God's special blessing for you will be your tongue!'" Al-Junayd used to say: "I cannot help crying, whenever I [remember] these words uttered by al-Sari." Al-Shibli said: "Gratitude is when you see the Benefactor, not His beneficence." It is said that gratitude is preserving what one has and chasing after what is lost. Abu ʿUthman [al-Hiri] said: "The common people are grateful to the One Who feeds and clothes them, whereas the elect are grateful for the [subtle] meanings that enter their hearts."

It is said that David – upon him be peace – said: "O my God, how can I thank You, when my very gratitude toward You is a beneficence that comes from You?" Then God revealed to him: "Now you have really thanked Me!" Moses – upon him be peace – said in his intimate conversation [with God]: "My God, You created Adam with Your hand and did this and did that ... How can I thank You?" God answered: "He knows that [all] this comes from Me, so his knowledge of this is his [best] gratitude to Me!" It is related that someone had an intimate friend, whom the ruler threw into prison. He wrote to his friend from there. The friend responded, saying: "Be grateful to God Most High!" Then the man was beaten [in prison] and wrote about this to his friend, who responded to him, saying: "Be grateful to God Most High!" Then they brought to that man a Zoroastrian with diarrhea who was put in shackles in such a way that one shackle was attached to the Zoroastrian's foot and the other to the foot of the man. The Zoroastrian would get up many times during the night. Therefore, he was forced to stand over him until he finished his business. The man wrote about this to his friend, who responded, saying: "Be grateful to God!" The other replied: "How long will you be saying this? Is there a trial that is worse that this?"//251 The friend wrote back to him, saying: "If the girdle [of the infidel][233] that he wears was put around your waist just as the shackle he wears was put around your foot, what would you do then?!" It is said that a man came to Sahl b. ʿAbdallah [al-Tustari] and said: "A thief broke into my house and stole my possessions!" Sahl replied: "Be grateful to God Most High! If the other thief, that is Satan, had entered your heart and corrupted your faith, what would you have done then?!"

It is said that the gratitude of the eyes is that you hide a fault that you see in your friend, while the gratitude of the ears is that you hide a faulty word that you hear from him. It is also said that gratitude is taking delight in praising Him for what one has not deserved.

---

232 Al-Sari al-Saqati was al-Junayd's uncle. See *IM*, pp. 50–52.
233 Non-Muslims who lived in lands under Muslim rule were required to display certain marks (such as a girdle), which indicated their status as a protected minority.

I heard al-Sulami say: I heard Muhammad b. al-Husayn say: I heard al-Husayn b. Yahya say: I heard Jaʿfar say: I heard al-Junayd say: "Whenever [my uncle] al-Sari [al-Saqati] would want me to benefit from him, he would ask me: 'Abu ʾl-Qasim, what is gratitude?' I would answer: 'It is when you are not using anything of His beneficence to disobey Him!' He would ask me: 'When did you learn this?' I would answer: 'During my studying with you.'"

It is said that Hasan b. ʿAli[234] once clung to a column [in the mosque of Mecca] and said: "My God, you have bestowed blessings on me, and You do not find me grateful! You have tested me, and You do not find me patient! Yet, despite my being ungrateful, You have not withheld Your blessings from me and You have not prolonged my hardship despite my being impatient! My God, nothing but generosity comes from the Generous One!" It is said: "If your hand is not long enough to repay [a blessing], you should [at least] stretch your tongue in giving thanks!" It is also said that four acts bring no fruit to those who do them: telling a secret to a deaf man, bestowing blessings on the one who is ungrateful, sowing seeds in a salt marsh, and lighting a lamp in broad daylight.

It is said that when the prophet Idris[235] – upon whom be peace – received tidings of forgiveness [from God], he asked [God] for a [long] life. When he was asked about this [wish], he answered: "[I need it] in order to give my gratitude to Him, for prior to this I was working [to secure His] forgiveness." At that moment, an angel extended its wing and carried him to heaven. It is said that one of the prophets – peace be upon them – passed by a small stone, from which much water was gushing forth. When he wondered at that, God made it speak to him and say: "Since the moment I heard God Most High say: 'A [hell]fire, whose fuel is men and stones',[236] I cannot help weeping out of fear!" The prophet then prayed to God to protect that stone, whereupon God Most High//252 revealed to him: "I have already protected it from the hellfire." The prophet went on. When he returned, he found that water continued to gush forth from it. When he wondered about that, God gave the stone [the gift of] speech. He asked it: "Why do you keep weeping, after God has forgiven you?" It answered: "That weeping was out of sadness and fear. Now I am weeping out of gratitude and joy!"

It is said that the grateful person is always in the presence of increase, because he constantly bears witness to [God's] blessing, for God Most High said: "If you are grateful, surely I will increase you."[237] And the one who is patient is with God Most High, because he finds himself in the presence of the One Who

---

234 A grandson of the Prophet by his cousin ʿAli and his daughter Fatima. The Shiʿites consider him their second imam. He died in 49/669.
235 A prophetic figure mentioned in the Qurʾan, 19:57 and 21:85, who is usually identified with the Biblical Elijah or Enoch.
236 Q. 66:6.
237 Q. 14:7.

puts him to test, for God – may He be blessed – said: "Verily, God is with the patient."[238]

It is recounted that a delegation [of Bedouin tribes] came to ʿUmar b. ʿAbd al-ʿAziz – may God be pleased with him. Among them was a youth. When he started to speak, ʿUmar [interrupted him], saying: "[Let] the elders [speak first]!" The youth objected to him saying: "O Commander of the Faithful, if this matter[239] were to be determined based on one's age, then there are among Muslims those who are older than you!" ʿUmar ordered him to speak. He said: "We are not a delegation of desire;[240] nor are we a delegation of fear.[241] As for desire, your generosity has already fulfilled it. As for fear, your justice has protected us from it." ʿUmar asked him: "Who then are you?" The youth answered: "We are a delegation of gratitude. We have come here to thank you and then to depart." They [the Bedouin] recited [the following]:

> It's a pity that my gratitude is silent about
> Your deeds; however your goodness speaks for itself
> I see your good deed, yet I conceal it
> I am therefore like a thief, who steals from the hand of
> The generous man.

It is said that God Most High revealed to Moses – peace be upon him: "I will have mercy upon My servants, both those who are tested by adversity and those who are spared from it!" He asked God: "Why those who are spared from it?" He answered: "Because they are not grateful enough for My saving them from it!" It is said: "Praise is due [to God] for [the gift of] breath and gratitude is due for the blessings of the senses." It is also said: "Praise begins with Him, while gratitude is your following that which comes from Him." According to an authentic report [from the Prophet]: "Among the first ones to be invited to Paradise are those who have been grateful to God for any state [He has put them into]." It is also said: "Praise is due for what [God] averts [from you], while gratitude is due for the good He does [to you]."

It is related that one Sufi said: "During one of my journeys I saw an old man of very advanced age.//253 I asked him about his condition. He answered: 'Early in my life I fell in love with my cousin, who reciprocated my feelings. Eventually, we got married. On the night of our wedding we said: "Let's spend this night giving thanks to God Most High for uniting us!" So we spent that night in prayer, paying no attention to each other. When the second night came, we made the same [pledge], and for seventy or eighty years we have done so every night. Isn't it so, my lady?' 'It is just as my husband says,' answered the old lady."

---

238 Q. 2:153, 8:46, etc.
239 That is, leadership of the Muslim community.
240 That is, one that seeks some benefit from the Caliph.
241 That is, one that came to the Caliph out of fear.

Certainty (*yaqin*)

God Most High said: "who have certainty in what has been sent down to thee and what has been sent down before thee, and have faith in the Hereafter."[242] The master and imam Abu Bakr Muhammad b. al-Hasan b. Furak told us: Abu Bakr Ahmad b. Mahmud b. Khurrazadh al-Ahwazi told us at Ahwaz: Ahmad b. Sahl b. Ayyub told us: Khalid (that is, Ibn Zayd)[243] told us: Sufyan al-Thawri told us on the authority of Sharik b. ʿAbdallah, on the authority of Sufyan b. ʿUyayna, on the authority of Sulayman al-Taymi, on the authority of Khaythama, on the authority of ʿAbdallah b. Masʿud, who said that the Prophet – may God bless and greet him – said: "Do not be pleased, when God's displeasure has befallen someone; do not praise anyone for the bounty that comes from God – may He be great and exalted; do not blame anyone for what God Most High has withheld from you! For God's sustenance is not given to you by the desire of the one who desires [something for you], nor is it repelled from you by the hatred of the one who hates [you]. Verily, God Most High in His justice and fairness has placed [all] pleasure and delight into satisfaction and certainty, whereas He has placed [all] sorrow and worry into doubt and displeasure."

Shaykh Abu ʿAbd al-Rahman al-Sulami told us: Abu Jaʿfar Muhammad b. Ahmad b. Saʿid al-Razi told us: ʿAyyash b. Hamza told us: Ahmad b. Abi ʾl-Hawari told us: Abu ʿAbdallah al-Antaki said: "When even the smallest [particle of] certainty enters one's heart, it fills the heart with light and expels whatever doubt there is in it. Consequently, the heart becomes filled with gratitude to and fear of God Most High." It is related that Abu Jaʿfar al-Haddad said: "Once Abu Turab al-Nakhshabi saw me in the desert, as I was sitting next to a pond. It had been sixteen days since I had eaten or drunk anything. He asked me why I was sitting like that. I told him: 'I am [vacillating] between knowledge and certainty, waiting to see which of them will prevail, so that I may follow it.' He meant to say: 'If knowledge prevails in me, I will drink, and if certainty, I will pass on [without drinking].' [Abu Turab] told me: 'A great future awaits you!'" Abu ʿUthman al-Hiri said: "Certainty is not to concern oneself with the morrow."//254 Sahl b. ʿAbdallah [al-Tustari] said: "Certainty comes from the abundance and true realization of faith." He also said: "Certainty is a branch of faith, which is slightly lower than the ultimate confirmation of [the truth] of faith (*tasdiq*)."[244]

A Sufi said: "Certainty is the knowledge deposited [by God] in the heart." He implied that it is not acquired [but given]. Sahl said: "Unveiling is the beginning of certainty. That is why one of the pious ancestors said: 'Even if the veil is lifted, this will not increase my certainty.' Then come direct witnessing and contemplation [of God] (*muʿayana wa-mushahada*)." Abu ʿAbdallah b. Khafif said: "Certainty is the true realization by the innermost heart of the realities of the Unseen." Abu Bakr b. Tahir said: "Knowledge is acquired by way

---

242 Q. 2:2–4.
243 Or, "Ibn Yazid".
244 According to scholarly consensus, *tasdiq* constitutes the pinnacle of faith.

of opposing doubts, whereas certainty presupposes no doubt [whatsoever]." He thus referred to both acquired knowledge and that that comes by way of intuition. The knowledge of this folk [Sufis] is like this: in the beginning it is acquired, and in the end it comes by way of intuition.

I heard Muhammad b. al-Husayn say that one Sufi said: "The first of the mystical stations is knowledge (maʿrifa), then certainty, then confirmation (tasdiq), then sincerity (ikhlas), then [direct] witnessing (shahada), then [full] obedience (taʿa); and faith (iman) is the word that combines all these." This individual implied that the first duty [of the faithful] is to know God – praise be to Him. This knowledge can only be obtained by fulfilling its conditions. They begin with the correct vision; then, once the proofs begin to follow one upon the other, clear evidence is obtained, and one begins [to see] the succession of [divine] lights and acquires an inner vision; then one is no longer in need of contemplating any further proofs [of God's existence]. This is the state of certainty. This is followed by the ultimate confirmation from the True Reality – may He be praised – that what He promised would happen in the future in response to His servant's plea will indeed happen, as was promised. Because the confirmation is the [belief by the servant] in what [God] has promised [him]. After this comes sincerity in [the servant's] fulfillment of God's requirements. Then [God] shows His response [in the form] of a beatific vision, which is followed by the [servant's] acts of obedience, as was prescribed to him and [his] denudation of what was proscribed to him. This is exactly what the imam Abu Bakr Muhammad b. Furak alluded to, when I heard him say: "What the tongue utters is nothing but what overflows the heart." Sahl b. ʿAbdallah said: "When the heart finds solace in something other than God Most High, it is barred from smelling the fragrance of certainty." Dhu ʾl-Nun al-Misri said: "Certainty prompts the servant to cut short his hopes [for things of this world]; cutting short one's hopes, in turn, prompts him to [embrace] renunciation;//255 renunciation produces wisdom, and wisdom produces desire to ponder upon one's fate in the Hereafter."

I heard Muhammad b. al-Husayn – may God have mercy on him – say: I heard Abu ʾl-ʿAbbas al-Baghdadi say: I heard Dhu ʾl-Nun al-Misri say: "There are three signs of certainty: reducing one's association with people in public; avoiding praise of people for what they give [one], and restraining oneself from censuring them when they deny [one's request]. There are three signs of utmost certainty (yaqin al-yaqin): looking toward God Most High in everything; having recourse to Him in every matter; and seeking His aid in every condition." Al-Junayd – may God have mercy on him – said: "Certainty is the constant presence in the heart of the knowledge that is not subject to fluctuation, change or vacillation." Ibn ʿAtaʾ said: "People attain certainty to the same degree as they attain fear of God. The root of fear of God is opposing that which is prohibited [by Him], while opposing that which is prohibited is the same as opposing one's soul. To the extent to which they depart from their souls, they arrive at certainty."

A Sufi said: "Certainty is but unveiling, and unveiling may be of three kinds: unveiling by means of good tidings; unveiling by means of the demonstration of [divine] Power; and unveiling by means of [receiving] the true realities of faith." Know that in the language of this folk [Sufis] "unveiling" means the appearance of something to the heart that takes full possession of it without leaving any room for doubt. Sometimes by "unveiling" they imply the state that is experienced by a person who is neither awake nor asleep. The Sufis occasionally refer to this state as "confirmation".

I heard the imam Abu Bakr b. Furak say: "I asked Abu ʿUthman al-Maghribi about something he had said. He answered: 'I saw certain people in such and such state.' I asked him: 'Did you see them with your own eyes or by unveiling?' He answered: 'By unveiling.'" ʿAmir b. ʿAbd Qays said: "Even if the veil were to be removed, my certainty would not increase." It is said that certainty is direct vision by means of the strength of one's faith. It is also said that certainty is the cessation of acts of opposition [to the divine Will].//256 Al-Junayd – may God have mercy on him – said: "Certainty is the removal of doubts through witnessing the Unseen."

I heard the master Abu ʿAli al-Daqqaq comment on the words of the Prophet – may God bless and greet him – about ʿIsa b. Maryam – peace be upon him: "Had his certainty been greater, he would have walked through the air as I did." [According to Abu ʿAli,] the Prophet alluded to his own state during the Night of Ascension,[245] because one of the subtle mysteries of the Ascension is that the Prophet – may God bless and greet him – said: "I saw Buraq[246] stay behind me, while I continued to walk on."

I heard Muhammad b. al-Husayn say: I heard Ahmad b. ʿAli b. Jaʿfar say: I heard Ibrahim b. Fatik say: I heard al-Junayd say: "I heard that someone asked al-Sari about certitude. He answered: 'It is your tranquility in the face of thoughts that swarm in your breast, because you have become certain that your own actions will neither benefit you, nor divert from you what has been predestined for you [by God].'" I also heard him [Muhammad b. al-Husayn] say: I heard ʿAbdallah b. ʿAli say: I heard Abu Jaʿfar al-Isbahani say: I heard ʿAli b. Sahl say: "[Being in the] presence [of God] is better than certitude, because presence implies permanent states, while certitude comes and goes." It seems that he considered certitude as the beginning stage of presence, the latter being the continuation of the former. It also seems that he implied that there can be certitude that is not followed by presence, while there can be no presence that is not preceded by certitude. This is why al-Nuri said: "Certitude is nothing other than witnessing [God]." He meant that in the process of witnessing one acquires complete certitude, for one who has no trust in what comes from God Most High can never witness Him.

Abu Bakr al-Warraq said: "Certitude is the foundation of the heart by which one's faith is perfected. One knows God through certitude, while the intellect

---

245 See the entry "al-Israʾ wa ʾl-miʿradj" in *EI*.
246 The fabulous mount that, according to Islamic tradition, brought Muhammad from Mecca to Jerusalem. See the previous note.

keeps one away from God Most High." Al-Junayd said: "Thanks to certainty some people walk on water and the best of them are those who die of thirst through their certitude." I heard Shaykh Abu ʿAbd al-Rahman al-Sulami say: I heard al-Husayn b. Yahya say: I heard Jaʿfar al-Khuldi say: I heard Ibrahim al-Khawwas say: "Once, in the middle of a trackless desert I met a youth, who was as beautiful as an ingot of silver. I asked him about his destination. He said that he was heading to Mecca. 'Without provisions, camel or money?', I asked him. He told me: 'O you whose certainty is weak! How can the One Who preserves the heavens and the earth be incapable of delivering me to Mecca without any provisions?' Afterwards, when I arrived in Mecca, I met//257 him going around the Kaʿba and saying:

> O my eye keep on crying incessantly,
> O my soul perish of grief,
> Do not love anyone except Him Who is glorious and everlasting!

"When he saw me, he asked: 'O shaykh, is your certitude still as weak as it was before?'" I also heard him [al-Sulami] say: I heard Mansur b. ʿAbdallah say: I heard al-Nahrajuri say: "When the servant has realized fully the true essence of certainty, his afflictions become his blessings and his comfort becomes his afflictions."

Abu Bakr al-Warraq said that certitude can be of three kinds – namely, the certitude of good tidings [from God], the certitude of [divine] proofs, and the certitude of witnessing [God]. Abu Turab al-Nakhshabi said: "Once I saw a young lad walking across the desert with no provisions. I said to myself: 'If he has no certitude, he will surely perish.' I then told him: 'How can you be in such a place with no provisions?' He replied: 'O shaykh, raise your head. Do you see anyone but God – may He be great and exalted?' I told him: 'Now you can go wherever you wish!'"

I heard Muhammd b. al-Husayn say: I heard Abu Nasr al-Isbahani say: I heard Muhammad b. ʿIsa say: I heard Abu Saʿid al-Kharraz say: "Knowledge is what makes you act and certitude is what brings you [to your goal]." I also heard him say: I heard Abu Bakr al-Razi say: I heard Abu ʿUthman al-Adami say: I heard Ibrahim al-Khawwas say: "I looked for a livelihood that would allow me to eat licit food. So I took to fishing. One day a fish swam into my net. I took it out and threw the net into the water once again. Another fish was trapped in it. I took it out and cast the net [into the water] once again. Suddenly, I heard a voice saying: 'Couldn't you find a livelihood other than going after those who mention My name, then killing them?!' I tore my net apart and abandoned fishing forthwith."

Patience (*sabr*)

God – may He be great and exalted – said: "And be patient; yet is thy patience with the help of God."[247]//258

---

247 Q. 16:127; 16:129, according to Arberry's translation.

ʿAli b. Ahmad al-Ahwazi informed us: Ahmad b. ʿUbayd al-Basri informed us: Ahmad b. ʿAli al-Kharraz informed us: Usayd b. Zayd told us: Masʿud b. Saʿd told us on the authority of al-Zayyat, on the authority of Abu Hurayra, on the authority of ʿAʾisha – may God be pleased with her – who recounted the following words of the Messenger of God – may God bless and greet him: "Patience is to be exercised at the first attack." ʿAli b. Ahmad informed us: Ahmad b. ʿUbayd informed us: Ahmad b. ʿUmar told us: Muhammad b. Mirdas told us: Yusuf b. ʿAtiyya told us on the authority of ʿAtaʾ b. Abi Maymuna, on the authority of Anas b. Malik – may God be pleased with him – that the Messenger of God – may God bless and greet him – said: "Patience is to be exercised at the first shock."

Patience can be of different sorts: patience with what one has acquired through one's own deeds and patience with what one has not acquired through one's deeds. Patience with what one has acquired can be of two kinds: endurance of that which God Most High has commanded and endurance of that which He has prohibited. As for patience with what one has not acquired through one's deeds, it is one's endurance of the hardships decreed for one by God, which cause one's suffering.

I heard Shaykh Abu ʿAbd al-Rahman al-Sulami say: I heard al-Husayn b. Yahya say: I heard Jaʿfar b. Muhammad say: I heard al-Junayd say: "The journey from this world to the next is simple for the believer – relinquishing [God's] creatures in order to be with God is difficult, while journey from one's self to God Most High is even more difficult. However, patience with God is the most difficult of all." Someone asked al-Junayd about patience. He answered: "It is drinking down a bitter cup without a grimace." ʿAli b. Abi Talib – may God be pleased with him – said: "Patience in relation to faith is like the head in relation to [the rest of] the body."

Abu ʾl-Qasim al-Hakim said that the words of God Most High "And be patient"[248] mean a command to worship [Him] (ʿibada), while His words "Yet is thy patience only with the help of God"[249] mean [absolute] servanthood (ʿubudiyya). He who has risen from the degree of 'for You' to the degree of 'by You' has advanced from worship to [absolute] servanthood."[250] The Prophet – may God greet him and bless him – said: "By You I live and by You I die."//259 I heard Shaykh Abu ʿAbd al-Rahman al-Sulami say: I heard Abu Jaʿfar al-Razi say: I heard ʿAyyash[251] say: I heard Ahmad say: I asked Abu Sulayman [al-Darani] about patience. He answered: "By God, if we cannot endure what we like, how, then, can we endure what we dislike?!" Dhu ʾl-Nun said: "Patience is staying away from acts of disobedience, keeping quiet while sipping the agonies of

---

248 Q. 16:127; 16:128, according to Arberry's translation.
249 Q. 16:127; 16:128, according to Arberry's translation.
250 That is, at the first stage, the servant seeks to please God by serving Him faithfully in expectation of reward in the Hereafter; at the second stage, the servant performs his worship through and by God, meaning that God becomes his sole "raison d'être", as it were.
251 Or "ʿAbbas".

misfortune, and showing contentment when poverty invades the arena of [your] livelihood." Ibn ʿAtaʾ said: "Patience is to show good manners in the face of misfortune." It is also said that patience is "self-annihilation in misfortune without showing signs of discontent".

Abu ʿUthman [al-Hiri] said: "One is most steadfast, when one has accustomed oneself to enduring the attacks of all manner of adversities." It is said that patience is to behave in adversity in the same way one behaves [in times of] well-being. Abu ʿUthman said: "The best reward for [one's] worship is the reward for [one's] patience. There's no higher reward. For God Most High said: 'We shall recompense those who were patient their wage, according to the best they did.'"[252] ʿAmr b. ʿUthman [al-Hiri] said: "Patience is to hold on to God Most High – may He be praised – and a quiet and welcoming acceptance of the afflictions He inflicts [on you]." [Ibrahim] al-Khawwas said: "Patience is holding on to the commands of the Book and the [Prophet's] custom." Yahya b. Muʿadh [al-Razi] said: "The patience of lovers [of God] (*muhibbin*) is greater than the patience of [world] renouncers (*zahidin*). I cannot fathom, how they can persevere!" They [Sufis] recite the following:

> Patience is praiseworthy under all circumstances, except patience toward
> You,[253] for this is not praiseworthy.

Ruwaym [b. Ahmad] said: "Patience is giving up complaint." Dhu ʾl-Nun said: "Patience is seeking help [only] from God Most High." I heard the master Abu ʿAli al-Daqqaq – may God have mercy on him – say: "Patience is like its name." Shaykh Abu ʿAbd al-Rahman al-Sulami recited to me: Abu Bakr al-Razi recited to me: Ibn ʿAtaʾ recited to me [the following verse] that he composed:

> I will be patient in order to please You, even though my sorrow kills me
> It suffices me that You are pleased, even though my patience kills me.

Abu ʿAbdallah b. Khafif said: "There are three types of patience: one who aspires to be patient; one who is patient; and one whose patience has no limit." ʿAli b. Abi Talib – may God be pleased with him – said: "Patience is a beast of burden that never tires."//260 I heard Muhammad b. al-Husayn: I heard ʿAli b. ʿAbdallah al-Basri, who said: "Someone came to al-Shibli and asked him: 'Which patience is most difficult for those who are patient?' He answered: 'Patience in God – may He be great and exalted.' The man said: 'No.' Al-Shibli said: 'Patience for [the sake of] God.' The man said: 'No.' Al-Shibli said: 'Patience with God.' The man said: 'No.' 'What is it, then?' asked al-Shibli. 'Patience without God,'[254] answered the man. Al-Shibli let out such a loud scream that it would seem that he nearly gave up the ghost." I also heard him [Muhammad b. al-Husayn] say: I

---

252 Q. 16:96; 16:98, according to Arberry's translation.
253 Or, perhaps, "from You".
254 That is, enduring something without God's assistance.

heard Muhammad b. ʿAbdallah b. Shadhan say: I heard Muhammad al-Jurayri say: "Patience is making no distinction between a state of blessing and a state of suffering; in either of them, the servant's mind remains unperturbed. To be patient is to remain unperturbed during a trial, while experiencing the hardships of suffering." One Sufi recited:

> I was patient and did not reveal my love for You to my patience
> I concealed what You had done to me from my patience
> Out of fear that my soul would secretly complain of my passion to
> My tears, and they would flow without my noticing it.

I heard the master Abu ʿAli al-Daqqaq – may God have mercy on him – say: "Those who are patient have won the best of all things in both worlds: they have found themselves in [the state of] togetherness with God, for God Most High said: 'Surely, God is with the patient.'"[255] It is said regarding the meaning of God Most High's words, "O believers, be patient and persevere in your patience and hold on to God",[256] that patience is lower than persevering in patience, while persevering in patience is lower than holding on to God. It is therefore said: "Be patient with your souls in obeying God Most High; persevere in patience with your hearts, while facing misfortunes for the sake of God; hold on to God with your innermost selves in striving to God." And it is also said: "Be patient for the sake of God; persevere in patience by God; and hold on to God [by being] with Him."

It is said that God Most High revealed to David – upon whom be peace – [the following words]: "Imitate My character traits, for one of them is that I am the Most Patient." It is said: "Gulp down patience in abundance, for if it kills you, you will die as a martyr, and if it lets you live, you will live in glory." It is said: "Patience for the sake of God is suffering; patience by God is subsisting [in Him]; patience in God is a trial; patience with God is faithfulness [toward Him], and patience without God is harshness [toward you]."//261

They recite [the following verse]:

> Patience without you is blameworthy in its consequences,
> Whereas patience in all else is praiseworthy.

They also recite:

> How can I be patient without one who resides so close to me as my right
> hand to my left one
> Men may trifle with many things, however, I have seen how love
> trifles with them.

---

255 Q. 2:153; 2:148, according to Arberry's translation.
256 Q. 3:200.

It is said: "Patient perseverance in seeking [something] predicts success, while patience in persevering trials promises deliverance." I heard Mansur b. Khalaf – may God have mercy on him – say: "A man was stripped for flogging with a whip. When brought back to prison [after the flogging], he called over one of the inmates and spat something into his palm. This turned out to be bits of silver. They asked him about it. He answered: 'I had two *dirhams* in my mouth. Among those present there was someone who watched me. I did not want him to see me crying out, so I kept biting these *dirhams* until they were pulverized in my mouth." It is said: "Your [spiritual] state is your stronghold, and everything other than God Most High is your enemy. So be steadfast in the stronghold of your state." It is said: "Patient perseverance is being patient in being patient, until one patience drowns in the other and patience becomes incapable of patience." They say about this:

> He patiently persevered in patience, so that patience appealed to him for help
> The lover then called out to patience: "Patience!"

Once al-Shibli was confined to a lunatic asylum. A group of people came to visit him. He asked them: "Who are you?" They answered: "We are those who love you and we have come to visit you." He started to throw stones at them and they ran away. He then said: "O liars! If you were really those who love me, you would have been patient, when I tried you." According to a transmitted report, [God said]: "I always see what those who are tested forbear for My sake." God Most High [also] said: "And be thou patient under the judgement of thy Lord: surely thou art before Our eyes."[257] A Sufi said: "When I was in Mecca, I saw a poor man[258] circumambulating the House [of God].[259] He took a scrap of paper out of his pocket, looked at it, and walked on. He did the same the next day. For several days I watched him doing the same. Finally, one day he completed another circumambulation, looked at the paper, stepped back [from the Ka'ba] and suddenly fell down dead. I took the paper out of his pocket. It said: 'And be thou patient under the judgement of thy Lord: surely thou art before Our eyes.'"[260]//262

It is related that a beardless youth was seen striking an old man in the face with his sandal. Someone asked him: "Aren't you ashamed? How can you beat this old man on his cheeks in such a way?" "His sin is great," answered the young man. They asked: "What is that?" He answered: "This man claims that he desires me, yet he has not seen me for three nights!" Someone said: "When I arrived in India, I came across a one-eyed man nicknamed 'So-and-so the Patient'." I asked people about his story. They said: "When this man was in the

---

257 Q. 52:48; 52:47, according to Arberry's translation.
258 That is, another Sufi.
259 That is, the Ka'ba.
260 See note 257.

prime of his youth, a friend of his set out on a journey. The man came to bid him farewell. [When he started to cry] one of his eyes shed tears, while the other remained dry. He said to the eye that did not cry: 'Why didn't you weep at the departure of my friend? I will now deprive you of seeing this world!' He closed his eye and has not opened it for sixty years."

Someone commented on the words of God Most High, "So be thou patient with a sweet patience",[261] that "sweet patience" here refers to someone who has just been struck with an affliction without anyone taking notice of him [suffering it]. ʿUmar b. al-Khattab – may God have mercy on him – said: "If patience and gratitude were two camels, I would not care which one of them I rode." Whenever Ibn Shubruma[262] found himself afflicted by trials, he used to say: "[These are but] clouds that will [soon] disperse." According to one report, when someone asked the Prophet – may God bless and greet him – about faith (*iman*), he answered: "Patience and generosity." Shaykh Abu ʿAbd al-Rahman al-Sulami – may God have mercy on him – said: Muhammad b. Ahmad b. Tahir al-Sufi informed us: Muhammad b. ʿAli al-Tijani told us: Muhammad b. Ismaʿil al-Bukhari told us: Musa b. Ismaʿil told us: Suwayd b. Hatim told us: ʿAbdallah b. ʿUbayd told us on the authority of ʿUmayr, who related this on the authority of his father, on the authority of his grandfather, who said that when the Prophet – may God bless and greet him – was asked about faith, he answered: "Patience and generosity."

Someone asked al-Sari [al-Saqati] about patience. As he began his speech, a scorpion crawled up his foot and stung it repeatedly with its tail. Yet he remained still. When asked why he did not brush it away, he answered: "I was ashamed before God Most High to discourse on patience, while myself being incapable of remaining patient." In one report it is said: "The poor who are patient will sit near God on the Day of Resurrection." God Most High revealed to one of His prophets: "I afflicted My servant with My trial, so he called upon Me. I was slow in answering him, so he complained to Me. Then I asked him: 'My servant! How can I have mercy on you [by relieving you] from something with which I have mercy on you?'"[263]//263

Ibn ʿUyayna commented on God's words, "We appointed from among them leaders guiding by Our command, when they endured patiently",[264] saying: "When they grasped the root of this affair,[265] We appointed from among them

---

261 Q. 70:5.
262 Son (or grandson) of a Companion of the Prophet named Shubruma, he was famous as a transmitter of *hadith* and a jurist, and, at one time, the chief judge of Kufa. Ibn Shubruma was also known for his sharp wit and tongue, and his maxims are often quoted in later Arabic literature. He died in 144/761.
263 That is, trials are a necessary precondition for patience, which will be richly rewarded by God in the Hereafter. By failing to be patient, the servant deprives himself of enjoying God's mercy in the future life.
264 Q. 32:24.
265 That is, divine command equals religion, of which patience is the root.

leaders." I heard the master Abu ʿAli al-Daqqaq say: "The definition of patience is that you do not resist the [divine] decree; showing [signs] of affliction upon one's face does not necessarily invalidate patience, for God Most High said to Job: 'Surely, We found him a patient man. How excellent a servant he was. He always turned [to Us].'"[266] And this is in spite of the fact that [he complained to God elsewhere], saying "Affliction has visited me."[267] I also heard him [al-Daqqaq] say: "God extracted this phrase, namely 'Affliction has visited me', from Job so that it may serve as a respite for the weak ones of this [Muslim] community." One Sufi said: "[God] said 'We found him a patient man (*sabir*).' He did not say 'most patient' (*sabur*), because he was not patient in all conditions; from time to time he took delight in his affliction and enjoyed it. Whenever he took delight in his affliction he was no longer patient. This is why [God] did not call him 'most patient'."

I heard the master Abu ʿAli al-Daqqaq – may God have mercy on him – say: "The true essence of patience is to emerge from affliction in the same state that you entered it. Like Job – peace be upon him – when he said at the end of his affliction: 'Affliction has visited me, and Thou art the most merciful of the merciful.'[268] He preserved the proper manner of speech, because he made an allusion by saying 'Thou are the most merciful of the merciful', instead of saying explicitly '[God] have mercy on me'."

Know that there are two kinds of patience: the patience of the worshipers (*ʿabidin*) and the patience of lovers [of God] (*muhibbin*). As for the patience of the worshipers, it is best that it be preserved; as for the patience of the lovers, it is best that it be abandoned. They have this meaning in mind when they recite:

On the day of separation it became clear that his resolve
To be patient was but an idle illusion.

The master Abu ʿAli implied the same meaning when he said: "Jacob//264 – peace be upon him – woke up after he had promised himself to be patient, saying: '[Come] sweet patience',[269] that is, 'Mine is sweet patience', and yet even before evening had come, he uttered: 'Ah, woe is me for Joseph!'"[270]

Awareness [of God] (*muraqaba*)[271]

God Most High said: "God is watchful over everything."[272] Abu Nuʿaym ʿAbd al-Malik b. al-Hasan b. Muhammad told us: Abu ʿAwana Yaʿqub b. Ishaq

---

266 Q. 38:44.
267 Q. 21:83.
268 Q. 21:83.
269 Q. 12:83.
270 Q. 12:84.
271 This Sufi term may mean both "self-examination" by the Sufi of his inner thoughts and intentions and his constant awareness of God's observing him. See, e.g., Chittick, *Sufi Path of Knowledge*, p. 348.
272 Q. 33:52.

informed us: Yusuf b. Saʿid b. Muslim told us: Khalid b. Yazid told us: Ismaʿil b. Abi Khalid told us on the authority of Qays b. Abi Hazim, on the authority of Jarir b. ʿAbdallah al-Bajali: "[The Archangel] Gabriel came to the Prophet – may God bless and greet him – in the image of a man and asked: 'Muhammad, what is faith (*iman*)?' He answered: 'To believe in God and His angels, His books, His messengers, and [His] decree (*qadar*) – be it good or bad, sweet or bitter [for you].' The man said: 'You have spoken the truth.' He [al-Bajali] said: 'We were surprised that someone would declare the Prophet – may God bless and greet him – to be truthful, for he [first] asked him a question, [then] declared his answer to be truthful.' The man then said: 'Tell me, what is Islam[273]?' The Prophet answered: 'Islam is to perform your prayer(s), give alms, fast [during the month] of Ramadan, and to perform the pilgrimage to the House [of God].' The man said: 'You have spoken the truth.' He then said: 'Tell me what is doing the beautiful (*ihsan*)[274]?' The Prophet answered: 'To worship God as if you see Him, for even though you may not see Him, He [always] sees you.'" [Here the Prophet] alluded to the state of awareness [of God], for awareness is the servant's knowledge that [his] Lord – praise be to Him – is always watching him. The servant's perseverance in this knowledge is nothing but his awareness of his Lord, which is the source of all good for him. He will arrive at this stage only after he has completed the stage of self-scrutiny (*muhasaba*). For when he takes account of what he has done in the past, corrects his [inner] state in the present, follows the path of Truth, takes good care of his heart in dealing with God Most High, stays with God Most High in every breath he makes, and observes God Most High in all his states, he will then realize that God – praise be to Him – is watching over him, that He is close to his heart, that He knows [all] his states, watches [all] his actions and hears [all] he says. Whosoever neglects all of this is shut off from attaining God, not to mention from the true realities of closeness [with Him].

I heard Shaykh Abu ʿAbd al-Rahman al-Sulami – may God have mercy on him – say: I heard Abu Bakr al-Razi say: I heard al-Jurayri say: "Whosoever has not firmly established [God-fearing] piety and [constant] awareness between himself and God Most High will never attain unveiling and witnessing." I heard the master Abu ʿAli al-Daqqaq – may God have mercy on him – say://265 "A ruler once had a vizier. One day, when the vizier was standing before him, he turned to one of the ruler's slaves present there, not out of suspicion but because of a noise or movement that he sensed from them. It so happened that at that very moment the ruler looked at the vizier. The latter was afraid that the ruler would imagine that he looked at them out of suspicion, therefore he continued to look sideways. From that day on, whenever the vizier entered in the ruler's presence he would always look to the side, so that the ruler thought that this was part of his inborn character. Now, this is one creature's

---

273 That is, submission to God.
274 This word is sometimes translated as "beneficence".

awareness of another creature. What, then, should be the servant's awareness of his [divine] Master?"

I heard a Sufi say: "One ruler had a slave, whom he liked more than his other slaves, although he was neither more valuable, nor more handsome than the rest. When people asked him about this, he decided to show them that that slave's service was superior to that of his other slaves. One day he was riding with his entourage. In the distance was a snow-capped mountain. The ruler looked at the mountain, then lowered his head. [Suddenly,] the slave urged his horse to run and galloped off. The people [in the entourage] did not know why he did so. After a short while the slave returned carrying with him some ice. The ruler asked him: 'How did you know that I wanted ice?' The slave replied: 'You glanced at it [the mountain], and the glance of the ruler is always for a purpose.' The ruler said: 'I have singled him out for favor and liking, because for everyone there is an occupation, and his occupation is to take note of my glances and to be aware of my moods.'"

A Sufi said: "Whosoever is aware of God in his thoughts, God will protect his limbs [from any sin]." Someone asked Abu 'l-Husayn b. Hind: "When does the shepherd chase his sheep away from the pastures of perdition by the staff of protection?" He answered: "When he knows that he is [himself] being watched." It is related that Ibn 'Umar[275] – may God be pleased with him – was on a journey, when he saw a slave tending some sheep. Ibn 'Umar asked him whether he would sell him one sheep. The slave answered: "These sheep are not mine." Ibn 'Umar told him: "Then tell the owner that it was taken by a wolf." The slave exclaimed: "And how about God?" From that time on, Ibn 'Umar would always say: "That slave said: 'How about God?'"

Al-Junayd said: "He who has achieved perfection in awareness fears the loss of favor only from his Lord and no one else." One Sufi master had many disciples. However, he would always single out one of them for his favors and affection over anyone else. When some folk asked him about this, he said: "I will explain this to you." He gave each of his disciples a bird and instructed them: "Slaughter this bird so that no one can see [you doing this]." The disciples went away. When they returned each of them brought with him a slaughtered bird. Only [the master's favorite disciple] brought back his bird alive. The master asked him why he did not kill it. He answered: "You ordered me to slaughter it, so that no one would see this. However, I could not find a place where no one would see me." The master said: "This is why I singled him out for my favor and affection!"

Dhu 'l-Nun al-Misri said: "One sign of awareness is to give preference to what is preferred by God Most High and to glorify what God Most High glorifies, while denigrating what God Most High denigrates."//266 Al-Nasrabadhi said: "Hope prompts you to obedience; fear [of God] distances you from disobedience; awareness [of God] leads to the paths of true realities." I heard Muhammad b.

---

275 'Abdallah b. 'Umar, son of the second rightly guided caliph 'Umar. One of the most prominent personalities in the first generation of the Muslims, he died in 74/693.

al-Husayn say: Abu ʾl-ʿAbbas al-Baghdadi said: I asked Jaʿfar b. Nusayr about awareness [of God]. He answered: "[It is] watching over your innermost self, because of your awareness that God – praise be to Him – watches [your] every thought." I also heard him say: I heard Abu ʾl-Hasan al-Farisi say: I heard al-Jurayri say: "This cause of ours [Sufis] rests on two foundations: you accustom your soul to be aware of God Most High and you know that [the Divine Law] is visible in your actions." I also heard him [Muhammad b. al-Husayn] say: I heard Abu ʾl-Qasim al-Baghdadi say: I heard al-Murtaʿish say: "Awareness [of God] is watching over your innermost heart by taking note of the Unseen with every breath and every phrase." Ibn ʿAtaʾ was asked what was the best act of obedience [to God]. He answered: "Being constantly aware of God." Ibrahim al-Khawwas said: "Watchfulness brings about awareness [of God], and awareness brings about the dedication to God Most High of one's innermost self and one's outward [actions]."

I heard Shaykh Abu ʿAbd al-Rahman al-Sulami – may God have mercy on him – say: I heard Abu ʿUthman al-Maghribi say: "The best things that man has come to observe as he travels along this [Sufi] path are: self-scrutiny, awareness [of God], and guiding his actions by the knowledge [of the Divine Law]." I also heard him say: I heard ʿAbdallah al-Razi say: I heard Abu ʿUthman [al-Maghribi] say: "Abu Hafs [al-Haddad] told me: 'When you preside [over an assembly of students], make sure to exhort your own heart and soul. Do not allow their attending your lecture to beguile you, for they are aware of your exterior, whereas God is aware of your interior.'" I heard him say: I heard Muhammad b. ʿAbdallah say: I heard Abu Jaʿfar al-Saydalani say: I heard Abu Saʿid al-Kharraz say: "One of my masters told me: 'You must watch over your innermost self and be aware [of God].' One day, as I was traveling in the desert, I heard a noise behind me that frightened me. I wanted to turn around [to see what it was]. However, I did not. Then I saw something [hovering] over my shoulder. I kept watching over my inner self, and it finally went away. I turned around, and saw a huge lion."

Al-Wasiti said: "The best act of obedience [to God] is watching over the moments." This means that one should not look beyond the limit set [to one by God]; that one should not be aware of anyone but one's Lord; and that one should keep company only with one's own [mystical] moment (*waqt*).

Satisfaction (*rida*)

God Most High said: "God is well-pleased with them and they are well-pleased with Him."[276]

ʿAli b. Ahmad al-Ahwazi – may God have mercy on him – informed us: Ahmad b. ʿUbayd al-Basri told us: al-Kuraymi[277] told us: "Yaʿqub b. Ismaʿil al-Sallal told us: Abu ʿAsim al-ʿAbbadani told us on the authority of al-Fadl b.

---

276 Q. 5:119; cf. 9:100; 9:97 according to Arberry's translation.
277 In another reading, "al-Kudaymi".

'Isa al-Raqashi, on the authority of Muhammad b. al-Munkadir, on the authority of Jabir, who related that the Messenger of God – may God bless and greet him – said: "When the people of Paradise will gather together, a light will shine on them from the gate of Paradise. They will raise their heads and see their Lord Most High looking down upon them. He will say: 'O people of Paradise, ask of Me!' They will say: 'We desire that You be pleased with us.' God Most High will reply: 'My pleasure has settled you in this abode of mine and bestowed My mercy upon you! The time has come, ask Me again!' They will say: 'We ask you for more!'" He [the Prophet] said: "They will be given noble steeds made of rubies with reins studded with green emeralds and rubies. They will ride upon these steeds, which will, with each step, set their hooves as far as their eye can see. Then God – praise be to Him – will command that trees with fruit upon them be brought there. Then maidens of Paradise (*houries*) will come to them, saying: 'We are the blessed ones, who are free from any fault; we are also eternal, we never die; we are mates for noble believing folk.' Then God – praise be to Him – will order piles of white sweet-smelling musk to be delivered and they will be stimulated by a fragrant wind called 'the Arouser' (*muthir*) until they reach the Garden of Eden, which is the very heart of Paradise. The angels will announce: 'O our Lord, the folk have arrived!' and God will say: 'Welcome to the truthful ones, welcome to the obedient ones!'" He [the Prophet] said: "The veil will be lifted for them and they will see God – may He be great and exalted – and they will enjoy the light of the All-Compassionate so that they will no longer see one another. God will tell [the angels]: 'Return them to their palaces with precious gifts!'" He [the Prophet] said: "They will be brought back, and will be able to see one another." The Messenger of God – may God bless and greet him – said: "This is what God Most High meant, when he said: 'Hospitality[278] from One All-Forgiving, One All-Compassionate.'"[279]

The Iraqis and the Khurasanians disagree regarding satisfaction: is it a mystical state or a mystical station?[280] The Khurasanians say that satisfaction is a station, and that it is the ultimate point of [the station of] trust in God (*tawakkul*). That is, it is one of those things that a servant of God acquires through his own effort. The Iraqis, on the other hand, say that satisfaction is a state and that it is not acquired by the servant. It is a phenomenon that descends upon the heart of the servant and dwells in it as all other states.//268 One can combine these two teachings and say: "At the beginning [of the Sufi path], the servant acquires satisfaction, so it is a station, while in the end it becomes a state, and, therefore, can no longer be acquired. When different people discourse about satisfaction, each one conveys his own state and his own share of experience. This is why they differ from one another when they discuss it, for their experiences and their portions of it are diverse. As for religious knowledge (*'ilm*), it stipulates

---

278 Or "provision".
279 Q. 41:32.
280 For a discussion of the differences between mystical states and stations see *IM*, pp. 303–309.

unconditionally that the person who is satisfied with God's [will] should never oppose what has been decreed for him [by God]."

I heard the master Abu ʿAli al-Daqqaq say: "Satisfaction is not that you remain immune to affliction; it is that you do not oppose [divine] judgement and decree. Know that it is incumbent upon the servant to be satisfied with the [divine] decree, with which he has been ordered [by God] to be satisfied. For not everything that constitutes [the divine] decree requires or permits the servant's satisfaction – for instance, disobedience and various trials [prescribed by God] to the Muslim community. The Sufi masters have said: "Satisfaction is the greatest gate of God." They imply that he who is graced by satisfaction will receive God's most perfect welcome and will be granted the highest proximity [with Him]. I heard Muhammad b. al-Husayn – may God have mercy on him – say: Abu Jaʿfar al-Razi informed us: al-ʿAbbas b. Hamza said: Ibn Abi ʾl-Hawari told us: ʿAbd al-Wahid b. Zayd said: "Satisfaction is the greatest door of God and Paradise on earth."

Know that the servant will never be satisfied with God – praise be to Him – until after God – praise be to Him – is satisfied with him, for God – may He be great and exalted – said: "God is well-pleased with them and they are well-pleased with him."[281] I heard the master Abu ʿAli al-Daqqaq say: "A disciple asked his master: 'Does the servant know whether God Most High is satisfied with him?' The master answered: 'No, how can he know that, when His satisfaction [belongs to] the Unknown (*ghayb*)?' The disciple objected, saying: 'Yes, he can know that.' The master asked how that could be. The disciple answered: 'If I find my heart satisfied with God Most High, I learn that He too is satisfied with me!' The master said: 'You have spoken well, young man!'"

It is said that Moses – peace be upon him – said: "My God, show me an action that I could perform in order to satisfy You." God answered: "You will be unable to bear it." Moses – peace be upon him – prostrated himself before God and implored Him. Then God, Most High revealed to him: "O son of ʿImran, My satisfaction lies in your satisfaction with My decree!"

Shaykh Abu ʿAbd al-Rahman – may God have mercy on him – said: Abu Jaʿfar al-Razi said: al-ʿAbbas b. Hamza said: Ibn Abi ʾl-Hawari said: I heard Abu Sulayman al-Darani//269 say: "When the servant has abandoned his passions, he will be satisfied." I also heard him [al-Sulami] say: "Whoever wants to attain the abode of satisfaction must adhere to that which satisfies God." Muhammad b. Khafif said: "There are two kinds of satisfaction: satisfaction with Him and satisfaction with what comes from Him. Satisfaction with Him is when one is satisfied with His arrangement of affairs, while satisfaction with that which comes from Him is [satisfaction] with His decree." I heard the master Abu ʿAli al-Daqqaq say: "The path of the travelers is longer, because it is the path of self-discipline. The path of the elect is shorter, but it is more difficult because it presupposes that you act to satisfy Him and that you are satisfied with His

---

281 Q. 5:119; cf. 9:100, 9:97, according to Arberry's translation.

decree." Ruwaym [b. Ahmad] said: "Satisfaction is that God has placed Gehenna[282] to one's right side, yet one does not ask God to move it to his left side."

Abu Bakr b. Tahir said: "Satisfaction is removing loathing from one's heart, so that there will be nothing in it except happiness and joy." Al-Wasiti said: "Make use of satisfaction to your uttermost, but do not let satisfaction make use of you, lest you may become veiled [from God] by its sweetness, and by your vision of it from the True Reality of that which you contemplate." Know that al-Wasiti's phrase is of great importance. It contains a warning about a hidden danger that awaits this folk.[283] Their preoccupation with [spiritual] states may veil them from the One Who brings about these states. A person who delights in his [state of] satisfaction and whose heart takes pleasure in it, may become veiled by his state from contemplating the Real. Likewise, al-Wasiti said: "Beware of indulging in the acts of piety! They are a deadly poison."

Ibn Khafif said: "Satisfaction is the heart's preoccupation with divine decrees and its agreement with what pleases God and that which He has chosen for it." Someone asked Rabi'a al-'Adawiyya: "When will the servant [of God] be satisfied?" She said: "When he rejoices at afflictions as much as he rejoices at bounty." Al-Shibli said in the presence of al-Junayd: "There's no power or might except by God!" Al-Junayd told him: "These words of yours show a soul gripped with distress and your distress comes from your abandoning satisfaction with God's decree." Al-Shibli fell silent. Abu Sulayman al-Darani said: "[True] satisfaction is when you do not ask God Most High for Paradise nor seek refuge in Him from the hellfire."

I heard Muhammad b. al-Husayn say: I heard Abu 'l-'Abbas al-Baghdadi say: I heard Muhammad b. Ahmad b. Sahl say: I heard Sa'id b. 'Uthman say: I heard Dhu 'l-Nun al-Misri//270 – may God have mercy on him – say: "There are three signs of satisfaction: "Giving up [your] free choice in anticipation of the [passing of] divine decree; feeling no bitterness after the decree has been passed; and [experiencing] the excitement of love [of God] in the middle of affliction." I also heard him [Muhammad b. al-Husayn] say: I heard Muhammad b. Ja'far al-Baghdadi say: I heard Isma'il b. Muhammad al-Saffar say: I heard Muhammad b. Yazid al-Mubarrad say: "Someone told al-Husayn b. Ali b. Abi Talib[284] – may God be pleased with both of them – that Abu Dharr[285] once said: 'I like poverty more than wealth and I like illness more than health.' He [al-Husayn] answered: 'May God have mercy on Abu Dharr! As for me, I say: "He who puts his trust in that which was predetermined for him by God Most High, can desire only that which God – may He be great and exalted – has predetermined for him."'"

---

282 A place of torment, hell. This term is derived from the name of the valley of Hinnom near Jerusalem, where refuse was burned in Biblical times.
283 That is, the Sufis.
284 The younger son of the fourth rightly guided caliph 'Ali and the third imam of the Twelver Shi'ites. Soon after he made a bid for power following the death of the first Umayyad caliph Mu'awiyya, he and his supporters were killed by an Umayyad army at Kerbela, Iraq, in 60/680.
285 A Companion of the Prophet who was famous for his frugality and austerity of character.

Al-Fudayl b. ʿIyad told Bishr al-Hafi: "Satisfaction is better than renunciation of this world, because he who is satisfied never aspires to anything above his station." Someone asked Abu ʿUthman [al-Hiri] about the words of the Prophet – may God bless and greet him, "I ask You to grant me satisfaction after [Your] decree has been passed [on me]." He answered: "Because satisfaction in anticipation of the decree is just a resolve to be satisfied, whereas satisfaction after [the passing of] the decree is [true] satisfaction." I heard Shaykh Abu ʿAbd al-Rahman al-Sulami – may God have mercy on him – say: I heard ʿAbdallah al-Razi say: I heard Ibn Abi Hassan al-Anmati say: I heard Ahmad b. Abi ʾl-Hawari say: I heard Abu Sulayman [al-Darani] say: "I hope to come to learn at least a small portion of satisfaction: when He throws me into the hellfire, I will be satisfied with this." Abu ʿUmar al-Dimashqi said: "Satisfaction is to abandon anxiety over [the workings of] the divine command, whatever it might be." Al-Junayd said: "Satisfaction is abandoning [your] free choice." Ibn ʿAtaʾ said: "Satisfaction is directing [your] heart toward God Most High's pre-eternal choice [of destiny] for His servant and giving up resentment." Ruwaym [b. Ahmad] said: "Satisfaction is accepting divine decrees with joy." Al-Muhasibi said: "Satisfaction is the tranquility of the heart in the face of the stream of divine decrees." Al-Nuri said: "Satisfaction is that [your] heart rejoices after having tasted the bitterness of the divine verdict."

I heard Muhammad b. al-Husayn say: I heard Abu ʾl-Husayn al-Farisi say: I heard al-Jurayri say: "Whoever is satisfied without measure, God Most High will raise him above his limit." I also heard him say: I heard Ahmad b. ʿAli say: I heard al-Hasan b. al-ʿAlawayh[286] say: Abu Turab al-Nakhshabi said: "He whose heart puts any value on this world will never attain satisfaction." Shaykh Abu ʿAbd al-Rahman al-Sulami informed us: Abu ʿAmr b. Hamdan informed us://271 ʿAbdallah b. Shiruya[287] told us: Bishr b. al-Hakam told us: ʿAbd al-ʿAziz b. Muhammad told us on the authority of Yazid b. al-Hadi, on the authority of Muhammad b. Ibrahim, on the authority of ʿAmir b. Saʿd, on the authority of al-ʿAbbas b. ʿAbd al-Muttalib, who said that the Messenger of God – may God bless and greet him – said: "He who is satisfied with God as his Lord has tasted the flavor of faith."

It is said that ʿUmar b. al-Khattab wrote a letter to Abu Musa al-Ashʿari[288] – may God be pleased with both of them – saying: "All goodness lies in satisfaction. Be satisfied, if you can; if not, then endure patiently." It is said that ʿUtba al-Ghulam spent the entire night until dawn saying: "If You punish me, I love You, and if You have mercy on me, I love You." I heard the master Abu ʿAli al-Daqqaq say: "Man is made of potter's clay and clay has nothing in it that would allow it to oppose the verdict of God Most High." Abu ʿUthman al-Hiri said: "For forty years God – may He be great and exalted – has never placed me

---

286 Or "al-ʿAlluya".
287 Or, "al-Shitriyya".
288 A Companion of the Prophet and military commander, he died after 42/662.

in a state that I dislike; nor has He transferred me from that state to a state that I would resent." I heard the master Abu ʿAli al-Daqqaq say: "A man was angry with a slave of his. The slave asked another person to intercede on his behalf with the other man. The master pardoned him, yet the slave burst into tears. The intercessor asked him: 'Why are you crying? Your master has pardoned you.' The master answered [instead of him]: 'He wants to obtain my satisfaction, but there is no way for him to achieve this. This is why he cries.'"

Servanthood (ʿubudiyya)

God – may He be great and exalted – said: "Serve thy Lord, until the Certainty[289] comes to thee."[290] Abu ʾl-Hasan al-Ahwazi – may God have mercy on him – informed us: Ahmad b. ʿUbayd al-Saffar informed us: ʿUbayd b. Sharik told us: Yahya told us: Malik told us on the authority of Habib[291] b. ʿAbd al-Rahman, on the authority of Hafs b. ʿAsim b. ʿUmar b. al-Khattab, on the authority of Abu Saʿid al-Khudri and Abu Hurayra that the Messenger of God – may God bless and greet him – said: "Seven are those whom God will shade with His shade on the day there will be no shade but His: a just leader (imam ʿadil), a youth raised in the service of God Most High, a man whose heart remains attached to the mosque from the moment he leaves it until he comes back to it, two men who love each other for the sake of God and who come together and take leave of one another in this condition, a man who remembers God Most High in private, his eyes overflowing with tears, a man who responds to a beautiful woman who tries to seduce him, saying: 'I fear God, Lord of the worlds', and a man who gives alms in such secrecy that his left hand does not know what his right hand gives."//272

I heard the master Abu ʿAli al-Daqqaq – may God have mercy on him – say: "Servanthood is more complete than worship (ʿibada); first comes worship, then servanthood, then servitude (ʿubuda). Worship belongs to the common believers; servanthood to the elect; and servitude to the elect of the elect." I also heard him say: "Worship belongs to those who possess certitude; servanthood belongs to those who possess the essence of certainty; and servitude belongs to those who possess the True Reality of certainty." He also said: "Worship is for those who strive [on the path of God] (mujahadat); servanthood is for those who subject themselves to strictures (mukabadat); and servitude is a sign of those who witness God (mushahadat). One who does not spare his soul for the sake of God is a worshiper; one who does not withhold his heart for the sake of God is a servant; and one who generously gives God his spirit is a possessor of servitude." They say: "Servanthood is practicing acts of obedience in the most ample manner, while seeing the shortcomings of your actions and keeping in mind that whatever virtues you might possess have been predetermined by God's decree." It is said:

---

289 Usually understood as death.
290 Q. 15:99.
291 Or "Khubayb".

"Servanthood is giving up your personal choice in favor of what has been foreordained for you by divine decrees." It is also said: "Servanthood is freeing yourself from your power and might, and recognizing the grants and blessings that He bestows upon you." It is also said: "Servanthood is embracing whatever God has commanded for you and departing from what He has prohibited for you." Someone asked Muhammad b. Khafif about the correct servanthood. He answered: "When the servant places his burden upon his Master and patiently bears with Him its afflictions."

I heard Shaykh Abu 'Abd al-Rahman al-Sulami – may God have mercy on him – say: I heard Abu 'l-'Abbas al-Baghdadi say: I heard Ja'far b. Muhammad b. Nusayr say: I heard Ibn Masruq say: I heard Sahl b. 'Abdallah [al-Tustari] say: "One can never achieve true servanthood without enduring four things: hunger, nakedness, poverty, and humiliation." They say: "Servanthood is to give oneself fully to God and to place one's burdens upon Him." They also say: "One of the signs of servanthood is giving up one's own planning and watching [the workings of] divine decrees."

Dhu 'l-Nun al-Misri said: "Servanthood is that you remain His servant at all times, while He remains your Lord at all times." Al-Jurayri said: "Servants of [God's] bounties are many. However, servants of the Bounty-Giver are very rare indeed."//273 The master Abu 'Ali al-Daqqaq said: "You are the servant of whoever holds you in his bondage. If you are in the bondage of your soul, then you are its servant; if you are in the bondage of this world of yours, then you are its servant." The Messenger of God – may God bless and greet him – said: "A plague be on the slaves of *dirhams*, a plague be on the slaves of *dinars*; a plague be on the wearers of embroidered garments!" Abu Zayn[292] saw a man and asked him: "What is your trade?" He answered: "I serve[293] donkeys." Abu Zayn answered: "May God Most High destroy your donkeys, so that you become a servant of God, not a servant of donkeys!"

I heard Shaykh Abu 'Abd al-Rahman al-Sulami say: I heard my grandfather Abu 'Amr b. Nujayd say: "No man can take even one step along the path of servanthood until he sees his deeds as hypocrisy and his spiritual states as pretensions." I also heard him say: I heard 'Abdallah al-Mu'allim say: I heard 'Abdallah al-Munazil say: "A person remains a slave of God as long as he does not seek a servant for himself. If he begins to seek a servant for himself, he falls from the rank of servanthood and abandons its manners." I also heard him say: I heard Muhammad b. al-Husayn say: I heard Ja'far b. Nusayr say: I heard Ibn Masruq say: I heard Sahl b. 'Abdallah [al-Tustari] say: "One will not achieve true service [of God] until one has reached a stage at which one shows neither signs of poverty while being destitute nor signs of well-being while being wealthy." It is said: "Servanthood is bearing witness to the divine lordship."

---

292 Or "Abu Yazid [al-Bistami]".
293 That is, "I provide."

I heard the master Abu ʿAli al-Daqqaq – may God have mercy on him – say: I heard al-Nasrabadhi say: "The worth of the servant corresponds to the worth of the object of his service. Likewise, the virtue of the one who knows corresponds to the virtue of the object of his knowledge." Abu Hafs [al-Haddad] said: "Servanthood is the adornment of the servant. Whoever abandons it, forfeits this adornment." I heard Muhammad b. al-Husayn – may God have mercy on him – say: I heard Abu Jaʿfar al-Razi say: I heard ʿAbbas b. Hamza say: I heard Ahmad b. Abi ʾl-Hawari say: I heard al-Nibaji say: "The root of servanthood is in three things: you must not oppose any of His rulings; you must not withhold anything from Him; you must never be heard asking for something from someone other than Him. I also heard him [Muhammad b. al-Husayn] say: I heard Abu ʾl-Husayn al-Farisi say: I heard Ibn ʿAtaʾ say: "Servanthood consists of four traits: being faithful to one's vows; observing the limits [established by God]; satisfaction with what you have; and bearing patiently that which you have not." I also heard him say: I heard Muhammad b. Shadhan say: I heard al-Kattani say: I heard ʿAmr b. ʿUthman al-Makki say: "Among the many pious men who resided in Mecca and elsewhere and among those who came to us [in Mecca] during the pilgrimage season I have met no one as passionate in his striving (*ijtihad*) and more persevering in worship than al-Muzani[294] – may God have mercy on him. Nor have I ever seen someone as respectful of the commands of God Most High or someone as strict with himself and as generous to others."//274

I heard the master Abu ʿAli al-Daqqaq say: "Nothing is nobler than servanthood. Nor is there a more perfect name for the believer than [being called 'servant']. This is the reason why God – glory to him – said about the Prophet – may God bless and greet him – on the night of his ascension to heaven – which was his greatest moment in his entire worldly life: 'Glory be to Him, Who carried His servant by night from the Holy Mosque [to the Further Mosque].'[295] The Most High also said: 'And then revealed to His servant what He revealed.'[296] If there were a name greater than 'servant' God would definitely have called him by it." With this meaning in mind they recite:

ʿAmr, to avenge me is a duty of my Zahra, anyone who hears and sees knows this
Call me by no name but a slave of her, for it is my noblest name!

One Sufi said: "There are only two things [that prevent you from achieving servanthood]: when you find repose in things that you like, and when you rely on your own actions. Once you have shed these two things, you have given servanthood its due." Al-Wasiti said: "Beware of the delight of giving [to others],

---

294 Ibrahim b. Yahya al-Muzani was a foremost disciple and exponent of the great jurisprudent al-Shafiʿi. He lived and died in Egypt in 264/878.
295 Q. 17:1.
296 Q. 53:10.

for it may become a veiling for the people of purity."²⁹⁷ Abu ʿAli al-Juzjani said: "Satisfaction [with God] is servanthood's courtyard; patience is its door; and relegating all power to God (*tafwid*) is its house. You raise your voice at the door,²⁹⁸ hurry through the courtyard, and then have rest in the house." I heard the master Abu ʿAli al-Daqqaq say: "Just as Lordship is a property of the Real – glory be to Him – which never ceases, so is servanthood a property of God's servant which stays with him as long as he is alive." A Sufi recited:

> If you ask me, I will say: "I am his servant."
> If you ask him, he will say: "Here's my slave."

I heard Shaykh Abu ʿAbd al-Rahman al-Sulami say: I heard al-Nasrabadhi say: "Acts of worship that are performed in search of [God's] pardon and forgiveness for their flaws are closer [to their goal] than those that are performed out of desire for compensation and reward." I also heard him say: I heard al-Nasrabadhi say: "Servanthood is shedding the awareness of your service in witnessing the One being served." I also heard him say: I heard Abu Bakr Muhammad b. ʿAbdallah b. Shadhan say: I heard al-Jurayri say: "Servanthood is abandoning all preoccupations and preoccupying yourself with the preoccupation²⁹⁹ that is the root of repose."//275

Desire (*irada*)

God – may He be great and exalted – said: "And do not drive away those who call upon their Lord at morning and evening desiring His countenance."³⁰⁰ ʿAli b. Ahmad b. ʿAbdan informed us: Ahmad b. ʿUbayd informed us: Hisham b. ʿAli told us: al-Hakam b. Aslam told us: Ismaʿil b. Jaʿfar told us on the authority of Humayd on the authority of Anas [b. Malik] – may God be pleased with him – who said that the Prophet – may God bless and greet him – said: "When God desires good for His servant, He puts him to use." Someone asked him: "How does He put him to use?" The Prophet responded: "He gives him success in performing a pious work before death."

Desire is the beginning of the path of the wayfarers and the name of the first station of those who aspire to God Most High. This feature is called "desire" because desire precedes every matter. If the servant of God does not desire something, he will not do it. Since this is the beginning for those who travel on the path to God – may He be great and exalted – it is called "desire" by analogy with the desire that precedes all matters. "One who desires" (*murid*)³⁰¹ derives his name from "desire" (*irada*) in the same way as "one who knows" (*ʿalim*) derives his name from "knowledge" (*ʿilm*), for both belong to [the category of] derivative

---

297 That is, to the Sufis.
298 In order to be let in.
299 That is, the service of God.
300 Q. 6:52.
301 This term is usually rendered into English as "[Sufi] disciple", or "aspirant".

names. However, according to the usage of this [Sufi] community, the *murid* is someone who has no desire; he who has not stripped himself from desire, cannot be counted among *murids*. Yet, in the regular usage, he who has no desire cannot be considered to be of those who desire (*murid*). Sufis have spoken much about desire, each one speaking according to what has manifested in his heart. The majority of Sufi masters say: "Desire is giving up what people are accustomed to, and the custom of most people is to race in the fields of forgetfulness, the drives of their passions, and to reside in the domain of their desire." However, the [Sufi] *murid* has rid himself from all of those qualities. His abandoning them is a sign and proof of the soundness of [his] desire. This condition is called "desire", which is the abandonment of [one's] habits, for the abandonment of [one's] habits is the sign of desire. The True Reality of desire is that your heart rushes forth in search of God – praise be to Him. It is therefore said that desire is "the anguish that reduces any fear to insignificance".//276

I heard the master Abu 'Ali al-Daqqaq – may God have mercy on him – recount on the authority of Mimshadh al-Dinawari, who said: "When I learned how serious the conditions of the poor[302] are, I ceased joking with any of them. Once a poor man came to me and said: 'Master, I wish you could prepare a sweetmeat for me.' Suddenly, the words 'desire' (*irada*) and 'sweetmeat' (*'asida*) flew from my tongue in a jesting way. [On hearing this] the poor man withdrew, without me taking notice of that. I ordered the sweetmeat to be prepared, then started to look for the man, but could not find him. Later on, I learned what had happened to him. I was told that he left [my house] immediately saying to himself: 'Desire (*irada*) and sweetmeat (*'asida*), desire (*irada*) and sweetmeat (*'asida*) ...' He wandered about aimlessly until he entered the desert, where he kept repeating these words until he died."

A Sufi master said: "I was alone in the desert and became depressed. So I cried: 'Human beings, talk to me!', 'Jinns, talk to me!' Suddenly I heard a voice, asking me: 'What do you desire?' I said: 'I desire God Most High!' The voice said: 'Why do you desire God?', meaning that someone who called on the jinns and human beings to talk to him could not possibly have desired God – may He be great and exalted." He who desires, keeps aspiring [to Him] day and night. Outwardly he is characterized by self-exertion, while inwardly he is engaged in struggle [against his ego]. He abandons the bed of repose and is preoccupied [with worship] at all times; he bears hardships, carries heavy burdens, seeks to improve his moral qualities, practices [self-imposed] strictures, copes with all kind of terrors and leaves behind all [false] appearances. Of this state it is said:

> I passed the night in the desert, fearing neither lion nor wolf
> My longing overwhelmed me and I wandered hastily through the night,
> For my passionate desire granted me no respite.

---

302 That is, "Sufis".

I heard the master Abu ʿAli al-Daqqaq say: "Desire is anguish in your innermost self, a sting in your heart, a torment in your soul, and a stirring in your inner being; it is fires raging in human hearts." I heard Muhammad b. al-Husayn say: I heard Muhammad b. ʿAbdallah say: I heard Abu Bakr al-Sabbak say: I heard Yusuf b. al-Husayn say: "There was a pact between Abu Sulayman [al-Darani] and Ahmad b. Abi ʾl-Hawari, according to which Ahmad was not supposed to disobey anything that Abu Sulayman might command him to do. Once he came to Abu Sulayman, when he was lecturing to his students. He told his teacher: 'The oven is hot. What do you command?' Abu Sulayman did not respond. When he repeated the same phrase two or three times, Abu Sulayman told him in a fit of anger: 'Then go and sit in it!' He forgot about Ahmad for a while, then remembered, and told [his students]: 'Go look for Ahmad, for he is in the oven. He made a pledge never to disobey me.' When they saw him sitting in the oven, they noticed that not a single hair on him was burned."

I heard the master Abu ʿAli al-Daqqaq say: "In my early youth I strove hard to achieve [true] desire. I used to say to myself: 'If I only knew what the meaning of desire is!'" It is said that those who desire [God] have the following qualities: loving supererogatory acts of piety; dispensing sincere advice to [the members of the community]; feeling comfortable in retreat; being patient in the face of divine decrees, no matter how harsh; always obeying the divine command; feeling ashamed under the gaze of God; seeking any means that can bring them closer to God; being happy in humility; giving the heart no rest until it attains its Lord. Abu Bakr al-Warraq said: "Those who desire face three evils: marriage, taking down *hadith*, and journeying abroad." Someone asked him: "Why did you stop writing down *hadith*?" He answered: "They prevented me from keeping up my desire." Hatim al-Asamm said: "If you see an aspirant (*murid*), who desires something other than the True Object of his desire (*murad*), know that he has exposed his depravity."

I heard Muhammad b. al-Husayn say: I heard Abu Bakr al-Razi say: I heard al-Kattani say: "Three things are required of the *murid*: sleeping only when overcome [by sleep]; eating only when overcome by need; and speaking only when absolutely necessary." I also heard him [Muhammad b. al-Husayn] say: I heard Husayn b. Ahmad b. Jaʿfar say: I heard Jaʿfar b. Nusayr say: I heard al-Junayd say: "When God Most High desires something good for the *murid*, He places him among the Sufis and shields him from the company of Qurʾan reciters.[303] I also heard him say: I heard al-Raqqi[304] say: I heard al-Daqqaq say: "The ultimate stage of desire is when you point toward God Most High and find Him where you pointed to." I asked him: "What renders desire unnecessary?" He answered: "When you can find Him without pointing."

I heard Muhammad b. ʿAbdallah al-Sufi say: I heard ʿAyyash b. Abi ʾl-Sahw[305] say: I heard Abu Bakr al-Daqqaq say: "The *murid* cannot be called that until the

---

303 Because they make the recitation of the Qurʾan their source of livelihood.
304 Or "al-Duqqi".
305 Or "al-Sakhr".

angel on his left side[306] has been unable write anything down [against him] for twenty years. Abu 'Uthman al-Hiri said: "If one lacks proper desire from the outset, one's estrangement [from God] will only increase with the passage of days." He also said: "When the *murid* hears something of the Sufi sciences and acts according to it, he thereby allows wisdom to enter his heart and settle there until the end of his days. He himself benefits from this [wisdom], and when he discourses about it, all those who listen to him benefit as well. As for the person who hears something of the Sufi sciences, but fails to act according to it, it [what he hears] is like a story that is remembered for a few days and then forgotten." Al-Wasiti said: "The first station of the *murid* is to desire God – may He be praised – which he achieves by abandoning his own desire." Yahya b. Mu'adh said: "The most difficult thing for the *murids* is to keep company with those who oppose them." I heard Shaykh Abu 'Abd al-Rahman al-Sulami say: I heard Abu 'l-Qasim al-Razi say: I heard Yusuf b. al-Husayn say: "When you see a *murid* who practices concessions[307] and engages in gainful employment, [know that] nothing good will come out of him." I also heard him [al-Razi?] say: I heard Muhammad b. al-Husayn say: I heard Ja'far al-Khuldi say: "Someone asked al-Junayd: 'Why should the *murids* listen to pious stories?' He answered: 'Pious stories are like God's legions. He strengthens their hearts with them.' Someone asked him whether he had any evidence [to support his statement]. He answered: 'Yes, God – may He be great and exalted – said: "And all that We relate to thee of the tidings of the messengers is only that wherewith We [seek to] strengthen thy heart."[308] I also heard him say: I heard Muhammad b. Khalid say: I heard Ja'far [al-Khuldi] say: I heard al-Junayd say: "The true *murid* is in no need of the learning of the scholars ('*ulama*')."

As for the difference between one who desires (*murid*) and one who is desired [by God] (*murad*), it is that every *murid* is, in essence, a *murad*. For if he were not desired by God Most High (*murad*) to desire Him, he would not be one who desires (*murid*). In other words, nothing can happen unless God Most High desires it, therefore one who desires (*murid*) is not other than he who is desired (*murad*). For God – praise be to Him – singles this person out for His desire and bestows upon him the desire [for Him]. However, this folk[309] still differentiate between *murid* and *murad*. The *murid* is the beginner [on the path to God], while the *murad* is the one who has reached [its] end. The *murid* is one who is placed in the middle of exhausting works (*ta'ab*) and cast into the strictures of hard labor. For the *murad*, on the other hand, [divine] command is sufficient in any hardship he goes through. Whereas the *murid* has to exert himself strenuously, the *murad* is assisted [by God] and is put at ease.

---

306 That is, the one who records his evil deeds, as opposed to the angel on his right side that records his good deeds.
307 That is, who does not exert himself to his full capacity in observing the Divine Law.
308 Q. 11:120; 11:121, according to Arberry's translation.
309 That is, the Sufis.

God Most High treats the travelers [on the Sufi path] differently. Most of them are granted success in their striving and, after much strenuous self-exertion, arrive at sublime matters. However, many of them are shown these sublime matters already at the beginning [of their path]. Thus they reach the heights that many of those who practice arduous self-discipline don't. Yet, most of those who are assisted by God's companionship choose to return to the arduous self-exertions in order to undertake their share of the hardships (which has so far eluded them) that characterize the practitioners of arduous self-discipline. I heard the master Abu ʿAli al-Daqqaq say: "The *murid* carries [the load of hardship], while the *murad* is carried [to his goal]." I also heard him say: "Moses – peace be upon him – was a *murid*, because he said: "Lord, open my breast [to truth]."³¹⁰ Our Prophet – may God bless and greet him – was a *murad*, because God Most High said of him: "Did We not expand thy breast for thee and lift from thee thy burden, the burden that weighed down thy back? Did We not exalt thy fame?"³¹¹ Likewise, Moses – peace be upon him – asked: "Oh my Lord, show me, that I may behold Thee!" God said: "Thou shalt not see Me!"³¹² On the other hand, God told our Prophet – may God bless and greet him: "Hast thou not regarded thy Lord, how He has stretched out the shadow?"³¹³ According to Abu ʿAli, the intention of the phrases "Hast thou not regarded thy Lord" and "how He has stretched out the shadow" was to conceal the story's [true] meaning³¹⁴ and to show the strength of [the Prophet's] state.

When someone asked al-Junayd about the *murid* and the *murad*, he answered: "The *murid* is governed by religious science (ʿilm), whereas the *murad* stays under God's protection – praise be to Him. Therefore the *murid* walks, while the *murad* flies. Can a walker overtake the flyer?" It is related that Dhu ʾl-Nun sent a messenger to Abu Yazid, saying: "Tell him: 'How long will this sleep and indolence last? The caravan has passed by!'" Abu Yazid told [the messenger]: "Say to my brother Dhu ʾl-Nun: 'The [true] man is he who sleeps through the entire night, then awakes at the caravan's destination before it arrives there.'" Dhu ʾl-Nun said: "Congratulations to him! These are the words that our present condition does not allow us to utter!"

Uprightness (*istiqama*)

God Most High said: "Those who have said 'Our Lord is God' have then become upright."³¹⁵ The imam Abu Bakr Muhammad b. al-Hasan b. Furak – may God have mercy on him – said: ʿAbdallah b. Jaʿfar b. Ahmad al-Isbahani told us: Abu Bishr Yunus b. Habib said: Abu Dawud al-Tayalisi said: Shuʿba said on the

---

310 Q. 20:25; 20:26, according to Arberry's translation.
311 Q. 94:1–4.
312 Q. 7:143; 7:138, according to Arberry's translation.
313 Q. 25:45; 25:47, according to Arberry's translation.
314 That is, the fact that the Prophet could see God.
315 Q. 41:30; 41:31, according to Arberry's translation.

authority of al-A'mash, on the authority of Salim b. Abi al-Ja'd, on the authority of Thawban, a client (*mawla*) of the Prophet – may God bless and greet him – that he said: "Be upright! Though you will never be able to do this fully. Know that the best part of your religion is prayer, and only the [true] believer is capable of preserving his [ritual] purity."

Uprightness is a degree that perfects and completes all affairs. Thanks to it good deeds and their proper order are achieved. He who is not upright in his spiritual state has wasted his striving and his efforts are all in vain. God Most High said: "And be not as a woman who breaks her thread, after it is firmly spun, into fibers."[316]//280 One who has no uprightness among his qualities will not be able to advance from one [mystical] station to another. Nor can he build his way [to God] on a sound foundation. It is necessary for one who embarks [on the Sufi path] to be upright in the rules pertaining to the beginnings [of it]. Likewise, each [perfected] gnostic must practice uprightness in the manners pertaining to the end [of the path]. A sign of steadfastness for the beginners is that their deeds are not marred by laxity. For those in the middle a sign of their uprightness is that their progress along the path presupposes no pausing. As for those who have attained the end of the path their sign is that their progress is not impeded by any veils.

I heard the master Abu 'Ali al-Daqqaq – may God have mercy on him – say: "Uprightness has three degrees: setting things right (*taqwim*) by disciplining one's self; seeking uprightness (*iqama*) by refining one's heart; and remaining upright (*istiqama*) by bringing one's innermost self near God. Abu Bakr – may God be pleased with him – said about God's words "And then they have become upright"[317] that they mean that "They do not associate anyone or anything with God" (*lam yushriku*). 'Umar said that these words mean that "They do not swindle like foxes". The commentary of the Trustworthy One[318] points to the observance of the foundations of God's oneness (*tawhid*), whereas 'Umar's commentary implies an attempt to find an explanation (*talab al-ta'wil*) and keeping the conditions of one's pacts [with God]. Ibn 'Ata' said that these words mean: "They have become upright by dedicating their hearts exclusively to God Most High." Abu 'Ali al-Juzjani said: "Be a seeker of uprightness, not a seeker of [divine] beneficence (*karama*), because your lower self prompts you toward seeking beneficence, whereas your Lord – may He be great and exalted – demands that you seek uprightness."

I heard Shaykh Abu 'Abd al-Rahman al-Sulami say: I heard Abu 'Ali al-Shabbuwi say: "I saw the Prophet – may God bless and greet him – in a dream and I said: 'It is reported that you, Messenger of God, said that the chapter of Hud[319] has made your hair turn white. What was it that made your hair turn

---

316 Q. 16:92; 16:94, according to Arberry's translation.
317 Q. 16:92.
318 An epithet of Abu Bakr (*al-siddiq*).
319 Q. 11.

white: the stories of the prophets of the past and of the destruction of nations?' He answered: 'No, it was [God's command] "Be upright, as you have been commanded!"'[320] It is said that only the greatest of men are capable of maintaining uprightness, because it means the abandonment of one's habits and departure//281 from habitual routines and customs, while standing before God Most High in full truthfulness and sincerity. This is why the Messenger of God – may God bless and greet him – said: "Be upright! Though you will never be able to do this fully." Al-Wasiti said: "Uprightness is the property that completes all virtues and the loss of which makes them turn ugly." It is told that al-Shibli – may God have mercy on him – said: "Uprightness means that you expect the Resurrection to occur at any moment." It is said that uprightness in one's speech means to forsake backbiting; uprightness in one's deeds means to abandon innovations in religion (bid'a); uprightness in one's good works means to avoid laxity; and uprightness in one's spiritual states means to rid oneself of the veil.

I heard the master Abu Bakr Muhammad b. al-Hasan b. Furak say: "The letter 'S' in the word 'to be upright' (istiqama) implies asking.[321] Therefore, it means that they ask God Most High to render them upright in their declaration of God's oneness, then make them faithful in their commitment and their keeping the boundaries [of God's Law]." The master said: "Know that steadfastness necessitates the continual flow of divine graces (karamat), for God Most High said: 'Would that they be upright on the way, we would give them to drink of water copiously.'[322] He did not say: 'We shall let them drink of water' (saqaynahum), He said: 'We would give them water to drink in abundance (asqaynahum).'" The Arabs say: "We shall give him water to drink", implying the continuity of the action.

I heard Muhammad b. al-Husayn – may God have mercy on him – say: I heard al-Husayn b. Ahmad say: I heard Abu al-'Abbas al-Farghani say: I heard al-Junayd say: "Once I met a young Sufi disciple in the desert sitting under an acacia tree. I asked him what made him sit there. He answered: 'It is something that I lost [here].' I left him where he was and continued on my way. When I was returning from my pilgrimage, I found that youth again, except this time he sat closer to the tree. I asked him: 'Why are you sitting here?' He answered: 'I have found what I was looking for on this spot, so I have decided to stay here.'" Al-Junayd commented: "I do not know what is more noble: his perseverance in seeking the state that he lost or his perseverance in sticking to the place where he found what he was looking for."

---

320 Q. 11:112; 11:114, according to Arberry's translation.
321 The tenth form of the verb qama "to be straight" connotes the process of asking – that is, "to seek to be/or to remain upright".
322 Q. 72:16.

Sincerity (*ikhlas*)

God Most High said: "Belongs not sincere religion to God?"[323] ʿAli b. Ahmad al-Ahwazi informed us: Ahmad b. ʿUbayd al-Basri told us//282: Jaʿfar b. Ahmad al-Faryabi told us: Abu Talut told us: Haniʾ b. ʿAbd al-Rahman b. Abi ʿAbla al-ʿUqayli told us on the authority of Ibrahim b. Abi ʿAbla al-ʿUqayli, who said: ʿAtiyya b. Washshaj [Wassaj] told me on the authority of Anas b. Malik – may God be pleased with him – who said: "The Messenger of God – may God bless and greet him – said: 'There are three things that prevent the heart of the believer from being unfaithful: being sincere to God in his actions, counseling those in power, and always holding on to the community of Muslims.'" The master [Abu ʿAli al-Daqqaq] said: "Sincerity means making God – praise be to Him – the sole object of one's worship." By worship he meant seeking closeness to God – praise be to Him – to the exclusion of everything else, such as making a show [of one's piety] for other people, seeking their praise and taking delight in it, or any other thing [that distracts one] from getting closer to God Most High. It is true that sincerity is to protect one's actions from being observed by people. It is also true that sincerity means pious concealment [of one's good deeds] from being observed by people. According to an authentic tradition, "The Prophet – may God bless and greet him – said on the authority of Gabriel, who spoke on the authority of God Most High – praise be to Him – Who said: 'Sincerity is the greatest mystery that I have deposited in the hearts of those servants of Mine whom I love.'"

I asked Shaykh Abu ʿAbd al-Rahman al-Sulami – may God have mercy on him – about sincerity. He answered: I asked ʿAli b. Saʿid and Ahmad b. Zakariya about sincerity. They said: We asked ʿAli b. Ibrahim al-Shaqiqi about sincerity. He answered: I asked Muhammd b. Jaʿfar al-Khassaf about sincerity. He answered: I asked Ahmad b. Bashshar about sincerity. He answered: I asked Abu Yaʿqub al-Shariti about sincerity. He answered: I asked Ahmad b. Ghassan about sincerity. He answered: I asked ʿAbd al-Wahid b. Zayd about sincerity.[324] He answered: I asked al-Hasan [al-Basri] about sincerity. He answered: I asked Hudhayfa about sincerity. He answered: I asked the Prophet – may God bless and greet him – about sincerity. He answered: I asked Gabriel about sincerity. He answered: I asked the Lord of greatness about sincerity. He answered: "This is one of My mysteries, which I have deposited into the hearts of those servants whom I love."//283

I heard the master Abu ʿAli al-Daqqaq say: "Sincerity is to protect one's action from being observed by people. As for truthfulness (*sidq*), it is cleansing oneself of being aware of one's self. The sincere one is free of self-conceit, while the truthful one is free from self-glorification." Dhu ʾl-Nun al-Misri said: "Sincerity is only perfected by being truthful in it and by constant forbearance

---

323 Q. 39:3.
324 See *IM*, pp. 16–18.

in it. As for truthfulness, it is only perfected by being sincere and constant in it." Abu Ya'qub al-Susi said: "As long as people notice sincerity in their sincerity, their sincerity is in need of sincerity." Dhu ʾl-Nun said: "Sincerity has three signs: when the praise and blame of the common folk become equal in your eyes; when you become oblivious of your good deeds as you are doing them; and when you forget about your reward [for your good deeds] in the Hereafter."

I heard Shaykh Abu 'Abd al-Rahman al-Sulami – may God have mercy on him – say: I heard Abu 'Uthman al-Maghribi say: "Sincerity is something in which your lower soul never finds pleasure. This is the sincerity of the ordinary folk. As for the sincerity of the elect, it is something that happens to them without them knowing it. Thus they show acts of obedience [to God], while remaining unaware of them, nor seeing or counting them. This is the sincerity of the elect." Abu Bakr al-Daqqaq said: "The major flaw of the sincere one is that he is aware of his sincerity. When God Most High wants to render his sincerity pure, he removes from his sincerity his awareness of being sincere. He thus becomes sincere through God (*mukhlas*), not sincere on his own accord (*mukhlis*). Sahl [al-Tustari] said: "No one knows hypocrisy better than the sincere one (*mukhlis*)."

I heard Abu Hatim al-Sijistani say: I heard 'Abdallah b. 'Ali say: I heard al-Wajihi say: I heard Abu 'Ali al-Rudhbari say: Ruwaym told me that Abu Sa'id al-Kharraz said: "The hypocrisy of the divine gnostics (*'arifin*) is better than the sincerity of the beginners on the Sufi path (*muridin*)." Dhu ʾl-Nun al-Misri said: "Sincerity is that which is protected from the corruption by the Enemy[325]." Abu 'Uthman [al-Hiri] said: "Sincerity is to forget about creatures through constantly gazing on the Creator." Hudhayfa al-Mar'ashi said: "Sincerity is when the servant's outward actions are the same as his [inner] thoughts." It is said: "Sincerity is that by which one seeks God – may He be praised – and by which one strives to be truthful." It is also said that sincerity is when one remains blind to one's own good deeds.

I heard Muhammad b. al-Husayn – may God have mercy on him – say: I heard Abu ʾl-Husayn al-Farisi say://284 I heard Muhammad b. al-Husayn say: I heard 'Ali b. 'Abd al-Hamid: I heard al-Sari [al-Saqati] say: "One who adorns himself for other people with something that is not [part of his character] will fall from the sight of God Most High." I also heard him [Muhammad b. al-Husayn] say: I heard 'Ali b. Bundar al-Sufi say: I heard 'Abdallah b. Mahmud say: I heard Muhammad b. 'Abd Rabbihi say: al-Fudayl [b. 'Iyad] said: "Abandoning good works for the sake of people is hypocrisy; doing them for the sake of people is polytheism; sincerity is that God absolves you from both." Al-Junayd said: "Sincerity is a secret between God and His servant. Even the recording angel[326] knows nothing of it so that he cannot write it down; nor does Satan know of it so that he cannot corrupt it; nor is his passion aware of it, so that it will not influence him." Ruwaym said: "Sincerity in one's deeds is that the one who performs them

---

325 That is, Satan.
326 That is, the angel who records man's every deed.

seeks no compensation for them in either this world or the Hereafter, nor does he ask for a reward in either of these two realms."

Someone asked Sahl b. ʿAbdallah [al-Tustari]: "What is the hardest thing for one's lower soul?" He answered: "Sincerity, for the soul has no share in it." Someone asked a Sufi about sincerity. He answered: "It is that you ask no one but God – may He be great and exalted – to be the witness of your good deeds." One Sufi related: "One day I entered Sahl b. ʿAbdallah's house on Friday before the prayer. Suddenly, I saw a snake in his house, so I paused at the porch. He told me: 'Come in! One cannot attain the True Reality of faith if one is afraid of anything on this earth [other than God]!' He then asked me: 'Would you like to perform the prayer in a congregational mosque?' I said: '[Yes,] but the [closest] mosque is at a distance of a one day and one night journey from here.' He took me by the hand, and in a matter of minutes we found ourselves at the mosque. We entered it and performed our Friday prayer, then came out and watched the members of the congregation leaving the mosque. Sahl said: 'There are so many people who say "There's no deity but God", yet so few of them are sincere.'"

Hamza b. Yusuf al-Jurjani informed us: Muhammad b. Muhammad b. ʿAbd al-Rahim told us: Abu Talib Muhammad b. Zakariya al-Muqaddasi told us: Abu Qirsafa Muhammad b. ʿAbd al-Wahhab al-ʿAsqalani told us: Zakariya b. Nafiʿ told us: Muhammad b. Yazid al-Qaratisi told us on the authority of Ismaʿil b. Abi Khalid, on the authority of Makhul, who said: "Anyone who has remained sincere for forty days will see wisdom flowing from the springs of his heart to his tongue." I heard Shaykh Abu ʿAbd al-Rahman al-Sulami – may God have mercy on him – say: I heard Muhammad b. ʿAbdallah b. Shadhan say: I heard ʿAbd al-Razzaq say: I heard Yusuf b. al-Husayn say: "The greatest thing in this world is sincerity. How many times did I try to remove hypocrisy from my heart, yet it sprang up there again in new guise."//285 I also heard him [al-Sulami] say: I heard al-Nasrabadhi say: I heard Abu ʾl-Jahm say: I heard Ibn Abi ʾl-Hawari say: I heard Abu Sulayman [al-Darani] say: "When you are sincere, Satan's whisperings and hypocrisy will fall away from you!"

Truthfulness (*sidq*)

God Most High said: "O believers, fear God, and be with the truthful ones."[327] The master Abu Bakr Muhammad b. Furak – may God have mercy on him – informed us: ʿAbdallah b. Jaʿfar b. Ahmad al-Isbahani told us: Abu Bishr Yunus b. Habib told us: Abu Dawud al-Tayalisi told us: Shuʿba told us on the authority of Mansur, on the authority of Abu Waʾil, on the authority of ʿAbdallah b. Masʿud, who heard that the Prophet – may God bless and greet him – said: "The servant of God, who is truthful and who constantly aspires to remain trustworthy, will be recorded in the Book of God as a trustful one (*siddiq*), whereas the servant

---

327 Q. 9:119; 9:120, according to Arberry's translation.

of God who lies and aspires to keep lying, will be recorded into the Book of God as a liar (*kadhdhab*).

The master [Abu ʿAli al-Daqqaq] said: "Truthfulness is the foundation of this affair[328]." Through it its perfection is effected and its correct order is achieved. It comes immediately after the rank of prophethood, for God Most High said: "And with those whom God has blessed: the prophets and truthful ones."[329] The word "trustworthy" (*sadiq*) is derived from the word "truth" (*sidq*), whereas the word "truthful" is the emphatic form of it – that is, one whose truth is abundant, who is dominated by truth – in the same way as the words *khimmir* and *sikkir* are emphatic forms for "drunkard". The minimal requirement for truthfulness is that one's outward actions and inward thoughts are equal. That is, the "trustworthy" is one who speaks truth, whereas the "truthful" is one who is veracious in his words, deeds, and spiritual states. Ahmad b. Khadrawayh said: "Whoever wishes God Most High to be with him should be truthful, for God Most High said: 'Surely, God is with the truthful ones.'"[330]

I heard Shaykh Abu ʿAbd al-Rahman al-Sulami – may God have mercy on him – say: I heard Mansur b. ʿAbdallah say: I heard al-Farghani say: I heard al-Junayd say: "The trustworthy one (*sadiq*) undergoes change forty times a day, while the hypocrite remains in one and the same state for forty years." Abu Sulayman al-Darani said: "If the truthful one desired to describe that which resides in his heart, he would have no need to move his tongue."[331] It is said: "Truthfulness means to speak the truth, even if this means your destruction." It is also said: "Truthfulness is when [your] innermost thoughts are in harmony with your speech." Al-Qannad said: "Truthfulness (*sidq*) is preventing your mouth (*shidq*) from uttering things that are prohibited [by God]." ʿAbd al-Wahid b. Zayd[332] said: "Truthfulness is to be loyal to God – praise be to Him – in [all your] actions."

I heard Muhammad b. al-Husayn say: I heard Abu ʾl-ʿAbbas al-Baghdadi say: I heard Jaʿfar b. Nusayr say: I heard al-Jurayri say: I heard Sahl b. ʿAbdallah say: "Anyone who conceals his true thoughts from himself or from others will never gain a whiff of truthfulness." Abu Saʿid al-Qurashi said: "The truthful one is he who is ready to die without being ashamed of exposing his innermost secrets, for God Most High said: 'Long for death, when you speak truly.'"[333]

I heard the master Abu ʿAli al-Daqqaq – may God have mercy on him – say: I heard Abu ʿAli al-Thaqafi say that one day ʿAbdallah b. Munazil told him: "Abu ʿAli, get ready for death, for there's no escape from it." Abu ʿAli responded saying: "And you, ʿAbdallah, get ready for death, for there's no escape from it."

---

328 That is, the Sufi path.
329 Q. 4:69; 4:71, according to Arberry's translation.
330 Q. 2:153.
331 That is, because being truthful in his words and deeds, he would have nothing new to impart to his listeners.
332 On him see *IM*, pp. 16–18.
333 Q. 2:94; 2:88, according to Arberry's translation.

On hearing this, ʿAbdallah stretched his hand, put his head on it, as if it were a pillow, and said: "I am already dead!" Abu ʿAli fell silent, because he was unable to match what ʿAbdallah had just done, for Abu ʿAli still had attachments [to this world], whereas ʿAbdallah had rid himself completely of them all.

I heard Shaykh Abu ʿAbd al-Rahman al-Sulami – may God have mercy on him – say: "Abu ʾl-ʿAbbas al-Dinawari was preaching [to a crowd], when suddenly an old woman who was there let out a shout. Abu ʾl-ʿAbbas told her: 'Die now!' She rose up, made a few steps, then turned to him saying, 'I have died', and she fell dead." Al-Wasiti said: "Sincerity is when one's declaration of [God's] unity is tied with one's intention to act [according to it]." It is said that ʿAbd al-Wahid b. Zayd asked one of his students, whose body had become emaciated: "Son, have you been fasting constantly?" He answered: "I do not perpetuate the breaking of my fast (*iftar*)." [ʿAbd al-Wahid] then asked: "Do you stay wake all night?" [The youth] answered: "I do not perpetuate my sleep." ʿAbd al-Wahid then asked: "So what, then, has emaciated you?" The youth answered: "[My] never-ending desire, and my never-ending concealment of it." ʿAbd al-Wahid exclaimed: "Be silent! How dare you!" On hearing this the youth sprang to his feet, walked a couple of steps, said "Oh, my God, if I am sincere, take me!", and fell down dead.

It is related that Abu ʿAmr al-Zajjaji said: "My mother died and I inherited a house from her. I sold it//287 for fifty *dinars* and went on the *hajj*. When I reached [the ruins of] Babel, I came across an overseer of the canals (*ahad al-qanaqina*),[334] who asked me: 'What do you have with you?' I said to myself: 'Truthfulness is [always] better' and told him that I had fifty *dinars*. He said: 'Give them to me!' I handed over [my] purse to him. He counted them [the *dinars*] and there were indeed fifty *dinars*. He said: 'Take them back. Your truthfulness has impressed me!' He then dismounted his horse and told me: 'Take it and ride!' I said: 'No, I do not want to!' However, he said that I must and he eventually prevailed over me. When I mounted the horse, he said: 'I will be following you.' And indeed after one year he caught up with me and stayed with me until he died."

I heard Muhammad b. al-Husayn – may God have mercy on him – say: I heard Mansur b. ʿAbdallah say: I heard Jaʿfar al-Khawwas say: I heard Ibrahim al-Khawwas say: "You will never see the truthful man except performing his obligations or engaging in a good deed." I also heard him [Muhammad b. al-Husayn] say: I heard Abu ʾl-Husayn b. Miqsam say: I heard Jaʿfar al-Khawwas say: I heard al-Junayd say: "The true essence of truthfulness is when you speak truth in a situation from which only a lie can rescue you." It is said: "Three things never elude the truthful: sweetness [of character], awe [of God], and grace."

---

334 The meaning of this word is not quite clear; it may also mean "an expert on finding water" or something along these lines.

It is related that God – praise be to Him – revealed [the following words to David] – peace be upon him: "David, whoever has trust in me in his innermost self, I will make him trustworthy in the eyes of [My] creatures." It is related that Ibrahim b. Dawha and Ibrahim Sitanba were about to enter the desert. Ibrahim b. Sitanba said: "Abandon any [mundane] attachments that [still] remain with you!" Ibrahim b. Dawha said: "I have already abandoned everything except one *dinar*." Ibrahim b. Sitanba exclaimed: "Ibrahim, do not keep my innermost self preoccupied [with it]! Give up all the attachments that [still] remain with you!" Ibrahim b. Dawha said: "So, I threw that *dinar* away." However, he kept saying: "Ibrahim, abandon any attachments that you [still] have!" [Ibrahim b. Dawha] said: "[Suddenly] I remembered that I had [spare] sandal thongs with me. So I threw them away and [from then on] whenever I was in need of a sandal thong on that journey, I immediately found one." [On seeing this], Ibrahim b. Sitanba said: "This is what happens when you deal with God Most High truthfully!"

Dhu 'l-Nun al-Misri – may God have mercy on him – said: "Truthfulness is the sword of God that cuts through everything it falls on." Sahl b. ʿAbdallah [al-Tustari] said: "When the truthful begin to talk to themselves,[335] they are beginning to betray their truthfulness." When someone asked Fath al-Mawsili about truthfulness, he thrust his hand into the blacksmith's forge, brought out a piece of [hot] iron//288 and held it in his palm, saying "This is truthfulness!" Yusuf b. Asbat said: "One night spent dealing with God truthfully is dearer to me than wielding my sword for the sake of God Most High."

I heard the master Abu ʿAli al-Daqqaq saying: "Truthfulness means being with other people in the same way as you consider yourself to be or considering yourself to be as you are [in yourself]." Someone asked al-Harith al-Muhasibi about the signs of truthfulness. He answered: "The truthful person would be unperturbed if any respect for him disappeared from the hearts of people as long as his own heart remained virtuous. He would not want even one grain's worth of his good deeds to be known to people; and yet, he would not mind if people were to observe any of his wrongdoing. For if he were to mind this, this would mean that he desired his worth to increase in the eyes of other people. And this [desire] is not among the features of the truthful."

A Sufi said: "If you do not fulfill your perpetual obligation (*fard daʾim*), your occasional obligation (*fard muʾaqqat*) will not be accepted from you."[336] Someone asked him about the meaning of "perpetual obligation". He answered: "Truthfulness." It is said: "If you seek God in truthfulness, He will grant you a mirror in which you will see all the marvels of this world and the Hereafter." It is said: "Hold on to truthfulness when you fear that it will harm you, for [in reality] it will benefit you. Give up a lie when you think that it will benefit you, for [in

---

335 Or "to their souls" – that is, when they stop saying publicly what they think.
336 According to a commentator, the former denotes an obligation that is required at all times, such as faith, whereas the latter refers to obligations due at particular times, such as daytime fasting during the month of Ramadan.

reality] it will harm you." It is said: "Everything is something. However, the friendship of a liar is nothing." It is said: "The sign of the liar is that he makes plenty of promises, when there is no one around to take him up on them." Ibn Sirin said: "Words are so broad that they absolve the intelligent man of lying."[337] It is also said: "A trustworthy (saduq) merchant will never be destitute."

Shame (haya)

God Most High said: "Does he not know that God sees?"[338]//289 Abu Bakr Muhammad b. ʿAbdus al-Hiri al-Muzakki informed us: Abu Sahl Ahmad b. Muhammad b. Ziyad al-Nahwi in Baghdad informed us: Ibrahim b. Muhammad b. al-Haytham told us: Musa b. al-Hayyan told us: al-Muqaddami told us on the authority of ʿUbaydallah b. ʿUmar, on the authority of Nafiʿ, on the authority of Ibn ʿUmar – may God be pleased with both of them – that: the Messenger of God – may God bless and greet him – said: "Shame is part of faith." Abu Saʿid Muhammad b. Ibrahim al-Ismaʿili informed us: Abu ʿUthman ʿAmr b. ʿAbdallah al-Basri told us: Abu Ahmad Muhammad b. ʿAbd al-Wahhab told us: Yaʿla b. ʿUbayd told us: Aban b. Ishaq told us on the authority of al-Sabbah b. Muhammad, on the authority of Murra al-Hamdani, on the authority of [ʿAbdallah] Ibn Masʿud – may God be pleased with him – that the Prophet of God – may God bless and greet him – told his Companions one day: "Be ashamed in the eyes of God as it befits Him!" They answered: "We are ashamed, the Prophet of God. Praise be to God!" He answered: "It is not that! He who feels himself ashamed in the eyes of God as it befits Him must guard his head from that which occurs to it and his stomach from that which it contains; and he must constantly remember death and afflictions. He who seeks the Hereafter must abandon the adornments of this life. Only he who has done all this is ashamed in the eyes of God as it befits Him."

I heard Shaykh Abu ʿAbd al-Rahman al-Sulami say: Abu Nasr al-Waziri told us: Muhammad b. ʿAbdallah b. Muhammad told us: al-Ghallabi told us: Muhammad b. Makhlad told us that his father said: "A wise man said: 'Renew [your] shame by keeping company with the One in the presence of Whom all others feel ashamed of themselves!'" I also heard him [al-Sulami] say: I heard Abu Bakr al-Razi say: I heard Ibn ʿAtaʾ say: "The greatest knowledge is awe and shame. When they disappear from [one's heart] nothing good remains there." I also heard him say: I heard Abu ʾl-Faraj al-Warathani say: I heard Muhammad b. Ahmad b. Yaʿqub say: Muhammad b. ʿAbd al-Malik said: I heard Dhu ʾl-Nun al-Misri say: "Shame is the presence of awe [of God] in your heart as a result of your consternation over your past transgressions against your Lord Most High." Dhu ʾl-Nin al-Misri also said: "Love makes [one] speak, shame silences, and fear

---

337 That is, the multiple meanings of words makes lying unnecessary, if one knows how to use them.
338 Q. 96:14.

unsettles." Abu ʿUthman [al-Hiri] said: "He who discourses about shame, without being ashamed in the eyes of God – may He be great and exalted – is being led on step by step (*mustadraj*)."

I heard Abu Bakr b. Ishkib say: al-Hasan b. al-Haddad came to ʿAbdallah b. Munazil, who asked where he came from. He answered: "From a meeting of Abu ʾl-Qasim the Preacher (*al-mudhakkir*)." "What was he speaking about?" asked ʿAbdallah. Al-Hasan said that he was speaking about shame. ʿAbdallah exclaimed: "How odd! How can one who is not ashamed of himself in the eyes of God Most High speak about shame?"[339]//290. I heard Muhammad b. al-Husayn say: I heard Abu ʾl-ʿAbbas al-Baghdadi say: I heard Ahmad b. Salih say: I heard Muhammad b. ʿAbdun say: I heard Abu ʾl-ʿAbbas al-Muʾaddib say: al-Sari said: "Shame and intimacy knock on the door of the heart. If they find there renunciation (*zuhd*) and scrupulousness (*waraʿ*), they settle down. If not they walk away." I also heard him [Muhammad b. al-Husayn] say: I heard Muhammad b. ʿAbdallah b. Shadhan say: I heard al-Jurayri say: "The first generation of people traded religion among themselves (*taʿamal*) until it grew thin. The second generation traded fidelity among themselves until it disappeared. The third generation traded chivalry among themselves until it disappeared as well. The fourth generation traded shame among themselves until shame disappeared. Now people have started to trade desire [for Paradise] and fear [of punishment in the Hereafter] ..."

They say about the words of God Most High, "For she [the wife of Potiphar] desired him and he would have taken her, but that he saw the proof of his Lord",[340] that the "proof" here was that she put a piece of cloth over the face of an idol [stationed] in a corner of her house. Yusuf – peace be upon him – asked her: "What are you doing?" She answered: "I am ashamed of him." Then Yusuf – peace be upon him – said: "And I am even more ashamed of myself before God Most High!" They say about the words of God Most High, "One of the women came to him [Moses] walking with shyness",[341] that she was embarrassed before him, because she was offering him hospitality and was embarrassed that Moses might not accept it. This is the kind of shame that is associated with generosity. I heard Muhammad b. al-Husayn – may God have mercy on him – say: I heard ʿAbdallah b. al-Husayn say: I heard Abu Muhammad al-Baladhuri say: I heard Abu ʿAbdallah al-ʿUmari say: I heard Ahmad b. Abi ʾl-Hawari say: I heard Abu Sulayman al-Darani say: "God Most High said: 'My servant, as long as you are ashamed before Me, I will make people forget your sins and I will make all corners of the earth forget your sins. I will erase all your transgressions from the Mother of the Books[342] and will not take you to account on the Day of Judgement.'"

---

339 He apparently referred to a preacher who had made preaching a source of his livelihood – a practice that was condemned by many Sufi masters. See *IM*, pp. 23–25 and 50.
340 Q. 12:24.
341 Q. 28:25.
342 That is, the book in which the destinies of all human beings are inscribed.

A man was seen praying outside the mosque. Someone asked him: "Why can't you enter the mosque and pray there?" He answered: "I am ashamed to enter God's house after I have disobeyed Him!" They say: "One of the signs of those who possess shame is that one will never see them in a shameful condition." A Sufi said: "Once we were traveling by night and entered a thicket. There we came upon a sleeping man, whose horse was grazing at his head. We woke him up and asked him: 'Aren't you afraid of sleeping in such a scary place that is full of wild beasts?' He raised his head and said: 'I would be ashamed before God Most High if I were to be afraid of anyone other than Him!' He then put his head down and fell back to sleep."//291

God – praise be to Him – revealed to Jesus – peace be upon him: "Admonish yourself. If you heed the admonishment, then admonish others. If not, then be ashamed before Me, when you admonish others!" It is said that there are different kinds of shame. One is the shame of transgression, as in the case with Adam – peace be upon him. When God asked him, "Are you fleeing from Me?", he answered, "No, I am fleeing from shame before You!" Another is the shame of falling short (*taqsir*), as in the case of the angels, who told [God]: "We have not worshiped You as You deserve [to be worshiped]!" Another type of shame is the shame of reverence (*ijlal*). It was characteristic of [the angel] Israfil – peace be upon him – who wrapped himself in his wings out of shame before God – may He be great and exalted! There's also the shame of generosity, which pertained to the Prophet – may God bless and greet him – for he was ashamed to ask [the people of his] community (*umma*) to leave him alone. Therefore God Most High [had to] say: "[And when you have had the meal, disperse,] neither lingering for idle talk."[343] Another type of shame is the shame of embarrassment, which was characteristic of ʿAli – may God be pleased with him – when he asked (bearing in mind the status of [the Prophet's daughter] Fatima – may God be pleased with her) al-Miqdad b. al-Aswad to ask the Messenger of God – may God bless and greet him – for a ruling concerning the emission of the sperm resulting from foreplay. Then there is the shame of humility, which was characteristic of Moses – peace be upon him – when he said: "When I need something from this world, I am ashamed to ask You [for it], my Lord!" To which God – may He be great and exalted – responded, saying: "Ask Me, even for salt for the dough of your bread and the fodder for your sheep!" Finally, there is the shame of [divine] beneficence. This is the shame of the Lord – praise be to Him – when He gives His servant a sealed book, after he has crossed the bridge leading to the Hereafter. In this book it is written: "You did what you did and I was ashamed of showing it to you. Go now, for I have forgiven you!" I heard the master Abu ʿAli al-Daqqaq say regarding this issue that Yahya b. Muʿadh said: "Praise be the [Lord] Who is ashamed of His sinning servant."

I heard Muhammad b. al-Husayn say: I heard ʿAbdallah b. Ahmad b. Jaʿfar say: I heard Zanjawayh al-Labbad say: I heard ʿAli b. al-Husayn al-Hilali say: I

---

343 Q. 33:53.

heard Ibrahim b. al-Ash'ath say: I heard al-Fudayl b. 'Iyad say: "There are five signs of wretchedness [in mankind]: the coarseness of the heart, the ruthlessness of the eye, the paucity of shame, desire for this world, and expecting too much of it." In a revealed book it is said: "My servant is unjust to Me. When he calls upon Me, I am embarrassed to turn him down. And yet he disobeys Me without being ashamed before Me!"[344]

Yahya b. Mu'adh said: "If a man is ashamed before God Most High while being obedient, God will be ashamed of [punishing] him, when he sins."//292 Know that shame is like melting, for they say that shame melts man's innards under the gaze of His Master. It is said: "Shame is the contraction of the heart, when it seeks to exalt its Lord." It is also said: "When a man sits to preach to other people, his two [recording] angels[345] tell him: 'Admonish yourself as you admonish others, or else be ashamed before your Master, for He always watches you!'" Someone asked al-Junayd about shame. He answered: "When you see both the favors of your God and your shortcomings there emerges between them the state known as 'shame'." Al-Wasiti said: "A man cannot feel the brand of shame until he has transgressed one of God's laws or violated one of his pacts [with Him]." Al-Wasiti also said: "Sweat streams forth from a man who feels shame, for this is a blessing that God puts into him. As long as any trace [of his soul's influence] remains in him, he is barred from being ashamed."

I heard the master Abu 'Ali al-Daqqaq – may God have mercy on him – say: "Shame is the abandoning of all [personal] pretensions before God – may He be great and exalted!" I heard Muhammad b. al-Husayn say: I heard Muhammad b. 'Abdallah al-Sufi – may God have mercy on him – say: I heard Abu 'l-'Abbas b. al-Walid al-Zawzani say: I heard Muhammad b. Ahmad al-Juzjani say: I heard Abu Bakr al-Warraq say: "Occasionally, I would pray two prayers to God Most High then come away ashamed as if I have robbed someone."

Freedom (*hurriyya*)

God – may He be great and exalted – said: "[They] prefer others to themselves even though poverty be their portion."[346] He[347] explained: "They have preferred others to themselves, because they have freed themselves from that which they have given up and preferred."

'Ali b. Ahmad al-Ahwazi informed us: Ahmad b. 'Ubayd al-Basri informed us: Ibn Abi Qammash told us: Muhammad b. Salih b. al-Nattah told us: Nu'aym b. Muwarri' b. Tawba told us on the authority of Isma'il al-Makki, on the authority of 'Amr b. Dinar, on the authority of Tawus, on the authority of ['Abdallah] Ibn 'Abbas, who said that the Messenger of God – may God bless

---

344 I have not been able to identify this Biblical reference.
345 According to an Islamic belief, each person is always accompanied by two angels, one of which records his/her good deeds, the other his/her bad deeds.
346 Q. 59:9.
347 That is, al-Qushayri.

and greet him – said: "What satisfies each one of you is what he is content with. For everything will end up in the four cubits and a span,³⁴⁸//293 because all things eventually come to an end."

He³⁴⁹ said: "Freedom means that the servant of God does not allow himself to become enslaved by [other] creatures, nor is he subject to the power of originated things (*mukawwanat*). The sign of its soundness is that his heart is no longer capable of distinguishing different things to such an extent that everything he sees looks equal to him." Haritha³⁵⁰ – may God be pleased with him – said to the Messenger of God – may God bless and greet him: "I have relinquished this world and now its stones and gold are equal to me." I heard the master Abu ʿAli al-Daqqaq – may God have mercy on him – say: "Whoever comes into this world free from it departs for the next world being free from it." I heard Muhammad b. al-Husayn say: I heard Abu Muhammad al-Maraghi say on the authority of al-Raqqi³⁵¹ that al-Daqqaq³⁵² said: "Whoever lives in this world being free from it will live in the next world being free from it."

Know that the True Reality of freedom lies in the perfection of one's servanthood (*ʿubudiyya*). When one's servanthood before God is sincere, one's freedom is cleansed from attachment to anything other than God. Those who fathom that the servant may occasionally remove the bridle of servanthood and turn his sight away from [God's] commands and prohibitions in the realm of the Divine Law (*dar al-taklif*), while being of sound mind, [are deluded,] for this is nothing but forfeiting one's religion.

God – praise be to Him – said to His Prophet – may God bless and greet him: "Serve thy Lord until the Certitude comes to you."³⁵³ All commentators agree that [the Certitude] here means one's appointed time [of death] (*ajal*). When the folk (*qawm*)³⁵⁴ speak of freedom they imply that one is not bound by any mundane attachments or fleeting things of this world nor those of the Hereafter. This man devotes himself solely to God and is subject to neither the transitory things of this world, nor to the fulfillment of his desires, nor to the promptings of aspirations; he has no requests, no goals, no need, and no fortune.

Someone asked al-Shibli: "Don't you know that God Most High is merciful?" He answered: "Yes, of course, but since I learned about His mercifulness, I have never asked Him to have mercy on me!"//294 The station of freedom is very rare. I heard the master Abu ʿAli [al-Daqqaq] – may God have mercy on him – say: Abu ʾl-ʿAbbas al-Sayyari used to say: "If using words other than the Qurʾan in one's prayer were to be permitted, they should have been the following:

---

348 That is, the size of a grave.
349 See note 347.
350 A Companion of the Prophet.
351 Or "al-Duqqi".
352 Or "al-Zaqqaq".
353 Q. 15:99.
354 That is, "Sufis".

I wish that the fate (*zaman*) grant me something that is [hardly] possible:
That my eyes would fall on the face of a free man (*hurr*)!"

The Sufi masters have discoursed profusely on freedom. Thus, al-Husayn b. Mansur [al-Hallaj] said: "Whoever aspires to freedom, let him devote himself constantly to the service [of God]!" Someone asked al-Junayd's opinion about someone whose debt to this world does not exceed the amount of moisture one can squeeze out of a date stone. He answered: "A slave who has signed a manumission contract with his owner remains a slave while he owes even one *dirham* [to his owner]." I heard Abu ʿAbd al-Rahman al-Sulami say: I heard Abu Bakr al-Razi say: I heard Abu ʿUmar al-Anmati say: I heard al-Junayd say: "You will never attain sincere freedom until there remains even one bit of true servanthood that you owe to Him." Bishr al-Hafi said: "Whoever wants to taste the flavor of freedom and to find rest from servanthood must purify the secret (*sarira*) between himself and God Most High."

Al-Husayn b. Mansur said: "When the servant has fulfilled all the stations of servanthood, he becomes free of the hardship of servanthood. He then [becomes capable of] acquiring servanthood without any effort or self-exertion on his part. This is the station of the prophets and the truthful (*siddiqun*)." That is, he is being borne (*mahmul*) [toward his goal]; no difficulty attaches itself to his heart, even though [outwardly] he remains adorned by [the injunctions of] the Divine Law.[355]

Shaykh Abu ʿAbd al-Rahman [al-Sulami] recited to us: Abu Bakr al-Razi recited to us: Mansur al-Faqih ("the Jurist") recited to us:

No free man remains among mankind, not a single one,
Nor is one found among the jinn!
The free of these two communities have departed
And the sweetness of life has grown bitter!

Know that the greatest kind of freedom lies in serving the poor.[356] I heard the master Abu ʿAli al-Daqqaq – may God have mercy on him – say: "God Most High revealed to [the prophet] David – peace be upon him: 'If you see anyone who seeks Me, be his servant!'" The Prophet – may God bless and greet him – said: "The master of a people is their servant." I heard Muhammad b. al-Husayn – may God have mercy on him – say: I heard Muhammad b. Ibrahim b. al-Fadl say: I heard Muhammad b. al-Rumi say: I heard Yahya b. Muʿadh say: "The children of this world are served by slave boys and slave girls, whereas the children of the next world are served by the righteous and the free." I also heard him [Muhammad b. al-Husayn] say: I heard ʿAbdallah b. ʿUthman b. Yahya say: I heard ʿAli b. Muhammad al-Misri say: I heard Yusuf b. Musa say: I heard Ibn

---

355 That is, even though everyone continues to see him exerting himself in fulfilling the injunctions of the *shariʿa*.
356 That is, the Sufis.

Khubayq say: I heard Muhammad b. ʿAbdallah say: I heard Ibrahim b. Adham say: "One who is noble and free withdraws from this world before he is removed from it [by God]." Ibrahim b. Adham also said: "Keep the company of none except one who is noble and free: he will listen, but will not speak [to others]."

Remembrance (*dhikr*)

God Most High said: "O believers, remember God oft."[357] Abu ʾl-Husayn ʿAli b. Muhammad b. ʿAbdallah b. Bashran informed us in Baghdad: Abu ʿAli al-Husayn b. Safwan al-Bardhaʿi informed us: Abu Bakr b. ʿAbdallah b. Muhammad b. Abi ʾl-Dunya told us: Harun b. Maʿruf said: Anas b. ʿIyad told us: ʿAbdallah b. Saʿid b. Abi Hind told us on the authority of Ziyad b. Abi Ziyad, on the authority of Abu Bahriyya, on the authority of Abu ʾl-Dardaʾ – may God be pleased with him – that the Messenger of God – may God bless and greet him – said: "Have I not told you of the best of your works, the purest of them in your Lord's eyes and the ones that are the most exalted in your ranks? They are better than giving gold and silver in charity and fighting your enemy and striking their necks as they are striking yours? They asked him: 'What is it, O Messenger of God?' He answered: 'Remembering God Most High!'"

Abu Nuʿyam ʿAbd al-Malik b. al-Hasan informed us: Yaʿqub b. Ishaq b. Ibrahim said: al-Dayri[358] told us on the authority of ʿAbd al-Razzaq, on the authority of Maʿmar the authority of al-Zuhri, on the authority of Thabit, on the authority of Anas [b. Malik], who said that the Messenger of God – may God bless and greet him – said: "The Hour of Judgement will not come upon one who is saying: 'God! God!'" ʿAli b. Ahmad b. ʿAbdan said: Ahmad b. ʿUbayd said: Muʿadh//296 said: My father said on the authority of Humayd, on the authority of Anas b. Malik, that the Messenger of God – may God bless and greet him – said: "The Hour of Judgement will not come until no one on this earth will be saying: 'God! God!'"

The master said: "Remembrance is a powerful pillar of the path to God – praise be to Him! Indeed, it is the very foundation of this path, for one can only reach God by constantly remembering His name."

There are two types of remembrance; the remembrance of the tongue and the remembrance of the heart. The continual remembrance of the tongue eventually brings the servant to the remembrance of the heart. The true effect, however, lies in the remembrance of the heart. If the servant is able to perform remembrance with both his tongue and his heart, he has achieved perfection in both his personal state and his wayfaring. I heard Abu ʿAli al-Daqqaq – may God have mercy on him – say: "Remembrance is the mandate (*manshur*) of sainthood. He who is given access to the remembrance is given the mandate, whereas he who is denied remembrance is banished [from the proximity of God]." It is said

---

357 Q. 33:41.
358 Or "al-Dabari".

that at the beginning of his wayfaring al-Shibli would go down into a cellar carrying with him a bundle of sticks. Whenever negligence entered his heart he would beat himself with a stick until he broke it upon himself. Sometimes, he ran out of the sticks before evening came, so he would strike his hands and feet against the wall. It is said the remembrance of God by the heart is the sword of the seekers with which they fight against their enemies and ward off any faults that assail them. When an affliction overcomes the servant of God, his heart should seek refuge with God Most High, and all that he abhors will be diverted from him.

Someone asked al-Wasiti about remembrance. He answered: "It is to depart from the arena of negligence to the vast expanse of witnessing [God], which is ruled by intense fear and love of Him." I heard Shaykh Abu ʿAbd al-Rahman al-Sulami say: I heard ʿAbdallah b. al-Husayn say: I heard Abu Muhammad al-Baladhuri say: I heard ʿAbd al-Rahman b. Bakr say: I heard Dhu ʾl-Nun al-Misri say: "He who mentions God Most High honestly, will forget about anything else through his remembrance. God will then protect him from everything and will recompense him for everything [he has missed]." I also heard him [al-Sulami] say: I heard ʿAbdallah al-Muʿallim say: I heard Ahmad al-Masjidi say://297 "Someone asked Abu ʿUthman [al-Hiri]: 'We remember God Most High, but we find no sweetness in our hearts as a result of this.' He answered: 'Give praise to God Most High that He at least has adorned your limbs with acts of obedience!'"

According to a well-known tradition from the Messenger of God – may God bless and greet him – he said: "When you pass by the gardens of Paradise, alight and graze there!" [His followers] asked him: "What are the gardens of Paradise?" He answered: "The gatherings at which God is remembered."

Abu ʾl-Hasan ʿAli b. Bakkar[359] informed us in Baghdad: Abu ʿAli b. Safwan told us: Ibn Abi ʾl-Dunya said: al-Haytham b. Kharija said: Ismaʿil b. ʿAyyash said on the authority of ʿUmar b. ʿAbdallah that Khalid b. ʿAbdallah b. Safwan told him on the authority of Jabir b. ʿAbdallah, who said: "The Messenger of God – may God bless and greet him – came out to us and said: 'O people, alight and graze in the gardens of Paradise!' We asked him: 'O Messenger of God, what are the gardens of Paradise?' He answered: 'The gathering at which God is remembered. So, go forth, morning and evening, and remember God. Let anyone who wishes to know his standing with God see what standing God has with him! For God – praise be to Him – grants everyone the same standing as one oneself grants to Him!'"

I heard Muhammad b. al-Husayn say: I heard Muhammad al-Farraʾ say: I heard al-Shibli say: "Does not God – may He be exalted – say: 'I am in the company of he who remembers Me'? What benefit did you reap from the companionship of God Most High?"

I heard him [Muhammad b. al-Husayn] say: I heard ʿAbdallah b. Musa al-Salami say: I heard al-Shibli reciting the following in his session:

---

359 Or "Bishr".

> I remembered Your name not because I had forgotten You even for one instant
> The easiest part of remembrance is to remember You with my tongue
> I almost died even without ecstasy actually overcoming me
> My heart trembles, overwhelmed with love
> And my ecstasy showed me that You are with me
> I witnessed Your presence everywhere
> Then I addressed one who was present without uttering a word
> And noticed one whom I knew without actually seeing him!

One of the characteristics of remembrance is that it is not confined to appointed times. Actually, the servant of God is enjoined to remember God at all times as [his religious] duty//298 or as a recommendation. As for the prayer, in spite of its being the noblest of all acts of worship, it can be said during appointed times only, while the remembrance of God in the heart [is recommended] in all states and conditions.

God Most High said: "And [men] who remember God standing and sitting and [lying] on their sides."[360] I heard the imam Abu Bakr b. Furak – may God have mercy on him – say: " 'Standing' here means 'remembering Him as it befits Him', while 'sitting' means 'abandoning any pretension vis-à-vis Him.' " I heard Shaykh Abu ʿAbd al-Rahman al-Sulami ask the master Abu ʿAli al-Daqqaq: "What is more perfect: remembrance or [rational] contemplation (*fikr*)?" The master, in turn, asked him: "And what do you think about this?" Shaykh Abu ʿAbd al-Rahman al-Sulami said: "In my view, remembrance is more perfect than contemplation, for God – praise be to Him – attributed remembrance to Himself, while He never did the same for contemplation. And anything that is attributed to God – praise be to Him – is always better than that which is attributed to His creatures." The master Abu ʿAli al-Daqqaq – may God have mercy on him – approved that answer.

I heard Shaykh Abu ʿAbd al-Rahman al-Sulami – may God have mercy on him – say: I heard Muhammad b. ʿAbdallah say: I heard al-Kattani say: "If remembering Him was not imposed on me [as a duty], I would not remember Him at all out of my awe for Him – for how can someone as lowly as me remember Him without cleansing his mouth one thousand times as a penance for mentioning Him?!"

I heard the master Abu ʿAli al-Daqqaq – may God have mercy on him – recite the following:

> I cannot remember your name without having my heart,
> my innermost self, and my spirit restrain me whenever even one thought of you visits me
> As if an invisible watcher from you tells me: "Beware!" "Woe onto you!"
> "Beware of this recollection!"

---

360 Q. 3:191; 3:187, according to Arberry's translation.

One of the characteristics of remembrance is that God always reciprocates one's remembrance of Him, for God Most High said: "Remember Me and I will remember you."[361] According to a sound tradition, Gabriel – peace be upon him – said to the Messenger of God – may God bless and greet him – that God Most High said: "I have given your community something that I have not given to any other community." The Messenger asked: "What is that, Gabriel?" He answered: "God Most High said: 'Remember Me and I will remember you!' He has not said that to any other community." It is said: "The angel of death asks the permission of the one who recollects [God] before seizing his spirit."//299

According to one of the [holy] books, Moses – peace be upon him – said: "Where do you reside, my Lord?" God Most High revealed to him: "In the heart of My faithful servant." This implies the dwelling of remembrance [of God], for God Most High is far removed from any notion of residing or dwelling. This "residence" means only the affirmation and appropriation [of God's name by the servant]. I heard Muhammad b. al-Husayn – may God have mercy on him – say: I heard ʿAbdallah b. ʿAli say: I heard Faris say: I heard al-Thawri say: I heard Dhu ʾl-Nun say, when I asked him about remembrance: "It means the absence of the one who remembers from his act of remembrance." He then recited the following [verse]:

> I multiply my remembrance of you not because I have forgotten you
> Remembrance simply flows from my tongue!

Sahl b. ʿAbdallah [al-Tustari] said: "Not a single day passes without the Majestic One calling out: 'O My servant, you have not treated Me justly, for I remember you, while you forget Me. I invite you to be with Me, while you go to visit others. I ward off afflictions from you, while you keep sinning. O son of Adam, what will you say tomorrow, when you come to see Me?!'" Abu Sulayman al-Darani said: "In Paradise there are tracts of land. Whenever anyone remembers God's name, angels begin to plant trees there. Every now and then an angel stops planting. When asked why he stopped, he answers: 'My [human] counterpart has grown lax [in his remembrance].'"

Al-Hasan [al-Basri] said: "Seek pleasure in three things: the [ritual] prayer, the remembrance of God's name, and in the recitation of the Qurʾan. If you find pleasure in these, fine. If not, then know that the door is shut." Hamid al-Aswad said: "Once I traveled with Ibrahim al-Khawwas. We came to a place that was teeming with snakes. He put down his water-skin and sat down. I, too, sat down. Then night came, the air grew cool, and the snakes came out [in great numbers]. I called upon the master, who said: 'Remember God!' As soon as I started remembering God, the snakes withdrew and did not return. So we sat for a while, until the air grew even cooler and the snakes came out again. I again called upon the master, and he said: 'Remember God!' I started remembering God, and

---

361 Q. 2:152; 2:147, according to Arberry's translation.

the snakes withdrew and did not return. After a while I called upon him again, and he said the same to me. So I kept remembering God until morning came. When we woke up, he stood up and walked on, and I followed him. Suddenly, a big snake fell out of his bedroll, into which it had slipped during the night. I asked him: 'Didn't you notice that snake?' He answered: 'No, it's been a while since I slept so well as last night!'" Abu ʿUthman [al-Hiri] said: "One cannot appreciate the desolation of negligence, until one has tasted the flavor of intimacy induced by remembrance of God."//300

I heard Muhammad b. al-Husayn say: I heard ʿAbd al-Rahman b. ʿAbdallah al-Dhubyani say: I heard al-Jurayri say: I heard al-Junayd say: I heard al-Sari say: "In one of the books revealed by God it is said: 'Whenever the remembrance of Me dominates My servant, he is enamored of Me (ʿashiqani) and I am enamored of him (ʿashiqtuh).'" He [al-Sari] also said: "God Most High revealed to David – peace be upon him: 'Rejoice in Me and take pleasure in remembering Me!'" [Sufyan] al-Thawri said: "Everyone has his own punishment. The punishment of the divine gnostic (ʿarif bi-ʾllah) is to be deprived of the remembrance of God." In the Gospels it is said: "Remember Me when you are angry and I will remember you when I am angry, for My helping you is better for you than your helping yourself." Someone asked a monk: "Are you fasting?" He answered: "I am fasting by remembering Him. Whenever I remember anyone other than Him, I break my fast." If remembrance of God takes hold of one's heart, each time a devil seeks to approach it he is seized by a fit of writhing, in the same way as man is seized by a fit of writhing whenever a devil tries to draw near him. Then the devils converge upon their fellow devil and ask: "What has happened [to you]?" And they hear the answer: "Men have overcome him!"

Sahl [al-Tustari] said: "I know of no sin more heinous than forgetting the Lord Most High." It is also said that the angels cannot carry a silent remembrance of God up to Him, because it is a secret between the servant and His God, may He be great and exalted. A Sufi related: "I was told about a man who practiced remembrance of God in the woods. So I came to see him. As he was sitting there, a huge lion attacked him and tore off a piece of his flesh from him. We both fainted. When we regained consciousness, I asked him about what had just happened. He answered: 'God has appointed this lion to watch over me. Each time I become lax [in my remembrance of Him] it takes a bite out of me, as you have just seen.'"

I heard Shaykh Abu ʿAbd al-Rahman al-Sulami say: I heard al-Husayn b. Yahya say: I heard Jaʿfar b. Nusayr say: I heard al-Jurayri say: "There was among us a man who was constantly repeating the name of God, "Allah, Allah." One day a branch from a tree fell upon his head, splitting it open. As his blood fell upon the ground, it formed the words: 'God, God (Allah).'"

Chivalry (futuwwa)

God Most High said: "They[362] were [chivalrous] young men (fitya) who believed in their Lord, and We increased them in guidance."[363]//301.

The master [al-Qushayri] said: "The foundation of chivalry is that the servant of God always exerts himself in the service of others." The Prophet – may God bless and greet him – said: "God Most High attends consistently to the needs of His servant as long as His servant attends to the needs of his fellow Muslims." 'Ali b. Ahmad b. 'Abdan reported the same story to us. He said: Ahmad b. 'Ubayd informed us: Isma'il b. al-Fadl told us: Ya'qub b. Humayd b. Kasib told us: Ibn Abi Hazim related this to us on the authority of 'Abdallah b. 'Amir al-Aslami, on the authority of 'Abd al-Rahman b. Hurmuz al-A'raj on the authority of Abu Hurayra, on the authority of Zayd b. Thabit – may God be pleased with both of them – that the Messenger of God – may God bless and greet him – said: "God Most High attends consistently to the needs of His servant as long as His servant attends to the needs of his fellow Muslims."

I heard the master Abu 'Ali al-Daqqaq say: "No one has achieved perfection in chivalry, except the Messenger of God – may God bless and greet him – for on the Day of Judgement everyone will be saying, 'Me, Me', except the Messenger of God, who will be saying: 'My community, my community!'" I heard Shaykh Abu 'Abd al-Rahman al-Sulami – may God have mercy on him – say: I heard Muhammad b. al-Husayn say: I heard Abu Ja'far al-Farghani say: I heard al-Junayd say: "Chivalry resides in Syria, eloquence in Iraq, and truthfulness in Khurasan." I also heard him [al-Sulami] say: I heard 'Abdallah b. Muhammad al-Razi say: I heard Muhammad b. Nasr b. Mansur al-Sa'igh say: I heard Muhammad b. Mardawayh say: I heard al-Fudayl [b. 'Iyad] say: "Chivalry means forgetting the faults of your brothers."

It is said: "Chivalry is when you do not consider yourself superior to others." Abu Bakr al-Warraq said: "The chivalrous person has no enemies whatsoever." Muhammad b. 'Ali al-Tirmidhi said: "Chivalry means that you are your own enemy before God."[364] It is also said: "The chivalrous person cannot be an enemy to anyone [but himself]." I heard the master Abu 'Ali al-Daqqaq – may God have mercy on him – say: I heard al-Nasrabadhi say: "The Men of the Cave were called '[chivalrous] young men',[365] because they believed in their Lord without any intermediary." It is said that the chivalrous person is one who has broken idols, for God Most High said: "We heard a [chivalrous] young man named Abraham making mention of them [the idols of his people]";[366] He also said: "He broke them [the idols] into fragments."[367] The idol of every person is his own self, therefore he who refuses to obey his passions is chivalrous in truth.//302

---

362 That is, "the Men of the Cave" mentioned in Chapter/sura 18 of Qur'an.
363 Q. 18:13; 18:12, according to Arberry's translation.
364 That is, you are always the first to acknowledge your failings before God.
365 See note 362.
366 Q. 21:60; 21:61, according to Arberry's translation.
367 Q. 21:58; 21:59, according to Arberry's translation.

Al-Harith al-Muhasibi said: "Chivalry means that you act justly, while not demanding justice for your own self." ʿAmr b. ʿUthman al-Makki said: "Chivalry means having good moral character." Someone asked al-Junayd about chivalry. He answered: "It is that you neither avoid the poor, nor confront the rich." Al-Nasrabadhi said: "Manliness (*muruwa*)[368] is part of chivalry. It means turning away from both worlds in disdain."[369] Muhammad b. ʿAli al-Tirmidhi said: "Chivalry means that the permanent and the transitory are equal in your eyes."

I heard Muhammad b. al-Husayn – may God have mercy on him – say: I heard ʿAli b. ʿUmar al-Hafiz say: I heard Abu Ismaʿil b. Ziyad say: I heard ʿAbdallah b. Ahmad b. Hanbal say: "Someone asked my father about chivalry. He answered: 'Abandoning what you are longing for, for what you dread.'" Someone asked a Sufi about chivalry. He answered: "It means that you do not care whether the guest whom you entertain at your table is a friend of God or an unbeliever." I heard one learned man say: "A Magian asked hospitality from Abraham, the Friend of God – peace be upon him. Abraham told him: 'Only if you embrace Islam!'[370] The Magian walked away. At that moment, God Most High revealed to him the following: 'For fifty years I have fed him despite his unbelief. Couldn't you have offered him a morsel without asking him to change his religion?' On hearing this, Abraham – peace be upon him – rushed after the Magian until he caught up with him. He then apologized before him. When the Magian asked him about the cause [of his change of heart], he explained what had happened to him, whereupon the Magian embraced Islam."

Al-Junayd said: "Chivalry means keeping trouble [away from others] and spending magnanimously [on them]." Sahl b. ʿAbdallah [al-Tustari] said: "Chivalry means holding on to the custom of the Prophet." It is said: "Chivalry is being faithful and observing the limits [set by God]." It is said: "Chivalry is a virtue that you perform without attributing it to yourself." It is said: "Chivalry is that you do not hide from those who seek your assistance." It is said: "Chivalry is that you neither hoard [wealth] nor seek excuses [not to give it away to those in need]." It is said: "Chivalry is showing [your gratitude for God's bounty] and hiding the hardship [inflicted upon you by God]." It is said: "Chivalry is when you invite ten guests [for a meal] and care not whether eleven or nine actually come." It is said: "Chivalry is never giving preference [for one thing or person over the other]."

I heard Shaykh Abu ʿAbd al-Rahman al-Sulami – may God have mercy on him – say: I heard Ahmad b. Khadrawayh say to his wife, Umm ʿAli: "I want to throw a feast and to invite to it the clever bandit of honor (ʿayyar shatir) who is head of the [chivalrous] young men (raʾs al-fityan)[371] in our town." The wife

---

368 On this noble quality of character, see the article "Muruʾa" in *EI*.
369 That is, this world and the Hereafter.
370 According to the Qurʾan, Abraham's religion was neither Judaism nor Christianity, but "submission" to God, or Islam.
371 The ʿayyars (ʿayyarun) were members of local urban militias in Muslim cities and towns, who adhered to a specific code of honor. For details see Bosworth, *The Mediaeval Islamic Underworld*.

responded: "It is inappropriate for the likes of you to invite [chivalrous] young men to your house." However, he persisted [in his wish],//303 and his wife told him: "If you want to do this, then have all your sheep, cows and donkeys slaughtered and laid one after another from the door of that man's house to your own door." Ahmad b. Khadrawayh asked her: "Well, I understand [why I should slaughter] the sheep and the cows. But what do the donkeys have to do with this?" The wife answered: "If you decide to invite a [chivalrous] young man to your house, you should make sure that all the dogs of your neighborhood should partake of your feast as well!"

It is related that one Sufi invited his friends to his house for a meal. Among them was a Sufi shaykh from Shiraz.[372] After the feast they tried to perform [Sufi] recitation (samaʿ), but were suddenly overcome by sleep. The shaykh from Shiraz asked the host what could have caused it. He said: "I do not know! I have carefully ascertained the propriety of all food,[373] except the eggplants. I forgot to ask about where they had come from." When they woke up next morning, they [went to] the eggplant vendor and interrogated him. He told them: "I had no eggplants in my store, so I stole them from such-and-such place and sold them." So they brought the man to the owner of that land in order to resolve this issue. When they came to the owner, he exclaimed: "Are you asking me about the one thousand eggplants which were stolen from me?! I am giving him [as a gift] this plot of land, two oxen, a donkey and plow as gifts so that he will not have to do such a thing again!"

It is said that a man married a woman, who suddenly became ill with smallpox right on the night of consummation. [After seeing this] the bridegroom declared that his eyesight had weakened; then he said that he had become completely blind. So the bride was brought to his house and stayed in it for twenty years until she died. All of a sudden, the man opened his eyes. When someone asked him about this, he answered: "I was never blind, I simply feigned blindness in order not to upset her [the wife]." On hearing that, someone told him: "You have indeed surpassed all [chivalrous] young men!"

Dhu ʾl-Nun al-Misri said: "He who seeks to acquire exquisite manners, should follow the example of the water-carriers of Baghdad." Someone asked him: "What about them?" He said: "When I was brought before the caliph on the accusations of heresy,[374] I saw a water-carrier in a turban, who wore an Egyptian-style cloth; he had in his hand several clay pitchers. I asked them whether he was a personal water-carrier of the caliph, but was told that he was an ordinary water-carrier, who served the common folk. So I took one of his pitchers and drank from it. Then I asked one of my companions to give him one *dinar*.

---

372 A province in south-western Iran.
373 That is, he made sure that the food came from religiously sound sources.
374 Dhu ʾl-Nun was said to have adhered to the doctrine of the uncreated Qurʾan, which was contrary to the state supported doctrine that held it to be created.

However, he did not take it, saying: 'You are a prisoner. It is contrary to the code of chivalry to take anything from you!'"

One of our late friends – may God have mercy on him – said: "It is contrary to the chivalric code of honor to earn a profit from one's friends." There was a [chivalrous] young man named Ahmad b. Sahl al-Tajir.[375] I bought a piece of white cloth from him. He charged me exactly what he himself had paid for it. I asked him why he had not surcharged me for it. He answered: "I will take the price of it from you, but I will not burden you with debt [to me],[376] because I am not afraid of looking better in your eyes than I actually am. However, I will not earn any profit from you, for it is contrary to the code of chivalry to earn profit from one's friend."//304 It is said that a man who had made claims of chivalry traveled from Nishapur to Nasa,[377] where someone invited him for a meal along with a group of [chivalrous] young men. When they had finished their feast, a slave girl came to pour water for them to wash their hands. The man from Nishapur retracted his hands, saying: "It is not allowed by the code of chivalry for a girl to pour water for men!" One of those present remarked: "I have come to this house for many years, yet I have never taken any notice of whether it was a man or a woman who poured water for us to wash our hands!"

I heard Mansur al-Maghribi say: "Someone wanted to put the bandit of honor (*ayyar*) named Nuh al-Naysaburi to a test. He sold him a slave girl dressed as a young man, stipulating that she indeed was a young man. The girl was very beautiful. Nuh purchased her thinking that she was indeed a young man. She stayed with him for many months. Someone asked her: "Did he know that you were a girl?" She answered: "No, he has never touched me, since he considered me to be a young man."

It is related that a chivalrous man was asked to hand over to the ruler (*sultan*) the youth who served him. He declined. He received one thousand lashes and yet he still did not surrender the youth. It so happened that on that same night he had a nocturnal emission. It was very cold outside, yet, when he woke up, he performed a full ablution with cold water.[378] Someone told him: "You have put your life in danger!" He answered: "I would have been ashamed before God Most High that I was able to endure one thousand lashes for the sake of a creature and not to endure the harshness of washing [myself] with cold water for His sake!"

A group of [chivalrous] young men came to visit a man who was famous for his chivalry. [When they arrived], the man called out, saying: "[Servant-]boy, bring the tray [with food]!" However, the boy did not bring anything. The man kept calling on him again and again ... The visitors looked at one another and said: "It is contrary to [the rules of] chivalry that someone would employ a person who fails to bring the tray after being asked so many times!" [When the

---

375 That is, "the Merchant".
376 That is, "if I were to give it to you without any charge".
377 A city in Khurasan.
378 A nocturnal emission requires major ablution under the Islamic law.

servant finally appeared], the host asked him: "Why have you tarried so long with the tray?" The boy answered: "There was an ant on it, and it is contrary to [the rules of] chivalry to bring out the tray to the men of chivalry when there is an ant on it, nor is it appropriate to toss it off the tray. So I tarried, until the ant finally crawled off the tray on its own." The visitors told the boy: "You did everything right, boy! You are therefore the kind to serve men of chivalry!"

It is related that a certain man was spending a night in Medina after the pilgrimage [season]. He dreamed that his purse was stolen. He came out [of his room] and saw Jaʿfar al-Sadiq.[379] The man accosted him and demanded: "You took my purse?" "What was in it?" asked Jaʿfar. "One thousand *dinars*," answered the man. Jaʿfar took him to his house and weighed out one thousand *dinars* for him. When the man returned to his house and entered it, he discovered his purse, which he thought had been stolen from him. So the man went back to Jaʿfar to apologize and to return his money to him. However, the latter refused to accept it, saying: "When I give something to someone, I never claim it back!" The man asked one of those present who he was. They told him that it was Jaʿfar al-Sadiq.//305

Shaqiq al-Balkhi asked Jaʿfar b. Muhammad [al-Sadiq] about chivalry. The latter inquired: "And what do you say?" Shaqiq said: "If we are given something, we are grateful, and if we are denied something, we persevere." Jaʿfar exclaimed: "That is what the dogs here in Medina also do!" Shaqiq inquired: "O son of the Messenger's daughter, what, then, do you regard as chivalry?" He answered: "If we are given something, we prefer [to give it to someone else], and if we are denied we are grateful!"

I heard Shaykh Abu ʿAbd al-Rahman al-Sulami – may God have mercy on him – say: I heard Abu Bakr al-Razi say: I heard al-Jurayri say: "One evening Shaykh Abu ʾl-ʿAbbas b. Masruq invited us to his house. On our way we met a friend of ours and told him: 'Come with us as the Shaykh's guests!' 'But he didn't invite me,' said our friend. We told him: 'We shall ask permission on your behalf in the same way as the Messenger of God – may God bless and greet him – asked permission on behalf of ʿAʾisha – may God be pleased with her.' So we took him with us. When we arrived at the door of the Shaykh's house, we informed about our conversation. He said: 'You [the friend] must have given me a special place in your heart, if you have decided to visit me without invitation. I therefore owe you one thing. You cannot proceed to your place without first stepping on my cheek.' He kept persuading the man, then placed one of his cheeks on the floor. The guest was led up to him and gently put his foot on his other cheek. The Shaykh kept dragging his face against the floor until he reached his seat."

Know that it is a condition of chivalry to conceal the faults of one's friends, especially those of them that elicit the glee of their enemies. I heard Abu ʿAbd al-Rahman al-Sulami often say to al-Nasrabadhi: "ʿAli, our singer,[380] drinks [wine]

---

379 The sixth *imam* of the Shiʿites, who was renowned for his piety and humility.
380 That is, the performer of Sufi poetry during Sufi gatherings.

during the night and comes to your [Sufi] gathering during the day." But al-Nasrabadhi would not listen to these rumors until one day he happened to be walking in the company of one of those who had mentioned to him these things about ʿAli. All of a sudden they found ʿAli lying on the ground, drunk. As al-Nasrabadhi was washing his mouth, his companion told him: "How often have we told the Shaykh about his [drinking], but he would not listen?! Here's ʿAli in the very condition that we described!" On hearing this, al-Nasrabadhi turned to the scold and told him: "Put him on your shoulders and carry him to his house!" The scold was unable to disobey the Shaykh's command. I also heard him [al-Sulami] say: I heard Abu ʿAli al-Farisi say: I heard al-Murtaʿish say: "Abu Hafs and I and some other folk went to see a sick friend of ours whom we had frequented. Abu Hafs asked the sick man: 'Would you like to recover?' The man said: 'Yes.' He [Abu Hafs] then told//306 his companions: 'Take his burden from him!' The sick man suddenly stood up and came out with us. The next morning, however, all of us became bedridden and had ourselves to receive visits from our friends."

Spiritual insight (*firasa*)

God Most High said: "Surely in that are signs for those who discern [marks]."[381] They say that [God] thereby meant "those who have spiritual insight". Shaykh Abu ʿAbd al-Rahman al-Sulami – may God have mercy on him – informed us: Ahmad b. ʿAli b. al-Hasan al-Razi informed us: Muhammad b. Ahmad b. al-Sakan informed us: Musa b. Dawud told us: Muhammad b. Kathir al-Kufi told us: ʿAmr b. Qays related on the authority of ʿAtiyya, on the authority of Abu Saʿid al-Khudri that the Messenger of God – may God bless and greet him – said: "Beware of the insight of the faithful [person], for he sees with the light of God – may He be great and exalted!"

Insight is a phenomenon that descends into the heart and expels everything there that opposes it; thus it takes possession of the heart. Etymologically it is derived from the phrase "the prey (*farisa*) of the wild animal". The human heart is incapable of opposing insight, no matter how hard it tries. The strength of insight corresponds to the strength of one's faith: the stronger one's faith, the stronger one's insight. Abu Saʿid al-Kharraz said: "He who sees with the light of insight, sees with the light of God; the substance of his knowledge comes from God unmixed with either negligence or forgetfulness. The decree of God thus flows freely from the tongue of His [faithful] servant." His phrase "he [the servant] sees by the light of God" means that he sees by a light which God has bestowed specifically upon him. Al-Wasiti said: "Insights are flashes of light that illuminate the heart; they are a firmly established knowledge that carries the hearts of men into the realms of the Unseen, from one realm to the other until they begin to see things in such a way as God – praise be to Him

---

381 Q. 15:75.

– wants them to see these things; they thus speak straight from their innermost hearts."

It is related that Abu ʾl-Hasan al-Daylami said: "Once I came to Antioch in order to meet a black man, who was said to have been able to speak about secret truths (*asrar*). I stayed there until he finally descended from the mountain Lukam carrying some licit provisions for sale. I had not eaten for a few days and was very hungry. So I asked him how much he wanted for the provisions that he had with him and made him believe that I wanted to purchase them from him. He told me: 'Sit here! When we sell something of these [provisions], we shall give you //307 some of our proceeds, so that you could purchase something for you [to eat].' I left him for another [vendor] in order to convince him that I wanted to find a better bargain. After a while I returned to him saying: 'If you intend to sell this, then tell me: how much does it cost?' He replied saying: 'You have not eaten for two days. Now, sit down: if I sell something, I'll give you [enough] of it to purchase some [food].' So I sat down for a while. Indeed, when he sold something [of his goods], he gave me the money and left. I followed him. He turned to me and said: 'If you have a need, then present it to God Most High. If, however, you ask something to please your own soul, then you will be denied the fulfillment of your wish.'"

I heard Muhammad b. al-Husayn – may God have mercy on him – say: I heard Muhammad b. ʿAbdallah say: I heard al-Kattani say: "Insight is the unveiling of certainty and the direct vision of the Unseen, which is one of the stations of faith." It is related that al-Shafiʿi[382] and Muhammad b. al-Husayn – may God have mercy on both of them – were in the Sacred Mosque [of Mecca], when a stranger entered it. Muhammad b. al-Husayn said, "My insight tells me that he is a carpenter", whereas al-Shafiʿi said, "My insight tells me that he is a blacksmith." So they approached him and queried him [about his profession]. He answered: "One time I was a blacksmith, but now I work as a carpenter."

Abu Saʿid al-Kharraz said: "The seeker of hidden [realities] (*mustanbit*) is constantly contemplating the Unseen. He does not forget it even for one moment and nothing is concealed from him. He is the one whom God Most High mentioned [in the following verse]: 'Those of them who seek [hidden truths], would have known the matter.'"[383]

The one who discerns [signs] (*mutawassim*) knows what is [hidden] in the secret recesses of hearts by means of evidential proofs and signs. God Most High said, "Surely in that are signs for those who discern [marks]",[384] that is, "for the ones who know the signs that God manifests to the two groups: His friends and His enemies".

The one who has insight sees by the light of God Most High. It consists of the flashes of light that shine in his heart. By means of these flashes he grasps the

---

382 A renowned Muslim scholar, who established the Shafiʿi school of law.
383 Q. 4:83; 4:85, according to Arberry's translation.
384 Q. 15:75.

meanings [of things]. Such a person belongs to the elite of the faithful, who are better endowed [than those who discern marks]; they are the "ones who are learned [in the science of] the Book", in accord with God's words: "Be learned in [the science of] the Book",[385] namely, scholars and wise men, who are adorned by the virtues of God in their thought and in their morals. They are no longer in need of communication with [God's] creatures, nor of paying any attention and being preoccupied with them.//308

It is related that Abu 'l-Qasim al-Munadi, a famous Sufi master from Nishapur, fell ill. [His friends] Abu 'l-Hasan al-Bushanji and al-Hasan al-Haddad went to visit him. En route they bought a half *dirham* worth of apples for him on credit. When they brought the apples to him and sat [next to his bed], Abu 'l-Qasim said: "What is the darkness [around you]?" They left, asking one another: "What have we done?" After thinking about what had happened they said: "Perhaps it is that we have not paid for the apples?" So, they gave the vendor [the price of the apples], and then returned to him [al-Munadi]. As soon as he saw them, he exclaimed: "This is strange! How can one get rid of this darkness so quickly? Tell me about your affair!" So they told him their story. He said: "Yes, each of you relied on the other to pay the price [of the apples], while the vendor was too embarrassed to ask you for money. So, the debt was never settled and I was the cause of it. Therefore, I saw that when I observed you." That man, Abu 'l-Qasim al-Munadi, used to go to the marketplace every day to cry his wares. As soon as he earned an amount sufficient for his needs, which could be a *daniq*[386] or half a *dirham*, he would leave the market and return to his primary occupation (*ra's waqtih*) and to the scrutiny of his heart.

Al-Husayn b. Mansur said: "When God takes possession of man's heart, He bestows upon it [divine] secrets, which it contemplates and communicates [to others]." When someone asked a Sufi master about insight, he answered: "It is when spirits circulate in the sphere of divine majesty (*malakut*), [where] they observe the meanings hidden in the Unseen. Then they speak about the secrets of the created world on the basis of direct witnessing (*mushahada*), not on the basis of guess or supposition." It is related that Zakariya al-Shakhtani had an affair with a certain woman before his repentance.[387] One day, after he had already become one of the best disciples of Abu 'Uthman al-Hiri, he was standing by his side. At that moment, a thought about that woman visited him. [Immediately], Abu 'Uthman raised his head and told him: "Aren't you ashamed?"

The master and imam [al-Qushayri] – may God have mercy on him – related: "At the beginning of my discipleship under the master Abu 'Ali al-Daqqaq – may God be pleased with him – I used to hold teaching sessions at the Mutarriz mosque [in Nishapur]. At some point, I asked his permission to take leave in order to visit [the city of] Nasa. He granted my request. One day, as he and I

---

385 Q. 3:79; 3:74, according to Arberry's translation.
386 A small coin worth one-sixth of a *dirham*.
387 Namely, before he entered the Sufi path.

were walking together on the way to his teaching session, it occurred to me: 'If only he could replace me in my teaching sessions during my absence.' At that moment, he turned to me and said: 'I will replace you in your teaching session during your absence.' I walked a little further. Then it occurred to me that he was not well and that it would be difficult for him to stand in for me for two days per week. I thought: 'Perhaps he should teach my session only once a week?' Again he turned to me and said: 'If I am unable to teach for you two days a week, I will replace you [in your session] only once a week.' I walked a little further, and then another matter occurred to me. Again he turned to me and said exactly what that matter was about."

I heard Shaykh Abu ʿAbd al-Rahman al-Sulami – may God have mercy on him – say: I heard my grandfather Abu ʿAmr b. Nujayd say: "Shah al-Kirmani[388] was possessed of a sharp insight, which never failed him. He would say: 'Whoever turns his eyes away from illicit things restrains himself from passionate drives (*shahawat*), reinforces his inner self with constant self-scrutiny (*muraqaba*) and his outward [behavior] with conformity to the Prophet's custom,//309 and accustoms himself to eating only licit food, will never fail in his insight.'" Someone asked Abu ʾl-Husayn al-Nuri: "Where do possessors of insight derive it from?" He answered with the following words of God Most High: "I [God] breathed My spirit in him."[389] One who has a greater portion of this [divine] light is distinguished by a sounder witnessing and truer insight in his judgement. Don't you see that God's breathing His spirit into him[390] necessitated His demand [for the angels] to prostrate themselves before him, in accordance with God's statement: 'When I have shaped him, and breathed My spirit in him, fall you [angels] down, bowing before him.'"[391] These statements of Abu ʾl-Husayn al-Nuri are somewhat ambiguous in that he mentioned the breathing of the spirit not for the sake of confirming the beliefs of those misguided individuals who think that the spirits are eternal. [On the contrary,] something that is subject to breathing, unification and separation is also liable to influence and change, which are the properties of originated entities. God Most High – praise be to Him – has favored the faithful with the [faculty] of vision and with lights, which enable them to have insights. They are none other than knowledge, which is confirmed by the Prophet – may God bless and greet him – who said: "For he [the faithful] sees with the light of God",[392] that is, God Most High has distinguished the faithful person with knowledge and vision, which has set him apart from all other [created] forms. Thus, calling knowledge and vision "lights" is not an innovation,[393] nor is it a mistake to describe this as "breathing", although [in this particular case the process of] creation is intended.

---

388 On him see al-Sulami, *Tabaqat*, pp. 183–185. He died around 299/911–912.
389 Q. 15:29.
390 That is, Adam.
391 Q. 15:29.
392 See p. 242.
393 Since it was mentioned by the Prophet.

Al-Husayn b. Mansur said: "The person with insight hits his target with the first shot; he is not diverted [from it] by a far-fetched interpretation (*ta'wil*), guessing or presupposition." It is said: "The insight of the beginners (*muridun*) is a guess that requires verification (*tahqiq*), whereas the insight of the gnostics (*'arifun*) is the verification that requires the True Reality (*haqiqa*)." Ahmad b. 'Asim al-Antaki said: "If you attend the gathering of the truthful (*ahl al-sidq*), be truthful with them, for they are the spies of hearts. They enter your hearts and leave them without you taking notice." I heard Muhammad b. al-Husayn – may God have mercy on him – say: I heard Mansur b. 'Abdallah say: I heard [Ja'far] al-Khuldi say: I heard Abu Ja'far al-Haddad say: "Insight is that something occurs to you without any opposition. However, when your occurrence encounters an opposing thought, it is just a transient idea and self-suggestion (*hadith al-nafs*)."

It is said that Abu 'Abdallah al-Razi, who resided in Nishapur,//310 related the following: "Ibn al-Anbari presented me with a woolen garment. [Later on], I noticed that [Abu Bakr] al-Shibli wore on his head an elegant cap (*qalansuwa*), which matched my garment. In my heart I wished that I would have both: the garment and the cap. When al-Shibli rose to leave the gathering, he turned toward me and I followed him, for it was his habit, whenever he wanted me to follow him, to turn toward me [as an invitation]. When we entered his house, he told me: 'Take off this woolen garment!' So I took it off. He folded it and threw his cap on top of it. He then called for fire and burned both of them."

Abu Hafs al-Naysaburi said: "One should not claim to possess insight. At the same time, one should beware of other people's insight, for the Prophet – may God bless and greet him – said: 'Beware of the insight of the faithful [person].' He [the Prophet] did not say: 'Practice insight!' How can claims to insight be appropriate for those who are expected to be wary of it?" Abu 'l-'Abbas b. Masruq said: "Once I went to see an old man, who was a companion of ours, after he had fallen ill. I found him in a state of abject destitution, and said to myself: 'How does this man make a living?' He exclaimed: 'Abu 'l-'Abbas, cast away these lowly thoughts, for God has hidden gifts [that He gives to His servants]!'" Al-Zabidi[394] related: "Once I was in a mosque in Baghdad with a group of the poor.[395] Nothing was given to us [as alms] for several days, so I came to [Ibrahim] al-Khawwas to ask him for something. As soon as he saw me, he inquired: 'Does God know of the need that has brought you to me?' I answered: 'Of course!' 'Then keep quiet and do not exhibit it to any of His creatures!' I returned [to the mosque], and, before long, I was given in alms more than I needed."

It is said that one day Sahl b. 'Abdallah [al-Tustari] was in the congregational mosque [of Basra]. Suddenly, a dove [fell on the floor] overcome by extreme heat and exhaustion. Sahl exclaimed: "Shah al-Kirmani has just died, by God's leave." Those who were in the mosque wrote that down, and indeed it was exactly as he

---

394 Or, "al-Zubayri".
395 That is, Sufis.

said. Once the famous [shaykh] Abu ʿAbdallah al-Turughandhi[396] was traveling to Tus.[397] When he reached [the city of] Kharw, he asked his companion to purchase some bread. The companion bought the amount that was sufficient for the two of them. However, al-Turughandhi asked him to purchase more. So the companion deliberately purchased food enough for ten men, as if he could not believe that the shaykh's words made any sense at all. He[398] said: "When we climbed the mountain, we encountered a group of men who had been tied up by thieves. They had not eaten anything for days, so they asked us for food. The shaykh then said: 'Prepare a table for them!'"

The shaykh and imam [al-Qushayri] said: "One day, I was sitting next to the master and imam Abu ʿAli [al-Daqqaq]. There was talk of how Shaykh Abu ʿAbd al-Rahman al-Sulami – may God have mercy on him – used to follow the custom of the [common] Sufi folk by rising up [in ecstasy] during a session of music and invocation (*samaʿ*).[399] The master Abu ʿAli exclaimed: 'It is better to keep quiet about a person like him being in such a state!' In the same gathering he told me: 'Go to al-Sulami. You will find him sitting in his library. On top of his books there will be a small square red volume//311 with the poetry of al-Husayn b. Mansur [al-Hallaj]. Take this volume, without saying anything to him, then bring it to me.' It was midday, when the heat was strong. So I came to him, as he was sitting in his library and the volume was indeed in the place mentioned by Abu ʿAli. When I sat down, Shaykh Abu ʿAbd al-Rahman al-Sulami began to speak. He said: 'There once was a man who used to censure one scholar for his [uncontrollable] movements during Sufi music sessions. Once that same man was seen in the privacy of his house, whirling around like a person in a state of ecstasy (*mutawajid*). When someone asked him about that, he responded: "There was a problem that I was unable to resolve. Suddenly, it became clear to me. I was unable to control my joy, so I rose up and began to whirl around!" He was told: "This is exactly what they [Sufis] experience!"' When I saw that everything [in the library] was exactly as the master Abu ʿAli told me, and when Shaykh Abu ʿAbd al-Rahman al-Sulami uttered exactly the same words that the master Abu ʿAli had said earlier,[400] I was completely bewildered and asked myself: 'How should I behave in this situation between those two?' I mulled over this matter in my thoughts and decided: 'There's nothing left for me but truth!' Then I told [al-Sulami]: 'The master Abu ʿAli described this volume to me and told me to bring it to him without asking your permission. On the one hand, I am afraid of you; on the other, I cannot disobey his orders. What will you command me to do?' He brought out a six-part volume of sayings by al-Husayn [b. Mansur], which included his own book titled *al-Sayhur fi naqd al-duhur*, and instructed

---

396 Or "al-Turughbadhi".
397 A city in Iran near present-day Mashhad (Meshhed).
398 Probably the companion, but the identity of the speaker is not quite clear from the context.
399 On *samaʿ* see *IM*, pp. 322–325.
400 That is, that one should not publicly discuss the ecstatic behavior of fellow Sufis.

me: 'Take this to him [Abu ʿAli] and tell him that I have studied this volume and quoted some poems from it in my own writings.' So I left."

It is related that al-Hasan al-Haddad – may God have mercy on him – said: "I was in the company of Abu ʾl-Qasim al-Munadi, when he hosted a group of Sufis. He asked me to go out and bring them something [to eat]. I rejoiced at his request, since he [thereby] permitted me to provide for the needs of the Sufis, despite the fact that he knew that I myself was poor. So I took a basket and left. When I reached the road [called] 'Sayyar', I saw an imposing looking elder. I greeted him and said: 'A group of Sufis have gathered in such-and-such place. Would you like to show them your noble character traits?' He ordered some bread, meat and grapes to be brought from his shop. When I reached the door of Abu ʾl-Qasim al-Munadi's house, he called from behind the door saying: 'Take this back to where you took it from!' So I returned to the elder and said: 'They [the Sufis] were not there. I assume that they must have left [while I was looking for food].'" So I returned everything to the elder, then I went to the marketplace, where I was given some food. I carried it with me [to al-Munadi's house]. [This time] he bade me to come in. I recounted my story to him. He said: 'Yes, that man's [nickname] is "Ibn Sayyar."[401] He is one of the governor's men. If you join//312 the Sufis, then give them what you have [now], not what you had earlier!'"

Abu ʾl-Husayn al-Qarafi related: "I paid a visit to Abu ʾl-Khayr al-Tinati. When I was about to bid him farewell, he accompanied me to the gate of the mosque and said: 'Abu ʾl-Husayn, I know that you never carry any provisions with you. However, you should take these two apples with you.' I took and put them in my pocket, whereupon I went on my way. For three days nothing came my way, so I took out one of the apples and ate it. When I wanted to reach for the second, I discovered that both apples were in my pocket. So, I ate them time and again, and they kept returning until I finally reached the gates of Mosul.[402] I said to myself: 'These apples are breaching my state of reliance [on God] (*tawakkul*), for they have become my provision!' So I took them out of my pocket for the last time and looked around. I saw a pauper wrapped in a cloak, who cried out: 'I crave an apple!' So I gave him the apples. As I was walking on, it occurred to me that the shaykh[403] actually sent them to him, while I was but their keeper on the way. I went back looking for the pauper, but could not find him."

I heard Muhammad b. al-Husayn say: I heard ʿAbdallah b. ʿAli say: I heard Abu ʿAmr b. ʿAlwan say: "There was a youth among the companions of al-Junayd, who was able to read other people's thoughts. When al-Junayd learned about this, he asked him: 'What is it that people say about you?' The youth told al-Junayd: 'Think of something!' 'I have done so!' said al-Junayd. The youth told him: 'You

---

401 Literally, "Son of the Sayyar [district]" – that is, someone who was apparently put in charge of it by the local ruler.
402 In present-day Iraq.
403 That is, al-Qarafi.

thought of such-and-such.' Al-Junayd denied that. The youth said: 'Think again!' He did. The youth said: 'You thought of such-and-such.' Al-Junayd denied that again. The same thing happened for the third time. The youth exclaimed: 'This is odd! You are trustworthy and I know [what] my heart [tells me].' Al-Junayd then said: 'You were right all three times, but I wished to test you in order to see if your heart would change.'"

I heard him [Muhammad b. al-Husayn] say: I heard Abu ʿAbdallah al-Razi say: "When Ibn al-Raqqi[404] became ill, someone brought him a cup of medicine and he took it. He then said: 'Today a [grave] incident has happened in this kingdom.[405] I won't eat or drink until I know what it is.' In a few days, the news arrived that the Qarmati [army] entered Mecca on that same day and massacred many people there."[406] I heard Shaykh Abu ʿAbd al-Rahman al-Sulami – may God have mercy on him – say: I heard Abu ʿUthman al-Maghribi say: "When this story was mentioned to Ibn al-Katib, he said: 'This is strange indeed!' I [Abu ʿUthman] told him: 'There's nothing strange about it!' Then Abu ʿAli b. al-Katib queried me: 'And what events are taking place in Mecca today?' I answered: 'The tribes [named] Talha and Hasan are fighting each other. The Talha tribe is headed by a black man wearing a red turban. [Also] today there hovers over Mecca a huge cloud equal in size to the Meccan sanctuary.' Abu ʿAli wrote to Mecca and things there turned out to be exactly as I had told him."

It is related that Anas b. Malik[407] – may God be pleased with him – said: "Once I came to ʿUthman b. ʿAffan[408] – may God be pleased with him – after I had met a woman on the road and admired her beauty. ʿUthman – may God be pleased with him – said: 'One of you has come to me today with traces of adultery in his eyes?' I asked him: 'Can there be [prophetic] inspiration after [the death of] the Messenger of God – may God bless and greet him?' He answered: 'No. However, there can still be perspicacity, irrefutable proof, and a veracious insight!'" Abu Saʿid al-Kharraz said: "Once I entered the Sacred Mosque [of Mecca] and saw a Sufi wearing two cloaks asking people for alms. I said to myself: 'Men like him are a burden on people.' He looked at me and said: 'God knows what is in your souls, so be fearful of Him!'[409] In my heart I begged his forgiveness and he responded, saying: 'It is He Who accepts repentance from His servants.'[410]"

It is related that Ibrahim al-Khawwas said: "Once I was in the Medina congregational mosque in Baghdad with a group of Sufis. There came to us an

---

404 Or "Ibn al-Barqi".
405 That is, the Caliphate.
406 For details, see Halm, *The Empire of the Mahdi*, pp. 247–264.
407 A close companion and servant of the Prophet, who died around 91–93/709–711. He distinguished himself as a prolific *hadith* transmitter.
408 The third of the so-called "rightly-guided" caliphs (successors to the Prophet), who was assassinated in 35/655.
409 Q. 2:235.
410 Q. 42:25; 42:24, according to Arberry's translation.

elegant looking young man, who emitted a sweet smell and had beautiful hair and handsome face. I told my companions: 'It has occurred to me that he is a Jew!' My companions resented [my saying] that. Then both the young man and I went out of the mosque, but [after a while] the young man came back to them and asked: 'What did that shaykh say about me?' They were too ashamed to tell him. However, he insisted and they [finally] told him: 'He said that you were a Jew.' The young man came to me, prostrated himself before me, and embraced Islam. When he was asked why he had done this, he said: 'In our [Jewish] books we read that the insight of the veracious one never fails him. So I said to myself: "I will test the Muslims." I began to watch them closely until I said to myself: "If there be a veracious person in their midst, he will be found among the Sufis (*fi hadhihi 'l-ta'ifa*), for they utter the words of God – praise be upon Him. So I concealed my true identity from them (*labistu 'alayhim*). However, when this shaykh saw me and perceived my [true identity through his insight], I realized that he indeed was a veracious one."' That young man subsequently became a great Sufi master."

I heard Shaykh Abu 'Abd al-Rahman al-Sulami – may God have mercy on him – say: I heard 'Abdallah//314 b. Ibrahim b. al-'Ala' say: I heard Muhammad b. Dawud say: "We were with al-Jurayri, when he asked: 'Is there a man among you, whom God – praise be to Him – would inform about an event that is about to take place in His Kingdom, before He actually had it take place?' We answered 'No, there isn't!' He then said: 'Weep then for the hearts that receive nothing from God Most High!'" Abu Musa al-Daylami[411] said that he asked 'Abd al-Rahman b. Yahya about trust in God (*tawakkul*). He answered: "It is when you push your hand up to the elbow into the mouth of a great serpent, fearing nothing but God Most High." He continued: "I then went to Abu Yazid [al-Bistami] in order to ask him about trust in God. When I knocked on his door, he inquired: 'Don't the words of 'Abd al-Rahman suffice you?' When I asked him to open the door, he replied: 'Since you have come to me not as a guest [but as an enquirer], the answer has come to you from behind the door.' He would not open the door, so I went away and waited one year before returning to him. He said to me: 'Welcome! [This time] you have come to me as a guest.' I stayed with him for one month. [During that time] he would tell me every single thing that occurred to me in my heart. When he was about to bid farewell to me, I begged him: 'Teach me a useful lesson (*fa'ida*)!' He said: 'My mother told me that when she was pregnant with me, she could only reach her hand for food that was licit. Whenever she was given a suspicious food,[412] her hand could not touch it.'"

Ibrahim al-Khawwas said: "Once I traveled [across] the desert, where I suffered much hardship. When I was finally able to reach Mecca, I felt proud of myself. Suddenly, an old woman called out to me, saying: 'Ibrahim, I was with

---

411 Or "al-Daybuli".
412 That is, the food the provenance of which was in doubt.

you in the desert, but I never dared to talk to you then for fear of distracting your inner self [from your goal]. Now, cast away these evil whisperings (*wasawis*)!'"

It is said that al-Farghani used to go on hajj every year. Each time he would pass Nishapur without stopping by Abu 'Uthman al-Hiri's house. He related: "[Eventually] I [decided to] visit him. I greeted him. However, he did not return my greetings. I said to myself: 'A Muslim comes to him and gives him his greetings, but he does not greet him in return?!' Abu 'Uthman replied: '[A Muslim] like this one, who goes on hajj, leaving his mother [in distress] and showing no reverence to her?' So I returned to Farghana[413] and looked after my mother until she died. After that I went to Abu 'Uthman again. When I entered his house, he received me and seated me next to himself." So al-Farghani stayed with Abu 'Uthman, who entrusted him with looking after his mount until he [Abu 'Uthman] died.

Khayr al-Nassaj said: "I was sitting in my house one day, when it suddenly occurred to me that al-Junayd was waiting at the door. I brushed this thought aside. However, it came to me a second time, then a third time. So I finally came out, and indeed there was al-Junayd, who asked me: 'Why did not you come out at the first thought?'" Muhammad b. al-Husayn al-Bistami said://315 "When I came to Abu 'Uthman al-Maghribi, I said to myself: 'Perhaps he would like me to bring something to him [as a gift]?' Abu 'Uthman responded: 'Not only do people want me to take something from them, they also want me to beg this from them!'" A Sufi recounted: "I was in Baghdad, when it occurred to me that al-Murta'ish would bring me fifteen *dirhams* so that I could buy a water-skin, a rope and [a pair of] sandals in order to go into the desert. Soon there was a knock on the door. When I opened the door, I saw al-Murta'ish with a cloth purse. He told me: 'Take this!' I said: 'My lord, I do not want it!' 'How much did you want?' he asked me. 'Fifteen *dirhams*.' He said: 'Here's fifteen *dirhams*!'"

A Sufi said about God's words, "Is he who was dead and We gave him life, [and appointed for him a light to walk by among the people as one of those who are in the depth of darkness?]"[414] that they mean, "Is he whose intellect was dead, but whom God Most High has revived with the light of insight and to whom He has given the light of [divine] revelation and direct contemplation [of divine mysteries] like a man who walks negligently among the negligent folk (*ahl al-ghafla*)?" It is said: "He whose insight is sound ascends to the stage of witnessing (*mushahada*)." I heard Shaykh Abu 'Abd al-Rahman al-Sulami say: I heard Muhammad b. al-Husayn al-Baghdadi say: I heard Ja'far b. Muhammad b. Nusayr say: I heard Abu 'l-'Abbas b. Masruq say: "Once a Sufi master (*shaykh*) came to us. He discoursed beautifully to us about this affair [of ours].[415] He was well spoken and showed excellent judgement. In one of his discourses he told us: 'Tell me about everything that might occur to you.' Suddenly, it occurred to me

---

413 In present-day Uzbekistan.
414 Q. 6:122.
415 That is, Sufism.

that he was a Jew. My thought grew stronger and stronger and persisted until I decided to share it with al-Jurayri, who resented it. So I decided to inform that man about it. I told him: 'You tell us to let you know about any thought that might occur to us. It has occurred to me that you are a Jew!' He fell silent, then raised his head and said: 'You have spoken the truth. I bear witness that there is no deity but God and that Muhammad is His messenger.' He then said: 'I have practiced all religious denominations, saying to myself: "If there is any truth among this community,[416] then it should be among this folk."[417] So I mingled with you in order to test you, and now [I am convinced that] you are truthful.' He became a good Muslim."

It is reported that al-Sari [al-Saqti] used to say to al-Junayd: "Go preach to people!" Al-Junayd recounted: "At that time, in my heart there was fear of speaking in public, because I was not sure that I was worthy of it. One night, which happened to be a Friday night, in my dream I saw the Prophet – may God bless and greet him – who instructed me: 'Go preach to people!' When I woke up, I went to al-Sari's house before he had woken up and knocked on his door. He inquired: 'So you did not believe me until you were told [to do this by the Prophet]?'" Next day, al-Junayd came to the Friday mosque and sat before the people. Immediately word got around that al-Junayd sat [in the mosque] in order to preach to people. A Christian youth in disguise approached him and said: "Master, what is the meaning of the words of the Messenger of God – may God bless and greet him: 'Beware of the insight of the faithful [person], for he sees with the light of God Most High.' Al-Junayd bowed his head for a moment, then raised it and said: "Embrace Islam! The time has come for you to become a Muslim!" So the youth became a Muslim.

Moral character (*khuluq*)

God Most High said: "Surely, thou [the Prophet] art of a good moral character."[418] ʿAli b. Ahmad al-Ahwazi informed us: Abu ʾl-Hasan al-Saffar al-Basri informed us: Hisham b. Muhammad b. Ghalib told us: Muʿalla b. Mahdi told us: Bashshar b. Ibrahim al-Numayri told us: Ghaylan b. Jarir told us on the authority of Anas [b. Malik], who said: "Someone asked the Messenger of God, 'Which of the faithful have the best faith?' He answered: 'Those of them who have the best moral character.'"

Thus, a good moral character is the servant's greatest virtue, one by means of which the true essence of men is known. One who is hidden by his outward complexion (*khalq*) reveals himself through his moral character. I heard the master Abu ʿAli al-Daqqaq – may God have mercy on him – say: "God Most High favored His Prophet – may God bless and greet him – with many excellent

---

416 That is, the Muslims.
417 That is, the Sufis.
418 Q. 68:4.

qualities. However, none of them is more praiseworthy than his good moral character, for God Most High said: 'Surely, thou [the Prophet] art upon a good character.'" Al-Wasiti said: "He [God] attributed a good moral character to him [the Prophet] because he gave away both worlds,[419] while being content with God Most High." Al-Wasiti also said that "good moral character" means that one shows no enmity toward anyone, nor is shown any enmity by anyone due to one's intimate knowledge of God Most High.//317 Al-Husayn b. Mansur [al-Hallaj] said: "The meaning of this [verse] is that one remains unperturbed when one is harshly treated by [God's] creatures, after having witnessed [their] Creator." Abu Saʿid al-Kharraz said: "[Good character] means that you have no concern other than God Most High."

I heard Shaykh Abu ʿAbd al-Rahman al-Sulami say: I heard al-Husayn b. Ahmad b. Jaʿfar say: I heard al-Kattani say: "Sufism is good moral character. Whoever surpasses you in moral character has also surpassed you in Sufism." It is said of Ibn ʿUmar[420] – may God be pleased with both of them[421] – that he said: "If you hear me say to a slave: 'May God disgrace you!' then consider him to be a free man!" Al-Fudayl said: "He who has shown every [possible] virtue, yet has mistreated his chicken, should not be considered to be among the virtuous." It is said that whenever Ibn ʿUmar – may God be pleased with both of them – saw a slave of his performing his prayer diligently, he would manumit him. When [all his servants] learned about this character trait of his, they began to perform prayer diligently to impress him so that he would manumit them. When someone mentioned this to him, he said: "When someone deceives us for the sake of God, we allow ourselves to be deceived."

I heard Muhammad b. al-Husayn say: I heard Muhammad b. ʿAbdallah al-Razi say: I heard Abu Muhammad al-Jurayri say: I heard al-Junayd say: I heard al-Harith al-Muhasibi say: "We have abandoned three things: decent appearance accompanied by self-restraint, nice words accompanied by trustworthiness, and good brotherhood accompanied by dependability."[422] I also heard him [Muhammad b. al-Husayn] say: I heard ʿAbdallah b. Muhammad al-Razi say: "Good moral character consists of denigrating your actions toward Him and exalting His actions toward you." Someone asked al-Ahnaf:[423] "Who taught you [your] moral character?" He answered: "Qays b. ʿAsim al-Minqari."[424] "How far did his moral character extend?" asked the inquirer. Al-Ahnaf said: "He was sitting in his house, when his slave girl brought a skewer with sizzling pieces of meat. It fell from her hand on one of his infant sons, who died instantly. The

---

419 That is, this world and the Hereafter.
420 ʿAbdallah, son of the second "rightly guided" caliph ʿUmar, who died in 73/693.
421 ʿAbdallah and his father ʿUmar b. al-Khattab.
422 Namely, one's words and appearances are no longer supported by one's actions.
423 Al-Ahnaf b. Qays, a leader of the powerful Tamim tribe under the Umayyads, who was famous for his poetic talent, nobility of character, and sagacity; he died in 67/687.
424 A leader of the Muqaʿis tribe (a subdivision of the Tamim), who was renowned for his generosity and leniency towards his enemies; he died in 47/667.

slave girl was overcome with agony. Qays told her: 'Fear not, you are now a free woman for God's sake!'"

Shah al-Kirmani said: "A sign of the good moral character is that you do not harm others, while bearing patiently the distress they inflict on you."//318 The Messenger of God – may God bless and greet him – said: "You will never make people happy by your wealth. Therefore make them happy by a friendly expression on your face and by [your] good moral character." Someone asked Dhu ʾl-Nun al-Misri: "Who has the greatest share of troubles?" He answered: "Those who have the worst moral character." Wahb [b. Munabbih] said: "If one is able to maintain a good moral character for forty days, God will make it part of his natural disposition (*tabiʿa*)." Al-Hasan al-Basri said about the words of God Most High, "Purify thy robes, [O Prophet]",[425] that they mean "Improve your moral character".

A certain ascetic had a ewe. [One day] he saw that one of its legs was missing. He asked who had done this.[426] One of his slaves admitted that he had. The ascetic asked him: "Why?" The man said: "I wanted you to be distressed over it." The ascetic told him: "No, I will not distress the One who ordered you to do so! Go, you are free now!" Someone asked Ibrahim b. Adham: "Have you ever found delight in [something of] this world?" He answered: "Yes, twice. The first time, when I was sitting and a stranger came and urinated on me. The second time, when I was sitting and a stranger came and slapped me round the face." It is related that whenever boys saw Uways al-Qarani,[427] they would pelt him with stones. In response, he would just tell them: "If you have to do this, then use small stones, lest you break my legs and prevent me from performing my prayers."

One day al-Ahnaf b. Qays found himself followed by a stranger, who was insulting him. When he approached his neighborhood, he stopped and said: "Young man, if you have something more [to say], do it now before the halfwits of my neighborhood hear you and respond to you [in kind]." Someone asked Hatim al-Asamm: "Should a man put up with others?" He answered: "Yes, except himself." It is related that the Commander of the Faithful ʿAli b. Abi Talib – may God be pleased with him – called a servant of his, who did not respond to his call. He called him again and again, but the servant still would not respond. So ʿAli went to him and found him lying down. ʿAli asked him: "Didn't you hear me?" The servant answered that he did. "Then what made you ignore my call?" He answered: "I feel safe from your punishment, so I [allowed myself to be] lazy." ʿAli told him: "Go. You are now free for the sake of God Most High!"

---

425 Q. 74:4.
426 That is, cut off one the ewe's legs.
427 A younger contemporary of the Prophet who is said to have embraced his teaching without ever meeting him in person. Sources describe him as an impoverished and ragged figure, who chose to live a life of solitude and privation. He is said to have been killed fighting on ʿAli's side against the army of Muʿawiyya b. Abi Sufyan in 37/657.

It is said that Maʿruf al-Karkhi went down to the Tigris in order to perform his ablutions. He laid down his Qurʾan and his cloak. A woman came along and took them. Maʿruf caught up with her and said: "Sister, I am Maʿruf. Don't be afraid of me. Do you have a son who can read?" She replied: "No." "And [your] husband?" "No," said the woman. Maʿruf told her: "Then give me the Qurʾan back and keep the cloak." Once thieves broke impudently into Shaykh Abu ʿAbd al-Rahman al-Sulami's house and stole everything they could find. I heard one of our companions recount [the following story]: "I heard Shaykh Abu ʿAbd al-Rahman al-Sulami say: 'I was passing through the marketplace one day when I saw my cloak on a vendor.[428] I turned away from him and left.'"

I hear Shaykh Abu Hatim al-Sijistani say: I heard Abu Nasr al-Sarraj al-Tusi say: I heard al-Wajihi say: al-Jurayri said: "When I came back from Mecca – may God protect it – the first thing I did was to go to al-Junayd, so as to save him the trouble [of visiting me]. I greeted him, then went to my house. When I was praying the morning prayer in the mosque the following day, I discovered that he was also praying in the row behind me. I told him: 'Didn't I come to you the other day in order to save you the trouble?' He said: 'That was your munificence, while [praying behind you after the *hajj*] is your due.'" Someone asked Abu Hafs [al-Haddad] about good moral character. He said: "This is what God – may He be great and exalted – bestowed upon His Prophet – may God bless and greet him – when He said: 'Embrace forgiveness and bid to that which is honorable.'"[429] It is said: "Good moral character is that you be close to people, while being a stranger to what occurs among them."[430]

It is said: "Good moral character is that you accept harsh treatment from your fellow creatures and God's decree with neither vexation, nor anxiety." It is related that Abu Dharr[431] was watering his camels at a pond, when a stranger rushed in and broke open [a side] of the pond. Abu Dharr first sat down, then lay down. When someone asked him about this, he answered: "The Messenger of God – may God bless and greet him – commanded us to sit down whenever we are angry and, should [our] anger persist, to lie down." In the Gospel it is said: "O My servant, remember Me when you are angry, and I will remember you when I am angry!" A woman shouted to Malik b. Dinar: "You hypocrite!" He answered: "Woman, you have found a name for me that the people of Basra have missed [thus far]!"

Luqman[432] said to his son: "There are three men whose true character makes itself known on three instances: a prudent man at the time of anger; a valiant man at the time of war; and a brother at the time when someone is in need of him."

---

428 Or auctioneer (*man yazid*).
429 Q. 7:199; 7:197, according to Arberry's translation.
430 That is, to their quarrels and disputes.
431 A pious and frugal Companion of the Prophet who died in 31 or 32/652 or 653.
432 A legendary hero and sage of pre-Islamic Arabia, who appears in the Qurʾan as a wise father giving pious admonitions to his son.

Moses – peace be upon him – said: "My God, I plea that I be ascribed no qualities that I do not possess!" God – praise be to Him – revealed to him: "I have not done this for Myself. How can I do this for you?"//320 Yahya b. Ziyad al-Harithi owned a troublesome slave. Someone asked him: "Why do you retain this slave?" He answered: "In order to learn temperance through him." It is said that in the words of God Most High: "He [God] has lavished on you His blessings, outward and inward."[433] "Outward" here means [man's] creation [by God][434] while "inward" means [God's] purifying [man's] moral character. Al-Fudayl said: "I'd rather have a good-natured sinner than bad-natured worshiper as my companion." It is said that good moral character consists of taking adversity in one's stride (*bi-husn al-mudara*).

It is related that Ibrahim b. Adham was traveling in a desert, when he encountered a soldier, who asked him: "Where is the closest settlement?" Ibrahim b. Adham pointed toward the graveyard, whereupon the soldier struck him on the head and wounded him. When the soldier finally let him go, he was told that [he had beaten] Ibrahim b. Adham, the [famous] ascetic from Khurasan. When the soldier returned to apologize before him, Ibrahim told him: "When you struck me, I asked God Most High to [admit] you to Paradise." The soldier inquired why he had done that. Ibrahim told him: "Because I knew that God would reward me for this. However, I did not want my portion to be good at your expense and your portion to be bad because of me!"

It is related that a man invited Abu 'Uthman al-Hiri to dinner. When he came to the man's door, the latter told him: "Sir, this is not a good time for you to enter [my house]. I regret it, but you must leave." When Abu 'Uthman reached his home, the man caught up with him and repeated his apologies and said: "Sir, I regret [turning you back]. You may come now." Abu 'Uthman took off and went [to the man's house]. When he came to the door of the man's house, the man said the same as he did the first time. He did the same the third and fourth times. Time and again, Abu 'Uthman came back to the man's door only to be sent away. Finally, the man told him that he simply wanted to test him. He apologized profusely and praised Abu 'Uthman highly [for his perseverance]. However, Abu 'Uthman told him: "Do not praise me for a character trait that you commonly find among dogs, for when a dog is called, it comes, and when it is yelled at, it runs away." It is related that Abu 'Uthman was crossing a street one day, when someone dumped a bucket of ashes on him. His companions were very angry and began to curse the person who dumped the ashes. However, Abu 'Uthman told them: "Don't say a word! He who has deserved the [hell]fire, yet has managed to get away with just ashes, has no right to be angry!"

It is related that a Sufi was staying in Ja'far b. Hanzala's house. The latter did his utmost to serve him well. The Sufi//321 used to tell him: "What a wonderful man you are, were it not for the fact that you are Jewish!" To which

---

433 Q. 31:20; 31:19, according to Arberry's translation.
434 Q. 7:10; 15:26–29.

Ja'far responded: "My religious creed (*'aqidati*) has no effect on my service of your needs! Therefore, pray for a cure for yourself and for guidance for me!" It is said that 'Abdallah al-Khayyat [the Taylor] had a Magian as his customer. 'Abdallah sewed clothes for him and the Magian paid him with counterfeit money. One day, when 'Abdallah left his shop on an errand, the Magian came with his counterfeit money and tried to give it to 'Abdallah's apprentice. When the apprentice refused to accept it, the Magian paid him genuine money. When 'Abdallah came back to his shop, he asked the apprentice: "Where's the Magian's shirt?" The apprentice told him what had happened. 'Abdallah exclaimed: "You have done a terrible thing! For a long time he has done business with me with [such counterfeit] money. I have been patient with him throughout and tossed his money into a well, so that he would not cheat other folk with it!"

It is said that bad moral character oppresses the heart of its possessor, because it leaves no room there for anything other than his [selfish] desires. It thus becomes like a small house, which is barely enough for its tenant. It is said that one sign of good character is that you are not annoyed by whoever prays by your side [during the ritual prayer]. As for bad character, it consists of paying attention to the bad character of others. Someone asked the Messenger of God – may God bless and greet him – about bad luck, he said: "Bad character!"

Abu 'l-Hasan 'Ali al-Ahwazi informed us: Abu 'l-Hasan al-Saffar al-Basri told us: Mu'adh b. al-Muthanna told us: Yahya b. Ma'na[435] told us: Marwan al-Fazari told us: Yazid b. Kaysan told us on the authority of Abu Hazim, on the authority of Abu Hurayra – may God be pleased with him – that someone asked the Messenger of God: "Messenger of God, pray to God Most High against polytheists!" He answered: "I was sent [by God] as a mercy, not as a punishment!"

Munificence (*jud*) and generosity (*sakha'*)

God – may He be great and exalted – said: "They prefer others above themselves, even though poverty is their portion."[436] 'Ali b. Ahmad b. 'Abdan informed us: Ahmad b. 'Ubayd informed us: al-Hasan b. al-'Abbas//322 told us: Sahl told us: Sa'id b. Muslim told us on the authority of Yahya b. Sa'id, on the authority of Muhammad b. Ibrahim, on the authority of 'Alqama that 'A'isha[437] – may God be pleased with her – said that the Messenger of God – may God bless and greet him – said: "The generous are close to God Most High, close to people, close to Paradise and far from the [hell]fire, while the miserly are far from God Most High, far from people, far from Paradise, and close to the [hell]fire. God loves the generous ignoramus (*jahil*) more than the miserly worshiper."

The master [al-Qushayri] said: "In the parlance of the folk[438] there's no difference between munificence and generosity. God – praise be to Him – on the

---

435 Or "al-Mu'in".
436 Q. 59:9.
437 The third (and favorite) wife of the Prophet, who died in 58/678.
438 That is, Sufis.

other hand, is not described as "generous" or "munificent", for lack of an appropriate precedent [in the Qurʾan or the Sunna]. The true essence of generosity is that one has no difficulty giving [to others]. According to the folk, generosity is the first step, which is followed by munificence and, finally, preferring others to oneself (*ithar*). He who gives away a portion and saves a portion for himself is generous. He who gives away a lot and saves a little for himself is munificent. He who suffers from shortage, yet gives away his bare minimum to someone else, is one who gives preference to others over himself. Likewise, I heard the master Abu ʿAli al-Daqqaq – may God have mercy on him – say that Asmaʾ b. Kharija said: "I hate to turn down anyone who approaches me with a need, because if he is noble, I guard his honor,[439] while if he is base I guard my honor from him." It is related that Muwarriq al-ʿIjli was very sophisticated in showing friendship toward his companions.[440] He would leave one thousand *dirhams* with them and say: "Keep this for me until I come back." After a while he would send them a note saying: "These *dirhams* are yours [to spend]."

A man from Manbij[441] met another man from Medina and inquired about him. When he was told that the man had come from Medina, he told him: "A man from your city named al-Hakam b. ʿAbd al-Muttalib came to us and made us rich." The man from Medina asked: "How come? He came to you with nothing but a hair-shirt on his back?" The man from Manbij replied: "He did not enrich us with money. Rather, he taught us generosity. We started to give to one another, until all of us grew rich." I heard the master Abu ʿAli al-Daqqaq say: "When Ghulam al-Khalil slandered the Sufis [of Baghdad] before the caliph,[442] he ordered them to be beheaded. Al-Junayd [avoided this trial] by presenting himself as a jurist (*faqih*), for he indeed issued legal rulings according to the juridical school [named after] Abu//323 Thawr,[443] while others, including al-Shahham, al-Raqqam, and al-Nuri, were arrested. When leather mats were spread for their beheading, al-Nuri stepped forward. The executioner asked him: 'Do you know what you are stepping forward for?' Al-Nuri responded that he did. The executioner then asked him: 'Then what makes you hurry?' Al-Nuri answered: 'I'd rather my companions live another moment.' The executioner was perplexed and reported the matter to the caliph, who sent the Sufis over to the judge to investigate their affair. The judge posed several legal questions to Abu ʾl-Husayn al-Nuri, who answered them all. He then proceeded to say [the following]: 'God has servants who, when they stand, they stand for the sake of God; when they speak, they speak for the sake of God.' He said other things as well that made the

---

439 By fulfilling his need.
440 Literally, "his brothers" (*ikhwanuh*).
441 An ancient town in Syria, located north-west of Aleppo.
442 See *IM*, pp. 61–62.
443 Ibrahim b. Khalid Abu Thawr (d. 240/854), a prominent jurist, who adhered closely to the school of law founded by al-Shafiʿi. However, his opinions were sufficiently different from those of al-Shafiʿi to consider him to be the founder of an independent school of law.

judge weep. He then sent the following note to the caliph: 'If these folk are heretics, then there's not a single [faithful] Muslim on the face of the earth.'"

It is related that ʿAli b. al-Fudayl[444] used to buy his goods from neighborhood merchants. Someone told him: "You could buy [the same goods] cheaper if you shopped at the [city] market!" He answered: "These merchants have settled in our neighborhood in the hope of serving our needs." It is related that someone sent [as a gift] a slave girl to Jabala, when he had his companions with him. He said: "It would be an ugly thing if I were to accept her for myself in your presence. At the same time, I hate to privilege one of you by [giving] her to him, for all of you have a right to her and to [being] honored [by me]. This girl cannot be divided [among you]." There were eighty people there. So he ordered that each of them be given a slave girl or a slave boy. It is said that ʿUbaydallah b. Abi Bakra[445] felt thirsty while on the road. He asked for water at the house of a woman. The woman brought out a cup and stood behind the door, saying: "Stay away from the door and let one of your slaves come and get it. I am a [modest] Arab woman, but my servant died a few days ago."[446] ʿUbaydallah drank the water and told his slave: "Give her ten thousand *dirhams*." The woman said: "May God be Glorified! Are you ridiculing me?" ʿUbaydallah said [to his slave]: "Take twenty thousand *dirhams* to her." She said: "I ask God Most High (to grant you) good health." ʿUbaydallah exclaimed: "Boy, give her thirty thousand *dirhams*!" On hearing that she slammed the door before him and cried: "Shame on you!" But the boy [finally] brought her thirty thousand *dirhams* and she accepted it. Before nightfall she was receiving numerous suitors.

It is said that munificence is acting on first impulse (*al-khatir al-awwal*). I heard one of the companions of Abu ʾl-Hasan al-Bushanji – may God have mercy on him – say: "One Abu ʾl-Hasan al-Bushanji was in the outhouse. [Suddenly] he called a disciple of his and asked him to take the shirt off his back and to present it to so-and-so. Someone asked him: 'Couldn't you wait until you came out of the outhouse?' He answered: 'I do not trust myself not to change my mind//324 about [giving away] my shirt!'"

Someone asked Qays b. Saʿd b. ʿUbada: "Have you ever seen anyone more generous than yourself?" He answered: "Yes. One day in the desert we came upon the camp of a Bedouin woman. When her husband arrived, she told him: 'Two guests have come to stay with us.' He then brought a she-camel, slaughtered it and said: 'This is for you!' The next day he brought another one and slaughtered it, saying 'This is for you!' We objected: 'We have eaten only a little of the one you slaughtered the other day!' He responded: 'I do not give yesterday's food to my guests!' We stayed with him two or three more days, because it was raining, and he continued to do this [every day]. When we were about to depart, we left

---

444 That is, son of the famous ascetic al-Fudayl b. ʿIyad.
445 The Arab military commander and governor of the Persian province of Sistan under the Umayyads. He died in 79/698.
446 And therefore could not bring water to her guests.

one hundred *dinars* in his tent, saying to his wife: 'Apologize to him on our behalf.' We continued our journey. At midday, we saw the man behind us shouting: 'Stop, you ignoble riders! You have paid me for my hospitality!' When he approached us, he said: 'Take this [money] back, or else I will stab you with my spear!' So we took the money and left, while he recited [the following]:

> Your robbing [me] of the reward due to me for what I have given you
> Is enough to humiliate me [for the rest of my life]!"

I heard Shaykh Abu ʿAbd al-Rahman al-Sulami – may God have mercy on him – say: "Abu ʿAbdallah al-Rudhbari came to visit one of his friends. The friend was not at home and the door of his house was shut. He exclaimed: 'Here's a Sufi, whose door is locked! Break the lock! Break the lock!' He then ordered everything he could find in the man's house and yard to be taken to the marketplace and sold. Al-Rudhbari and his companions sold all this, bought the things that they wanted from the proceeds, and returned to his house. When the owner of the house returned, he could not utter a single word. His wife came after him, wearing a cloak. When she entered the house, she threw off her garment and exclaimed: 'This, too, is part of our property, so go and sell it as well!' The husband asked her: 'Why are you giving this away on your own accord?' She answered: 'Hush! A master like him [al-Rudhbari] confronts us and passes his judgement on us in this manner, yet we are still trying to hide something from him?'"

Bishr b. al-Harith [al-Hafi] said: "Seeing a miser hardens one's heart." It is said that Qays b. Saʿd b. ʿUbada fell ill. His friends tarried in visiting him, so he asked what was wrong with them. He was told: "They [are not coming] because they are ashamed of the debts they owe you." He exclaimed: "May God curse the money that prevents friends from visiting [one of their own]!" He then//325 asked the town crier to announce: "Whoever owes anything to Qays is now free from it!" By the nightfall the porch of his house was broken by all those who came to visit him. Someone said to ʿAbdallah b. Jaʿfar: "You give generously when asked, yet you give no ground to someone who opposes you." He answered: "I am generous with my money, yet I am stingy with my intellect." It is said that ʿAbdallah b. Jaʿfar once went to inspect his property in the countryside. He stopped at a date palm grove where a black slave boy was working. When food was brought to the slave boy, a dog came from outside the garden and approached the boy. He threw a piece of bread to it, and it ate it. He threw it another piece of bread, then a third one, and the dog ate them, as ʿAbdallah b. Jaʿfar was looking on. He then asked the boy: "How much food do you get every day?" The boy answered: "Just what you have seen!" Jaʿfar asked him: "Why did you prefer the dog over yourself?" The boy responded: "This is not an area that dogs normally frequent. This dog must have come from afar, so I did not want to turn it away." ʿAbdallah b. Jaʿfar asked him: "How will you manage [without food]?" The boy said: "I will persevere through the rest of the day." ʿAbdallah exclaimed: "I have been reproached for being too generous! However, this boy is more generous than I!" So he purchased the date palm grove, the boy and all the tools that were there, then manumitted the boy and gave all this [property] to him."

It is related that a man went one day to visit a friend of his. When he knocked on his door, the friend came out and asked him: "Why have you come?" The man answered: "Because of a four-hundred *dirham* debt that I am saddled with." The friend went inside, weighed out four hundred *dirhams* and brought them out to him. He then returned home in tears. His wife asked him: "Why could you not find an excuse [not to give him the money], if giving [it to him] is so hard for you?" The man said: "I am weeping only because I was unable to perceive his need so that he had to reveal it to me!" Mutarrif b. al-Shikhkhir said: "Whenever one of you is in need of my assistance, let him deliver it to me in writing, for I hate to see the humiliation of need on anyone's face." A man, who wanted to embarrass ʿAbdallah b. al-ʿAbbas, visited the prominent people of the city and told them: "Ibn al-ʿAbbas invites you to have dinner with him tonight!" So, the notables came to him and filled his entire house. He asked what was going on and was told the story. He immediately proceeded to order fruit, bread, and various dishes to be bought. In this way, he managed to salvage the situation. When the feast was over, he asked his household managers: "Do we have [enough money] to offer this [hospitality] every day?" They said: "Yes [we do]." He then said: "Then let's entertain all of them here every day!"

I heard Shaykh Abu ʿAbd al-Rahman al-Sulami – may God have mercy on him – say: the master Abu Sahl//326 al-Suʿluki was performing his ablutions in his courtyard, when a man approached him and asked for alms. He had nothing with him at that time, so he said: "Wait until I am finished." The man waited. When al-Suʿluki finished [his ablutions], he said: "Take this [valuable] bottle and go!" The man took the bottle and left. Al-Suʿluki waited until he knew that the man was far away, then cried out: "A man entered [my house] and took the bottle!" [His family] went out searching for the man, but could not catch up with him. Al-Suʿluki did that because his household used to reproach him for his excessive generosity. I also heard him [al-Sulami] say: "The master Abu Sahl [al-Suʿluki] gave his robe to a certain man in [the middle of] the winter. Since he had no other robe, he had to put on a woman's robe whenever he went out to teach [his classes]. Once a delegation of distinguished men arrived from Fars.[447] It included all kinds of famous scholars: jurists, theologians (*mutakallimun*), grammarians, and so on. The ruler of the city,[448] Abu ʾl-Hasan, sent for Abu Sahl, ordering him to ride out to meet the delegation. He put on a woolen tunic over his woman's robe and rode out. [When the ruler saw him], he exclaimed: 'He has humiliated me in front of the entire city by riding out in the woman's robe!' However, when Sahl started to debate them, his arguments proved to be superior to theirs in every field of knowledge they represented."

---

447 A province in Iran.
448 That is, Nishapur.

I also heard him [al-Sulami] say: "The master Abu Sahl [al-Su'luki] never handed alms to anyone directly. Rather, he would cast it on the ground, so that the beggar would pick the alms from the ground, saying: 'This world is of so little worth that, for the love of it, I do not want to see my hand putting anything into the hand of another man.' However, [the Prophet] – may God bless and greet him – said: 'The upper hand[449] is better than the lower hand[450].'"

Abu Marthad – may God have mercy on him – was a generous person. Once a poet praised him in his verse. Abu Marthad told him: "I have nothing to give you [for your poem]. However, you should take me to the judge and claim that I owe you ten thousand *dirhams*, and I will confirm this. Then have me put into prison. My family will not allow me to be in prison for long." The poet did as he was told, and by the end of that same day he received ten thousand *dirhams*, while Abu Marthad was released from prison. It is related that a man asked al-Hasan b. 'Ali b. Abi Talib – may God be pleased with him – for some charity and the latter gave him fifty thousand *dirhams* and five thousand *dinars*. He then said: "Bring a porter to carry this money for you!" When the man brought a porter, al-Hasan gave the man his shawl, saying: "The porter's wages are also on me!"

A woman asked Layth b. Sa'd[451] for a bowl of honey. He ordered her an entire skin full of honey. When someone asked him about that, he replied: "She asked according to her need, while I gave according to my benefaction!" A Sufi related: "One day I was performing the morning prayer in the mosque of al-Ash'ath[452] at Kufa. I came there in search of one of my debtors. When //327 I completed my prayer, someone put in front of me a suit of clothes and a pair of sandals. When I asked what it was, I was told that al-Ash'ath had just returned from Mecca and ordered [such presents] to be given to the entire congregation of his mosque. I told them: 'I have come here in search of my debtor, so I do not belong to this congregation.' They told me: 'This is to be given to all those who have come to the mosque.'" It is related that when the hour of al-Shafi'i's – may God be pleased with him – death drew near, he said: "Tell so-and-so to wash my body!" However, the man happened to be away. When he came back [from his trip], he was told about this. The man then asked for al-Shafi'i's ledger, and found that al-Shafi'i had a debt of seventy-thousand *dirhams*. He settled that debt, saying: "This is my washing of his [body]!" It is related that when al-Shafi'i came from Sanaa[453] to Mecca, he had with him ten thousand *dinars*. Someone told him to purchase a slave girl [to serve him] with this money. He set up a tent outside Mecca and put the *dinars* [on his robe] and began to give away these *dinars*. He would give a fistful of them to anyone who came to see him. By

---

449 That is, the hand of the giver.
450 That is, the hand of the taker.
451 A famous *hadith* collector and jurist, who lived and died in Egypt in 175/791.
452 A tribal leader from Hadramawt, who took an active part in the conquest of Iraq. He later settled in Kufa, where he died in 40/661.
453 The capital city of present-day Yemen.

midday, he stood up and shook out his robe: there was not a single piece left on him.

It is related that al-Sari [al-Saqati] left his house on a festival day and encountered a man of importance, to whom he gave only a cursory greeting. He was told: "This is a man of importance!" He answered: "Yes, I recognized him. However, a well-attested tradition has it that whenever two Muslims meet, one hundred divine blessings are divided between them, of which ninety go to the more cheerful one. So, I wanted him to receive the larger portion [of the blessings]. It is related that the Commander of the Faithful ʿAli b. Abi Talib – may God be pleased with him – was found weeping one day. When asked what made him cry, he told: "Not a single guest has come over in the past seven days. I am afraid that God Most High may have decided to humiliate me!" It is related that Malik b. Anas[454] – may God be pleased with him – said: "The tax of any house is that [its owner] should set aside a room for guests [in it]."

Concerning the words of God Most High, "Hast thou received the story of the honored guests of Abraham?"[455] the guests are called "honored" because Abraham attended upon them himself, and the guest of an honorable person (*karim*) is also honorable. Ibrahim b. al-Junayd said: "There are four things that the noble person should not be remiss in, even if he be a prince: standing up from his place when his father enters [the room], serving his guests [personally], serving a scholar from whom you have learned, and asking [men of learning] about what he does not know."

Ibn ʿAbbas – may God be pleased with him – said concerning the words of God Most High, "There is no fault in you that you eat//328 whether in groups or separately",[456] that it means: "They [the Companions of the Prophet] felt uneasy when any one of them would eat alone, so God gave them permission to do that." It is related that one day ʿAbdallah b. ʿAmir b. Kurayz[457] offered hospitality to a man. He entertained him very well. However, when the guest was about to depart, his servants did not help him [with his preparations]. When someone reprimanded him, he answered: "They never help anyone who leaves us!" ʿAbdallah b. Bakawayh the Sufi recited to us the following verse of al-Mutanabbi:[458]

If you leave a company who could prevent you from departing
Then they are the ones that are leaving!

ʿAbdallah b. Mubarak said: "Being generous with regard to what other people possess[459] is better than being generous in giving away [one's own possessions]."

---

454 A famous early jurist, founder of the Maliki legal school of Sunni Islam; he died in 179/796.
455 Q. 51:24.
456 Q. 24:61.
457 Governor of Basra (d. 59/680) under ʿUthman and Muʿawiyya, who was renowned for his generosity.
458 A great Arab poet, who died in 354/955.
459 That is, being happy at the sight of other people's wealth.

A Sufi recounted: "On a very cold day I came to visit Bishr b. al-Harith. He had no clothes on him and sat there trembling [from cold]. I told him: 'Abu Nasr, on a day like this people put on extra clothing! Why do you have so little [clothing on you]?' He answered: 'I have remembered the poor and their plight. Since I have nothing to bestow on them, I have decided to keep their company in enduring this cold!'"

I heard Shaykh Abu ʿAbd al-Rahman al-Sulami – may God have mercy on him – say: "I heard Abu Bakr al-Razi say: I heard [Abu ʿAli] al-Daqqaq say: "Generosity lies not in the wealthy giving to the indigent (muʿdam). Generosity lies in the indigent giving to the wealthy!"

Jealousy (*ghayra*)

God Most High said: "My Lord has only forbidden indecencies, the inward and the outward."[460] Abu Bakr Muhammad b. Ahmad b. ʿAbdus al-Muzakki informed us: Abu Ahmad Hamza b. al-ʿAbbas al-Bazzaz informed us in Baghdad: Muhammad b. Ghalib b. Harb told us: ʿAbdallah b. Muslim told us: Muhammad b. al-Furat told us on the authority of Ibrahim al-Hajari, on the authority of Abu ʾl-Ahwas, on the authority of ʿAbdallah b. Masʿud, who said: "The Messenger of God – may God bless and greet him – said: 'No one is more jealous than God Most High. Out of His jealousy He has forbidden indecencies, the inward and the outward.'"//329 ʿAli b. Ahmad al-Ahwazi informed us: Ahmad b. ʿUbayd al-Saffar informed us: Abu ʾl-Husayn b. Bunan told us: ʿAbdallah b. Rajaʾ told us: Harb b. Shaddad told us: Yahya b. Abi Kathir told us on the authority of Abu Salama that Abu Hurayra – may God be pleased with him – told them that the Messenger of God – may God bless and greet him – said: "God is jealous and the believer is jealous. The jealousy of God Most High is aroused when the believing servant commits an act prohibited by God."

Jealousy (*ghayra*) is resentment against sharing [something] with another (*ghayr*). When God – praise be to Him – is called "jealous" this means He is not pleased with sharing with anyone the obedience of His servant that rightfully belongs to Him [alone]. It is related that one day the verse "When thou recitest the Koran, We place between thee, and those who do not believe in the world to come, a curtain obstructing"[461] was recited before al-Sari. He asked his companions: "Do you know what this curtain is? It is the curtain of jealousy. No one is more jealous than God Most High." By saying "the curtain of jealousy" al-Sari meant that God never imparts the true religion to the unbelievers. The master Abu ʿAli al-Daqqaq – may God have mercy on him – used to say: "God Most High has attached to the feet of those remiss in worshiping Him the weights of abandonment (*khidhlan*); He has chosen them for banishment from Himself and removed them from His closeness, causing them to fall behind [in their worship]." They recite:

---

460 Q. 7:33; 7:31, according to Arberry's translation.
461 Q. 17:45; 17:46, according to Arberry's translation.

I long for the one I have passion for; however, how can I protect myself
From the [jealous] slander of [my] friends?

They also say about this situation: "[He is] a sick man whom no one comes to visit and a desiring one whom no one desires." I heard the master Abu ʿAli al-Daqqaq – may God have mercy on him – say: I heard al-ʿAbbas al-Zawzani say: "I was blessed with a good start [on the path of God], because I knew [the distance] between me and the goal I have aspired to reach. One night, in a dream, I saw myself falling from the peak of the mountain I had aspired to reach. I was saddened by this. Then a slumber came over me and I saw a man who told me: 'Oh ʿAbbas, God did not want you to attain//330 the goal you aspired to. However, a wisdom was revealed to your tongue.' He proceeded to say: 'When I woke up, I was entrusted with the words of wisdom.'"

I heard the master Abu ʿAli al-Daqqaq – may God have mercy on him – say: "There was a Sufi master (*shaykh*), who experienced [his] state and moment with God. He went into hiding and was not seen among the poor.[462] After a while he came back in a mystical state (*waqt*) that was different from the one he was in before. When he was asked about what had happened, he answered: 'Alas, a veil has come down …'" The master Abu ʿAli al-Daqqaq – may God have mercy on him – used to say, when, during a Sufi session, something irritating entered the hearts of those present: "This is the jealousy of God – praise be to Him." Abu ʿAli meant that the purity of the mystical moment (*waqt*) he was experiencing eluded his companions. They imply this sense when they recite:

She wanted to visit us, but when she looked into a mirror, her beautiful
face prevented her from coming.

Someone asked a Sufi: "Do you wish to see Him?" He said: "No." They asked him: "Why not?" He answered: "This beauty is too lofty to be seen by someone like me!"

They have this meaning in mind, when they recite:

I envy my eyes when they look at you, so I lower them: seeing you
strutting around in all your beauty makes me jealous of you for you!

Someone asked al-Shibli: "When do you find rest [from jealousy]?" He answered: "When I find no one else [in the entire world] who remembers (*dhakir*) Him!" I heard the master Abu ʿAli al-Daqqaq – may God have mercy on him – mention the words of the Prophet – may God bless and greet him – after he had purchased a horse from a Bedouin. The Bedouin then asked him to rescind their transaction and the Prophet agreed to that. The Bedouin told him: "May God Most High give you a long life! Who are you?" The Prophet – may God bless and greet him – said: "A man of the Quraysh." One of the Companions present there exclaimed:

---

462 That is, the Sufis.

"How rude of you not to recognize your Prophet!" [Abu ʿAli al-Daqqaq] – may God have mercy on him – commented: "The Prophet said: '[I am] a man of the Quraysh' out of jealousy, because otherwise he would have been obligated to answer to everyone who asked him who he was. However, God – praise be to Him – [prevented him from doing this] by casting the aforementioned words on the tongue of the Companion."

Some people say that jealousy is an attribute of beginners on the Sufi path and that one with the [genuine] knowledge of divine oneness (*tawhid*) can display no jealousy. Such a person is incapable of exercising his own choice, for he has no authority over what happens in the Kingdom [of God]. It is God Most High Who has authority over everything and determines things as He pleases.//331 I heard Shaykh Abu ʿAbd al-Rahman al-Sulami – may God have mercy on him – say: I heard Abu ʿUthman al-Maghribi say: "Jealousy pertains to beginners, not to those who have attained [divine] realities (*haqaʾiq*). I also heard him [al-Sulami] say: I heard Abu Nasr al-Isbahani say: I heard al-Shibli say: "There are two types of jealousy: one, when human beings are jealous of one another; and the other, when God is jealous of [His servants'] hearts." Al-Shibli also said: "God is also jealous of the breaths of His servants lest they be wasted on something other than God Most High. One must conclude that there are two types of jealousy: God's being jealous of His servant, meaning that He keeps him away from His creatures out of His envy for him; and the servant's being jealous of God, meaning that he devotes all his spiritual states and breaths to no one but God Most High. One should not say: "I am jealous of God." Rather one should say: "I am jealous for the sake of God." Thus, being jealous of God Most High is nothing but ignorance which may lead to the abandonment of faith. As for jealousy for the sake of God, it demands [of His servant] the maintenance of His rights and purifying his deeds for His sake.

Know that it is God's custom with regard to His friends to throw them into confusion each time they rely on something other [than Him], take notice of something other, or cleave to something else with their hearts. He is jealous of their hearts to such an extent that He brings them [the hearts] back to Himself, faithful to Him, empty of anything [other than Him] that they may have relied on, noticed or cleaved to. As in the case of Adam – peace be upon him: no sooner had he set his mind on staying in the garden of Paradise forever, than God expelled him from it. The same happened to Abraham – peace be upon him – when he delighted in his son Ishmael – peace be upon him. God ordered him to sacrifice him, so that he would banish him from his heart. "When they both surrendered, and he flung him upon his brow",[463] his heart was purified of his [love of] his son and God commanded him to make a substitute sacrifice [of a ram].

I heard Shaykh Abu ʿAbd al-Rahman al-Sulami – may God have mercy on him – say: I heard Abu Zayd al-Marwazi – may God have mercy on him – say: I heard Ibrahim b. Shayban say: I heard Muhammad b. Hassan say: "One day,

---

463 Qurʾan 37:103, 37:104, according to Arberry's translation.

when I was wandering in the mountains of Lebanon, a young man came upon me. His skin was burned by the hot desert winds and sandstorms. When he saw me, he suddenly turned away and fled. I followed him, asking him to share a [wise] word with me. He told me: 'Beware, for He is jealous. He dislikes seeing anything other than Him in the heart of His servant!'" I heard Shaykh Abu ʿAbd al-Rahman al-Sulami – may God have mercy on him – say: "Al-Nasrabadhi said: 'God Most High is jealous. Part of His jealousy is that He has made no road to Himself other than Himself.'"

It is said that God – praise be to Him – revealed to one of His prophets: "When so-and-so is in need of Me, I too am in need of him. If he satisfies My need, I will satisfy his." That prophet – peace be upon him – then said in his intimate dialogue (*munajat*) with God: "My God, how can you have a need?" He answered: "That man's heart found support in something other than Me. May he empty his heart of that thing, so that I could satisfy his need!"//332 It is related that in his dream Abu Yazid al-Bistami saw a band of houris. He gazed upon them, whereupon he was deprived of his [mystical] moment with God. After that he saw the houris in his dream once again. However, this time he paid no attention to them, saying: "You are nothing but distractions (*shawaghil*)!"

It is related that when Rabiʿa al-ʿAdawiyya fell ill, someone asked her: "What is the cause of your illness?" She answered: "My heart was attracted to Paradise, so He chastised me for that. However, He is benevolent [toward His servants].[464] I will never do this again!" It is related that al-Sari [al-Saqati] said: "I was looking for a friend of mine for a long time. One day, when I was traveling through some mountains, I came across a group of people afflicted with various diseases and blindness. I asked them what they were doing there. They told me: 'There's a man [in the cave] up there. Once a year he comes out and prays for these [sick] people, whereupon they are cured [of their afflictions].' So I waited until he came out. He prayed for them, and they indeed were cured. I followed him and caught up with him, saying: 'I have an inner illness. How can I treat it?' He responded: 'Sari, leave me alone, for God Most High is jealous. When he sees you rely on someone other than Him, your status in His eyes will be diminished!'"

The master [Abu ʿAli al-Daqqaq] said: "Some Sufis grow jealous when they observe other people remember God Most High mechanically. They are unable to tolerate this sight and are aggravated by it." I heard the master Abu ʿAli al-Daqqaq – may God have mercy on him – say: "One day, a Bedouin entered the mosque of the Messenger of God and urinated in it. The Companions rushed toward him in order to throw him out [of the mosque]." Abu ʿAli commented on this episode, saying: "True, the Bedouin misbehaved. However, the Companions were ashamed and embarrassed at the sight of that depravity. The same is true of the servant of God. Once he has realized the greatness of God's majesty, he suffers each time he hears someone remembering God mechanically or performing an act of obedience to Him without showing proper reverence [for Him]." It is

---

464 That is, "He has pardoned me".

related that a son of Abu Bakr al-Shibli named Abu ᵓl-Hasan died. His mother cut her hair as a sign of mourning for him. As for al-Shibli, he went to the public bath and shaved off his beard. When he started to receive condolences, everyone who came to him asked: "Abu Bakr, what have you done?" He would say: "I have done this in solidarity with my wife." One of the visitors pressed him, asking "Abu Bakr, tell me the truth. Why have you done this?" He responded: "I knew that the people who would come to extend their condolences to me would mention God's name vainly, when they would say: 'May God Most High recompense you [for your loss]!' So I sacrificed my beard to [avert their attention and] prevent their mention of God's name in vain."

[Abu ᵓl-Husayn] al-Nuri on hearing a muezzin[465] [summon people to the prayer] would exclaim: "A curse and deadly poison!" Or he would hear a dog bark and say: "Here I am [God], at Your service!" Someone told him, "Isn't this apostasy? How can one tell a believer who utters the profession of faith that [his words are] 'A curse and deadly poison'? Or how can one say 'Here I am [God], at your service' to a barking dog?" Al-Nuri responded: "As for the muezzin, he mentioned God's name mechanically (ʿala raᵓs al-ghafla). As for the dog, didn't God Most High say: 'Nothing is, that does not proclaim His praise [but you do not understand their extolling].' "[466] One day al-Shibli was performing the call to the prayer. After he had uttered the profession of faith[467] twice, he [paused] and said: "Had You not ordered me to do so, I would never have mentioned anyone else along with You!" One man heard another say: "May God be exalted (jalla ᵓllah)!" He told him: "I would rather you exalt Him above [your exaltation]!" A Sufi related that he heard Abu ᵓl-Hasan al-Khazafani – may God have mercy on him – say: "I utter the words 'There is no deity but God' from the bottom of my heart, while I utter the words 'Muhammad is the Messenger of God' from my earlobe."[468] Those of you who see only the outward meaning of these words might imagine that al-Khazafani has degraded the Divine Law (sharʿ). However, this thought is incorrect, because in reality attributing something other than God to the [absolute and unique] majesty of God – praise be to Him – is itself a degrading [of Him]."

Friendship with God (*wilaya*)[469]

God Most High said: "Surely God's friends – no fear be on them, neither shall they sorrow."[470] Hamza b. Yusuf al-Sahmi – may God have mercy on him –

---

465 The person who calls the congregation to a prayer.
466 Q. 17:44; 17:45, according to Arberry's translation.
467 Namely, that there is no deity but God and that Muhammad is His Messenger.
468 That is, "Simply because I was commanded by God to do so."
469 For a detailed discussion of this term, which is often rendered into English as "sainthood", see Cornell, *Realm of the Saint*, pp. xvii–xliv, *et passim*. The term may connote both a holy person's proximity to God and God's patronage vis-à-vis His elected servants.
470 Q. 10:62; 10:64, according to Arberry's translation.

informed us: ʿAbdallah b. ʿAdi al-Hafiz told us: Abu Bakr Muhammad b. Harun b. Humayd told us: Muhammad b. Harun al-Muqri[471] told us: Hammad al-Khayyat told us on the authority of ʿAbd al-Wahid b. Maymun, a client of ʿUrwa, on the authority of ʿUrwa,//334 on the authority of ʿAʾisha – may God be pleased with her – that the Prophet – may God bless and greet him – said: "God Most High says: 'Whoever has caused harm to a friend of mine (*walī*) has [thereby] declared war against me. My servant approaches Me by performing the obligations that I have imposed on him. He draws even nearer to Me by performing supererogatory acts of piety (*nawāfil*) until I love him. Nothing that I do makes Me more hesitant than having to seize the spirit of My faithful servant, because he dreads death, while I loathe causing harm to him. However, there is no escape [for him] from it.'"[472]

"Friend" has two meanings. One of them implies passivity[473] – namely, "one whose affairs are managed (*yatawalla*) by God – praise be to Him". As God Most High says: "He [God] manages the affairs of the righteous."[474] That is, God does not entrust the affairs of His servant to him for a single moment; He Himself is in charge of his affairs. The second meaning implies an intensity of action on the part of the actor.[475] That is, the "friend" (*walī*) is one who is thoroughly engaged in worshiping and obeying God to such an extent that his virtuous acts follow one upon the other without being interrupted by any [tinge] of disobedience. Both meanings must apply in order for the friend of God to be a [genuine] friend. He must fulfill his obligations toward God Most High meticulously and exhaustively, while God, in turn, protects him constantly [from any disobedience] in good or bad times. One of the conditions of being a friend of God is to enjoy His protection (*mahfuz*), in the same way as one of the conditions of being a prophet is to be infallible (*maʿsum*). Anyone who violates the Divine Law is deluded and deceived.

I heard the master Abu ʿAli al-Daqqaq – may God have mercy on him – say: "Abu Yazid al-Bistami decided to visit a man who had the reputation of being a friend of God. When he arrived at the mosque where the man used to pray, he sat down and waited until the man came out. When the man was coming out, he spat. Abu Yazid left immediately without even greeting the man. He said: 'This man cannot be trusted with maintaining the rules prescribed by the Divine Law. How can he be privy to God's [intimate] secrets?!'"

---

471 Or "al-Maqqari".
472 For a full version of this famous *hadith qudsi* (a report in which God speaks in the first person with the Prophet as the transmitter), see Chittick, *The Sufi Path of Knowledge*, pp. 325–331 and idem, *The Self-Disclosure*, "Index of Terms" under "obligatory and supererogatory [acts]".
473 That is, grammatically it is an intensifying adjective formed on the pattern *faʿīl*, substituting for the form *mafʿūl* (passive participle) that implies the passivity of the subject.
474 Q. 7:196.
475 This meaning is derived from the same adjectival form *faʿīl* which may also connote the intensity of action. It takes here the meaning of *fāʿil* (the active participle).

Sufis disagree as to whether a friend of God may or may not know that he is one. Some claim that this is not possible, saying: "The friend of God always looks upon himself with humility. Whenever he manifests divine graces (*karamat*),[476] he becomes frightened, because he believes that this is but a [divine] ruse (*makr*).[477] Therefore, he is constantly seized with fear as he is afraid of diminishing his rank [in the eyes of God] and of his eventual state being contrary to his current one."[478] Such people consider fidelity [to the principles of friendship] until the very end to be one of its preconditions. Sufi masters of this group//335 have told many stories to illustrate this idea and it has numerous supporters among them. If we were to recount them all, we would forfeit our goal of concision. One of those masters whom we have known to have adhered to this idea was imam Abu Bakr b. Furak – may God have mercy on him.[479]

However, there are those who claim: "It is possible that the friend of God is aware of being one and, therefore, constant fidelity [to the principles of friendship with God] is not a precondition for retaining the status of the friend in the Hereafter." If this is indeed the case, then the friend of God can receive divine graces[480] from God by which God lets him know that he is assured of a favorable outcome [in the Hereafter]. Thus one must acknowledge the possibility of divine graces being bestowed on [God's] friends. Even though the fear of the unfavorable outcome [in the Hereafter] may depart from his heart, his condition of awe, reverence and exaltation of God is more perfect and stronger than such a fear in any case. For even a small amount of reverence and awe is more comforting for the hearts of men than an abundance of fear. When the Prophet – may God bless and greet him – said: "Ten of my Companions will be in Paradise", those ten no doubt believed the Messenger of God – may God bless and greet him – and were confident of the good outcome for them [in the Hereafter]. Yet, this [realization] did not detract from their [righteous] state [in this life].

One of the conditions of a proper understanding of prophethood is the acknowledgement of the definition of [prophetic] miracles, which includes the realization of their veracity. A friend of God, when he manifests divine graces,[481] can always distinguish them from the miracles [pertaining to the prophets]. When he observes something like this, he realizes that he is on the true path at that moment. So, it is permissible for him to believe that he will maintain the same state in the Hereafter. This realization is itself a divine grace for him. Thus, the doctrine of divine graces [granted to] saints is correct. This is confirmed by

---

476 That is, whenever he happens to work miracles.
477 That is, he thinks that God is testing him.
478 That is, he is aware that his present status as a friend of God does not guarantee his being among the blessed in the Hereafter.
479 A famous theologian of the Ash'arite school, who lived in Nishapur; he died 406/1015, probably poisoned by members of a rival theological school.
480 That is, miracles.
481 That is, saintly miracles, which do not have the same status as prophetic miracles.

numerous stories transmitted by this group,[482] as we shall mention in the chapter on the divine graces, God willing. Among the Sufi masters whom we met, the master Abu ʿAli al-Daqqaq – may God have mercy on him – used to adhere to this [latter] opinion.

It is said that Ibrahim b. Adham once asked a certain man: "Would you like to be a friend of God?" He said: "Yes." Ibrahim b. Adham told him: "[Then] desire not anything of this world and the next one, dedicate yourself fully to God Most High and turn your face toward God, so that He would turn His face to you and make you a friend of His." Yahya b. Muʿadh described the friends of God in the following manner: "They are those of His servants who have been clothed with intimacy [with Him] after suffering [for His sake] (*mukabada*). They have been granted rest after striving for His sake through arriving at the station of friendship [with Him]." I heard Shaykh Abu ʿAbd al-Rahman al-Sulami – may God have mercy on him – say: I heard Mansur b. ʿAbdallah//336 say: I heard my paternal uncle (*ʿammi*) al-Bistami say: I heard my father say: I heard Abu Yazid say: "God's friends are His brides and no one looks at brides except their family. They are wrapped up in the covers of intimacy [with Him]. No one sees them in either this world or the next." I heard Abu Bakr al-Saydalani (the Pharmacist), who was a righteous man, say: "In the graveyard of al-Hira,[483] I was often repairing the tombstone of Abu Bakr al-Tamastani and engraving his name on it. Continually, the tombstone was dug out and stolen, while all other tombs in the vicinity remained intact. I was surprised by this and asked Abu ʿAli al-Daqqaq – may God have mercy on him – about it one day. He responded: 'That master chose to remain anonymous in this world, whereas you want to make his grave known by a tombstone that you constructed [for this purpose]. However, God – praise be to Him – chose to conceal his grave, as he chose to remain anonymous [in this world].'" Abu ʿUthman al-Maghribi said: "A friend of God might become renowned (*mashhur*), but he will never be seduced (*maftun*) [by this]."

I heard Shaykh Abu ʿAbd al-Rahman al-Sulami – may God have mercy on him – say: I heard al-Nasrabadhi say: "Friends of God have no demands; they remain weak and anonymous." He [al-Sulami] also said: "The furthest reaches (*nihayat*) of the friends of God are the beginnings (*bidayat*) of the prophets." Sahl b. ʿAbdallah [al-Tustari] said: "The friend of God is he whose actions always coincide [with the will of God]." Yahya b. Muʿadh said: "The friend of God shows no pretense, nor can he be hypocritical. How few peers such a person may have!"

Abu ʿAli al-Juzjani said: "The friend of God annihilates his own state, while remaining in the contemplation of God – praise be to Him. God takes possession of his guidance so that the lights of His guidance would descend on him without interruption. He thus becomes completely oblivious of himself and resides with

---

482 That is, the Sufis.
483 A city in lower Iraq, south-west of present-day Najaf.

no one but God." Abu Yazid [al-Bistami] said: "The shares (*huzuz*) allotted [by God] to [His] friends differ from each other in accordance with four [divine] names. Each group [acts] according to the name [assigned] to it. These names are: 'The First', 'The Last', 'The Outward', and 'The Inward'. When a friend of God becomes oblivious of these names, after having been clothed with them, he achieves perfection. One whose allotted share is the divine name 'Outward' contemplates the marvels of God's power; one whose allotted share is the name 'Inward' contemplates the divine lights that appear in the innermost hearts [of men]; one whose allotted share is the name 'First' occupies himself with the things of the past; while one whose allotted share is the name 'Last' is attached (*murtabit*) to the things that will happen in the future. Each friend receives the manifestation of his name according to his ability, except for those whom God – praise be to Him – has, in His goodness, taken under His [personal] protection by putting Himself in his place." The words of Abu Yazid indicate that God has some elect [friends] (*khawass*) who rise above those divisions [according to the divine names]. They are concerned neither with recollecting past things, nor thinking about things to come; nor are they captivated by any [worldly] calamities (*tawariq*). They are//337 the folk of divine realities, whose creaturely features have been completely erased. God Most High had them in mind, when He said: "Thou would have thought them awake, as they lay sleeping."[484]

Yahya b. Mu'adh said: "The friend of God is His sweet basil which He planted in this earth of His. When the veracious ones (*siddiqun*) inhale it, its fragrance reaches their hearts and they begin to long for their Master and to increase their acts of worship according to their different natural predispositions." Someone asked [Abu Bakr] al-Wasiti: "How is the friend of God nurtured in his friendship [with Him]?" He answered: "In the beginning, through his acts of worship and devotion and in his maturity through God's concealing from him His kind nature. He then drags him back to the attributes and qualities which were assigned to him from eternity, and, after that, He makes him taste [the sweetness of His presence] by sustaining him in all his states."

It is said that the friend of God is distinguished by three features: his constant preoccupation (*shughl*) with God; his recourse (*firar*) to God [under any circumstances]; and his concern (*hamm*) with God [at all times]. [Abu Sa'id] al-Kharraz said: "When God Most High decides to make someone His friend, He opens for him the door of the recollection [of His name]. When he has tasted the sweetness of recollection, He opens for him the door of proximity [to Him]. He then elevates him to intimate conversations [with Him] and seats him on the throne of [divine] unity. After that, He raises the veils [that have separated him from God] and allows him to enter the abode of unicity (*fardaniyya*) by revealing to him the [divine] glory and magnificence. When his eyes have fallen on the [divine] glory and magnificence, his 'I' disappears completely and he becomes a

---

484 Q. 18:18.

non-existent entity deprived of any power. He then falls under God's exalted protection, free from any pretensions to selfhood."

I heard Muhammad b. al-Husayn – may God have mercy on him – say: I heard Mansur b. ʿAbdallah say: I heard Abu ʿAli al-Rudhbari say: I heard Abu Turab al-Nakhshabi say: "Whenever one's heart becomes accustomed to turning away from God, it inevitably declares war on His friends. It is said that one of the features of the friends of God is that they have no fear, for fear implies an anticipation of some dreaded event to occur in the future or an apprehension that one might somehow miss a thing that one loves. The friend of God, on the other hand, is the son of his moment, who has no future to be afraid of." Just as he has no fear, the friend has no hope either, for hope implies expecting an agreeable thing to occur or a dreaded thing to be averted sometime in the future. Likewise, the friend of God feels no sorrow, for sorrow is but a hardship that resides in the heart. How can one feel sorrow while basking in the light of satisfaction (*rida*) and enjoying the coolness of complete compliance [with the divine will]? Didn't God Most High say: "Surely God's friends – no fear be on them, neither shall they sorrow."[485] //338

Supplicatory prayer (*duʿaʾ*)

God Most High said: "Call on your Lord, humbly and secretly."[486] He – may He be great and exalted – also said: "Your Lord has said: 'Call upon Me and I will answer you.'"[487] ʿAli b. Ahmad b. ʿAbdan informed us: Abu ʾl-Hasan al-Saffar al-Basri informed us: Muhammad b. Ahmad al-ʿUdi told us: Kamil told us: Ibn Lahiʿa told us: Khalid b. Yazid said on the authority of Saʿid b. Abi Hilal, on the authority of Anas b. Malik that the Messenger of God – may God bless and greet him – said: "Supplicatory prayer is the core of worship [of God]." Supplicatory prayer is the key to every need. It is the resting place of all those in need, the recourse of the disturbed, and a respite for those who aspire. God Most High – praise be to Him – censured those who abandon prayer, when He said: "They [the hypocrites] keep their hands shut."[488] They say that this means "They do not stretch them to Us in supplication."

Sahl b. ʿAbdallah [al-Tustari] said: "God Most High fashioned His creatures and commanded: 'Speak to Me in secret; if you don't do this, then look toward Me; if you don't do this, then listen to Me; and if you don't do any of this, at least wait at My door; and if you don't do this either, then submit your needs to Me.'" I heard the master Abu ʿAli al-Daqqaq – may God have mercy on him – say: Sahl b. ʿAbdallah said: "The prayer most likely to be answered [by God] is that of one's spiritual state (*hal*). The prayer of the spiritual state is the prayer

---

485 Q. 10:62; 10:64, according to Arberry's translation.
486 Q. 7:55; 7:53, according to Arberry's translation.
487 Q. 40:60; 40:62, according to Arberry's translation.
488 Q. 9:67.

of a man who is forced to pray to God in order to fulfill his need." Hamza b. Yusuf al-Sahmi – may God have mercy on him – informed us: I heard Abu ʿAbdallah al-Makanisi say: "I was with al-Junayd one day, when a woman came to him. She said: 'Pray to God so that my son be returned to me. For I have a son, who has gone missing.' Al-Junayd told her: 'Go away and be patient!' She came back after a while, and pleaded with him once again. Again, he told her: 'Go away and be patient!' She left only to return again and again, but al-Junayd would keep saying: 'Go away and be patient!' Finally, she exclaimed: 'My patience has come to an end. I am no longer able to persevere. Pray to God on my behalf!' Al-Junayd told her: 'If this is true, then go away, for your son has returned!' Indeed, she went home and found her son there. She then returned in order to thank him for this. Someone asked al-Junayd: 'How could you possibly have known this?' He answered: 'Didn't God Most High say: "He Who answers the constrained, when he calls unto Him, and removes the evil".'"[489]//339

People disagree as to whether it is better to pray for something or to keep silent and be satisfied [with their condition]. The first group says: "Supplicatory prayer is itself an act of worship, for the Prophet – may God bless and greet him – said, 'Supplicatory prayer is the core of worship [of God]', therefore the performance of worship is better than refraining from it. Besides, this is a right due to God Most High. Even though God may not answer the servant's prayer and he will not receive what he has asked for, he has still given his Lord what is due to Him. For prayer is nothing but an expression of the need inherent in the state of servanthood (*ʿubudiyya*)." Abu Hazim al-Aʿraj said: "Being deprived of prayer is harder for me than [my prayer] not being answered." Another group argues that silence and passivity in the face of divine decree are more perfect [states] and satisfaction with the divine choice is more appropriate [for the servant]. This is why al-Wasiti said: "Choosing what has been for you in pre-eternity is better than opposing the divine decree of the moment (*waqt*) [by praying to God]." The Prophet – may God bless and greet him – said, quoting God's communication: "I will give a better reward to the servant whose recollection of My [name] prevents him from asking Me for something over those who ask something of Me." Others say: "The servant should pray to God with his tongue, while maintaining satisfaction [with His decree] in his heart. In this way, he should combine both."

The most appropriate stance is to say that moments vary: in certain circumstances (*ahwal*) prayer is preferable to silence and constitutes the proper behavior (*adab*), while in others silence is preferable to prayer and constitutes the proper behavior. The servant realizes this with every [new] moment, for the knowledge of each moment takes place as moments flow. Whenever the servant's heart finds a sign pointing to prayer, then prayer is preferable and whenever it finds a sign pointing to silence, then silence is preferable. One should also say: "While in the state of prayer, the servant must not be neglectful of contemplating His Lord Most High. He is also required to monitor his spiritual state. If his prayer leads to

---

489 Q. 27:62.

the expansion (*bast*)⁴⁹⁰ of his current moment, than prayer is preferable for him. However, if, during his prayer, his heart feels something like an irritation (*zajr*) and contraction (*qabd*), then abandoning prayer at that moment is preferred. If his heart finds neither expansion nor an irritation, then his praying or not praying is equal for him. If in this moment in time he is preoccupied with [exoteric] knowledge (*ʿilm*),⁴⁹¹ then prayer is preferable for him, since it is [part of] worship. However, if in this moment in time he is preoccupied with [esoteric] knowledge (*maʿrifa*), a mystical state and silence, then silence is preferable for him. It is also appropriate to say: "For anything that benefits the Muslims and gives God His due, prayer is always preferable. As for anything that benefits the servant's own self, silence is better."

According to a transmitted report: "When a servant whom God – praise be to Him – loves prays to Him, He says: 'Gabriel, do not fulfill the need of My servant just yet, for I love to listen to his voice.' However, when a servant whom God dislikes prays to God, He says://340 'Gabriel, fulfill his need [immediately], for I abhor his voice!'" It is related that Yahya b. Saʿid al-Qattan – may God have mercy on him – saw God – praise be to Him – in a dream and asked Him: "I pray so much to You, my God. However, You do not answer me!" God responded: "Yahya, this is because I love to listen to your voice!" The Prophet – may God bless and greet him – said: "By the One Who holds my soul in his hand, when the servant with whom God is angry prays to Him, He turns away from him. When the servant prays to God once again, He turns away from Him again. The servant prays for the third time, and again God turns away from him. When the servant prays to Him for the fourth time, God Most High says to His angels: 'My servant has refused to pray to anyone other than Me, therefore I have answered his prayer.'"

Abu ʾl-Husayn ʿAli b. Muhammad b. ʿAbdallah b. Bashran informed us in Baghdad: Abu ʿAmr ʿUthman b. Ahmad, nicknamed "Ibn al-Sammak", told us: Muhammad b. ʿAbd Ribbihi al-Hadrami said: Bishr b. ʿAbd al-Malik informed us: Musa b. al-Hajjaj told us: Malik b. Dinar said: al-Hasan [al-Basri] told us on the authority of Anas b. Malik – may God be pleased with him – who said: "In the time of the Messenger of God – may God bless and greet him – there lived a man who brought goods [for sale] from Syria to Medina and from there back to Syria. He traveled alone, not with any caravan, putting his trust in God – may He be great and exalted. Once, as he was traveling from Syria to Medina he was confronted by a robber riding a horse. The robber ordered him to stop. The merchant stopped and told the robber: 'Take my merchandise and leave me alone!' The robber responded: 'I already have your merchandise. However, I want your soul as well!' The merchant said: 'Why do you need my soul? Take my merchandise and leave me alone!' However, the robber repeated what he had

---

490 See the chapter on "expansion" (*bast*) and "contraction" (*qabd*) (pages 79–81).
491 That is, the knowledge of the external aspects of religion (*zahir*) as opposed to the realization of its internal meaning (*batin*).

just said, to which the merchant responded: 'Then wait until I perform my ablutions, my ritual prayer, and my supplicatory prayer.' The robber said: 'Do as you see fit.' The merchant rose, performed his ablution, his ritual prayer of four prostrations, whereupon he raised his hands to the sky and uttered: 'O the Loving One, O the Loving One! You are the possessor of the magnificent throne [of the Universe], the One in Whom all things originate and to Whom they return, You, Who does whatever He pleases! I implore you by the light [emanating from] Your face, the light that fills all the corners of this Universe, I implore you by Your power, with which You have predetermined the fate of Your creation and Your mercy which has encompassed everything. There's no deity but You! O [my] succor, come to my rescue.' (And he repeated this three times.) As soon as he completed his supplicatory prayer, there appeared a rider dressed all in green on a grey horse. He held in his hand a spear made of light. When the robber saw the rider, he abandoned the merchant and rode toward the rider. When he approached him, the rider charged him and dealt him a blow that threw him from his horse. Then he came up to the merchant and told him: 'Rise and kill him!' The merchant asked him: 'Who are you? I have never killed anyone in my entire life and I abhor killing anyone!' Then the rider returned//341 to the robber and killed him. Then he came to the merchant once again and said: 'Know that I am an angel from the third heaven. When you uttered your prayer for the first time, we heard a noise at the gates of the heavens. We [angels] said to each other: 'Something has happened!' When you prayed the second time, the gates of the heavens were thrown open and there appeared sparks of fire from behind them.' When you prayed for the third time, Gabriel – peace be upon him – fell from [the upper heaven], screaming: 'Who will come to the rescue of this distressed one?' So I asked my Lord to entrust me with his [the robber's] killing. Know, O servant of God, that whoever prays to Him with a prayer like yours at the time of distress, hardship or any other affliction, God Most High will surely relieve him from it and come to his rescue.' So, the merchant returned to Medina safe and sound, and went to the Prophet – may God bless and greet him – to tell him the story of what had happened. The Prophet – may God bless and greet him – told him: 'God – may He be great and exalted – has dictated to you His Most Beautiful Names. Whoever implores Him with them will receive His answer, and whoever asks something of Him by them, his request will be granted.'"

Part of the proper conduct in supplicatory prayer is the continual attentiveness of the heart so that it shall not be neglectful. It is related that the Prophet – may God bless and greet him – said: "God Most High will never answer the prayer of a servant whose heart is heedless." Another condition is that the supplicant's food be lawful (halal), for the Prophet – may God bless and greet him – said: "Obtain your livelihood properly and your supplicatory prayer will be answered." It is said that supplicatory prayer is a key whose ridges are made of a lawful morsel. Yahya b. Mu'adh used to pray, saying: "O my God, how can I, who disobey You, ask You for something [in prayer]? And how can I not ask You, Who are ever generous?" It is related that Moses – peace be upon him – passed by a man who was humbly making his supplicatory prayer. Moses said: "My God, if only I had the power [to fulfill] his need, I would have done so!" Then God Most High revealed to him: "I am more compassionate toward him than you, for when he prays to Me his heart is preoccupied with his sheep and goats. I do not answer the prayer of a servant whose heart is preoccupied with someone other than Me." Moses – peace be upon him – mentioned this to the man. He then turned himself wholly to God Most High, and his need was fulfilled [by God]. Some people told Ja'far al-Sadiq: "What is wrong with us? We pray, but our prayers are not answered?" He responded: "Because you pray to the One Whom you do not know!"

I heard the master Abu 'Ali al-Daqqaq say: "Ya'qub b. Layth[492] developed an ailment which eluded his physicians. He was told: 'In your realm there's a righteous man named Sahl b. 'Abdallah [al-Tustari]. If he were to pray for you, God – praise be to Him – may answer his prayer.' So [Ya'qub b. Layth] summoned Sahl to his court and told him: 'Pray to God – may He be great and exalted – on my behalf.' Sahl told him: 'How can my prayer on your behalf be answered,//342 when you unjustly hold people in your prisons?' So Ya'qub released all the prisoners he had held. Sahl prayed: 'O God, You have already shown him the humiliation of being disobedient [toward You]. Now show him the power of being obedient [to You] by removing his affliction!' [Thereupon] Ya'qub recovered from his illness. He offered a great deal of money to Sahl, but the latter refused to accept it. Someone told him: 'You should have accepted this money in order to give it to the poor!' Sahl cast his glance on some desert pebbles and they turned into jewels. He then asked his companions: 'How can a man [like myself] who has been granted such power stand in need of Ya'qub b. Layth's money?'"

It is related that Salih al-Murri used to say: "If one keeps knocking on the door persistently, it will eventually open for one." To this Rabi'a [al-'Adawiyya] responded, saying: "For how long will you continue saying this? Has the door ever been closed, so that one had to request that it be opened?" Salih replied: "An old man [like myself] has shown ignorance (*jahila*), while a woman has shown [true] knowledge (*'alimat*)." I heard Shaykh Abu 'Abd al-Rahman al-Sulami – may God have mercy on him – say: I heard Abu Bakr al-Razi say: I heard Abu Bakr al-Harbi say: I heard al-Sari [al-Saqati] say: "One day I attended a gathering at Ma'ruf al-Karkhi's house. A man came to him and said: 'Abu Mahfuz, can you pray to God Most High that my purse be returned to me?' There was one thousand *dinars* in it and it was stolen [from me]. Ma'ruf did not say a word. The man asked him once again. He did not say a word. The man asked again. Finally, Ma'ruf responded, saying: 'What should I say? [God,] return to this man what You have withheld from Your prophets and Your elect ones (*asfiya*)?' However,

---

492 Ya'qub b. Layth al-Saffar ("the Coppersmith"), the leader of a popular rebellion against the 'Abbasids in eastern Iran, who was able to assert his control over part of eastern Iran and Afghanistan; he died in 265/879.

the man kept pleading, 'Pray to God Most High on my behalf!' until Maʿruf finally said: 'O my God, choose what's best for him!'"

It is related that al-Layth said: "One day I met ʿUqba b. Nafiʿ.[493] He was blind. After a while I met him again. This time he could see. I asked him: 'How was your sight restored?' He answered: 'Someone came to me in a dream and told me: "Say: 'O Near One (*ya qarib*)! O One Who answers! O One Who hears the prayer! O One Who is kind to anyone He wishes! Return my eyesight to me!'" I said this and God – may He be great and exalted – returned my eyesight to me!'"

I heard the master Abu ʿAli al-Daqqaq say: "When I first returned from Marv to Nishapur, I was afflicted with a pain in my eye. For several days, I was unable to sleep. One morning I was finally overcome with slumber and heard a voice saying: 'Shall not God suffice His servant?'[494] When I woke up, both my eyesore and my pain were gone. Since then, I have never been afflicted by any eye pain." It is related that Muhammad b. Khuzayma said: "When Ahmad b. Hanbal[495] died, I was//343 in Alexandria. I was overcome with sadness. Then, in a dream I saw Ahmad b. Hanbal walking proudly. I asked him: 'Abu ʿAbdallah, whence this [proud] gait?' He responded: 'This is the gait of the servants of God in the abode of peace.' I asked: 'What has God – may He be great and exalted – done with you?' He answered: 'He pardoned me, placed a crown on my head and golden sandals on my feet. God told me: "Ahmad, this is [a reward for] your saying that the Qurʾan is My speech!" He then added: "Ahmad, pray to Me with the prayer that has come to you from Sufyan al-Thawri and which you used to utter while you were in that world!" So I said: "O Lord of everything! By Your power over everything, pardon me for everything and question me not about anything [I have done]!" God then said: "Ahmad, this is Paradise. Enter!" And I entered it.'"

It is related that a youth once clutched the cover of the Kaʿba saying: "O my God, You have no partner to whom one may turn [for help], nor a vizier whom one may bribe [to gain access to You]. If I obey You, it is only due to Your good grace, so all praise still belongs to You. If, on the other hand, I disobey, I do so out of my own ignorance, so that You have a clear proof against me. Yet, although Your proof against me is firmly established and the proof [of my innocence] is invalid in Your eyes, You have still pardoned me!" [Suddenly], he heard a voice saying: "This youth is safe from the hellfire." They say: "[The object of] supplicatory prayer is to present one's need to God Most High. Yet, the Lord will still do as He pleases." They say: "The prayer of the ordinary people is their words; the prayer of ascetics (*zuhhad*) is their deeds; and the prayer of divine

---

493 A prominent military commander, who directed the Arab conquest of North Africa. He fell in a battle against a Berber-Byzantine force in 63/683. ʿUqba's real historical personality is obscured by a thick layer of legends associated with his name.

494 Q. 39:36.

495 The famous *hadith* collector and transmitter who founded the Hanbali religio-political school in Baghdad. He died there in 241/855.

gnostics (*'arifun*) is their spiritual states." They also say: "The best prayer is one that springs from [one's] sorrows." A Sufi said: "If you have asked God for something, and He grants your request, ask Him immediately for Paradise, for this may be the day when all your requests are being granted." They say: "The tongues of the beginners [on the Sufi path] are overflowing with supplicatory prayers, whereas the tongues of those who have attained true realities (*mutahaqqiqun*) are devoid of them." When someone asked al-Wasiti to make a prayer, he said: "I am afraid that if I pray, I will be told: 'If you are asking Us for something that We have already predetermined for you, you are thereby mistrusting Us. And if you ask Us for something that we have not predetermined for you, then your praise of Us is false. If, on the other hand, you remain content, We shall bestow upon you the things that We have decreed for you from eternity.'"

It is related that 'Abdallah b. Munazil said: "I have not prayed for fifty years and do not wish anyone else to pray on my behalf." They say: "Prayer is the ladder of the sinful." They say: "Prayer is an exchange of messages. As long as this exchange is maintained, all is well." They also say: "The sinful make their prayers with their tears."//344 I heard the master Abu 'Ali al-Daqqaq – may God have mercy on him – say: "When the sinner weeps, he sends a message to God – may He be great and exalted." About this they recite the following [verse]:

The tears of the young man reveal what he is trying to conceal
And his sighs show what is hidden in his heart.

A Sufi said: "Praying is the abandoning of sins." They say: "Prayer is the tongue of passionate longing for the Beloved." They say: "Obtaining permission to pray [from God] is better for the servant than having his supplication granted." Al-Kattani said: "God Most High casts apologies on the tongue of the believer only in order to open the door of His pardon for him." This means: "Supplicatory prayer puts you in the presence of God, whereas [God's] granting [your request] leads to [your] departure [from Him]. Therefore, standing at [God's] door [in supplication] is better than leaving [Him] after [your request] is granted." They say: "Prayer means addressing God Most High with the tongue of humility and shame (*haya*')." They say: "One of the conditions of prayer is to accept [divine] decrees with contentment." They say: "How can you expect [God] to answer your prayer, when you have cluttered its passage with your sinful deeds?" Someone asked a Sufi to pray on his behalf. He answered: "You are already distancing yourself enough from God by putting an intermediary between you and Him."

I heard Hamza b. Yusuf al-Sahmi say: I heard Abu 'l-Fath Nasr b. Ahmad b. 'Abd al-Malik say: I heard 'Abd al-Rahman b. Ahmad say: I heard my father relate: "A woman came to [the shaykh] Baqi b. Makhlad[496] and told him: 'The

---

496 A celebrated transmitter of *hadith* and exegete of Cordova, who died in 276/889.

Christians[497] have captured my son. [I cannot ransom him] because I have no property except my house, which I cannot sell. If only you could direct me to someone who could ransom him, for I have no rest or consolation and cannot distinguish day from night.' Baqi told her: 'Fine. Go [back home] and I will look into this matter, God willing.' The shaykh then bowed his head and moved his lips. We waited a few days. Then, after a while, the woman returned bringing her son with her. She called out to the shaykh, saying: 'He returned home safely and has a story to tell you!' The young man said: 'I was a captive of a Christian ruler along with other prisoners. The ruler had a man who was charged with making us work every day. He used to take us into the desert to do some work, then bring us back in chains. As we were coming back from our work after sunset accompanied by our guard, the chains on my legs suddenly broke open and fell on the ground.' He then mentioned the exact date and time when this happened and they coincided with those during which the woman came to Baqi and he made his [silent] prayer. The young man continued: 'Our guard rushed to me shouting: "You have broken your chain!" I told him: "No, it simply fell from my legs!" The guard was bewildered. He called his comrades, who brought a blacksmith with them and put me back in chains. As soon as I took a few steps, the chain dropped from my legs once again. Now they were all bewildered. They called for some of their monks, who asked me: "Do you have a mother?" I said: "Yes." They told me: "Her prayer [on your behalf] has been answered. God – may He be great and exalted – has released you from bondage, and we can no longer keep you in chains." So they gave me some provisions and an escort, who took me back to Muslim territory.'"

Poverty (*faqr*)

God Most High said: "For the poor who are restrained in the way of God, and are unable to journey in the land; the ignorant man supposes them rich because of their abstinence, but thou shalt know them by their mark – they do not beg of people in a demanding way. And whatever good you expend, surely God has knowledge of it."[498]

Abu ʿAbdallah al-Husayn b. Shujaʿ b. al-Hasan[499] b. Musa al-Bazzaz informed us in Baghdad: Abu Bakr Muhammad b. Jaʿfar b. Muhammad b. al-Haytham al-Anbari informed us: Jaʿfar b. Muhammad al-Saʾigh told us: Qabisa told us: Sufyan [al-Thawri] told us on the authority of Muhammad b. ʿAmr b. ʿAlqama, on the authority of Abu Salama, on the authority of Abu Hurayra, on the authority of the Prophet – may God bless and greet him – who said: "The poor will enter Paradise five hundred years before the rich, which is half a day [according to the

---

497 *Al-Rum*, literally "the Byzantines"; this term in al-Andalus was applied to the Romance-speaking Christians of the northern part of the country.
498 Q. 2:273; 2:274, according to Arberry's translation.
499 Or "al-Husayn".

reckoning of the Qurʾan]."⁵⁰⁰ Abu Bakr Muhammad b. ʿAbdus al-Hiri informed us in Baghdad: Abu Ahmad Hamza b. al-ʿAbbas al-Bazzaz told us in Baghdad: Muhammad b. Ghalib b. Harb told us: Muhammad b. Salama told us: Muhammad b. Abi ʾl-Furat told us on the authority of Ibrahim al-Hajari on the authority of Abu ʾl-Ahwas, on the authority of ʿAbdallah [b. al-ʿAbbas] that the Messenger of God – may God bless and greet him – said: "The indigent is not he who wanders around in the hope of getting a morsel or two or a date or two." Someone asked him: "Who, then, is the indigent one, Messenger of God?" He answered: "He is one who cannot find that which satisfies his need, yet is leery of begging [people for alms]//346 and [his poverty] is inconspicuous, therefore no one gives him any charity."

The master [Abu ʾl-Qasim al-Qushayri] said: "He meant that 'being ashamed of begging people [for alms]' actually implies 'being ashamed before God Most High to beg people [for alms]', not 'being ashamed of begging people [for alms]'."

Poverty is the hallmark of the friends of God (*awliyaʾ*), a decoration of the pure (*asfiyaʾ*), and the special feature with which God – praise be to Him – distinguishes His elect ones from among the righteous and the prophets. The poor are the elect servants of God – may He be glorified and exalted – and the carriers of His secrets among His creatures. By means of them God protects His creatures and due to their blessings He bestows livelihood upon them. The poor are the patient ones, who will sit next to God Most High on the Day of Judgement, as related in a report transmitted from the Prophet – may God bless and greet him.

The master Abu ʿAbd al-Rahman al-Sulami informed us: Ibrahim b. Ahmad b. Muhammad b. Rajaʾ al-Fazari told us: ʿAbdallah b. Muhammad b. Jaʿfar b. Ahmad b. Khushaysh al-Baghdadi told us: ʿUthman b. Maʿbad told us: ʿUmar b. Rashid told us on the authority of Malik [b. Anas], on the authority of Nafiʿ, on the authority of [ʿAbdallah] b. ʿUmar, on the authority of ʿUmar b. al-Khattab – may God be pleased with him – that the Messenger of God – may God bless and greet him – said: "There is a key to everything and the key to Paradise is love of the indigent, for the poor are the patient ones, who will sit next to God Most High on the Day of Judgement." It is related that someone brought ten thousand *dinars* to Ibrahim b. Adham. However, he refused to accept them, saying: "Do you want to erase my name from the roster of the poor by ten thousand *dinars*? I will never do this!" Muʿadh al-Nasafi said: "God Most High will never destroy a people, no matter what they do, unless they hold the poor in contempt and humiliate them!" It is said: "If the poor in God had no other virtue except their desire that the Muslims enjoy the abundance of provisions and their availability to all, this would be sufficient for them. Then they would need to purchase these

---

500 According to Islamic theology, time in the Hereafter will be different from that of this world; see Q. 22:47.

provisions, while the rich would have to sell them. If this is the case with the ordinary poor, what would then be the status of the elect among them?"

I heard Shaykh Abu ʿAbd al-Rahman al-Sulami say: I heard ʿAbd al-Wahid b. Bakr say: I heard Abu Bakr b. Samʿan say: I heard Abu Bakr b. Masʿud say: "Someone asked Yahya b. Muʿadh about poverty. He answered: 'Its True Reality is that the servant of God is independent of anything except God and its mark is not being in need of any provisions.'" I also heard him [al-Sulami] say: I heard Mansur b. ʿAbdallah say: I heard Ibrahim al-Qassar say: "Poverty is a clothing that brings about contentment (*rida*), if one has realized its true meaning."//347 A poor man from Zuzan came to the master Abu ʿAli al-Daqqaq in the year 394 [1003] or 395 [1004]. He was wearing a hair-shirt and a hat made of wool. One of Abu ʿAli's companions asked him mockingly: "How much did you pay for this wool?" He answered: "I bought it with this world [of ours]. However, if I were offered the Hereafter for it, I would not sell it!" I heard the master Abu ʿAli al-Daqqaq say: "A poor man stood up during a [Sufi] gathering and begged for charity, saying: 'I have gone hungry for three days!' One of the Sufi masters who was there exclaimed: 'You lie! Poverty is a secret [between you and] God. He does not entrust His secret to someone who divulges it to whomever he wishes!'"

I heard Muhammad b. al-Husayn say: I heard Muhammad b. al-Farraʾ say: I heard Abu Zakariya al-Nakhshabi say: I heard Hamdun al-Qassar say: "When Satan and his troops get together, nothing makes them more happy than three things: when someone murders a believing Muslim, when someone dies in the state of unbelief, and when [they see a man whose] heart dreads poverty." I also heard him [al-Sulami] say: I heard ʿAbdallah b. ʿAtaʾ say: I heard Abu Jaʿfar al-Farghani say: I heard al-Junayd say: "O poor ones, you are known thanks to God and you are being honored because of Him. However, how will you fare with God when you find yourselves alone with Him?" I heard Shaykh Abu ʿAbd al-Rahman al-Sulami say: I heard Muhammad b. al-Hasan al-Baghdadi say: I heard Muhammad b. ʿAbdallah al-Farghani say: I heard someone ask al-Junayd: "Which state is better: being in need of God Most High – praise be to Him – or being satisfied with God Most High?" Al-Junayd responded: "When one's need in God – may He be great and exalted – is sound, then one's complete satisfaction with God Most High is sound too. Therefore, you should not ask which of them is better, for one cannot be perfected without the other." I also heard him [al-Sulami] say: I heard Mansur b. ʿAbdallah say: I heard Abu Jaʿfar [al-Farghani] say: I heard Ruwaym [b. Ahmad] say, when asked about the characteristic feature of the poor person: "Placing oneself under the commands of God Most High."//348 It is said that the poor are distinguished by three character traits: protecting one's secret heart [from evil influences], performing one's religious duty (*fard*), and maintaining one's poverty.

Someone asked Abu Saʿid al-Kharraz: "Why does the beneficence of the rich not reach the poor?" He answered: "For three reasons: their wealth is illegal, their giving is not approved by God, and because the poor are meant to suffer."

God – may He be great and exalted – revealed to Moses – peace be upon him: "When you see the poor, beg them in the same way you beg the rich. If you do not do this, then you can bury everything I have taught you under the dust." It is related that Abu 'l-Darda'[501] said: "I'd rather fall from the wall of a castle and be smashed to pieces than attend a gathering of the rich, because I heard the Messenger of God – may God bless and greet him – say: 'Beware of sitting together with the dead.' Someone asked him who were 'the dead'. He responded: 'The rich.'" Someone complained to al-Rabi' b. Khuthaym about high prices. He responded: "We are not worthy of being starved by God. He only starves His friends (awliya')." Ibrahim b. Adham said: "We sought poverty but got wealth, whereas other people sought wealth but got only poverty." I heard Muhammad b. al-Husayn say: I heard Ahmad b. 'Ali say: I heard al-Hasan b. 'Alawayh say: "Someone asked Yahya b. Mu'adh about poverty. He answered: 'It is nothing but fear of poverty.'" Someone asked [a Sufi]: "What is wealth?" He answered: "It is trust (amn) in God Most High." I also heard him [Muhammad b. al-Husayn] say: I heard Abu Bakr al-Razi say: I heard al-Jurayri say: I heard al-Karini[502] say: "The poor person who is sincere shuns wealth lest he becomes rich and spoils his poverty, whereas the wealthy one shuns poverty lest it comes and deprives him of his wealth." Someone asked Abu Hafs: "How does the poor one approach his Lord – may He be great and exalted –?" He responded: "The poor one has nothing but poverty with which to approach his Lord."//349 It is said that God Most High revealed the following to Moses – peace be upon him: "Would you like to have all the good works of the whole of mankind on the Day of Judgement?" He answered: "Yes." God said: "[Then you must] visit the sick and clear lice from the clothing of the poor." So Moses – peace be upon him – made a habit for himself of spending seven days of each month delousing the garments of the poor and visiting the sick.

Sahl b. 'Abdallah [al-Tustari] said: "There are five things that constitute the [true] core of everyone's soul: a poor man who shows himself to be free from want, a hungry man who shows himself to be satiated, a sad man who shows happiness, a man who shows love to his adversary, and a man who fasts during the day and keeps vigil during the night without showing weakness." Bishr b. al-Harith said: "The best station is [to be able to] withstand poverty until your grave." Dhu 'l-Nun said: "God's displeasure with His servant becomes evident when he [the servant] is afraid of poverty." Al-Shibli said: "The minimal indication of true poverty is this: when the servant who is offered the entire world decides to give it out as charity. If, however, after that he says to himself, 'I should have saved some of it [at least for] one day', his poverty is insincere." I heard the master Abu 'Ali al-Daqqaq say: "People dispute what is better: poverty or wealth. In my opinion, it is best when one is given enough to sustain himself (kifayatah), whereupon one perseveres with this [for the rest of one's life]."

---

501 A Companion of the Prophet, who was renowned for his asceticism and frugality.
502 Or "al-Karnabi".

I heard Muhammad b. al-Husayn say: I heard Abu ʿAbdallah al-Razi say: I heard Abu Muhammad b. Yasin say: "I asked Ibn al-Jallaʾ about poverty. He fell silent until everyone else had left, then walked away himself only to return [to me] after a short while. He then said: '[When you asked,] I had four *daniqs*[503] on me and was thus ashamed before God – may He be great and exalted – to converse about poverty. So I left and gave them away.' He then sat down and began to converse about poverty." I also heard him [Muhammad b. al-Husayn] say: I heard ʿAbdallah b. Muhammad al-Dimashqi say: Ibrahim b. al-Muwallad said: "I asked Ibn al-Jallaʾ: 'When does the poor one [consider himself deserving] of his name?' He responded: 'When he rids himself of any trace of it.' I asked him: 'How can this be?'//350 He said: 'When he has it, it does not belong to him, and when he does not have it, it belongs to him!'" They say: "True poverty is that the poor one in his poverty is not satisfied with anything, except He for Whom he has [true] need." ʿAbdallah b. al-Mubarak said: "To appear rich while being poor is better than poverty itself."

I heard Muhammad b. ʿAbdallah al-Sufi say: I heard Hilal b. Muhammad say: I heard al-Naqqash say: I heard Bunan al-Misri say: "One day, as I was sitting in Mecca, I saw a youth in front of me. A man approached him who was carrying a purse full of *dirhams*. He placed it in front of him, to which the youth responded, saying: 'I do not need this!' The man told him: 'Then give this [money] to the indigent (*masakin*).' When the evening came, I saw the youth in the valley begging. I told him: 'You should have saved at least some of that [money] for yourself!' He answered: 'At that time, I was not sure I would still be alive now!'"

I heard Shaykh Abu ʿAbd al-Rahman al-Sulami say: I heard ʿAli b. Bundar al-Sayrafi say: I heard Mahfuz say: I heard Abu Hafs [al-Haddad] say: "The best way for the servant to reach his Master is to be in need of Him in all his [spiritual] states, to follow the custom [of His prophet] in all his deeds, and to eat nothing but licit food." I also heard him [al-Sulami] say: I heard al-Husayn b. Ahmad say: I heard al-Murtaʿish say: "The aspirations of the poor should not run ahead of his feet." I also heard him say: I heard Abu ʾl-Faraj al-Warathani say: I heard Fatima, sister of Abu ʿAli al-Rudhbari, say: I heard Abu ʿAli al-Rudhbari say: "There were four individuals [who were unique in terms of poverty] during their time. One would not accept anything from either his brethren or the rulers. This was Yusuf b. Asbat. He inherited seventy thousand *dirhams* from his father, yet accepted none of it. He used to weave palm-leaf mats with his own hands. Another one – Abu Ishaq al-Fazari – used to accept [donations] from his brethren or the rulers. Whatever he accepted from his brethren he used to spend on those folks who concealed their poverty and refused to move [in order to collect charity]; whatever he accepted from the rulers he used to bring to the deserving ones from among the inhabitants of Tarsus.[504] The third was ʿAbdallah b. al-Mubarak. He would never accept [donations] from the rulers and whatever

---

503 A coin worth one-sixth of a *dinar*.
504 An ancient city in present-day Turkey, some 240 miles south-east of the capital Ankara.

he accepted from his brethren, he would reimburse them in kind. The fourth was Makhlad b. al-Husayn.//351 He would accept [donations] from the rulers, but not from his brethren, saying: 'The ruler does no one a favor [by his generosity], while the brethren do.'"

I heard the master Abu ʿAli al-Daqqaq say: "A transmitted report says: 'Whoever humbles himself to a rich man because of his wealth has lost two-thirds of his faith.' This is because a man [acts] by his heart, by his tongue and by his soul. Therefore, whenever he humbles himself to a rich man by his soul and his tongue he has lost two-thirds of his faith; and whenever he assumes his superiority by his heart, while also humbling himself to him by his soul and his tongue, he has lost his faith in its entirety." It is said: "The minimal requirements for the poor man in his poverty are four: a knowledge that guides him; a scrupulous discernment (waraʿ) that keeps him away [from the forbidden]; a certainty (yaqin) that leads him [to his goal]; and a remembrance [of God] (dhikr) that brings about his intimacy [with God]." It is also said: "He who aspires after the honor bestowed by poverty will die poor, while he who aspires after poverty in order not to be distracted from God Most High [by mundane things], will die rich."

Al-Muzayyin said: "There used to be more paths to God than the stars of the sky. Of these only one has remained – that of poverty, for it is the soundest of them all." I heard Muhammad b. al-Husayn say: I heard al-Husayn b. Yusuf al-Qazwini say: I heard Ibrahim b. al-Muwallad say: I heard al-Hasan b. ʿAli say: I heard al-Nuri say: "The sign of the poor is that he remains quiet at the time of scarcity and gives whatever he has to others at the time of plenty." I also heard him [Muhammad b. al-Husayn] say: I heard Mansur b. ʿAbdallah say: "Someone asked al-Shibli about the true essence of poverty. He answered: 'It is that the servant of God finds satisfaction in nothing but God – may He be great and exalted.'" I also heard him [Muhammad b. al-Husayn] say: I heard Mansur b. Khalaf al-Maghribi say: Abu Sahl al-Khashshab the Elder (al-kabir) said: "Poverty is [both] poverty and submissiveness." I responded, saying, "On the contrary, it is poverty and greatness", to which he responded, saying, "Poverty and [a plot of] land [in which you will be buried]", to which I responded, saying, "On the contrary, it is poverty and a throne [in the presence of God]". I heard the master Abu ʿAli al-Daqqaq say: "Someone asked me about the meaning of the words of the Prophet – may God bless and greet him: 'Poverty is close to unbelief.' I answered: 'The virtue and strength of a thing is in inverse proportion to the harm it brings. Whatever possesses the most virtue //352 has the most harmful effect as its opposite. For instance, faith is the noblest of all qualities, yet it has unbelief as its opposite. Since the danger inherent in poverty is that it may turn into unbelief, it leaves no doubt that it [poverty] is the noblest of all attributes.'"

I heard Shaykh Abu ʿAbd al-Rahman al-Sulami say: I heard Abu Nasr al-Harawi say: I heard al-Murtaʿish say: I heard al-Junayd say: "If you meet a poor man, treat him with kindness not with knowledge, for kindness pleases him, whereas knowledge alienates him." I asked him: "Abu ʾl-Qasim, how can knowledge alienate the poor man?" He answered: "Yes, if the poor man is sincere in his poverty, then your presenting him with your knowledge will melt him in the same way the fire melts [a piece of] lead." I also heard him [al-Sulami] say: "I heard ʿAbdallah al-Razi say: I heard Muzaffar al-Qirmisini say: "The poor one has no need of God." The master Abu ʾl-Qasim [al-Qushayri] said: "This expression may be somewhat confusing for those who hear it, if they are ignorant of the aim of this folk.[505] The speaker implied that [the servant of God] should abandon any demands, give up his own free choice and be satisfied with God's – praise be to Him – decrees in his regard."

Ibn Khafif said: "Poverty means a lack of any property and the abandonment of the attributes of one's own self." Abu Hafs [al-Haddad] said: "One's poverty is not perfect until giving [to others] becomes more agreeable to one than receiving. Generosity is not when the wealthy one gives something to the indigent one. It is when the indigent one gives something to the wealthy one." I heard Muhammad b. al-Husayn say: I heard ʿAbd al-Wahid b. Bakr say: I heard al-Duqqi say: I heard Ibn al-Jallaʾ say: "If humility were not an honorable quality in the eyes of God, then the poor would swagger when they walk." Yusuf b. Asbat said: "For forty years I have had only one shirt." One of them [Sufis] said: "[In a dream] I saw the [event of the] Day of Judgement. It was announced: 'May Malik b. Dinar and Muhamad b. Wasiʿ be brought into Paradise!' As I was watching I wondered which one of them would enter first. It was Muhammad b. Wasiʿ. I asked why he preceded [Malik b. Dinar] and was told://353 'He had only one shirt, whereas Malik had two!'" Muhammad al-Musuhi said: "The poor one has no need for anything [in this world]." Someone asked Sahl b. ʿAbdallah [al-Tustari]: "When can the poor one enjoy repose?" He answered: "Only when he expects nothing for himself in any given moment (*waqt*)." Some folk mentioned poverty and wealth in the presence of Yahya b. Muʿadh. He said: "[On the Day of Judgement] one will weigh neither poverty nor wealth. What will be weighed is patience and gratitude. Then it will be said: 'He was grateful [to God] and patient.'"

It is related that God Most High said to one of His prophets – peace be upon them: "If you want to know whether I am satisfied with you, look to what extent the poor are satisfied with you." Abu Bakr al-Zaqqaq said: "One whose poverty is devoid of fear of God (*tuqa*) eats food that is wholly illicit." It is related that during gatherings at Sufyan al-Thawri's house the poor were treated as if they were princes. I heard Shaykh Abu ʿAbd al-Rahman al-Sulami say: I heard Muhammad b Ahmad al-Farraʾ say: I heard Abu Bakr b. Tahir say: "Among the character traits of the poor is that they have no desire [for things] of this world. If one of them does have it, it should never exceed what is sufficient for him (*kifayatuh*)." He then said: "ʿAbdallah b. Ibrahim b. al-ʿAlaʾ recited to me: Ahmad b. ʿAtaʾ recited to me:

---

505 That is, the Sufis.

They told [me]: 'Tomorrow is a holiday. What will you wear?'
I answered: 'The garment of the one who pours out love in abundant gulps!'
Poverty and patience are my two garments underneath which is a heart that sees its intimate companion on Fridays and holidays
The best garment in which to meet your beloved on the day of visitation is one that he has clad you with
Time for me is nothing but [incessant] mourning, when you are not with me, O my hope!
And my holiday is whenever I can see and hear you!"

They say that these verses belong to Abu ʿAli al-Rudhbari. Abu Bakr al-Misri said, when asked about the poor man who is sincere: "It is he who has nothing and is not inclined to [acquire] anything." Dhu ʾl-Nun al-Misri said://354 "In my eyes, a constant need of God Most High that is tainted by confusion (*takhlit*) is still better than constant serenity that is tainted by self-conceit."

I heard Abu ʿAbdallah al-Shirazi say: I heard ʿAbd al-Wahid b. Ahmad say: I heard Abu Bakr al-Jawwal say: I heard Abu ʿAbdallah al-Husri say: "For twenty years Abu Jaʿfar al-Haddad used to work, making one *dinar* per day. He would then spend it on the poor and fast. Between the sunset and evening prayer he would go around from door to door seeking charity." I heard Muhammad b. al-Husayn say: I heard Abu ʿAli al-Husayn b. Yusuf al-Qazwini say: I heard Ibrahim b. al-Muwallad say: I heard al-Hasan b. ʿAli say: I heard [Abu ʾl-Husayn] al-Nuri say: "One of the marks of the poor is to remain content in times of want and to spend lavishly [on others] during times of plenty." I also heard him [Muhammad b. al-Husayn] say: I heard Mansur b. ʿAbdallah say: I heard Muhammad b. ʿAli al-Kattani say: "There was a youth with us in Mecca who wore tattered rags. He never attended our gatherings or sat with us [during our conversations]. I developed affection for him in my heart. One day I came into possession of two hundred *dirhams* that came from a lawful source (*halal*). I took them with me and put them on the edge of his prayer mat and said: 'This has come to me from a lawful source. Spend this [money] on whatever you want.' He looked at me askance and then revealed to me what was concealed from me, saying: 'I bought [this opportunity] to be in the presence with God Most High for seventy thousand *dinars*, not to count my other properties and estates. And you want to cheat me out of these [two hundred *dirhams*]?' He stood up and scattered the money. I sat there crouching as I was trying to gather it from the ground. I have never witnessed the like of the dignity with which he left, nor the like of the ignominy with which I was trying to gather up the money."

Abu ʿAbdallah b. Khafif said: "For forty years I have been unable to pay the alms due at the end of Ramadan,[506] yet I have enjoyed a great prestige both among the common folk and the elite." I heard Shaykh Abu ʿAbdallah b.

---

506 Because he had no taxable property.

Bakawayh al-Sufi say: I heard Abu ʿAbdallah b. Khafif telling this story. I also heard him [Muhammad b. al-Husayn] say: I heard Abu Ahmad al-Saghir (the Younger) say: "I asked Abu ʿAbdallah b. Khafif about a poor man who went hungry for three days, whereupon he went out asking for alms: 'How would you describe him?' He said: 'This is greedy! [One should tell such people:] "Eat and be quiet!" When a poor man behaves like this, he has disgraced all of you!'" I heard Muhammad b. al-Husayn say: I heard ʿAbdallah b. ʿAli al-Sufi say: I heard al-Duqqi say, when he was asked about the bad manners of the poor before God in their affairs. He responded: "It is when they stoop down from [the search of] true realities (*haqiqa*) to [the search of] received knowledge (*ʿilm*)." I also heard him [Muhammad b. al-Husayn] say: I heard Muhammad b. ʿAbdallah al-Tabari say: I heard Khayr al-Nassaj say: "[One day] I entered a mosque and found a poor man there. When he saw me, he approached me, saying: 'O master, have mercy on me, for my affliction is great indeed!' I asked him what his affliction was. He told me: 'I have not been able to experience any affliction and I have been in good health!' I looked at him and, lo, he was immediately showered with [the good things of] this world.'" I also heard him [Muhammad b. al-Husayn] say: I heard Muhammad b. Muhammad b. Ahmad say: I heard Abu Bakr b. al-Warraq say: "May God bless the poor in this world and the next one!" Someone asked him [Abu Bakr] what he meant by this. He answered: "The ruler in this world cannot impose any property tax on him, while the All-Powerful One cannot call him to account in the Hereafter."

Sufism (*tasawwuf*)

The praise of purity (*safaʾ*)[507] is on everybody's tongue, while its opposite, impurity, deserves [nothing but] blame. ʿAbdallah b. Yusuf al-Isbahani informed us: ʿAbdallah b. Yahya al-Talhi informed us: al-Husayn b. Jaʿfar told us: ʿAbdallah b. Nawfal told us: Abu Bakr b. ʿAyyash told us on the authority of Ziyad b. Abi Ziyad, on the authority of Abu Juhayfa,[508] who said: "The Messenger of God – may God bless and greet him – came out to us one day with the color [of his face] changed, saying: 'Purity has disappeared from this world, leaving nothing but impurity. Therefore, today death is a blessing for every [faithful] Muslim!'"

With time, this name came to be applied to the entire group. They began to say: "[This is] 'a man of purity' (*rajul sufi*) with [the word] *sufiyya* being the plural." As for the one who aspires to reach this [condition], he came to be called *mutasawwif*, with *mutasawwifa* for its plural. No evidence for such an etymological analogy can be found in the Arabic language. It is more likely that it is a nickname of sorts. There are also those who claim that it is derived from the word "wool" (*suf*); therefore, the verb *tasawwaf* would mean "to wear wool", in the same

---

507 According to an etymology popular in some Sufi circles, the word *tasawwuf* is derived from the Arabic root SFW with the general meaning of "being pure"; see *IM*, p. 5.
508 Or "Abu Hujayfa".

manner as the verb *taqammas* means "to wear a shirt (*qamis*)". This is possible. However, this folk are not unique in wearing wool.//356 There are also those who argue that the Sufis derive their name from the covered room (*suffa*)[509] [adjacent to] the mosque of the Messenger of God – may God bless and greet him. However, the word "Sufi" could not possibly have derived from *suffa*. [The same is true of] those who derive the word "Sufi" from "purity" (*safa*); this, too, is far-fetched from the linguistic point of view. There are those who argue that it is derived from the word "row" (*saff*), meaning that they [Sufis] are in the front row [before God] with their hearts. This meaning is correct in principle, albeit the language disallows that it be derived from the word *saff*. In all, however, this group is too renowned to need any justification by attributing itself to any [particular] word or etymology. People have had much debate over the meaning of "Sufism" and "Sufi". Each one of them has spoken from his own experience (*ma waqaʿ lah*), so we cannot exhaust this topic without violating our [stated] principle of being concise. We therefore will limit ourselves to mentioning some of what they have said without going into details, God willing.

I heard Muhammad b. Ahmad b. Yahya al-Sufi say: I heard ʿAbdallah b. ʿAli al-Tamimi say: "Someone asked Abu Muhammad al-Jurayri about Sufism: 'It means assuming every sublime moral character trait and giving up every lowly one.'" I heard ʿAbdallah b. Yusuf al-Isbahani say: I heard my father say: I heard Abu ʿAbdallah Muhammad b. ʿAmmar al-Hamadani say: I heard Abu Muhammad al-Maraghi say: "Someone asked my master about Sufism. He answered: 'I heard that when al-Junayd was asked about it, he responded: "It means that God causes you to die for yourself, while endowing you with a life in Him."'" I heard Shaykh Abu ʿAbd al-Rahman al-Sulami say: I heard ʿAbd al-Wahid al-Farisi say: I heard Abu ʾl-Fatik say: I heard al-Husayn b. Mansur say, when someone asked him about "Sufi": "He is solitary in his essence: no one accepts him and he accepts no one."[510] I also heard him [al-Sulami] say: I heard ʿAbdallah b. Muhammad say: I heard Jaʿfar b. Muhammad b. Nusayr say: I heard Abu ʿAli al-Warraq say: I heard Abu Hamza al-Baghdadi say: "One sign of the sincere Sufi is that he is poor after having been wealthy, that he shows humility after having been glorified, and that he seeks anonymity after having experienced fame. As for the sign of the false Sufi, he enriches himself with [the things of] this world after having been poor, aspires to glory after having been humiliated, and seeks fame after anonymity."

Someone asked ʿAmr b. ʿUthman al-Makki about Sufism. He answered: "It is that the servant of God's behavior in each moment (*waqt*) is most appropriate for that particular moment." Muhammad b. ʿAli al-Qassab said: "Sufism means a noble moral character trait that a noble person shows in a noble moment in time

---

509 This word is sometimes translated as "bench"; but is more likely to apply to a portico or vestibule attached to the mosque, where a number of indigent Muslim were sheltered and fed by the Prophet.
510 That is, he belongs exclusively to God.

(*waqt*) in the presence of a noble company." Someone asked Samnun [al-Muhibb] about Sufism. He responded: "It means that you own nothing and nothing owns you."//357 Someone asked Ruwaym [b. Ahmad] about Sufism. He answered: "Turning yourself over to God Most High, so that He may do with you what He wants." Someone asked al-Junayd about Sufism. He answered: "Remaining with God Most High without any [physical] attachment (*ʿalaqa*)." I heard ʿAbdallah b. Yusuf al-Isbahani say: I heard Abu Nasr al-Sarraj al-Tusi say: Muhammad b. al-Fadl informed me: I heard ʿAli b. ʿAbd al-Rahman al-Wasiti say: I heard Ruwaym b. Ahmad al-Baghdadi say: "Sufism rests on three characteristics: sticking to poverty and being in need of God [alone]; achieving perfection in generosity and altruism (*ithar*);[511] relinquishing resistance [to divine decrees] and [your] free choice." Maʿruf al-Karkhi said: "Sufism means grasping divine realities (*haqaʾiq*) and despairing (*yaʾs*) of what the hands of men hold." Hamdun al-Qassar said: "Keep the company of the Sufis. They find excuses for your errors, while not glorifying you for your good deeds." Someone asked [Abu Saʿid] al-Kharraz about the Sufis. He answered: "They are a folk who are provided for [by God] until they rejoice and who are deprived [by God] until they are lost [to themselves]. Then they are summoned from the depth of [divine] mysteries [by a voice saying]: 'Come on! Weep over us!'" Al-Junayd said: "Sufism is a struggle with no truce." He also said: "They are the inhabitants of one household, which no one but they can enter." He also said: "Sufism is the recollection of God at a gathering [of like-minded people], ecstasy at the hearing [of this recollection], and action in compliance with the Divine Law." He also said: "The Sufi is like a [fertile] soil: [all manner of] base things (*qabih*) are cast onto it, yet it produces nothing except beautiful (*malih*) things." He also said: "He [the Sufi] is like the earth which is trampled upon by both the righteous and the evildoers; he is [also] like the cloud which casts its shade on all things; or like the raindrop that quenches everyone's thirst." He also said: "If you see a Sufi who is concerned about his appearance, you should know that his inner self is rotten (*kharab*)."

Sahl al-Tustari said: "The Sufi is he who does not care if his blood be spilled and his property taken away from him." Al-Nuri said: "One of the signs of a [true] Sufi is [his] contentment during times of scarcity and generosity to others during times of plenty."//358 Al-Kattani said: "Sufism (*tasawwuf*) is but good morals (*khuluq*); whoever surpasses you in good morals surpasses you in purity (*safaʾ*)." Abu ʿAli al-Rudhbari said: "Sufism is a vigil at the door of the Beloved, even when you are being chased away." He also said: "[Sufism] is the purity of nearness [with God], after the filth of banishment." It is also said: "There's nothing more repugnant (*qabih*) than a niggardly Sufi (*sufi shahih*)." It is also said: "Sufism is an empty hand and a beautiful heart." Al-Shibli said: "Sufism is to sit with God [unperturbed] by any concern." Ibn Mansur[512] said: "The Sufi is one who is appointed (*mushir*) by God Most High, while other creatures are

---

511 Literally, "in preferring others to yourself".
512 Or "Abu Mansur"; probably "al-Husayn b. Mansur al-Hallaj".

pointers to (*asharu*) God Most High." Al-Shibli said: "The Sufi is he who cuts himself off from creatures to attach himself to God, for God Most High said [to Moses], 'I have chosen thee for My service',[513] thereby cutting you off from all else; He then said to [Moses]: 'Thou shalt not see Me.'"[514] Al-Shibli also said: "Sufis are children in the lap of God." He also said: "Sufism is a lightning that burns everything (*barqa muhriqa*)." He also said: "Sufism is a guarantee against paying heed to creatures." Ruwaym said: "The Sufis are on the right track as long as they quarrel with one another.[515] As soon as they make peace, they go astray." Al-Jurayri said: "Sufism is scrutinizing one's spiritual states and maintaining proper manners (*adab*)." Al-Muzayyin said: "Sufism is [full] obedience to God." Abu Turab al-Nakhshabi said: "The Sufi is not sullied by anything and is purified by everything." It is said: "The Sufi is not exhausted by [his] quest and undisturbed by mundane things." I heard Abu Hatim al-Sijistani say: I heard Abu Nasr al-Sarraj [al-Tusi] say: "Someone asked Dhu 'l-Nun//359 al-Misri about the Sufis. He answered: 'They are the folk who have chosen God – may He be great and exalted – over all else, and who God – may He be great and exalted – has chosen over everyone else.'" [Abu Bakr] al-Wasiti – may God have mercy on him – said: "At the beginning, the [Sufi] folk were guided by clear evidence (*isharat*), which later turned into mere motions (*harakat*), and now they are left with nothing but regrets (*hasarat*)." Someone asked al-Nuri about "Sufi". He answered: "It is one who has heard [divine commands] and who has chosen to observe them." I heard Abu Hatim al-Sijistani – may God have mercy on him – say: I heard Abu Nasr al-Sarraj say: "I asked al-Husri: 'What do you think about "Sufi"?' He answered: 'It is he whom the earth cannot carry and whom the sky cannot shade.'" The master Abu 'l-Qasim [al-Qushayri]: said: "He [al-Husri] referred to the [spiritual] state of 'erasure' (*mahw*)."[516] It is said: "The Sufi is he who, when presented with two good states or two moral qualities, always opts for the better of the two."

Someone asked al-Shibli: "Why are the Sufis (*sufiyya*) called so?" He answered: "Because the traces of their [lower] selves still persist in them. Otherwise, they would have no name at all." I heard Abu Hatim al-Sijistani say: I heard Abu Nasr al-Sarraj say: "Someone asked Ibn al-Jalla' about the meaning of 'Sufi'. He answered: 'We do not know him through the definitions of ordinary knowledge. However, we know that he is one who is poor and deprived of any means of sustenance (*asbab*), and who remains with God Most High no matter where he is, yet God – praise be to Him – does not bar him from knowing any place. Such a person is called "Sufi".'" One Sufi said: "Sufism means that you lose your social status (*jah*) and blacken your face in this world and the next." Abu Ya'qub al-Mazabili said: "Sufism is a state in which human attributes are

---

513 Q. 20:41; 20:44, according to Arberry's translation.
514 Q. 7:143; 7:138, according to Arberry's translation.
515 That is, as long as they are eager to correct each other in their pursuit of godliness.
516 That is, one in which the Sufi loses his identity and joins God.

dissolved." Abu Hasan al-Sirawani said: "The [true] Sufi concerns himself with divine visitations (*waridat*), not with litanies (*award*)."

I heard the master Abu 'Ali al-Daqqaq – may God have mercy on him – say: "The best thing that has been uttered regarding this matter is the following: 'This path is not appropriate except for those with whose spirits God cleans the dunghills (*mazabil*).'" This is why Abu 'Ali once said: "If the poor one had nothing except for his spirit which he would offer to the dog guarding this door, the dog would not even look at it." The master Abu Sahl al-Suʿluki said: "Sufism is an aversion to (*iʿrad*) any opposition (*iʿtirad*) [to God's will]."//360 Al-Husri said: "The Sufi does not exist after his absence and is not absent after his existence." The master al-Qushayri commented: "This statement is complicated. By saying that 'he [Sufi] does not exist after his absence', he implied that when the Sufi's faults (*afat*) fall away from him, they never return. As for his statement 'he is not absent after his existence', it means that if he is preoccupied with God and nothing else, he retains his [high] status [in the eyes of God], while the rest of God's creatures lose theirs, and that things of this world (*hadithat*) have no impact on him." It is said: "The Sufi is completely effaced by the glimpses of the Divine." It is also said: "The Sufi is forced to act (*maqhur*) according to God's dispensations and is protected [from error] by [his] acts of worship." It is said: "The Sufi is not subject to change. If, however, he undergoes any change, it smears him not."

I heard Shaykh Abu 'Abd al-Rahman al-Sulami – may God have mercy on him – say: I heard al-Husayn b. Ahmad al-Razi say: I heard Abu Bakr al-Misri say: I heard al-Kharraz say: "I was in the mosque of Kairouan[517] during the Friday prayer, when I observed a man going around, saying: 'Show me charity! I was a Sufi, but have now become weak.' I offered him some charity, but he told me: 'Go away and leave me alone! This is not what I ask for!' And he refused my donation."

Good manners (*adab*)

God Most High said: "His eyes [the Prophet's] swerved not, nor swept astray."[518] They say: "[This means that] he [the Prophet] observed the manners of [being in] the presence [of God] (*adab*)." God Most High also said: "[Believers,] guard yourselves and your families against the Fire."[519] According to Ibn 'Abbas's interpretation, this means: "Instruct them and teach them proper manners."

'Ali b. Ahmad al-Ahwazi informed us: Abu ʾl-Hasan al-Saffar al-Basri informed us: Ghannam said: 'Abd al-Samad b. al-Nuʿman said: 'Abd al-Malik b. al-Husayn told us on the authority of 'Abd al-Malik b. 'Umayr, on the authority of Musʿab b. Shayba, on the authority of 'Aʾisha – may God be pleased with her

---

517 An ancient mosque and religious college located in present-day Tunisia.
518 Q. 53:17.
519 Q. 66:6.

– who transmitted this from the Prophet//361 – may God bless and greet him – that he said: "It is the right of every child that its parent give it a good name, a good wet-nurse, and teach it good manners." It is related that Saʿid b. al-Musayyib said: "Whoever does not know his obligations toward God – may He be great and exalted – and fails to comply (*yataʾaddab*) with God's commands and prohibitions, is barred from good manners (*adab*)." It is related that the Prophet – may God bless and greet him – said: "God – may He be great and exalted – has instructed me in good manners and His instruction was excellent."

In truth, good manners is the combination of all virtuous character traits. The well-mannered person is one who has combined in himself all good character traits. Hence the word *maʾdaba*, which means "a gathering of well-mannered people". I heard the master Abu ʿAli al-Daqqaq – may God be pleased with him – say: "The servant of God reaches Paradise by being obedient [toward Him], and he reaches God Himself by means of his good manners." I also heard him say: "I saw how someone tried to stretch his hand toward his nose in order to pick it during the prayer, but his hand was stopped." The master [al-Qushayri] said: "He must have said this about himself, for no one but he himself could have known that his hand was stopped." The master Abu ʿAli – may God have mercy on him – made a vow not to lean against anything. One day, I met him at a gathering and tried to put a cushion behind his back, because I saw that he had nothing to lean against. He discreetly moved away from my cushion. I thought that he was wary of the cushion because it was not covered by a cloth or rug. However, he told me: "I want no support whatsoever." After that I kept watching him [for a while] and indeed he never leaned against anything.

I heard Abu Hatim al-Sijistani say: I heard Abu Nasr al-Sarraj say: I heard Ahmad b. Muhammad al-Basri say: I heard al-Jalajili al-Basri say: "The declaration of the unity of God (*tawhid*) is an obligation that requires faith; therefore a person without faith (*iman*) cannot declare God's unity. Faith is an obligation that requires [the observance of the] Divine Law (*shariʿa*); therefore a person without the Divine Law can have neither faith nor the declaration of the unity of God. The Divine Law is an obligation that requires good manners; therefore a person who has no manners can have neither the Divine Law, nor faith, nor the declaration of the unity of God."

Ibn ʿAtaʾ said: "Good manners means that you stick to good deeds." Someone inquired of him what this meant. He answered: "This means that you treat God properly both inwardly and outwardly. If you do this, you are a well-mannered person (*adib*), even though you are not an Arab."[520]//362. He then recited the following:

> When she spoke, she showed the utmost eloquence (*malaha*)
> And when she kept silent, she showed the utmost elegance (*malih*).

---

[520] According to a commonly held belief, the Arabs had an "inborn" ability to show "good manners" (*adab*) under any circumstances.

Muhammad b. al-Husayn informed us: I heard ʿAbdallah al-Razi say: I heard al-Jurayri say: "For twenty years I have not stretched my legs even in a solitary retreat (*khalwa*), for one should observe good manners in the presence of God." I heard the master Abu ʿAli al-Daqqaq – may God have mercy on him – say: "Whoever associates himself with rulers without showing good manners will be killed through his ignorance." It is related that someone asked Ibn Sirin: "What kind of good manners brings one closest to God Most High?" He answered: "Acknowledging His Lordship (*rububiyatuh*), showing obedience to Him through one's deeds, praising God in good times and being patient in bad ones." Yahya b. Muʿadh said: "If the divine gnostic misbehaves with the object of his knowledge (*maʿrufuh*),[521] he will perish along with the doomed."

I heard the master Abu ʿAli al-Daqqaq – may God have mercy on him – say: "Abandoning good manners necessitates expulsion. When one misbehaves on the carpet [in the living room], one is banished to the door; when one misbehaves at the door, one will be banished to the barnyard." Someone asked al-Hasan al-Basri: "Much has been said about the knowledge of good manners. Which of them are most beneficial in this world and most effective [in securing reward] in the Hereafter?" He answered: "Being knowledgeable in matters of religion. Renouncing this world, and being aware of your obligations toward God – may He be great and exalted." Yahya b. Muʿadh said: "One who has shown good manners toward God Most High will become one of His beloved." Sahl [al-Tustari] said: "The folk (*qawm*)[522] seek God's help in fulfilling His commands and are steadfast in observing good manners toward Him." It is related that Ibn al-Mubarak said: "We need a small amount of good manners more than we need a great deal of knowledge." I heard Muhammad b. al-Husayn say: I heard Muhammad b. Ahmad b. Saʿid say: I heard al-ʿAbbas b. Hamza say: Ahmad b. Abi ʾl-Hawari told us: al-Walid b. ʿUtba said: Ibn al-Mubarak said: "We kept seeking good manners even after those who could have taught them to us were all gone." They say: "There are three character traits that preclude estrangement [from God]//363: avoiding those who hold suspicious beliefs (*ahl al-rayb*), [observing] good manners, and causing no harm to others."

Shaykh Abu ʿAbdallah al-Maghribi – may God be pleased with him – recited to me the following verses pertaining to this matter:

Three things adorn the stranger in his wanderings
They are good manners, then good morals, and, thirdly,
Keeping away from that which is suspicious.

When Abu Hafs [al-Haddad] arrived in Baghdad, al-Junayd told him: "You have instructed your followers in manners [suitable] for sultans!" Abu Hafs answered: "Beautiful outward manners are a sign of beautiful manners on the

---

521 That is, God.
522 That is, the Sufis.

inside!" ʿAbdallah b. al-Mubarak is said to have said: "Good manners for the gnostic is what repentance is for the beginner [on the Sufi path]." I heard Mansur b. Khalaf al-Maghribi say: "Someone said to a Sufi: 'You have bad manners!' He answered: 'No, I do not have bad manners!' He was then asked: 'Who taught you manners?' He answered: 'The Sufis!'"

I heard Abu Hatim al-Sijistani say: I heard Abu Nasr al-Tusi al-Sarraj say: "With respect to manners people can be divided into three categories: the people of this world, most of whose manners have to do with eloquence, rhetoric, and the study of various sciences, names of rulers, and poetry of the Arabs; the second category comprises the men of religion, who acquire their manners through the subjugation of their [base] souls, restraining their members [from prohibited things], observing the norms of the Divine Law, and abandoning passions and appetites; the third category comprises the elite (*khususiyya*); their manners consist of purifying their hearts, scrutinizing their inner thoughts, being faithful to their pacts, observing [the conditions of] every [spiritual] moment (*waqt*), paying little attention to tempting thoughts, and observing the rules of proper behavior in their striving [toward God], during the time of being in the presence [of God], and while traversing the stations of proximity [with Him]."

It is recounted that Sahl b. ʿAbdallah said: "Whoever has succeeded in forcing himself to observe good manners will be sincere in his worship of God." It is said: "No one can attain perfection in good manners except for the prophets and the veracious ones (*siddiqun*)." ʿAbdallah b. al-Mubarak said: "Much has been said about good manners. We simply say: 'It is [nothing but] the knowledge of your soul.'" Al-Shibli said: "Speaking profusely in the presence of God – praise be to Him – is [a sign of] bad manners." Dhu ʾl-Nun al-Misri said: "The manners of the divine gnostic (*ʿarif*) are superior to any other kind of manners, because his heart is instructed in good manners by the object of his knowledge." A Sufi said: "God – praise be to Him – said: 'When I allow someone to stay in the presence of My names and attributes, I always impose//364 proper manners upon him; when, however, I decide to reveal to him the True Reality of My essence (*haqiqat dhati*), I impose perdition (*atab*) upon him. So, choose what you like best: good manners or perdition!'"

It is said that one day Ibn ʿAtaʾ pushed his leg in the middle of the circle of his companions, saying: "Violating the rules of proper behavior amidst its upholders is itself [a sign] of proper behavior!" This statement is justified by the following report: "The Prophet – may God bless and greet him – was with Abu Bakr and ʿUmar, when ʿUthman entered [the room]. The Prophet covered up his thigh, saying: 'How can I not be ashamed before a man, before whom even the angels feel ashamed?'" The Prophet – may God bless and greet him – thereby indicated that despite ʿUthman's bashfulness, which the Prophet held in high regard, his relations with Abu Bakr and ʿUmar were more intimate. A similar meaning is conveyed by the following verses:

I behave with restraint and modesty; however, when I find myself in the company of trustworthy and honorable people
I let myself loose and behave naturally, speaking what I want without any bashfulness.

Al-Junayd said: "When one's love [of God] is true, the rules of proper behavior fall away." On the other hand, Abu ʿUthman [al-Hiri] said: "When one's love [of God] has proved to be true, one must nevertheless be meticulous in observing good manners." Al-Nuri said: "He who does not observe the rules of proper behavior in his mystical moment (*waqt*), his moment will turn into spite (*maqt*)." Dhu ʾl-Nun al-Misri said: "When the seeker (*murid*) leaves the bounds of proper behavior, he will return to where he came from." I heard the master Abu ʿAli al-Daqqaq – may God have mercy on him – say the following about the words of God – may He be great and exalted: "Job, when he called unto his Lord, said: 'Behold, affliction has visited me, and Thou art the most merciful of the merciful.'[523] He [Job] did not say, 'Have mercy on me!', because he wanted to observe the proper rules of address. The same is true of Jesus – peace be upon him – who said: 'And if Thou chastisest them, they art Thy servants'[524] and 'If indeed I said it, Thou knowest it.'[525] He [Jesus] did not simply claim: 'I did not say [such a thing]' in order to observe the rules of proper behavior in the presence [of God].'"

I heard Muhammad b. ʿAbdallah al-Sufi – may God have mercy on him – say: I heard Abu ʾl-Tayyib b. al-Farkhan say: I heard al-Junayd say: "One righteous man came to me on a Friday and asked me: 'Send with me one of your poor folk [to my house]. He [may] bring me joy and eat something with me.' I looked around and saw a poor man, in whom I observed the marks of dire need. I called on him//365 and said: 'Go with this old man and bring him joy!' The poor man departed. Soon afterwards, the old man came to me and said: 'Abu ʾl-Qasim, that poor man ate nothing but a small morsel, then left my house!' I asked him: 'Perhaps you said some harsh word to him?' The old man said: 'No, I said nothing!' I looked around and saw the poor man sitting nearby. I asked him: 'Why did not you make him happy [by sharing his meal with him]?' He said: 'My lord, I traveled from Kufa to Baghdad without eating anything en route. I did not want to appear ill-mannered in your presence [by asking you for food]. When you called on me, I was glad, because the invitation came from you [without my request]. So I followed [the old man] as if I was heading for Paradise. When I sat at his table, he gave me a piece of food, saying: "Eat it! I love [sharing] this dish [with you] more than ten thousand *dirhams*!" When I heard him say this, I realized that his intentions were mean (*danʾ al-himma*), so I decided not to eat his food.'" Al-Junayd then said [to the host]: "Didn't I tell you that you misbehaved toward

---

523 Q. 21:83.
524 Q. 5:118; in this passage the Qurʾanic Jesus disowns his misguided followers (i.e., the Christians), who deified him and his mother.
525 Q. 5:116.

this [poor] man?" The host exclaimed: "Abu ʾl-Qasim, I repent!" So, al-Junayd told the poor man to go back with the old man and to fill [his heart] with joy.

The rules of travel (*safar*)

God – may He be great and exalted – said: "It is He Who conveys you on the land and the sea."[526] ʿAli Ahmad b. ʿAbdan informed us: Ahmad b. ʿUbayd al-Basri informed us: Muhammad b. al-Faraj al-Azraq told us: Hajjaj told us: Ibn Jurayj said: Abu ʾl-Zubayr informed us that ʿAli al-Azdi informed him that Ibn ʿUmar related to them: "When the Messenger of God – may God bless and greet him – mounted a camel in order to set out on a journey, he would say 'God is the greatest' (*Allah akbar*) three times, whereupon he would add: 'Glory be to Him Who has subjugated this [beast] to us, and we ourselves were not equal to it; surely unto God we are turning.'[527] He would then proceed saying: 'O God, in this journey we plead that You grant us righteousness and piety and only the deeds that please You! O God, make our journey easy for us! O God, You are our companion in this journey and our representative with our family [that we are leaving behind]. O God, I take refuge in You against the hardships of this journey, the worries of the return and the evil eye in our property and family.' And when he returned, he would repeat the same words: 'We are coming back repentant, and praising our Lord!'"

The master [al-Qushayri] said: "Since most folks of this group (*taʾifa*)[528] recommend travel, we have dedicated a special chapter of this epistle to it. For it is indeed one of their greatest achievements. Yet, even within this group people still disagree as to whether [one should] travel. Some even//366 give preference to staying in one place over travel. They would not travel unless this is a [religious] obligation (*fard*), such as, for example, the performance of the pilgrimage. Among those who preferred staying put were al-Junayd, Sahl b. ʿAbdallah [al-Tustari], Abu Yazid al-Bistami, Abu Hafs [al-Haddad], and some others. Others, however, had chosen travel and remained committed to it until they departed from this world, for instance, Abu ʿAbdallah al-Maghribi, Ibrahim b. Adham, and so on.

Many of them traveled extensively at the beginning [of their Sufi calling], then, toward the end of their lives, they settled down and stayed put. This is the case with Abu ʿUthman al-Hiri, al-Shibli, and others. Each of them had principles upon which he built his progress [to God]. Know that travel can be divided into two parts: travel with your body, which implies moving from one place to another; travel with your heart, which implies rising from one attribute to another. One sees many who travel with their bodies, while those who travel with their hearts are few.

I heard the master Abu ʿAli al-Daqqaq – may God have mercy on him – say: "In a village called 'Farakhk' near [the city of] Nishapur there lived a Sufi master,

---

526 Q. 10:22.
527 Q. 43:13–14.
528 That is, the Sufis.

who had written a number of books on Sufi science. Someone once asked him: 'Shaykh, have you ever traveled?' He, in turn, asked: '[Are you asking about] travel in the earth or travel in the heavens? As for the former, the answer is no; as for latter, yes.'" I also heard him [al-Daqqaq] – may God have mercy on him – say: "One day, when I resided in Merv, a Sufi came to me, saying: 'I have traveled a long way in order to meet you!' I told him: 'Had you parted ways with your lower soul, one step would have sufficed for you.'" Stories about the travels of the Sufis vary according to the different types and spiritual states they represent. I heard Shaykh Abu ʿAbd al-Rahman al-Sulami – may God have mercy on him – say: I heard Muhammad b. ʿAli al-ʿAlawi say: I heard Jaʿfar b. Muhammad say: I heard Ahnaf al-Hamadhani say: "Once I was alone in the desert completely exhausted. So, I raised my hands and pleaded: 'O Lord, I am weak and sick, so I ask for Your hospitality!' Suddenly, in my heart I felt as if someone asked me: 'Who invited you?' I answered: 'O Lord, isn't it a domain (*mamlaka*) that can accommodate an uninvited guest?' All of a sudden I heard a voice behind me; when I turned around, I saw a Bedouin riding a camel. He asked me: 'Foreigner, where are you headed?' 'To Mecca.' 'Did He invite you?' I said: 'I don't know.' He told me: 'Didn't God say: "Only if he [a pilgrim] is able to make his way there."'[529] I told him: 'This is a vast domain that can accommodate an uninvited guest.' He told me: 'What a splendid uninvited guest you are!//367 Do you know how to manage a camel?' I said that I did. He then dismounted from his camel and gave it to me, saying: 'Ride it!'"

I heard Muhammad b. ʿAbdallah al-Sufi say: I heard Muhammad b. Ahmad al-Najjar say: I heard al-Kattani say, when some Sufi asked him for pious advice: "Strive to be a guest of some mosque every night and to die only between two stations!"[530] It is related that al-Husri used to say: "To sit down once is better than to make one thousand pilgrimages!" He meant a sitting down that produces a deep concentration of [spiritual] energy (*hamm*) in such a way as to witness God (*shuhud*). Upon my life![531] Such a sitting is indeed better than a thousand pilgrimages performed in the state of absence from God! I heard Muhammad b. Ahmad al-Sufi – may God have mercy on him – say: I heard ʿAbdallah b. ʿAli al-Tamimi say: "It is related that Muhammad b. Ismaʿil al-Farghani recounted: 'Abu Bakr al-Zaqqaq, al-Kattani and I traveled together for some twenty years without mixing with or befriending anyone else. Whenever we arrived at a town which had a [respected] master (*shaykh*) we would go to greet him and would sit with him until nightfall. We would then go to a [local] mosque. Al-Kattani would perform his prayers from the beginning of the night, during which time he would recite the entire Qurʾan. Al-Zaqqaq would sit [throughout the night] facing the direction of prayer (*qibla*), while I would lie on my back and immerse

---

529 That is, to journey to Mecca in order to perform the rites of the pilgrimage. See Q. 3:97; 3:91, according to Arberry's translation.
530 That is, on the way from one place to the next.
531 This is, apparently, the voice of the author (al-Qushayri).

myself in contemplation. When morning came, we would perform the morning prayer with the ritual ablution of the evening prayer.[532] If someone happened to sleep in the mosque during that night, we would consider him to be better than ourselves.'"

I heard Muhammad b. al-Husayn – may God have mercy on him – say: I heard ʿAbdallah b. ʿAli say: I heard ʿIsa al-Qassar say that someone asked Ruwaym [b. Ahmad] about the rules of travel. He answered: "The traveler's aspiration should not outstrip his steps and his resting place should be the place where his heart has stopped." It is related that Malik b. Dinar said: "God Most High revealed to Moses – peace be upon him: 'Take a pair of sandals of iron and an iron staff. Then travel the earth, seeking wise traditions and admonitions until the sandals are worn out and the staff is broken.'" It is related that Abu ʿAbdallah al-Maghribi always traveled with his companions. Throughout [his journeys] he would maintain the state of ritual consecration (*muhrim*);[533] whenever he happened to violate it, he would re-consecrate himself again. Yet, his ritual garment would never become dirty, and his hair and nails would not grow at all. His companions used to walk behind him during the night. Whenever one of them strayed from the path, he would call out, saying: "To your right, so-and-so!" or "To your left, so-and-so!" He would never stretch his hand to anything ordinary people wanted. His meal consisted of a root of some plant which had to be plucked out of the ground [in order] to feed him.//368 They say: "If you say to your companion, 'Stand up, let's go!' and he would ask you 'Where?', he is no longer your companion." They have this idea in mind when they recite:

When someone seeks their help [in battle] they never ask the caller:
"To which fight?" or "To what place?"

It is related that Abu ʿAli al-Ribati said: "I used to travel with ʿAbdallah al-Marwazi. Before I met him, he used to travel in the desert with neither provisions nor a mount. When I attached myself to him, he asked me: 'Would you like me or you to be in charge (*amir*)?' I answered: 'Rather yourself.' He then asked me: 'Will you obey [me]?' I said: 'Yes.' He took a bag, filled it with provisions and put it on his back. When I asked him to give it to me to carry, he told me: 'I am in charge here, and you are to obey me!' When the night came, it rained, so he stayed over me holding a cover to protect me from the rain. I kept saying to myself: 'I wish I had died rather than tell him: "You will be in charge!"'

---

532 That is, during the night they would preserve their ritual purity intact by engaging in acts of devotion.

533 The state of ritual purity required of all pilgrims during their stay on the Meccan precincts in the pilgrimage season. This state (*ihram*) requires, among other things, that the pilgrims do not trim their hair or clip their nails. It also requires wearing a simple garment consisting of two pieces of white unsewn fabric.

He then told me: 'If you want to accompany someone in his travels, you should treat him the way I have treated you.'"

A youth came to visit Abu 'Ali al-Rudhbari. When he was about to leave, he said: "Would the master say something [wise to me]?" Abu 'Ali responded: "Young man, [the Sufis of old] never got together at a [prearranged] appointment (maw'id), nor dispersed after taking each other's council (mashura)."[534]

Al-Muzayyin the Elder said: "One day I was traveling with Ibrahim al-Khawwas on one of his journeys. All of a sudden, I saw a scorpion crawling toward his thigh. I got up to kill it. However, he stopped me, saying: 'Leave it alone! Everything is in need of us, only we are not in need of anything.'" Abu 'Abdallah al-Nasibini said: "I traveled for thirty years without ever patching my [Sufi] garment (muraqqa'),[535] heading for a place in which I knew I would meet a friend, and without ever allowing anyone to carry anything for me."

Know that after this folk have observed [all] the rules of proper behavior in the presence of God by exerting themselves strenuously (mujahadat), they have desired to add something else to this. So they have added the injunction to travel in order to force their lower souls to abandon the things that they [souls] enjoy and to part ways with acquired knowledge in order to remain with God without any link or means. One thing that they have not given up is their [mystical] prayers (awrad). [Sufi masters] say: "Dispensations from required obligations (rukhas)[536] apply only to those who travel out of necessity. [They do not apply to us], since travels for us are neither a job nor a necessity."//369

I heard Abu Sadiq b. Habib say: I heard al-Nasrabadhi say: "One day, I lost my strength in the desert and lost any hope [of survival]. Suddenly my gaze fell upon the moon and I saw [the following words of God] inscribed on it: 'God will suffice you.'[537] I regained my strength and from that time on this saying was bestowed upon me." Abu Ya'qub al-Susi said: "In his journey the traveler needs four things: a knowledge that guides him, scrupulous piety that restrains him [from the forbidden], an [ecstatic] state that carries him along, and a good moral character that protects him." They say: "Travel (safar) is named by this name, because it reveals (yusfir) the [true] character of men." When al-Kattani learned that a Sufi went to Yemen, then returned, he would order [his followers] to keep away from him. He did so because at that time many of them [Sufis] used to travel to Yemen to seek comfort (rifq). It is related that Ibrahim al-Khawwas never took anything with him on his journeys. The only things that he never parted with were a needle and a bowl. He used the needle to mend his robe when it was torn in order to conceal his private parts; as for the bowl, he used it for his ablutions. This is why he considered them neither an attachment [to this world] nor a source of comfort.

---

534 That is, they had never planned anything in advance, allowing God to guide them in their movements.
535 This patched ragged robe was a symbol of the Sufi lifestyle.
536 Such dispensations (e.g., exemption from fasting and daily prayers) applied to ordinary travelers.
537 Q. 2:137; 2:131, according to Arberry's translation.

It is related that Abu 'Abdallah al-Razi said: "I left [the city of] Tarsus[538] barefoot. I was accompanied by a friend of mine. When we came to a village in Syria, a Sufi brought me a pair of sandals, but I refused to accept them. My friend exclaimed: 'Put them on! I have been sick, so God has rewarded you with this on my account!' I asked him about his condition. He answered: 'I took off my sandals [at the beginning of our journey] in order to show solidarity with you, as required by the rules of companionship.'" It is related that Ibrahim al-Khawwas was once traveling with three other people. They came across a mosque in the desert and decided to spend a night there. The mosque had no door and it was very cold outside. So they slept there. When they woke up they saw al-Khawwas standing at the entrance. They asked him what he was doing. He answered: "I was afraid that you might get cold." So he stood there all night long. It is related that al-Kattani asked his mother to allow him to perform a pilgrimage [to Mecca]. She gave him her permission and he departed. When he was traveling in the desert, his robe was soiled with his urine. He said to himself: "My condition (*hali*) is now flawed." So he returned. When he knocked on the door of his house, his mother answered him and opened the door. He noticed that [all that time] she had been sitting next to the door. He asked her why she was doing this. She answered: "After you had left, I made a vow not to leave this spot until I saw you again."

I heard Muhammad b. al-Husayn say: I heard 'Abdallah b. Muhammad al-Dimashqi say: I heard/370 Ibrahim b. al-Muwallad say: I heard Ibrahim al-Qassar say: "I have traveled for thirty years in order to incline people's hearts to the poor."[539] A man came to Dawud al-Ta'i and said: "Abu Sulayman, my soul has been prompting me to meet you for a long time." Dawud answered: "On the contrary, when the bodies are quiet and the hearts are calm, the meeting is always easier!" I heard Abu Nasr al-Sufi, a companion of al-Nasrabadhi, say: "I disembarked from the sea in the region of Oman. As I was walking across the marketplace I felt hunger. I reached a food store and saw there a roasted lamb and all kinds of sweetmeats. I approached a man and asked him: 'Buy me some of it!' He asked me: 'Why? Do I owe you anything or am I in your debt?' I insisted, saying: 'You must buy some of it for me!' Another man saw me and said: 'Leave him alone, young man! I, not he, am the one who is obligated to buy you whatever you want! So make your request to me and choose what you want!' He then purchased for me what I wanted and left." Abu 'l-Hasan al-Misri related: "On my journey from Tripoli[540] I came across al-Sijzi.[541] We went on for days without eating anything. One day I saw a discarded gourd and began to eat it. The shaykh [al-Sijzi] stared at me, but said nothing. He did not touch it. So I cast the gourd away, for I realized that he disapproved of what I was doing. On

---

538 In present-day Turkey.
539 That is, to the Sufis.
540 A city in present-day Lebanon.
541 Or "al-Shajari", according to another reading.

that day we were given five *dinars*. We came to a village and I said to myself: 'Now the shaykh will no doubt purchase some [food] for us.' However, he went on without buying anything. He then said: 'You probably thought: "Well now, we are walking hungry, and he has not purchased anything [for us]." We shall approach a village called "Yahudiyya" where a man and his family live. When we enter the village, he will play host to us and I will give him that money, so that he can spend it on both us and his family.' So, we came there and he gave that man those *dinars*, so that he could spend them. When we were about to leave [that place], he told me: 'Where are you headed, Abu 'l-Hasan?' I told him: 'I want to continue with you!' He answered: 'You have betrayed me on account of a gourd, and you still want to accompany me? No way!' And he refused to have me as his companion."

I heard Muhammad b. 'Abdallah al-Shirazi – may God have mercy on him – say: I heard Abu Ahmad the Younger say: I heard Abu 'Abdallah b. Khafif say: "When I was young, I met a Sufi,//371 who saw signs of privation and hunger on me. He brought me to his house and served me meat cooked in groats. However, the meat was spoiled, so I ate the gravy, but avoided the meat because of its condition. He gave me a morsel, and I ate it against my wish. When he gave me another one, I was overcome with nausea. When he noticed that in me, he was embarrassed and I myself was embarrassed for his sake. I left immediately and set out on a journey. I sent someone to my mother to break the news [of my departure] and to fetch my patched robe for me. My mother did not object to my decision; on the contrary, she was pleased with my departure. So I left from al-Qadisiyya[542] with a group of Sufis. We lost our way, used up all our provisions and prepared to die. We reached a Bedouin encampment, but found nothing there. We were so desperate that we purchased a dog from the Bedouin for many *dinars*. We roasted it and I was given a morsel of its flesh. When I was about to eat it, I contemplated my plight and realized that it was the consequence of the embarrassment of that Sufi [who had fed me]. So I repented and fell silent. Then the Bedouin showed us the way and we departed. I performed my pilgrimage and when I returned, I apologized to that Sufi."

Companionship (*suhba*)

God – may He be great and exalted – said: "And when the two[543] were in the Cave, he said to his companion, 'Sorrow not; surely God is with us.'"[544] When God – praise be to Him – bestowed companionship upon [Abu Bakr] al-Siddiq, He made it clear that [the Prophet] did so out of compassion because he said:

---

542 A town in present-day Iraq.
543 This verse is usually interpreted as a reference to the Prophet's flight from Mecca to Medina, during which he was accompanied by Abu Bakr; the two were pursued by their Meccan foes and hid themselves in a cave.
544 Q. 9:40.

"Sorrow not; surely God is with us." For a noble person always shows compassion toward the one who accompanies him.

ʿAli b. Ahmad al-Ahwazi – may God have mercy on him – informed us: Ahmad b. ʿUbayd al-Basri informed us: Yahya b. Muhammad al-Jayyani told us: ʿUthman b. ʿAbdallah al-Qurashi told us on the authority of Nuʿaym b. Salim, on the authority of Anas b. Malik, who said that the Messenger of God – may God bless and greet him – said: "When do I meet my beloved friends (*ahbabi*)?" His companions replied: "By our father and mother! Aren't we then your beloved friends?" He answered: "You are my Companions (*ashabi*); as for my beloved friends, they are those who have trusted me without ever seeing me. Therefore my passion for them is greater!"

Companionship can be of three kinds: companionship with someone who stands above you [in rank]; this is but service (*khidma*). [The second type is] companionship with someone who is below you; it requires that the follower be treated with compassion and kindness and the one who is followed to be treated with compliance and respect. [And the third type is] the companionship of peers and equals, which rests on giving preference [to them over yourself] (*ithar*) and spiritual chivalry. When one accompanies a master,//372 whose [spiritual] rank (*rutba*) is equal to one's own, one should abandon any opposition to him, while interpreting everything that comes from him in a positive vein. I heard a companion of Mansur b. Khalaf al-Maghribi ask him: "How many years have you accompanied Abu ʿUthman al-Maghribi?" He looked askance at him and said: "I wasn't his companion; rather I served him for some time." When you have someone of an inferior station as your companion, you would violate the rules of proper companionship were you not to alert him to a deficiency of his spiritual state. It is about this that Abu ʾl-Khayr al-Tinati wrote to Jaʿfar b. Muhammad Nusayr, saying: "The burden of the ignorance of the poor rests on you alone, because you are too preoccupied with your own self to instruct them in good manners, thereby allowing them to persist in ignorance." If, on the other hand, you accompany someone of an equal rank, then your approach is that of being blind toward his faults and interpreting, as far as possible, everything you see from him in a positive way. If you are unable to find any [favorable] interpretation, then blame and recriminate yourself.

I heard the master Abu ʿAli al-Daqqaq – may God have mercy on him – say: Ahmad b. Abi ʾl-Hawari said: I told Abu Sulayman al-Darani: "So-and-so is of little import to me." Abu Sulayman responded: "He is of little import to me as well. However, we may be mistaken about our own status. That is, we may not be from among the righteous (*salihun*) and thus do not love them!" It is related that a certain man accompanied Ibrahim b. Adham. When they were about to part ways, the man asked Ibrahim: "If you have found any fault with me, let me know what it is!" Ibrahim answered: "I have found no fault with you, because I have been looking at you with an eye of affection and therefore have seen only good in you. Therefore, ask someone else about your faults." It is with this meaning in mind that they recite the following verses:

The eye of contentment is blind to any fault,
While the eye of spite reveals every error.

It is related that Ibrahim b. Shayban said: "We have never accompanied anyone who said: 'My sandals.'"[545] I heard Abu Hatim al-Sufi say: I heard Abu Nasr al-Sarraj say: "Abu Ahmad al-Qalanisi, who was a teacher of al-Junayd, said: 'I accompanied some folk from Basra, who treated me with much honor. One day I asked them, 'Where's my waist-cloth?', and, lo, I fell from their grace.'"//372 I heard Abu Hatim say: I heard Abu Nasr al-Sarraj say: I heard Zaqqaq[546] say: "I have kept company with this folk[547] for forty years and I have seen them always showing friendship toward one another or friendship toward those who love them. He who does not accompany his deeds by piety and scrupulousness eats nothing but what is totally illicit." I heard the master Abu ʿAli al-Daqqaq say: "A certain man told Sahl b. ʿAbdallah [al-Tustari]: 'Abu Muhammad, I want to be your companion.' He asked him: 'If one of us dies, who will be the companion of the survivor?' The other man answered: 'God.' Sahl said: 'Then let us accompany Him now!'" A man accompanied another man for some time. One of them then decided to part ways with his companion and asked him permission [to leave]. To this, the companion replied: "Only on the condition that your next companion be superior to us. And if this is the case, then you should still not be his companion, since you chose us as your first companion." The other man then said: "The desire to leave has disappeared from my heart."

I heard Abu Hatim al-Sufi say: I heard Abu Nasr al-Sarraj say: I heard al-Duqqi say: I heard al-Kattani say: "A certain man used to be my companion. However, my heart disagreed with him. I gave him a present in order to remove this dislike from my heart. However, it remained there. So I took that man to my house and told him: 'Place your foot on my cheek!' He refused. I told him that he must do this. I then made a vow that he should not remove his foot from my cheek until God removed this dislike from my heart. When this [feeling] was removed, I told him: 'Now, you can raise your foot!'" Ibrahim b. Adham used [to earn his living] as a seasonal harvester and an orchard watchman, spending [everything] he had earned on his companions. He kept company with a group of his companions, working during the day and spending the money he earned on them. They used to get together during the night after having fasted during the day. Ibrahim was usually late from his work, so they said: "Let's break our fast without him. Perhaps he will be joining us sooner because of that." So they broke their fast and fell asleep. When Ibrahim returned, he found them fast asleep. He said: "Poor things! Perhaps they had nothing to eat!" So he took some flour that was at that place and kneaded it. He then lit the fire and threw some

---

545 That is, a true companion must always use the plural of the first person to refer to his possessions, indicating his willingness to share them with his friends.
546 Or "al-Duqqi", according to an alternative reading.
547 That is, the Sufis.

ashes on the bread dough. When they woke up, they found him blowing on the fire with his beard and moustache pressed against the floor. They asked him what he was doing. He answered: "I thought you had no food to break your fast with and had fallen asleep, so I wanted to wake you up only when the dough was ready to be baked."//374 They said to each other: "Look what we have done and how he treats us after that!" It is related that before taking someone as his companion Ibrahim b. Adham would lay down three conditions for him – namely, that it would be him who served [his companion], that he would utter the call to the prayer, and that he would receive the same portion of any worldly sustenance God might provide. One day a companion of his told him: "What if I am not capable of this?" Ibrahim answered: "I liked his honesty." Yusuf b. al-Husayn said: "I asked Dhu 'l-Nun: 'Who should I keep company with?' He answered: 'Anyone from whom you do not hide anything that God Most High knows about you.'" Sahl b. ʿAbdallah told someone: "If you are afraid of wild beasts, you cannot be my companion."

I heard Muhammad b. al-Husayn say: I heard Muhammad b. al-Hasan al-ʿAlawi say: ʿAbd al-Rahman b. Hamdan told us: al-Qasim b. Munabbih told us: I heard Bishr b. al-Harith say: "When you keep company with an evil folk, you begin to think ill of even the elect ones (*akhyar*)." Al-Junayd recounted, saying: "When Abu Hafs [al-Haddad] arrived at Baghdad, he had with him a bald man who never uttered a word. I asked [other] companions of Abu Hafs about him. They said: 'This man spent one hundred thousand *dirhams* on Abu Hafs, then borrowed another one hundred thousand to spend on him. Yet, Abu Hafs will not permit him to utter a single word!'" Dhu 'l-Nun said: "Do not keep company with God, unless you obey Him; do not keep company with [His] creatures unless you dispense advice to them; do not keep company with your lower self unless you oppose it, and do not keep company with the Devil unless you show enmity toward him." Someone asked Dhu 'l-Nun: "Who should I keep company with?" He answered: "With someone who will pay visits to you when you fall ill and someone who will repent on your behalf when you sin." I heard the master Abu ʿAli al-Daqqaq – may God have mercy on him – say: "A tree that grows by itself and is not cultivated by anyone will bring forth leaves but no fruit. Likewise, a disciple (*murid*) who has no master to study with – nothing [good] will come out of him." The master Abu ʿAli [al-Daqqaq] used to say: "I took this [Sufi] path from al-Nasrabadhi, who took it from al-Shibli, who took it from al-Junayd, who took it from al-Sari [al-Saqati], who took it from Maʿruf al-Karkhi, who took it from Dawud al-Taʾi, who studied under the Successors [of the Prophet's Companions]." I also heard him [al-Daqqaq] say: "I would never come to al-Nasrabadhi's teaching sessions without first making a full ablution."

The master Abu 'l-Qasim al-Qushayri said: "As a beginner I would never enter into the presence of my master Abu ʿAli//375 unless I was fasting. I would also perform a full ablution. How many times did I come to the door of his school only to turn back out of my lack of resolve to enter [his house]? When I overcame my timidity and entered the school, I would be overcome by a sense of numbness in the middle of it to such an extent that one could stick a needle into me without my taking notice of it. When I had an issue [to discuss] I had no need to move my tongue in order to ask him about it, for no sooner than I found myself in his presence, he would start to explain it [to me]. Many a time I witnessed this phenomenon on his part. Sometimes I would think to myself: 'If God were to send a messenger to His creatures during my lifetime, could I possibly have felt for him the same respect that I had for Abu ʿAli – may God have mercy on him?' I could not imagine that this was possible at all. Throughout my attendance of his teaching sessions and being in his presence, after a [spiritual] bond (wasla) had formed between us, not for a single moment until his very death did a thought of disputing [his opinion] cross my mind."

Hamza b. Yusuf al-Sahmi al-Jurjani – may God have mercy on him – informed us: Muhammad b. Ahmad al-ʿAbdi informed us: ʿAbu ʿAwana informed us: Yusuf told us: Khalaf b. Tamim Abu ʾl-Ahwas told us on the authority of Muhammad b. Nadr al-Harithi, who said: "God – praise be to him – revealed to Moses – peace be upon him: 'Be alert and seek companions for yourself. Rid yourself of any companion who does not rejoice in obeying you and never keep company with him, for he will make your heart harden and will be your adversary. Multiply your thoughts of Me and you will deserve My gratefulness and the abundance of My grace.'"

I heard Shaykh Abu ʿAbd al-Rahman al-Sulami – may God have mercy on Him – say: ʿAbdallah b. al-Muʿallim said: I heard Abu Bakr al-Tamastani say: "Be God's companions, and if you are not able, then keep company with God's companions, so that the blessings of their companionship brings you to the companionship of God."

The Oneness of God (tawhid)[548]

God – may He be great and exalted – said: "Your God is one God."[549] Imam Abu Bakr Muhammad b. al-Hasan b. Furak – may God be pleased with him – informed us: Ahmad b. Mahmud b. Khurrazadh told us: Masih[550] b. Hatim al-ʿUqli told us: al-Hajabi//376 ʿAbdallah b. ʿAbd al-Wahhab told us: Hammad b. Zayd told us on the authority of Saʿid b. Saʿd b. Hatim al-ʿAtaki, on the authority of Ibn Abi Sadaqa, on the authority of Muhammad b. Sirin, on the authority of Abu Hurayra, who said: "The Messenger of God – may God bless and greet him – said: 'Once, in the previous epoch, there lived among us a man who had done no good whatsoever except declare God's oneness. He told his family: "When I die, burn me up, grind me into ashes, and scatter half of them over the land and the other half over the sea on a windy day!" [When he died],

---

548 This term means simultaneously "oneness [of God]" and "declaration or affirmation of God's oneness".
549 Q. 2:163; 2:158, according to Arberry's translation.
550 Or "Musabbih".

they did as he told them. God – may He be great and exalted – said to the wind: "Bring me what you have taken!" and the man appeared before him. God asked him: "What prompted you to do what you did?" The man answered: "[I did that], because I was ashamed of You!" So, God pardoned him.'"

"Oneness" means to declare that a certain thing is one. Knowing that a certain thing is one is also "oneness". They [Arabs] say, "I have rendered you one", meaning "I have described you as singularity (*wahdaniyya*)". Likewise, they [Arabs] say, "I have rendered you courageous", meaning "I have described you as being courageous". From the linguistic point of view, it [is derived from the verbs] *wahada* and *yahidu* ("he was/is one"). Its derivatives are *wáhid*, *wahd*, and *wahíd* with the meaning "being one and alone". Its synonym is [the verb] *farada* ("to be single") with its derivatives *fárid*, *fard*, and *faríd* ("being single or sole"). The root of the word *ahad* ("one") is *wahd* ("being one"); the letter *waw* of the root has turned into the *hamza*, because the consonant *waw* when it is followed by the vowel *a* (*fatha*) may [occasionally] convert into the *hamza*. The same happens to the *waw*, when it is followed by the vowels *i* (*kasra*) and *u* (*damma*), for example "charming woman" (*imra'a asma'*), which was [initially pronounced] *imra'a wasma'* – a derivative of the noun *wasama* ("charm").

From the theological viewpoint, God's being one means that He is not subject to addition or subtraction. This is different from your saying, "One man", because that man may have a hand or a leg missing – that is, he is subject to subtraction. On the other hand, God – praise be to Him – is essentially one (*ahadiyyu 'l-dhat*), which is contrary to the usage of this word[551] when it is applied to the carrier [of a multitude of qualities and parts].[552] One of those who has attained truth (*ahl al-tahqiq*) said: "God's being one means the denial of any multiplicity in His essence; the denial of any resemblance [between] His True Reality and attributes [and those of His creatures]; and the denial of any partner (*sharik*) in His deeds and creations."

There are three types of [the declaration of divine] oneness. The first is [the affirmation of] oneness by God to God, which means that He knows that He is one and He declares Himself to be one. The second is [the declaration of] oneness by God – praise be to Him – to His creatures, which means that He commands His servant that he affirm [His oneness] and that He creates the awareness of His oneness in him. The third is [the declaration of] oneness by God's creatures to God – praise be to Him – which means that the servant knows that God – may He be great and exalted – is one and then affirms and declares that He is one.//377 This, in a nutshell, is the definition of [the declaration of] oneness.

Sufi masters disagree about the meaning of oneness. I heard Shaykh Abu 'Abd al-Rahman al-Sulami – may God have mercy on him – say: I heard

---

551 That is, "one".
552 According to a medieval commentator, al-Qushayri implies that the word "one" is true of God alone, since in the case of other objects "oneness" is applied metaphorically because their essences always consist of multiple parts and faculties.

Muhammad b. ʿAbdallah b. Shadhan say: I heard Yusuf b. al-Husayn say: I heard Dhu ʾl-Nun al-Misri say, when he was asked about [the declaration of] oneness: "It is that you know that the power of God Most High resides in all things without admixture, that He creates all things without any manipulation, that He is the cause of everything He produces, and that His act of creation is not caused [by anything]. Whatever you may imagine, God is totally different from it." I also heard him say: I heard Ahmad b. Muhammad b. Zakariyya say: I heard Ahmad b. ʿAtaʾ say: I heard ʿAbdallah b. Salih say: al-Jurayri said: "The knowledge of oneness can be articulated only with the tongue of oneness." Someone asked al-Junayd about oneness. He answered that it is: "To assert the oneness of the One, while truly realizing His unicity (*tahqiq wahdaniyatih*) and perfecting His singularity (*ahadiyatih*) [by stating] that He is the One, 'Who has not begotten and has not been begotten',[553] while denying that He [may] have any counterparts, equals or semblances and divesting Him of any similarity (*tashbih*), quality, image, or likeness, [as stated in the Qurʾan]: 'Like Him there is naught; He is the All-Hearing, All-Seeing.'"[554] Al-Junayd also said: "Those possessors of intellects who have arrived at its utmost realization, have arrived at bewilderment (*hayra*)."[555]

I heard Muhammad b. al-Husayn say: I heard Abu ʾl-Hasan b. Miqsam[556] say: I heard Jaʿfar b. Muhammad say: I heard al-Junayd say, when asked about oneness: "It is a reality in which all outward traces (*rusum*) disappear and all knowledge passes away, while God Most High remains as He always has been." Al-Husri said: "Our principles in regard to oneness are five: the removal of the temporary, the assertion of the [absolute] singularity of the Eternal, the flight from the loved ones, the departure from the native land, and the forgetfulness of what is known and unknown."//378 I heard Mansur b. Khalaf al-Maghribi say: "Once I found myself in the courtyard of the Friday mosque in Baghdad – that is, the mosque of [the caliph] al-Mansur – while al-Husri was discoursing about oneness. [Suddenly] I noticed two angels ascending to the sky. One of them said to the other: 'What this man says is but [theological] science (*ʿilm*)[557], whereas [the true declaration] oneness is something else.'" He [Mansur] was [probably] in the state between wakefulness and sleep. Faris said: "Oneness means giving up any [earthly] means under the influence of [an overwhelming] spiritual state, while returning to them, as commanded [by the Divine Law]; [it also] means the realization that good deeds cannot change one's assigned portion [in the Hereafter], be it salvation or perdition." Someone inquired of al-Junayd about the [doctrine of] oneness pertaining to the [spiritual] elite (*tawhid al-khass*). He answered: "It means that the servant appears before God – praise be to Him – as

---

553 Q. 112:3.
554 Q. 42:11; 42:9, according to Arberry's translation.
555 Because of the subtlety of the notion of God being absolutely transcendent, while being simultaneously ascribed, in the Qurʾan, human-like characteristics.
556 Or "al-Muqassim".
557 According to another version of the text, "the science of oneness".

a soulless body (*shabah*) that is moved by nothing except the workings of His predetermination (*tadbir*), which flow through the channels of the divine decrees (*ahkam*) emanating from His power (*qudra*), which [in turn] emerges from the depths of His oneness; [as a consequence] he [the servant] is annihilated – in the proximity to God – from his own self, from the call of this world to him, and from his response [to this call] through the realities of divine existence and unicity (*wahdaniyya*) and [loses] his own sensations and actions. This is because God – praise be to Him – now has placed him in the station which He wishes for him, which means that the servant's current state returns to its very beginning, and he becomes what he was before he was."[558] Someone asked al-Bushanji about oneness. He said: "It is neither likening the Divine Essence [to creatures], nor stripping It of any attributes."[559]

I heard Shaykh Abu ʿAbd al-Rahman al-Sulami say: I heard Mansur b. ʿAbdallah say: I heard Abu ʾl-Husayn[560] al-ʿAnbari say: I heard Sahl b. ʿAbdallah say, when asked about the essence of God – may He be great and exalted: "The essence of God is described by [religious] knowledge, [yet] it cannot be grasped by any comprehension nor seen by the [human] sights in this world. It is found in the realities of faith without having any limit, being subject to human grasp, or dwelling in any creature. It will be seen by the [human] sights in the Hereafter plainly in its royal might and power. Creatures are barred from knowing its inner reality (*kunh*), yet it shows itself to them by means of its signs (*ayatuh*). The hearts know it, while the intellects cannot grasp it. The faithful look at it with their eyes, yet they cannot ever comprehend or grasp it."

Al-Junayd said: "The best thing one has ever said about oneness is the words of Abu Bakr al-Siddiq – may God be pleased with him: 'Praise be to Him Who has granted His creatures access to the knowledge of Himself only through their inability (*ʿajz*) to know Him!'"//379

The master Abu ʾl-Qasim [al-Qushayri] said: [Abu Bakr] al-Siddiq – may God be pleased with him – did not mean that God cannot be known. According to those who have attained the True Reality (*muhaqqiqun*), the inability [to know God] can only pertain to something that exists; it cannot apply to something that has no existence. Thus, for a paralyzed person sitting (*quʿud*) is not possible,[561] for it requires of him neither an assumption [of this state], nor any action, because the state of sitting already resides in him. Likewise, one who knows God (*ʿarif*) is incapable of [the act of] knowing God, for this knowledge already resides in

---

558 A reference to the primordial covenant between God and the human race, which was then forgotten by human beings as they became distracted from it by the drives and temptations of their lower souls and the allure of this world. For details see Böwering, *Mystical Vision*, pp. 147–157, 175–184 *et passim*.
559 This is a typical Ashʿari position that is supposed to represent the "middle path" between what was seen as an excessive "anthropomorphism" of the Hanbalites and a denial of divine attributes by their opponents, the Muʿtazilis.
560 Or "al-Hasan".
561 That is, he is already in the state of permanent sitting.

him, since, in his case, it is a necessity. And this folk[562] believe that, in the end, knowledge of God – praise be to Him – is a necessity for all of them. At the beginning [of the Sufi path], knowledge of God, even if it is true, is [always] acquired (*kasbiyya*). However, al-Siddiq – may God be pleased with him – counted it for nothing in regard to the necessary knowledge. For him, it was like [the light of] a lamp at the rise of the sun, when its rays encompass it.

I heard Muhammad b. al-Husayn say: I heard Ahmad b. Sa'id al-Basri in Kufa say: I heard Ibn al-A'rabi say: al-Junayd said: "The [knowledge of] oneness that is peculiar to the Sufis consists in the singling out (*ifrad*) of the eternal (*qidam*) from the temporary (*hadath*), leaving your homeland, giving up on things that please you, and abandoning what is known and what is unknown until God – praise be to Him – replaces everything [for you]." Yusuf b. al-Husayn said: "One who has fallen into the seas of oneness will only grow more thirsty with the passage of time." Al-Junayd said: "The knowledge of [divine] oneness is different from His existence and His existence is distinct from His knowledge." He also said: "The knowledge of [divine] oneness rolled up its carpets[563] twenty years ago, while people keep discoursing around its edges."

I heard Muhammad b. al-Husayn say: I heard Muhammad b. Ahmad al-Isbahani say: "A man stopped before al-Husayn b. Mansur and said: 'Who is this God about Whom everyone talks?' He answered: 'He is the origin of all creatures, Who Himself has no origin.'" I also heard him [Muhammad b. al-Husayn] say: I heard Mansur b. 'Abdallah say: I heard al-Shibli say: "One who has learned a dust-speck worth of the knowledge of [divine] oneness will not be able to carry even a bedbug [worth of weight in addition], because of the great weight of his load." I heard Abu Hatim al-Sijistani say: I heard Abu Nasr al-Sarraj say: "Someone asked al-Shibli://380 'Tell us about pure oneness with the tongue of exceptional truth (*haqq mufarrad*)!' He exclaimed: 'Woe to you! Whoever speaks about oneness by using ordinary expressions (*'ibara*) is a heretic (*mulhid*); whoever makes [allegorical] allusions (*ashara*) to it is a dualist; whoever points to it [with a gesture] is a worshiper of idols; whoever utters (*nataqa*) it plainly is reckless (*ghafil*); whoever keeps silent about it is ignorant; whoever fathoms that he has arrived at its realization is vain; whoever thinks that he has come close to it is in fact far from it; whoever thinks that he has found it in his ecstasy will lose it. And each time you think that you are able to discern its meaning by your imagination and attain its significance by your intellect in the most perfect manner, it comes back to you rejected, temporal and transient like yourselves.'"

Yusuf b. al-Husayn said: "The [declaration of] oneness of the spiritual elite means that the servant stands in the presence of God most High with his innermost self, his ecstatic state of finding (*wajd*),[564] and his heart, while being subject to the workings of His predetermination and the decree emanating from

---

562 That is, the Sufis.
563 That is, "left", "disappeared".
564 That is, a state that is engendered by a direct encounter with God.

His power, drowned in the seas of [divine] oneness through the annihilation from (*fanaʾ ʿan*) his own self and loss of any perception. Then God – praise be to Him – places him in the station that He wants of him, so that he would be as he was before he was, being moved by nothing except divine commands." They say: "[The declaration of] oneness belongs to God, and creatures are superfluous (*tufayli*)." They say: "Oneness means the dropping of all personal and possessive prounouns; you cannot say: 'mine', 'with me', 'from me', 'to me'." Someone asked Abu Bakr al-Tamastani about oneness. He answered: "[The declaration of] oneness, the one who declares it, and the One who is declared are one. These three, then." Ruwaym [b. Ahmad] said: "[The declaration of] oneness is the erasure of the traces of humanity and bringing forth [those of] divinity."

When Abu ʿAli al-Daqqaq was approaching the end of his life and suffering from ailments, I heard him say: "One of the signs of [divine] help is [that the awareness of divine] oneness is preserved [in you] at the time of the passing of divine decrees." He then proceeded to explain his statement by pointing to his own condition: "God cuts you piece by piece with the scissors of [His] power [thereby] executing His decrees in your regard, while you remain grateful and full of gratitude to Him." Al-Shibli said: "Whoever imagines that he has attained [divine] oneness has not smelt even a whiff of it." Abu Saʿid al-Kharraz said: "The first station of someone who has found and truly realized the knowledge of oneness is that any awareness of [mundane] things vanishes from his heart and he is left alone with God – may He be great and exalted."//381 Al-Shibli asked a certain man: "Do you know why your [declaration of] oneness is incomplete?" He exclaimed: "No, I don't!" Al-Shibli said: "Because you are seeking it through your own self!"

Ibn ʿAtaʾ said: "One sign of a true [declaration] of oneness is losing consciousness of it, which means that a person who performs it becomes one [with God]." They say: "There are people, who [in their declaration of divine oneness][565] are granted the vision of [divine] actions; they can see all temporal occurrences through God Most High. Others are granted the vision of the True Reality; they lose consciousness of anything aside from Him and witness the mystery (*sirr*) of a [complete and undifferentiated] unity (*jamʿ*) within their own innermost mystery, while their outward aspect continues to witness dispersion (*tafriqa*)."[566]

I heard Muhammad b. ʿAbdallah al-Sufi say: I heard ʿAli b. Muhammad al-Qazwini say: I heard al-Qunfudh[567] say: "When someone asked al-Junayd about [the declaration of] unity, he said: 'I heard someone recite the following:

He sang to me from my heart and I sang to him as he did to me
We were wherever they were and they were wherever we were.'

---

565 This phrase is omitted from some versions of the text.
566 That is, the dispersion of divine attributes in the things and phenomena of the empirical world.
567 In another reading, "al-Qannad".

[On hearing this] someone exclaimed: 'So the Qur'an and the sacred tradition (*akhbar*) have perished?!' He answered: 'No. However, a man who declares divine oneness avails himself of the simplest and clearest words!'"

How some Sufis [of old] behaved at the time of their departure from this world (*ahwaluhum 'inda 'l-khuruj min al-dunya*)

God Most High said: "[The Godfearing] whom the angels take while they are goodly."[568] That is, for those who better their souls by devoting themselves [fully to God] returning to their Master is easy.

'Abdallah b. Yusuf al-Isbahani informed us: Abu 'l-Hasan 'Ali b. Muhammad b. 'Uqba al-Shaybani said in Kufa: al-Khadir b. Aban al-Hashimi told us: Abu Hudba told us on the authority of Anas b. Malik that the Messenger of God – may God bless and greet him – said: "When the servant of God is overcome with pain and agony of death, his members greet each other, saying: 'Peace be upon you! You separate yourself from me and I separate myself from you until the Day of Judgement.'"

Shaykh Abu 'Abd al-Rahman al-Sulami informed us: Abu 'l-'Abbas al-Asamm told us: al-Khadir b. Aban al-Hashimi told us: Sawwar told us: Ja'far told us on the authority of Thabit, on the authority of Anas that the Prophet – may God bless and greet him – came to see a youth who was dying. He asked him: "How do you feel?" He answered: "I place my hope//382 in God Most High and am afraid of my sins." The Messenger of God – may God bless and greet him – said: "When these two things come together in the heart of a faithful servant of God at such a moment, God will inevitably grant him what he hopes for and render him from what he is afraid of."

Know that the conditions of Sufis at the time of dying vary. Some are overwhelmed by awe (*hayba*), while others experience hope (*raja'*). To others things are revealed that bring them serenity (*sukun*) and a beautiful trust [in the favorable outcome in the Hereafter]. Abu Muhammad al-Jurayri recounted: "I was with al-Junayd at the time of his death. It was a Friday [that coincided with] the New Year's Day.[569] He was reading the [entire] Qur'an until he finished it. I asked him: 'Abu 'l-Qasim, [you are doing this] even in this condition?' He answered: 'For whom would be this more appropriate than myself – one whose page is about to be turned!'" I heard Abu Hatim al-Sijistani say: I heard Abu Nasr al-Sarraj say: I came to know that Abu Muhammad al-Harawi said: "I was with al-Shibli on the night he died. Throughout that night he kept reciting the following verses:

> Every house[570] You reside in needs no lamps
> Your face to which we aspire will be our evidence
> On that day all people will bring their evidences [to God]."

---

568 Q. 16:32; 16:34, according to Arberry's translation.
569 The first day of the Persian new year which, at that time, was celebrated around mid-June.
570 That is, in the heart of every believer, according to a commentator.

It is related that ʿAbdallah b. Munazil said: "Hamdun al-Qassar admonished his companions not to leave him among women at the time of his death." When Bishr al-Hafi was about to die, someone asked him: "Abu Nasr, it looks as if you like life?" He responded: "Entering in the presence of God – may He be great and exalted – is hard." Whenever Sufyan al-Thawri was getting ready to set out on a journey, his companions would ask him: "Did you leave us instructions as to what we should do?" He would say: "If you find death, buy it for me!" However, when his time drew near, he exclaimed: "I used to long for this, but, lo, it is hard!" When death came to al-Hasan b. ʿAli b. Abi Talib, he wept. Someone asked him why he was weeping. He answered: "I am entering into the presence of a master (*sayyid*) Whom I have never seen before!" When death came to Bilal,[571] his wife cried: "What a painful affliction!" He objected, saying: "On the contrary, what a happy occasion! Tomorrow I will meet my beloved – Muhammad and his host (*hizb*)!"//383 On his deathbed ʿAbdallah b. Mubarak opened his eyes and laughed, saying: "[This is indeed a mighty triumph], and for the like of this let the workers work!"[572] It is related that [during his life] Makhul al-Shami was often overwhelmed with sadness. However, when people came to visit him on his deathbed, they found him laughing. When they inquired of him about that, he answered: "Why should I not laugh, when I am about to depart from what I have always been on guard against and am soon to approach that which I have always looked forward to and hoped for!" Ruwaym related: "I was present at the death of Abu Saʿid al-Kharraz, who recited the following with his last breath:

> The hearts of the [divine] gnostics long for remembrance [of God]
> And during the moments of their intimate conversations [with God]
> (*munajat*) they always think about the mystery (*sirr*)[573]
> They were given wine-cups that bring sure death
> So that they become oblivious of this world like a drunkard
> Their aspirations (*humum*) roam around an encampment
> In which God's beloved shine like resplendent stars
> While their mortal bodies on the earth have already been destroyed by their love of Him,
> Their spirits, draped in veils, rise to heavens
> They will not rest until they find themselves close to their Beloved
> And will not flinch, when they encounter a calamity or harm."

Someone told al-Junayd that Abu Saʿid al-Kharraz often fell into ecstasy on the eve of his death. He commented: "It was not surprising, for his spirit was longing for departure!" When a Sufi was about to die, he said [to his servant]:

---

571 An Ethiopian slave from Mecca, who became a close Companion of the Prophet; he was renowned for his beautiful voice and served as the one who performed the call to prayer for the first Muslim community. He died in Syria at the time of the Muslim conquests.
572 Q. 37:61; 37:59, according to Arberry's translation.
573 This word may denote both "mystery" and the mystic's "innermost self".

"Shackle me and rub my cheeks with dust!" He then exclaimed: "The time of departure has come; I am not free from sin and there's no excuse that I could produce to exonerate myself, nor is there any power with which I could help myself. There's only You to help me, only You to help me!" He then issued a loud cry and died. [Suddenly,] those who were there heard a voice saying: "The servant has surrendered himself to his Master, and the Master has accepted him!" Someone asked Dhu 'l-Nun on his death bed: "What do you desire?" He answered: "To know Him for one instant before I die!" Someone told a Sufi in his death agony: "Say 'God!'" He exclaimed: "How long will you be telling me: 'Say "God!"', while I have been burned by Him!'"

Someone related: "I was with Mimshadh al-Dinawari, when a poor man came and said: 'Peace be upon you!' Those present returned his greeting. He then said: 'Is there around here a clean place in which one could die?' They showed him such a place, near which there was a water spring. The man performed his ritual ablution and a prayer [at the spring], then proceeded to the place that they had showed him. He then stretched his feet and died." I heard Shaykh Abu 'Abd al-Rahman al-Sulami say: "One day Abu 'l-'Abbas al-Dinawari was delivering a sermon in his gathering. Suddenly, a woman yelled out of ecstasy. He told her: 'Die!' She stood up and went away. When she reached the door,//384 she turned toward him and said, 'I have just died', and she fell on the floor, dead." A Sufi recounted: "I was with Mimshadh al-Dinawari at the time of his death. He was asked: 'How do you find your illness?' He answered: 'You'd better ask my illness how it finds me!' He was told: 'Say: "There's no deity but God!"'" He turned his face to the wall and said: 'You have annihilated my entire self (*kulli*) in Your entirety (*kullika*). This is the reward of one who loves You!'" Someone asked Abu Muhammad al-Dabili, when he was about to die: "Say: 'There is no deity but God!'" He answered: "We already know this and have been annihilated [in God] through it." He then recited:

> He clothed Himself in the robe of desolation when I longed after Him and
> Turned away from me, because He did not want me to be His servant.

On his death bed al-Shibli was told: "Say: 'There's no deity, but God!'" [Instead], he recited the following:

> The king of his love said: 'I accept no bribes!'
> Ask him – may I be his ransom – why he insists on killing me!

I heard Muhammad b. Ahmad al-Sufi say: I heard 'Abdallah b. 'Ali al-Tamimi say: I heard Ahmad b. 'Ata' say: I heard a certain Sufi say: "When Yahya al-Istakhri was on his death bed, one of us told him: 'Say: "I bear witness that there's no deity, but God."' Yahya sat erect, then took one of those present by the hand and said: say: 'I bear witness that there's no deity, but God.' He then took another one by the hand [and said the same thing], until he made everyone who was there bear witness. After that he died." Fatima, the sister of Abu 'Ali al-Rudhbari, related: "When the death hour of my brother Abu ʿAli al-Rudhbari drew nigh, his head was resting in my lap. He opened his eyes and said: 'The gates of the heaven are open, the gardens of Paradise are in blossom and a [heavenly] voice tells me: "Abu ʿAli, we have bestowed upon you the highest rank, even though you may not have wished it [for yourself]."' He then recited the following:

> By Your Truth! I have [tried to gaze] upon anyone else but You
> With an eye of passionate love, until I have finally seen You
> With my weakening sight I see how You torment me
> And how [Your] cheek shows itself from Your [sweet] harvest.

I heard a Sufi say: "When Ahmad b. Nasr – may God have mercy on him – was on his death bed, someone told him://385 'Say: "I bear witness that there's no deity, but God."' He looked at the man and said: 'Be respectful!' (*bihurmati ma-kun*, in Persian)." One Sufi recounted: "I saw a Sufi, a stranger, who was about to give up his spirit. His face was covered with flies. I sat next to him and brushed the flies from his face. He opened his eyes and said: 'Who is that? For so many years I have been waiting for a moment that will belong to me and no one else. It has finally come, and here come you and intrude yourself onto it! Go away, may God protect you!'" Abu ʿImran al-Istakhri said: "I saw Abu Turab [al-Nakhshabi] in the desert standing upright, dead. Nothing propped him up!"

I heard Abu Hatim al-Sijistani say: I heard Abu Nasr al-Sarraj say: "The cause of Abu ʾl-Husayn al-Nuri's death was that he heard the following verse:

> In my love of you I have kept frequenting a place
> Which bewilders those hearts that settle there.

"Al-Nuri fell into ecstasy and wandered into a field where he came upon a bed of freshly cut reeds. Their stems were sharp as swords. He walked over them [in ecstasy] repeating the [above] line of poetry until the next day, blood gushing out of [the wounds on] his feet. [Finally, he] fell on the floor as a drunkard. His feet swelled up and he died. It is said that on his bed he was asked to say: 'There's no deity, but God.' He responded: 'Am I not returning to Him?'"

It is related that Ibrahim al-Khawwas came down with diarrhea in the congregational mosque of Rayy[574]. Once, after having relieved himself, he entered water[575] in order to perform an ablution. It was then that his soul departed. I heard Mansur al-Maghribi relate that Yusuf b. al-Husayn finally came to visit him in his illness after many days of absence and neglect. When he saw al-Khawwas, he asked him whether he would like anything. Al-Khawwas said: "Yes, I would like a piece of fried liver." The master Abu ʾl-Qasim [al-Qushayri] commented: "Perhaps there is a hint in this phrase, implying: 'I would like a heart that is compassionate toward the poor and a liver that is fried and burned to feed a

---

574 An ancient Persian city, now in ruins, which lies some five miles south-east of Tehran, Iran.
575 Probably an ablution pond located near or in the mosque.

stranger.' He [al-Khawwas] thereby showed his displeasure with Yusuf b. al-Husayn for neglecting to visit with him." It is related that the cause of Ibn ʿAtaʾ [al-Adami's] death was that he was once brought before the vizier [Hamid], who spoke harshly to him. Ibn ʿAtaʾ told him: "Be quiet, man!" The vizier ordered the guards to beat him on his head with his shoes, and he died because of it. I heard Muhammad b. Ahmad b. Muhammad al-Sufi say: I heard ʿAbdallah b. ʿAli al-Tamimi say: I heard Abu Bakr al-Duqqi say: "We were with Abu Bakr al-Zaqqaq one morning. [Suddenly,] he said: 'My God, for how long will You keep me//386 here?' Before the time of the first morning prayer came, he was dead." It is related that Abu ʿAli al-Rudhbari said: "One day I met a youth in the desert. When he saw me, he exclaimed: 'Isn't it enough for Him that He has enflamed me with His love so as to make me sick?' I then saw him giving up his spirit. I told him, 'Say: "There's no deity, but God"', to which he responded, saying:

> O One from Whom, although He torments me, I have no escape
> O One, Who has installed Himself in my heart for ever and ever!"

Someone told al-Junayd: "Say: 'There's no deity, but God.'" He responded, saying: "I have not forgotten Him, so that I should be reminded to remember Him!" He then recited the following:

> He is present in my heart, He resides there
> I have not forgotten Him, so that I should be reminded about Him
> He is my master and my support
> And my portion from Him is great indeed!

I heard Muhammad b. Ahmad al-Sufi say: I heard ʿAbdallah b. ʿAli al-Tamimi say: I asked a servant of al-Shibli, Jaʿfar b. Nusayr Bakran al-Dinawari, about things that he saw from him. He related the following on his authority: "[Once] I[576] owed a *dirham* that was improperly obtained. [To expiate my sin] I had given away thousands of *dirhams* in the name of its owner, so that I could set my mind at ease on this account." [On his death bed] al-Shibli told me: "Give me the ablution for prayer." I gave him the ablution. However, I forgot to run water through his beard. At that time, he had lost his ability to speak, therefore he grabbed me by the hand and rubbed through his beard. After that he expired." After Jaʿfar had related this [about al-Shibli], he burst into tears, saying: "What can you say about a man who did not neglect a single rule of the Divine Law even on his death bed?!" I heard ʿAbdallah b. Yusuf al-Isbahani say: I heard Abu ʾl-Hasan ʿAbdallah al-Tarsusi: I heard ʿAllush[577] al-Dinawari say: I heard al-Muzayyin the Elder say: "Once, when I was in Mecca, I was overcome by agitation. So, I left Mecca for Medina. When I reached the well of Maymuna, I

---

576 That is, al-Shibli, as quoted by his servant.
577 Or "ʿAllus".

came across a youth who lay prostrated on the ground. When I approached him, I saw that he was about to expire. I told him: 'Say: "There's no deity but God!"' He opened his eyes and recited the following:

> If I die, my heart is filled with passion,
> For the noble men perish by the illness of passion.

He then issued a shriek and expired. I washed him, wrapped him up in a shroud, and prayed over him. After I had buried him, my desire for travel suddenly subsided and I returned to Mecca."

Someone asked a Sufi: "Do you love death?" He answered: "It is better to go to someone from whom you hope to see good than to stay with someone from whose evil you cannot be protected." It is related that al-Junayd said: "I was with my master Ibn al-Karnabi, when he was giving up his soul. I raised my eyes to the sky [in prayer for him]. However, he told me: 'Not yet.' Then I lowered my gaze, to which he responded, saying: 'Not yet.' That is, he was still too near you//387 for you to look at the sky or to the earth. He [Ibn al-Karnabi] had not yet reached his place." I heard Abu Hatim al-Sijistani say: I heard Abu Nasr [al-Sarraj] al-Tusi say: I heard one of our companions say: "Abu Yazid said at his death: 'I remember You only after I have neglected You, and You take my soul only after I have slackened [in my worship of You].'"

I heard Abu Hatim al-Sijistani say: I heard Abu Nasr al-Sarraj say: I heard al-Wajihi say: I heard Abu ʿAli al-Rudhbari say: "One day I arrived in Egypt only to find a large crowd of people. They told me: 'We have just accompanied the funeral bier of a youth who died after he had heard the following verses:

> Great is the longing of the servant that prompts him to seek a glimpse of You.'

[After he had heard this], he issued a shriek and expired."

It is related that a group of people came to visit Mimshadh al-Dinawari on his death bed. They asked him: "How has God treated you?" He answered: "For thirty years I have been shown Paradise and things that are in it, yet I have not given it even one glance!" At his death agony they asked him: "How does your heart feel?" He answered: "It's been thirty years since I lost my heart!" I heard Muhammad b. Ahmad b. Muhammad al-Sufi say: I heard ʿAbdallah b. ʿAli al-Tamimi say: I heard al-Wajihi say: "Ibn Bunan died because a certain spiritual state entered his heart, as a result of which he began to roam aimlessly. When some people found him in the middle of the desert of the Israelites lying on the sand, he opened his eyes and said: 'Graze here! This is the grazing ground of the beloved [of God] (*ahbab*).' After that his spirit departed."

Abu Yaʿqub al-Nahrajuri said: "When I was in Mecca, a Sufi came to me carrying one *dinar* and said: 'If I die tomorrow, use half of this [*dinar*] to dig a grave [for me] and another half to perform funeral rites on me.' I thought to myself: 'This man has gone mad; probably the penury of the Hijaz has afflicted him.' When the next day came, he began to circumambulate the Kaʿba. He made a few steps, then stretched himself on the ground. I said [to myself]: 'Here it is: he is trying to fake death!' However, when I came up to him and tried to move him, I discovered that he was indeed dead. I then buried him, as he requested." When the condition of Abu ʿUthman al-Hiri deteriorated, his son Abu Bakr tore his shirt. Abu ʿUthman opened his eyes and told him: "My son, violating the [Prophet's] custom outwardly results in hypocrisy within your inner self." It is related that Ibn ʿAtaʾ came to al-Junayd at the time of his death. He greeted him, but al-Junayd was slow in giving his reply. Finally, he returned the greeting, adding: "Excuse me. I was reciting my prayers (*wird*)." After that he expired.

Abu ʿAli al-Rudhbari related: "A Sufi who came to us died. When I put him in the grave,//388 I opened his face before covering him with earth so that God – may He be great and exalted – could extend His mercy on him as a stranger.[578] Suddenly, he opened his eyes and said: 'Abu ʿAli, are you pampering me before Him, Who has already pampered me?' I inquired of him: 'Sir, how can you live after death?' He said: 'No, I am alive, for everyone who loves God – may He be great and exalted – is alive, so that I can help you, O Rudhbari, tomorrow[579] with my status (*jahi*) [in the eyes of God].'"

It is related that Ibn Sahl al-Isbahani said: "Do you really think I will die like any ordinary person – getting sick and receiving visits [from friends]. [No,] I will simply be called upon and it will be said: 'ʿAli!', and I will answer [the call]." One day, as he was out walking, he uttered: "Here I am, God!" and expired. I heard Muhammad b. ʿAbdallah al-Sufi say: I heard Abu ʿAbdallah b. Khafif say: I heard Abu ʾl-Hasan al-Muzayyin say: "When Abu Yaʿqub al-Nahrajuri came to his final end, I told him, as he was experiencing the agony of death: 'Say: "There's no deity, but God."' He smiled at me and answered: 'Are you talking to me?! By the majesty of the One Who will never taste death, nothing is left between Him and myself, except the veil of majesty.' As soon as he uttered that, his light went out." Al-Muzayyin, who recounted this story, then said, grabbing his beard: 'A cupper[580] like myself [had the cheek] to ask God's friends [like him] to utter the profession of faith (*shahada*)?! What a shame!'" He would always weep, when he told this story. Abu ʾl-Husayn al-Maliki said: "I kept the company of Khayr al-Nassaj[581] for many years. Eight days before his death he told me: 'I will die on Thursday around the sunset prayer. I will be buried on Friday before the [Friday] prayer. You may forget this. [Please] do not forget!' Abu ʾl-Husayn said: 'I forgot about it until that Friday. Then I met someone who informed me about his death. I went out to

---

578 That is, the fact that he died far from his home was supposed to improve his fate in the Hereafter.
579 That is, when you yourself die.
580 His nickname, "Muzayyin", indicates that he was a barber; barbers often served as cuppers as well.
581 A famous Sufi of Baghdad, who died in 322/934.

join his funeral procession, only to find some people, who told me: 'He will be buried after the prayer.' I walked on and encountered the funeral procession that had left [his house] before the prayer, as he told me. I asked one of those who were with him at his death [about his condition]. He said: 'At first, he lost consciousness, then came to himself and turned in the direction of [God's] House[582], saying: "Wait, may God protect you! You are a servant under orders (ʿabd maʾmur) and I am a servant under orders. That which you have been ordered to do will not elude you. However, that which I have been ordered may elude me." He then asked for water to perform his ablutions, after which he prayed. He then stretched out and his eyes grew dull.' Someone saw him in a dream after his death and asked him about his condition. He answered: 'Don't ask. However, I have finally rid myself of this filthy world of yours!'"

Abu ʾl-Husayn al-Himsi, the author of the "Book of Delectation of Mysteries", mentioned that when Sahl b. ʿAbdallah [al-Tustari] died, people flocked to his funeral procession in great numbers. In that city[583] there was a Jew, some seventy years old. When he heard the commotion, //389 he went out to see what it was. When he saw the funeral procession, he exclaimed: "Do you see what I see?" They answered: "No, we don't." He then said: "I see crowds descending from the heavens in order to touch the bier of the deceased." He then uttered the [Muslim] profession of faith and embraced Islam. He became a good Muslim.

I heard Shaykh Abu ʿAbd al-Rahman al-Sulami say: I heard Mansur b. ʿAbdallah say: I heard Abu Jaʿfar b. Qays in Egypt say: I heard Abu Saʿid al-Kharraz say: "Once I was in Mecca. As I was whiling away my day at the gate of Banu Shayba, I noticed a youth with a handsome face, lying there dead. As I was looking at his face, he smiled and said to me: 'O Abu Saʿid, don't you know that the beloved [of God] are alive even though they have died?! They simply move from one domain to another!'" I also heard him [al-Sulami] say: I heard Abu Bakr al-Razi say: I heard al-Jurayri say that [some people] asked Dhu ʾl-Nun for a pious advice as he was lying on his death bed. He responded, saying: "Don't distract me, for I am enjoying the beauties of His kindness!" I also heard him say: I heard ʿAbdallah b. Muhammad al-Razi say: I heard Abu ʿUthman al-Hiri say that some people asked Abu Hafs [al-Haddad] as he was lying on his death bed: "Admonish us!" He answered: "I do not have enough strength to speak." However, he eventually gathered strength, and I asked him: "Tell me [what you want], so that I could pass on your words [to others]!" He said: "My admonition is this: May every heart be abased by each mistake it commits!"

Divine gnosis (al-maʿrifa [bi-llah])

God Most High said: "They measured God not with His true measure."[584] It is written in a commentary that this means: "They have not known God as He

---

582 That is, the Kaʿba.
583 That is, Basra.
584 Q. 6:91.

should be known." ʿAbd al-Rahman b. Muhammad b. ʿAbdallah al-ʿAdl: informed us: Muhammad b. Qasim al-ʿAtaki said: Muhammad b. Ashras said: Sulayman b. ʿIsa al-Shajari,[585] said on the authority of ʿAbbad b. Kathir, on the authority of Hanzala, on the authority of Abu Sufyan, on the authority of al-Qasim b. Muhammad, on the authority of ʿAʾisha – may God be pleased with her – that the Prophet – may God bless and greet him – said: "The support of the house is its foundation and the support of the faith is the knowledge of God Most High, certitude, and a restraining intelligence." [ʿAʾisha] asked him: "By my mother and my father, what is the restraining intelligence?" He answered: "Refraining from disobedience to God and eagerness to obey Him." The master [Abu ʾl-Qasim al-Qushayri] said: "According to scholars (ʿulamaʾ), 'gnosis' (maʿrifa) means 'knowledge' (ʿilm). Thus, all knowledge is gnosis and all gnosis is knowledge. Each person who is cognizant of God (ʿarif) is a knower (ʿalim). In the usage of this folk, gnosis is the attribute of one who is cognizant of God//390 – praise be to Him – and His names and attributes, and of one who has put his trust in God Most High in his everyday behavior and who has rid himself of bad morals and transgressions. He then proceeds to reside at the door [of God's mercy] with his heart toiling constantly, whereupon he becomes endeared to God Most High and trusts Him in everything he experiences; the whisperings of his [low] self abandon him and thoughts about anyone else [but God] never enter his heart. Thus, when he becomes a stranger to all other creatures, completely innocent of any faults of his [lower] soul, and free from any recourse to or concern for other [than God], he enters into an uninterrupted intimate conversation with God Most High and accepts nothing except what is true. After that, he begins to speak on behalf of God – praise be to Him – Who imparts to him (taʿrif) the mysteries of the dispensations of His foreordained decrees. It is then that he is called a 'gnostic' and his state is called 'gnosis'. In brief, the more estranged he is from his own self, the more he knows his Lord. Sufi masters have discoursed profusely about gnosis, each speaking from his own experience and things he has discovered in his own mystical moment."

I heard the master Abu ʿAli al-Daqqaq – may God have mercy on him – say: "Among the signs of divine gnosis is awe of Him; the more you have gnosis, the greater is your awe." He also said: "Gnosis brings tranquility to your heart; the more gnosis you have, the greater is your tranquility." I heard the master Abu ʿAbd al-Rahman al-Sulami say: I heard Ahmad b. Muhammad b. Zayd say: I heard al-Shibli say: "The gnostic has no attachment, the lover has no complaint, the servant has no [selfish] pretension, the one who fears [God] has no rest, and no one has escape from God." I also heard him [al-Sulami] say: I heard Muhammad b. Muhammad b. ʿAbd al-Wahhab say: I heard al-Shibli say, when someone asked him about gnosis: "It begins with God Most High, and the rest of it has no end." I heard him [al-Sulami] say: I heard my father say: I heard Abu

---

585 Or "al-Sijzi".

ʾl-ʿAbbas al-Dinawari say: Abu Hafs [al-Haddad] said: "Since I acquired the gnosis of God Most High, neither truth nor falsehood have ever entered my heart."

The master Abu ʾl-Qasim [al-Qushayri] commented: "What Abu Hafs said is somewhat problematic. What it most likely means is that, in the opinion of this folk, gnosis renders the servant completely oblivious of himself due to his preoccupation with the remembrance of God – praise be upon Him: he witnesses no one but God – may He be great and exalted – and turns to no one else but Him. Just as the intelligent person (ʿaqil) turns to his heart, his thinking abilities, and his memory in dealing with matters and spiritual conditions that present themselves to him, the Sufi gnostic turns to his Lord. If he has been preoccupied with nothing but his Lord, he has not turned to his heart. So, how can a certain idea enter the heart of someone who has no heart?//391 This is the difference between someone who lives through his heart and someone who lives through his Lord."

Someone asked Abu Yazid [al-Bistami] about gnosis. He answered, [quoting the Queen of Sheba]: "Kings, when they enter a city, disorder it and make the mighty ones of its inhabitants abased."[586] The master [al-Qushayri] said: "This is the meaning of Abu Hafs' allusion." Abu Yazid said: "[All] people possess [spiritual] states, whereas the gnostic possesses none, because his personal characteristics (rusum) are totally erased, his personality (huwiyya) is fully annihilated by the personality of the Other, and his qualities are rendered nonexistent by the qualities of the Other." Al-Wasiti said: "Man's gnosis is imperfect as long as he is content with God and is in need of Him." The master said: "Being in need of God and content with Him are signs of the servant's sobriety (sahw) and of the persistence of his personal characteristics, because they are part of his attributes. The gnostic, on the other hand, is completely erased by the object of his gnosis (maʿruf). How can he have any [need] at all when he is fully consumed by His existence and submerged in the contemplation of Him? He is oblivious of [his] being, deprived of any sense of his personal traits." Al-Wasiti also said about this: "Whoever knows God Most High falls silent, because he becomes mute and subdued." The Prophet – may God bless and greet him – said: "I cannot count your praises." These are the characteristics of those who have attained the furthest reaches. As for those who have not yet reached this limit, they have discoursed profusely about divine gnosis.

Muhammad b. al-Husayn informed us: Abu Jaʿfar Muhammad b. Ahmad b. Saʿid al-Razi told us: ʿAyyash[587] b. Hamza told us: I heard Ahmad b. Abi ʾl-Hawari say: I heard Ahmad b. ʿAsim al-Antaki say: "Whoever knows God most is most afraid of Him." A Sufi said: "Whoever has known God Most High is disgusted with existence, for despite its breadth this world has become too narrow for him." It is said: "Whoever knows God attains a pure livelihood and a good life;

---

586 Q. 27:34.
587 Or "ʿAbbas".

everyone is in awe of him, while he himself fears no creature, because he becomes God's intimate friend." It is also said: "Whoever knows God loses desire for things of this world; he is neither attached nor detached."//392 It is said: "Gnosis demands both humility and exaltation (ta'zim) in the same way as the declaration of [God's] oneness demands both contentment and surrender [to God]." Ruwaym [b. Ahmad] said: "Gnosis for the gnostic is like a mirror; whenever he looks into it, his Master appears to him." Dhu 'l-Nun al-Misri said: "Friendship with the gnostic is like friendship with God Most High. He treats you with gentleness and shows kindness to you, thereby imitating God's moral qualities." Someone asked Ibn Yazdaniyar: "When will the gnostic witness God – praise be to him?" He responded: "When the witness appears, the perceptions will be annihilated, the senses will fade away, and sincerity will disappear."[588] Al-Husayn b. Mansur said: "When the servant reaches the station of gnosis, God will dictate to him all his thoughts and protect his innermost mystery (sirr), so that not a single thought about something apart from God will enter his mind." He also said: "One of the signs of the gnostic is that he is empty of any thought about this world and the next one." Sahl b. 'Abdallah [al-Tustari] said: "Gnosis has two goals: confusion (dahash) and bewilderment."[589] I heard Muhammad b. al-Husayn say: I heard Muhammad b. Ahmad b. Sa'id say: I heard Muhammad b. Ahmad b. Sahl say: I heard Sa'id b. 'Uthman say: I heard Dhu 'l-Nun al-Misri say: "The person who knows God Most High is the most bewildered of all in regard to Him." I also heard him [Muhammad b. al-Husayn] say: I heard Abu Bakr al-Razi say: I heard Abu 'Umar al-Antaki say: "A man asked al-Junayd: 'Some possessors of gnosis say that abandoning movements [in the service of God] (harakat) is part of piety and righteousness.' Al-Junayd responded, saying: 'These are the words of those who profess the giving up of acts of worship. I consider this a grave [sin] ('azim). A person who steals and commits adultery is better than one who says such things. The divine gnostics borrow their works from God Most High and with them they return to Him. Were I to live one thousand years, I would not fall short in my pious works by an iota!'"

Someone asked Abu Yazid al-Bistami: "How did you acquire this gnosis of yours?" He answered: "By an empty stomach and a naked body." Abu Ya'qub al-Nahrajuri related: I asked Abu Ya'qub al-Susi: "Can the gnostic miss any-thing//393 except God – may He be great and exalted?" He responded, saying: "Does he see anything but God to miss it?" I asked him: "How does he see things?" He answered: "He sees them with the eye of [self-]annihilation and cessation (zawal)." Abu Yazid [al-Bistami] said: "The gnostic is a flyer, whereas the ascetic is a walker." It is said: "The eyes of the gnostic are weeping, while his heart is laughing." Al-Junayd said: "One cannot be a gnostic until one has

---

588 Gramlich, in his German translation of the "Epistle" (p. 432), suggests that one should read *ihsas* ("sensation") instead of *ikhlas*, but all the Arabic texts I have consulted have the latter.
589 On bewilderment and confusion as the marks of true gnosis, see Chittick, *The Sufi Path*, "Index" under "bewilderment".

become like the earth, which is trampled upon by both the righteous and the sinners, or like the cloud which casts its shadow on everything, or like the rain that quenches the thirst of those it loves and those it does not love." Yahya b. Muʿadh said: "When the gnostic leaves this world he cannot get enough of two things: weeping over his lot and praising his Lord – may He be great and exalted." Abu Yazid said: "The gnostics acquire their gnosis by abandoning what belongs to them and keeping what is due to Him."

I heard Shaykh Abu ʿAbd al-Rahman al-Sulami say: I heard Abu ʾl-Husayn al-Farisi say: I heard Yusuf b. ʿAli say: "No one can become a [true] gnostic unless when given the wealth equal to that of [king] Solomon – peace be upon him – he would not be distracted from God for the blink of an eye." I also heard him say: I heard Abu ʾl-Husayn al-Farisi say: I heard Ibn ʿAtaʾ say: "Gnosis rests on three pillars: awe, humility, and intimacy." I also heard him say: I heard Muhammad b. ʿAbdallah b. Shadhan say: I heard Yusuf b. al-Husayn say: "Someone asked Dhu ʾl-Nun: 'How have you acquired knowledge of your Lord?' He responded: 'I have come to know my Lord through my Lord. Were it not for my Lord, I would not have known Him.'" They say: "The scholar serves as an example for other people, whereas the gnostic serves as their guide." Al-Shibli said: "The gnostic takes no notice of anything other than Him; nor speaks anything that God has not spoken, nor does he see his protector in anyone but God Most High." They say: "The gnostic finds intimacy in the recollection of God, and God estranges him from [the rest of] His creatures; the gnostic needs God, and God makes him independent from His creatures; he shows humility toward God Most High, and God gives him a high position among His creatures." Abu ʾl-Tayyib al-Samarri said: "Gnosis is God's appearance in the innermost souls [of His servants] through enlightening them with a constant stream of lights." It is said: "The gnostic stands above the things he says, whereas the scholar stands below the things he says." Abu Sulayman al-Darani said: "God unveils [His mysteries] to the gnostic, while he sleeps in his bed, while He does not unveil//394 anything to any other person, even though he may be standing in prayer." Al-Junayd said: "The gnostic is someone on behalf of whose innermost soul God speaks, while he remains silent." Dhu ʾl-Nun al-Misri said: "Everyone and everything has a punishment of his or its own; the punishment of the gnostic is when he ceases the recollection of God Most High."

I heard Abu Hatim al-Sijistani say: I heard Abu Nasr al-Sarraj say: I heard al-Wajihi say: I heard Abu ʿAli al-Rudhbari say: I heard Ruwaym say: "The hypocrisy of the gnostics is better than the sincerity of the aspirants (*muridun*)." Abu Bakr al-Warraq said: "The silence of the gnostic is more beneficial; while his speech is sweeter and more pleasant." Dhu ʾl-Nun al-Misri said: "The ascetics[590] (*zuhhad*) are the kings of the Hereafter, while they themselves are but the poor [in the service of] the gnostics." Someone asked al-Junayd about the gnostic. He

---

590 This term can also be translated as "world-renouncers".

said: "The color of the water is the same as the color of its vessel." That is, [his condition is determined] by the command of his mystical moment (*waqtuh*). Someone asked Abu Yazid about the gnostic. He answered: "[It is he who] sees only God in his sleep and during his waking hours; he agrees with no one but God and contemplates no one but God Most High."

I heard Muhammad b. al-Husayn say: I heard ʿAbdallah b. Muhammad al-Dimashqi say that someone asked a Sufi master how he got to know God Most High. He answered: "By a flash that entered the tongue [of someone who] had lost the common ability to differentiate among things and by a word that appeared on the tongue [of someone] who had perished and been lost [to this world]." [The speaker reported here about a direct encounter with God], while at the same time manifesting a mystery that veils [the true state of things]. [In other words,] God has made Himself apparent by that which He has manifested, while at the same time concealing Himself by that which He has veiled.[591] He is He in that in which He has made His appearance and He is not He in that in which He concealed Himself. He then proceeded to recite the following:

> You spoke without saying a word, yet this is still nothing but speech
> Your speech consists of words, yet it is different from the [usual] speech
> You presented yourself to my sight, so that I could hide myself, after you had been hiding
> You darted a lightning at me, that is, you spoke as if you were throwing lightning bolts.

I heard him [Muhammad b. al-Husayn] say: I heard ʿAli b. Bundar al-Sirafi say: I heard al-Jurayri say that someone asked Abu Turab about the characteristics of the gnostic. He answered: "He is one whom nothing can sully, while everything is purified by him." I also heard him say: I heard Abu ʿUthman al-Maghribi say: "The gnostic is someone upon whom the light of knowledge falls, so that he might observe the marvels of the unseen through it." //395 I heard the master Abu ʿAli al-Daqqaq say: "The gnostic is lost in the sea of veracious realization (*tahqiq*), or, as one of them put it: 'Gnosis is the waves of the sea that plunge down, then rise only to collapse again.'" Someone asked Yahya b. Muʿadh [al-Razi] about the gnostic. He said: "This is someone who is both present and absent (*kaʾin baʾin*)."[592] On another occasion he said: "[This is someone] who is here, yet separate." Dhu ʾl-Nun said: "The gnostic is distinguished by three [signs]: the light of his gnosis does not extinguish the light of his piety; he does not adhere to an inner knowledge that may contradict an outward [religious] injunction; and the plenitude of divine graces does not push him towards violating any of God's

---

591 This complicated statement is deemed to convey the dynamics of concealment and revelation that the Sufis ascribed to God, who is immanently present in this world, while at the same time being transcendent to it and thus unknown and unknowable to His creatures.

592 According to a commentary, he is present with creatures in his body, yet far from them in his heart.

prohibitions – may He be great and exalted." It is said: "One cannot be [considered] a gnostic if one discourses about gnosis in front of the inhabitants of the Hereafter, not to mention the inhabitants of this world." Abu Saʿid al-Kharraz said: "Gnosis springs from the spring of [divine] grace and exerting oneself [for the sake of God]." I heard Muhammad b. al-Husayn say: I heard Muhammad b. ʿAbdallah say: I heard Jaʿfar say that someone asked al-Junayd about Dhu ʾl-Nun's statement concerning the [distinguishing] characteristic of the gnostic: "He was here, but has already left." Al-Junayd commented, saying: "He is not confined by any state, and no [mystical] station veils him from advancing through other stations; when he finds himself with people belonging to any particular station, he experiences exactly what they experience and he discourses on its particularities in such a way that they benefit from his discourses." I heard him [Muhammad b. al-Husayn] say: I heard ʿAbdallah al-Razi say: I heard Muhammad b. al-Fadl say: "Gnosis is the heart's life with God Most High." I also heard him say: I heard Ahmad b. ʿAli b. Jaʿfar say: I heard al-Kattani say that someone asked Abu Saʿid al-Kharraz: "Can the gnostic reach a state in which weeping becomes a burden for him?" He responded: "Yes, weeping [is necessary] during their [gnostics'] travel to God Most High. However, once they have arrived at the true realities of closeness [with God] and tasted the victuals of union with Him through His grace, weeping no longer remains with them."//396

Love (mahabba)

God – may He be great and exalted – said: "O believers, whosoever of you turns from their religion, God will assuredly bring forth a people [instead of you] whom He loves, and who love Him."[593] Abu Nuʿaym ʿAbd al-Malik b. Husayn informed us: Abu ʿAwana Yaʿqub b. Ishaq told us: al-Sulami told us: ʿAbd al-Razzaq told us on the authority of Maʿmar, on the authority of Humam[594] b. Munabbih, on the authority of Abu Hurayra that the Messenger of God – may God bless and greet him – said: "Whoever loves to meet God, God, too, will love to meet him; and whoever does not love to meet Him, God, too, will not love to meet him." Abu al-Husayn ʿAli b. Ahmad b. ʿAbdan informed us: Ahmad b. ʿUbayd al-Saffar al-Basri told us: ʿAbdallah b. Ayyub told us: al-Hasan b. Musa told us: Haytham b. Kharija told us: al-Husayn b. Yahya told us on the authority of Sadaqa al-Dimashqi, on the authority of Hisham al-Kattani, on the authority of Anas b. Malik, on the authority of the Prophet – may God bless and greet him, who related this from Gabriel – peace be upon him, who related this from God Most High – praise be to Him: "Whoever has denigrated a friend of mine, has declared war on Me; I do not hesitate in anything more than taking the soul of my faithful servant, who abhors death, while I abhor harming him; yet, there's no escape for him from this. The servant does not draw near Me by anything that I love more than

---

593 Q. 5:54; 5:56, according to Arberry's translation.
594 Or "Hammam".

his fulfillment of the duties that I have imposed upon him. My servant keeps drawing ever closer to me by [performing] supererogatory acts of worship (*nawafil*) until I love him; and whomever I love, I become his hearing, his sight, his hand, and his support."

ʿAli b. Ahmad b. ʿAbdan informed us: Ahmad b. ʿUbayd informed us: ʿUbayd b. Sharik informed us: Yahya told us: Malik [b. Anas] told us on the authority of Suhayl b. Abi Salih, on the authority of his father, on the authority of Abu Hurayra that the Prophet – may God bless and greet him – said: "When God – may He be great and exalted – loves a servant of His, he tells Gabriel: 'Gabriel, I love so-and-so, so love him, too!' And Gabriel loves him. Then Gabriel announces to the inhabitants of heaven that God Most High loves so-and-so and tells them to love him, and they love him too. Then Gabriel makes him a great welcome on the earth. And when God loathes someone ..." Malik said: "I believe that he [the Prophet] said the same thing regarding loathing."//397

The master [al-Qushayri] said: "Love is a noble state, as God has attested to His servant, when he informed him about His love of him. [In the Qurʾan] God is described as loving His servant and the servant is described as loving God – praise be to Him." According to the terminology of the scholars "love" is "desire". However, according to the parlance of this folk[595] "love" is not "desire", for "desire" cannot apply to the eternal. O God, let "desire" not be understood [by them] except as drawing near and exalting Him! We shall briefly mention just some approaches to this issue, God willing. God's love toward His servant is but His desire to bestow special favors (*inʿam*) upon him. Likewise, His mercy (*rahma*) toward His servant is but His desire to [bestow] favors upon him. However, mercy is more specific than desire, while love is more specific than mercy. God Most High's desire to deliver recompense and favors to [His] servant is named "mercy", while His desire to single him out for nearness [to Him] and lofty [spiritual] states is named "love".

God's desire – praise be to Him – is but one quality. However, its names differ in accordance with the different objects of its application. When it applies to punishment it is named "wrath"; when it applies to all His favors [toward His servants] it is named "mercy"; and when it applies to the special favors among them, it is named "love". Some Sufis say that God's love toward His servant is his praise of Him and his lauding of Him for [His] beneficence (*jamil*). Thus, the meaning of "love" according to this teaching goes back to Him and His speech, and His speech is eternal.[596] Others argue that God's love toward His servant belongs to His attributes of actions, which is a special grace (*ihsan*) with which God meets His servant and a special state to which God elevates him. As one of them said: "[God's] mercy toward His servant is His showing beneficence toward

---

595 That is, the Sufis.
596 That is, God's love for His servant, which consists of endowing the latter with gratitude, was pre-determined from eternity in divine foreknowledge (= His "speech"), which pertains to the divine essence.

him." As for the earlier generations [of the Sufis], they said that love was one of the [divine] attributes of goodness (*khayriyya*). Although they used this word, they refrained from explaining it in detail. As regards that which goes beyond this summary – namely, the known characteristics of love pertaining to creatures, such as an inclination to a certain thing or seeking intimacy with a certain thing, as is the case with the human lover and his beloved – the Eternal One is far too exalted for this.

As for the servant's love of God, it is a state that he finds in his heart that is too subtle for any expression. Such a state may move the servant to exalt Him, to seek His satisfaction, to be impatient, and to long passionately for Him, to be restless without Him, and to find intimacy with Him in his heart by remembering Him. The servant's love of God – praise be to Him – involves neither an inclination nor a limit. How can this be otherwise, when His everlasting Essence is too holy to allow any contact, grasp or comprehension? It is better for the lover to be in the state of full engrossment in his beloved than to be in a state characterized//398 by any limitation. Love, as such, cannot be described or defined by any clear and understandable description or definition.[597] Usually, an exhaustive discussion [of it] is required when something is [so] complex. However, when the confusion disappears, there is no longer any need to delve into explanations.

People have suggested numerous explanations of love and have discoursed profusely about [the meaning of] its root in the [Arabic] language. Some argue that *hubb* (love) is a name that denotes the purity of affection (*safaʾ al-mawadda*), because the Arabs say *habab al-asnan*[598] about white and fresh-looking teeth. They also say *habab*[599] about things that appear on the surface of the water during a heavy rain. Hence *mahabba*[600] means the "boiling" or "stirring" of the heart when it is thirsty and its passionate longing for meeting its beloved. They also say that *hubb* is derived from [the phrase] *habab al-maʾ* with the meaning of its [water's] "center" and that it was called thus because of the centrality of love to the heart's preoccupations. Others say that it is derived from [the words] *luzum* and *thabat*,[601] [because the Arabs] say: *ahabba al-baʿir*, "the camel has kneeled and refused to stand up". Likewise, the lover persists in remembering his beloved in his heart. They also say that *hubb* is derived from *hibb*, which means "earring". The poet said:

The snake, menacingly flicking its tongue, stayed close to him
As if it were an earring, overhearing a secret conversation.

---

597 According to an alternative reading, "Love cannot be described or defined by a description or a definition that is clear and conducive to [our] comprehension."
598 Literally, "teeth that are covered with streaks of saliva".
599 Literally, "bubbles" or "ripples".
600 "Love."
601 Namely, "persistence" and "stubbornness".

The earring was called *hibb*, because of being constantly attached to the ear or because of its constant movement and agitation. Both these meanings are true about love (*hubb*). They also say that it comes from [the word] *habb*, which is the plural of *habba*.[602] The "kernel" of the heart is that which sustains it, so it was named *hubb* due to its importance, because [the words] *habb* and *hubb* are similar to [the words] ʿ*amr* and ʿ*umr*.[603] They also say that *hubb* comes from *hibba*, which is the seed of the desert. *Hubb* was called so because it is the seed of life in the same way as the seed is the life[604] of all vegetation. It is also said that *hubb* denotes four pieces of wood on which the [earthenware] jar is placed. Love is called thus because of the disdain and humiliation that the lover tolerates from his beloved.//399 They say that *hubb* is the jar filled with water, because it contains what is poured into it and can take no more than what is already there. Likewise, the heart is brimming with love that leaves no room for anyone but the beloved.

As for the sayings of Sufi masters about this matter, one of them said: "[Love is] a constant longing of the enraptured heart" (*al-mayl al-daʾim bi-ʾl-qalb al-haʾim*). They say: "Love is giving preference to the beloved over all other attachments." They say: "[It is] to agree with the beloved in his presence and his absence." They say: "[It is] erasing the lover's attributes and fixing the beloved in his [lover's] essence." They say: "[It is] the heart's compliance with the will of its Lord." They say: "[It is] the fear of [displaying] irreverence (*tark al-hurma*) accompanied by the constancy of service." Abu Yazid al-Bistami said: "Love means denigrating your own efforts and exaggerating whatever your beloved does, no matter how small it is." Sahl [al-Tustari] said: "Love means to embrace obedience and part ways with disobedience." When someone asked al-Junayd about love, he answered: "[It is] the substitution of the attributes of the lover for those of the beloved." He [al-Junayd] thus alluded to the remembrance of the beloved that takes possession of the lover to such an extent that only the remembrance of the attributes of the beloved remains and he becomes totally oblivious of his own attributes and no longer perceives them. Abu ʿAli al-Rudhbari said: "Love means compliance." Abu ʿAbdallah al-Qurashi said: "True love means giving yourself fully to the one you love, so that there would be nothing in you that belongs to you." Al-Shibli said: "Love is named *mahabba* because it erases (*tamhu*) everything from the [lover's] heart except the beloved." Ibn ʿAtaʾ said: "Love means constant [self-]reproach."

I heard Abu ʿAli al-Daqqaq – may God have mercy on him – say: "Love is pleasure (*ladhdha*) and the site of the [divine] reality (*haqiqa*) is puzzlement (*dahash*)." I also heard him say: "Loving desire (ʿ*ishq*) means to transgress the limit (*mujawazat al-hadd*), and God – praise be to Him – cannot be described as a transgressor of the limit, so loving desire cannot be attributed to Him. Were the loves of the entire created world brought together in one and the same person,

---

602 That is, "kernel," "the innermost [part]".
603 In that both have the same meaning, despite the different vowels in their first syllable.
604 Literally, "the core".

he would still be unable to love God – praise be to Him – as He deserves. Therefore one cannot say that someone has transgressed the limit in his love of God. So, God Himself is not described as possessing loving desire (*ya'shaq*), nor should the servant describe Him as such. Thus, loving passion is [totally] negated://400 neither the servant nor God – praise be to Him – uses it to describe the other."

I heard Shaykh Abu 'Abd al-Rahman al-Sulami say: I heard Mansur b. 'Abdallah say: I heard al-Shibli say: "Love means that you are jealous of someone who may love your beloved as much as you do." I heard him [al-Sulami] say: I heard Abu 'l-Husayn al-Farisi say: I heard Ibn 'Ata' say about love: "[It is] the stems that are planted in the heart; they bring fruit according to the strength of [one's] understanding (*'uqul*)." I also heard him say: I heard al-Nasrabadhi say: "One love demands that blood be spared and another that it be spilt." I heard Muhammad b. 'Ali al-'Alawi say: I heard Ja'far say: I heard Samnun say: "Lovers of God Most High have removed nobility from this world and the Hereafter, because the Prophet – may God bless and greet Him – said: 'Man is always with the one he loves' and they [the lovers] are always with God Most High." Yahya b. Mu'adh said: "Love is something that is neither decreased by coarseness [of character], nor increased by righteousness (*birr*)." He also said: "A man who claims to be in love [with God] is insincere if he does not observe the limits set by Him." Al-Junayd said: "When love is true, the rules of proper behavior disappear." I heard the master Abu 'Ali [al-Daqqaq] recite the following verses pertinent to this matter:

When love between folk is pure and their affection lasts,
[Their] praise [of each other] turns ugly.

[Likewise, Abu 'Ali] used to say: "You will not see a compassionate father who [excessively] honors his son in talking to him. When other people address him [formally], the father just says: "Hey, so-and-so!" Al-Kattani said: "Love is giving preference to the beloved over oneself."

I heard Muhammad b. al-Husayn say: I heard Abu Sa'id al-Arrajani say: I heard Bundar b. al-Husayn relate: "Someone saw Majnun of the Banu 'Amir [tribe][605] in a dream and asked him: 'What has God done to you?' He answered: 'He pardoned me and set me as an argument against all those who claim love.'" Abu Ya'qub al-Susi related: "True love means that the servant of God forgets the earthly portion (*hazz*) allotted to him by Him and then also forgets that he needs it." Al-Husayn b. Mansur [al-Hallaj] said: "True love means that you remain with your beloved divested of all your own attributes." I heard Shaykh Abu 'Abd al-Rahman al-Sulami say: "Someone said to al-Nasrabadhi: 'You have no part in the love [of God].' He responded: 'They[606] have been sincere [in their

---

605 A hero of Arabian folklore, who came to exemplify unrequited and tragic love. He is also known as the "Majnun of Layla", after the name of his beloved.
606 That is, those who love God.

love]. However, I have received only their sorrows. See how I am being consumed by this!'"//401 I heard him [al-Sulami] say: Al-Nasrabadhi said: "Love means avoiding any distractions under any circumstances." He then recited the following:

> While some in their long-lasting passion may [occasionally] taste diversion
> I, however, because of Layla[607] have never tasted it
> The most I have experienced since meeting her are
> My desires, which are not real, like the flashes of a lightning.

Muhammad b. al-Fadl said: "Love means that the heart is devoid of any other love, except the love of the beloved." Al-Junayd said: "Love is an abundance of desire that is never requited (*al-mayl bila nayl*)." It is said: "Love is a confusion that settles in the heart on account of the beloved." They also say: "Love is a trial that settles in the heart because [of its aspiration toward] the beloved." Ibn ʿAtaʾ recited:

> I planted a stem of passion for the people of love
> For no one before me had ever known what passion is
> It covered the stem with leaves and rendered its leaning[608] ripe
> Then it yielded to me the bitterness of a sweet fruit
> The passion of all the lovers of [the world], if they were to trace it back
> Comes from this source [of mine].

They say: "Love's beginning is deception, while its end is death." I heard the master Abu ʿAli al-Daqqaq – may God have mercy on him – comment on the words of the Prophet – may God bless and greet him – "Your love of something makes you blind and mute" as follows: "It makes one blind to others out of jealousy and to the beloved out of awe [of him]." He then proceeded to recite the following:

> When [I came out and] he appeared before me, I was so terrified by his [giant] stature
> That I reverted to the state of someone who never wanted to go.

I heard Shaykh Abu ʿAbd al-Rahman al-Sulami say: Ahmad b. ʿAtaʾ said: I heard Ibrahim b. Fatik say: I heard al-Junayd say: I heard al-Harith al-Muhasibi say: "Love means you are inclined toward someone in your entirety, then you give preference to this someone over yourself, your spirit and your possessions, then you comply with his wishes openly and secretly, whereupon you acquire the awareness of your love's imperfection." I heard him [al-Sulami] say: I heard Ahmad b. ʿAtaʾ say: I heard ʿAbbas b. ʿIsam say://402 I heard al-Junayd say: I

---

607 See note 605.
608 A word play on the meaning of the word *sabwa*, which denotes both "longing for something" and "the leaning of a tree".

heard al-Sari [al-Saqati] say: "Love between two is incomplete until one of them can say to the other: 'I!'" Al-Shibli said: "The lover perishes if he keeps silent, whereas the gnostic perishes if he does not keep silent." It is said: "Love is a flame in the heart that burns down everything except what the beloved wishes." It is also said: "Love means to exert oneself to the utmost degree, while allowing the beloved do as he pleases." Al-Nuri said: "Love means tearing down all veils and unveiling all secrets." Abu Ya'qub al-Susi said: "Love is imperfect until the lover abandons the vision of his love for the one whom he loves by annihilating the very awareness of his love." Ja'far recounted that al-Junayd said: "Al-Sari gave me a piece of paper, saying 'This is better for you than seven hundred [pious] stories or the choicest [prophetic] reports.' It read:

> When I said that I loved her, she told me: 'You have lied to me! Don't I see that
> The members [of your body] are still covered [with flesh]?'
> It is not [true] love until the heart sticks to your bowels
> And until you are so emaciated that you are unable to respond to someone who calls on you
> And until you are wasted away so that your passion has left you nothing
> But a naked eyeball with which you pray and seek intimacy [with your beloved]!"

Ibn Masruq related: "I saw Samnun [al-Muhibb] speaking about love; all the lamps in the mosque [where he was speaking] broke up!" I heard Muhammad b. al-Husayn say: I heard Ahmad b. 'Ali say: I heard Ibrahim b. Fatik say: "I heard Samnun as he was holding a session in the mosque and discoursing about love. A small bird approached him and began to draw nearer and nearer, until it finally perched on his hand. Then it began to strike the floor with its beak until blood flowed from it. After that it expired." Al-Junayd said: "Each love has its object,[609] and when the object disappears, love disappears with it." It is related that al-Shibli was confined to a lunatic asylum.[610] A group of people came to visit him. He asked them: "Who are you?" They replied: "Abu Bakr, we are those who love you!" He then started to throw rocks at them and they ran away. He exclaimed: "If you claim that you love me, you should patiently tolerate the harm that I cause you!" Al-Shibli recited:

> O the Benevolent Master, [my] love of You resides in my innards//403
> O You, who remove sleep from my eyelids, You know well what has happened to me.

I heard Shaykh Abu 'Abd al-Rahman al-Sulami say: I heard Mansur b. 'Abdallah say: I heard al-Nahrajuri say: I heard 'Ali b. 'Ubayd say: Yahya b. Mu'adh wrote

---

609 In an alternative reading, "each love has its compensation".
610 According to an oft-cited story, he was placed there for his ecstatic utterances that scandalized the public.

to Abu Yazid [al-Bistami], saying: "I have become drunk after drinking too much from the cup of His love." Abu Yazid wrote back to him, saying: "Someone else has drunk the seas that are on earth and in heaven and yet has not quenched his thirst and his tongue is sticking out [of his mouth] as he utters: 'Is there any more?'"[611]

They recite the following:

I wonder at someone who says: "I remember my intimate friend."
Did I forget [him], so that I have to remember what I forgot?
When I remember you, I die, only to live again soon after
And were it not for my trust in you, I would have never lived again
I live thanks to my aspiration [toward you] and I die because of [my] passionate longing
How often have I lived and died because of you!
I have drunk [the wine of] love one cup after another
Yet, the wine has not run out and my thirst has not been quenched!

It is related that God Most High revealed the following to Jesus – peace be upon him: "Verily, when I search the heart of a servant of mine and do not find there love of this world and the next, I fill it with love of Me." I saw this written by the hand of my master Abu 'Ali al-Daqqaq – may God have mercy on him: "In one of the revealed books it is said: 'My servant, I render what is due to you by loving you, so render what is due to Me by loving Me!'" 'Abdallah b. al-Mubarak said: "Whoever is endowed with a portion of [divine] love, while not being endowed with an equal portion of [divine] fear, is deluded." It is said: "Love is that which erases every trace of you." It is also said: "Love is an intoxication, whose possessor will not get sober until he witnesses his beloved." As for the intoxication that happens during the witnessing, it eludes any description. They recite:

The circling of the cup [of wine] made my companions drunk,
While I was intoxicated with the one who passed it around.

The master Abu 'Ali al-Daqqaq was fond of reciting the following line:

I have two types of intoxication, while my boon-companions have only one
It is something that distinguishes me from among them.

Ibn 'Ata' said: "Love is a constant [self-]recrimination." The master Abu 'Ali al-Daqqaq had a slave girl named Fayruz. He loved her for the many services she rendered to him. I heard him say: "One day Fayruz was pestering me and lashing me repeatedly with her tongue. Abu 'l-Hasan al-Qari' reprimanded her,

---

611 Q. 50:30; this passage describes the condition of sinners in Hell.

saying: 'Why are you pestering the shaykh?' She answered: 'Because I love him!'"
Yahya b. Mu'adh said: "A mustard seed's worth of love, in my opinion, is better than seventy years of worship without love."//404 It is related that a youth recited the following verse to [a crowd of] people on a feast day:

> Whoever wants to die out of loving passion, let him die!
> For there's no good in loving passion without death!

He then hurled himself from a high roof and fell onto earth dead. It is related that a man from India had a loving passion for a slave girl. When she was about to depart, the man came to bid her farewell. Tears poured from one of his eyes, but the other remained dry. He then shut the eye that did not cry and kept it shut for eighty-four years as a punishment for it for not crying at the departure of his beloved. About this they recite the following:

> One of my eyes shed tears on the morning of the separation,
> While the other was stingy in its weeping
> So I punished the one that withheld tears by shutting it on the day
> we finally reunited.

A Sufi related: "We were with Dhu 'l-Nun al-Misri one day, discussing love. He exclaimed: "Refrain from this issue! If your souls fail to understand it properly, they might lay claims to it." He then recited the following:

> Fear and sadness are better for the evildoer, when he practices devotion,
> While love is appropriate for the one who fears God and is free from any defilement.

Yahya b. Mu'adh said: "Whoever discusses [divine] love amidst those who do not understand it, makes false claims." It is related that a man claimed that he was madly in love with someone. The young man[612] told him: "How come [you love me], while my brother's face is more handsome and more perfect [than mine]?" The man raised his head and turned [to the brother]. They both were standing on the roof [of a house] and the young man pushed him from the roof, exclaiming: "This is the recompense of someone who claims that he loves us, yet looks at someone else!"

Samnun [al-Muhibb] used to elevate love above divine gnosis, while the majority [of Sufis] give preference to gnosis over love. According to those who have attained the truth (*muhaqqiqun*), love is an immersion into pleasure, while gnosis is witnessing [God] in perplexity (*hayra*) and being annihilated in awe [of Him]. Abu Bakr al-Kattani said: "A discussion of the issue of love occurred in Mecca during the pilgrimage season. [Sufi] masters discoursed about it, al-Junayd being the youngest of all. They asked him: 'Tell us what you think, Iraqi!' He lowered his head and tears streamed from his eyes. He then uttered: 'When the

---

612 Apparently, the object of his affection.

servant of God forgets about himself, becomes united with the recollection of his Lord, renders what is due to Him, and watches Him with his heart, [then] the lights of His essence incinerate his heart, his drinking from the cup of affection becomes pure, and the Mighty One unveils the curtains of His mystery before him. [Afer that] if he talks, he talks through God; if he utters [a word], it is from God; if he moves, he moves by God's command; if he rests, he rests with God; he is thus, through God, for God and with God.' The [Sufi] masters burst into tears and said: 'Nothing can be added to this! May God empower you, O the crown of the [divine] gnostics!'" It is related that God revealed to David – peace be upon him: "David, I have prohibited that love for any one else but Me enter the hearts of men!"

Hamza b. Yusuf al-Sahmi informed us: Muhammad b. Ahmad b. al-Qasim informed us: Humayyim b. Humam told us: Ibrahim b. al-Harith informed us: ʿAbd al-Rahman b. ʿAffan told us: Muhammad b. Ayyub told us: Abu ʾl-ʿAbbas, the servant of Fudayl b. ʿIyad told us: "When al-Fudayl's urine was suppressed, he raised his hands and exclaimed: 'My God, by my love of You, release me from this!' And before we could move, he was cured!" It is said: "Love is giving preference [to the lover over oneself], as the wife of al-ʿAziz[613] said, when she erred in her affair, 'I solicited him, but he is a truthful man',[614] while at the beginning she was saying, 'What is the recompense of him who proposes evil against thy folk, but he should be imprisoned, or a painful chastisement?'[615] Thus, at the beginning she ascribed sin to him. However, in the end she accused herself of infidelity." I [al-Qushayri] heard the master Abu ʿAli [al-Daqqaq] relate this. It is related that Abu Saʿid al-Kharraz said: "In a dream I saw the Prophet – may God bless and greet him – and asked him: 'Messenger of God, forgive me, for my love of God has distracted me from loving you!' He exclaimed: 'O the blessed one! Whoever loves God Most High, loves me [as well]!'" In one of her intimate conversations with God, Rabiʿa [al-ʿAdawiyya] said: "My God, can you burn with fire a heart that loves You?" She heard a voice saying: "We have not done so. Do not think ill of Us!" They say that [the word] "love" (*hubb*) has two letters, *haʾ* and *baʾ*, because one who is in love abandons both his spirit (*ruh*) and his body (*badan*).[616]

The consensus of the sayings of the Sufis [regarding this matter] is this: love is compliance [with the will of God], while the strongest compliance is that of the heart. Love necessitates the rejection of any difference [between its object and subject]; the lover always remains with his beloved, as confirmed by the following report. The imam Abu Bakr b. Furak – may God have mercy on him – told us: the judge Ahmad b. Mahmud b. Khurrazadh informed us: al-Hasan b. Hammad b. Fadala told us: Yahya b. Habib told us: Marhum b. ʿAbd al-ʿAziz told us on

---

613 The Biblical Potiphar of the story of Joseph.
614 Q. 12:51.
615 Q. 12:25.
616 The word *ruh* ends in the letter *haʾ*, while the word *badan* begins with *baʾ*.

the authority of Sufyan al-Thawri, on the authority of al-Aʿmash, on the authority of Waʾil, on the authority of Abu Musa al-Ashʿari that someone told the Prophet – may God bless and greet him://406 "Can a man love someone without attaching himself to him?" The Prophet answered: "Man is [always] with one whom he loves." I heard Shaykh Abu ʿAbd al-Rahman al-Sulami say: I heard ʿAbdallah al-Razi say: I heard Abu ʿUthman al-Hiri say: I heard Abu Hafs [al-Haddad] say: "Most damage to the [Sufi's spiritual] states comes from three things: the transgression of the gnostics, the infidelity of the lovers, and the falsehood of the aspirants. Abu ʿUthman explained: "the transgression of the gnostics" means that they turn their sight, tongue and hearing toward the affairs and delights of this world; "the infidelity of the lovers" is that they choose their passion over against contentment with God – may He be great and exalted – in whatever befalls them; and "the falsehood of the aspirants" is that they remember and watch creatures more than they remember and watch God – may He be great and exalted!

I also heard him [al-Sulami] say: I heard Abu Bakr al-Razi say: I heard Abu ʾl-Qasim al-Jawhari say: I heard Abu ʿAli Mimshad b. Saʿid al-ʿUkbari say: "A male swallow sought the affection of a female one under the dome of Solomon's palace. She rejected his courtship, and he told her: 'How can you reject me? If you wish, I will collapse this dome upon Solomon!' Solomon – peace be upon him – summoned him and asked: 'What caused you to say such a thing?' The male swallow replied: 'O prophet of God! One cannot blame the lovers for the things they say!' Solomon said: 'You have spoken the truth!'"

Passionate longing (*shawq*)

God – may He be great and exalted – said: "Who so looks to encounter God, God's term is coming."[617] ʿAli b. Ahmad b. ʿAbdan al-Ahwazi informed us: Ahmad b. ʿUbayd al-Basri informed us: Ibn Abi Qammash informed us: Ismaʿil b. Zurara informed us: on the authority of Hammad b. Zayd: ʿAtaʾ b. al-Saʾib informed us on the authority of his father: "[Once] ʿAmmar b. Yasir[618] was performing a prayer with us. He cut it short, and I asked him: 'Why did you make it lighter [than usual], Abu Yaqzan?' He answered: 'No harm for me in that! I prayed to God with the [supplicatory] prayers that I heard from the Messenger of God – may God bless and greet him.' When he finished his prayer, one of those present followed him and asked him about that prayer. He answered: 'My God, by Your knowledge of the Unseen and by Your power over Your creatures, let me live a life that You know is best for me//407 and let me die a death that You know is best for me! My God, I ask that You grant me fear of You inwardly and outwardly, and I ask that you grant me a truthful word in both contentment

---

617 Q. 29:5.
618 A Companion of the Prophet and a partisan of ʿAli, who was killed at the battle of Siffin in 37/657.

and anger, I ask that You grant me the just mean in wealth and poverty, I ask that You grant me a never-ending bliss and an incessant joy! I ask that You grant me satisfaction with Your judgement and a pleasant life after death. I ask that You grant me the vision of Your noble face and passionate longing for a meeting with You without a harmful affliction nor a misleading temptation. My God, adorn us with the adornment of faith! My God, place us among those who walk on the right path!'"

The master [al-Qushayri] said: "Passionate longing is the heart's desire to meet its beloved; it is equal to the amount of love. I heard the master Abu ʿAli al-Daqqaq making a distinction between passionate longing (*shawq*) and yearning (*ishtiyaq*), when he said: "Passionate longing subsides after the meeting and vision [of the beloved], and yearning completely disappears after the meeting." About this they recite the following:

> No sooner than a gaze is deflected by his sight,
> It returns to him full of passion.

I heard Shaykh Abu ʿAbd al-Rahman al-Sulami say: I heard al-Nasrabadhi say: "All creatures possess the station of passionate longing, while they do not possess yearning, because whoever enters the state of yearning loses his mind, leaving no trace or constancy (*qarar*) behind him." It is related that Ahmad b. Hamid al-Aswad came to ʿAbdallah b. Munazil and said: "I saw in a dream that you will die in a year. Shouldn't you prepare for the departure?" ʿAbdallah b. Munazil responded to him, saying: "You have given us a long time! Will I [be able] to live for one year? I found consolation in that verse of al-Thaqafi (he meant Abu ʿAli [al-Thaqafi]):

> O you, who bemoans his passionate longing due to the long separation,
> Be patient, perhaps you will meet the one you love tomorrow!"

Abu ʿUthman [al-Hiri] said: "A sign of passionate longing is to lovingly welcome death with relief." Yahya b. Muʿadh said: "One of the signs of passionate longing is the weaning of one's members from temptations (*shahawat*)." I heard the master Abu ʿAli al-Daqqaq say: "David – peace be upon him – went out into the desert all on his own and God revealed to him: 'Why do I see you all alone, David?' He answered: 'My God,//408 my heart has preferred longing for Your company over itself and barred me from keeping the company of creatures!' Then God Most High revealed to him: 'Go back to them! You have come to me as a runaway slave, whereas I have recorded you into the Guarded Tablet as a great hero!'" It is related that there once was an old woman, one of whose relatives returned from a trip. Her family displayed joy [at his arrival], whereas the old woman started to cry. They asked her: "What makes you cry?" She answered: "The arrival of this youth reminded me of the day on which [we shall be brought] before God Most High."

Someone asked Ibn ʿAtaʾ about passionate longing. He answered: "The burning of the intestines, the inflammation of the hearts, and the shredding of the livers." He was also asked: "What is greater: loving passion, or love?" He answered: "Love, because loving passion is born out of it." One Sufi said: "Loving passion is an inflammation that begins in the folds of the intestines and occurs as a result of separation. It dies down as the meeting draws near. When the innermost selves are dominated by the contemplation of the beloved, they are no longer subject to passionate longing." A Sufi was asked whether he had experienced passionate longing. He answered: "No, for passionate longing is after someone who is absent, whereas He is [always] present." I heard the master Abu ʿAli al-Daqqaq say about the words of God – may He be great and exalted, "I [Moses] have hastened to Thee, O my Lord, only that I may satisfy Thee",[619] that it means "[I hastened] out of passionate longing for Thee"; however, he concealed it[620] by the word "satisfaction". I also heard him – may God Most High have mercy on him – say: "One of the signs of passionate longing is that the one who stands on the carpet of well-being (ʿawafi) desires death, as happened to Joseph – peace be upon him. When he was thrown into a well, he did not say: '[God] let me die!'; nor did he say this when he was thrown into [Pharaoh's] prison. Only when his parents came to him, his brothers prostrated themselves before him and sovereignty and bliss were perfected for him, did he say: 'Receive me to Thee [after my death] in true submission!'"[621] They have this meaning in mind when they recite:

> We experience the utmost joy; however, only through you is our joy complete
> Shame on us for our condition, O my beloved people, for you are absent, whereas we are present.

They also recited about this:

> Someone rejoices at the new festival, while there's no joy in it for me
> My joy would only be complete, if my beloved were to be present here.//409

Ibn Khafif said: "Loving passion is the repose of the hearts in the ecstatic encounter [with God] (*wajd*) and the love of an intimate meeting [with Him]." Abu Yazid [al-Bistami] said: "God has servants who, if He were to bar them from seeing Him in Paradise, would seek to escape from Paradise, in the same way as the inhabitants of the hellfire seek to escape from it."

Muhammad b. ʿAbdallah al-Sufi informed us: Abu ʾl-ʿAbbas al-Hashimi informed us at Baydaʾ[622]: Muhammad b. ʿAbdallah al-Khuzaʿi told us: ʿAbdallah al-Ansari said: I heard al-Husayn al-Ansari say: "In a dream I saw that the Day of Judgement had arrived and there was a man standing under God's throne.

---

619 Q. 20:84.
620 That is, the passionate longing.
621 Q. 12:101.
622 The names of several Iranian cities and towns.

God – praise be to Him – asked: 'My angels, who is this?' They answered that God knew best. He then said: 'This is Maʿruf al-Karkhi. He is intoxicated with the love of Me and will only come to when he meets Me!'" In another version of the story of this dream God says: "This is Maʿruf al-Karkhi. He left this world longing for God, and God – may He be great and exalted – permitted him to gaze at Him." Faris said: "The hearts of those who long passionately for God are enlightened by the light of God Most High. When their passionate longing is stirred, this light fills both the heavens and the earth. God then introduces them to His angels, saying: 'These ones are passionately longing for Me. I want you to bear witness that I passionately long for them even more than they do.'"

I heard the master Abu ʿAli al-Daqqaq say the following about the words of the Prophet – peace be upon him: "I ask that You grant me passionate longing for a meeting with Me." "Passionate longing consists of one hundred parts, of which ninety-nine belong to Him, and one is distributed among all mankind. He wanted even this part for Himself as well, being jealous that even a splinter of passionate longing might belong to someone else." It is said: "The passionate longing of those who are near to God is more perfect than the passionate longing of those who are still veiled [from Him]." Therefore, they recite the following:

> The worst affliction is passionate longing on a day when the tents
> [of the lovers] are close to one another.

It is said: "Those who experience passionate longing are gulping the sweetness of death when it arrives, because the pleasure of the arrival [in His presence] (*wusul*) unveiled to them is sweeter than honey [to them]." I heard Muhammad b. al-Husayn say: I heard ʿAbdallah b. ʿAli say: I heard Jaʿfar say: I heard al-Junayd say: I heard al-Sari [al-Saqati] say: "Passionate longing is the greatest station for the gnostic, when he has realized its True Reality (*tahaqqaq*); and when he has realized it, he forgets everything that distracts him from the One for Whom he is longing."//410 Abu ʿUthman al-Hiri commented on the words of God Most High, "God's term is coming",[623] saying: "This is the solace of those who passionately long for Him."

It is related that God Most High revealed to David – peace be upon him: "Tell the young men of Israel: 'Why are you busying yourselves with something other than Me, while I have passionate longing for you? Whence this rudeness?!'" It is also related that God – may He be great and exalted – revealed to David – peace be upon him: "If only those who turn their backs on Me knew how I aspire to them, how I seek their company, and how passionately I want them to abandon their disobedience, they would have died of passionate longing for Me and the joints of their bodies would have been severed from one another because of [their] love for Me. This is what I wish for those who turn their backs on Me. What, then, will I wish for those who turn to Me?!" It is recorded in the Torah:

---

623 Q. 29:5.

"We have passionate longing for you, yet you long not for Us; We frighten you, yet you are not afraid [of Us]; We lament for you, yet you voice no lament [for Us]."

I heard the master Abu ʿAli al-Daqqaq say: "Shuʿayb[624] wept until he became blind. God – may He be great and exalted – restored his eye-sight. He then wept more until he turned blind again. God – may He be great and exalted – restored his eye-sight once again. Again, he wept until he turned blind. Then God Most High revealed to him: 'If you were weeping for the sake of Paradise, I have already allowed you to enter it; if you were weeping for the fear of Hell, I have already exonerated you from it.' Shuʿyab said: 'No, I [wept] out of passionate longing for You.' God revealed to him: 'This is why I made my prophet and interlocutor (*kalimi*)[625] serve you for ten years!'"

It is said: "Whoever longs for God, all things long for him." According to a [prophetic] report, "Paradise longs for three [individuals]: ʿAli, ʿAmmar [b. Yasir][626] and Salman [al-Farisi]."[627] I heard the master Abu ʿAli al-Daqqaq say: "One Sufi master said: 'I came to the marketplace where all things longed for me, while I remained free from them.'"

I heard the master Abu ʿAbd al-Rahman al-Sulami say: I heard ʿAbdallah b. Jaʿfar say: I heard Muhammad b. ʿUmar al-Ramli say: Muhammad b. Jaʿfar the imam told us: Ishaq b. Ibrahim told us: Marhum told us: I heard Malik b. Dinar say: "I found the following in the Torah: 'We have a passionate longing for you, but you long not for Us; We play the flute for you, but you dance not.'" //411 I heard Muhammad b. ʿAbdallah al-Sufi say: I heard Muhammad b. Farhan say: I heard al-Junayd say, when someone asked him why the lover weeps when he meets his beloved: "[He weeps] out of joy [at meeting] him and because of the strength of his longing for him. I have heard that two brothers [met] and embraced each other. One of them exclaimed: 'O passionate longing!', while the other cried: 'O [painful] ecstasy!'"

On how [God] protects the hearts of Sufi masters and on [the necessity of] not opposing them [in anything they do]

God Most High said regarding the story about Moses and al-Khadir[628] – peace be upon them both: "Shall I follow thee so that thou teachest me, of what thou hast been taught, right judgement?"[629] The master [al-Qushayri] commented: "When

---

624 An Arabian prophet mentioned in the Qurʾan (11:91); he was sent to the "People of the Thicket", whose identity remains a moot point. Shuʿyab is sometimes identified by Qurʾan commentators as Jethro, the father-in-law of Moses, mentioned in Exodus (for example, 3:1; 4:18.)
625 That is, Moses, to whom God spoke directly; see Q. 27:28.
626 A Companion of the Prophet, who sided with ʿAli and was killed at the Battle of Siffin in 37/657.
627 A famous Companion of the Prophet, who died in 35/655.
628 Q. 18:60–78.
629 Q. 18:66.

he [Moses] wanted to accompany al-Khadir, he observed the rules of proper behavior. At first, he asked the permission to be a companion, to which al-Khadir replied by setting a condition for him that he [Moses] not contradict him in anything, nor oppose any of his judgements. When Moses – peace be upon him – disagreed with him, he [al-Khadir] forgave him. He did the same another time. However, when it came to the third time – three being the last number of the small amount and the first of the large one – he sought separation [from him], saying: 'This is the parting between me and thee.'"[630]

Al-Hasan al-Ahwazi informed us: Ahmad b. ʿUbayd al-Basri told us: Abu Salim al-Qazzaz told us: Yazid b. Bayan told us: Abu ʾl-Rajaʾ[631] told us on the authority of Anas b. Malik, who said that the Messenger of God – may God bless and greet him – said: "A young man does not honor an old man without God Most High appointing someone who will honor him when he gets old." I heard the master Abu ʿAli al-Daqqaq – may God have mercy on him – say: "The beginning of every separation is controversy (*mukhalafa*)." He implied that whoever opposes his master has forfeited his spiritual path (*tariqa*) and the [spiritual] bond between them is broken, although they may continue to share the same space. Whoever has accompanied a Sufi master, then opposed him in his heart, has violated the pact of companionship, which requires repentance from him. At the same time, some Sufi masters say: "Disobedience toward masters cannot be expiated by any repentance." I heard the master Abu ʿAbd al-Rahman al-Sulami say: "I set out to Marv when my master Abu Sahl al-Suʿluki was still alive. Before I departed, he used to hold a teaching session on Friday mornings during which [attendees] read the text of the Qurʾan, taking turns. When I returned, I found out that he had discontinued that session in order to give room to the lecture session taught by Abu ʾl-Ghafani. I was perplexed by this and kept saying to myself: 'He has replaced the session of Qurʾan recitation with a lecture session!' One day, he told me: ʿAbd al-Rahman, what do people say about me?' I told him: 'They say that you discontinued the session of Qurʾan recitation in order to set up a lecture session!' He told me: 'Whoever asks his teacher "why?" will not prosper.'" It is known that al-Junayd said: "One day I came to al-Sari [al-Saqati] and he ordered me to do something. I fulfilled the task quickly, and when I came back he gave me a piece of paper, saying: 'This is for your fulfilling your task for me quickly!' I read the paper, which said: 'I heard a camel driver sing this in the desert:

> I weep and do you know what makes me weep? I weep out of fear that you will abandon me, that my bond with you will be severed and that you will desert me.'"

It is related that Abu ʾl-Hasan al-Hamadani al-ʿAlawi said: "One night I was with Jaʿfar al-Khuldi. [Earlier] at home, I had ordered that a chicken be broiled in the

---

630 Q. 18:78.
631 According to an alternative reading, "Abu Rahhal".

oven, and I was thinking of it. Ja'far invited me to spend that night with him, but I found an excuse not to, and returned home. [When I came home,] the chicken was taken out of the oven and placed before me. [All of a sudden] a dog entered [the house] through the door and carried the chicken off, because those who were there were distracted [by something]. Then they brought out to us the gravy in which the chicken was cooked. It became entangled in the hem of the servant's garment and spilled over. When I woke up next day, I went to Ja'far. As soon as his gaze fell on me, he said: 'When someone does not protect the hearts of [his] masters, God empowers a dog to punish him!'" I heard Shaykh Abu 'Abd al-Rahman al-Sulami say: I heard 'Abdallah b. 'Ali al-Tusi say: I heard Abu 'Abdallah al-Dinawari say: I heard al-Hasan al-Damaghani say: I heard 'Ammi al-Bistami[632] relate on the authority of his father that Shaqiq al-Balkhi and Abu Turab al-Nakhshabi came to Abu Yazid al-Bistami. A table cloth [with food] was brought out for them and [there came] a youth who served Abu Yazid. [Shaqiq and Abu Turab] invited him to eat with them. He told them: "I am fasting." Shaqiq told him: "Eat and you will receive a month's worth of fasting as your reward!" However, he declined. Shaqiq then said: "Eat, and you will receive a year's worth of fasting as your reward!" He again declined. Then Abu Yazid exclaimed: "Leave him alone, for he has [now] fallen from God's grace!" [Indeed,] in a year that youth was caught as he was trying to steal something, and his hand was chopped off. I heard the master Abu 'Ali al-Daqqaq say: "Sahl b. 'Abdallah [al-Tustari] ascribed friendship with God (*wilaya*) to a man who was a baker in Basra. One of Sahl b. 'Abdallah's friends heard about this and aspired to see that man. He set out for//413 Basra and went to the baker's shop. He observed the baker baking bread with his head covered with a veil,[633] as was the custom of bakers. [The visitor] said to himself: 'If he were a friend of God his hair would not be burned even without the veil.' He then greeted the baker and asked him about something. However, the baker told him: 'You thought ill of me, so do not bother to talk to me now!' and he refused to talk to him."

I heard the master Abu 'Abd al-Rahman al-Sulami say: I heard 'Abdallah al-Razi say that he heard Abu 'Uthman al-Hiri praise Muhammad b. al-Fadl al-Balkhi. Al-Razi aspired to see him and came to visit him. However, [when he met al-Balkhi] he did not find him to be as he had expected. He returned to Abu 'Uthman and the latter asked him: "How did you find him?" He answered: "I did not find him to be as I expected him to be." Abu 'Uthman told him: "You thought ill of him, and when one thinks ill of another, one is barred from his virtues. Go back to him with respect." So 'Abdallah returned to him [with respect] and [this time] benefited from his visit. It is related that 'Amr b. 'Uthman al-Makki saw al-Husayn b. Mansur [al-Hallaj] write something and asked him what it was. He answered: "With this I can compete with (*u'arid*) the Qur'an!" [On hearing this,] 'Amr b. 'Uthman cursed him and abandoned him.

---

632 That is, "my paternal uncle".
633 To protect his face and hair from the intense heat of the oven.

Sufi masters say: "What happened to him [al-Hallaj]⁶³⁴ long after that was because of the curse of that master."⁶³⁵

I heard the master Abu ʿAli al-Daqqaq – may God Most high have mercy on him – say: "When the inhabitants of Balkh expelled Muhammad b. al-Fadl from their city, he cursed them, saying: 'God, deprive them of sincerity!' From that time on, not a single veracious person has come from Balkh." I heard Ahmad b. Yahya al-Abiwardi say: "Whoever has won the satisfaction of his master will not receive his reward during his lifetime, so that his praise for that master would not leave his heart. Only when the master dies will God – may He be great and exalted – show him the reward due to him from the master's satisfaction. However, when someone's master is dissatisfied with him, he too will not receive the recompense for this dissatisfaction as long as his master is alive in order that the master may have no pity on him, for by their nature masters are all-forgiving. Only when the master dies will the disciple [who earned his dissatisfaction] be recompensed."

Listening to music (samaʿ)

God – may He be great and exalted – said: "So give thou good tidings to My servants who give ear to the Word and follow the fairest of it."⁶³⁶ The definite article of "the Word" implies that it has an all-comprehensive and universal [meaning], as indicated by His praise of those who follow "the fairest" of it. God Most High said: "They shall walk with joy in a green meadow."⁶³⁷ According to one interpretation, ["walking with joy"] means listening to music. Know that "listening to music" is permissible, when it means the perception of beautiful sounds and pleasant melodies, when the listener//414 does not intend anything that is prohibited, when he does not listen to anything that is condemned by the Divine Law, when he allows no free rein to his passions, and is not seduced by the amusement that resides in it.

There is no disagreement that poems were recited before the Messenger of God – may God bless and greet him – and that he listened to them, without condemning those who recited them. If he allowed listening to this poetry without musical accompaniment, [there is no reason why his] judgement would be different, if it were to be listened to when musical accompaniment takes place. This much is obvious. [Furthermore] the listener should have an abundant desire to perform acts of obedience [to God] and remember the [high spiritual] ranks that God Most High has established for His Godfearing servants, so that this would make him free from any lapses and immediately bring pure divine visitations to his heart, [all of] which is laudable from the standpoint of religion and preferred from the viewpoint of the Divine Law.

---

634 He was executed in Baghdad in 309/922 on charges of heresy.
635 That is, ʿAmr al-Makki.
636 Q. 39:17–18.
637 Q. 30:15.

In the statements of the Messenger of God – may God bless and greet him – there are some things that resemble poetry, although he may not have intended it to be such. Abu ʾl-Hasan ʿAli b. Ahmad al-Ahwazi informed us: Ahmad b. ʿUbayd al-Saffar informed us: al-Harith b. Abi Usama told us: Abu ʾl-Nadr told us: Shuʿba told us on the authority of Humayd, who said: I heard Anas [b. Malik] say: "The [Prophet's] Helpers[638] (*ansar*) were digging the ditch,[639] chanting the following:

> We have pledged our allegiance to Muhammad in [his] struggle (*jihad*)
> As long as we are alive.

"The Messenger – may God bless and greet him – responded to them, saying: 'O God, there's no life except that of the Hereafter, be benevolent to the Helpers and the Emigrants!'" Although this phrase of the Messenger – may God bless and greet him – is not composed according to a poetic meter, it is still close to poetry. The first Muslims and the great scholars [of the subsequent generations] used to listen to the chanting of poetry. Among those of them who allowed it was Malik b. Anas, and all the people of the Hijaz allowed singing (*ghinaʾ*). As for the songs of the camel drivers (*hidaʾ*), all of them agreed that it was permissible. Reports and traditions to this effect are abundant. It is related that Ibn Jurayj permitted listening to music. Someone asked him: "When you will be brought [before God] on the Day of Judgement with your good and evil deeds, on which side will your [allowing] of music be?" He answered, "Neither among the good, nor among the evil", implying that it is allowed (*mubah*).[640] As for al-Shafiʿi,[641] he did not prohibit it, although he considered it to be reprehensible for the common folk. However, if someone makes singing his profession or listens to it constantly by way of entertainment, then his testimony [in court] is to be rejected. While al-Shafiʿi considered listening to music among those things that diminish one's manhood, he nevertheless did not attribute it to [the category of] actions prohibited [by the Law].//415

However, we are not talking here about this kind of listening, for this group[642] occupies too high a rank to listen to music for the sake of entertainment, or to sit at a music session negligently, or to busy their hearts with any nonsense (*laghw*), or to listen to music in an unsuitable manner. Many reports concerning

---

638 The Prophet's followers in Medina, as opposed to the Emigrants, who left Mecca to follow him to Medina.
639 In anticipation of the siege of Medina by the hostile Meccan force and its allies, the Prophet ordered a ditch to be dug around the vulnerable parts of the city.
640 One of the intermediate categories of Islamic law that fall in between acts that are strictly prohibited and strongly commanded. Being "allowed" means that a certain act is neither religiously reprehensible, nor laudable, but is tolerated.
641 A great legal scholar, who established one of the four major schools of Sunni law. The author of the present book, al-Qushayri, adhered to the Shafiʿi legal school.
642 The Sufis.

the permissibility of listening to music are reported on the authority of Ibn ʿUmar.⁶⁴³ The same is true of ʿAbdallah b. Jaʿfar b. Abi Talib and ʿUmar [b. al-Khattab] – may God be pleased with all of them – who [also] transmitted reports about the singing of caravan drivers. Poems were recited in the presence of the Prophet – may God bless and greet him – and he did not prohibit it. It is also related that he himself asked for [some] poems to be recited [to him]. It is also well known and obvious that [once] he entered the house of ʿAʾisha – may God be pleased with her – when two of [her] slave girls were singing there, yet he did not prohibit them [from singing].

Shaykh Abu ʿAbd al-Rahman al-Sulami informed us: Muhammad b. Jaʿfar b. Muhammad b. Matar informed us: al-Hubab b. Muhammad al-Tustari told us: Abu ʾl-Ashʿath informed us: Muhammad b. Bakr al-Bursani told us: Shuʿba told us on the authority of Hisham b. ʿUrwa, on the authority of his father, on the authority of ʿAʾisha – may God be pleased with her – that she related that Abu Bakr al-Siddiq⁶⁴⁴ – may God be pleased with him – came to her, when two singing-girls were singing about how the Helpers were fighting each other at the Battle of Buʿath.⁶⁴⁵ Abu Bakr said twice: "The flute of the Devil!" while the Prophet – may God bless and greet him – said: "Leave them⁶⁴⁶ alone, Abu Bakr! Each folk has its own festival, and our festival is today!" ʿAli b. Ahmad al-Ahwazi informed us: Ahmad b. ʿUbayd informed us: ʿUthman b. ʿUmar al-Dabbi told us: Abu Kamil told us: Abu ʿAwana told us on the authority of al-Ajlah, on the authority of Abu Zubayr, on the authority of ʿAʾisha – may God be pleased with her – that she arranged a marriage for a female relative of hers on the Helpers' side. The Prophet – may God bless and greet him – came and asked: "Have you taken the bride to the bridegroom?" ʿAʾisha said that they had. The Prophet asked: "Did you send anyone who would sing [for them]?" She said no. The Prophet said: "The Helpers like love songs. You should have sent [them] someone who would recite this [poem]:

> We have come to you, we have come to you
> Greet us and we shall greet you!"//416

The master and imam Abu Bakr Muhammad b. al-Hasan b. Furak – may God be pleased with him – informed us: Ahmad b. Mahmud b. Khurrazadh told us: al-Hasan b. al-Harith al-Ahwazi said: Saʿid told us on the authority of Sadaqa bint Abi ʿImran that she said: ʿAlqama b. Marthad told us on the authority of Zadhan, on the authority of al-Baraʾ b. ʿAzib, who said that he heard the Messenger of God – may God bless and greet him – say: "Adorn the Qurʾan with

---

643 Son of the second caliph ʿUmar b. al-Khattab.
644 The first caliph and ʿAʾisha's father.
645 This battle occurred in 617 C.E. between the two major Medinan tribes, Aws and Khazraj, whose members later invited Muhammad to arbitrate between them and became his first Medinan followers.
646 That is, the two singing girls.

your voices, for a beautiful voice makes the Qurʾan more beautiful." ʿAli b. Ahmad b. ʿAbdan al-Ahwazi informed us: Ahmad b. ʿUbayd told us: ʿUthman b. ʿUmar al-Dabbi informed us: Abu ʾl-Rabiʿ told us: ʿAbd al-Salam b. Hashim told us: ʿAbdallah b. Muharrir,[647] on the authority of Qatada, on the authority of Anas b. Malik, said that the Messenger of God – may God bless and greet him – said: "Everything has its adornment, and the adornment of the Qurʾan is a beautiful voice." ʿAli b. Ahmad al-Ahwazi informed us: Ahmad b. ʿUbayd informed us: Yunus al-Karimi[648] told us: al-Dahhaq b. Makhlad Abu ʿAsim told us: Shabib b. Bishr al-Halabi told us on the authority of Anas b. Malik that the Messenger of God – may God bless and greet him – said: "Two sounds are cursed: the sound of wailing at the time of an affliction; and the sound of the flute at the time of happiness (niʿma)."[649] The meaning of the words [of the Messenger] imply his allowing [of listening to music] on certain occasions, so any specific [and hard-and-fast] ruling[650] in this regard should be considered invalid. Reports about this matter are numerous. If we continue to recount such stories further, we shall depart from our goal of being concise. It is told that a certain man recited the following verses in front of the Messenger of God – may God bless and greet him:

> She appeared and her cheek-bones shone like a piece of jet jewelry
> She turned around, and I said to her with my heart all ablaze:
> "Woe unto both of you,[651] is there upon me a sin for my love [of her]?"

The Messenger of God – may God bless and greet him – said: "No!" God Most High bestowed a beautiful voice on some people as a blessing, saying: "He increases creation as He wills."[652] Some interpreters say that among these things is a beautiful voice.//417 At the same time God – praise be to Him – condemned an ugly voice, saying: "The most hideous of voices is the ass's."[653] One cannot ignore [the fact] that the hearts [of people] take pleasure in nice voices and find a repose in them. Thus, a child is calmed by a nice voice and a camel endures the hardships of a journey and the heaviness of its burden when [the caravan driver] sings his song for it. God Most High said: "Do they not consider how the camel was created?"[654] Ismaʿil b. ʿUlayya related: "I used to stroll with al-Shafiʿi – may God have mercy on him – in the heat of the midday. As we were passing a certain place, we heard a person recite something. Al-Shafiʿi told me: 'Let's go there [to listen]!' He then asked me: 'Did this amuse you?' I said: 'No.' He then

---

647 Or "al-Muharraz".
648 Or "al-Kudaymi".
649 According to another version of the text, the last word should be read as *naghama* – that is, "singing".
650 That is, one that absolutely prohibits the practice in question.
651 That is, her cheek-bones.
652 Q. 35:1.
653 Q. 31:19; 31:17, according to Arberry's translation.
654 Q. 88:17.

told me: 'You have no perception!'" The Messenger of God said: "God Most High does not like to listen to anything more than listening to a prophet who sings (*yataghanni*) the Qur'an." ʿAli b. Ahmad al-Ahwazi informed us: Ahmad b. ʿUbayd informed us: Ibn Mulhan told us: Yahya b. Bukayr told us: al-Layth told us on the authority of ʿUqayl, on the authority of Ibn Shihab, who said that Abu Salama informed him on the authority of Abu Hurayra that the Messenger of God – may God bless and greet him – said: "God Most High does not like to listen to anything more than to a prophet who publicly sings the Qur'an."

It is related that the jinn, human beings, birds and beasts used to listen to David – peace be upon him – when he recited the Psalms. They used to carry away four hundred funeral biers from his reciting session with bodies of those who had died while listening to his recitation. The Messenger of God – may God bless and greet him – said to Abu Musa al-Ashʿari:[655] "I was given one of the psalms that used to belong to the tribe of David."//418 Muʿadh b. Jabal said to the Messenger of God – may God bless and greet him: "If I knew that you would listen [to my recitation], I would make it [sound] very beautiful." Abu Hatim al-Sijistani informed us: ʿAbdallah b. ʿAli al-Sarraj informed us: Abu Bakr Muhammad b. Dawud al-Dinawari al-Duqqi[656] related: "I was in the desert, where I came across a Bedouin tribe. A man from that tribe hosted me. There I saw a black slave in shackles and some dead camels lying in the yard. The slave told me: 'This night you are a guest and you are [thus] held dear by my master. Intercede before him on my behalf and he will not turn you down.' I told the host: 'I will not eat any of your food until you free this slave!' The host exclaimed: 'This slave has impoverished me and ruined my property!' I asked him what he had done. The host said: 'He has a beautiful voice. I used to live off the work of these camels. This slave put a very heavy load on them and sang to them [so beautifully] that they ran three days' worth of distance in just one day. When he finally unloaded them, they died immediately. However, I grant your wish.' And he removed the shackles from the slave. In the morning, I wished to listen to his voice. I asked [the host] for that, and he ordered the slave to sing to a camel that was near a well, drinking. When the slave started to sing, the camel rushed forth headlong and tore up his rope. I do not think I have ever heard a more beautiful voice. I fell unconscious [and lay there] until the host gave a sign to him to fall silent."

I heard Shaykh Abu ʿAbd al-Rahman al-Sulami say: I heard Muhammad b. ʿAbdallah b. ʿAbd al-ʿAziz say: I heard Abu ʿAmr[657] al-Anmati say: I heard al-Junayd say, when someone asked him: "Why is a man [usually] quiet, but becomes agitated when he hears music?" He answered: "God Most High addressed [disembodied human] souls during the primordial pact, saying: 'Am I

---

655 A distinguished Companion of the Prophet and military leader of the early Muslim community who died around 42/662.
656 Or "al-Raqqi".
657 Or "ʿAbu ʿUmar".

not your Lord?' They answered: 'Yes, we testify',[658] and the spirits [of human beings] fully absorbed the sound of these words, so whenever they listen to music, the remembrance of that [original act of] hearing agitates them." I heard the master Abu 'Ali al-Daqqaq say: "Listening to music is prohibited for the common folk because they still remain under the influence of their [lower] souls; it is permitted for ascetics (*zuhhad*) because they engage in the spiritual struggle [against their base instincts]; it is recommended (*mustahabb*) to our companions[659] because they enliven their hearts [through it]."//419 I heard Abu Hatim al-Sijistani say: I heard Abu Nasr al-Sufi say: I heard al-Wajihi say: I heard Abu 'Ali al-Rudhbari say that al-Harith al-Muhasibi used to say: "There are three things that one enjoys when one happens to have them; they, however, have eluded us. [They are:] A beautiful face, when it is accompanied by self-restraint; a beautiful voice, when it is accompanied by piety; and a beautiful friendship, when it is accompanied by fidelity."

Someone asked Dhu 'l-Nun about a beautiful voice. He answered: "[Beautiful] speeches and [subtle] gestures that God Most High has placed in every righteous man and woman." When he was asked about listening to music another time, he responded: "[This is] a divine visitation (*warid*) that excites the hearts [to seek] God. Whoever heeds it in truth (*bi-haqq*), attains truth (*tahaqqaq*), and whoever heeds it with his lower soul, apostatizes (*tazandaq*)." Ja'far b. Nusayr related on the authority of al-Junayd that the latter said: "[Divine] mercy (*rahma*) descends upon the poor in three places: when they listen to music, for they hear it only through a true aspiration and speak only out of an ecstatic encounter [with God]; when they eat their food, for they eat it only out of a true need; and during a discussion of religious matters, for they mention only the [pious] character traits of God's friends (*awliya*)." I heard Muhammad b. al-Husayn say: I heard al-Husayn b. Ahmad b. Ja'far say: I heard Abu Bakr Mimshadh al-Dinawari say: I heard al-Junayd say: "Listening to music is a temptation (*fitna*) for someone who seeks it, and a repose for someone who suddenly encounters it." It is also related that al-Junayd said: "Listening to music requires three things: time (*zaman*), a place (*makan*), and friends (*ikhwan*)."

Someone asked al-Shibli about listening to music. He answered: "Its outward aspect is temptation (*fitna*), while its inward aspect is exhortation ('*ibra*). Whoever understands its subtle allusion is granted the listening that brings exhortation; if not, he falls victim to [its] temptation and sets himself up for a trial." They say: "Listening to music is allowed only to one whose soul is dead and whose heart is still living. The soul of such a person is slaughtered by the sword of spiritual self-exertion and his heart is enlivened by the light of compliance [with God's will]." Someone inquired of Abu Ya'qub al-Nahrajuri about listening to music. He answered: "This is a state that brings about the return to the [divine] mysteries through the burning [of one's self]."//420 They say: "Listening to music is a

---

658 Q. 7:172.
659 That is, the Sufis.

delicious nourishment for the spirits of [divine] gnostics." I heard the master Abu ʿAli al-Daqqaq say: "Listening to music is [man's] nature (*tabʿ*), unless it comes from [obeying] the Divine Law; it is violation, unless it comes from a true [aspiration]; and it is temptation, unless it comes from pious exhortation." They say: "Listening to music is of two types. [The first type is] listening to music by way of religious learning and sobriety. One who takes part in it must have knowledge of [divine] names and attributes, or else he will fall into pure unbelief. [The other type is] listening to music by way of a spiritual state. One who takes part in it must eliminate all his human attributes and purify himself from all mundane attachments and traces by manifesting the characteristics of the True Reality." Ahmad b. Abi ʾl-Hawari related: "I asked Abu Sulayman [al-Darani] about listening to music." He said: "I like it more when it comes from two rather than one." Someone asked Abu ʾl-Husayn al-Nuri about "Sufi". He responded: "It is he who listens to music and chooses means."[660] Once someone asked Abu ʿAli al-Rudhbari about listening to music. He answered: "If only we could make it pure step by step!"

I heard Shaykh Abu ʿAbd al-Rahman al-Sulami say: I heard Abu ʿUthman al-Maghribi say: "Whoever lays claim to listening to music without listening to the voices of birds, the creaking of the door, or the rattling of winds is a false pretender." I heard Abu Hatim al-Sijistani say: I heard Abu Nasr al-Sarraj al-Tusi say: I heard Abu ʾl-Tayyib Ahmad b. Muqatil al-ʿAkki say: Jaʿfar [al-Khuldi] related: "Ibn Ziri,[661] a companion of al-Junayd, was a distinguished Sufi master. He used to frequent places where listening to music took place. If he liked it, he would spread his garment on the floor and say: 'The Sufi is wherever his heart is.' If he did not like it, he would say, 'Listening to music is only for those who possess hearts (*arbab al-qulub*)', then walk away, taking his sandals with him."[662] I heard Muhammad b. al-Husayn – may God have mercy on him – say: I heard ʿAbd al-Wahid b. Bakr say: I heard ʿAbdallah b. ʿAbd al-Majid say: "Someone asked Ruwaym [b. Ahmad] about the ecstasy the Sufis experience (*wajd*) during listening to music. He answered: 'They witness realities that are hidden from others. They point to them, exclaiming: "[Come] to me!" "[Come] to me!" Then a veil falls and their joy turns into grief; some of them tear their clothes, others scream, still others weep – each in accord with what was allotted to him.'" I heard Muhammad b. Ahmad b. Muhammad al-Tamimi say: I heard ʿAbdallah b. ʿAli say: I heard al-Husri say in one of his lectures: "What do I do with a listening that ceases when the one who listens [himself] ceases to be? This is why your listening must be permanent, and not interrupted."//421 He [ʿAbdallah b. ʿAli] also said that al-Husri said: "[The listener] must have a

---

660 That is, one who carefully selects his means of livelihood in order to avoid things that are unlawful.
661 Or "Ibn Zizi".
662 This phrase may be interpreted as a veiled criticism of the participants in the session that he disliked.

permanent thirst and a permanent drinking, for whenever his drinking increases, his thirst increases as well." According to Mujahid,[663] God's words "They shall walk with joy in a green meadow"[664] mean [that they[665] will be] listening to the maidens of Paradise singing with pleasant voices: "We are eternal, we shall never die; we are blessed, we shall never suffer!" They say: "Listening is a call and ecstasy is aspiration [in response] to it."

I heard Muhammad b. al-Husayn say: I heard Abu ʿUthman al-Maghribi say: "The hearts of the people of the [divine] Truth are always present and their ears are always open." I also heard him say: I heard the master Abu Sahl al-Suʿluki say: "The listener is hovering between veiling (*istitar*) and manifestation (*tajalli*). The veiling necessitates inflammation, while the manifestation brings about relief. Out of the veiling originate the movements of the aspirants (*muridun*), while out of the manifestation originates the repose of those who have arrived [at their goal] (*wasilun*). This is the site of uprightness and stability. This is a characteristic of [divine] presence which allows nothing but humility under the passage of awe-inspiring divine visitations. God Most High said [about this]: 'When they were in its presence they said, "Be silent!" ' "[666]

Abu ʿUthman al-Hiri said: "Listening has three faces. One of them [is turned] to the aspirants and beginners, who seek to attain noble spiritual states through it, and in which they may be subject to temptation and hypocrisy. The second face belongs to the veracious ones, who seek to intensify their spiritual states. They listen only to that which agrees with their mystical moments. The third face belongs to the people of uprightness from among the gnostics. They leave God Most High to choose whatever movement or repose may enter their hearts." I heard the master Abu ʿAbd al-Rahman al-Sulami – may God have mercy on him – say: I heard Abu ʾl-Faraj al-Shirazi say: I heard Abu ʿAli al-Rudhbari say: Abu Saʿid al-Kharraz said: "When someone feels that during 'understanding' – that is, during a listening session – he is overwhelmed and his movements take control over him, the sign of his [sincerity]//422 is that his ecstasy makes the listening session in which he participates more beautiful." Shaykh Abu ʿAbd al-Rahman al-Sulami said that when this statement was mentioned to Abu ʿUthman al-Maghribi, he said: "This is just the minor part of this [state]. The real sign [of his sincerity] is that there remains in his session not a single sincere individual who does not feel affection for him, while there also remains no pretender who does not feel alienated from him."

Bundar b. al-Husayn said: "Listening [may occur] according to three different modes. There are those who listen by their [lower] nature, then those who listen by their spiritual state, and those who listen truly.[667] Those who listen by their

---

663 A renowned Qurʾan interpreter, whose work laid the foundations of Qurʾanic exegesis. He died between 100/718 and 104/722.
664 Q. 30:15; 30:14, according to Arberry's translation.
665 That is, the blessed.
666 Q. 46:29.
667 Or "by God" (*bi ʾl-haqq*).

nature can be found both among the commoners and the elite, since human nature is innately prone to a beautiful voice. Those who listen by their spiritual state expect to remember such things as reproach, speech, arrival, departure, proximity, distance, and regrets that someone is gone or desire to see someone arrive [as well as] faithfulness to an agreement, fulfillment of a promise or its violation, remembrance of anxiety or passion, fear of separation or the joy of meeting or the threat of departure and so on. As for those who listen truly, they listen by and for God Most High. They cannot be described by the states that are associated with human passions, for the passions pertain to imperfection and deficiency. Rather, such listeners listen truly and genuinely, not out of any [mundane] need or aspiration. They say that those who listen belong to three classes. First are the children of divine realities who in their listening resort to God's – praise be to Him – addressing them. The second class are those who address God Most High in their hearts by the words that they listen to. They strive to achieve truthfulness in what they point toward God with. The third type are the poor ones who have absolutely no possessions and who have severed all ties with this world and its sins. They listen freely and willingly with their hearts, and they are the closest of all of them to salvation."

I heard Muhammad b. al-Husayn say: I heard Abu Bakr al-Razi say: I heard Abu ʿAli al-Rudhbari say, when asked about listening: "[It is] the unveiling of the innermost selves for the vision of the Beloved." When someone asked [Ibrahim] al-Khawwas, "Why should anyone be stirred by listening to anything other than the Qurʾan, whereas this[668] does not happen to him when he listens to the Qurʾan?", he answered: "Because listening to the Qurʾan is but a shock (*sadma*), so no one is capable of moving during it due to the strength of its overpowering force. Listening to regular speech, on the other hand, results in a relief and repose, so one can move during it."//423 I heard Muhammad b. al-Husayn say: I heard ʿAbdallah b. Muhammad b. ʿAbd al-Rahman al-Razi say: I heard al-Junayd say: "When you see an aspirant who loves listening, know that he still has traces of vanity (*batala*) in him." I also heard him [Muhammad b. al-Husayn] say: I heard ʿAli b. ʿAbdallah al-Baghdadi say: I heard Abu Saʿid al-Ramli say: Sahl b. ʿAbdallah [al-Tustari] said: "Listening to music is a knowledge that God Most High has reserved for Himself. No one but He knows it."

Ahmad b. Muqatil al-ʿAkki related: "When Dhu ʾl-Nun al-Misri entered Baghdad, [local] Sufis gathered around him. Among them was a singer (*qawwal*). The Sufis asked Dhu ʾl-Nun's permission to have him [the singer] perform something for them. He gave them [his] permission, and the singer began to recite:

> Even a little amount of [my] passion for you has caused me [great] pain
> What would happen, if it were to take full control over me?
> You have brought together in my heart a passion that used to be shared with others

---

668 That is, the stirring.

Have you no sympathy for one who is broken by mourning,
who weeps, while one who is free [from affliction] is laughing?!

[On hearing this] Dhu 'l-Nun stood up and fell on his face, blood streaming from his forehead onto the ground. Then one of the Sufis also stood up and displayed ecstatic behavior. Dhu 'l-Nun told him, '[The All-Compassionate] Who sees thee when thou standest',[669] and the man sat down." I heard the master Abu ʿAli al-Daqqaq say about this story: "Dhu 'l-Nun was able to perceive [the true motive of] that man and to let him know that this was not his place,[670] whereas the man was fair enough to accept this from him when he sat down."

I heard Muhammad b. Ahmad b. Muhammad al-Tamimi say: I heard ʿAbdallah b. ʿAli al-Sufi say: I heard al-Duqqi[671] say: I heard Ibn al-Jallaʾ say: "In the Maghrib, there were two [Sufi] masters, who had [numerous] companions and disciples. One was named Jabala, the other Zurayq. One day, Zurayq and his companions came to visit Jabala. One of the companions of Zurayq recited a passage [from the Qurʾan]. On hearing it a companion of Jabala issued a cry and died. The next morning, Jabala asked Zurayq: 'Where is the man who recited yesterday? Let him read again.' The man read a verse [from the Qurʾan]. A companion of Jabala issued a cry and the reciter died. Jabala commented: 'One for one, but the one who started is more at fault!'" Someone asked Ibrahim al-Maristani about movement during a listening session. He responded: "I have heard that Moses – peace be upon him – was sermonizing among the Children of Israel. One of his listeners tore up his shirt [out of ecstasy]. God Most High then revealed to Moses: 'Tell him: "Tear up your heart, not your clothing for Me!"'" Abu ʿAli al-Maghazili asked al-Shibli: "From time to time, a verse from the Book of God – may He be great and exalted – reaches my ears that urges me to abandon [mundane] affairs and to turn away from this world. However, after a while, I return to my original state and to people.//424 Al-Shibli responded: "That which draws you to Him is His sympathy and kindness for you from Him, while that which returns you to yourself is His pity for you from Him, because it is not appropriate for you to divest yourself of all ability and power, when you turn to Him." I heard Abu Hatim al-Sijistani say: I heard Abu Nasr al-Sarraj say: I heard Ahmad b. Muqatil al-ʿAkki say: "I was in a mosque with al-Shibli one night during the month of Ramadan. He and I were praying behind the imam of that mosque, when the imam recited: 'If We willed, We could take away what We have revealed to thee.'[672] Al-Shibli issued a loud shriek and trembled so [violently] that I said to myself that he was about to give up his spirit. He then exclaimed: 'He says such things to His loved ones!' And he kept repeating this many times."

---

669 Q. 26:218.
670 Or "his station" (*maqamuh*).
671 In another version, "al-Raqqi".
672 Q. 17:86; 17:87, according to Arberry's translation.

It is related that al-Junayd said: "One day I came to al-Sari [al-Saqati] and found a man lying unconscious there. I asked him what had happened to him. He answered: 'He heard a verse from the Book of God Most High.' I said: 'It should be recited to him one more time.' This was done and he came to. Al-Sari asked me: 'Where did you learn this?' I answered: 'The eye[sight] of Jacob was gone because of Joseph's shirt, but it also returned to him due to it.' Al-Sari approved my answer." I heard Abu Hatim al-Sijistani say: I heard Abu Nasr al-Sarraj say: I heard 'Abd al-Wahid b. 'Alwan say: "A young companion of al-Junayd used to issue a loud shriek each time he heard a remembrance of God's name (*dhikr*). Al-Junayd [finally] told him: 'If you do this one more time, you will no longer be my companion!' From then on, each time he heard something [of recollection], he would grow pale and try to restrain himself so that [sweat] would begin to drip from his hair and body. One day, he issued a cry and expired." I heard Abu Hatim al-Sijistani say: I heard Abu Nasr al-Sarraj say: "One of my [Sufi] brothers recounted to me on the authority of Abu 'l-Husayn al-Darraj, saying: 'I left Baghdad in order to meet Yusuf b. al-Husayn al-Razi. When I came to Rayy,[673] I began asking about his residence. Each person I asked would tell me: "What business do you have with this heretic (*zindiq*)?" They were so upset thereby, that I decided to go back. I spent that night in a mosque, thinking: "Since I have come to this city anyway, the least I can do is to visit him!" So I kept inquiring about his whereabouts until I was finally led to his mosque. He was sitting in the *mihrab* with a book-stand in front of him on which there was a copy of the Qur'an. He was reading from it. And lo and behold, he was an imposing master with a handsome face and a beautiful beard. I approached him and greeted him. He returned my greetings. He asked me: "Where [are you] from?" I answered: "From Baghdad. I wanted to visit [you], master." He inquired: "If you were in a strange city and someone were to propose to you, 'Stay with me and I will buy you either a house or a slave girl' would this have possibly prevented you from visiting me?" I said: "Sir, God most High has not tested me with anything like this! Had this happened I would not have known what to do!" He said: "Are you good enough to recite anything?" I said yes, and recited://425

> I saw you building assiduously on my property
> [However,] were you a man of sound judgement
> You would have smashed that which you were building!

When he heard this, he closed the copy of the Qur'an and started to weep until both his beard and his clothing were soaked [with his tears] and I felt pity for him on account of the abundance of his weeping. He then told me: "My son, do not blame the people of Rayy for saying: 'Yusuf b. al-Husayn is a heretic.' Since the time of the prayer I was reading the Qur'an without a single tear dropping from my eye, whereas I felt as if it were the Day of Judgement, because of that verse!"'"

---

673 That is, the native city of al-Razi, as his name ("he of Rayy") indicates.

I heard Muhammad b. Ahmad b. Muhammad al-Sufi say: I heard ʿAbdallah b. ʿAli al-Tusi say: I heard al-Duqqi[674] say: I heard al-Darraj say: "As Ibn al-Fuwati and I were walking along the Tigris between Basra and Ubulla, we came upon a beautiful castle with a watchtower. Upon it was a man with a slave girl, who was singing the following:

On the path of God there is a love that is bestowed on me for you
You change (*tatalawwan*) with every new day, but it is more appropriate for you not to be like that.

Listening underneath the watchtower, was a young man with a leather [begging] bowl, dressed in a patched robe.[675] He exclaimed: 'O girl, by the life of your master, sing once again: "You change with every day, but it is more for you not to be like that."' She repeated this line. The young man said [again]: 'Repeat!' She did. The dervish exclaimed: 'This, by God, is my [constant] change[676] with God!' He then issued a loud cry and his spirit departed. The owner of the castle told the slave girl: 'You are now free for the sake of God Most High!' The people of Basra came over and, when they had finished burying him and praying over him, the owner of the castle stood up and exclaimed: 'Don't you know me, [people]! Bear witness that I give up all I have for the sake of God and that all my slaves are now free!' He then girded himself with a waist-cloth, put on a [shabby] robe, gave away his castle as charity and left. No one has seen his face or heard any news about him ever since."

I heard Muhammad b. Ahmad b. Muhammad al-Sufi say: I heard ʿAbdallah b. ʿAli al-Tusi say: I heard Yahya b. al-Rida al-ʿAlawi say: "When Abu Hulman[677] al-Dimashqi heard a pilgrim performing a circumambulation of the Kaʿba recite: 'O wild thyme!' (*ya saʿtar barri*), he lost conscience and fell down. When he came to, someone asked him about this. He answered: 'I thought that he was saying: "Strive and you will see My goodness! (*isaʿ tara birri*)."'" ʿUtba al-Ghulam heard a man say: "Praise be to the Lord of the heavens, truly, the lover is in distress!" ʿUtba uttered, "You have spoken the truth!", while another man, on hearing this same phrase, said, "You have lied!" Each one heard, according to his [own spiritual] state. I heard Abu Hatim al-Sijistani say: I heard Abu Nasr al-Sarraj say: I heard Abu ʾl-Hasan//426 ʿAli b. Muhammad al-Sufi[678] say: I heard Ruwaym [b. Ahmad] say, when someone asked him about how Sufi masters behave during

---

674 Or "al-Raqqi".
675 That is, the usual attributes of an itinerant dervish.
676 In the sense of "vacillation".
677 This is, obviously, a mistake; his correct name is Abu Hulman al-Farisi. Active in the early 4th/10th century, he was considered to be the founder of a heretical group known as "hulmaniyya". Abu Hulman and his followers espoused a heretical doctrine, according to which God can dwell and be contemplated in beautiful people and objects. He was also known for his predilection for listening to music.
678 Or "al-Sayrafi".

listening sessions. He answered: "As if they were a flock of sheep attacked by a wolf." It is related that Abu Saʿid al-Kharraz said: "I saw ʿAli b. al-Muwaffaq say during a listening session: 'Let me stand!' They raised him; he stood up and behaved ecstatically, whereupon he said: 'I am dancing master! (*shaykh zaffan*.)'" They say that al-Duqqi[679] kept vigil all night until dawn, reciting the following verse, while all those who were present wept. This is this verse:

> By God, give back the heart of a distressed one
> For whose beloved there's no substitute.

I heard Muhammad b. Ahmad al-Tamimi say: I heard ʿAbdallah b. ʿAli al-Sufi say: I heard ʿAli b. al-Husayn b. Ahmad at Basra[680] say: I heard my father say: "I served Sahl b. ʿAbdallah [al-Tustari] for many years without ever seeing him changing his condition during a listening session, whether this be a recollection of God's name or a recitation of the Qurʾan. However, at the end of his life, when he heard [the Qurʾanic verse] 'Today no ransom shall be taken from you',[681] I saw him grow pale and tremble so that he nearly fell down. When he returned to his original state of sobriety (*sahw*), I asked him about this. He answered: 'My dear (*habibi*), we have grown weak!'" Ibn Salim[682] related: "I saw him another time, when [the verse] 'That day, the [true] Kingdom shall belong to the All-Merciful'[683] was read in his presence. His condition changed and he nearly fell. I inquired him about this, and he answered: 'We have become weak!'" This is a feature of the outstanding [masters]: whenever a divine visitation (*warid*) descends on them, no matter how powerful it may be, they prove to be stronger than it.

I heard the master Abu ʿAbd al-Rahman al-Sulami say: "I went to visit Abu ʿUthman al-Maghribi, when someone was drawing water from a well by using a pulley. Abu ʿUthman asked me: 'Abu ʿAbd al-Rahman, do you know what the pulley says?' I said: 'No.' He said: 'It says: "God, God ..."'" I heard Muhammad b. ʿAbdallah al-Sufi say: I heard ʿAli b. Tahir say: I heard ʿAbdallah b. Sahl say: I heard Ruwaym say: It is related that ʿAli b. Abi Talib – may God be pleased with him – said to his companions, when he heard the sound of a [church] bell: "Do you know what it says?" They answered: "No." He said: "It says: 'Praise be to God, truly, truly; the Master is eternal, the One who abides.'" I heard Muhammad b. Ahmad al-Tamimi say: I heard ʿAbdallah b. ʿAli say: I heard Ahmad b. ʿAli al-Karakhi al-Wajihi say: "A group of Sufis used to gather at the house of al-Hasan//427 al-Qazzaz. They were accompanied by singers, whose singing made them ecstatic. When Mimshadh al-Dinawari [once] observed them, they fell

---

679 Or "al-Raqqi".
680 His correct name is Abu ʾl-Hasan Ahmad b. Muhammad b. Salim (Ibn Salim) al-Basri (d. 356/967), the foremost follower, along with his father, of the renowned Sufi master Sahl al-Tustari.
681 Q. 57:15; 57:14, according to Arberry's translation.
682 See note 680.
683 Q. 25:26.

silent. He told them: 'Go back to what you were doing! Were all the musical instruments of this world assembled in my ear, this would not affect my concentration [on God] (*hamm*), nor would this cure my present condition!'" According to the same line of transmission, al-Wajihi said: "In this business of ours[684] we have reached a point that is similar to the edge of a sword. If we were to incline [here] even this much, we would fall into the hellfire." Khayr al-Nassaj said: "Moses, the son of ʿImran[685] – may God bless them both – was preaching to a group of people. One of them screamed. When Moses scolded him, God Most High revealed to him: 'It is because of My kindness that they weep; it is because of their love of Me that they expose themselves [to censure]; it is because of their ecstasy in [finding] Me that they scream! Why, then, do you denounce My servants?'"

Al-Shibli heard someone call: "A dozen cucumbers (*khiyar*) are for one *daniq*[686]!" He issued a cry, saying: "If the virtuous ones (*khiyar*) are one *daniq* for a dozen, what would be the price of the evil ones?!"[687] They say: "When the maidens of Paradise begin to sing, the trees of Paradise blossom." It is related that ʿAwn b. ʿAbdallah ordered a slave girl with a beautiful voice to sing a sad melody to make people cry.

Someone inquired of Abu Sulayman al-Darani about listening to music. He responded: "Each heart that longs for a beautiful voice is weak and must be treated in the same way one treats a child when one wants it to sleep." Abu Sulayman then added: "A beautiful voice does not introduce anything into the heart. Rather it sets in motion something that already resides there." Ibn Abi ʾl-Hawari commented: "By God, Abu Sulayman spoke truth!" Al-Jurayri said [about the Qurʾanic verse]: "Be you [knowledgeable] masters."[688] This means, "[Be] those who listen to God and speak through Him."

Someone asked a Sufi about listening to music. He answered: "Flashes of lighting that glitter, then fade away; lights that appear then disappear. How sweet they are when they remain with someone even for the blink of an eye!" He then recited:

A thought entered into his innermost heart as if it were a lightning bolt that flashed, then disappeared.

They say: "Every [human] limb has a part in listening to music. When a part of it falls on the eye, it weeps; when a part of it falls on the tongue, it cries out; when a part of it falls on the hand, it tears clothes apart and beats the breast; when a part of it falls on the leg, it dances." It is related that when a Persian king died,

---

684 That is, the Sufi path.
685 The Biblical ʿAmram.
686 A small coin equal to one-sixth of a *dirham*.
687 A pun based on the Arabic homonym *khiyar*, which denotes both the "virtuous ones" and the "cucumbers".
688 Q. 3:79; 3:74, according to Arberry's translation.

he left behind a small son. When his subjects wanted to pledge their fealty to him,[689] they asked [themselves]: "How//428 can we determine [the extent of] his knowledge and cleverness?" They then agreed to bring a singer and have him sing something. If the son were to listen attentively, they would know that he was intelligent. So they brought a singer. As soon as he sang something, the suckling laughed. They kissed the ground before him and pledged their fealty to him.

I heard the master Abu ʿAli al-Daqqaq say: "Abu ʿAmr b. Nujayd, al-Nasrabadhi and [Sufis of] their generation assembled in a certain place. Al-Nasrabadhi said: 'I believe that when a group of people gather together, it is better that only one person should speak, while the rest should remain silent rather than engage in backbiting on somebody's account.' Abu ʿAmr retorted: 'Even if you had been backbiting for thirty years, this is still better[690] for you than displaying something you do not really feel at the time of listening.'" I heard the master Abu ʿAli al-Daqqaq – may God have mercy on him – say: "There are three groups of people as far as listening is concerned: the one who aspires to listen (*mutasammiʿ*), the one who listens (*mustamiʿ*), and the [real] listener (*samiʿ*). The first listens according to his mystical moment (*waqt*); the second, according to his [overall] spiritual state (*hal*); and the third listens in truth (*bi-haqq*)." Repeatedly, I asked the master Abu ʿAli al-Daqqaq – may God Most High have mercy on him – for a concession regarding listening to music. However, he kept referring me to things that one must avoid [in it]. Then, after a long companionship [between us] he [finally] said: "Sufi masters say: 'If your heart is attached to God – praise be upon Him – then there's no harm in it!'" Abu ʾl-Hasan ʿAli b. Ahmad al-Ahwazi informed us: Ahmad b. ʿUbayd al-Basri informed us: Ismaʿil b. al-Fadl told us: Yahya b. Yaʿla al-Razi told us: Hafs b. ʿUmar al-ʿUmari told us: Abu ʿAmr ʿUthman b. Badr told us: Harun b. Hamza[691] told us on the authority of al-Ghadafiri,[692] on the authority of Saʿid b. Jubayr, on the authority of [ʿAbdallah] Ibn ʿAbbas – may God be pleased with both of them – that God – praise be to Him – revealed to Moses – peace be upon him: "I have placed in you ten thousand listening faculties, so that you can hear My words, and ten thousand tongues, so that you can respond to Me. However, you are most beloved and close to Me when you multiply your blessings for Muhammad – may God bless and greet him!" It is related that a Sufi saw the Prophet – may God bless and greet him – in a dream. He said: "Mistakes in this [matter] are [especially] numerous." He meant listening to music. I heard Shaykh Abu ʿAbd al-Rahman al-Sulami say: I heard Muhammad b. ʿAbdallah b. Shadhan say: I heard Abu Bakr al-Nihawandi say: I heard ʿAli al-Saʾih say: I heard Abu ʾl-Harith al-Awlasi say: "As I was resting on a roof, in a dream I saw the Devil – may God curse him

---

689 That is, the son.
690 Literally, "more conducive to salvation".
691 Or "Harun Abu Hamza".
692 Or "al-ʿUdhafir".

– on one of the roofs of [the town of] Awlas. On his right was a group of people and on his left was another one. They were dressed in clean clothes. He said to one group: 'Sing!' They sang and performed melodically. The beauty of their singing scared me so that I decided to hurl myself off the roof. He then said [to them]: 'Dance!' and they danced in the most beautiful manner. He then told me: 'Abu ʾl-Harith, I have not found a better way to gain access to you than this!'"

I heard Muhammad b. al-Husayn say: I heard ʿAbdallah b. ʿAli say: "One night//429 I was with al-Shibli – may God have mercy on him. When a singer sang something, al-Shibli issued a shriek and behaved ecstatically, while sitting. Someone asked him: 'Abu Bakr, what's wrong with you? You are sitting in the midst of a [listening] session!' He rose in ecstasy and recited:

I have two intoxications, whereas my boon-companions have just one
This is the [only] thing that singles me out among them."

I also heard him [Muhammad b. al-Husayn] say: I heard Mansur b. ʿAbdallah al-Isbahani say: I heard Abu ʿAli al-Rudhbari say: "As I was passing by a castle [one day], I saw a youth with a handsome face lying on the ground. He was surrounded by a group of people. I inquired about him. They said: 'As he was passing by this castle, [he heard] a slave girl sing:

Great is the resolution of a servant that impels [him] to see you
Isn't it enough for [his] eye to see someone who has already seen you?

He let out a shriek and expired.'"

Miracles of God's friends (*karamat al-awliyaʾ*)

The master Abu ʾl-Qasim [al-Qushayri] says that it is possible for God's friends to display miracles.[693] The proof of the [miracle's] possibility is that it is something that can be conceived by the intellect and that its occurrence does not lead to the suspension of any basic principle. One must ascribe to God – praise be to Him – the ability to originate it, and, since it can be made possible by God – praise be to Him – then there is nothing that can negate the possibility of it taking place. When someone displays miracles, this is a sign of his being truthful in his spiritual states. [Conversely,] they cannot be displayed by someone who is insincere. One evidence of this is that the Eternal One – praise be to Him – has informed us by means of a [persuasive] argument that it is something that can be conceived [by our intellects], so that we could discern between one who is truthful in his spiritual states and one who is insincere. This can only be done through singling out the friend of God by [granting him] something that the imposter in his

---

[693] One should bear in mind that in Islamic theology saintly miracles (*karamat*) are clearly distinguished from prophetic ones (*muʿjizat*), the latter being the exclusive prerogative of the prophets. For details, see the article "Karama" in *EI*.

pretensions cannot possibly have. The miracle, as we have pointed out, is precisely this very thing.

The miracle must be a matter that breaks the habitual order [of events] (ʿada) during the period when the [divinely ordained] religious obligation (taklif) is in force.[694] It is displayed by an individual who is characterized by saintliness in order to ascertain the truthfulness of his spiritual state. Those who have attained the [divine] truth (ahl al-haqq) have discoursed profusely regarding the difference between prophetic and saintly miracles. The imam Abu Ishaq al-Isfaraini – may God have mercy on him – argued that prophetic miracles (muʿjizat) [serve as] demonstrations of the truthfulness of the prophets and a proof of [their] prophetic mission, which is unique to prophets. Likewise, a sound intellect serves as a proof of the learned man being a learned man; it cannot be found in anyone who is not learned. He [al-Isfaraini] also taught that saintly miracles resemble [God's] answering [somebody's] prayer (ijabat al-daʿwa). As for the kind of miracles that the prophets have, this is not the case.//430

The imam Abu Bakr b. Furak – may God have mercy on him – used to argue that prophetic miracles are proofs of truthfulness. In his words, when the miracle worker claims prophethood, prophetic miracles [are meant to] demonstrate his veracity. When, however, the miracle worker claims sainthood (wilaya), the miracle [only] demonstrates the truthfulness of his spiritual state. It is, therefore, called karama, not muʿjiza. Although the former is a type of the latter, there is a difference [between them]. [Abu Bakr] – may God have mercy on him – used to argue that the difference between prophetic and saintly miracles is that the prophets are commanded to display miracles, whereas the friend of God must hide and conceal them. The prophet [Muhammad] – may God bless and greet him – laid claim to this[695] and spoke unequivocally about it. As for the friend of God, he does not lay claim to it, nor does he speak unequivocally about his miracles due to the possibility that this is but a ruse [on the part of God] (makr).

The judge Abu Bakr al-Ashʿari, the prodigy of his age in his field,[696] argued that prophetic miracles are characteristic of the prophets, while saintly miracles pertain to God's friends. God's friends cannot display prophetic miracles, because one of the conditions of the prophetic miracles is that they should be associated with a claim of prophethood. The prophetic miracle cannot be such in and of itself. It must meet a wide variety of definitions. If one of these conditions is not fulfilled, it cannot be a prophetic miracle. One of these conditions is a claim of prophethood, while God's friend cannot lay claim to prophethood. Therefore that which he displays cannot be a prophetic miracle. This is a doctrine that we rely on, teach and believe in. All or almost all of the conditions of the prophetic

---

694 Namely, between now and the Day of Judgement, when all divine ordinances concerning this world will be suspended.
695 That is, his prophetic mission.
696 A renowned representative of the Ashʿarite school of speculative theology, who is better known as Abu Bakr al-Baqillani (d. 403/1013).

miracle are found in the saintly miracle, except this one. The saintly miracle is, without any doubt, an originated event (*muhdath*), for what is eternal cannot be attributed to any [created thing]. It is an [act of] disrupting the established order of things, which takes place during the time when religious obligation is in force. It is displayed by a servant of God as a sign of his special status and privilege [bestowed upon him by God]. It may happen to him as a result of his wish and supplication, but it may not happen to him either. Occasionally, it may take place irrespective of his wish. The friend of God has not been commanded to call people to himself. However, if He [God] reveals any of this to a person who deserves it, then it becomes possible.

Those who have attained the truth have disagreed over whether it is permissible that the friend of God know if he is one. The imam Abu Bakr b. Furak – may God have mercy on him – used to argue that it was not permissible, because this would deprive him of fear of God and instill in him a sense of security. However, the master Abu ʿAli al-Daqqaq – may God have mercy on him – used to argue that this is permissible. We prefer his position and uphold it.//431 This does not necessarily apply to all the friends of God – namely, that each of them would know that he is one of them. Some of them may know this, while others may not. Whenever someone learns that he is a friend of God, this is but a miracle unique to him. When a certain friend of God performs a miracle, this does not mean that all other friends of God ought necessarily to perform it as well. Moreover, if a friend of God fails to display a miracle during his lifetime, its lack does not impugn his status as a friend of God. The case of the prophets is different. They must perform miracles, because a prophet is sent to creatures and people who need to know the veracity [of his claim], which can only be accomplished by means of a miracle. The case of the friend of God is the opposite of this, because neither he nor the people [around him] ought to know that he is a friend of God.

Ten of the Companions of the Messenger of God – may God bless and greet him – trusted him when he said that they would be among the inhabitants of Paradise. As for the opinion of those who argue that this is not possible, because [the promise] would divest them of the fear of God, it does not really matter, because those who were promised would still be afraid of [God's] changing His decree in the Hereafter. The awe, respect and reverence of God – praise be to Him – that they found in their hearts only increased, resulting in a great deal of fear [of Him]. Know that the friend of God must not find repose in a saintly miracle, nor even take notice of it. When they[697] experience anything of this sort it only [strengthens] their certitude and increases their [spiritual] insight (*basira*), because they realize that this is an action [coming] from God and they see in it a proof of the soundness of their [religious] convictions. In all, acknowledging the possibility of performance of saintly miracles by the friends of God is an obligation. This is held by the majority of the learned (*ahl al-maʿrifa*). Thanks to

---

697 Namely, friends of God.

the abundance of sound reports and stories about various types [of miracles], the awareness of their existence and of their manifestation through God's friends has become firmly established and free from any doubt. Whoever has kept the company of the Sufis and heard their reports and stories will have not even the slightest doubt concerning this thesis. Among its proofs found in the Qur'an is the story of a companion of Solomon – peace be upon him – who said: "I will bring it [the throne] to thee, before even thy glance returns to thee."[698] Yet, he was not a prophet. There is also a sound report about the Commander of the Faithful 'Umar b. al-Khattab – may God be pleased with him – according to which he exclaimed, "O Sariya, [watch out for] the mountain!" during his Friday sermon and [according to which] the voice of 'Umar reached Sariya,//432 putting him on guard against the ambush of the enemy on a mountain at that same time.[699]

One may then ask: "How is it possible that some saintly miracles may surpass the miracles performed by [God's] messengers? And how it is possible [thereby] to give preference to the friends of God over the prophets – peace be upon them?" [In response] one should say: "These saintly miracles follow the prophetic miracles of our Prophet – may God bless and greet him – because no one who is not truthful in his religion can display a saintly miracle. Each prophet whose saintly miracle was manifested through a member of his community can count it among his prophetic miracles. For if this messenger had not been truthful [in his message], no saintly miracle would have been manifested by any of his followers. As for the rank of the friends of God, it is lower than that of the prophets – peace be upon them – according to the consensus reached [by the scholars]. When someone asked Abu Yazid al-Bistami about this issue, he answered: "What the prophets receive is like a water-skin full of honey from which a single drop of honey has fallen. This drop is similar to what all the friends of God possess and that which remains in the container is similar to what our Prophet – may God bless and greet him – possesses."

Section (fasl)

These saintly miracles may come in response to a prayer, such as the appearance of food at a time of need without any visible means; or the appearance of water

---

698 Q. 27:40; this is a reference to the Qur'anic encounter between Solomon and Bilqis (the Queen of Sheba of the Biblical tradition) during which a person in Solomon's entourage offers to miraculously transfer Bilqis' throne to Solomon's palace. In the later exegetical tradition, the unnamed companion was identified as Asaf b. Barakhya, a confidant and minister to King Solomon.

699 A story that is often mentioned in Sufi sources as a proof of the possibility of miracles. According to it, the second caliph was preaching to a congregation in Medina, when he suddenly interrupted his sermon and uttered the aforementioned phrase addressed to a field commander Sariya b. Zunaym al-Du'ili (d. ca. 30/650). It was miraculously heard by the addressee, who was fighting a Persian force at the city of Nihawand, and warned him of the impending attack of a Persian contingent hiding on a local mountain.

at the time of drought; or enabling [someone] to traverse a [great] distance in a short time; or an escape from an enemy; or hearing the speech of an invisible speaker, and other kinds of things that break the established order [of things]. Know, that today it is definitely and surely known that among the many things that God has preordained some may never appear in the form of saintly miracles under any circumstances. These include the origination of a human being without two parents, the transformation of an inanimate matter into a beast or an animal, and so on and so forth.

Section

If someone asks, "What is the meaning of 'friend of God' (*walī*)?", they say: "There are two possibilities." First, it may be [formed on the pattern of the passive participle] *faʿīl* as the intensification of the meaning of [the active participle] *fāʿil*, as in [the words] *ʿalīm* ("very knowledgeable"), *qadīr* ("very powerful"), and so on. In this case, its meaning would be "one whose acts of piety followed one upon the other without being interrupted by any disobedience." It is also possible that it is [formed on the pattern] *faʿīl* implying the passivity [of the subject], as in *qatīl* in the sense of "one who is killed" (*maqtūl*) or *jarīh* in the sense of "one who is wounded" (*majrūh*). That is, *walī* is one whom God – praise be to Him – has taken (*yatawallā*) under His protection and care at all times and incessantly (*ʿala ʾl-tawālī*). God does not create for him [the phenomenon of] abandonment (*khidhlān*),[700] which may have rendered him capable of disobedience. Rather, His assistance to His friend is incessant, which enables him to remain obedient [all the time]. As God Most High said: "He [God] takes into His protection the righteous."[701] //433

Section

If someone asks, "Can a friend of God be protected from sin (*maʿṣūm*)?", they say: "If [one implies] necessarily and essentially, as is said about the prophets, then the answer is no. If, however, [one means] that [they are] divinely protected and do not persist in any sins, even though [they may occasionally] display minor faults, failings and slippages, then this quality can be included into their description." Someone asked al-Junayd: "Abu ʾl-Qasim, can a gnostic commit adultery?" He lowered his head and remained silent for a while, then raised his head and said: "God's commandment is a destiny decreed."[702]

Section

If someone asks, "Can fear abandon the friends of God?", they [should] answer: "Fear dominates the greatest among them, yet what we have said earlier about

---

700 That is, God protects His friend from any error at all times.
701 Q. 7: 196.
702 Q. 33:38.

this is not impossible, if rare." Al-Sari al-Saqati said: "If someone were to enter a garden with many trees and on each tree were a bird saying in a clear [Arabic] language: 'Peace be upon you, O friend of God!' and he would not fear this to be a ruse of God (*makr*), he has already been deceived." Stories such as this abound among the Sufis.

Section

If someone asks, "Is it possible to see God – praise be upon Him – in this world by means of a saintly miracle?", the answer is: "The best opinion about this is that [such a vision] is not possible, due to a consensus [reached by scholars] regarding this matter." I heard the imam Abu Bakr b. Furak – may God be pleased with him – relate on the authority of Abu ʾl-Hasan al-Ashʿari[703] that the latter expounded two teachings concerning this matter in his big book [devoted to] the vision [of God].

Section

If someone asks, "Is it possible that a person might be a friend of God now, but will change this status at the end of his life?", they say: "Those who consider the favorable outcome [of one's life] among the conditions of sainthood do not allow this." Others, however, argue that one can be a true believer at present, even though one's state might change later on; therefore, it is not impossible that one may be a true and sincere friend of God at the moment, then change one's status. We opt for this view.//434 It is possible for the miracles of a friend of God to include his knowledge that he is assured a favorable outcome [in the Hereafter] which will remain unchanged until his death. This issue is relevant to what we have already mentioned regarding the friend of God knowing that he is one.

Section

If someone asks, "Can the fear of [divine] ruse leave the friend of God?", they say: "When he is detached from his surroundings, snatched from his consciousness and removed from his sense perception by his spiritual state, consumed completely by that which has taken possession of him, [fear disappears]. For fear is an attribute of those who are present."[704]

Section

If someone asks, "What [feature] dominates the friend of God in his state of sobriety?", they say: "[First,] his sincerity in observing the rights of God – praise

---

703 A renowned Sunni theologian who founded the Ashʿarite school of speculative theology, which gradually became dominant among the Sunnis; he died in Baghdad in 324/935.
704 That is, those who retain their self-consciousness.

be to Him – then his friendliness and compassion toward other people in all his states, then the extension of his mercy to entire mankind, then his constant forbearance toward them and [his dealing with them] with gentleness. He constantly beseeches God – may He be great and exalted – to show benevolence toward them, while not asking [anything] from them. He applies his spiritual energy (*himma*) toward the salvation of mankind and seeks not to avenge himself on them. He abstains from being resentful toward God's creatures, keeps his hands away from their property, displays no greed at all in any manner, and withholds his tongue from saying evil things about them. He guards himself from seeing their failings and shows no adversity toward anyone in this world and the next."

Know that one of the greatest miracles that the friends of God enjoy is [God's] assistance in [performing] acts of obedience [toward Him] and [divine] protection from disobedience and opposition [to the divine will]. Among the Qurʾanic proofs of the existence of saintly miracles is that which God – praise be to Him – said about Mary – peace be upon her – who was neither a prophet, nor a messenger of God: "Whenever Zachariah went in to her [Mary] in the Sanctuary, he found her provisioned."[705] He would ask her: "How come this to thee?" and Mary would answer: "From God."[706] Another proof is the words of God – praise be to Him – [addressed to Mary]: "Shake also to thee the palm-trunk, and there shall come tumbling upon thee dates fresh and ripe."[707] And that was not the season for dates. Likewise, the story of the sleepers of the cave and the miraculous deeds they displayed, such as their dog talking to them and so forth.[708] To the same category belongs the story of Dhu ʾl-Qarnayn,[709] whom God – praise be to Him – empowered like no one else. To the same category belongs the story of al-Khadir – peace be upon him – and the miracles that he manifested, such as the construction of the wall and so forth, as well as his knowledge of what was concealed from Moses – peace be upon him.[710] All these deeds that broke the established custom were attributed to al-Khadir – peace be upon him – despite the fact that he was not a prophet, only a friend of God.[711]

Among other reports pertaining to this theme is the story of Jurayj the Monk. Abu Nuʿaym//435 ʿAbd al-Malik b. al-Hasan al-Isfaraini informed us: Abu ʿAwana Yaʿqub b. Ibrahim b. Ishaq informed us: ʿAmmar b. Rajaʾ told us: Wahb b. Jarir told us: My father told me: I heard Muhammad b. Sirin relate on the authority of Abu Hurayra that the Messenger of God – may God bless and

---

705 Q. 3:37; 3:33, according to Arberry's translation.
706 Q. 3:37.
707 Q. 19:25.
708 Q. 18:9–27.
709 A Qurʾanic personage, who is traditionally identified with Alexander the Great; see Q. 18:83–98.
710 The story of Moses and his mysterious companion, traditionally identified as al-Khadir (Elijah), whose inexplicable behavior confounded the Hebrew prophet. See Q. 18:65–82.
711 However, some Muslim scholars consider al-Khadir to be a prophet.

greet him – said:⁷¹² "Only three individuals spoke from the cradle: Jesus son of Mary, an infant at the time of Jurayj, and one more infant. As for Jesus, you already know about him. As for Jurayj, he was a pious man of the Children of Israel. He had a mother. One day, as he was praying, his mother felt a strong longing for him and called upon him: 'Jurayj!' He asked: 'My Lord, is it better [for me] to pray or to come to her?' So, he continued his prayer. She called upon him once again, and he said the same thing and continued his prayer. His mother found this hard to bear and said: 'My God, do not let him die until You have shown him the faces of prostitutes!' There was among the Children of Israel a prostitute. She told them: 'I will seduce Jurayj, so that he would commit fornication.' She then came to him, but was unable to achieve anything. There was a shepherd, who used to spend the night at the foot of Jurayj's retreat. When Jurayj rejected her, she endeavored to attract the shepherd to herself. He came to her, and [after a while] she gave birth to a child, whereupon she said: 'This child of mine is from Jurayj!' The Children of Israel came to Jurayj, destroyed his retreat, and upbraided him. He prayed and made a supplication. He then punched the boy with his hand." Muhammad [b. Sirin] continued: Abu Hurayra said: "I was looking at the Prophet – may God bless and greet him – when he said, 'With his hand'⁷¹³ [then added]: 'Boy, who is your father?' The boy answered: 'The shepherd!' [The Children of Israel] regretted what they had done and apologized before him, saying: 'We shall build for you a retreat of gold' – or perhaps they said 'silver'. However, he declined and he rebuilt it as it had been before.

As for another infant [who spoke from the cradle], there was a lady with a suckling child. [Once] there passed by her a young man with a handsome face and beautiful complexion. She exclaimed: 'My God, make my child be like that!' The child then spoke, saying: 'My God, don't make me be like that!'" Muhammad b. Sirin said: "I was watching the Prophet – may God bless and greet him – as he was recounting the words of the suckling child. Then, there passed by them a woman who was said to have stolen, fornicated and was punished [for that]. The mother exclaimed: 'God, do not make my child be like that!' The child, however, said: 'God, make me be like her!' Its mother inquired it about that. It answered: 'This young man is a tyrant, and for the woman, although they say about her that she has fornicated, she in fact has not; although they say that she has stolen she has not. She has simply kept saying: 'God is sufficient for me!'"//436 This report is related in the *Sahih*.⁷¹⁴

---

712 Following this, al-Qushayri provides an alternative chain of transmission of the same prophetic report, which is: "Abu ʿAwana said: al-Sanʿani told me: Abu ʿUmama said: Al-Husayn b. Muhammad al-Muruwadhi said: Jarir b. Hazim said to us, on the authority of Muhammad b. Sirin, on the authority of Abu Hurayra: ..."

713 Probably, Abu Hurayra refers to the Prophet's gesturing as he recounted the story.

714 One of the two most respected collections of "sound" reports going back to the Prophet and his Companions. It was assembled by a famous traditionalist, al-Bukhari, who died in 256/870.

To the same category belongs the story of the cave, which is well known and which is recorded in the collections of sound [prophetic] reports. Abu Nuʿaym ʿAbd al-Malik b. al-Hasan al-Isfaraini informed us: Abu ʿAwana Yaʿqub b. Ibrahim told us: Muhammad b. ʿAwn,[715] Yazid b. ʿAbd al-Samad al-Dimashqi, ʿAbd al-Karim b. al-Haytham al-Dayrʿaquli and Abu ʾl-Khasib b. al-Mustanir al-Massisi told us: Abu ʾl-Yaman told us: Shuʿayb told us on the authority of al-Zuhri, on the authority of Salim, on the authority of his father, who said that the Messenger of God – may God bless and greet him – said: "A long time ago, three men set out on a journey. When night came, they found refuge in a cave. When they entered it, a big rock fell from the mountain and blocked them in the cave. They said: 'By God, there is no rescue for us from this rock unless we appeal to God Most High by means of our good deeds!' One of them said: 'I had two very elderly parents. I would never give an evening drink to either my family or my livestock before first offering it to them. One day, my search for firewood prevented [me from coming home before dark], and I only arrived at home, when they were already asleep. I milked [one of my animals] to prepare their evening drink. However, when I came to them, they were already asleep. I was reluctant to wake them up, while at the same time unwilling to offer an evening drink to either my family or my livestock. So, I stood with a cup in hand waiting for them to wake up until the break of dawn. They [finally] woke up and drank their evening drink. My God, if I did this seeking Your pleasure, relieve us from our plight!' A crack opened in the rock, but the opening was not wide enough for them to get out through it." The Messenger of God – may God bless and greet him – continued: "The second man said: 'My God, I had a cousin whom I loved more than any other human being. I tried to instill in her affection for me. However, she turned me down. Finally, one year she had fallen on hard times and came to me. I gave her one hundred and twenty *dinars* on the condition that she would become mine. So she came to me and as I was about to make her mine she told me: 'It is not allowed for you to break the seal unless you have the right [to do so]!' So I shunned from sleeping with her and walked away from her, leaving with her all the gold that I had given her. My God, if I did that seeking Your pleasure, relieve us from our plight!' The rock cracked wider, but they [still] were unable to get out of the cave." The Messenger of God – may God bless and greet him – said: "The third man uttered: 'My God, I used to hire some laborers and paid them their wages, except for one man, who left without collecting his wages. I invested his wages with a profit. He came to me after a while and said: "ʿAbdallah, pay me my wages!" I told him: "Everything that you see – the camels, the sheep, the cows and the slaves, is your wages!" He exclaimed: "ʿAbdallah, don't make fun of me!" I told him: "I do not make fun of you!" So he took everything [I had] and left nothing behind! My God, if I did this seeking Your pleasure, relieve us from our plight!' The rock cracked open, they got out of the cave and went on their way."//437 This is a sound report accepted by all.

---

715 Or "Muhammad b. ʿAwf".

To the same category belongs the report from the Messenger of God – may God bless and greet him – that a cow spoke to him. Abu Nuʿaym al-Isfaraini informed us: Abu ʿAwana informed us: Yunus b. ʿAbd al-Aʿla informed us: Ibn Wahb informed us: Yunus b. Yazid informed us on the authority of Ibn Shihab, who said: Saʿid b. Musayyb told us on the authority of Abu Hurayra that the Prophet – may God bless and greet him – said: "[Once] a man was driving his cow, which he had loaded with certain goods. The cow turned to him and said: 'I was not created for this! I was created to plow.' The people [in the audience] exclaimed [in disbelief]: 'Praise be to God!' The Prophet – may God bless and greet him – said: 'I believe this – I and Abu Bakr and ʿUmar.'" To the same category belongs the report about Uways al-Qarani[716] and about his state and story as witnessed by ʿUmar b. al-Khattab – may God be pleased with him. Subsequently, he met Harim b. Hayyan and they greeted each other without having any prior knowledge of one another. All these are conditions that are contrary to the customary order of things. We have skipped a detailed explanation of the Uways story, because it is widely known.

Miracles have been displayed by the pious ancestors (*salaf*), including the Companions [of the Prophet] and the generation that followed them, as well as those who came in their wake. They are abundant indeed. Many books were written about this matter, and we shall mention only a few of them for the sake of brevity, God willing. Thus, [it is related] that Ibn ʿUmar[717] was once on a journey when he met a group of people standing on the road for fear of a lion. He chased the lion away from the road then told them: "God has given power over man to things that he fears. Were he afraid of no one but God, no one would have power over him." This is a well-known report. It is related that the Messenger of God – may God bless and greet him – sent al-ʿAlaʾ b. al-Hadrami on a raid. Between him and his goal there was a patch of sea. He implored God by His greatest name and his troops walked over the water. It is related that when ʿAbbad[718] b. Bishr and Usayd b. Hudayr [b. Imruʾ al-Qays] left the Messenger of God's house [one night]; [as they walked] the tip of the staff of one of them glowed, showing them the way as if it were a lamp. It is related that a large bowl [of food] was [once] standing in front of Salman and Abu ʾl-Dardaʾ.[719] It praised God and they both heard this praise. It is related that the Prophet – may God bless and greet him – said: "How many a person with disheveled hair, covered with dust, with nothing but two pieces of clothing to his

---

716 A semi-legendary figure whose visit to ʿUmar was predicted by the prophet Muhammad, who had held Uways in high regard. Although the Prophet and Uways never met, they are said to have communicated telepathically.
717 Son of the second caliph ʿUmar b. al-Khattab. A prominent and highly respected member of the first Muslim community in his own right, he took an active part in the Muslim conquests. He died at a very advanced age in 73/693.
718 Or "ʿAttab b. Bashir", according to another reading.
719 Two prominent Companions of the Prophet, who were renowned for their loyalty to him and their piety.

name, unnoticed, who pleads to God has his plea is granted!"//438 The Prophet did not specify what exactly such a person may plead to God for. Since these reports are well known, we have not provided chains of transmission for them.

It is related that Sahl b. ʿAbdallah said: "Whoever has renounced this world for forty days truthfully and with a sincere heart will display miracles. If he fails to display them, it is because he is not sincere in his renunciation." Someone asked Sahl: "How will he display miracles?" He answered: "He takes what he wants, how he wants, and from wherever he wants." ʿAli b. Ahmad b. ʿAbdan informed us: Ahmad b. ʿUbayd al-Saffar told us: Abu Muslim told us: ʿAmr b. Marzuq told us: ʿAbd al-ʿAziz b. Abi Salama al-Majashun told us: Wahb b. Kaysan told us on the authority of Ibn ʿUmar, on the authority of Abu Hurayra, who said that the Prophet – may God bless and greet him – said: "As a man was saying his prayers, he heard thunder in a cloud. He then heard a voice in the cloud, saying: 'Water the garden of so-and-so!' The cloud moved to a certain plot and discharged its water onto it. The man followed the cloud and came upon another man, who was praying in his garden. The [first] man asked the other what his name was and he gave him his name. The [first] man asked: 'What will you do with the harvest of this garden of yours?' The [second] man asked [in turn]: 'Why are you asking about this?' The [first] man said: 'I heard a voice from a cloud, saying: "Water the garden of so-and-so!"' The [second] man said: 'Since you have asked, I will divide it into three parts. I will keep one-third for myself and my wife, one-third I will return to the garden itself,[720] and one-third I will set aside for the poor and the travelers.'"

I heard Abu Hatim al-Sijistani say: I heard Abu Nasr al-Sarraj say: "When we arrived in Tustar,[721] we saw on the property [that used to belong to] Sahl b. ʿAbdallah [al-Tustari] a house that the locals called 'the house of the lions' (*bayt al-sibaʿ*). We asked them about it. They answered: 'Lions used to come to Sahl. He would take them to this house and play host to them, feeding them with meat. He then let them go.'" Abu Nasr al-Sarraj said: "The entire population of Tustar were in agreement about this, despite their great number and no one denied it." I heard Muhammad b. Ahmad b. Muhammad al-Tamimi say: I heard ʿAbdallah b. ʿAli al-Sufi//439 say: I heard Hamza b. ʿAbdallah al-ʿAlawi say: "[One day] I went to see Abu ʾl-Khayr al-Tinati. I made a vow to myself to greet him and to leave without eating anything at his place. After I had left his house and walked some distance, I suddenly saw him [walking] behind me with a tray full of food. He said: 'Eat this, young man! You have already fulfilled your pledge!'" Abu ʾl-Khayr al-Tinati was famous for miracles. Ibrahim al-Raqqi recounted: "I set out to offer my greetings to him. He performed his sunset prayer, during which he made a mistake in reciting the 'Opening'.[722] I said to myself: 'My journey was in vain.' After I greeted him, I went outside to perform my ablutions. A lion

---

720 Perhaps in order to offset its maintenance costs?
721 Tustar (or Shushtar), a town in south-western Iran.
722 That is, the first chapter of the Qurʾan (*al-Fatiha*), which is recited during each prayer.

rushed toward me and I returned to Abu ʾl-Khayr, saying: 'A lion rushed toward me!' He went outside and shouted at the lion: 'Didn't I tell you not to accost my guests?' The lion retreated and I performed my ablutions. When I came back to him, he said: 'You are preoccupied with putting externals in order, and you are afraid of the lion, whereas we are preoccupied with putting [our] hearts in order and the lion is afraid of us!'"

Jaʿfar al-Khuldi had a ring-stone. One day he dropped it into the Tigris. He knew a well-tested prayer by which to return lost things. He uttered it and found his ring-stone amidst the papers that he was leafing through. I heard Abu Hatim al-Sijistani say: I heard Abu Nasr al-Sarraj say that [the words of] this prayer are: "O the One who brings together all people 'on the Day wherein is no doubt',[723] bring me together with what I have lost!" Abu Nasr al-Sarraj said: "Abu ʾl-Tayyb al-ʿAkki showed me a volume that contained [the names of] those who offered this prayer over something that they lost and then found again. It consisted of many pages." I asked Ahmad al-Tabarani al-Sarakhsi – may God have mercy on him: "Have you ever displayed any miracles?" He answered: "During my novitiate (*iradati*), at the beginning of my path [to God], I occasionally searched for a stone with which to cleanse myself after defecating and could not find one. I would then draw something out of the air and it would turn out to be a precious stone (*jawhar*). I would cleanse myself with it and throw it away." He then asked: "What is the importance of miracles? Their intended purpose is to strengthen [one's] faith in God's Oneness. He who sees nothing in this existence except God does not care whether he contemplates an ordinary event or an event that is contrary to the customary order [of things]."

I heard Muhammad b. Ahmad al-Sufi say: I heard ʿAbdallah b. ʿAli say: I heard Abu ʾl-Hasan[724] al-Basri say: "At ʿAbbadan[725] there was a poor black man who used to frequent the [local] ruins. I took something with me and sought him out. When his eyes fell on me, he smiled and pointed with his hand toward the earth. I saw that the entire earth was covered with shining gold. He told me: 'Give what you have brought!' I gave it to him. However, his [spiritual] state frightened me so, that I ran away from him." I heard Mansur al-Maghribi say: I heard Ahmad b. ʿAtaʾ al-Rudhbari say: "I used to be//440 excessively concerned with the matter of ritual purity (*tahara*). One night I felt oppressed due to the large amount of water I poured [over myself], while performing my ablutions. My heart would not rest. [Finally,] I said: 'My Lord, I seek Your forgiveness!' I then heard a voice saying: 'Forgiveness lies in knowledge!' And my sickness disappeared."

I heard Mansur al-Maghribi say: "I saw him [al-Rudhbari] one day sitting on a plain rock in the desert that was covered with the dung of goats and sheep. I

---

723 Q. 3:9.
724 Or "Abu ʾl-Khayr al-Basri".
725 An island in the mouth of Shatt al-ʿArab, which served as a refuge for early Muslim ascetics; see *IM*, pp. 17–18.

asked him: 'Master, this is the dung of goats and sheep!' He responded, saying: 'Legal scholars (*fuqaha*ʾ) hold different opinions regarding this matter.'" I heard Abu Hatim al-Sijistani say: I heard Abu Nasr al-Sarraj say: I heard al-Husayn b. Ahmad al-Razi say: I heard Abu Sulayman al-Khawwas say: "One day I was riding a donkey. It was pestered by flies and kept shaking its head. As I was beating its head with a stick that I held in my hand, the donkey raised his head and uttered: 'Keep beating! You yourself will be beaten on your head!'" Al-Husayn [b. Ahmad al-Razi] asked Abu Sulayman: "Did it indeed happen to you?" He answered: "Yes, it did, [exactly] as you have heard!" It is related that Ibn ʿAtaʾ [al-Adami] said: I heard Abu ʾl-Husayn al-Nuri say: "Some of these miracles have occurred to me. I took a cane from some boys, and entered [in the river] between two boats, saying: 'By Your greatness, if a three-pound fish does not come to me, I will drown myself!' And indeed a fish weighing three pounds came out to me." When al-Junayd heard this story, he said: "It would have been better for him that a snake come out of the water to bite him!" I heard Shaykh Abu ʿAbd al-Rahman al-Sulami say: I heard Abu ʾl-Fath Yusuf b. ʿUmar al-Zahid al-Qawwas at Baghdad say: Muhammad b. ʿAtiya said: ʿAbd al-Kabir b. Ahmad told us: I heard Abu Bakr al-Saʾigh say: I heard Abu Jaʿfar al-Haddad, the teacher of al-Junayd, say: "Once, when I was in Mecca my hair had grown long and I had no iron instrument to trim my hair with. So I went to a barber in whom I discerned signs of a good nature and asked him: 'Will you cut my hair for the sake of God Most High?' He said: 'Yes, with pleasure!' There was [in his shop] a wealthy man. The barber pushed him aside, sat me down instead and cut my hair. He then gave me a pouch with *dirhams* and told me: 'Spend this on some of your needs!' I took it and made a decision to pay him back as soon as God bestowed something on me. I entered the mosque, where I was greeted by a companion of mine who told me: 'One of your [Sufi] brothers brought with him from Basra a purse with three hundred *dinars* that was given to you by another [Sufi] brother of yours.' I took the purse and brought it to the barber, saying: 'This is three hundred *dinars*. Spend them on some of your needs!' He told me: 'Aren't you ashamed of yourself, master? [First] you tell me to cut your hair for the sake of God Most High, and then you want me to charge a fee for it! Leave, may God pardon you!'"//441 I heard Abu Hatim al-Sijistani say: I heard Abu Nasr al-Sarraj say: I heard Ibn Salim say: "When Ishaq b. Ahmad died, Sahl b. ʿAbdallah [al-Tustari] went to visit him in his retreat, where he found a basket woven of palm leaves. In it there were two bottles. One contained a red substance, the other a white one. He also found there a scrap of gold and a scrap of silver. Sahl threw both scraps into the Tigris and poured the content of both bottles into the dust. Now Ishaq was in debt." Ibn Salim continued: "I asked Sahl: 'What was in those two bottles?' He said: 'If you pour a *dirham* worth of its weight from one of these bottles on several units (*mathaqil*) of copper, it will turn into gold, and if you pour a *dinar* worth of its weight on several units of lead, it will turn into silver.' I asked him: 'Would it have been held against him if he had settled his debt with this?' Sahl answered: 'Friend, he was afraid for his faith.'" It is related that one night al-Nuri went out to the bank of the Tigris and found out that its two banks drew together [to allow him to cross it]. He walked away, saying: "By Your greatness, I will only cross it in a boat!"

I heard Abu Hatim al-Sijistani say: I heard Abu Nasr al-Sarraj say: al-Wajihi dictated to me a story about Muhammad b. Yusuf al-Banna'. He said: "Abu Turab al-Nakhshabi displayed many miracles. Once I traveled with him in a company of forty other people. At one point we were afflicted by starvation. Abu Turab veered off the road and returned with a bunch of bananas. All of us partook of it, except a young man who did not eat any of it. Abu Turab told him to eat. He answered: 'I have made a vow to give up [the quest for] any sort of assured livelihood (maʿlumat), yet you have provided me with one. I part company with you from now on!' Abu Turab told him: 'Then keep up your vow!'" Abu Nasr al-Sarraj related on the authority of Abu Yazid [al-Bistami], who said: "Once Abu ʿAli al-Sindi – who was his teacher – came to see me with a sack in his hand. When he emptied its contents, it turned out to be full of jewels. I asked him where he obtained this. He answered: 'I was in a valley over there when I saw this shining like a lamp, so I took it with me.' I asked him: 'What was your [mystical] moment (waqtuka), when you entered that valley?' He answered: 'It was the moment in which the spiritual state I had been in began to weaken.'" Someone told Abu Yazid: "So-and-so walked all the way to Mecca in a single night!" He responded: "Satan – may God curse him – walks from East to West in an hour!" //442 He was told: "So-and-so walks on water and flies in the air!" He retorted: "Birds, too, fly in the air and fish flow across the water!" Sahl b. ʿAbdallah [al-Tustari] said: "The greatest miracle is that you change even one of the blameworthy traits of your moral character."

I heard Muhammad b. Ahmad b. Muhammad al-Tamimi say: I heard ʿAbdallah b. ʿAli al-Sufi say: I heard Ibn Salim say: "A man named ʿAbd al-Rahman b. Ahmad used to keep company with Sahl b. ʿAbdallah [al-Tustari]. Once, he told Sahl: 'When I perform my ritual ablutions before the prayer, [ablution] water streams from me as two branches: one of gold and the other of silver.' Sahl retorted: 'Don't you know that when little children cry, they are given rattles [of dried poppy heads] in order to be distracted.'" I heard Abu Hatim al-Sijistani say: I heard Abu Nasr al-Sarraj say: Jaʿfar b. Muhammad informed us: al-Junayd told me: "One day I went to see al-Sari [al-Saqati]. He told me: 'A bird used to come here every day. I would crumble some bread for it and it would eat from my hand. One day it came, but did not perch on my hand. I thought to myself: "What might be the cause of this?" I remembered that I had eaten meat with spices. I said to myself: "I will never eat it again and I repent from having done this." And the bird perched on my hand and ate [some bread].'"

Abu ʿUmar[726] al-Anmati related: "I was in the desert with my master, when it started to rain. We found refuge in a mosque. Its roof was leaking, so we climbed up to the roof with a board to fix the roof. However, the board was too short to

---

726 Or "ʿAmr", according to an alternative reading.

reach the wall. My master told me: 'Stretch it!' I [managed to] stretch it and it covered the wall from one edge to the other." I heard Muhammad b. ᶜAbdallah al-Sufi say: I heard Muhammad b. Ahmad al-Najjar say: I heard al-Duqqi[727] say: I heard Abu Bakr al-Daqqaq say: "As I was wandering in the desert of the Children of Israel, it occurred to me that the knowledge of the True Reality (ᶜilm al-haqiqa) is different from the Divine Law (al-shariᶜa). [Suddenly] I heard a voice from beneath a tree, saying: 'Each truth that does not conform to the Divine Law is but unbelief!'" A Sufi related: "I was with Khayr al-Nassaj, when a certain man came to him and said: 'Master, I saw you the other day selling yarn for two *dirhams*. I followed you and stole them from the fold of your loincloth. Suddenly, my hand became//443 paralyzed with two *dirhams* clasped in my fist!' Khayr laughed and pointed his hand at the hand of the man and it opened. He then said: 'Go and purchase something for your family with these *dirhams*. And never do anything like this again!'" It is related that Ahmad b. Muhammad al-Sulami said: "One day I went to see Dhu ᵓl-Nun al-Misri and saw before him a golden basin. Burning around it was a mixture of aromatic incenses and ambergris. He told me: 'You are one of those who enter into the presence of kings, when they feel generous!' He gave me one *dirham* with which I was able to pay all my expenses all the way to Balkh."[728] It is related that Abu Saᶜid al-Kharraz said: "During one of my travels, there appeared before me something to eat every three days. This sufficed me. Once, however, three days passed by without anything presenting itself for me and I grew weak. As I sat down, I heard a voice saying: 'What do you like best: power or means?' 'Power,' I replied. Instantly, I stood up and for twelve days I walked without eating anything. Yet, I was not exhausted."

Al-Murtaᶜish related: I heard [Ibrahim] al-Khawwas say: "I had been wandering across the desert for many days on end [until] a stranger approached and greeted me. He asked me whether I was lost. I said: 'Yes.' He told me: 'Why don't I show you the way?' He then walked a few steps in front of me, whereupon he disappeared from my sight. I found myself on the thoroughfare. From that moment on, I experienced neither hunger nor thirst in my journey." I heard Muhammad b. ᶜAbdallah al-Sufi say: I heard ᶜUmar b. Yahya al-Ardabili say: I heard al-Duqqi[729] say: I heard Ibn al-Jallaᵓ relate to me: "After my father died, he kept laughing [while lying] on the washing litter. No one dared to wash his body, because they thought he was still alive. Finally, one of his close followers came and washed him." I heard Muhammad b. Ahmad al-Tamimi say: I heard ᶜAbdallah b. ᶜAli say: I heard Talha al-Qasaᵓiri[730] say: I heard al-Manihi, a companion of Sahl b. ᶜAbdallah [al-Tustari], relate: "Sahl used to abstain from food for eighty days. Whenever he ate, he grew weaker, while when he went hungry he grew stronger. At the beginning of the month of Ramadan Abu ᶜUbayd al-Busri would

---

727 Or "al-Raqqi", according to another version.
728 An ancient city in northern Afghanistan.
729 Or "al-Raqqi", according to an alternative reading.
730 Or, according to another reading, "al-Ghadaᵓiri".

come to his wife and tell her: 'Seal the door of my room with clay and throw me each night a loaf of bread through that small window!' On the day of the festival [of the breaking of the fast] we would open the door, his wife would come into his room and would discover thirty loaves of bread in one of its corners. Although he did not eat, drink or sleep [for the entire month], he would not miss a single cycle of his prayer."//444

Abu ʾl-Harith al-Awlasi said: "For thirty years I lived with my tongue listening to no one but my innermost self. After that [my] condition changed so that my innermost self would listen to no one but my Lord!" Muhammad b. ʿAbdallah al-Sufi told us: Abu ʾl-Hasan, a servant of Shaʿwana, said: I heard ʿAli b. Salim say: "At the end of his life, Sahl b. ʿAbdallah was afflicted by a paralysis. When the time of the prayer came, his hands and feet would be loosened, and, after he had fulfilled his religious duty, they would return to their original [paralyzed] state." Abu ʿImran al-Wasiti related: "[Our] ship sank, and my wife and I kept afloat on a board. Under these circumstances she gave birth to a girl. She called upon me, saying: 'Thirst is killing me!' I told her: 'God sees our condition!' I raised my head and saw a man [suspended] in the middle of the air. In his hand was a chain of gold to which a ruby cup was attached. He told us: 'Drink [this]!' I seized the cup and we both drank from it. The water was more fragrant than musk, colder than ice and sweeter than honey. I asked him: 'Who are you – may God have mercy on you?' He said: 'I am a servant of your Master!' I asked him how he attained such a [lofty] rank. He answered: 'I abandoned [all] my desires for the sake of His pleasure and He seated me on the air.' He then disappeared from my sight and I have not seen him since."

Muhammad b. ʿAbdallah al-Sufi informed us: Bakran b. Ahmad al-Jili told us: I heard Yusuf b. al-Husayn say: I heard Dhu ʾl-Nun say: "At the Kaʿba I observed a young man, who repeatedly bowed and prostrated himself [in prayer]. I approached and said: 'You are making a lot of prayers!' He responded: 'I am waiting for my Lord's permission to depart!' Then I saw a piece of paper that read: "From the Glorious and All-Forgiving One to My sincere servant. Leave, for I have forgiven thee thy former and latter sins.' "[731] A Sufi related: "I was in the city of the Messenger of God[732] – may God bless and greet him – in his mosque, exchanging [stories about] God's signs[733] with a group of other people. Near us was a blind man, listening. He then approached us and said: 'I enjoyed your speeches. Know, that I had a little daughter and other children and that I [used to earn my livelihood] by gathering firewood at a certain place. One day, I went there and saw a young man dressed in a linen shirt with sandals on his feet. I thought that he must have lost his way. I came up to him in order to steal his clothes. I told him to take off the clothes that he had on himself. He told me: "Go away, may God protect you!" I persisted, repeating my demand three times,

---

731 Q. 48:2.
732 That is, Medina.
733 That is, the miracles of the friends of God.

until he finally said: "So be it?" I said: "So be it!" He pointed at my eyes with his finger from some distance away and my eyes flowed out. I cried out: "By God, who are you?" He said: "Ibrahim al-Khawwas."'" Dhu 'l-Nun related: "Once I was on board a ship, when a piece of expensive fabric was stolen. People suspected a certain man of doing that. I said: 'Leave him alone until I have a friendly chat//445 with him.' This young man was sleeping wrapped in his cloak. When he stuck his head out of his cloak, Dhu 'l-Nun asked him about this matter. The young man exclaimed: 'How can you tell me this? My Lord, I implore You that not a single fish shall come out [of the sea] without bringing a jewel with it!' And I indeed saw fish appearing on the surface of the sea, each carrying a jewel in its mouth. The young man then threw himself into the sea and walked all the way across the sea to the shore."

Ibrahim al-Khawas related: "Once I went into the desert. In the middle of it I met a Christian girdled with the belt [of protection] (*zunnar*).[734] He requested that he be my companion, and we traveled together for seven days. He told me: 'O monk of the monotheists (*hanafiyya*),[735] show your hospitality, for we are hungry!' I said: 'My God, do not let me be disgraced before this unbeliever!' I then saw a tray with food, roast meat, dates and a pitcher full of water. We ate, drank and walked for seven more days. This time I spoke before him, saying: 'O monk of the Christians, show me what you can! For it's now your turn!' He leaned upon his staff and said a prayer, and, lo, there appeared before us two trays with twice the food that was on my tray. I was bewildered, grew pale and refused to eat. He persisted, but I did not respond to him until he finally said: 'I have two good tidings for you. First, I bear witness that there is no deity but God and that Muhammad is His messenger.' And he untied his belt. As for the second, I prayed: 'My God, if this servant of Yours has any worth in Your eyes, give me such-and-such.' And He did. We then ate, and walked forth. We[736] then performed a pilgrimage. We stayed in Mecca for one year, whereupon he died and was buried in its vicinity."

Muhammad b. al-Mubarak al-Suri said: "As Ibrahim b. Adham and I were on our way to Jerusalem, there came the afternoon time and we made a halt under a pomegranate tree. After we had offered several prayers, we heard a voice from under the tree, saying: 'Abu Ishaq, honor us by partaking something of us.' Ibrahim lowered his head. The voice spoke [to] us three times, then said [to me]: 'Muhammad, intercede before him on my behalf, so that he would partake something of us!' I said: 'Abu Ishaq, you have heard [it].' He stood up and plucked two pomegranates. He ate one and gave me the other. I ate it and it was sour. The tree [itself] was short. However, when we passed it by on our way back, it was a tall tree with sweet pomegranates. It started to bear fruit twice a year and people

---

734 The belt symbolized the dependent status of Jewish and Christian minorities under Muslim rule.
735 That is, the Muslims.
736 Another reading has "he".

named it 'the Pomegranate Tree of the Worshipers'. Worshipers used to seek shelter in its shade." I heard Muhammad b. 'Abdallah al-Sufi say: I heard Muhammad b. al-Farhan say: I heard al-Junayd say: I heard Abu Ja'far al-Khassaf say: Jabir al-Rahbi told me: "The people of al-Rahba[737] often expressed to me their rejection of saintly miracles. One day I rode into Rahba sitting on a lion,//446 and asked them: 'Where are those who accuse the friends of God of lying?' From that time on they have left me alone."

I heard Mansur al-Maghribi say: "A Sufi saw al-Khadir – peace be upon him – and asked him: 'Have you ever seen anyone who is above yourself?' He answered: 'Yes, 'Abd al-Razzaq b. Humam used to relate prophetic reports at Medina, and [many] people gathered around him to listen. I saw [nearby] a young man [sitting] with his head upon his knees, and exclaimed: 'Hey you, 'Abd al-Razzaq relates the reports of the Messenger of God – may God bless and greet him. How come you are not listening to him?' He said: 'He relates from the person who is dead,[738] whereas I am never absent from God!'[739] I asked him: 'If things are like you say, who am I?' He raised his head and said: 'You are my brother Abu 'l-'Abbas al-Khadir.' I then realized that God has servants whom I do not know.'" Ibrahim b. Adham had a companion named Yahya, who worshiped God in a room that had neither a ladder nor a staircase. Whenever he needed to perform an ablution, he would go to the door of his room and utter: 'There's no power nor strength save in God!' He would then fly through the air, like a bird. After he performed his ablutions, he would [again] say: 'There's no power nor strength save in God' and would return to his room." Muhammad b. 'Abdallah al-Sufi informed us: I heard 'Umar b. Muhammad b. Ahmad al-Shirazi at Basra say: I heard Abu Muhammad Ja'far al-Hadhdha' at Shiraz say: "I studied under Abu 'Umar al-Istakhri. Whenever a question would occur to me, I would set out for Istakhr.[740] Sometimes he would resolve it for me without me even asking him about it and sometimes I would ask him and he would answer. Once I was prevented from making a journey [to Istakhr]. However, when a question entered my mind he would respond to me from Istakhr and dealt with the matter that had presented itself to me."

Someone related: "A poor man[741] died in a dark room. When we wanted to wash his body, we had to look for a lamp. [Suddenly,] a light appeared through a small window and illuminated the house. We washed him, and when we were done the light disappeared as if it had never been there." Adam b. Abi Iyas related: "When we resided at 'Asqalan,[742] a young man would come to us and converse with us. When we finished our discussion, he would stand and pray [with us].

---

737 An ancient city, now in ruins, on the right bank of the river Euphrates in present-day Syria.
738 That is, the prophet Muhammad.
739 Who is eternal.
740 An ancient city in the province of Fars, Iran.
741 That is, a Sufi.
742 Heb. "Ashkelon", a coastal city in present-day Israel–Palestine.

One day he bid us farewell, saying that he wanted to go to Alexandria.[743] I left with him and offered him a few *dirhams*, but he refused to take them. When I insisted, he threw a handful of sand into his leather bowl and added some sea water to it. He then told me: 'Eat it!' I looked [into it] and, lo, it was a gruel with lots of sugar in it. He then said: 'Does someone who has such a stature//447 with God need your petty change?' He then recited the following:

> By the right of passionate love, O those who love me consider the speech of my impassioned encounter (*wujudi*) with God, which this encounter has rendered unintelligible
> It is forbidden for the heart captivated by passion to find solace in anything else!"

Someone else recited the following:

> In neither the heart nor the soul [of the lover] is there any empty space for the beloved to see
> He is my aspiration, my desire and my joy
> And it is through him, as long as I live, that my life is [full of] delight
> When sickness happens to enter my heart
> I will not be able to find any healer for it apart from him.

Ibrahim al-Ajurri related: "A Jew came to me to demand a debt that I had owed him. At that moment I was sitting next to a kiln for baking bricks (*ajurr*).[744] The Jew told me: 'Ibrahim, show me a miracle that would make me become a Muslim!' I asked him: 'Will you do it?' He said that he would. I told him: 'Take off your outer garment!' When he took it off, I wrapped it up and put my own garment around it. After that I threw all this into the kiln and entered the kiln, drawing the clothing out of the blaze. I went out through the other door and, lo and behold, my garment preserved its original form, undamaged, whereas his turned into a bunch of ashes. So, that Jew embraced Islam." It is related that Habib al-ʿAjami was seen at Basra on the Day of Provisioning [oneself] with Water (*yawm al-tarwiya*) and at the Day of the [Plain of] ʿArafat (*yawm ʿarafa*).[745] I heard Muhammad b. ʿAbdallah al-Sufi say: I heard Ahmad b. Muhammad b. ʿAbdallah al-Farghani say: "ʿAbbas b. al-Muhtadi married a certain woman. On the night after the wedding, however, he found himself seized with remorse. When he tried to approach [his wife], he was forcefully kept from her (*zujira ʿanha*) in such a way as he could not sleep with her. So he left her, and in three days it turned out that she already had a husband."[746] The master and imam [al-Qushayri] commented:

---

743 A major city in Egypt.
744 Al-Ajurri's name indicates that he earned his living making and baking bricks.
745 These are two consecutive days during the pilgrimage season, namely, the 8th and the 9th of the month of Dhu ʾl-Hijja; before proceeding to the Plain of ʿArafat from the vicinity of Mecca, the pilgrims provided themselves with water for the journey on the next day.
746 The implication here is that her husband might have been absent (in a travel or battle) for a long time. In such cases a judgement is issued allowing the deserted wife to remarry.

"This is a true miracle, because [his] religious knowledge guarded him [from the sin of cohabiting with a woman who had a living husband]!"

It is related that al-Fudayl b. ʿIyad once found himself on one of the mountains around [the valley of Mina].[747] He said: "If only a friend of God would order this mountain to tremble, it would surely tremble. When the mountain moved, he said: 'Stand still! I don't want you to do this!' And the mountain was still!"//448 ʿAbd al-Wahid b. Zayd[748] asked Abu ʿAsim al-Basri: "How did you behave when al-Hajjaj[749] summoned you?" He said: "I was in my room, when they knocked on my door[750] and came in. I gave myself a push and found myself on the mountain of Abu Qubays near Mecca!" ʿAbd al-Wahid asked him: "How did you eat?" He answered: "Every time I wanted to break my fast, an old woman would climb up to me with two loaves of bread, which I used to eat while in Basra." ʿAbd al-Wahid commented: "God Most High ordered this [entire] world to serve Abu ʿAsim." It is related that when ʿAmir b. ʿAbd Qays[751] received his military stipend, he would give of it to everyone who met him on his way. Once at home, he would throw the money on the floor and its amount would be the same as he had received, nothing missing. I heard Abu ʿAbdallah al-Shirazi say: I heard Abu Ahmad al-Kabir say: I heard Abu ʿAbdallah b. Khafif say: I heard Abu ʿAmr al-Zajjaji say: "When I was about to set out on a pilgrimage, I went to al-Junayd, who gave me a real *dirham*.[752] I tied it up in my waist-cloth. [En route] each time I entered a house I found friends there, so I never needed that *dirham*. When I returned to Baghdad and came to al-Junayd, he stretched his hand and told me: 'Give [it to me]!' He then asked me: 'How was it?' I answered: 'The ordinance was fulfilled!'" Abu Jaʿfar al-Aʿwar recounted: "I was with Dhu ʾl-Nun al-Misri. We were trading stories about how things obey [the orders of] the friends of God. Dhu ʾl-Nun said: 'One sign of [such] obedience is that I tell this couch to walk around and visit [all] four corners of this house, then to return to its place.' He did [as he had said], and indeed the couch walked around, visiting [all] four corners of the house, then returned to its place. Among us was a youth, who burst into tears, then died instantaneously."

It is related that Wasil al-Ahdab was reading [the verse]: "And in heaven is your provision, and that [which] you are promised."[753] He exclaimed: "My

---

747 An area near Mecca that serves as a station on the pilgrimage route.
748 On him, see *IM*, pp. 16–18.
749 Al-Hajjaj b. Yusuf al-Thaqafi (d. 95/714), a talented military commander and statesman under the early Umayyad caliphs (especially, ʿAbd al-Malik), who was notorious for his cruelty and "ruthless efficiency", which earned him an unfavorable reputation in later Muslim literature and folk-lore, especially under the ʿAbbasids. Fiercely loyal to the Umayyad dynasty, he persecuted anyone who dared to raise their voice against its rule.
750 The context of the story and Abu ʿAsim's name indicate that he resided in Basra at that time.
751 An early ascetic (d. around 50/670), who is said to have deliberately imitated the world denouncing attitudes of Christian monks.
752 Namely, one whose weight and composition met the state standard.
753 Q. 51:22.

provision is in heaven, and I have been searching for it here on earth. By God, I will not search for it anymore!" He settled in some ruins and spent two days there. Nothing was given to him and he felt great distress. On the third day, a palm-leaf basket full of dates appeared before him. He had a brother, whose intention was even stronger [than his]. When the brother joined him, there appeared before them two baskets. This condition of theirs persisted until death separated them.//449 A Sufi related: "I watched over Ibrahim b. Adham in the garden that he was guarding.[754] When he was overcome with slumber, there appeared a snake with a bunch of narcissus in its mouth and fanned over him with it." It is related: "As a group of people was traveling with Ayyub al-Sakhtiyani they despaired of finding water. Ayyub asked [them]: 'Will you keep my secret as long as I am alive?' They answered: 'Yes!' Ayyub spun around and, lo, water gushed forth [from the ground] and we drank of it. When we arrived in Basra, Hammad b. Zayd told this story. ʿAbd al-Wahid b. Zayd [confirmed it], saying: 'I witnessed that with him on that day!'"

Bakr b. ʿAbd al-Rahman said: "We were with Dhu ʾl-Nun al-Misri in the desert. We found shelter under a tree of the Umm Ghaylan species.[755] I said: 'How wonderful this place would be if there were dates here!' Dhu ʾl-Nun smiled and said: 'Do you [really] want dates?' He shook the tree and uttered: 'I adjure you by Him Who originated you and made you a tree, shower fresh dates upon us!' He shook it again and fresh dates showered down. We ate them and were satiated [with them]. After we took a nap and woke up, we shook the tree [again], but it showered us with thorns!" Abu ʾl-Qasim b. Marwan al-Nihawandi related: "[Once] Abu Bakr al-Warraq and I were walking along the sea shore towards Saydaʾ[756] with Abu Saʿid al-Kharraz. He saw somebody [walking] in the distance and said: 'Sit down! This person must be a friend of God!' Soon a young man with a handsome face came by. He was carrying a [begging] leather-bowl and an inkpot and wearing a patched frock. Abu Saʿid turned to him in order to reprimand his carrying [both] the inkpot and the beggar's bowl[757] and said: 'O young man, what are the paths to God Most High?' He answered: 'Abu Saʿid, I know two paths to God: the common and the elect. You are on the common path. As for the elect path, let me show it to you.' He then walked over the water until he vanished from our sight." Abu Saʿid left perplexed. Al-Junayd narrated: "I went to the al-Shuniziya[758] mosque and saw there a group of Sufis discussing the signs of God. One of them said: 'I knew a man who could order this column to become half gold and half silver, and it would be [as he said].'" Al-Junayd said: "I looked [at it] and it indeed was half gold and half silver!" It is related that when

---

754 According to a legend, he earned his livelihood as a night watchman guarding gardens and fields.
755 A species of the acacia tree common to the arid desert.
756 Ancient "Sidon"; a coastal city in present-day Lebanon.
757 Because one was an attribute of a scholar, the other one of a mendicant dervish.
758 A mosque and cemetery in the western part of Baghdad.

Sufyan al-Thawri went on a pilgrimage with Shayban al-Ra'i, they encountered a lion. Sufyan cried: 'Do you see this lion?' 'Don't be afraid,' Shayban told him. He then took the lion by the ear and rubbed it, after which the lion wagged its tail. Sufyan asked him: 'Isn't it but vainglory?' Shayban retorted, saying: 'If it were not for the fear of vainglory, I would have put my possessions on its back, so that it would carry it all the way to Mecca!'"//450

It is related that after al-Sari [al-Saqati] had abandoned his business, his sister supported him from the proceeds she earned by selling the yarn she spun. One day she came late to his house. He asked her why she was late. She answered: "Because my yarn does not sell. People say it is of poor quality." [That night] al-Sari refrained from eating her food. When his sister came back to him after a while, she saw an old woman cleaning his house. She [also] brought him two loaves of bread every day. The sister was saddened and complained to Ahmad b. Hanbal,[759] who, in turn, mentioned this to al-Sari. The latter said: "When I refrained from eating her food, God assigned this world to support and serve me." Muhammad b. 'Abdallah al-Sufi informed us: 'Ali b. Harun told us: 'Ali b. Abi Muhammad al-Tamimi told us: Ja'far b. al-Qasim al-Khawwas told us: Ahmad b. Muhammad al-Tusi told us: Muhammad b. Mansur al-Tusi told us: "I was with Abu Mahfuz Ma'ruf al-Karkhi and he prayed for me. When I returned to him the next day, I noticed a scar on his face. Somebody asked him: 'Abu Mahfuz, we were with you the other day, and there was no scar on your face then! What, then, is this?' 'Ask about what concerns you!' retorted al-Karkhi. The man [persisted], saying: 'By the One Whom you worship, tell [me what happened]!' Al-Karkhi related: 'Last night, after I had prayed here, I wanted to circumambulate the Ka'ba. I went to Mecca, performed my circumambulations, and went over to Zamzam[760] in order to drink of its water. I slipped at the door and hurt my face, as you can see.'"

It is related that 'Utba al-Ghulam used to sit, saying: "O turtledove! If you are more obedient to God – may He be great and exalted – than I, then come and perch on my hand!" And the turtledove did indeed come [to him] and perched on his hand. Abu 'Ali al-Razi related: "One day as I was walking along the Euphrates, I felt a craving for fresh fish. All of a sudden, the water pushed out a fish toward me and a man came running and asked: 'Shall I grill it for you?' I said 'Yes', then sat down and ate it." It is related that Ibrahim b. Adham was traveling with a company [of people], when a lion confronted them. They cried: "Abu Ishaq, a lion has confronted us!" Ibrahim came and said [to the lion]: "Lion, if you have been commanded to do something to us, then go ahead. If not, leave!" The lion left and the people continued on their way. Hamid al-Aswad related: "I

---

759 Ibn Hanbal, the founder of the Hanbali legal and theological school, was generally well disposed toward his Sufi contemporaries, although he reserved the right to criticize what he considered to be their "excesses". For details, see Michael Cooperson, "Ahmad Ibn Hanbal and Bishr al-Hafi: A case study in biographical traditions", *Studia Islamica* 86/2 (1997), pp. 71–101.

760 The sacred well located in the Meccan sanctuary.

was in the desert with [Ibrahim] al-Khawwas. When we set up a camp for the night under a tree, a lion approached us. I climbed up the tree and stayed there until morning, sleepless, whereas Ibrahim al-Khawwas [continued to] sleep. The lion sniffed him from head to foot, then walked away.//451 We spent the second night in a mosque of a village. [While there] a gnat descended on Ibrahim's face and bit him. He groaned. I said: 'This is strange. The other night you were not afraid of a lion, while tonight you scream from [the bite of] a gnat!' He said: 'Last night, my spiritual state was one with God – may He be great and exalted – while tonight it is one in which I am on my own.'" It is related that ʿAtaʾ al-Azraq's wife gave him two *dirhams* that she had earned spinning yarn, so that he would buy some flour for them. After he left the house, he encountered a slave girl crying. He asked her what had happened to her. She answered: "My owner had given me two *dirhams* so that I would buy something [for him], but I lost them and am now afraid that he will beat me." ʿAtaʾ gave her [his] two *dirhams* and went away. He sat at the shop of a friend of his, [who earned his living] cutting teakwood and mentioned to him what had happened to him and [said] that he was afraid of his wife's bad temper. His friend told him: "Take some of the sawdust from the sack over there; maybe it will help you to heat your house, for at the moment I am unable to assist you in any other way." So he took the sack [to his house], opened the door and threw in the bag. He then shut the door [and went] to the mosque, where he stayed until the dark in order for his family to be overcome with sleep and for his wife not [to be able] to vent her anger at him. When he opened the door, he found them[761] baking bread. He asked them where the bread had come from. They said: "From the flour that was in the sack. Don't ever buy any other flour!" He exclaimed: "I will do that, God willing!"

I heard Shaykh Abu ʿAbd al-Rahman al-Sulami say: I heard Mansur b. ʿAbdallah say: I heard Jaʿfar b. Barakat say: "I used to sit in a session with some Sufis. [Once] I received one *dinar* and wanted to give it to them. However, it occurred to me that I might need it myself. [Suddenly] I felt a toothache and had to have one of my teeth pulled. Then I felt that my other tooth was aching and I had to have it pulled too. I heard a voice saying: 'If you do not give them that *dinar*, not a single tooth will be left in your mouth!'" The master [al-Qushayri] said: "As far as miracles are concerned, this one is more perfect than if he had received many *dinars* contrary to the customary order [of things]." Abu Sulayman al-Darani related: "ʿAmir b. [ʿAbd] Qays set out for Damascus, carrying a water-skin. When he wished, water poured from it so he could make his ablution;//452 when he wished, milk poured from it, so he could drink it."

ʿUthman b. ʿAbi ʾl-ʿAtika related: "We were on a raid into Byzantine lands. [Our] commander dispatched a detachment to a certain location and set a certain day for it [to return to its headquarters]. The day came, but the detachment did

---

761 That is, his family.

not arrive. In the mean time Abu Muslim⁷⁶² was performing his prayer with his lance thrust into the earth in front of him.⁷⁶³ [Suddenly] a bird perched on the head of his lance, saying: 'The detachment is safe and sound. It will return to you on such-and-such day, at such-and-such time.' Abu Muslim asked it: 'Who are you, may God Most High have mercy on you?' It answered: 'I am one who expels sorrow from the hearts of the faithful!' Abu Muslim went to the commander and informed him about this. When the day mentioned by the bird arrived, the detachment came back, as it had foretold." A Sufi related: "When we were on board a ship, a sick man who was with us died. We performed burial rites over him and wanted to throw him into the sea. [Suddenly] the sea dried up and the ship ran aground. We went out, dug a grave for him and buried him [there]. When we had finished, the water rose, the ship was lifted, and we continued on our way." It is related that when the people of Basra were starving, Habib al-ʿAjami bought some food on credit and distributed it among the needy. He then took his purse and put it under his head. When the creditors came demanding money [from him], he took the purse and it turned out to be full of *dirhams*. With these he settled the debts that he owed to them. It is related that Ibrahim b. Adham wanted to board a ship, but [the crew] refused to allow him [to board] unless he paid them one *dinar*. He performed two cycles of prayer on the shore saying, "My God, they have asked me for something I do not have", and the sand before him turned into *dinars*.

Muhammad b. ʿAbdallah al-Sufi told us: ʿAbd al-ʿAziz b. al-Fadl told us: Muhammad b. Ahmad al-Marwazi told us: ʿAbdallah b. Sulayman told us: Abu Hamza Nasr b. al-Faraj, the servant of Abu Muʿawiya al-Aswad lost his eyesight. However, each time he wanted to recite the Qurʾan, he would unroll the scroll and God would return his eyesight to him. As soon as he rolled the scroll up, his eyesight would leave him. Ahmad b. al-Haytham al-Mutatayyib⁷⁶⁴ said: Bishr al-Hafi said: "Tell Maʿruf al-Karkhi://453 'I will come to you after I have prayed.' I delivered the message and waited for him. We prayed the midday prayer. However, he did not come. We then prayed the afternoon and sunset prayers [but he did not come]. I said to myself: 'Praise be to God, a person like Bishr should say something and not do it! It is impossible that he won't do it.' So I waited on the roof of the mosque near the water-trough. Late at night Bishr finally came with his prayer rug on his head. He approached the Tigris and walked over the water. I jumped off the roof and kissed his hands and feet, saying: 'Pray to God for me!' He prayed for me, then said: 'Keep my secret!' I did not speak about this until he died." I heard ʿAbdallah al-Shirazi say: Abu ʾl-Faraj al-Warathani told us: I heard ʿAli b. Yaʿqub say at Damascus: I heard Abu Bakr Muhammad b. Ahmad say: I heard Qasim al-Juʿi say: "I saw a man circumambulate

---

762 Abu Muslim al-Khawlani (d. 62/682), a Yemeni warrior of the second generation of Muslims, who was renowned for his asceticism and piety.
763 Indicating the direction of Mecca toward which the canonical prayers must be performed.
764 Or "al-Mutatabbib".

the Kaʿba, who repeated one and the same prayer: 'My God, You have fulfilled everyone's need, but You have not fulfilled my need!' I asked him: 'What is it with you? You say one and the same prayer!' He answered: 'I will tell you. Know that I was one of seven men from different lands, who joined the holy war [against the Byzantines]. The Byzantines captured us and took us with them in order to execute us. [Suddenly] I saw how seven doors were opened in the sky. At each of them stood a beautiful maiden of Paradise. One of us stepped forward and his head was cut off. I saw a maiden of Paradise descend to the earth with a kerchief in her hand and receive his spirit. Thus the heads of six men were cut off. Then one of the Byzantines asked that I be given to him [as a slave]. [The last] maiden exclaimed: "O you, the deprived one (*mahrum*), what a thing you have missed!" The doors [in the sky] were closed and I, my friend, am now having regrets and grieving for what I have missed!'" Qasim al-Juʿi added: "I consider him to be the best of them all, because he saw something they did not see and directed his passion [toward God] after they had died." I also heard him [al-Shirazi] say: I heard Abu ʾl-Najm Ahmad b. al-Husayn in Khuzistan say: I heard Abu Bakr al-Kattani say: "As I was traveling to Mecca in the middle of the year, I came upon a large purse lined with sparkling *dinars*. I decided to take it with me in order to distribute it among Mecca's poor, but a voice told me: 'If you take it, We shall deprive you of your [state of] poverty!'"

Muhammad b. ʿAbdallah al-Sufi informed us: Ahmad b. Yusuf al-Khayyat told us: I heard Abu ʿAli al-Rudhbari say: I heard al-ʿAbbas al-Sharqi say: "We were on the road to Mecca together with Abu Turab al-Nakhshabi. He veered off to the side of the road and//454 a young companion of his told him: 'I am thirsty.' Abu Turab stomped the ground with his foot and there appeared a spring with cold, sweet water. The youth said: 'I would like to drink it with a cup.' Abu Turab struck his hand upon the ground and gave the youth a cup of white glass that was the nicest I had ever seen. The youth drank and gave it to us to drink, and the cup remained with us until we reached Mecca. One day Abu Turab asked me: 'What do your companions say about these matters which God generously grants to [some of] His servants?' I said: 'I have not seen anyone who would not believe in them.' He said: 'Whoever does not believe in them is an unbeliever. I inquired of you in the sense of [their] inner states.' I said: 'I am not aware of them speaking about this.' He commented: 'Your companions hold that they[765] are a deception on the part of God. However, this is not the case. They become a deception only when one relies on them. As for those who do not seek them and who do not rely upon them, [they have attained] the degree of the men of God (*rabbaniyun*).'" Muhammad b. ʿAbdallah al-Sufi told us: Abu ʾl-Faraj al-Warathani told us: I heard Muhammad b. ʿAli b. al-Husayn al-Muqri at Tarsus[766] say: I heard Abu ʿAbdallah b. al-Jallaʾ say: "We were in Sari al-Saqati's room in Baghdad. After some part of the night had passed, he put on a clean

---

765 That is, saintly miracles.
766 An ancient city in Cilicia, in present-day Turkey.

shirt, trousers, a cloak and sandals, then prepared to leave. I asked where he was going at such a [late] time. He answered: 'I will visit Fath al-Mawsili.' As he was walking through the streets of Baghdad, a night patrol seized him and jailed him. The next day, an order was issued that he should be flogged along with the other prisoners. When the executioner raised his hand to strike him, it stopped [in mid-air] and he was unable to move it. They told the executioner: 'Beat!' He answered: 'In front of me stands a [Sufi] master, who [keeps] telling [me], "Do not beat him!", and I cannot move my hand.' They investigated who that man was, and it turned out to be Fath al-Mawsili. So they did not beat him."[767]

Shaykh Abu ʿAbd al-Rahman al-Sulami informed us: Abu ʾl-Harith al-Khattabi told us: Muhammad b. al-Fadl told us: ʿAli b. Muslim told us: Saʿid b. Yahya al-Basri told us: "Some people of the Quraysh [tribe] used to attend the sessions of ʿAbd al-Wahid b. Zayd. One day they came to him and said: 'We fear shortage and need.' He raised his face to the heavens and said: 'My God, I implore You with Your lofty name, with which You show [Your] generosity to whomever You will of Your friends and with which You instruct the pure ones among Your beloved [servants], that You bestow upon us our daily sustenance thereby cutting [out] Satan's bonds from our hearts and the hearts of these companions of ours. For You are the [All-]Compassionate Giver, Whose beneficence has no beginning and no end. Now, right now, my God!' Then I heard, by God, the clattering of the roof and *dinars* and *dirhams* showered upon us.//455 ʿAbd al-Wahid b. Zayd said: 'May God suffice you – may He be great and exalted – to the exclusion of everything else!' The people [of Quraysh] collected this [money]. Only ʿAbd al-Wahid b. Zayd took nothing [for himself]." I heard Abu ʿAbdallah al-Shirazi say: I heard Abu ʿAbdallah Muhammad b. ʿAli al-Juzi[768] at Jundishapur[769] say: I heard al-Kattani say: "[In Mecca] I met a Sufi, a stranger, whom I had not known before. He came up to the Kaʿba and said: 'O Lord, I do not know what those – he meant the people circumambulating the Kaʿba – are reciting!' Someone told him: 'Look at this sheet of paper!' [Suddenly] the sheet flew into the air and disappeared." I also heard him [al-Shirazi] say: I heard ʿAbd al-Wahid b. Bakr al-Warathani say: I heard Muhammad b. ʿAli b. al-Husayn al-Muqri at Tarsus say: I heard Abu ʿAbdallah b. al-Jallaʾ say: "One day, my mother had a craving for fish and asked my father to bring her one. My father went to the market and I followed him. He bought a fish and stood looking for someone to carry it for him. He saw a boy with another boy stop in front of him. The boy asked: 'Uncle, you want someone to carry it for you?' My father said: 'Yes.' The boy took the fish and walked along with us. We heard the call to the prayer. The boy said: 'The caller is calling to prayer. I need to make my ablution and pray, if you allow me. If not, you will [have to] carry the fish yourselves.' He put down the fish and left. My father said: 'We'd better put our trust in God

---

767 That is, Sari al-Saqati.
768 Or "al-Jawzi".
769 Or "Gondeshapur"; an ancient city in Khuzistan, Iran.

regarding this fish.' So we entered the mosque and prayed; when we came out we found the fish exactly as we left it. The boy picked up the fish and we went to our house. My father mentioned this [episode] to my mother, who said: 'Tell him to stay with us, so that we could eat all together.' We invited him, but he said that he was fasting. We told him: 'Then come back to us tonight!' He responded: 'I work as a porter only once a day, and I will not do it twice. However, I will now retire to the mosque and remain there until the sunset prayer. Then I will come by your place.' He then walked away. In the evening, the boy came to us and we ate together. When we were done, we showed him the place to make ablutions. We noticed that he preferred solitude and left him alone in the house. Now, one of our relatives had a paralytic daughter. She came to us walking later that night, and we asked her about [the change in] her condition.[770] She said that she prayed: 'Lord, for the sake of our guest, cure me! And, lo, I was able to stand up.' We went looking for the boy. The doors were locked as before, but we could not find the boy. My father commented: 'Among them[771] are [both] big and small!'"//456 I heard Muhammad b. al-Husayn say: Abu ʾl-Harith al-Khattabi said: Muhammad b. al-Fadl told us: ʿAli b. Muslim told us: Saʿid b. Yahya al-Basri told us: "I went to visit ʿAbd al-Wahid b. Zayd. He was sitting in the shade. I asked him: 'If you ask God to bestow your sustenance upon you, you hope that He will do this?' He answered: 'My Lord knows better about the well-being of His servants.' He took a handful of pebbles from the ground, then said: 'My God, if You want to make them gold, then do so!' And, by God, they became gold in his hand. He threw them at me, saying: 'Spend it [as charity]! There's nothing good in this world, except that [it prepares you] for the next one.'"

I heard Muhammad b. ʿAbdallah al-Sufi say: I heard al-Husayn b. Ahmad al-Farisi say: I heard al-Duqqi[772] say: I heard Ahmad b. Mansur say that the master Abu Yaʿqub al-Susi related: "As I was washing [the body of] a Sufi disciple [lying] on the washing bier, he grabbed me by the thumb. I told him: 'My son, let go of my hand. I know that you are not dead. This is nothing but a transition from one abode to another.' And he let go of my hand." I also heard him [Muhammad b. ʿAbdallah] say: I heard Abu Bakr al-Tarsusi say: I heard Ibrahim b. Shayban say: "A young man of proper [spiritual] aspiration (*irada*) attached himself to me. He died. My heart was very distraught on his account. When I started to wash his body, I wanted to wash his hands. Because of my grief, I began washing his left hand first. He pulled it away from me and gave me his right hand. I said: 'You are right, my son, and I am wrong.'" I also heard him say: I heard Abu ʾl-Najm al-Muqri al-Bardhaʿi at Shiraz say: I heard al-Duqqi[773] say: I heard Ahmad b. Mansur say: I heard Abu Yaʿqub al-Susi say: "In Mecca a Sufi novice came to me and said: 'Master, I will die tomorrow at noon. Take this

---

770 That is, she was now able to walk on her own.
771 That is, the friends of God.
772 Or "al-Raqqi".
773 Or "al-Raqqi".

dinar and spend half of it on digging a grave for me and the other half on my shroud.' The next day he came and performed a circumambulation of the Ka'ba. He then stepped back from it and died. I wrapped him in a shroud and put him in the grave. [Suddenly] he opened his eyes. I asked him: 'Is there life after death?' He answered: 'I am alive, for every lover of God is alive.'" I heard Shaykh Abu 'Abd al-Rahman al-Sulami say: I heard Muhammad b. al-Husayn al-Baghdadi say: I heard Abu 'Ali b. Wasif al-Mu'addib say: "One day, Sahl b. 'Abdallah [al-Tustari] was discoursing regarding the remembrance of God. He said: 'If one who remembers God in truth had the intention to revive the dead, he would do so.' He then rubbed a sick man with his hand, and the man was cured and stood up."

I heard Abu 'Abdallah al-Shirazi say: 'Ali b. Ibrahim b. Ahmad informed me: 'Uthman b. Ahmad told us: al-Hasan b. 'Amr told us: I heard Bishr b. al-Harith say://457 "When 'Amr b. 'Utba prayed, a cloud used to hover over his head and the lions would assemble around him wagging their tails." I heard him [al-Shirazi] say: I heard Abu 'Abdallah b. Muflih say: I heard al-Maghazili say: I heard al-Junayd say: "I had four *dirhams* and I went to see al-Sari. I said: 'Here are four *dirhams* that I brought you.' Al-Sari exclaimed: 'I give you good news that you will prosper, [my] boy! I was in need of four *dirhams* and I prayed: "My God, send them to me by means of someone who will prosper with You!"'" I also heard him [al-Shirazi] say: Ibrahim b. Ahmad al-Tabari told me: Ahmad b. Yusuf told us: Ahmad b. Ibrahim b. Yahya told us: my father told me: Abu Ibrahim al-Yamani told me: "We set out on a journey together with Ibrahim b. Adham and were walking along the seashore. We came across a thicket in which there was plenty of dry firewood. Nearby there was a fort. He said to Ibrahim b. Adham: 'What if we spend the night here and light a fire with this wood?' He agreed. We asked [the garrison of the fort] for fire and set up a campfire [with the dry firewood]. We had with us some bread that we took out in order to eat. One of us said: 'How wonderful are these coals. If only we had some meat to broil upon them!' Ibrahim b. Adham said: 'God Most High has the power to feed you!' Immediately, a lion appeared, chasing an ibex. When the ibex approached us, it fell and broke its neck. Ibrahim b. Adham stood up and cried: 'Slaughter it! God has fed you!' So we slaughtered it and broiled its meat, as the lion stood there watching." I heard Muhammad b. al-Husayn say: I heard Abu 'l-Qasim 'Abdallah b. 'Ali al-Shajari say: I heard Hamid al-Aswad say: "I was with Ibrahim al-Khawwas in the desert for seven days, with [our] condition remaining unchanged [all this time]. On the seventh day, however, I grew weak and sat down. He turned to me and asked: 'What has happened to you?' I said that I had grown weak. He asked me: 'What do you need most: food or water?' I said: 'Water.' He then said: 'Water is behind you.' I turned and indeed there was a spring with water that was like fresh milk. I drank and made my ablutions. Ibrahim watched but did not come near. When I was ready to go, I decided to take some of it with me. However, he said: 'Don't do this. This is not something you keep as provisions.'" I heard Abu 'Abdallah [al-Shirazi] say: I heard Abu

'Abdallah al-Dabbas al-Baghdadi say: I heard Fatima, the sister of Abu 'Ali al-Rudhbari say: I heard Zaytuna, the maid-servant of Abu 'l-Husayn al-Nuri,//458 who also served Abu Hamza [al-Baghdadi] and al-Junayd, relate: "It was a cold day. I asked al-Nuri whether I should bring him anything. He said: 'Yes.' I asked him what he wanted. He said [that he wanted] bread and milk, so I brought them to him. In front of him there were some extinct coals, which he kept stirring with his hand to keep it busy [with something]. When he started eating the bread, the milk began to stream down his arm [mixed] with the black [dust] of the coal. I said to myself: 'O Lord, how filthy Your friends are! There's no one among them who is clean!' When I left him and went outside, a woman grabbed me [in the street] and shouted: 'You stole a bundle of clothing from me!' They dragged me to the police officer. When al-Nuri was informed about this, he went to the police officer and told him: 'Don't detain her, for she is a friend of God Most High!' The officer said: 'But what can I do? That woman has brought charges [against her].' Then came a maid carrying the bundle of clothing that [the woman] was looking for. When al-Nuri brought the woman[774] home, he told her: 'And you [still] say: "How filthy Your friends are!"' The maid said: 'I have already repented before God Most High!'"

I heard Muhammad b. 'Abdallah al-Shirazi say: I heard Muhammad b. Faris al-Farisi say: I heard Abu 'l-Hasan Khayr al-Nassaj say: I heard [Ibrahim] al-Khawwas say: "On one of my journeys, I experienced such a [strong] thirst that I collapsed because of it. Suddenly, I felt water being splashed over my face. I opened my eyes and saw before me a handsome man, riding a brownish-gray horse. He gave me water to drink and told me: 'Be my co-rider!' After a short while, I found myself in the Hijaz. The man asked me: 'What do you see?' I told him: 'I see Medina!' He then said: 'Dismount, and go and greet the Messenger of God – may God bless and greet him. Tell him: "Your brother al-Khadir sends you his greetings!"'" I heard Shaykh Abu 'Abd al-Rahman al-Sulami say: I heard Muhammad b. al-Hasan al-Baghdadi say: Abu al-Hadid said: I heard al-Muzaffar al-Jassas say: "One night I was with Nasr al-Kharrat at a certain location. We were debating issues pertaining to [Sufi] knowledge. Al-Kharrat said: 'When someone remembers God, at the beginning of his remembrance he needs to know that his remembrance is by virtue of God Most High's remembering him [first], for his own remembrance comes from God's remembrance.' I disagreed with him and he said: 'If only al-Khadir – peace be upon him – were here he would bear witness to the correctness of my statement!' Suddenly, there appeared [before us] an old man suspended between the sky and the earth. He approached us and said: 'He has spoken the truth. One who remembers God Most High acquires his remembrance by virtue of God Most High's remembering him.' We then realized that that was al-Khadir – peace be upon him." I heard

---

774 It seems that the mode of the narrative is switched here from the first-person account of al-Nuri's maid to a third-person narrative only to return to the first-person mode again in the next sentence.

the master Abu ʿAli al-Daqqaq say: "A man went to Sahl b. ʿAbdallah [al-Tustari] and said: 'People say that you can walk on water.' Sahl said: 'Ask the muezzin of this quarter. He is a righteous man who won't lie.' The man asked him, and the muezzin said: 'I know nothing about it. However, a few days ago he went to the pond to make his ablution and fell into the water. If it had not been for me, he would have remained there.'" The master Abu ʿAli al-Daqqaq said://459 "Sahl did indeed possess the quality ascribed to him.[775] However, God – praise be to Him – wants to protect [the secrets of] His friends, so He used the story of the muezzin and the pond as a cover [to hide] the true state of Sahl. For Sahl did indeed display miracles."

Similar to this is the story narrated by Abu ʿUthman al-Maghribi, who said that he saw it written down by the hand of Abu ʾl-Hasan al-Jurjani. It said: "Once I decided to go to Egypt. It occurred to me that I should travel by ship. Then it occurred to me that I am well-known there, while I was leery of [mundane] fame. In the meantime, a ship was passing by. Something prompted me and I walked across the water until I caught up with it and entered it, as people were watching. However, no one said that this was contrary to the customary order of things, and I realized that the friend of God is always protected [by Him], even if his actions are obvious."

Some of the [miraculous] states of the master Abu ʿAli al-Daqqaq – may God be pleased with him – we witnessed with our own eyes. Thus, he was afflicted with an inflammation of the bladder and had to urinate several times during an hour, to the extent that he had to make more than one ablution to perform two cycles of canonical prayer. He would carry a bottle with him on the way to his teaching session and would use it several times along the way both coming and going. However, when he sat on his chair, lecturing, he would require no ablutions, even when the session lasted for a long time. We observed this [quality] in him for many years, although it did not occur to us during his lifetime that this was something that violated the customary order [of things]. Only after his death this thought visited me and I realized [what was going on]. Similar to this is a story about Sahl b. ʿAbdallah. At the end of his life he was afflicted with paralysis, yet his strength would return to him at the time of the [canonical] prayer and he would perform it standing. It is well known that ʿAbdallah al-Wazzan was paralyzed, yet when he experienced ecstasy while listening to music he would stand up and take part in it.

I heard Muhammad b. ʿAbdallah al-Sufi say: Ibrahim b. Muhammad al-Maliki told us: Yusuf b. Ahmad al-Baghdadi told us: Ahmad b. Abi ʾl-Hawari told us: "I went on pilgrimage with Abu Sulayman al-Darani. During our journey, I lost my water-skin. I told Abu Sulayman: 'I have lost the water-skin.' So we were left without water, and it was very cold. Abu Sulayman prayed: 'O You Who return that which was lost and Who guides away from error, return our loss to us!' All of a sudden, we heard someone shouting: 'Who has lost a water-skin?' I shouted:

---

775 That is, the ability to walk on the water.

'Me!' I took it. As we continued on our way, we wrapped ourselves up in fur due to the severe cold. We came across a man dressed in rags, who was dripping with sweat. Abu Sulayman told him: 'Come on, we shall share with you some of our [warm]//460 clothes!' The man responded: 'Abu Sulayman, how can you instruct us in [matters of] renunciation, while you suffer from cold? I have been traveling through this wasteland, yet I have never shivered nor trembled. During the cold season God has clothed me with the heat of His love, while during the summer He has clothed me with the cool taste of His love!' He then went away."

I also heard him [Muhammad b. ʿAbdallah al-Sufi] say: I heard Abu Bakr al-Takriti say: I heard Muhammad b. ʿAli al-Kattani say: I heard [Ibrahim] al-Khawwas say: "Once I was walking through the desert in the middle of the day. I arrived at a tree with [a spring of] water nearby and made camp there. Suddenly, I saw an enormous lion coming towards me. I surrendered myself [to my fate]. As the lion came close to me, [I saw that] it was limping. It groaned, knelt in front of me and put its paw onto my lap. I looked at it and discovered that it was swollen and smeared with pus and blood. I took a piece of wood and pierced the place swollen with pus. Then I tied a piece of cloth around its paw. The lion went away. It soon came back with [its] two cubs, which wagged their tails at me. They brought me a loaf of bread." I also heard him say: ʿAli al-Saʾih told us: Muhammad b. ʿAbdallah b. Matraf[776] told us: Muhammad b. al-Hasan al-ʿAsqalani told us: Ahmad b. Abi ʾl-Hawari told us: "Muhammad b. al-Sammak complained to us [about his health]. So we took [a sample of] his urine and headed to the doctor, who was a Christian. As we were traveling between al-Hira and Kufa[777] we came across a man with a handsome face, who emanated a pleasant smell and wore a clean garment. He asked us where we were going. We said: 'We are looking for so-and-so, the doctor, to show him Ibn al-Sammak's urine.' He exclaimed: 'You are seeking to help a friend of God by having recourse to an enemy of His! Smash this [bottle] against the ground and go back to Ibn al-Sammak. Tell him: "Put your hand on the place that hurts and say: 'With the truth We have sent it down, and with the truth it has come down.' " '[778] The man then disappeared from our sight. We returned to Ibn al-Sammak and told him about what had happened. He put his hand on the place that hurt him and said what the man had said. He was cured on the spot, and said: 'That was al-Khadir – peace be upon him!' "

I heard Muhammad b. al-Husayn say: I heard ʿAbd al-Rahman b. Muhammad al-Sufi say: I heard my uncle (ʿAmmi) al-Bistami say: "We were present at Abu Yazid al-Bistami's teaching session, when he said: 'Let's go and welcome a friend of God Most High!' We stood up and went. When we reached the city gate, we met Ibrahim b. Shayba al-Harawi. Abu Yazid told him: 'It occurred to me that I [should] come out to welcome you and intercede on your behalf with my

---

776 Or "al-Mutarrif".
777 Cities in lower Iraq.
778 Q. 17:105; 17:107, according to Arberry's translation.

Lord!'//461 'If you were to intercede on behalf of all creatures of this world, this would not be much,' responded Ibrahim b. Shayba, 'for they are but a piece of dirt!' Abu Yazid was perplexed by his response." The master [al-Qushayri] commented: "The miracle of Ibrahim, who made little of this world, is more perfect than that of Abu Yazid in so far as he demonstrated [supernatural] perspicacity and a stance with regard to intercession that corresponded to his spiritual state." I heard Shaykh Abu ʿAbd al-Rahman al-Sulami say: I heard Abu Bakr al-Razi say: I heard Yusuf b. al-Husayn say: I heard Dhu ʾl-Nun al-Misri say, when Salim al-Maghribi asked him about the cause of his repentance: "I left Egypt[779] for a village [in the countryside] and slept while on the road. When I woke up and opened my eyes, I noticed a blind [nestling] lark that had fallen out from a tree onto the ground. [Suddenly] the earth split open and there emerged from it two bowls, one gold and one silver. One of them contained sesame seeds, the other rosewater. The nestling ate from one and drank from the other. I said [to myself]: 'This is sufficient for me! I have repented.' And I kept standing at [God's] door until He finally received me."

It is related that ʿAbd al-Wahid b. Zayd was afflicted by palsy. When the time of [canonical] prayer arrived, he wanted to make his ablution. He cried: "Anybody here?" but no one responded to him. He was afraid that he would miss the time [of the prayer] and exclaimed: "Lord, set me free from my fetters, so that I can perform my ablution, and then it will be up to You how to deal with me!" He was cured and performed his ablutions. He then returned to his bed and reverted to his prior state. Abu Ayyub al-Hammal related: "Whenever Abu ʿAbdallah al-Daylami decided to make camp during his travels, he would lean up to his donkey and say in its ear: 'I would have wanted to tie you up. However, I won't tie you up and will send you to graze in the field. When we choose to depart, do come back!' When the time of departure came, the donkey would come back." It is said that Abu ʿAbdallah al-Daylami had arranged a marriage for his daughter and needed to supply her with dowry. He used to prepare a robe that he would sell for one *dinar* each time [he was in need]. So he prepared a robe and took it to a dealer. The dealer told him: "This is worth more than one *dinar*." They kept driving the price up until it reached one hundred *dinars* and al-Daylami was able to provide a dowry for his daughter. Al-Nadr b. Shumayl said: "I bought a waste-wrapper, then found out that it was too short. I asked my Lord to stretch it by one cubit." He added: "If I had asked for more, He would have given me more!" It is related that ʿAmir b. ʿAbd Qays asked [God] to make his ablutions easy for him during the winter. [From then on] whenever he brought [ablution water], it steamed. He also asked [God] to remove passion for women from his heart, so that he would pay no attention to them. Finally, he asked [God] to expel Satan from his heart. When he prayed, however, [God] did not grant his wish [this time].

---

779 *Misr*; the story-teller probably refers to Fustat, the first city founded in Egypt by its Muslim conquerors. It served as the residence of the Muslim governors of Egypt, and thus as its *de facto* capital.

Bishr b. al-Harith related: "I came home and found a man there. I asked him: 'Who are you? You entered my home without my permission!' The man said: 'I am your brother al-Khadir.' I asked him to pray for me. He said: 'May God make your obedience to Him easy!' I asked him: 'Say more!' He said: 'May He conceal your obedience from you!'"//462 Ibrahim al-Khawwas related: "During one of my journeys to Mecca, I entered some ruins at night. There I encountered a huge lion. I was scared. Then I heard a voice: 'Be steadfast! Around you are seventy thousand angels to protect you!'" Muhammad b. al-Husayn informed us: Abu 'l-Faraj al-Warathani informed us: I heard Abu 'l-Hasan 'Ali b. Muhammad al-Sirafi say: I heard Ja'far al-Daybuli say: "When al-Nuri went into a stream, a thief stole his clothes. He then brought them back, because his hand had withered. Al-Nuri said: 'He returned [our] clothes to us, and we return his hand to him.' After that he was cured." Al-Shibli related: "Once I made a vow not to eat anything except that which is permitted [by the Divine Law] (halal). One day, as I was wandering about in the desert, I came upon a fig tree. When I stretched my hand toward it, the tree called to me, saying: 'Keep your vow! Don't eat from me, for I belong to a Jew!'"

Abu 'Abdallah b. Khafif related: "On my way to the pilgrimage, I visited Baghdad. The vainglory of the Sufis had filled my head: I did not eat bread for forty days, did not go to see al-Junayd, then left [Baghdad] and drank no water until I reached [the town of] Zubala(h),[780] while maintaining my ritual purity.[781] [Suddenly] I saw a gazelle at the brim of a well, drinking. I was thirsty. When I approached the well, the gazelle fled, and lo, the water [level] in the well dropped to its very bottom. I walked on and exclaimed: 'My Lord, am I not of the same stature [in Your eyes] as this gazelle?' I heard [a voice] behind me, saying: 'We have tested you, and you have not showed [enough] patience!' I returned and, indeed, the well was full of water. I filled my water-skin with it and used it for drinking and ablutions all the way to Medina, but it was never exhausted. As I was drinking [from it], I heard a voice saying: 'The gazelle came with neither a water-skin, nor a rope, whereas you came with both a water-skin and a rope!' On my return from the pilgrimage [via Baghdad] I went to the [Baghdad] Friday mosque. When al-Junayd saw me, he said: 'If you had only been patient, water would have gushed forth from under your feet! If only you had just an hour's worth of patience!'" I heard Hamza b. Yusuf al-Sahmi al-Jurjani say: I heard [Abu] Ahmad b. 'Adi al-Hafiz say: I heard Ahmad b. Hamza at Fustat (Misr) say: 'Abd al-Wahhab, a pious man, told me: Muhammad b. Sa'id al-Basri related: "As I was walking in the streets of Basra, I saw a Bedouin driving a camel. As I was looking at him, the camel fell down dead and its saddle and baggage [also] fell on the ground. I was about to walk on, but, as I looked, I saw the Bedouin pray: 'The Causer of all causes, O the Master of all seekers, return to me what I have just lost//463 – the camel that carried the saddle and

---

780 A small town in lower Iraq.
781 Through constant praying.

the baggage!' And, lo, the camel stood up with both the saddle and the baggage upon its back!"

It is related that Shibl al-Marwazi had a strong appetite for meat and bought some of it for a half *dirham*. On the way, a kite snatched it from him. Shibl went into the mosque to pray. When he returned home, his wife served meat to him. "Where is this from?" he asked. She said: "Two kites had a fight and this fell down from them." Shibl exclaimed: "Praise be to God, Who has not forgotten Shibl, even though Shibl has often forgotten Him!" Muhammad b. ʿAbdallah al-Sufi informed us: ʿAbd al-Wahid b. Bakr al-Warathani told us: I heard Muhammad b. Dawud say: I heard Abu Bakr b. Muʿammar say: I heard Ibn Abi ʿUbayd al-Busri recount on the authority of his father: "My father once took part in a military campaign.[782] As he was riding together with his detachment, the colt he was riding died under him. He prayed: 'O Lord, lend it to us, so that we can return to Busra!' – he meant his [native] village. [All of sudden,] the colt stood up. After he took part in the campaign and returned home, he ordered me to unsaddle the colt. I said: 'It is sweating. If I take the saddle off it, it may catch a cold.' The father said: 'It is on loan, my son!' When I unsaddled the colt, it fell down dead." It is related that one Sufi used to be a grave-robber [before he repented]. Once a woman died. When people prayed over her, the grave-robber prayed with them in order to know where her grave was. When the night came, he dug the grave up. The woman exclaimed: "Praise be to God! A man who has been forgiven is taking the shroud of a woman who has been forgiven!" He said: "Suppose you have been forgiven, but what about me?" The woman said: "God has forgiven both myself and all those who prayed over me!" He said: "So I left her alone and replaced the earth on her grave." The man then repented and his repentance was good.

I heard Hamza b. Yusuf say: I heard Abu ʾl-Hasan Ismaʿil b. ʿAmr b. Kamil in Egypt say: I heard Abu Muhammad Nuʿman b. Musa al-Hiri at al-Hira[783] say: "I saw Dhu ʾl-Nun after two men had a fight. One of them was a sultan's retainer, the other a commoner. The commoner attacked the soldier and broke his tooth. The soldier grabbed him and cried: 'Let the commander settle between us!' As they were passing by Dhu ʾl-Nun, people told them: 'Go to the [Sufi] master!' They went to him and appraised him of what had happened. He took the tooth, moistened it with his saliva and put it back in the soldier's mouth, moving his lips [in prayer]. The tooth, by God's leave, held. The soldier kept examining his mouth only to discover that all his teeth were alike." Abu ʾl-Husayn Muhammad b. al-Husayn al-Qattan informed us at Baghdad: Abu ʿAli Ismaʿil b. Muhammad b. Ismaʿil al-Saffar told us: al-Hasan b. ʿArafa b. Yazid told us: ʿAbdallah b. Idris al-Awdi told us on the authority of Ismaʿil b. Abi Khalid, on the authority of Abu Sabra al-Nakhaʿi: "A man from Yemen was on his way [to

---

782 Probably against the Byzantines.
783 Thus in our text, but it is more likely that the man's name was "al-Jizi", from al-Jiza, a city in Egypt.

the Hijaz], when his donkey expired. He made an ablution, then performed two cycles of prayer and said://464 'My God, I have come to fight a holy war in order to win Your pleasure and I bear witness that You can revive the dead and resurrect those who are in the graves! Don't let me oblige anyone! Today I ask You to resurrect my donkey.' The donkey stood up and wiggled its ears."

I heard Hamza b. Yusuf say: I heard Abu Bakr al-Nabulusi say: I heard Abu Bakr al-Hamdhani say: "I stayed in the desert of the Hijaz for days on end, eating nothing. I was craving hot beans and bread that are made at Bab al-Taq,[784] but I said to myself: 'I am in [the middle of] the desert and there's a great distance between me and Iraq, so my wish will never be fulfilled.' Before I could finish my thought, a Bedouin cried from afar: 'Hot beans and bread!' I came up to him and asked: 'Do you [indeed] have hot beans and bread?' He said: 'Yes.' He spread out the waist-wrapper that was on him, took out beans and bread, and invited me to eat. I ate. He invited me to eat three times, and I ate. On the fourth time I said: 'For the sake of the One Who sent you to me, who are you?' He answered: 'I am al-Khadir.' Then he disappeared and I saw him no more."

I heard Shaykh Abu ʿAbd al-Rahman al-Sulami say: I heard Abu ʾl-ʿAbbas b. al-Khashshab al-Baghdadi say: I heard Abu Jaʿfar al-Haddad say: "I arrived at Thaʿlabiyya,[785] which lay in ruins. I had not eaten anything for seven days. I went inside the domed building. Then some Khurasanians came by, who were so exhausted [by their journey] that they threw themselves on the ground at the entrance to the building. Then a Bedouin came riding a she-camel and threw some dates before them. They started to eat and said nothing to me, while the Bedouin did not see me. After some time, the Bedouin returned and asked them: 'Is there anyone here beside you?' They said: 'Yes, there is a man inside this building.' He asked me: 'Who are you? Why did you not talk [to me]? On my way I encountered a man, who told me: "You have left behind a man whom you have not fed." I was unable to continue my journey and the road was made longer for me because I had to walk [extra] miles.' He put a lot of dates before me and left. I invited the Khurasanians to eat and they ate together with me." I heard Hamza b. Yusuf say: I heard Abu Tahir al-Raqqi say: I heard Ahmad b. ʿAtaʾ say: "A camel once spoke to me. On my way to Mecca I saw camels that carried litters on them. They were extending their necks in the night. I said: 'Praise be to the One Who could relieve them of that which they are carrying!' My own camel then turned to me and uttered: 'Say: "God is great!"' and I said: 'God is great!'"

I heard Muhammad b. ʿAbdallah al-Sufi say: I heard al-Hasan[786] b. Ahmad al-Farisi say: I heard al-Duqqi[787] say: I heard Abu Bakr b. Muʿammar say: I heard Abu Zurʿa al-Janbi say: "A certain woman tried to deceive me. She told me:

---

784 A district of Baghdad.
785 A way-station on the pilgrimage route to Mecca.
786 Or "al-Husayn".
787 Or "al-Raqqi".

'Won't you come into the house to visit a sick person?' When I came in, she locked the door. When I found no one there, I realized what she was up to. I prayed: 'My God, make her black!' And she was blackened. She was frightened and opened the door so that I could leave.//465 I then prayed: 'My God, return her to her [original] state!' And He returned her to her [original] state." I heard Hamza b. Yusuf say: I heard Abu Muhammad al-Ghitrifi say: I heard [Abu Nasr] al-Sarraj say: I heard Abu Sulayman al-Rumi say: I heard Khalil al-Haddad relate: "My son Muhammad went missing and we were losing our minds from grief. I went to Ma'ruf al-Karkhi and said: 'Abu Mahfuz, my son disappeared and his mother is losing her mind from grief!' He asked me what I wanted [him to do]. I said: 'Pray to God that He return him [to us].' He prayed: 'My God, the heaven and the earth are Yours and what lies between them is Yours also. Bring Muhammad [back]!'" Khalil continued, saying: "I went to the Damascus gate[788] and found him standing there. 'Where have you been, Muhammad?' I asked him. He said: 'My father, just a few moments ago I was in al-Anbar.'"[789]

The master Abu 'l-Qasim [al-Qushayri] said: "Know that stories of this sort are countless. If we were to add to them more than we have already mentioned we would go beyond the confines of brevity that we strive to achieve. What we have already mentioned suffices for this topic."

The vision of the Sufis (ru'yat al-qawm)

God Most High said: "For them[790] there are good tidings in the present life and in the life to come."[791] [Commentators] say: "This [means] the beautiful vision that the believer will see or that will be shown to him."

Abu 'l-Hasan al-Ahwazi informed us: Ahmad b. 'Ubayd al-Basri informed us: Ishaq b. Ibrahim al-Munqari told us: Mansur b. Abi Muzahim told us: Abu Bakr b. 'Ayyash told us on the authority of 'Asim, on the authority of Abu Salih, on the authority of Abu 'l-Darda', who said that someone questioned the Prophet – may God bless and greet him – about this verse, that is, "For them there are good tidings in the present life and in the life to come." The Prophet responded: "No one has asked me about this verse before. This [means] the beautiful vision that the believer will see or that will be shown to him."

Sayyid[792] Abu 'l-Hasan Muhammad b. al-Husayn al-'Alawi informed us: Abu 'Ali al-Husayn b. Muhammad [b.] Zayd informed us: 'Abdallah b. al-Walid told us on the authority of Sufyan [al-Thawri], on the authority of Yahya b. Sa'id, on the authority of Abu Salama, on the authority of Abu Qatada that the Messenger of God – may God bless and greet him – said: "Visionary dream

---

788 In Baghdad.
789 A city on the left bank of the Euphrates, some thirty-eight miles from Baghdad.
790 That is, the friends of God.
791 Q. 10:64.
792 An honorific title of a descendant of the Prophet.

(*ruʾya*) is from God, while dream (*hulm*) is from Satan. If one of you dreams a night dream that he dislikes, let him spit to his left and take refuge in God.⁷⁹³ In this case, it won't hurt him."//466

Abu Bakr Muhammad b. Ahmad ʿAbdus al-Muzakki informed us: Abu Ahmad Hamza b. al-ʿAbbas al-Bazzaz told us: ʿAyyash b. Muhammad b. Hatim told us: ʿAbdallah b. Musa told us: Israʾil told us on the authority of Abu Ishaq, on the authority of Abu ʾl-Ahwas, on the authority of Abu ʿUbayda, on the authority of ʿAbdallah b. Masʿud, who said that the Messenger of God – may God bless and greet him – said: "Whoever sees me in a dream has seen me, for Satan cannot appear in my form." The meaning of this report is this: This vision is a veracious one and its interpretation is truth, for vision is one type of miracle. The correct definition of vision is the thoughts that enter the heart and the states that take their shape in the imagination (*wahm*), when sleep does not entirely suppress perception. When a person is in a waking state, he believes that this was a true vision. However, for human beings this is but visual forms and imaginings that reside in their hearts. When their external perceptions abandon them, these imaginings are stripped of the knowledge both acquired and necessary, and then this state strengthens itself in the seer. However, when he wakes up, the states that he imagined weaken in comparison to his perception [of things] by means of his [physical] sight and by means of the necessary knowledge [granted to him]. The seer of dreams is like a person who sees by means of the light of a lamp, when the darkness falls. However, when the sun rises it outshines the light of the lamp, for the latter is weak in comparison to the light of the sun. Thus, the condition of dream is like that of someone in the lamplight, while the condition of someone who wakes up is like that of someone upon whom the day rises. One who has woken up remembers things that he was imagining while asleep. Now those stories and thoughts that enter the heart of the sleeper may occasionally come from Satan, occasionally from the promptings of the soul, and occasionally from the thoughts [dictated] by angels. Sometimes they come as notifications from God – may He be great and exalted – Who creates them directly in the heart of the seer. According to a [prophetic] report: "The most veracious of you in vision are the most veracious of you in speech."

Know that there are two kinds of sleep: the sleep of unconsciousness (*nawm ghafla*) and the sleep of habit (*nawm ʿada*). Such sleep is not praiseworthy; on the contrary, it is flawed, because it is the brother of death. A transmitted report says: "Sleep is the brother of death."//467 God – may He be great and exalted – said: "It is He Who recalls you by night and He knows what you work by day."⁷⁹⁴ God Most High also said: "God takes the souls at the time of their death, and that which has not died, in its sleep."⁷⁹⁵ They say: "If there were [any] good in sleep, there would be sleep in Paradise." They say: "When God cast sleep over

---

793 By saying chapter 114 of the Qurʾan.
794 Q. 6:60.
795 Q. 39:42.

Adam in Paradise, He extracted Eve from him, and all his trials happened to him when Eve was created."

I heard the master Abu ʿAli al-Daqqaq say: "When Abraham said to Ishmael – peace be upon both of them, 'My son, I see in a dream that I sacrifice thee',[796] Ishmael responded: 'This is the recompense of someone who falls asleep [in the presence of] his Beloved. If you had not slept, you would not have been commanded to slaughter your child!'" They say that God Most High revealed to David – peace be upon him: "Whoever falls asleep when the night comes, lies when he claims that he loves Me." Sleep is the opposite of knowledge. This is why al-Shibli said: "One sleep in a thousand years is an abomination." Al-Shibli said: "God looked at His creatures and said: 'Who sleeps is neglectful; who is neglectful is veiled [from God].'" Al-Shibli used to rub salt into his eyes, so that he would not fall asleep. It is with this meaning in mind that the Sufis recite:

How strange that a lover should fall asleep
For any sleep is forbidden to the lover!

They say: "The Sufi novice eats only when in need, sleeps only when overcome, and speaks only out of necessity." When Adam – peace be upon him – fell asleep in the presence of God, he was told: "This is Eve, so that you might rest in her."[797] This is the recompense of one who falls asleep in divine presence. They say: "If you are present with God, you do not sleep, for sleeping in God's presence is bad manners." They say: "If you are absent, you belong to the people of grief and affliction, and the afflicted one cannot be overtaken by sleep."

As for those who exert themselves [for God's sake], their sleep is a charity bestowed upon them by God. God – may He be great and exalted – is proud of a servant of His who falls asleep while praying. He says: "Look at My servant. He sleeps, but his spirit is with Me and his body is [prostrated] before Me!" The master [al-Qushayri] said: "That is, his spirit is in the state of intimate conversation [with God] (*najwa*) and his body is spread on the carpet of worship." They say: "If one sleeps in the state of ritual purity,[798] one's spirit then receives permission to circumambulate the throne [of God] and to prostrate itself before God – may He be great and exalted." God Most High said: "We appointed you sleep for rest."[799]//468 I heard the master Abu ʿAli al-Daqqaq say: "A man complained to a Sufi master that he slept too much. The master said: 'Go and thank God Most High for [your] health! How many a sick man is craving a wink of the sleep that you complain about!'" They say: "Nothing is harder on the Devil than the sleep of the sinner. He complains: 'When will he wake up and stand up, so he could disobey God?!'" They say: "The sinner's best state is when he is asleep. If he has no time, nothing will be held [by God] against him." I

---

796 Q. 37:102.
797 Q. 7:189; 7:188, according to Arberry's translation.
798 That is, after performing an ablution.
799 Q. 78:9.

heard the master Abu ʿAli al-Daqqaq say: "Shah al-Kirmani used to practice night vigils. Once he was overcome with sleep and saw God – praise be to Him – in a dream. From that time on, he would deliberately try to sleep [as much as possible]. When someone asked him about this, he recited:

> I found the joy of my heart in my sleep
> And I have come to love slumber and sleep!"

It is related that a man had two disciples who disagreed over an issue. One of them claimed: "Sleep is better, because a man does not disobey God in this state." The other said: "Wakefulness is better, because one knows God Most High in this state." They brought this issue to the master for arbitration. He said: "You who speak of the superiority of sleep, death is better for you than life. You who speak of the superiority of wakefulness, life is better for you than death." They say: "A certain man bought a slave girl. When the night came, he told her to make his bed. The slave girl asked him: 'My master, is there a master above you?' He said: 'Yes.' 'Does your master ever sleep?' asked the slave girl. He said 'No.' She then said: 'Aren't you ashamed to sleep, while your master doesn't?'" They say that a little girl asked Saʿid b. Jubayr: "Why don't you sleep?" He answered: "Gehenna does not allow me to sleep!" They say: "Malik b. Dinar's daughter asked him: "Why don't you sleep?" He answered: "Your father is afraid of a surprise attack by night!" It is related that when al-Rabiʿ b. Khuthaym died, a little girl asked her father: "Where has the pillar that used to stand in our neighbor's yard gone?" The father responded: "Our neighbor was a pious man who used to stand in prayer all night, from beginning to end." The girl thought that he was a pillar, because she would only climb up the roof of her house [to sleep] at night and [always] find him standing [there]. A Sufi related: "In [one's] sleep [one encounters] some realities that do not occur in [one's] waking state. Thus, in a dream a man can see the Elect One[800] – peace be upon him – [his] Companions, and the pious Muslims of the earlier generations (*salaf*), while he is unable to see them in his waking state. Likewise, he can see God in a dream, which is a great distinction."//469

It is related that Abu Bakr al-Ajurri saw God – praise be to Him – in a dream. God asked him: "Ask for what you need!" I said: "My God, pardon all sinners of the community of Muhammad – may God bless and greet him!" He said: "It is more appropriate that I do this rather than you. Ask for what you [yourself] need!" Al-Kattani related: "In a dream I saw the Prophet – may God bless and greet him. He said: 'Whoever adorns himself for the sake of people with something which, as God knows, he does not have, will be disgraced by God.' He also said: 'I saw the Prophet – may God bless and greet him – in a dream and asked him: "Pray to God that my heart will not die!" He said: 'Say forty times every day, "O Living, O Self-Sufficient", and God will enliven your heart!" Al-Hasan b.

---

800 An epithet of the Prophet (*al-mustafa*).

'Ali[801] – may God be pleased with both of them – saw Jesus son of Mary in a dream and asked him: "I want to make a seal-ring. What should I inscribe on it?" Jesus answered: "Inscribe on it: 'There is no deity but God, the King, the Manifest Truth.'[802] This is written at the end of the Gospel." It is related that Abu Yazid [al-Bistami] said: "I saw my Lord – may He be great and exalted – in a dream and asked Him: 'What is the path to You?' 'Abandon your [lower] soul, and come!'" Ahmad b. Khadrawayh[803] saw his Lord in a dream. He told him: "Everyone demands something from Me. Only Abu Yazid demands Me." Yahya b. Sa'id al-Qattan said: "I saw my Lord in a dream and said: 'O Lord, how many times have I prayed to You and You have not answered me!' Most High said: 'Yahya, I love hearing your voice!'" Bishr b. al-Harith said: "I saw the Commander of the Faithful 'Ali b. Abi Talib – may God be pleased with him – in a dream and said: 'O Commander of the Faithful, advise me!' He said: 'How beautiful is the inclination of the rich toward the poor in their search of the reward of God Most High! And how beautiful is the pride of the poor toward the rich in their reliance on God Most High!' I asked: 'O Commander of the Faithful, give me more!' He recited:

> You were dead, then became alive and soon you shall be dead [again]
> A residence in the abode of transience is hardly possible
> So build a residence [for yourself] in the abode of eternity!"

It is related that someone saw Sufyan al-Thawri in a dream and asked him: "What did God Most High do to you?" He answered: "He showed mercy to me." He was asked: "And what is the state of 'Abdallah b. al-Mubarak?" He answered: "He is one of those who enter into the presence of [their] Lord twice a day." I heard the master Abu 'Ali al-Daqqaq say that the master Abu Sahl al-Su'luki saw Abu Sahl//470 al-Zajjaji in a dream. [During his lifetime] the latter used to uphold the teaching about the eternity of punishment [for the sinners in the afterlife]. Al-Su'luki asked him: "What did God do to you?" Al-Zajjaji responded: "Things here are easier than we thought." Someone saw al-Hasan b. 'Isam al-Shaybani in a dream and asked him: "What did God do to you?" He said: "What can come from the Benevolent One except benevolence?" Someone saw a Sufi in a dream and asked him about his state. He recited:

> They took us to account and were precise,
> Then they treated us kindly and set us free!

Someone saw Habib al-'Ajami[804] in a dream and asked: "Are you dead, Habib al-'Ajami?" He said: "Far from it! My Persianhood ('ujma) has left me and I

---

801 The elder son of 'Ali b. Abi Talib, the cousin and brother-in-law of the Prophet.
802 Q. 24:25.
803 Or "Khidruya", according to the Persian pronunciation.
804 His last name can be translated as both "the Persian" and "the Barbarian"; as a generic term this word denotes anyone who speaks Arabic with a foreign accent. It has become a generic term for non-native speakers of Arabic.

reside in a bliss (*ni'ma*)." It is related that al-Hasan al-Basri entered the mosque in order to pray the sunset prayer. He found Habib al-'Ajami there serving as the prayer leader and he did not pray behind him, because he was afraid that Habib would mispronounce the [words of] the prayer due to the foreignness of his tongue.[805] On that night in a dream he saw someone who said: "Why didn't you pray behind him? Had you prayed behind him, all your prior sins would have been forgiven!" Someone saw Malik b. Anas in a dream and asked him: "What did God do to you?" He answered: "I was forgiven thanks to the words that 'Uthman b. 'Affan[806] – may God be pleased with him – uttered each time he saw a funeral procession: 'Praise be to the Living One Who never dies!'[807]" On the night of al-Hasan al-Basri's death someone saw in a dream that the gates of the heaven were opened and a crier announced: "Verily, al-Hasan al-Basri is coming to God Most High, Who is pleased with him!"

I heard Abu Bakr b. Ishkib say: I saw the master Abu Sahl al-Su'luki in a dream in a pleasant state and asked him: "Master, how did you attain this [state]?" He said: "By thinking well of my Lord!" Someone saw al-Jahiz[808] in a dream and asked him: "What did God do to you?" [In response] he recited:

Don't ever write with your hand anything that you won't be happy to see
On the Day of Judgement.

In a dream al-Junayd saw the Devil naked and asked him: "Aren't you ashamed of yourself before people?" He answered: "Those are not [real] people! The real people are in the al-Shuniziyya mosque. They emaciate my body and burn my liver!" Al-Junayd said: "When I woke up, I went to the mosque and saw a group of people with their heads on their knees, engrossed in contemplation. When they saw me, they said: 'May you not be deceived by the story of the evil one!'" After al-Nasrabadhi's death someone saw him at Mecca in a dream and asked him: "What did God Most High do to you?" He said: "I was reprimanded in the way the noble ones (*ashraf*) are reprimanded. Then a voice called on me, saying: 'Abu 'l-Qasim, is there unification after separation?' I said: 'No, O Possessor of Majesty!' And no sooner had they put me in the grave than I was with the One!"//471 It is related that someone saw Dhu 'l-Nun al-Misri in a dream and asked him: "What did God do to you?" He said: "In that life I asked Him to grant three of my wishes. He granted some of them and I hope that He will grant me the rest [in the afterlife]. [First,] I asked Him to grant me one of the ten [good] things

---

805 See note 804.
806 The third of the four "rightly guided" successors (caliphs) of the Prophet, who was murdered by a group of mutineers in 35/655.
807 It is not clear who uttered these words: someone who was present at Malik's funeral, or, perhaps, 'Uthman's words served as his intercession before God on behalf of all deceased.
808 A celebrated man of letters and prolific author from Basra, who adhered to the Mu'tazilite school of speculative theology; he died in 255/869. His works addressed a wide variety of themes from language and *belles-lettres* to politics and theology.

that Ridwan[809] holds in his hand and He gave it to me by Himself; [second, I asked Him] to torture me with ten tortures of which the hand of Malik[810] holds just one, and He did that Himself; [third, I asked Him] to endow me with [the ability to] recollect Him with the tongue of eternity."[811] It is related that someone saw al-Shibli in a dream after his death and asked him: "What did God Most High do to you?" He answered: "He did not take me to task for any of my claims, except one. One day I said: 'There is no greater loss than the loss of Paradise and entry into Hell.' God told me: 'What loss can be greater than the loss of meeting with Me?'"

I heard the master Abu 'Ali al-Daqqaq say: "Al-Jurayri saw al-Junayd in a dream [after his death] and asked him: 'How are you, Abu 'l-Qasim?' He answered: 'Gone are all those allegorical allusions (isharat), and all those unequivocal expressions ('ibarat) have vanished. Only those praises of God that we used to utter in the morning have benefited us [in the Hereafter]!'" Al-Nibaji said: "One day I had a craving for something. In a dream I heard a voice saying: 'Does it befit a free man seeking [God] (al-hurr al-murid) to humiliate himself before [His] servants, while he can receive everything he wants from his Master?'" Ibn al-Jalla' said: "I arrived in Medina destitute and hungry. I went to the grave [of the Prophet] and said: 'I am your guest, the prophet of God.' Then I fell asleep and, in my dream, saw the Prophet – may God bless and greet him. He gave me a loaf of bread and I ate half of it. When I woke up, I [still] held the other half in my hand." A Sufi related: "I saw the Prophet – may God bless and greet him – in a dream. He told me: 'Go visit Ibn 'Awn, for he loves God and His messenger!'" It is related that 'Utba al-Ghulam saw a beautiful maiden of Paradise (hawra') in a dream. She told him: "'Utba, I am in love with you. Be careful not to do anything that would stand between you and me!" 'Utba then told her: "I have divorced this world thrice and I will not return to it until I meet you!" I heard Mansur al-Maghribi say: "In Syria I saw a distinguished Sufi master who habitually kept to himself (inqibad). I was told: 'If you want this master to be friendly to you, greet him by saying: "May God endow you with the maidens of Paradise!" He will be pleased with you thanks to this greeting.' I asked them about the reason for that and was told that he had seen some maidens of Paradise in his dream and this [scene] remained in his heart. So I went to him and greeted him, saying: 'May God endow you with the maidens of Paradise!' And the master was friendly to me."//472 It is related that Ayyub al-Sakhtiyani saw a funeral procession of a sinner and hid in an entrance hall of a house lest he be required to offer a funeral prayer for it. A Sufi saw the deceased in a dream and asked: "What did God do to you?" He answered: "He pardoned me and said: 'Tell Ayyub al-Sakhtiyani:

---

809 The angel that guards the gates of Paradise, who dresses and serves the blessed, and draws away the veils that cover the face of God.
810 The angel of Hell who torments its inhabitants.
811 According a commentator, the first two wishes were granted in the Hereafter, while the last was granted in his earthly life.

"Say: If you possessed the treasures of my Lord's mercy, yet would you hold back for fear of expending."[812]" It is said that on the night Malik b. Dinar died [people] saw as if the gates of heaven had opened and a voice announced: "Verily, Malik b. Dinar has become a dweller in Paradise!" A Sufi recounted: "On the night that Dawud al-Ta'i died, I saw a light and angels, both ascending and descending. I asked [them]: 'What night is this?' They said: 'This is the night in which Dawud al-Ta'i died. Paradise has been decorated for the arrival of his spirit [amidst its inhabitants].'[813]"

The master Abu 'l-Qasim al-Qushayri said: "I saw the master Abu 'Ali al-Daqqaq in a dream [after his death] and asked: 'What did God do to you?' He answered: 'Forgiveness is not of great importance here and of the least importance among those present here is so-and-so' – and he mentioned his name. It occurred to me in my dream that the person he had in mind had unlawfully killed a man." It is related that when Kurz b. Wabra died, someone saw in a dream as if the inhabitants of the graves had come clad in new white garments. When the seer of the dream asked them what it was, he was told: "The inhabitants of the graves have put on new garments because Kurz b. Wabra is coming to [join] them." Someone saw Yusuf b. al-Husayn in a dream and asked him: "What did God do to you?" He said: "God has pardoned me." When [the dreamer] asked him why, he answered: "Because I had never mixed seriousness with joke." Someone saw Abu 'Abdallah al-Zarrad in a dream and asked him: "What did God Most High do to you?" He answered: "He stationed me [before Him] and pardoned me all the sins that I had committed to in my earthly life, except one, which I was too ashamed to admit. So he kept me standing and sweating until flesh started to fall off my face." The dreamer asked what his sin was. He said: "One day I looked at a handsome person and was too ashamed to mention it."

I heard Abu Sa'id al-Shahham say: "In a dream I saw the master and imam Abu 'l-Tayyib Sahl al-Su'luki[814] and told him: 'O master!' 'Forget about "the master"!' he responded. 'After all those [spiritual] states you experienced [in this life]?' I asked him. 'They were of no use to us,' he said. Then I asked him: 'What did God do to you?' He said: 'He pardoned me, thanks to the issues that the old and infirm folks used to question me about and to which I responded.'" I heard Abu Bakr al-Rashidi al-Faqih say: "In a dream I saw Muhammad al-Tusi al-Mu'allim who said://473 'Recite this to Abu Sa'id al-Saffar al-Mu'addib:

> We used to keep the pledge not to deviate from [our] passion
> But, by love's life, you have deviated, whereas we have not
> You have been distracted from us by the company of others
> And you have shown alienation [toward us], no we were not like this [before]

---

812 Q. 17:100; 17:103, according to Arberry's translation.
813 This last phrase is omitted from one of the versions of the text.
814 He was a prominent Shafi'i jurist, who was born in Isfahan and spent most of his life in Nishapur; he died either in 402/1011 or 404/1014.

May He Who directs affairs by His knowledge unite us after
death just as we used to be!'

"When I woke up, I recited this to Abu Sa'id al-Saffar, who told me: 'I used to visit his grave every Friday. However, I neglected to visit it this [last] Friday.'"

A Sufi related: "In a dream I saw the Messenger of God – may God bless and greet him – surrounded by a group of the poor.[815] While he was in that state, two angels descended from heaven. One of them had a basin in his hand, the other a pitcher. [One] placed the basin before the Messenger of God – may God bless and greet him – [while the other] washed his hands. The Messenger then ordered the two angels to wash the hands of the poor. After that, the basin was placed before me. One angel said to the other: 'Don't pour water on his hands, for he is not one of them.' I asked the Messenger of God: 'Has it not been reported that you said: "A man belongs to those he loves"?' He said: 'Yes, indeed.' I said: 'I love you and I love these poor ones!' The Messenger – may God bless and greet him – then commanded: 'Pour water on his hands, for he is one of them!'"

It is related that a Sufi was constantly calling: "Well-being! Well-being!" Someone asked him about the meaning of this prayer. He explained: "Initially, I worked as a porter. One day, I was carrying a heavy load of flour. I put it down in order to have some rest and said: 'O Lord, if You were to provide me with two loaves of bread without toil, I would be content with them!' Suddenly, there appeared two men who were quarreling with one another. When I stepped forward in order make peace between them, one of them struck me on the head with something in an attempt to strike his opponent. My face was bloodied. Then the local constable arrived and arrested them. When he saw me stained with blood, he thought that I too took part in the quarrel and put me in jail. I remained in the jail for some time, and each day two loaves of bread were brought to me. One night, in a dream I heard a voice saying: 'You asked for two loaves of bread every day without any exertion on your part. However, you did not ask for well-being, so God has given you what you asked for.' When I woke up, I uttered: 'Well-being! Well-being!' [All of a sudden] I heard that someone knocked on the door of the jail, crying: 'Where is 'Umar the Porter (al-Hammal)?' They then set me free and let me go."

Al-Kattani related: "One of our companions had an inflamed eye. Someone asked him why he was not treating it. He answered: 'I made a vow not to treat it until it heals on its own.' Then I [al-Kattani] saw in a dream that someone said: 'Had all the inhabitants of the hellfire made such a vow, we would have taken them out of the fire!'" It is related that al-Junayd said: "In a dream I saw myself preaching to people. An angel appeared before me and asked: 'What makes those close to God the closest to Him?' I answered: 'A secret deed measured by a trustworthy scale.'//474 The angel departed from me, saying: 'By God, this is

---

815 That is, Sufis.

indeed a blessed speech!'" A man said to al-ʿAlaʾ b. Ziyad: "In a dream I saw you among the inhabitants of Paradise!" He answered: "Perhaps Satan wanted to foist something on me, but I was rendered immune to it. So he dispatched a man to me whom he charged with achieving his goal of leading me astray!" Someone saw ʿAtaʾ al-Salami in a dream and told him: "[During your lifetime] you used to be constantly grief-stricken. What did God Most High do to you?" He answered: "By God, He replaced that with a long rest and constant joy!" The dreamer asked him: "What rank do you occupy?" He answered [quoting the Qurʾan]: "They are with those whom God has blessed, prophets, just men, the righteous ..."[816] Someone saw al-Awzaʿi[817] in a dream. He said: "I have not seen here a rank loftier than that of the scholars, followed by that of the sad ones." Al-Nibaji related: "In a dream I was told: 'Whoever entrusts God with his sustenance will see his moral character bettered, his soul generous in expending it, and tempting thoughts in his canonical prayer being rare.'" Someone saw Zubayda[818] and asked her: "What did God do to you?" She said: "He pardoned me." The dreamer asked: "[That is] because of the charitable donations you expended on the road to Mecca?" "No," she said. "This was but the fee that reverted to its [rightful] owners.[819] He pardoned me on account of my [sincere] intention." Someone saw Sufyan al-Thawri in a dream and asked him: "What did God do to you?" He answered: "My first step landed on the Bridge[820] and the second in Paradise." Ahmad b. Abi ʾl-Hawari related: "In a dream I saw a young woman of the beauty the like of which I had never seen. Her face radiated light. I asked her what had made her face so radiant. She answered: 'Do you remember the night on which you wept?' I said: 'Yes.' She said: 'A drop of your tears was brought to me. I rubbed it into my face and it became like this.'"

It is related that Yazid al-Raqashi[821] saw the Prophet – may God bless and greet him – in a dream and recited [some passages from] the Qurʾan to him, whereupon the Prophet asked: "This is the recitation, but where is the weeping?" Al-Junayd related: "In a dream I saw two angels descend from heaven. One of them asked: 'What is truthfulness (sidq)?' I answered: 'Being faithful to one's promise.' The second [angel] said, 'He has spoken truth', and they ascended [to heaven]." Someone saw Bishr al-Hafi in a dream and asked him: "What did God Most High do to you?" Bishr said: "He pardoned me and said: 'Bishr, aren't you

---

816 Q. 4:69; 4:71, according to Arberry's translation.
817 A renowned jurist from Syria under the Umayyads, who died in 157/774.
818 Zubayda bint Jaʿfar (216/832), wife of the caliph Harun al-Rashid, who was renowned for her piety and charitable activities, including the improvement of the pilgrimage road to Mecca.
819 Since the money she donated was, in the final account, extracted from the caliph's subjects, often unlawfully, the caliph's subjects were its rightful owners.
820 The bridge over Hell, which the righteous cross in the winking of an eye and which the wicked fall off of into the fire of Gehenna.
821 Yazid b. Aban al-Raqashi (d. 129/738) belonged to the circle of al-Hasan al-Basri and was famous for his world-renouncing attitude.

ashamed before Me, for having been so much afraid of Me?!'"//475 Someone saw Abu Sulayman al-Darani in a dream and asked him: "What did God do to you?" He answered: "He pardoned me. Nothing did more harm to me than the allegorical allusions of the Sufis!" ʿAli b. al-Muwaffaq said: "One day I was thinking about my family and the poverty that they were suffering. Then I saw in a dream a sheet of paper. Written on it was [the following]: 'In the name of God the Merciful, the Compassionate. O Ibn al-Muwaffaq, how can you be afraid of poverty, when I am your Lord?' At the end of the night, a man brought me a purse which contained five thousand *dinars* and told me: 'Take them, you of weak certitude!'" Al-Junayd related: "In a dream I saw myself standing in front of God Most High. He told me: 'Abu ʾl-Qasim, where do you get the words that you say?' I answered: 'I say nothing but truth.' He told me: 'You have spoken the truth!'" Abu Bakr al-Kattani said: "In a dream I saw a young man, the most handsome I had ever seen. I asked him who he was. 'I am the fear of God (*taqwa*),' he answered. 'Where do you reside,' I asked him. 'In the heart of every sad individual,' he answered. Then I turned and saw a black woman, as ugly as one can [possibly] be. I asked her who she was. She answered: 'I am laughter.' I asked her: 'Where do you reside?' 'In every cheerful, carefree heart,' she answered. When I woke up, I made a vow never to laugh, unless I am overcome [with laughter]." It is related that Abu ʿAbdallah b. Khafif said: "In a dream I saw the Messenger of God – may God bless and greet him. He told me: 'Whoever has known the path to God Most High, followed it and then deviated from it, will taste the punishment that no one in the world has ever suffered.'" Someone saw al-Shibli in a dream and asked him: "What did God Most High do to you?" He answered: "He interrogated me until I grew desperate. When He saw my desperation, He enveloped me in His mercy."

Abu ʿUthman al-Maghribi said: "In a dream, I heard a voice saying: 'Abu ʿUthman, fear God in poverty even in matters as unimportant as a sesame seed.'" It is related that Abu Saʿid had a son, who had predeceased him. Abu Saʿid saw him in a dream and told him: "My son, advise me!" The son said: "Father, do not deal with God in a cowardly manner!" "Tell me more," asked Abu Saʿid. The son said: "Do not contradict God in what He demands of you." "Tell me more," asked Abu Saʿid. The son said: "Don't set a shirt between you and God!" [After that,] Abu Saʿid did not wear a shirt for thirty years.//476 A Sufi used to say in his prayer: "My God, if something does no harm to You, while benefiting us, do not prevent it from [happening to] us." In a dream he was told: "If something neither harms you, nor benefits you – give it up!" Abu ʾl-Fadl al-Isbahani related: "In a dream I saw the Messenger of God – may God bless and greet him. I told him: 'Messenger of God, ask God not to deprive me of faith!' The Messenger – may God bless and greet him – said: 'This is something God Most High has already assured!'" Abu Saʿid al-Kharraz related: "In a dream I saw the Devil and raised my walking stick in order to hit him. [Suddenly] I heard a voice saying: 'He is not afraid of this. He is afraid of a light [of faith] that resides in the heart!'"

A Sufi related: "I used to direct my prayers to Rabi'a al-'Adawiyya.[822] Once I saw her in a dream saying: 'Your gifts come to us on the dishes of light wrapped up in the napkins of light!'" It is related that Sammak[823] b. Harb said: "When I went blind, I saw in a dream someone who told me: 'Go to the Euphrates, immerse yourself in it, then open your eyes!' I did so, and my eyesight returned to me." It is related that someone saw Bishr al-Hafi in a dream and asked him: "What did God do to you?" He said: "When I saw my Lord – may He be great and exalted – He told me: 'Welcome, Bishr! I took you to Myself on the day I took you to Myself and there's no one on the [entire] earth whom I love more!'"

Spiritual advice for Sufi novices (*wasaya li'l-muridin*)

The master and imam [al-Qushayri] said: "After we have mentioned some episodes from the biographies of the [Sufi] folk and complemented this with chapters on the stations [of the Sufi] path, we would like to complete this epistle with some spiritual advice (*wasiyya*)[824] for [Sufi] novices. We ask God Most High that He help them in properly executing this advice, that He not prevent them from fulfilling it, and that He not use it as an argument against us.[825] The first step of the [Sufi] novice on this [Sufi] path requires that he be sincere, so that he could build on a sound foundation. Sufi masters have said [about this]: "They were deprived of the arrival [in God's presence] (*wusul*), because they neglected the foundations (*usul*)." Likewise, I heard the master Abu 'Ali al-Daqqaq say: "The beginning [of the Sufi path] requires a sound belief that binds the servant and God Most High – one that is free from uncertainty and doubt, devoid of delusion and innovation, and derived from [irrefutable] proofs and arguments." It is revolting if the novice should espouse a teaching that does not belong to this [Sufi] path. If a Sufi happens to adhere to a teaching of those who deviate from the Sufi path,//477 this is but a result of his ignorance of the teachings of the followers of this path. For their arguments in support of their beliefs are clearer than anyone else's and the foundations of their teachings are firmer than the foundations of any other teaching. People [belong to two classes]: they are either adherents of received knowledge (*naql*) and transmitted reports (*athar*), or supporters of [rational] knowledge (*'aql*) and speculation (*fikr*). The masters of this community (*ta'ifa*) have risen above them all. What others consider to be unknown is but a manifest [truth] for them. The knowledge that other people can only aspire to is rendered real to them by God – praise be to Him. They are those who have arrived [in the presence of God], while the rest are guided by argumentative reasoning. They are as the poet described them:

---

822 The celebrated female mystic from Basra, who figures prominently in the Sufi lore; she died in 185/801; see *IM*, pp. 26–32.
823 Or "Simak".
824 This term can also be translated as, for example, "instruction", "bequest" and "counsel".
825 That is, in case they prove to be incorrect.

My night has turned to dawn thanks to your face
While its darkness spreads itself among people
They are enveloped with darkness
Whereas we roam in the bright shine of the day.

There has never been an age in the history of Islam without a master of this community who was proficient in the science of the oneness [of God]. There has never been a leader of the Sufis to whom the greatest scholars of his epoch would not subordinate themselves and pay obeisance and seek blessing of. Had they not had the distinction and special qualities to them, this would not have been so.

Once, as Ahmad b. Hanbal was sitting with al-Shafiʿi,[826] Shayban al-Raʿi[827] came to them. Ahmad said [to al-Shafiʿi]: "Abu ʿAbdallah, I'd like to draw your attention to his lack of knowledge,[828] so that he would busy himself with acquiring some of it." Al-Shafiʿi exclaimed: "Don't do this!" However, Ibn Hanbal did not desist. He asked Shayban: "What can you say about someone who forgot [to perform] one of the five [canonical] daily prayers and cannot remember which of them he forgot? Shayban, what do you think he should do?" Shayban replied: "Ahmad, that is a heart that was neglectful of God Most High. Therefore, it must be educated [in good manners], so that it would never ever be neglectful of its Master." [On hearing this] Ahmad [b. Hanbal] fainted. When he came to, al-Shafiʿi – may God have mercy on him – said: "Didn't I tell you to leave him alone?!" Shayban al-Raʿi was an illiterate man. If an illiterate Sufi like him had such a stature, one can only fathom what their leaders were like!//478 It is related that the teaching circle[829] of the great jurist named Abu ʿImran used to assemble [in the mosque] next to al-Shibli's teaching circle. Whenever al-Shibli spoke, the members of Abu ʿImran's circle would migrate to him. [One day] the members of al-Shibli's circle asked him a question about menstruation in order to embarrass him. [In response] al-Shibli mentioned [all] the teachings pertaining to this issue as well as disagreements over it. [On hearing this] Abu ʿImran stood up and kissed al-Shibli on the head saying: "Abu Bakr, I have heard ten statements about this issue which I have not heard before. Out of that which you said [about this issue], I knew only three teachings!" The jurist named Abu ʾl-ʿAbbas b. Surayj[830] was passing by the teaching circle of al-Junayd – may God have mercy on both of them – and heard him speak. Someone asked him what he thought about that speech. He answered: "I do not understand what he said, but I felt in his words the strength that an idle talker can never produce."

---

826 Both were the most distinguished scholars and jurists of their age, who founded legal schools named after them.
827 That is, Shayban "the Shepherd".
828 Ibn Hanbal apparently implied the knowledge of the transmitted [prophetic] reports and jurisprudence.
829 Before the emergence of religious colleges (*madrasa*) each distinguished scholar conducted his teaching session in a mosque, surrounded by the "circle" (*halqa*) of his disciples.
830 A distinguished Shafiʿi scholar who died in 306/918.

Someone asked ʿAbdallah b. Saʿid b. Kullab: "You have debated the teachings of every [scholar] you have heard. There is a man named al-Junayd. Go and see if you can challenge him." ʿAbdallah attended al-Junayd's circle. He asked al-Junayd about God's oneness (*tawhid*). When al-Junayd responded, ʿAbdallah became confused and asked him to repeat what he had said. Al-Junayd repeated the same point but used different words [to express it]. ʿAbdallah told him: "I am unable to grasp this; can you say this again for me?" Al-Junayd repeated this to him using different expressions. ʿAbdallah told him: "I am unable to grasp what you say. Can you dictate this for me?" Al-Junayd said: "If you [are ready to] traverse it,[831] I will dictate this to you." ʿAbdallah stood up, recognized his [al-Junayd's] superiority and acknowledged his exalted status. The foundations of this community are the soundest foundation, its leaders are the greatest and its scholars are the most learned of men. Therefore the novice who has faith in them, if he travels along [their] path and aspires toward their goals, will share in the unveilings of the unseen [that they witness] and will have no need in the meddling of anyone who does not belong to this community. If he aspires to the path of [pious] precedent and is not independent in his spiritual state, if he strives to depart from the domains of blind imitation in order to arrive at the true realization (*tahqiq*), then he must follow in the footsteps of its founders and tread the path of this generation [of Sufis], for they are better than anyone else. I heard Shaykh Abu ʿAbd al-Rahman al-Sulami say: I heard Abu Bakr al-Razi say: I heard al-Shibli say: "What do you think about knowledge compared to which the knowledge of the learned may seem doubtful?" I also heard Muhammad b. ʿAli b. Muhammad al-Mukharrimi say: I heard Muhammad b. ʿAbdallah al-Farghani say: I heard al-Junayd say: "Had I known that God has created a knowledge under the sun//479 that is nobler than what we together with our companions and brothers are teaching, I would have aspired and striven toward it!" After the seeker has established a pact between himself and God, he should obtain – either through his own realization (*tahqiq*) or by means of asking the religious authorities – the knowledge of the Divine Law that allows him to fulfill his religious duty. When the rulings of legal scholars vary, he should adopt the most comprehensive of them and seek to avoid any controversy. Dispensations from obligatory requirements (*rukhas*) are intended for the weak ones and those who seek to shirk [their duties] by referring to their [mundane] needs and concerns. As for this [Sufi] community, they have no concern except for observing the rights of God – praise be to Him. Therefore, they say that if a Sufi has taken recourse from the rank of the True Reality to a dispensation from the requirements of the Divine Law, he has departed from his pact with God and violated that which has existed between God Most High and himself. Now, the novice must be educated in good manners by a [Sufi] master. If he does not have one, he will never succeed. Abu Yazid said: "He who does not have a master,

---

831 That is, the Sufi path.

Satan is his leader." I heard the master Abu ʿAli al-Daqqaq say: "The tree that has grown on its own without a gardener will bring forth foliage, but will never bring any fruit. Likewise, if the novice has no master to take his teaching from breath after breath, then he worships nothing but his personal whims and will never achieve what he aspires to." If the novice wants to walk along the [right] path, he must seek refuge in God from any slip and abandon all errors – be they manifest or hidden, small or great. He must seek to obtain the pleasure of his adversaries, for he who fails to satisfy his adversary will not achieve anything on this [Sufi] path.

Thus they have proceeded until they have begun to cut all ties and preoccupations of this world, for this path rests on the emptiness of the heart [from all mundane preoccupations]. Al-Shibli told al-Husri at the beginning of his novitiate: "If something other than God Most High enters your mind from one Friday during which you visit me to the next, you are prohibited from visiting me." When the aspirant seeks to cut ties to this world, he should first abandon [his] property; property distracts one from God. There's no aspirant in this affair of ours[832] who remains attached to this world. If he does keep this attachment, //480 then it will soon drag him back to what he aspired to leave behind. And when he abandons property, he must also give up his [social] status (*jah*), for clinging to one's love of rank is a major obstacle. If the aspirant is concerned by other people accepting or rejecting him, nothing [good] will come out of him. The worst thing that can happen to the aspirant is that people begin to take notice of him [looking at him] with an approving eye and [seeking his] blessing. For the [common] folk have no inkling of all this, while the novice has not yet made right his aspiration [to God], so how can one seek to obtain his blessing? [Sufi] novices are required to abandon their renown, for it is a deadly poison to them. After the aspirant has given up his property and rank, he should make good his pact with God Most High and not oppose his master in anything that the latter prescribes to him. For opposition to one's master during one's novitiate is a grave deficiency, because one's initial state is the best indicator of [what will happen to him] during the rest of his life. One condition for success is that there should be no opposition to the master in his student's heart. If it occurs to the aspirant that he has any value or power in this world and the next, or that there's on the face of the earth someone who is more lowly than he, he has no right to [aspire to God]. For one must exert oneself in order to know one's Lord and not to seek power for oneself. There is a great difference between a person who aspires to God Most High and a person who aspires to self-aggrandizement, either in this life or the Hereafter. Next, the novice must preserve his secret from his ilk, except his master. If he has concealed even one breath from his master, he will have betrayed him in his right of companionship. Should he happen to disagree with what the master has commanded to him, he must confess this in front of his master immediately. He then should submit himself to the master's judgement as a

---

832 Namely, Sufism.

punishment for his transgression and objection. This may be an [expiatory] journey assigned to him by the master or [some other] penance, as the master sees fit.

The master has no right to overlook the failings of his novices, for this is but the forfeiture of the rights due to God Most High. As long as the novice retains any of his [mundane] attachments, the master is unable to instill in him the [proper] remembrance [of God], for he [the master] must first test him. When the master's heart bears witness to the novice's proper intention, the master must stipulate that the novice on the Sufi path should accept all the verdicts of God's decree [in his regard]. The master must also establish a pact with him [demanding] that he should not depart from this path despite any harm, humiliation, poverty, illness or pain that may afflict him and that his heart not be diverted to easy ways and have recourse to dispensations during the attacks of need and want. Nor should he prefer rest or be overcome with laziness, for coming to a halt for the aspirant is worse than becoming lax. The difference between them is that laxity means a departure and forfeiture of one's aspiration [to God], while a halt means resting from the [hardships] of travel in favor of the pleasures of laziness. Nothing good will come out of the novice who makes a halt at the beginning of his aspiration. Once the master has tested the novice, he instructs him in a method of remembrance as he sees fit and commands him to mention a certain name [of God] with his own tongue. He then orders that the heart of the aspirant recollect God alongside the tongue. He tells him: "Keep this remembrance with you//481 constantly as if you were always present with God in your heart. Nothing but this name should flow from your tongue, if you are capable of this." The master then orders that the aspirant always maintain ritual purity, that he should not sleep unless overwhelmed [by sleep], that he reduce the amount of his food bit by bit until he has grown accustomed to it. A report says: "He who allows his riding animal to perish on a journey traverses no distance nor has a back to carry [his goods on]." The master then orders the aspirant to seek solitude and retreat and, while in this state, spare no effort in banishing mundane thoughts and distracting promptings from his heart.

Know that no aspirant in this state at the beginning of his aspiration is free from evil whisperings that may corrupt his determination, especially when he possesses an adroit heart. Few are aspirants who do not encounter such states at the beginning of their progress. Such are temptations that the aspirants usually encounter. When the master observes adroitness in the aspirant, he must direct him to rational proofs, for there is no doubt that one who aspires toward [religious] knowledge rids himself by it from the evil whisperings that accost him. When the master discerns in his disciple the [necessary] strength and determination in following the [Sufi] path, he orders him to be patient and to constantly recollect [God's name] so that before long the lights of his acceptance [by God] would begin to shine in his heart and the suns of arrival [in God's presence] would rise in his innermost self. These rules apply only to few aspirants. In most cases, one has to treat them by referring them to speculative reasoning (*nazar*) and the witnessing of [divine] signs, provided that the aspirant has acquired the knowledge of the fundamentals of religion in accordance with the need that is peculiar to him.

Know that aspirants are particularly vulnerable to the temptations of this sort.[833] When they withdraw to a place where they engage in the remembrance [of God] or participate in listening to music and recitation and so on, they may hear whisperings in their souls or blameworthy thoughts might occur to them. They know for sure that God – praise be to Him – is far above all this. They have no doubt whatsoever that it is but falsehood, but it persists and they undergo severe suffering due to this, to the extent that they experience the ugliest of curses, the ugliest of insinuations, and the most repulsive of thoughts. The aspirant, however, is unable to utter them with his tongue, nor display them to anyone else. This is the worst thing that can happen to him. In this case, he should pay no attention to such thoughts, constantly remember [God] and pray to God, asking His protection from this.//482

These thoughts are not the whisperings of Satan. Rather they are the promptings of one's lower soul. However, if the servant of God pays no attention to them, they will soon come to an end. Part of the rules of proper behavior for the aspirant – indeed an obligation pertaining to his spiritual state – is that he should remain in the place where his aspiration started and not travel anywhere until the [Sufi] path has accepted him and his heart has arrived in the presence of his Lord. Travel at a wrong time for the aspirant is but deadly poison and not one of those who has traveled at a wrong time has ever attained the place he has hoped to reach. If God wishes good to the aspirant, he makes him firm from the very beginning. If, however, He wishes ill to the aspirant, He will keep sending him back to his initial state and profession. And if God wishes to test the aspirant, He will banish him to the wastelands of alienation from Him.

Now, this applies to the aspirant who is destined to reach his goal. There are, however, young men who are best suited for the path of outward service to the poor.[834] Such an individual is lower than them in his rank pertaining to the path. He and the likes of him are content to imitate the outward customs [of the Sufi folk]. They dedicate themselves to travels. The most they can achieve on this path is to journey [to different lands], to visit places to which people aspire, and to meet [Sufi] masters in a purely outward manner. Therefore they witness only the outward aspects of things and are content with that kind of travel. Such people should travel incessantly so that idleness would not prompt them to commit things that are prohibited [by the Divine Law]. For if a young man enjoys rest and idleness, he enters the arena of temptation (*fitna*).

It is very detrimental for the novice to find himself amidst an assembly of [advanced] Sufi masters and [their] companions. If one happens to be tested in this manner, one should show [great] respect for the Sufi masters, render services to those in their entourage, never oppose them and should make them feel at

---

833 Namely, doubt and devilish promptings.
834 Namely, the Sufis.

ease. One should also seek that the heart of a Sufi master not be alienated from him. In dealing with Sufi masters one must always take their part against oneself and never one's own part against them. One should always consider oneself indebted to each of them, while at the same time not considering them in any way indebted to oneself. The aspirant must never disagree with anyone. If he knows that he is right, he must keep silent and show his agreement with everyone. If the aspirant laughs, or is prone to anger and debate – nothing [good] will come out of him. If the aspirant finds himself amidst an assembly of Sufis – be this on the road or at gathering – he must not disagree with [any aspect of] their outward behavior – be it food, fasting, rest, or movement. If he feels disagreement with them in his innermost self and in his heart, he should keep his heart with God – may He be great and exalted. If, for instance, they invite him to eat, he should eat one or two morsels and not allow his lower soul revel in its appetite.//483

A constant and ostentatious recitation of [Sufi] litanies is not part of proper manners among the aspirants. The [Sufi] folk engage in the purification of their thoughts, improving their morals and banishing forgetfulness from their hearts [inwardly], not by multiplying the acts of piety. They, however, must observe all prescribed rites and follow [the prophetic] customs. As for the supererogatory prayers, a constant remembrance of God in one's heart is better for the aspirants. The aspirant's principal fortune is his [ability] to tolerate everyone in good spirit, to accept everything he encounters with contentment, to patiently withstand hardship and poverty, and to give up demands and opposition [toward anyone] in both little and big things that he receives as his allotted share. If he is incapable of tolerating these things, he must go back to the marketplace. For if he desires what the ordinary people desire, he must obtain it from wherever people obtain it – from the toil of his hand and the sweat of his brow. After the aspirant has adopted a constant remembrance of God and has gone into a retreat, he may find there things that he has not witnessed before – which may occur to him in his sleep, in his waking state and in a state between these two. He may hear speeches and contemplate images that contradict the customary order [of things]. He must never preoccupy himself with any of such things, nor find repose in them, nor anticipate their arrival. For all this is but distraction from God – praise be to Him. Under those conditions he must describe all this to his master, so that his [the aspirant's] heart would be emptied of this.

The master, in his turn, must protect his secret, keep it away from others and make it look unimportant in his [aspirant's] eyes. For all this is nothing but tests, and reliance on it is a ruse [on the part of God]. Therefore the aspirant should be on his guard against this and pay little attention to this, for it has little significance beyond this. Know that the most detrimental thing for the aspirant is that he may take delight in the signs of proximity and special favor that God – praise be to Him – casts into his innermost heart, as if He is saying: "I have bestowed special favor upon you and singled you out from among your peers." However, when he decides to reject such suggestions, he will find himself elevated above this [stage] by means of veridical unveilings that will manifest themselves to him. Books, however, cannot provide a [detailed] explanation of this.

If the aspirant cannot find someone who could instruct him in the place he lives, it is incumbent on him to travel to someone who is renowned//484 in his age for [his] guidance of novices. He must stay with this teacher and never leave the door of his house except for the canonical prayers. Know that one must give precedence to the knowledge of the Lord of the [Sacred] House[835] – praise be to Him – over visiting the [Sacred] House, for were it not for the knowledge of the Lord of the House, visiting His House would not have been required. Those young men from among Sufi novices who go on a pilgrimage without the advice of their masters are driven by the promptings of their lower souls. Even though they may display the outward signs of this [Sufi] path their travel [to the pilgrimage site] is without [any] foundation. One evidence of this is that the more they travel, the greater the detachment of their hearts is [from God]. Departing even a few steps from their own lower souls would have been more beneficial to them than a thousand journeys.

The aspirant who pays a visit to a Sufi master must observe certain conditions. He must show respect to the master upon his entry and look at him with humility. Should the master choose him for any service, he should consider it to be a great favor.

Section

The aspirant should not ascribe infallibility to Sufi masters. Instead he should concede their states to them [as they are], think well of them and observe the limits set by God Most High in everything that the master instructs him to do. [His] knowledge is sufficient to him in distinguishing right from wrong.

Section

Every aspirant in whose heart the things of this world retain any value and significance can be associated with aspiration [to God] only metaphorically. As long as there remains in his heart preference for the pleasant things that he has given up, while he performs an act of righteousness or deals with a certain individual, then he is faking his true state and there is a danger that he might return to this world. For the goal of the aspirant lies in cutting and abandoning all ties to it, and not striving to [ostentatious] works of righteousness. It is absolutely inappropriate that the aspirant should [first] give up his property and inheritance and then become a captive to his [new] profession. Instead, he should seek a state when having and not having make no difference to him, so that he would not shun any poor person on account of it nor oppress anyone, even a fire-worshiper.//485

---

835 That is, the Kaʿba.

Section

When the hearts of Sufi masters accept an aspirant, this is the clearest proof that he will achieve salvation. As for he whom the heart of a master has rejected, he will inevitably see the consequence of this, even though this may take some time. If someone is destined [by God] to show disrespect toward Sufi masters, he has already displayed an unmistakable sign of his wretchedness [in the Hereafter].

Section

Seeking the company of youth is one of the gravest afflictions on this path. It is the consensus of Sufi masters that if God has afflicted someone with this sin then this person has been humiliated and deserted not only by God – may He be great and exalted – but also by himself, even though God may have granted him thousands upon thousands of miracles. Even if he has attained the rank of the witnesses [of faith] (*shuhada*ʾ), as alluded in a transmitted report, isn't it [a fact] that the heart may become preoccupied by a [mere] creature? Even worse than this [affliction] is that the heart considers this too trivial and regards this as totally unimportant. [About this] God Most High said: "You reckoned it a light thing, and with God it is a grave thing."[836] Al-Wasiti said [about this]: "When God wants to humiliate His servant, He throws him among evil-smelling trash and corpses."

I heard Abu ʿAbdallah al-Sufi say: I heard Muhammad b. Ahmad al-Najjar say: I heard Abu ʿAbdallah al-Husri say: I heard Fath al-Mawsili say: "I kept company with thirty [Sufi] masters, who were considered to be among the Substitutes (*al-abdal*).[837] When I was about to leave them, each of them gave me one and the same advice: 'Stay away from the company of youth and do not mingle with them!'" There are, however, those who claim to have overcome the depravity pertaining to this issue[838] and who argue that this is but a test of the [human] spirit that does no harm. [As their proof] they recount the insinuations of those who teach about the "sign" (*shāhid*)[839] and the anecdotes about certain Sufi masters and the sinful behavior that they have exhibited, which it would have been more appropriate for them to conceal [from the public]. This kind of talk approximates to polytheism and amounts to [sheer] unbelief. So may the aspirant avoid the company of youths or mingling with them, for this easily opens the door//486 of [his] abandonment and rejection [by God]. Let us take refuge in God from evil behavior!

---

836 Q. 24:15; 24:14, according to Arberry's translation.
837 One of the most elevated ranks in the Sufi spiritual hierarchy. They were thus called for their ability to maintain their presence in several different places at the same time.
838 Namely, keeping company with youths.
839 Namely, a young boy or man, whom they consider to be a reflection of divine beauty (misguidedly, according to al-Qushayri).

Section

Another grave sin that may afflict the aspirant is the secret envy of his brothers that may penetrate his heart. It may occur as a result of the special treatment that God – may He be great and exalted – accords to his peers on this [Sufi] path and which He deprives him of. He should know that what happens is but portions [that God bestows upon His creatures] (*qisam*). The servant can purify himself from [envy] by finding his satisfaction in God's existence and eternal nature rather than in His generosity and grace. Whatever you see, O aspirant, has been predetermined by God – so carry His burden [patiently]. This is the custom that is followed by the cleverest of the seekers [of God].

Section

When the aspirant happens to find himself in a company of people, it is his obligation to give preference to every single one of them [over himself]. He should put above himself every person, regardless of whether that person is hungry or sated. He should seek instruction from anyone who displays signs of masterly features, even though he may be more knowledgeable than his teacher. He[840] can only arrive at this stage by divesting himself of his own power and capacity, and by being guided to it by God's might and beneficence.

Section

In regard to the aspirant's behavior at a listening session, it is never appropriate that he should move during it on his own accord. He can only be excused, if a divine visitation [commanding] movement descends upon him, in which case its intensity should not exceed the strength of the power (*ghalaba*) that overwhelms him. When this overwhelming power ceases, he must sit down and be still. If, however, he continues to move seeking pleasure in ecstasy without such an overwhelming power and necessity, then this is not right. When he has accustomed himself to this [rule] he holds [himself] back and does not display any [divine] realities imparted to him. The most he can hope for when he has attained such states is to take delight in them in his heart.

In general, movement takes a toll on everyone who engages in it and detracts from his spiritual state regardless of whether this is a master or an aspirant. The only exception is that it is dictated by one's [mystical] moment (*waqt*) or an overwhelming power that deprives one of one's [sense of] discernment (*tamyiz*).//487 However, when the master instructs the aspirant to move and he engages in this movement in accord with the master's instruction, then there is no harm in it, for the master is one who has authority over him. If [advanced] Sufis instruct the aspirant to join in their movements,[841] he should join them in

---

840 That is, the aspirant.
841 That is, in their dance and body postures.

what they are doing, and perform what is necessary in order to prevent their hearts from alienating themselves [from him]. Now, if his spiritual state is sincere, it will prevent the hearts of the [advanced] Sufis from questioning him when he joins them.

As to the throwing off of one's clothes [during a listening session], the aspirant has absolutely no right to take back anything that he has given away [in this manner], except when a Sufi master instructs him to do so. He then treats it as a loaned thing in his heart and takes it back only to give it away later without alienating the heart of the master. If the aspirant who has not done so before [finds himself among] a group of Sufis whose custom is to throw off their robes – and the aspirant knows that they return them [to one another] and there is no master among them to whom he could entrust his embarrassment and his uneasiness – it is best that he join in their custom and choose to cast his robe off before the singer,[842] even though they may take theirs back. He is also allowed not to cast it off, because he knows that they are accustomed to taking back what they have cast off [before the singer]. For the impropriety lies in their custom of taking back [their] robes and not in his opposing what they do. Nevertheless, the best way is to cast off [his robe] in accord with them, then not take it back. Under no circumstance should the aspirant make demands of the singer, for it is the sincerity of his [aspirant's] spiritual state that causes the singer to repeat certain things, while causing others to follow [him].

Whoever seeks blessing from the aspirant does injustice to him, for since he has little spiritual power, this may harm him. Therefore it is incumbent upon the aspirant not to display his [spiritual] status in front of anyone who ascribes to him blessing and [high] status.

Section

When the aspirant is tested by [worldly] renown, a secure and abundant livelihood, friendship with a youth, attraction to a woman or the [comforting] belief in an assured source of sustenance, and there is no master next to him who would suggest to him how to rid himself of this, then he should travel and move away from his place of residence, in order to distract his ego from this condition.//488 There is nothing more harmful for the heart of the aspirant than to achieve [worldly] renown before extinguishing his human nature.

One of the requirements of proper behavior is that the aspirant's knowledge of the [Sufi] path should not be ahead of his actual [spiritual] stage [along it]. Should he learn the ways of this [Sufi] community and imitate the acquisition of the knowledge of the issues and [spiritual] states that they face before actually realizing his true status [vis-à-vis them] and acting accordingly, his arrival at all these things will be delayed. That is why the Sufi masters say: "When the gnostic speaks [profusely] about [his] gnosis, consider him to be ignorant!" For this is

---

842 As a sign of gratitude and payment.

nothing but talking about mystical stations without [direct] knowledge [of them]. He whose knowledge is greater than his station is a possessor of [abstract] knowledge, not a traveler on the [Sufi] path.

Section

One of the requirements of proper manners is that aspirants should not seek prominence (*tasaddur*), nor have disciples and novices. For the aspirant (*murid*) who has become one to whom others aspire (*murad*) before ridding himself of his human nature and his failings is veiled from the True Reality. Therefore his instructions and teachings will benefit no one.

Section

When an aspirant renders services to [advanced] Sufis [he should know] that their inner thoughts[843] are their messengers to him. Therefore, the aspirant must not resist sincere striving in their service and the total dedication of his efforts [for their well-being] that his innermost soul commands him.

Section

If it is the aspirant's duty to render services to Sufis, he should bear it patiently if they are harsh to him. Even if he believes that he spares no effort in their service, while they never praise him [for that], he should apologize to them for his shortcomings and assert that it is he himself who is at fault, thereby soothing their hearts. [He should do this] even though he may know that he has nothing to be blamed for. Even though they may persist in being harsh toward him, he should exert himself in their service and in his solicitude [toward them]. I heard imam Abu Bakr b. Furak say: "As an adage has it: 'If you cannot be patient under the hammer, why then become an anvil?'" With this in mind the Sufis recite:

> I would occasionally come to him to submit my apologies to him
> For my sins even before I have done any wrong.//489

Section

The foundation and the essence of this matter[844] is the observance of the rules of the Divine Law, the guarding of one's hand from stretching to anything that is forbidden or ambiguous [under it], protecting one's senses from prohibited things, and avoiding forgetfulness of God Most High even for [the duration of] a single breath. If, in the time of need, one is not allowed to consider lawful as much as a sesame seed because of doubt about [its provenance], how [do you think] one should behave at a time of ease and free choice?

---

843 That is, "their wishes and desires", according to a commentator.
844 That is, Sufism.

It is the aspirant's duty to constantly exert himself in an effort to give up passionate desires (*shahawat*). For whoever follows his passion, forfeits his purity. One of the ugliest features in the aspirant is that he reverts to the passion which he previously gave up for the sake of God Most High.

Section

It is the aspirant's duty to keep his pact with God Most High. Breaking the pact while on the path of aspiration is [for the aspirant] like apostasy (*ridda*) for the people of outward [faith]. The aspirant should not, as far as possible, promise to God Most High anything of his own free choice, for the requirements of the Divine Law contain enough to satisfy anyone's ability [to worship God]. God said regarding certain folk: "[Monasticism][845] they invented – we did not prescribe it to them – only seeking the good pleasure of God; but they observed it not as it should be observed."[846]

Section

It is the aspirant's duty not to entertain high hopes [for the future], for the poor one[847] is the son of his [mystical] moment.[848] Nothing will come out of the aspirant who makes plans for the future, looks beyond his [condition] in the present moment and anticipates what might happen to him.

Section

It is the aspirant's duty that he has no [secure] sustenance, no matter how small, especially when he is in the company of Sufis. For the darkness of [secure] sustenance stifles the light of the [mystical] moment.

Section

It is the aspirant's duty – which applies to all those who travel along this [Sufi] path – not to accept any favors from women, not to mention actively seeking them.//490 This is the way of the masters of the Sufi community and what they have advised others to do.

---

845 This word appears only in some versions of the text; others omit it.
846 Q. 57:27; 57:29, according to Arberry's translation. This verse is a matter of controversy among Muslim exegetes, since it allows two diametrically opposed interpretations: one is favorable toward the Christian monks (in which case, one reads "We did not prescribe it for them except that [it arose] out of desire for the satisfaction of God"); the other is critical of their "innovation", as in the translation suggested by Arberry.
847 That is, the Sufi.
848 That is, he lives by the "here and now".

Section

It is the aspirant's duty to keep away from worldly people, for keeping company with them is a time-tested poison. They will benefit from him, while they will detract from his [spiritual] stature. God Most High said: "Obey not him whose heart We have made neglectful of Our remembrance."[849] Those who renounce the world (*zuhhad*) take money out of their purses in order to draw closer to God, whereas the pure ones[850] take the creatures [of this world] and [mundane] knowledge out of their hearts in order to attain to God's True Reality.

The master and imam Abu 'l-Qasim ʿAbd al-Karim b. Hawazin al-Qushayri – may God be pleased with him – said: "This is our advice to the aspirants. We ask that God the Generous grant them success and that He not hold it against us [in the Hereafter]. We have completed dictating this *Epistle* at the beginning of the year four hundred and thirty-eight.[851] We ask God the Generous not to make it an argument against us and not to punish us on account of it [in the Hereafter]. On the contrary, [we ask] that it serve for us as a means [to salvation] and a benefit. Verily, His grace is His wont and forgiveness is [always] ascribed to Him."

Praise be to God as is His due. May His graces, blessings and mercy be on His messenger, our master the virgin (*ummi*)[852] Prophet as well as upon his pure family and his elect and noble Companions! May God greet them all abundantly!

---

849 Q. 18:28; 18:27, according to Arberry's translation.
850 *Ahl al-safaʾ* – that is, the Sufis.
851 That is, 1046 C.E.
852 That is, one whose mission and teachings were original and unprecedented.

Glossary

ʿAbd: servant of God; worshiper

Abdal: lit. "substitutes"; members of the highest rank of the Sufi spiritual hierarchy; they were called so for their ability to maintain their presence in several different places at the same time

ʿAbid, pl., *ʿubbad*: [a devout] worshiper of God

Adab: good manners [in the presence of God or one's fellow human beings]

[*al-*]*Akhira*: the Hereafter as opposed to this life ([*al-*]*dunya*)

Akhlaq: a person's character traits, especially his or her manners and morals

ʿAlaqa(t): attachment(s) to this world and mundane things

ʿArif [*bi-ʾllah*], lit. "he who knows God"; gnostic; the highest category of Sufi masters; see also *maʿrifa*

Asbab, sing., *sabab*: means of existence and sustenance that may distract the Sufi from worshiping God as befits Him

Awba: a variant of *tawba*; "return to God after repenting before Him"; the ultimate stage of repentance (*tawba*)

Awliyaʾ, sing., *wali*: "friends of God" or "God's protegés"; advanced Sufi masters, who in Western literature are sometimes identified as the Muslim equivalent of Christian saints

ʿAyn al-yaqin: the essence of certainty; a state of absolute certainty experienced by the mystic; see also *yaqin* and *haqq al-yaqin*

ʿAyyar: bandit of honor; a member of urban militia, who adhered to a special code of honor; see also *futuwwa*

Balaʾ: affliction or trial to which God may subject His servant

Baqaʾ: the mystic's subsistence/survival in God following *fanaʾ*

Basira: inward vision; insight

Bast: expansion; a state of ease, confidence and joy experienced by the Sufi; see also *qabd*

Batin: see *zahir*

Bawadih/Hujum: "attacks" or "onslaughts" of mystical states upon the Sufi

Buʿd: distance from God as opposed to *qurb*

Bukaʾ: weeping, crying; a Sufi practice

Dhawq: "[direct] tasting" of the true realities behind the appearances of the empirical world

Dhikr: remembrance/recollection of God and his names

[*al-*]*Dunya*: see [*al-*]*Akhira*

Duʿaʾ: supplicatory prayer, as opposed to the canonical one; see also *sala(t)*

[*al-*]*Dunya*: this world and its "deceptive" trappings

Fanaʾ: the mystic's self-annihilation in God; see also *baqaʾ*

Faqr: poverty; a station of the mystical path

Farq: separation; the state of detachment from God; see also *jamʿ*

Fata/fityan: see *futuwwa*

Fikr, fikra: contemplation; self-scrutiny

Firasa: clairvoyance; supernatural perspicacity

Futuwwa: spiritual "chivalry" – a code of honor to be observed by the genuine Sufi, which enjoins him to be generous, to give preference to others over his own self, and to help the poor and needy

Ghafla: temporary forgetfulness of God and His commands

Ghafr: concealment, veil; the state of being barred from God

Ghayb: the unseen; the realm of divine mysteries that is closed to everyone but the most advanced Sufi gnostics

Ghayba: "absence from God" (both mental and devotional), as opposed to "being present with Him" (*hudur*)

Ghayra: "jealousy" of God toward His servants, namely His insistence that they turn to and seek help of no one but Him

Ghiba: backbiting; one of the sins to be avoided by the Sufis

Hadith: report about an action or saying of the Prophet

Hajis, pl., *hawajis*: the promptings of the lower soul; see also *khawatir* and *waswas*

Hal: spiritual state which the mystic experiences on his way to God; see also *maqam*

Haqiqa: True Reality; ultimate truth; the genuine state of affairs

[al-]Haqq: the Real; the True Reality; God

Haqq al-yaqin: truth of certainty; a state of certainty experienced by the mystic

Hasad: envy, in particular, being envious of somebody's more advanced spiritual state; a sin to be avoided by the Sufis

Hatif: invisible voice by which God communicates with His elect friends

Hawa, pl., *ahwaʾ*: urges and drives of one's lower soul (*nafs*)

Haya: shame before God

Hayba: awe and trepidation before God

Hayra; *tahayyur*: perplexity, bewilderment of the mystic in the face of ever-changing divine self-manifestations

Hudur: "being present with God" (with one's entire self), as opposed to "absence from God" (*ghayba*)

Hujum: see *bawadih*

Hulm: a variety of dream that may occasionally carry a negative connotation as opposed to *ruʾya*

Huzn: sadness and despondency; a Sufi virtue

ʿIbada / ʿubudiyya: worship of God, especially fulfilling one's obligations toward Him

ʿIbara: see *Ishara*

Iʿjab: complacency; self-conceit

Ikhlas: sincerity before God; a *sine qua non* of the Sufi path

Ikhtiyar: freedom of choice and the ability to choose among several options

Ilham: [divine] inspiration; revelation

ʿIlm al-yaqin: a variant of *yaqin*

Iman: faith; the middle/intermediate member of the famous Sufi triad: *islam* (external submission) – *iman* (internalization of faith) – *ihsan* (serving God as if you see Him; that is, acting in full compliance with His will)

Inaba: turning to God in repentance; an advanced stage of repentance (*tawba*)

Irada: aspiration to God; the state of turning to God and entering on the path leading to Him; see also *murid*

Ishara: indirect allusion as opposed to clear and unequivocal statement (*'ibara*)

'Ishq: the mystic's passionate longing [for God]

Istiqama: uprightness; moral rectitude

Jam': unification; the state of being in the presence of God

Jamal: [divine] beauty; the benign aspect of God as opposed to that of divine majesty (*jalal*)

Jihad: struggle against the drives and passions of one's low soul; fighting against an "infidel" enemy

Jud: generosity (usually of God to human beings)

Karama: saintly miracle – that is, one that is performed by a friend of God and not a prophet, whose miracle is called *mu'jiza*

Kashf: unveiling; the disclosure of true realities and secrets of being before the Sufi

Khadim: servant – and sometimes also disciple – of a Sufi master

Khalwa: retreat; isolation; a common Sufi practice

Khawatir, sing., *khatir*: secret thoughts – often blameworthy and distracting – that may visit or even assault the Sufi; they usually emanate from the Sufi's own lower soul that is in league with the Devil; see also *waswas*

Khawf: fear of God's wrath as opposed to *raja'*

Khidhlan: abandonment by God of His servant to punish him for his transgressions

Khirqa: Sufi cloak or robe; a piece of patched garment worn by the Sufi as an outward sign of his affiliation with the ascetic and mystical movement in Islam

Khuluq: good moral qualities

Khumul: humility; resignation

Khushuʿ: humility before God; see also *tawaduʿ*

Kibr/takabbur: pride as opposed to *khushuʿ* and *tawaduʿ*

Ladhdha: pleasure [in the presence of God]

Lawaʾih: the mystical experience of the "glimmings" of divine presence; see also *lawamiʿ* and *tawaliʿ*

Lawamiʿ: the mystical experience of the "flashes" of divine presence; see also *lawaʾih* and *tawaliʿ*

Mahabba/hubb: mystical love of God and loving relationship between God and man; see also *shawq* and *ʿishq*

Mahq: the experience of being "ground down" and obliterated by divine presence

Mahw: the experience of being "erased" and "annihilated" by divine presence

Makasib: "earnings"; something that one acquires by means of sincere worship of God; see *mawahib*

Makr: divine ruse; a test set by God for the Sufi

Malakut: the realm/sphere of divine majesty

Maqam: spiritual station [on the Sufi path]

Maʿrifa [bi-llah]: [divine] gnosis; the supersensory, revelatory knowledge of God and the world granted to the accomplished Sufi master; see also *ʿarif*

Mawahib: divine gifts and graces that are granted to God's servant "free of charge"

Muʿayana: direct contemplation [of God and divine realities] by the Sufi; see also *mushahada*

Muhaqqiq: one who has attained truth; truth-verifier; an accomplished mystic

Muhasaba: taking account of one's actions and thoughts; self-scrutiny

Muhibb/habib: lover/beloved; usually in reference to the mystic and his divine Beloved

Mujahada: self-exertion on the path of God; Sufi practices aimed at minimizing detrimental drives and promptings of the lower soul through abstention from the delights of this world and strict self-discipline

Muʿjiza: see *karama*

Mukabada: spiritual struggle; self-exertion on the path to God; see also *mujahada*

Mukashafa: see *kashf*

Mukhalafat al-nafs: "opposing one's soul"; resisting its self-centred drives and passions; see also *nafs*

Munazala: spiritual station; see also *maqam*

Muraqaba: awareness of God's presence by the Sufi and the concomitant self-scrutiny of his actions and thoughts

Murid: lit. "one who aspires"; aspirant; Sufi novice/disciple

Muruʾa: manliness; a code of chivalry and nobility of spirit practiced by the Sufis

Mushahada: direct witnessing of God and/or the true realities of existence; see also *muʿayana*

Mutasawwif, pl., *mutasawwifa*: Sufi(s) and those who try to imitate them

Nadam, nadama: remorse; a Sufi virtue

Nafas: bringing one's "breath" in compliance with the changing modes of divine existence – the utmost stage of the Sufi's spiritual journey

Nafs: appetitive soul; self

Nawafil: supererogatory acts of piety and worship – e.g., night vigils and additional prayers practiced by Sufis

Qabd: contraction; a state of distress and agony that may assault a Sufi; the opposite of *bast*

Qadaʾ: divine decree; predestination

Qalb: heart as an instrument of cognition and an arena of the mystic's encounter with God; it occupies the intermediate position in the triad *nafs–qalb–ruh*

Qanaʿa: contentment with God's decree and one's apportioned lot

Qurb: the state of proximity to God as opposed to *buʿd*

Qawm: [Sufi] folk; Sufis

Raghba: desire; aspiration

Rahba: horror before God

Rahbaniyya: monasticism

Raja': hope for God's grace and mercy as opposed to *khawf*

Rida: contentment; satisfaction with divine decree

Riya': hypocrisy; complacency; self-conceit

Riyada: ascetic exercise; self-exertion

Rububiyya: divine lordship

Ruh: spirit; the divine "spark" cast in the human body

Ru'ya: visionary experience; vision of God [in the Hereafter]

Sabr: patience in the face of adversity; a Sufi virtue

Sadiq: sincere one

Safa': purity

Safar: journey or travel undertaken by Sufis in search of masters or to fulfill the duty of *hajj*

Sahw: sobriety as opposed to "intoxication" (*sukr*) with a mystical state

Sakha': generosity (usually of human beings as opposed to *jud*)

Sakina: divine presence; Shekina

Sala(t): canonical prayer (there are five of them), as opposed to the supplicatory one; see also *du'a'*

Sama': listening to music; spiritual concert

Samt: silence; a Sufi virtue

Satr: concealment of/from God as opposed to His [self-]disclosure/revelation (*tajalli*)

Shahada: direct witnessing of God by the mystic; see also *mushahada*

Shahid: lit. "witness"; a sign of divine grace or presence that appears to the Sufi; also a youth, whose beauty was viewed by some Sufis as a reflection of divine perfection; the practice of gazing at "beardless young men" to gain a glimpse of divine beauty was condemned by many Sufi masters

Shahwa: desire; passion (usually base)

Shakur: the grateful one

Shari'a: the Divine Law

Shawq: loving passion; longing

Shaykh: lit. "elder"; a Sufi master

Shubha: lit. "that which is suspicious"; a thing the status of which is dubious from the viewpoint of the Divine Law

Shukr: gratitude or gratefulness, especially toward God

Siddiq: "one who is truthful and trustworthy" – an advanced Sufi master; also, an epithet of the first caliph Abu Bakr [al-Siddiq]

Sidq: truthfulness and sincerity before God; see also *ikhlas*

Sirr: the "heart of hearts" of the Sufi; the arena of his loving relation with God; see also *nafs* and *ruh*

Suʾ al-khuluq/suʾ al-adab: improper behavior before God and other people

Suhba: companionship among the Sufis, which usually involved the training of a younger Sufi (*murid*) or Sufis by a more advanced one known as *shaykh*

Sukr: "intoxication" with a mystical state; see *sahw*

Sunna: the [exemplary] custom of the Prophet

Taʿa: act of worship, piety and obedience to God

Tadbir: divine predestination of events; the ability to exercise one's free choice

Tafakkur/fikr/fikra: pious meditation; a spiritual practice current among the Sufis

Tafriqa: a vision or perception of the plurality of the empirical world; the opposite of *jamʿ*

Tahayyur: the state of bewilderment and perplexion

Tajalli: self-revelation/manifestation of God; see also *satr*

Talwin: "inconstancy" of one's spiritual states, when one is quickly succeeded by another; the opposite of stability or "fixity" (*tamkin*) of one's state

Tamkin: "stability" or "fixity"; the stabilization of one's spiritual state (*hal*); the opposite of *talwin*

Taqwa: fear of God and pious behavior springing from it; piety; righteousness

Tasarruf (tasrif): the ability to exercise freedom of choice and perform certain actions

Tasawwuf: putting on a woolen garment; Sufism

Tasdiq: confirmation

Taslim: surrender to God's will

Tasrif: see *Tasarruf*

Tawaduʿ: modesty and humbleness before God; see also *khushuʿ*

Tawajud: ecstatic behavior that was often associated with listening to music (*samaʿ*); see also *wajd* and *wujud*

Tawakkul: trust in God; a total reliance on God by the Sufi

Tawaliʿ: the mystical experience of the "dawnings" of divine presence; see also *lawaʾih* and *lawamiʿ*

Tawba/awba: lit. "return to God"; repentance; see also *inaba* and *awba*

Tawfiq: divine assistance

Tawhid: the doctrine that declares God to be one and only

ʿUbuda: see also *ʿibada* and *ʿubudiyya*

ʿUbudiyya: the state of servanthood before God; worship of God

ʿUjb: complacency; self-conceit; smugness

Uns: intimacy with God, as opposed to awe before Him (*hayba*)

ʿUzla: solitude; isolation: a Sufi exercise

Wajd: ecstatic rapture engendered by the mystic's encounter with the Divine Reality; see also *wujud*

Wahda: unicity/oneness of God

Wali/Walí: see *awliyaʾ*

Waqiʿa: spiritual event/state

Waqt: mystical moment in time; the eternal "here-and-now" of the Sufi

Waraʿ: scrupulousness in discerning between the licit and the forbidden under the Divine Law

Warid: occurrence; divine visitation

Wasiyya, pl., *wasaya*: spiritual advice; admonition

Waswas, pl., *wasawis*: devilish whisperings; secret thoughts that may distract the Sufi on his path to God; see also *khawatir*

Wilaya: the state of being a friend of God; see *awliyaʾ*

Wird, pl., *awrad*: prayer; supplication

Wujud: the act of "finding" of God by the mystic, which may throw him into ecstasy or induce a trance

Yaqin: certain, unshakeable knowledge of God and trust in Him; see also *ʿayn al-yaqin* and *haqq al-yaqin*

Zahid: pl., *zuhhad*: world-renouncer; ascetic

Zahir: the outward, external aspect of a certain thing or phenomenon as opposed to its inward, secret aspect (*batin*)

Zuhd: renunciation; abstention from the delights and allure of this world; asceticism

BIBLIOGRAPHY

Abbreviations

EI Encyclopaedia of Islam, 2nd. edition, vols. 1–11, E. J. Brill, Leiden, 1954–2004.
IM Knysh, Alexander, *Islamic Mysticism: A Short History*, E. J. Brill, Leiden, 2000.
Q. Arberry, Arthur J. (trans.), *The Koran Interpreted*, Simon and Schuster, New York, 1996.

Full titles of other cited works

Ahmad b. Hanbal, *Al-Musnad*, Bulaq, Cairo, 1313 A.H.
Anonymous, *Adab al-muluk: Ein Handbuch zur islamischen Mystik aus dem 4./10. Jahrhundert*, (ed.) Bernd Radtke, Franz Steiner, Beirut, 1991.
Baldick, Julian, *Mystical Islam: An Introduction to Sufism*, I. B. Tauris, London, 1989.
Edmund Bosworth, *The Mediaeval Islamic Underworld: The Banu Sasan in Arabic Society and Literature*, E. J. Brill, Leiden, 1976.
Böwering, Gerhard, *The Mystical Vision of Existence in Classical Islam*, Walter de Gruyter, Berlin and New York, 1980.
Chittick, William, *The Self-Disclosure of God: Principles of Ibn al-ʿArabi's Cosmology*, SUNY Press, Albany, N.Y., 1998.
—*The Sufi Path of Knowledge: Ibn al-ʿArabi's Metaphysics of Imagination*, SUNY Press, Albany, N.Y., 1989.
Cooperson, Michael, "Ahmad Ibn Hanbal and Bishr al-Hafi: A Case Study in Biographical Traditions", *Studia Islamica* 86/2 (1997).
Cornell, Vincent, *Realm of the Saint: Power and Authority in Moroccan Sufism*, University of Texas Press, Austin, 1998.
Ernst, Carl, *Words of Ecstasy in Sufism*, SUNY Press, Albany, N.Y., 1985.
Frank, Richard, *Beings and Their Attributes: The Teaching of the Basran School of the Muʿtazila in the Classical Period*, SUNY Press, Albany, N.Y., 1978.
Gimaret, Daniel, *Les Noms Divins en Islam*, Cerf, Paris, 1988.
Gramlich, Richard (trans.), *Das Sendschreiben al-Qušayris über das Sufitum*, Franz Steiner, Wiesbaden, 1989.
Halm, Heinz, *The Empire of the Mahdi* (trans. Michael Bonner), E. J. Brill, Leiden, 1996.
Harris, Rabia (trans.), *The Risalah: Principles of Sufism*, ed. by Laleh Bakhtiar, Kazi Publications, Chicago, IL, 2002.
Mojaddedi, Jawid, *The Biographical Tradition in Sufism*, Curzon Press, Richmond, Surrey, 2001.

al-Qushayri, *Lata'if al-isharat*, ed. by Ibrahim Basyuni, Dar al-kitab al-ʿarabi, Cairo, 1968.

—*Al-Risala al-qushayriyya*, ed. by ʿAbd al-Halim Mahmud and Mahmud b. al-Sharif, Dar al-kutub al-haditha, Cairo, 1966.

—*Al-Risala al-qushayriyya fi ʿilm al-tasawwuf*, with commentaries by Zakariya al-Ansari, Dar al-kutub al-ʿarabiyya al-kubra, Mustafa al-Babi al-Halabi, Cairo, 1276 A.H. (1859 C.E.).

—*Al-Risala al-qushayriyya*, with commentaries by Mustafa al-ʿArusi and Zakariya al-Ansari, ʿAbd al-Wakil al-Darubi and Tasin ʿArafa, Jamiʿ al-Darwishiyya, Damascus, no date.

—*Al-Risala al-qushayriyya fi ʿilm al-tasawwuf*, ed. by Muhammad ʿAbd al-Rahman al-Marʿashali, Dar ihyaʾ al-turath al-ʿarabi, Beirut, 1998.

al-Sarraj, *Kitab al-lumaʿ fi ʾl-tasawwuf*, ed. by Reynold A. Nicholson, E. J. Brill, Leiden, 1914.

al-Sulami, *Tabaqat al-sufiyya*, ed. by Johannes Pedersen, E. J. Brill, Leiden, 1960.

Schimmel, Annemarie, *Mystical Dimensions of Islam*, University of North Carolina Press, Chapel Hill, 1975.

van Ess, Josef, "Vision and Ascension: *Surat al-Najm* and Its Relationship with Muhammad's *miʿraj*" in *Journal of Qurʾanic Studies*, vol. 1/1 (1999).

von Schlegell, Barbara, *Principles of Sufism*, Mizan Press, Berkeley, 1990.

Wensinck, Arent, *Concordance et Indices de la Tradition Musulmane*, E. J. Brill, Leiden, 1936–1969.

Index

A

Aban b. Abi ʿAyyash Firuz al-ʿAbdi, Abu Ismaʿil (d. 138/755–6 or somewhat later)   174
Aban b. Ishaq al-Asadi al-Kufi al-Nahwi   226
Aban b. Thaʿlab [Taghlib] b. Riyah al-Jurayri al-Kufi al-Rabaʿi, Abu Saʿd (d. ca 141/758–9)   161
Abandonment [by God] (*khidhlan*)   264, 361, 411
ʿAbbad b. Bishr b. Waqsh al-Khazraji (killed in 12/633)   366
ʿAbbad b. Kathir   320
ʿAbbadan   34, 368
al-ʾAbbas b. ʾAbd al-Muttalib b. Hashim b. ʿAbd Manaf, Abu ʾl-Fadl (d. ca 32/653)   209
al-ʿAbbas b. (al-)Fadl al-Asqati (al-Isqati)   118, 125
(al-)ʿAbbas (or ʿAyyash) b. Hamza b. ʿAbdallah al-Naysaburi al-Waʿiz, Abu ʾl-Fadl (d. 288/901)   129, 159, 207, 212, 294, 321
ʿAbbas b. ʿIsam   135, 330
ʿAbbas b. al-Muhtadi al-Sufi, Abu ʾl-Fadl   133, 375
al-ʿAbbas al-Sharqi   381
ʿAbbas b. Tamim   151
al-ʿAbbas al-Zawzani   265
ʿAbd al-Aʿla b. Hammad b. Nasr al-Bahili, Abu Yahya al-maʿruf bi-ʾl-Narsi (or al-Qurashi) (d. 237/851)   125
ʿAbd al-ʿAziz b. ʿAbdallah b. Abi Salama Maymun al-Majashun, Abu ʿAbdallah (d. 164/780–1)   367
ʿAbd al-ʿAziz b. Abi Hazim Salama b. Dinar al-Muharibi (d. 184/800–1)   122
ʿAbd al-ʿAziz b. Abi Salama *see* ʿAbd al-ʿAziz b. ʿAbdallah b. Abi Salama
ʿAbd al-ʿAziz b. al-Fadl   26, 159, 380
ʿAbd al-ʿAziz b. Muʿawiyya b. ʿAbdallah al-Basri, Abu Khalid (d. 284/897–8)   122
ʿAbd al-ʿAziz b. Muhammad b. ʿUbayd b. Abi ʿUbayd al-Darawardi al-Madani, Abu Muhammad (d. ca 187/803)   209
ʿAbd al-ʿAziz al-Najrani   119
ʿAbd al-ʿAziz b. ʿUmayr   159
ʿAbd al-Kabir b. Ahmad   369
ʿAbd al-Karim b. al-Haytham b. Ziyad b. ʿImran al-Qattan al-Dayrʿaquli, Abu Yahya (d. 278/891–2)   365
ʿAbd al-Malik b. ʿAbd al-ʿAziz b. Jurayj al-Umawi al-Makki, Abu ʾl-Walid (d. 149–151/766–769)   297, 343

ʿAbd al-Malik b. al-Hasan b. Muhammad b. Ishaq al-Isfaraini, Abu Nuʿaym (d. 400/1009)   152, 202, 232, 363, 365
ʿAbd al-Malik b. (al-)Husayn al-Nakhaʿi al-Kufi, Abu Malik   292
ʿAbd al-Malik b. ʿUmayr b. Suwayd b. Haritha al-Qurashi al-Kufi, Abu ʿUmar al-maʿruf bi-ʾl-Qibti (d. ca 136/753–4)   292
ʿAbd-al-Rahim b. ʿAli al-Bazzaz al-Hafiz, Abu ʾl-Qasim   23
ʿAbd al-Rahman b. ʿAbdallah   45
ʿAbd al-Rahman b. ʿAbdallah al-Dhubyani   236
ʿAbd al-Rahman b. ʿAbdallah b. ʿUtba b. ʿAbdallah b. Masʿud al-Kufi al-Masʿudi (d. 165/781–2 or 160/776–7)   143
ʿAbd al-Rahman b. Abi Hatim Muhammad b. Idris b. al-Mundhir al-Tamimi al-Hanzali al-Razi (d. 327/938)   25
ʿAbd al-Rahman b. ʿAffan   334
ʿAbd al-Rahman b. Ahmad   279, 370
ʿAbd al-Rahman b. Ahmad b. Baqi b. Makhlad, Abu ʾl-Hasan   279
ʿAbd al-Rahman b. Ahmad al-Sufi   56
ʿAbd al-Rahman b. Bakr   233
ʿAbd al-Rahman b. Hamdan   305
ʿAbd al-Rahman b. Hurmuz al-Aʿraj al-Madani, Abu Dawud (d. 107/725–6)   237
ʿAbd al-Rahman b. Ibrahim b. Muhammad b. Yahya al-Muzakki, Abu ʾl-Hasan b. Abi Ishaq (d. 397/1006)   129, 155, 161
ʿAbd al-Rahman b. Muhammad b. ʿAbdallah al-ʿAdl   320
ʿAbd al-Rahman b. Muhammad al-Sufi   387
ʿAbd al-Rahman b. Saʿid b. Mawhab   145
ʿAbd al-Rahman b. Yahya al-Aswad al-Daybuli   250
ʿAbd al-Razzaq b. Hammam b. Nafiʿ al-Himyari, Abu Bakr (d. 211/826–7)   138, 222, 232, 325, 374
ʿAbd al-Samad b. al-Nuʿman al-Baghdadi al-Nasaʾi al-Bazzaz, Abu Muhammad (d. 216/831–2)   292
ʿAbd al-Samad b. Yazid al-Saʾigh al-maʿruf bi-Mardawayh, Abu ʿAbdallah (d. 235/850)   142
ʿAbd al-Wahhab   177, 389
ʿAbd al-Wahhab b. ʿAbd al-Majid b. al-Salt b. ʿUbaydallah al-Thaqafi al-Basri, Abu Muhammad (d. 194/810)   154
ʿAbd al-Wahid b. Ahmad   287
ʿAbd al-Wahid b. ʿAli *see* al-Sayyari, ʿAbd al-Wahid b. ʿAli

ʿAbd al-Wahid b. ʿAlwan, Abu ʿAmr   352
ʿAbd al-Wahid b. Bakr, Abu ʾl-Faraj al-Warathani al-Shirazi (d. 372/982–3)   10–11, 41, 48, 160, 180, 226, 282, 284, 286, 348, 382, 390
ʿAbd al-Wahid b. Maymun, Abu Hamza   269
ʿAbd al-Wahid b. Muhammad b. Shah al-Farisi al-Shirazi al-Isbahani, Abu ʾl-Husayn (d. ca 380/990)   289
ʿAbd al-Wahid b. Zayd al-Basri (d. ca 150/767, 177/793–4)   134, 136, 207, 220, 224, 377, 382–3, 388
ʿAbdallah b. (al-)ʿAbbas b. ʿAbd al-Muttalib al-Qurashi al-Hashimi, Abu ʾl-ʿAbbas (d. 68/687 or later)   5, 261, 281
ʿAbdallah b. ʿAbd al-Hamid   34
ʿAbdallah b. ʿAbd al-Majid al-Sufi   348
ʿAbdallah b. ʿAbd al-Wahhab al-Hajabi al-Basri, Abu Muhammad (d. 227–228/841–843)   306
ʿAbdallah b. ʿAdi b. ʿAbdallah b. Muhammad b. al-Mubarak al-Jurjani al-Hafiz, Abu Ahmad b. al-Qattan (d. 365/976)   39, 269
ʿAbdallah b. Ahmad b. Hanbal, Abu ʿAbd al-Rahman (d. 290/903)   238
ʿAbdallah b. Ahmad al-Istakhri, Abu Muhammad   158–9
ʿAbdallah b. Ahmad b. Jaʿfar b. Ahmad al-Shaybani al-Naysaburi, Abu Muhammad b. Abi Hamid (d. 372/983)   228–9
ʿAbdallah b. ʿAli b. Muhammad b. Yahya al-Tamimi see al-Sarraj, Abu Nasr
ʿAbdallah b. ʿAli al-Sijzi (or al-Shajari), Abu ʾl-Qasim   384
ʿAbdallah b. ʿAli al-Tamimi al-Sufi see al-Sarraj, Abu Nasr
ʿAbdallah b. ʿAli al-Tusi see al-Sarraj, Abu Nasr
ʿAbdallah b. ʿAli b. Yahya al-Tamimi (= ʿAbdallah b. ʿAli b. Muhammad b. Yahya) see al-Sarraj, Abu Nasr
ʿAbdallah b. ʿAmir al-Aslami al-Madani, Abu ʿAmir (d. 150/767 or 151/768)   237
ʿAbdallah b. ʿAmir b.Kurayz b. Rabiʿa al-Umawi, Abu ʿAbd al-Rahman (d. 59/680)   263
ʿAbdallah al-Ansari   337
ʿAbdallah b. ʿAtaʾ   282
ʿAbdallah b. ʿAwn b. Abi ʿAwn ʿAbd al-Malik b. Yazid al-Hilali al-Baghdadi al-Adami al-Kharraz, Abu Muhammad (d. probably 232/847)   398
ʿAbdallah b. Ayyub al-Qirabi   157, 175, 325
ʿAbdallah b. Bakawayh (Bakuya)   263
ʿAbdallah b. Burayda   129
ʿAbdallah al-Dinawari   341
ʿAbdallah b. al-Harith al-Ansari al-Basri, Abu ʾl-Walid   149
ʿAbdallah b. Hashim b. Hayyan al-ʿAbdi al-Tusi, Abu ʿAbd al-Rahman (d. 155/771 or later)   143

ʿAbdallah b. al-Husayn b. Balawayh (Baluya) al-Sufi, Abu ʾl-Qasim   37, 227, 233
ʿAbdallah b. Ibrahim b. al-ʿAlaʾ   250, 286
ʿAbdallah b. Ibrahim b. ʿAmir al-Ghifari al-Madani, Abu Muhammad   175
ʿAbdallah b. Idris b. Yazid b. ʿAbd al-Rahman b. al-Aswad al-Awdi al-Zaʿafiri al-Kufi, Abu Muhammad (d. 192/808)   390
ʿAbdallah b. Jaʿfar see ʿAbdallah b. Muhammad b. Jaʿfar
ʿAbdallah b. Jaʿfar b. Abi Talib b. ʿAbd al-Muttalib al-Hashimi (d. ca 80/699–700)   260, 344
ʿAbdallah b. Jaʿfar b. Ahmad b. Faris al-Isbahani, Abu Muhammad (d. 346/958)   178, 217, 222, 339
ʿAbdallah b. al-Jafʿar b. Ahmad b. Khushaysh al-Sayrafi al-Baghdadi, Abu ʾl-ʿAbbas (d. 318/930–1)   281
ʿAbdallah al-Kharraz see al-Kharraz, Abu Muhammad ʿAbdallah
ʿAbdallah al-Khayyat   257
ʿAbdallah b. Khubayq b. Sabiq al-Antaki, Abu Muhammad (d. 200/815–16)   41
ʿAbdallah b. Lahiʿa b. ʿUqba al-Hadrami al-Misri, Abu ʿAbd al-Rahman (d. 174/790)   273
ʿAbdallah al-Maghazili see al-Maghazili
ʿAbdallah b. Mahmud   221
ʿAbdallah b. Marwan (al-Khuzaʿi al-Basri?)   130
ʿAbdallah al-Marwazi (possibly Abu Muhammad ʿAbdallah b. Ahmad al-Ribati al-Marwazi?)   299
ʿAbdallah b. Masʿud see Ibn Masʿud, ʿAbdallah
ʿAbdallah al-Muʿallim see ʿAbdallah b. Muhammad b. Fadlawayh (Fadluya)
ʿAbdallah b. al-Mubarak, Abu ʿAbd al-Rahman (d. 181/797)   128, 136, 174, 186, 284, 295, 332, 396
ʿAbdallah b. Muhammad (al-Shaʿrani? possibly the same as below)   180, 228
ʿAbdallah b. Muhammad b. ʿAbdallah b. ʿAbd al-Rahman al-Razi al-maʿruf bi-ʾl-Shaʿrani, Abu Muhammad (d. 353/964)   35, 45, 69, 140, 142, 144–5, 163, 175, 180, 237, 253, 319, 350
ʿAbdallah b. Muhammad b. ʿAbd al-Rahman al-Razi see ʿAbdallah b. Muhammad b. ʿAbdallah b. ʿAbd al-Rahman al-Razi
ʿAbdallah b. Muhammad b. ʿAbd al-Wahhab see Abu Saʿid al-Qurashi
ʿAbdallah b. Muhammad b. Abi ʾl-Dunya see Ibn Abi ʾl-Dunya
ʿAbdallah b. Muhammad al-Dimashqi see Abu ʾl-Qasim ʿAbdallah b. Muhammad al-Dimashqi
ʿAbdallah b. Muhammad b. Fadlawayh (Fadluya) al-Muʿallim   63, 211, 233, 306
ʿAbdallah b. Muhammad b. Jaʿfar b. Hayyan al-Isbahani, Abu Muhammad, known as Abu ʾl-Shaykh (d. 369/979)   160

ʿAbdallah b. Muhammad al-Kharraz al-Razi *see* al-Kharraz, Abu Muhammad ʿAbdallah b. Muhammad
ʿAbdallah b. Muhammad b. Munazil al-Naysaburi, Abu Mahmud (d. 329–332/940–944)   43, 63, 166, 180, 211, 223, 227, 279, 313, 336
ʿAbdallah b. Muhammad al-Razi *see* ʿAbdallah b. Muhammad b. ʿAbdallah b. ʿAbd al-Rahman
ʿAbdallah b. Muhammad b. al-Samit   179
ʿAbdallah b. Muhammad al-Shaʿrani *see* ʿAbdallah b. Muhammad b. ʿAbd al-Rahman al-Razi
ʿAbdallah b. Muhammad b. Wasiʿ b. Jabir al-Azdi   166
ʿAbdallah b. Muharrir al-ʿAmiri al-Jazari al-Harrani (d. 150–160/767–777)   345
ʿAbdallah b. Munazil *see* ʿAbdallah b. Muhammad b. Munazil
ʿAbdallah b. Musa b. al-Husayn al-Salami, Abu ʾl-Hasan (d. 366/976–7 or 374/984–5)   5, 233, 393
ʿAbdallah b. Muslim   264
ʿAbdallah b. Nawfal   288
ʿAbdallah b. Qays *see* Abu Musa al-Ashʿari
ʿAbdallah b. Qays al-Sakuni al-Taraghimi al-Himsi, Abu Bahriya (d. 86–96/705–715)   232
ʿAbdallah b. Rajaʾ b. ʿAmr al-Basri, Abu ʿAmr (d. propably 219/834–5)   264
ʿAbdallah al-Razi *see* ʿAbdallah b. Muhammad b. ʿAbdallah b. ʿAbd al-Rahman
ʿAbdallah b. Sahl   117, 354
ʿAbdallah b. Saʿid b. Abi Hind al-Fazari al-Madani, Abu Bakr (d. 147/764–5)   232
ʿAbdallah b. Saʿid b. Kullab *see* Ibn Kullab
ʿAbdallah b. Salih   308
ʿAbdallah b. Shiruya   209
ʿAbdallah b. Shubruma b. al-Tufayl b. Hassan b. al-Mundhir b. Dirar b. ʿAmr al-Dabbi al-Kufi, Abu Shubruma (d. 144/761–2)   201
ʿAbdallah b. Sulayman   380
ʿAbdallah b. Tahir *see* Abu Bakr ʿAbdallah b. Tahir al-Abhari
ʿAbdallah b. ʿUbayd b. ʿUmayr b. Qatada al-Laythi al-Jundaʿi al-Makki, Abu Hashim (d. 113/731–2)   201
ʿAbdallah b. ʿUmar b. al-Khattab, Abu ʿAbd al-Rahman (d. 74/693–4)   204, 226, 253, 281, 344
ʿAbdallah b. ʿUthman b. Yahya   231
ʿAbdallah b. Wahb b. Muslim al-Qurashi al-Misri, Abu Muhammad (d. 197/813)   155, 366
ʿAbdallah b. al-Walid b. Maymun al-Umawi al-Makki, Abu Muhammad al-maʿruf bi-ʾl-ʿAdani   392
ʿAbdallah al-Wazzan   386
ʿAbdallah b. Yahya al-Talhi   288
ʿAbdallah b. Yusuf al-Isbahani, Abu Muhammad   24, 30, 36–7, 46, 138, 178, 288–90, 312, 316

ʿAbdallah b. Zayd b. ʿAmr b. Waʿil b. Malik, Abu Qilaba (d. 104/722 or 105/723–4)   171
al-Abhari *see* Abu Bakr ʿAbdallah b. Tahir al-Abhari
Abiward   20–1
Abraham   151, 168, 180, 182, 237–8, 263, 266, 394
Absence (*ghayba*)   91–3, 146
Abstention (*zuhd*)   130, 131, 134–8, 175, 194, 209, 227, 367, 387, 416
Abu ʾl-ʿAbbas (a servant of al-Fudayl b. ʿIyad)   334
Abu ʾl-ʿAbbas Ahmad b. Muhammad al-Dinawari (d. ca 340/951–2)   71, 160, 224, 314
Abu ʾl-ʿAbbas Ahmad b. Muhammad b. Masruq (d. 298–9/910–11)   23, 54, 241, 246, 250
Abu ʾl-ʿAbbas Ahmad b. ʿUmar b. Surayj al-Baghdadi al-Qadi (d. 306/918)   44, 63, 150, 404
Abu ʾl-ʿAbbas al-Asamm   312
Abu ʾl-ʿAbbas b. ʿAtaʾ *see* Ahmad b. ʿAtaʾ, Abu ʾl-ʿAbbas
Abu ʾl-ʿAbbas al-Baghdadi *see* Abu ʾl-ʿAbbas b. al-Khashshab *or* Abu ʾl-ʿAbbas Ahmad b. ʿUmar b. Surayj
Abu ʾl-ʿAbbas al-Damaghani, Ahmad b. Khalid (d. 280/893–4)   124
Abu ʾl-ʿAbbas al-Dinawari *see* Abu ʾl-ʿAbbas Ahmad b. Muhammad al-Dinawari
Abu ʾl-ʿAbbas al-Farghani al-Dimashqi al-Darir, Hajib b. Malik b. Arkin (d. 306/918–19)   219, 223
Abu ʾl-ʿAbbas al-Hashimi   337
Abu ʾl-ʿAbbas al-Karaji (or al-Karkhi)   70
Abu ʾl-ʿAbbas (b.) al-Khashshab, Muhammad b. al-Hasan (probably b. al-Husayn) b. Saʿid b. al-Khashshab al-Mukharrimi al-Baghdadi (d. 361/971–2)   13, 34, 40, 46, 51, 61, 118, 128–9, 150, 182, 194, 205, 208, 211, 223, 227, 391
Abu ʾl-ʿAbbas b. Masruq *see* Abu ʾl-ʿAbbas Ahmad b. Muhammad b. Masruq
Abu ʾl-ʿAbbas al-Muʿaddib   227
Abu ʾl-ʿAbbas al-Qass *see* Ahmad b. Abi Ahmad al-Tabari
Abu ʾl-ʿAbbas al-Qassab *see* al-Qassab, Abu ʾl-ʿAbbas Ahmad b. Muhammad
Abu ʾl-ʿAbbas al-Sayyad   53
Abu ʾl-ʿAbbas al-Sayyari *see* al-Sayyari, Abu ʾl-ʿAbbas
Abu ʾl-ʿAbbas b. Surayj *see* Abu ʾl-ʿAbbas Ahmad b. ʿUmar b. Surayj
Abu ʾl-ʿAbbas b. al-Walid *see* Abu ʾl-ʿAbbas al-Walid b. Ahmad
Abu ʾl-ʿAbbas al-Walid b. Ahmad b. Muhammad b. al-Walid b. Ziyad al-Zawzani (d. 376/986)   229
Abu ʿAbd al-Rahman al-Dirfash   159
Abu ʿAbdallah b. ʿAbdallah *see* Ibn Bakuya
Abu ʿAbdallah al-Antaki *see* Ahmad b. ʿAsim al-Antaki

Abu ʿAbdallah b. Bakawayh (Bakuya) *see* Ibn Bakawayh (Bakuya)
Abu ʿAbdallah al-Dabbas al-Baghdadi   384–5
Abu ʿAbdallah al-Daylami   388
Abu ʿAbdallah al-Farisi   40
Abu ʿAbdallah b. al-Jallaʾ *see* Ibn al-Jallaʿ
Abu ʿAbdallah al-Maghribi, Muhammad b. Ismaʿil (d. ca 299/911–12)   54, 66, 169, 297–9
Abu ʿAbdallah al-Makanisi   274
Abu ʿAbdallah b. Muflih   384
Abu ʿAbdallah al-Muqriʾ *see* Muhammad b. Ahmad b. Muhammad al-Muqriʿ
Abu ʿAbdallah b. Muslih   114
Abu ʿAbdallah al-Nasibini   300
Abu ʿAbdallah b. Qahraman   13
Abu ʿAbdallah al-Qurashi, Muhammad b. Saʿid   114, 181, 328
Abu ʿAbdallah al-Ramli, Muhammad b. ʿAbd al-ʿAziz b. Muhammad al-ʿUmari better known as Ibn al-Wasiti   123
Abu ʿAbdallah al-Razi *see* al-Husayn b. Ahmad b. Jaʿfar al-Razi
Abu ʿAbdallah al-Rudhabari *see* Ahmad b. ʿAtaʾ, Abu ʿAbdallah
Abu ʿAbdallah al-Shirazi *see* Ibn Khafif *or* Ibn Bakuya
Abu ʿAbdallah al-Sijzi (d. 255/868–9)   301
Abu ʿAbdallah al-Sufi *see* Ibn Bakuya, Abu ʿAbdallah
Abu ʿAbdallah al-Tarwaghandi   86
Abu ʿAbdallah al-ʿUmari   227
Abu Ahmad b. ʿAdi al-Hafiz *see* ʿAbdallah b. ʿAdi b. ʿAbdallah
Abu Ahmad Hamza al-Bazzaz *see* Hamza b. al-ʿAbbas
Abu Ahmad b. ʿIsa   63
Abu Ahmad the Junior (al-Saghir), al-Hasan b. ʿAli (d. 385/995–6 or 384/994–5)   70, 160, 288, 302
Abu Ahmad al-Kabir, al-Fadl b. Muhammad (d. 377/987–8)   376
Abu Ahmad al-Qalanisi *see* al-Qalanisi, Abu Ahmad
Abu ʾl-Ahwas *see* ʿAwf b. Malik b. Nadla *or* Khalaf b. Tamim
Abu ʿAli al-Balkhi *see* Abu ʿAli Saʿid b. Ahmad
Abu ʿAli al-Dallal   13
Abu ʿAli al-Daqqaq *see* al-Daqqaq, Abu ʿAli
Abu ʿAli al-Farisi   242
Abu ʿAli al-Juzjani *see* al-Juzjani
Abu ʿAli b. al-Katib *see* Ibn al-Katib
Abu ʿAli al-Razi   21, 378
Abu ʿAli al-Ribati   299
Abu ʿAli al-Rudhabari *see* al-Rudhabari, Abu ʿAli
Abu ʿAli al-Shabbuwi, Ahmad (or Muhammad) b. ʿUmar al-Marwazi   218
Abu ʿAli al-Sindi   370
Abu ʿAli al-Thaqafi *see* al-Thaqafi, Abu ʿAli

Abu ʿAli b. Wasif al-Muʿaddib   384
Abu ʿAmmar al-Husayn b. Hurayth b. al-Hasan al-Khuzaʿi al-Marwazi (d. 244/859)   21
Abu ʿAmr b. ʿAlwan (= Ibn Khalaf ʿAlwan b. ʿAlwan)   23, 248
Abu ʿAmr al-Bikandi   154
Abu ʿAmr al-Dimashqi *see* Abu ʿUmar al-Dimashqi
Abu ʿAmr b. Hamdan *see* Muhammad b. Ahmad b. Hamdan b. ʿAli
Abu ʿAmr (or Abu ʿUmar or Abu ʿImran) al-Istakhri, ʿAbd al-Rahim b. Musa   315, 374
Abu ʿAmr al-Jawlasti   36
Abd ʿAmr b. Matar = Abu ʿAmr Muhammad b. Jaʿfar b. Muhammad b. Matar al-Naysaburi (d. 360/971)   29, 175
Abu ʿAmr b. Nujayd *see* Ismaʿil b. Nujayd
Abu ʿAmr b. al-Sammak *see* Ibn al-Sammak, Abu ʿAmr ʿUthman b. Ahmad
Abu ʿAmr al-Zajjaji, Muhammad b. Ibrahim b. Yusuf b. Muhammad al-Naysaburi (d. 348/959–60)   67, 72, 224, 376
Abu ʾl-Ashʿath   344
Abu ʿAsim al-Basri al-ʿAbbadani al-Maraʿi, ʿAbdallah b. ʿUbaydallah   376
Abu ʾl-Aswad al-Duʿali (d. 69/688)   129
Abu ʿAwana al-Waddah b. ʿAbdallah al-Yashkuri al-Wasiti al-Bazzaz (d. 176/792)   344
Abu ʿAwana Yaʿqub (b. Ibrahim) b. Ishaq al-Isfarayini   202, 325, 363, 365
Abu Ayyub al-Hammal   388
Abu ʾl-Azhar al-Mayyafariqini   41
Abu Bahriya *see* ʿAbdallah b. Qays al-Sakuni
Abu Bakr ʿAbdallah b. Tahir al-Abhari (d. ca 330/941–2)   66, 193, 208, 286
Abu Bakr b. Abu ʿUthman   45
Abu Bakr b. ʿAffan   27
Abu Bakr b. Ahmad al-Balkhi   53
Abu Bakr al-Ajurri, Muhammad b. al-Husayn b. ʿAbdallah (d. 360/970)   395
Abu Bakr b. ʿAyyash b. Salim al-Asadi al-Kufi al-Muqriʾ (d. ca 193/808)   288, 392
Abu Bakr al-Balkhi *see* Abu Bakr b. Ahmad al-Balkhi
Abu Bakr al-Bardhaʿi   180
Abu Bakr b. Bint Muʿawiyya   27
Abu Bakr al-Farisi *see* al-Tamastani, Abu Bakr
Abu Bakr b. Furak *see* Abu Bakr Muhammad b. al-Hasan b. Furak
Abu Bakr al-Ghazzal   158
Abu Bakr al-Hamdhani   391
Abu Bakr al-Harbi, Muhammad b. Saʿid   22, 24, 155, 277
Abu Bakr al-Husayn b. ʿAli b. Yazdaniyar   67
Abu Bakr b. Ishkib   152, 227, 397
Abu Bakr al-Jawwal   287
Abu Bakr al-Kattani *see* al-Kattani, Abu Bakr
Abu Bakr al-Maraghi   175
Abu Bakr b. Masʿud   282

Abu Bakr al-Misri, Muhammad b. Ibrahim
 (d. 345/956–7)   65, 287, 292
Abu Bakr b. Muʿammar *see* Muhammad b. Muʿammar
Abu Bakr Muhammad b. Ahmad al-Balkhi   179, 380
Abu Bakr Muhammad b. al-Hasan b. Furak
 al-Ansari al-Isbahani (d. 406/1015)   8, 72, 111, 145, 159, 178, 193–5, 217–19, 222, 234, 270, 306, 334–5, 344, 358–9, 362, 414
Abu Bakr Muhammad b. Jaʿfar al-Baghdadi   21, 280
Abu Bakr Muhammad b. Shadhan *see* Muhammad
 b. ʿAbdallah b. Muhammad b. ʿAbd al-ʿAziz b. Shadhan
Abu Bakr al-Nabulusi   391
Abu Bakr al-Nihawandi   356
Abu Bakr al-Rashidi *see* al-Rashidi, Abu Bakr
Abu Bakr al-Razi *see* Muhammad b. ʿAbdallah b.
 Muhammad b. ʿAbd al-ʿAziz b. Shadhan
Abu Bakr al-Sabbak   215
Abu Bakr al-Saʿigh   369
Abu Bakr al-Saʿih   159
Abu Bakr b. Samʿan   282
Abu Bakr b. Shadhan *see* Muhammad b. ʿAbdallah
 b. Muhammad b. ʿAbd al-ʿAziz b. Shadhan
Abu Bakr al-Siddiq, ʿAbdallah b. ʿUthman b. ʿAmir
 (d. 13/634)   129, 140, 188, 218, 295, 302, 309–10, 344, 366
Abu Bakr b. Tahir *see* Abu Bakr ʿAbdallah b. Tahir
Abu Bakr al-Tarsusi   383
Abu Bakr b. ʿUthman (b. Abi ʿUthman al-Hiri?)   49
Abu Bakr al-Warraq *see* al-Warraq, Abu Bakr
Abu Bakr al-Wasiti *see* al-Wasiti, Abu Bakr
Abu Bakr al-Zaqqaq *see* al-Zaqqaq
Abu Bishr Yunus b. Habib *see* Yunus b. Habib
Abu ʾl-Dardaʾ ʿUwaymir b. Zayd al-Ansari
 al-Khazraji (d. 32/652–3)   148, 232, 283, 366, 392
Abu ʾl-Dawaniq   133
Abu Dawud al-Tayalisi, Sulayman b. Dawud b.
 Jarud (d. 203/818–19)   178, 217, 222
Abu Dharr Jundab b. Junada b. Sufyan al-Ghifari
 (d. 32/652–3)   129, 166, 208, 255
Abu Dujana   20
Abu ʾl-Fadl al-ʿAttar *see* Nasr b. Abi Nasr
 Muhammad
Abu ʾl-Fadl al-Isbahani   402
Abu ʾl-Faraj al-Shirazi *see* ʿAbd al-Wahid b. Bakr
Abu ʾl-Faraj al-Warathani *see* ʿAbd al-Wahid b. Bakr
Abu Farwa Yazid b. Sinan b. Yazid al-Tamimi
 al-Jazari al-Rahawi (d. 155/771)   134
Abu ʾl-Fatik *see* Ibrahim b. Fatik
Abu ʾl-Ghafani   340
Abu Habib Hamza *see* Hamza b. ʿAbdallah
Abu al-Hadid   385

Abu Hafs al-Naysaburi (al-Nisaburi) al-Haddad,
 ʿAmr (or ʿUmar) b. Salama (or: Salm, Salim,
 Aslam, Maslama, Muslim) (d. between
 265/874 and 270/879)   38–9, 45, 57, 62–3,
 92, 113, 116, 121, 126, 136, 142, 143, 144,
 147, 168, 205, 212, 242, 246, 255, 283, 284,
 286, 294, 297, 305, 319, 321, 335
Abu Hamza al-Baghdadi, Muhammad b. Ibrahim
 al-Bazzaz (d. 269/882–3 or 289/902)   57–8, 60, 105, 140, 183, 289, 385
Abu Hamza al-Khurasani (d. 290/903)   60–1, 186
Abu Hanifa al-Nuʿman b. Thabit (d. 150/767)
 29, 127, 140
Abu ʾl-Harith al-Awlasi, Fayd b. al-Khadir
 (d. 297/909–10)   356, 372
Abu ʾl-Harith al-Khattabi, ʿAli b. al-Qasim b. Ahmad
 b. Muhammad b. al-Khattab (d. 350/961)
 382–3
Abu ʾl-Hasan   261
Abu ʾl-Hasan (servant of Shaʿwana)   372
Abu ʾl-Hasan b. ʿAbdallah al-Fuwati al-Tarsusi
 24, 316
Abu ʾl-Hasan b. Abi ʾl-Hawari *see* Ibn Abi ʾl-Hawari
Abu ʾl-Hasan al-Ahwazi *see* ʿAli b. Ahmad b. ʿAbdan
Abu ʾl-Hasan al-ʿAlawi *see* Abu ʾl-Hasan
 al-Hamadhani
Abu ʾl-Hasan ʿAli b. Ahmad al-Ahwazi *see* ʿAli b.
 Ahmad b. ʿAbdan
Abu ʾl-Hasan ʿAli b. Muhammad al-Sayrafi   389
Abu ʾl-Hasan al-Damaghani   341
Abu ʾl-Hasan al-Farisi (possibly the same as Abu
 ʾl-Husayn al-Farisi?)   11, 32, 55, 126, 130,
 205, 209, 212, 221, 323, 329
Abu ʾl-Hasan al-Hamadhani al-ʿAlawi, Muhammad
 b. al-Husayn   243, 340, 392
Abu ʾl-Hasan b. Jahdam *see* ʿAli b. Jahdam
Abu ʾl-Hasan al-Jurjani   386
Abu ʾl-Hasan al-Khazafani (possibly = Abu ʾl-Hasan
 Muhammad b. al-Fadl b.ʿAli b. al-ʿAbbas b.
 al-Walid b. Bihzadhan al-Harbi al-Khazafi,
 d. 382/992   268
Abu ʾl-Hasan b. Miqsam *see* Abu ʾl-Hasan Ahmad
 b. Muhammad b. al-Hasan b. Yaʿqub
Abu ʾl-Hasan al-Misri *see* ʿAli b. Muhammad b.
 Ahmad b. al-Hasan al-Misri
Abu ʾl-Hasan al-Qariʿ   332
Abu ʾl-Hasan al-Qazwini *see* ʿAli b. Muhammad
 b. Mihruya
Abu ʾl-Hasan al-Saffar al-Basri   151, 188, 252,
 257, 273, 292
Abu ʾl-Hasan b. al-Saʿigh al-Dinawari, ʿAli b.
 Muhammad b. Sahl (d. 330/941–2)   59
Abu ʾl-Hasan al-Shaʿrani   42
Abu ʾl-Hasan al-Sirawani *see* al-Sirawani, Abu
 ʾl-Hasan ʿAli b. Jaʿfar
Abu Hashim Sahib al-Zaʿfarani al-Basri, ʿAmmar b.
 ʿUmara   157

Abu Hatim al-ʿAttar al-Basri 40
Abu Hatim al-Sijistani al-Sufi al-Tamimi,
   Muhammad b. Ahmad b. Muhammad b.
   Yahya 5, 7, 32, 115, 150, 159, 164, 180,
   221, 255, 289, 291, 293–5, 304, 310, 312,
   315–17, 323, 346, 347, 348, 351–3, 367–70
Abu Hazim al-Makki 257
Abu Hazim Salama b. Dinar al-Aʿraj (d. ca
   140/757–8) 176, 274
Abu Hudba 312
Abu Hujayfa Wahb b. ʿAbdallah al-Suwali, known
   as Wahb al-Khayr (d. ca 74/693–4) 288
Abu Hulman al-Dimashqi al-Farisi 353
Abu Hurayra ʿAbd al-Rahman b. Sahr al-Dawsi
   al-Yamani (d. probably 58/677–8 or
   59/678–9) 122, 129, 132, 138, 142, 152,
   155, 165, 173, 175, 197, 210, 237, 257, 264,
   280, 306, 325–6, 346, 363–4, 366–7
Abu ʾl-Husayn b. Ahmad al-ʿAttar al-Balkhi 31
Abu ʾl-Husayn ʿAli b. Hind al-Farisi al-Qurashi
   204
Abu ʾl-Husayn al-Basri 128
Abu ʾl-Husayn b. Bunan al-Misri (d. 310/922–3)
   66, 264
Abu ʾl-Husayn al-Damaghani, al-Hasan b. ʿAli b.
   Hanawayh (Hannuya) 6
Abu ʾl-Husayn al-Darraj, Saʿid b. al-Husayn
   (d. 320/932 or later) 352
Abu ʾl-Husayn b. Faris (Abu ʾl-Husayn Ahmad b.
   Faris b. Zakariya, d. 395/1004) 44
Abu ʾl-Husayn al-Farisi see Abu ʾl-Husayn al-Farisi,
   Muhammad b. Ahmad or Abu ʾl-Husayn ʿAli
   b. Hind al-Farisi
Abu ʾl-Husayn al-Farisi, Muhammad b. Ahmad b.
   Ibrahim 11, 55, 126, 179, 209, 212, 221,
   323, 329
Abu ʾl-Husayn al-Hajjaji see al-Hajjaji
Abu ʾl-Husayn al-Himsi 319
Abu ʾl-Husayn b. Hind see Abu ʾl-Husayn ʿAli b.
   Hind
Abu ʾl-Husayn al-Maliki 60, 318
Abu ʾl-Husayn al-Nuri see Al-Nuri, Abu ʾl-Husayn
   Ahmad b. Muhammad
Abu ʾl-Husayn al-Qarafi, ʿAli b. ʿUthman 248
Abu ʾl-Husayn al-Razi 40, 160
Abu ʾl-Husayn al-Warraq see al-Warraq, Abu
   ʾl-Husayn
Abu ʾl-Husayn al-Zanjani 126
Abu Ibrahim 161
Abu Ibrahim al-Yamani 384
Abu ʿImran al-Istakhri see Abu ʿAmr al-Istakhri
Abu ʿImran al-Kabir 57
Abu ʿImran al-Wasiti 372
Abu Iqal b. ʿAlwan al-Maghribi 86
Abu Ishaq ʿAmr b. ʿAbdallah b. ʿAli al-Sabiʿi
   al-Hamadhani al-Kufi (d. 127/745) 393

Abu Ishaq Ibrahim b. Muhammad al-Fazari
   (d. 186/802) 284
Abu Ishaq al-Isfaraini see al-Isfaraini
Abu Jaʿfar al-Aʿwar 376
Abu Jaʿfar al-Balkhi 174
Abu Jaʿfar al-Farghani, see al-Farghani, Abu Jaʿfar
   Muhammad b. ʿAbdallah
Abu Jaʿfar al-Haddad 182, 193, 246, 287, 369,
   391
Abu Jaʿfar Muhammad b. Yaʿqub b. al-Faraj al-Sufi
   al-Samiri al-maʿruf bi-Ibn al-Faraji (d. ca
   270/883) 180
Abu Jaʿfar b. Qays 319
Abu Jaʿfar al-Razi see Muhammad b. Ahmad b.
   Saʿid
Abu ʾl-Jahm 222
Abu Kamil Muzaffar b. Mudrik al-Khurasani
   (d. 207/822–3) 344
Abu Khabab al-Walid b. Bukayr al-Tamimi
   al-Tuhawi al-Kufi 188
Abu Khallad 134
Abu ʾl-Khasib b. al-Mustanir al-Massisi 365
Abu ʾl-Khayr al-Aqtaʿ al-Tinati, ʿAbbad b. ʿAbdallah
   (d. 349/960–1) 64, 159, 248, 303, 367
Abu ʾl-Khayr al-Basri 368
Abu ʾl-Khayr al-Tinati see Abu ʾl-Khayr al-Aqtaʿ
Abu Marthad Kannaz b. Husayn b. Yarbuʿ b. Tarif
   b. Khurshuba al-Ghanawi (d. 12/633–4)
   262
Abu Muʿadh al-Qazwini 13
Abu Muʿawiya al-Aswad 380
Abu Muʿawiyya al-Darir, Muhammad b. Khazim
   (or b. Muʿawiya) al-Tamimi al-Saʿdi al-Kufi
   (d. 195/810–11) 152, 155
Abu Muhammad b. Abi Hamid, see ʿAbdallah b.
   Ahmad b. Jaʿfar
Abu Muhammad al-Baladhuri, see Ahmad b.
   Ibrahim b. Hashim
Abu Muhammad al-Harawi 312
Abu Muhammad al-Istakhri, see ʿAbdallah b.
   Ahmad al-Istakhri
Abu Muhammad al-Maraghi 230, 289
Abu Muhammad b. Yasin 284
Abu Muqatil al-ʿAkki 82
Abu Musa al-Ashʿari, ʿAbdallah b. Qays (d. probably
   42/662–3) 209, 335, 346
Abu Musa al-Bastami see Abu Musa ʿIsa b. Adam
Abu Musa al-Daybuli (or al-Dabili) 178, 250
Abu Musa ʿIsa b. Adam b. ʿIsa al-Bastami
   (al-Bistami) 32, 272
Abu Muslim 367, 380
Abu Muslim al-Khawlani al-Yamani, ʿAbdallah b.
   Thuwab (d. 62/682) 380
Abu ʾl-Nadr Hashim b. al-Qasim b. Muslim b.
   Miqsam al-Laythi al-Baghdadi (d. 207/832 or
   205/821) 343

Abu Nadra al-Mundhir b. Malik b. Qutaʿa al-ʿAbdi 118
Abu ʾl-Najm al-Muqri al-Bardhaʿi 383
Abu Nasr al-Harawi 285
Abu Nasr al-Isbahani 43–4, 196, 266
Abu Nasr the Muezzin (al-Muʿadhdhin) 92
Abu Nasr al-Sufi 301, 347
Abu Nasr al-Tammar 160
Abu Nasr al-Tusi *see* al-Sarraj, Abu Nasr
Abu Nasr al-Waziri, Muhammad b. Tahir b. Muhammad b. al-Hasan b. al-Wazir (d. 365/976) 226
Abu Nuʿaym al-Isfaraini *see* ʿAbd al-Malik b. al-Hasan al-Isfaraini
Abu ʾl-Qasim ʿAbdallah b. al-Husayn *see* ʿAbdallah b. al-Husayn b. Baluya
Abu ʾl-Qasim ʿAbdallah b. Muhammad al-Dimashqi 62, 129, 144, 284, 301, 324
Abu ʾl-Qasim b. Abi Nizar 176
Abu ʾl-Qasim al-Baghdadi 205
Abu ʾl-Qasim al-Dimashqi *see* Abu ʾl-Qasim ʿAbdallah b. Muhammad al-Dimashqi
Abu ʾl-Qasim al-Hakim, Ishaq b. Muhammad b. Ismaʿil al-Samarqandi (d. 342/953) 143–4, 197
Abu ʾl-Qasim al-Jawhari 335
Abu ʾl-Qasim b. Marwan (or b. Mardan) al-Nihawandi 377
Abu ʾl-Qasim al-Mudhakkir 227
Abu ʾl-Qasim al-Munadi 244, 248
Abu ʾl-Qasim b. (Abi?) Musa 13, 146
Abu ʾl-Qasim b. Musa *see* Abu ʾl-Qasim b. (Abi?) Musa
Abu ʾl-Qasim al-Razi *see* Jaʿfar b. Ahmad b. Muhammad
Abu Qatada al-Harith b. Ribʿi b. Balduma al-Salami al-Madani (d. probably 54/673–4) 392
Abu Qilaba *see* ʿAbdallah b. Zayd b. ʿAmr
Abu Qirsafa Muhammad b. ʿAbd al-Wahhab al-ʿAsqalani 222
Abu Qubays 376
Abu ʾl-Rabiʿ al-Wasiti al-Aʿraj 30
Abu ʾl-Rabiʿ al-Zahrani *see* Sulayman b. Dawud al-ʿAtaki
Abu ʾl-Rajaʾ *see* Muhriz b. ʿAbdallah
Abu Sabra al-Nakhaʿi, ʿAbdallah b. ʿAbis 390
Abu Saʿd al-Malini *see* al-Malini
Abu Saʿdan (Saʿid) al-Taharti 187
Abu Sadiq b. Habib 300
Abu Sahl al-Khashshab al-Kabir 18, 24, 285
Abu Sahl al-Suʿluki *see* al-Suʿluki
Abu Saʿid b. al-Aʿrabi *see* Ibn al-Aʿrabi, Abu Saʿid
Abu Saʿid al-Arrajani 329
Abu Saʿid al-Kharraz *see* al-Kharraz, Abu Saʿid
Abu Saʿid al-Khudri *see* al-Khudri, Abu Saʿid

Abu Saʿid al-Qurashi, ʿAbdallah b. Muhammad b. ʿAbd al-Wahhab b. Nusayr al-Razi (d. 382/992–3) 56, 156, 223
Abu Saʿid al-Ramli 350
Abu Saʿid al-Saffar (al-Muʿaddib) 399–400
Abu Salama b. ʿAbd al-Rahman b. ʿAwf b. ʿAbd ʿAwf al-Zuhri al-Madani (d. probably 94/712–13) 138, 264, 280, 346, 392
Abu Salih Dhakwan al-Samman al-Zayyat al-Madani (d.101/719–20) 392
Abu Salih Hamdun *see* Hamdun al-Qassar
Abu Salim (?) Muhammad b. Yahya b. al-Mundhir al-Qazzaz 340
Abu Sufyan (al-)Tarif b. Shihab al-Saʿdi al-Basri al-Ashall 149, 320
Abu Sulayman al-Darani *see* al-Darani
Abu Sulayman al-Khawwas 369
Abu Sulayman al-Rumi 392
Abu Tahir al-Isfaraini 174
Abu Talut 220
Abu ʾl-Tayyib al-ʿAkki *see* Ahmad b. Muqatil al-ʿAkki
Abu ʾl-Tayyib b. Farkhan 296
Abu ʾl-Tayyib al-Maraghi 5
Abu ʾl-Tayyib al-Samarri 137, 323
Abu Thawr Ibrahim b. Khalid b. Abi ʾl-Yaman al-Kalbi (d. 240/854) 43, 258
Abu Turab al-Nakhshabi, ʿAskar b. Husayn (d. 245/859) 38, 40, 42, 51–2, 55, 60, 160, 180, 184, 193, 196, 209, 273, 291, 315, 324–5, 341, 370, 381
Abu ʿUbayd al-Busri, Muhammad b. Hassan (d.238/852–3, probably later) 47, 51–3, 371
Abu ʿUbayda ʿAmir b. ʿAbdallah b. al-Jarrah al-Qurashi (d. 18/639) 393
Abu Umama al-Bahili, Sudayy b. ʿAjlan b. Wahb (d. ca 86/705) 128, 138, 364
Abu ʿUmar ʿAli b. Muhammad b. ʿAli b. Bashshar b. Salman al-Anmati 23, 44, 117, 124, 168, 231, 346
Abu ʿUmar al-Anmati, *see* Abu ʿUmar ʿAli b. Muhammad b. ʿAli
Abu ʿUmar al-Antaki 322
Abu ʿUmar al-Dimashqi (also known as Abu ʿAmr al-Dimashqi) (d. 320/932) 47, 69, 144, 209
Abu ʿUmar al-Istakhri *see* Abu ʿAmr al-Istakhri
Abu ʿUthman al-Adami 196
Abu ʿUthman al-Baladi 28
Abu ʿUthman al-Hiri *see* al-Hiri, Abu ʿUthman
Abu ʿUthman al-Maghribi, Saʿid b. Sallam (d. 373/983) 8, 9, 45, 59, 72, 118, 121, 123, 150, 158, 195, 205, 221, 249, 251, 266, 271, 303, 324, 348–9, 354, 386, 402
Abu ʿUthman Saʿid b. Abu Saʿid *see* Saʿid b. Ahmad b. Muhammad b. Jaʿfar

Abu ʿUthman Saʿid b. Ahmad *see* Saʿid b. Ahmad b. Muhammad b. Jaʿfar
Abu Waʾil Shaqiq b. Salama al-Asadi al-Kufi (d. during the caliphate of ʿUmar 13–23/634–644)   222
Abu ʾl-Walid al-Tayalisi *see* Hisham b. ʿAbd al-Malik al-Bahili
Abu ʾl-Yaman al-Hakam b. Nafiʿ al-Bahrani al-Himsi (d. 211/826–7 or 222/837)   365
Abu Yaʿqub al-Aqtaʿ al-Basri   184
Abu Yaʿqub al-Mazabili (d. ca 290/903)   291
Abu Yaʿqub al-Nahrajuri *see* al-Nahrajuri
Abu Yaʿqub al-Shariti (or al-Shuruti)   220
Abu Yaʿqub al-Susi, Yusuf b. Hamdan   64, 124, 221, 300, 322, 329, 331, 383
Abu Yazid al-Bastami (or al-Bistami) b. Tayfur b. ʿIsa b. Surushan (d. probably 261/874–5) 32–3, 38, 93, 95, 118, 123, 127, 164, 177–9, 211, 217, 250, 267, 269, 271–2, 297, 317, 321–2, 324, 328, 332, 338, 341, 360, 370, 387–8, 396, 405
Abu Zakariya al-Nakhshabi   282
Abu Zayd Muhammad b. Ahmad b. ʿAbdallah b. Muhammad al-Fashani al-Marwazi al-Faqih, Abu Zayd (d. 371/982)   66, 266
Abu ʾl-Zubayr Muhammad b. Muslim b. Tadrus al-Asadi al-Makki (d. 126/743–4)   297
Abu Zurʿa al-Janbi   21, 51, 391
Actions *see* Deeds
Adam   13, 32, 116, 144, 147, 164, 171, 190, 228, 235, 245, 266, 394
Adam b. Abi Iyas, Abu ʾl-Hasan b. ʿAbd al-Rahman b. Muhammad al-ʿAsqalani (d. 220/835)   374
Admonition   228–9
Advice *see* Spiritual advice
Affirmation (ithbat)   96
Affliction/Trial (balaʾ)   3, 202, 206–8, 211, 226, 233, 235, 276–8, 394
Afghanistan   18, 31, 46, 174, 277, 371
Ahmad b. Abi Ahmad al-Tabari, Abu ʾl-Abbas (b.) al-Qass   42
Ahmad b. Abi ʾl-Hawari *see* Ibn Abi ʾl-Hawari
Ahmad b. Abi Rawh   157
Ahmad b. Abu Tahir al-Khurasani   129
Ahmad b. ʿAli, Abu ʾl-Husayn   64–5
Ahmad b. ʿAli al-Dimashqi   26
Ahmad b. ʿAli al-Hasan b. Shadhan al-Muqriʾ al-Tajir al-Hasnuyi, Abu Hamid (d. ca 340/951–2)   209, 242
Ahmad b. ʿAli b. Jaʿfar al-Qazzaz al-Jurjani, Abu ʾl-Qasim   56, 118, 125, 136, 182, 195, 325
Ahmad b. ʿAsim al-Antaki, Abu ʿAli (or Abu ʿAbdallah; d. 220/835)   41, 125, 150, 246, 321
Ahmad al-Aswad al-Dinawari   336

Ahmad b. ʿAtaʾ, Abu ʾl-ʿAbbas b. Muhammad b. Sahl b. ʿAtaʾ al-Adami (killed 309/921–2)   28, 56
Ahmad b. ʿAtaʾ, Abu ʿAbdallah al-Rudhabari (d. 369/980)   13–14, 55, 73, 286, 308, 330, 368, 391
Ahmad b. Bashshar b. ʿAbdallah b. ʿUmar b. ʿAmri al-Sirafi (al-Sayrafi)   220
Ahmad b. al-Fath   140
Ahmad b. Ghassan   220
Ahmad b. Hamid al-Aswad *see* Ahmad al-Aswad al-Dinawari
Ahmad b. Hamza   389
Ahmad b. Hanbal (d. 241/855)   26, 57, 132, 135, 137, 148, 278, 378, 404
Ahmad b. al-Haytham al-Mutatabbib   380
Ahmad b. al-Husayn   138
Ahmad b. al-Husayn, Abu ʾl-Najm   381
Ahmad b. Ibrahim b. Hashim al-Tusi al-Baladhuri al-Mudhakkir al-Hafiz al-Waʿiz, Abu Muhammad (killed 339/950–1)   227
Ahmad b. Ibrahim b. Yahya   384
Ahmad b. ʿIsa (possibly the same as al-Kharraz, Abu Saʿid Ahmad b. ʿIsa)   37, 53, 63, 155
Ahmad b. Ismaʿil al-Azdi   134
Ahmad b. Khadrawayh (Khidruya) al-Balkhi, Abu Hamid (d. 240/854–5)   19, 36, 38, 52–3, 119, 179, 223, 238–9
Ahmad b. Mahmud b. Khurrazadh al-Ahwazi, Abu Bakr   111, 193, 306, 334, 344
Ahmad b. Mansur   160, 383
Ahmad al-Masjidi   233
Ahmad b. Muhammad b. ʿAbdallah al-Farghani   160, 375
Ahmad b. Muhammad b. Ahmad b. Salim   158
Ahmad b. Muhammad b. Ahmad b. Salim al-Basri, Abu ʾl-Hasan (d. 356/967)   131, 293, 354
Ahmad b. Muhammad b. Ahmad b. Zakariya al-Taghlibi, Abu ʾl-ʿAbbas al-maʿruf bi-Ibn Abi Shaykh al-Khalanji   308
Ahmad b. Muhammad b. ʿAli b. Harun, Abu ʾl-ʿAbbas al-Bardaʿi
Ahmad b. Muhammad al-Basri *see* Ahmad b. Muhammad b. Ahmad b. Salim
Ahmad b. Muhammad al-Bukhari   31
Ahmad b. Muhammad b. Ibrahim al-Mahrajani, Abu Nuʿaym   143
Ahmad b. Muhammad b. Khurrazadh (or Khurzad) *see* Ahmad b. Mahmud b. Khurrazadh
Ahmad b. Muhammad al-Qirmisini   180
Ahmad b. Muhammad b. Salih b. ʿAbdallah al-Samarqandi, Abu Yahya   185
Ahmad b. Muhammad b. al-Sari b. Yahya b. Abi Darim al-Muhaddith al-Kufi al-Rafidi, Abu Bakr (d. 352/963)   37
Ahmad b. Muhammad al-Sulami   371

Ahmad b. Muhammad al-Thaghri (or al-Baghawi) 51
Ahmad b. Muhammad al-Tusi 378
Ahmad b. Muhammad b. Yahya al-Sufi (probably Muhammad b. Ahmad b. Muhammad b. Yahya, Abu Hatim al-Sijistani al-Sufi al-Tamimi) 131
Ahmad b. Muhammad b. Zakariya *see* Ahmad b. Muhammad b. Ahmad b. Zakariya
Ahmad b. Muhammad b. Zayd 320
Ahmad b. Muhammad b. Ziyad al-Nahwi 226
Ahmad b. Muqatil al-ʿAkki al-Baghdadi, Abu ʾl-Tayyib 348, 350–2
Ahmad b. Nasr 315
Ahmad b. Sahl b. Ayyub 193
Ahmad b. Sahl al-Tajir 240
Ahmad b. Saʿid b. Ahmad b. Muhammad b. Maʿdan al-Maʿdani al-Basri, Abu ʾl-ʿAbbas (d. 375/986) 310
Ahmad b. Salih *see* Ahmad b. Muhammad b. Salih
Ahmad al-Tabarani al-Sarakhsi 368
Ahmad b. Tulun (r. 254–270/868–884) 57
Ahmad b. ʿUbayd al-Saffar al-Basri, Abu ʾl-Hasan 111, 118, 122, 125, 138, 145, 148, 149, 155, 157, 161–2, 167, 171, 174, 179, 197, 205, 210, 213, 220, 229, 232, 237, 257, 264, 297, 303, 325–6, 335, 340, 343–6, 356, 367, 392
Ahmad b. ʿUbaydallah al-Basri 162, 175
Ahmad b. ʿUmar 197
Ahmad b. Yahya al-Abiwardi 342
Ahmad b. Yunus 125
Ahmad b. Yusuf b. Khalid al-Muhallabi al-Azdi al-Sulami al-Naysaburi better known as Hamdan, Abu ʾl-Hasan (d. 264/877–8) 138, 384
Ahmad b. Yusuf al-Khayyat 381
Ahmad b. Zakariya 111, 220
Ahnaf al-Hamadhani 298
al-Ahnaf b. Qays b. Muʿawiya b. Husayn al-Murri al-Saʿdi al-Minqari al-Tamimi (d. ca 72/691–2) 253–4
Ahwaz 114, 193
al-Ahwazi *see* ʿAli b. Ahmad b. ʿAbdan
ʿAʾisha 145, 151, 188, 197, 241, 257, 269, 292, 320, 344
al-Ajlah, Yahya b. ʿAbdallah b. Hujayya al-Kindi, Abu Hujayya (d. ca 145/762) 129, 344
Al-Ajurri *see* Abu Bakr al-Ajurri or Ibrahim al-Ajurri
al-Akhfash *see* Ahmad b. ʿImran b. Salama
al-ʿAkki *see* Abu Muqatil al-ʿAkki
al-ʿAlaʾ b. ʿAbdallah al-Hadrami (d. 21/641–2 or later) 366
al-ʿAlaʾ b. Zayd 148
al-ʿAlaʾ b. Ziyad b. Matar b. Shurayh al-ʿAdawi al-Basri, Abu Nasr (d. 94/712–13) 401

Aleppo 258
Alexandria 278, 375
ʿAli b. ʿAbd al-Hamid al-Jadaʿiri al-Halabi 221
ʿAli b. ʿAbd al-Rahim al-Wasiti *see* al-Qannad, Abu ʾl-Hasan
ʿAli b. ʿAbdallah al-Azdi al-Bariqi, Abu ʿAbdallah b. Abi ʾl-Walid 297
ʿAli b. ʿAbdallah al-Baghdadi *see* ʿAli b. ʿAbdallah b. Muhammad al-Baghdadi
ʿAli b. ʿAbdallah al-Basri 198
ʿAli b. ʿAbdallah b. Muhammad al-Baghdadi, Abu ʾl-Hasan (d. ca 380/990) 350
ʿAli b. Abi ʿAli b. ʿUtba b. Abi Lahab 167
ʿAli b. Abi Muhammad al-Tamimi 378
ʿAli b. Abi Talib (killed in 40/661) 131
ʿAli b. Abi Talib 197–8, 254, 262, 263, 313, 354, 396
ʿAli b. Ahmad b. ʿAbdan al-Ahwazi, Abu ʾl-Hasan (or Abu ʾl-Husayn, d. 415/1024) 111, 122, 125, 128, 138, 145, 148, 149, 151, 155, 157, 161–2, 167, 174, 179, 188, 197, 205, 213, 220, 229, 232, 237, 252, 257, 264, 273, 292, 303, 325–6, 335, 343–6, 356, 367
ʿAli al-ʿAttar *see* ʿAli b. al-Hasan b. Jaʿfar al-ʿAttar
ʿAli al-Azdi *see* ʿAli b. ʿAbdallah al-Azdi
ʿAli b. Bakkar al-Basri al-Zahid, Abu ʾl-Hasan (d. ca 199/814–5) 141
ʿAli b. Bakran 157
ʿAli b. Bashran *see* ʿAli b. Muhammad b. ʿAbdallah b. Bashran
ʿAli b. Bundar b. al-Husayn al-Sayrafi/al-Sirafi (al-Sufi), Abu ʾl-Hasan (d. 359/969–70) 221, 284, 324
ʿAli b. al-Fudayl b. ʿIyad al-Tamimi (d. 174/790–1) 259
ʿAli b. Harb b. Muhammad b. ʿAli al-Mawsili, Abu ʾl-Hasan (d. 260/873–4) 30, 152
ʿAli b. Harun 378
ʿAli b. al-Hasan 173
ʿAli b. al-Hasan b. Jaʿfar al-ʿAttar al-Bazzaz al-Makhrami al-maʿruf bi-Ibn al-ʿAttar, Abu ʾl-Husayn (d. 376/986) 131
ʿAli b. al-Hasan b. Musa al-Hilali al-Darabjirdi, Abu ʾl-Hasan b. Abi ʿIsa (d. 269/883) 228
ʿAli b. Hubaysh 155
ʿAli b. al-Husayn 138, 161
ʿAli b. al-Husayn b. ʿAli b. Abi Talib, known as Zayn al-ʿabidin (d. between 92/710 and 99/717) 92
ʿAli b. Husayn al-Arrajani 159
ʿAli b. Ibrahim b. Ahmad 384
ʿAli b. Ibrahim al-Haddad, Abu ʾl-Husayn 44
ʿAli b. Ibrahim al-Husri *see* al-Husri, Abu ʾl-Hasan ʿAli b. Ibrahim
ʿAli b. Ibrahim al-Qadi 159
ʿAli b. Ibrahim al-Shaqiqi 220

ʿAli b. Ibrahim al-ʿUkbari 145
ʿAli b. ʿIsa b. Dawud b. al-Jarrah (d. 334/946) 23, 117
ʿAli b. ʿIsa b. Mahan (d. 195/810) 31
ʿAli b. Jahdam see ʿAli b. ʿAbdallah b. al-Hasan b. Jahdam
ʿAli b. Khashram b. ʿAbd al-Rahman b. ʿAtaʾ b. Hilal 25
ʿAli b. Muhammad 38
ʿAli b. Muhammad b. ʿAbdallah b. Bashran al-Muʿaddil al-Umawi, Abu ʾl-Husayn (d. 415/1024) 232, 275
ʿAli b. Muhammad b. Ahmad b. al-Hasan al-Misri, Abu ʾl-Hasan (d. 338/950) 18, 61, 186, 231–2, 301
ʿAli b. Muhammad al-Dallal 22
ʿAli b. Muhammad b. Mihruya al-Qazwini, Abu ʾl-Hasan 60, 311–12
ʿAli b. Muhammad al-Misri see ʿAli b. Muhammad b. Ahmad b. al-Hasan
ʿAli b. Muhammad b. Muhammad b. ʿUqba al-Shaybani, Abu ʾl-Hasan 312
ʿAli b. Musa b. Jaʿfar al-Rida, Abu ʾl-Hasan (d. 203/818) 21–3
ʿAli b. Musa al-Taharti, Abu ʿAddallah (321/933) 130
ʿAli b. Mushir al-Qurashi al-Kufi, Abu ʾl-Hasan (d. 189/804–5) 161
ʿAli b. Muslim 382–3
ʿAli b. al-Muwaffaq al-Baghdadi, Abu ʾl-Hasan (d. 265/878–9) 354, 402
ʿAli b. al-Nahhas al-Misri 158
ʿAli al-Qawwal 72
ʿAli al-Razi 145
ʿAli b. Razin, Abu ʾl-Hasan 54
ʿAli b. Sahl b. al-Azhar al-Isbahani, Abu ʾl-Hasan (d. 307/919–20) 54–5, 195
ʿAli b. Saʿid al-Thaghri [al-Massisi] 73, 220
ʿAli b. Saʿih 356, 387
ʿAli b. Salim 372
ʿAli b. Shahmardhan 150
ʿAli b. Tahir 354
ʿAli b. ʿUbayd 331
ʿAli b. ʿUmar b. Ahmad b. Mahdi b. Masʿud al-Hafiz al-Daraqutni, Abu ʾl-Hasan (d. 385/995) 20, 238
ʿAli b. Yaʿqub b. Suwayd al-Warraq 380
ʿAli b. Yazid al-Faraʿidi, Abu ʾl-Hasan 128, 138, 162
ʿAli b. Zayd b. Judʿan al-Rawi 118
ʿAllus al-Dinawari 316
Allusion (ishara) 398
ʿAlqama b. Marthad al-Hadrami al-Kufi, Abu ʾl-Harith 344
ʿAlqama b. Qays b. ʿAbdallah b. Malik b. ʿAlqama al-Nakhaʿi al-Kufi, Abu Shubayl (d. 61/680–1 or later) 161
ʿAlwan b. ʿAlwan see Abu ʿAmr b. ʿAlwan

al-Aʿmash see Sulayman b. Mihran
al-ʿAmili, Bahaʾ al-din see Bahaʾ al-din al-ʿAmili
ʿAmir b. ʿAbd Qays (= ʿAmir b. ʿAbdallah b. ʿAbd Qays al-ʿAnbari) (d. 41–60/661–680) 195, 376, 388
ʿAmir b. Abi ʾl-Furat 142
ʿAmir b. Saʿd b. Abi Waqqas al-Zuhri al-Madani (d. 104/722–3) 209
ʿAmmar b. Rajaʿ 363
ʿAmmar b. Yasir b. ʿAmir al-Kinani al-Madhhiji, Abu ʾl-Yaqzan (killed in 37/657) 335, 339
ʿAmmi (Uncle) al-Bastami/al-Bistami, Abu ʿImran Musa b. ʿIsa al-maʿruf bi-ʿAmmi 32–3, 271, 341, 387
ʿAmr 212
ʿAmr b. ʿAbdallah al-Basri, Abu ʿUthman 226
ʿAmr b. Dinar al-Makki al-Jumahi al-Athram, Abu Muhammad (d. 125–126/742–744) 64, 229
ʿAmr b. Marzuq al-Bahili al-Basri, Abu ʿUthman (d. 224/838–9) 367
ʿAmr b. Qays al-Mulaʾi al-Kufi, Abu ʿAbdallah (d. 146/763–4) 242
ʿAmr b. Sinan 178
ʿAmr b. ʿUtba b. Farqad al-Sulami al-Kufi (killed in 32/652–3) 384
ʿAmr b. ʿUthman b. Kurayb b. Ghusas al-Makki, Abu ʿAbdallah (d. probably 291/904) 28, 50, 54, 67, 98, 212, 238, 289, 341
ʿAmram (ʿImran) 355
Anas b. ʿIyad al-Laythi al-Madani, Abu Damra (d. 200/815–16 or earlier) 232
Anas b. Malik b. al-Nadr b. Damdam b. Zayd al-Najjari al-Khazraji, Abu Hamza (d. ca 91–93/709–711) 111, 125, 149, 157, 161, 174, 179, 197, 213, 220, 232, 249, 252, 273, 275, 303, 312, 325, 340, 343, 345
[al-]Anbar 392
al-ʿAnbari, Abu ʾl-Hasan see ʿUmar b. Wasil al-Basri
Angel(s) 12, 60, 91, 106–7, 109, 127, 171, 191, 203, 206, 216, 221, 228, 235, 245, 275–6, 308, 338, 389, 393, 399–401
  see also Gabriel, Israfil, ʿIzraʿil, Malik, Michael, Ridwan
al-Anmati see Abu ʿUmar ʿAli b. Muhammad b. ʿAli b. Bashshar b. Salman or Ishaq b. Ibrahim b. Abi Hassan
Annihilation see Self-Annihilation [in God]
al-Ansari 13
al-Antaki see ʿAbdallah b. Khubayq or Ahmad b. ʿAsim or Abu ʿUmar al-Antaki
Antioch 41, 243
al-Aqtaʿ see Abu ʾl-Khayr al-Aqtaʿ or Abu Yaʿqub al-Aqtaʿ
Arabia 55, 255
ʿArafat (plain) 111, 178, 375
Armenia 67
Arrajan 71

al-Arrajani *see* Abu Saʿid al-Arrajani
Asaf b. Barakhya   360
Ascension to heaven (al-miʿraj)   8, 101, 212
Ascetic (zahid; pl. zuhhad)   17
Ascetic   18, 21, 135, 174, 254, 256, 322, 376
Asceticism *see* "Abstention" (zuhd)
al-Ashʿari, Abu ʾl-Hasan ʿAli b. Ismaʿil (d. 324/935–6)   362
Ashʿarite(s)   9, 11, 270, 358, 362
al-Ashʿath b. Qays b. Maʿdikarib al-Kindi, Abu Muhammad (d. ca 40/660–1)   262
ʿAsim b. Bahdala (or ʿAsim b. Abi ʾl-Najud) al-Asadi al-Kufi, Abu Bakr (d. 127/744–5 or 128/745–6)   178, 392
Asmaʾ b. Kharija b. Hisn b. Hudhayfa al-Fazari (d. ca 66/685–6)   258
al-Asmaʿi, Abu Saʿid ʿAbd al-Malik b. Qurayb b. Asmaʿ (d. ca 213/828)   172
Aspirant/[Sufi] novice (murid)   4, 49, 59, 68, 113, 213–17, 296, 305, 383, 394, 398, 402–16
ʿAsqalan/Ashkelon   374
al-Asqati *see* al-ʿAbbas b. Fadl al-Asqati
ʿAtaʾ b. Abi Maymuna Maniʿ al-Basri, Abu Muʿadh (d. 131/748–9)   197
ʿAtaʾ al-Azraq   379
ʿAtaʾ b. al-Saʿib b. Malik al-Thaqafi, Abu ʾl-Saʿib (d. 136/753–4)   335
ʿAtaʾ al-Salami al-ʿAbdi al-Basri (d. ca 140/796)   401
ʿAtaʾ b. Yasar al-Hilali al-Madani, Abu Muhammad (d. 107/725–6)   151, 155
al-ʿAtawi, Abu Bakr   45
ʿAtiyya b. Saʿd b. Junada al-ʿAwfi al-Jadali al-Kufi, Abu ʾl-Hasan (d. 111/729–30, possibly later)   242
Attachment(s) [to this world] (ʿalaqa(t))   290, 300
Attacks (bawadih/hujum)   100
al-ʿAttar *see* Abu ʾl-Husayn b. Ahmad al-ʿAttar or Nasr b. Muhammad b. Ahmad or Abu Hatim al-ʿAttar al-Basri or ʿAli b. al-Hasan b. Jaʿfar al-ʿAttar.
Awareness of God (muraqaba)   202–5, 213, 245
Awe (hayba)   81, 82, 93, 143, 234, 270, 312, 322–3, 333, 349, 359
ʿAwf b. Abi Jamila al-ʿAbdi al-Hajari al-Basri, Abu Sahl (d. 146/763–4 or 147/764–5)   173
ʿAwf b. Malik b. Nadla al-Jushami al-Kufi, Abu ʾl-Ahwas   264, 281, 393
Awlas   357
al-Awlasi *see* Abu ʾl-Harith al-Awlasi
ʿAwn b. ʿAbdallah b. ʿUtba b. Masʿud al-Hudhali (d. ca 115/733)   355
Aws   344
al-Awzaʿi, Abu ʿAmr ʿAbd al-Rahman b. ʿAmr b. Yuhmid (d. 157/774)   401
ʿAyyash b. Abi ʾl-Sawh   197, 215
ʿAyyash b. Muhammad b. Hatim   393

Ayyub b. Abi Tamima Kaysan al-Sakhtiyani al-Basri (d. ca 131/748, possibly earlier)   398
al-Aʿzab *see* Ibrahim b. ʿAli al-Aʿzab
al-Azdi *see* Shaqiq al-Balkhi

B

Backbiting (ghiba)   52, 139, 172–7, 219, 356
Bad/poor manners (suʾ al-khuluq/suʾ al-adab)   58, 60, 72, 159, 288, 295, 394
Baghdad   4–6, 8–11, 21–9, 42, 44–8, 50–1, 53–4, 60–5, 68, 73, 82, 86, 105, 130, 134, 153, 165, 168, 169, 174, 226, 232–3, 239, 246, 249, 251, 258, 264, 275, 278, 280–1, 294–6, 305, 308, 318, 342, 350, 352, 362, 369, 376–7, 381–2, 389–92
Baghshur   46
Baʿja b. Abdallah b. Badr al-Juhani (d. before 101/719–20, possibly 100/718–19)   122
Bakr b. ʿAbd al-Rahman   377
Bakr b. Sulaym al-Sawwaf   150
Bakran b. Ahmad al-Jili   372
Bakran al-Dinawari, Jaʿfar b. Nusayr (servant of al-Shibli)   61, 316
Balaam   147
Al-Baladhuri, Abu Muhammad *see* Ahmad b. Ibrahim b. Hashim
Balkh   18, 31, 37, 48, 53, 342, 371
Banu Shayba   150, 319
Baqi b. Makhlad b. Yazid al-Qurtubi, Abu ʿAbd al-Rahman (d. 276/889)   279–80
al-Baqillani, Abu Bakr Muhammad b. al-Tayyib b. Muhammad b. Jaʿfar al-Qasim (d. 403/1013)   358
Baraʾ b. ʿAzib b. al-Harith b. ʿAdi al-Madani, Abu ʿUmara (d. 72/691–2)   344
Barber   318, 369
al-Bardhaʿi (or al-Bardaʿi) *see* Abu Bakr al-Bardhaʿi or Abu ʾl-Najm al-Muqriʾ or Ahmad b. Muhammad b. ʿAli b. Harun or al-Husayn b. Safwan b. Ishaq
al-Barusi, Abu ʾl-Hasan Salm b. al-Hasan   42
Bashshar b. Ibrahim al-Numayri   252
Basil *see* Sweet Basil
Basra   8, 13, 27, 34, 41, 42, 117, 127–8, 131, 154, 158, 246, 255, 263, 304, 319, 341, 353, 369, 374, 375–7, 380, 389, 397, 403
Bastam/Bistam   38, 93, 127
Baydaʾ   337–8
Bazaar/Market-place (suq)   23, 40, 47, 61, 119, 163, 182, 184, 244, 259, 382
al-Bazzaz *see* ʿAbd al-Rahim b. ʿAli al-Bazzaz or Abu Hamza al-Baghdadi or ʿAli b. al-Hasan b. Jaʿfar al-ʿAttar or Hamza b. al-ʿAbbas al-Bazzaz or al-Husayn b. Shujaʿ b. al-Hasan
Beard   19, 30, 61, 64, 162, 268, 305, 316–19, 352
Bedouin (Bedouins)   97, 171, 179, 192, 259, 265, 267, 302, 346, 389–91

Beloved *see* Lover
al-Bikandi *see* Muhammad b. Muhammad b. al-Ashʿath
Bilal al-Khawwa 26
Bilal b. Rabah al-Habashi, Abu ʿAbdallah (d. 20/641, maybe earlier) 166, 188, 313
Bilqis (the Queen of Sheba) 360
Bishr b. ʿAbd al-Malik 275
Bishr b. al-Hakam b. Habib b. Mihran al-ʿAbdi al-Naysaburi, Abu ʿAbd al-Rahman (d. 238/852–3 or 237/851–2) 209
Bishr b. al-Harith b. ʿAbd al-Rahman b. ʿAtaʾ b. Hilal al-Hafi, Abu Nasr (d. 227/842) 25–7, 41, 53–4, 130–1, 137, 140, 145, 156, 160, 165, 175, 179, 185, 209, 231, 260, 263–4, 283, 305, 313, 378, 380, 384, 389, 396, 401–3
Bishr b. Musa al-Asadi 128, 138, 149
Breath (nafas) 105–6
Buʿath 344
Bukhara 39
al-Bukhari, Muhammad b. Ismaʿil *see* Muhammad b. Ismaʿil b. Ibrahim b. Mughira
Bunan b. ʿAbdallah al-Baghdadi al-Misri 284
Bunan b. Muhammad b. Hamdan b. Hamdan b. Saʿid al-Hammal, Abu ʾl-Hasan (d. 316/928) 57, 185
Bundar b. al-Husayn b. Muhammad b. Muhallab al-Shirazi al-Arrajani, Abu ʾl-Husayn 71, 329, 349
Buraq 195
Burd b. Sinan al-Shami al-Dimashqi, Abu ʾl-ʿAlaʾ (d. 135/752–3) 175
Bushanj 42
al-Bushanji, Abu ʾl-Hasan ʿAli b. Ahmad b. Sahl (d. 348/953) 6, 69–70, 116, 244, 259, 309
al-Busri, Abu ʿUbayd *see* Abu ʿUbayd al-Busri
Byzantine(s) 21, 146, 147, 173, 278, 379, 381, 390

C

Cairo 20
Camel 73, 163, 179, 180, 196, 259, 297, 298, 327, 345–6, 389–91
Camel-driver (hidaʾ) 340, 343
Canonical prayer (salat) 386, 388, 401
Central Asia 8, 30, 132
Certain knowledge (ʿilm al-yaqin) *see* Certainty
Certainty (yaqin) 107, 194–6, 285
Character traits/Moral character (akhlaq) 3, 20, 56, 90, 109, 119, 123, 172, 199, 238, 244, 248, 252–7, 282, 286–7, 289, 293–4, 300, 347, 370, 401
Chivalrious/gallant ones (fityan) 136, 237–42
Chivalry (futuwwa) 39, 69, 70, 90, 227, 237–42, 303
Christian/Christianity 2, 147, 188, 238, 252, 280, 373, 387, 414

Clothing 97, 154, 167, 181–2, 264, 282–3, 351–2, 366, 375, 385
Companionship (suhba) 302–6
Concealment (satr) 96, 97, 220, 224, 324
Contemplation/Self-scrutiny (fikr; tafakkur) 112, 193, 234, 251, 271, 403
Contentment/Satisfaction (qanaʿa/rida) 77–9, 175–7, 282, 290
Contraction (qabd) 79–82, 108, 275

D

al-Dabari, Abu Yaʿqub Ishaq b. Ibrahim b. ʿAbbad 232
al-Dabbas *see* Abu ʿAbdallah al-Dabbas
al-Dabili, Abu Muhammad 314
al-Dahhaq b. Makhlad b. al-Dahhak b. Muslim b. al-Dahhak al-Shaybani al-Basri, Abu ʿAsim al-Nabil (d. 211–13/826–29) 345
al-Dallal *see* ʿAli b. Muhammad al-Dallal
al-Damaghani *see* Abu ʾl-ʿAbbas al-Damaghani or Abu ʾl-Hasan al-Damaghani or Abu ʾl-Husayn al-Damaghani.
Damascus 35, 39, 47, 65, 68, 132, 159, 379–80, 392
Dandanaqan 42
al-Dandanaqani *see* Mansur b. ʿAmmar
Daniq *see* Money
al-Daqqaq, Abu ʿAli al-Hasan b. ʿAli b. Muhammad (d. 405/1015) 7, 13, 22, 24–6, 28, 29, 36, 44, 45, 58, 61, 62, 75–6, 78–80, 84–5, 87, 92, 96, 101, 104, 105–6, 113–14, 118, 120, 123–5, 131, 135, 137–8, 141–6, 151, 154, 156–8, 160, 162, 180–2, 195, 198–9, 202–3, 207–15, 217–18, 220–3, 228–32, 234, 237, 244, 247–8, 252, 258, 264–7, 269–71, 273, 277–9, 282–5, 292–4, 296–8, 303–5, 311, 320, 324, 328–30, 332, 334, 336–41, 342, 347–8, 351, 356, 359, 371, 385–6, 394–9, 403, 406
Daran 35
al-Darani, Abu Sulayman ʿAbd al-Rahman b. Ahmad b. ʿAtiya (d. 215/830) 35, 39, 41, 113, 121, 130, 135, 136, 145, 159, 162, 165, 170, 175, 183–4, 197, 207–9, 215, 222–3, 227, 235, 303, 323, 348, 355, 379, 386–7, 401–2
al-Daraqutni al-Hafiz *see* ʿAli b. ʿUmar b. Ahmad b. Mahdi
al-Darraj *see* Abu ʾl-Husayn al-Darraj
David 18, 116, 155, 170–1, 190, 199, 225, 231–2, 236, 334, 336, 338, 346, 394
Dawnings (tawaliʿ) 99–100
al-Dawraqi *see* Bashir b. ʿUqba
Dawud b. Muʿadh 158
Dawud b. Nusayr al-Taʾi al-Kufi, Abu Sulayman 22, 29, 140, 156, 301, 305, 399
Dawud al-Zahiri, Abu Sulayman b. ʿAli b. Khalaf al-Isbahani (d. 270/884) 48
al-Daybuli *see* Abu Musa al-Daybuli or Jaʿfar al-Daybuli

INDEX   441

al-Daylami, Abu ʾl-Hasan ʿAli b. Muhammad   243
Death   19, 208–10, 213, 226, 230, 235, 269, 312–19, 338, 393
Deeds/Actions/Works   109, 113, 139, 146, 174, 189, 192, 197, 211, 216–25, 266, 278–9, 284, 290, 293–4, 304, 365, 410
Demavend   61
Desire/Passion (irada; shahwa; shawq, ʿishq)   119, 123, 145, 156–60, 170, 184–6, 192–3, 206, 213–16, 224–9, 286–7, 326, 326, 328, 322, 415
Devil *see* Iblis
Dhakwan al-Samman *see* Abu Salih Dhakwan
Dhat ʿIrq   158
Dhu ʾl-Nun al-Misri, Abu ʾl-Fayd Thawban b. Ibrahim al-Ikhmimi (d. 245/860)   7, 10, 12, 19–20, 27, 33, 47, 51–3, 78, 93, 115–16, 120–1, 123, 125–6, 136, 140, 144, 148, 167, 168, 176, 180–1, 194, 197–8, 204, 208, 211, 217, 221, 225–6, 233, 235, 239, 254, 283, 287, 291, 295–6, 305, 308, 314, 319, 322–4, 333, 347, 350–1, 371–3, 376–7, 388, 390, 397
Dhu ʾl-Qarnayn   363
al-Dimashqi *see* Abu ʾl-Qasim ʿAbdallah b. Muhammad al-Dimashqi
Dinar *see* Money
al-Dinawari *see* ʿAbdallah al-Dinawari or Abu ʾl-ʿAbbas Ahmad b. Muhammad al-Dinawari *or* Abu ʾl-Hasan b. al-Saʿigh *or* Ahmad al-Aswad *or* Bakran al-Dinawari *or* al-Duqqi, Abu Bakr *or* al-Hasan al-Qazzaz *or* ʿIsa al-Qassar or al-Kisaʿi, Abu Bakr *or* Mimshadh al-Dinawari.
Direct tasting *see* Tasting (dhawq)
Dirham *see* Money
Discernment (waraʿ)   77, 86, 285
Distance (buʿd)   103–5
Dream (manam; hulm)   392–403
Drinking (dhawq) *see* Tasting (shurb)
Drunk/Drunkard   93–4, 153, 223, 313–15
Drunkenness (sukr)   93–4
al-Duqqi, Abu Bakr Muhammad b. Dawud al-Dinawari (d. 366/977, possibly earlier)   51, 57, 68, 69, 86, 215, 230, 286, 288, 304, 316, 346

E

Ecstasy (wajd; tawajud; wujud)   3–4, 83–6, 93, 108, 234, 247, 290, 310, 313–15, 337–9, 348–9, 351, 354–7, 412
Effeminate man (muhannath)   154, 175
Ego *see* Soul
Egypt   7, 19–20, 27, 49, 57, 59, 62, 66, 130, 169, 185, 212, 262, 317, 319, 375, 386, 388, 390
Elijah (Ilyas) *see* al-Khadir/al-Khidr
Enoch   191
Envy (hasad)   171–2, 412
Erasure (mahw)   96, 104, 291

Essence of certainty (ʿayn al-yaqin) *see* Certainty
Euphrates   374, 378, 392, 403
Eve   394
Expansion (bast)   79–82, 108, 275

F

al-Fadl b. ʿIsa b. Aban al-Raqashi al-Basri, Abu ʿIsa   205
al-Fadl b. Sadaqa   155
Faith (iman)   194, 201–3, 209, 226, 242, 266, 268, 293
al-Faraʿidi *see* ʿAli b. Yazid al-Faraʿidi
Farakhk   297
Farghana   58
al-Farghani, Abu ʾl-ʿAbbas *see* Abu ʾl-ʿAbbas al-Farghani
al-Farghani, Abu Bakr (320/932)   43, 46
al-Farghani, Abu Jaʿfar Muhammad b. ʿAbdallah   128, 182, 237, 251, 282, 405
Faris b. ʿIsa al-Dinawari al-Baghdadi, Abu ʾl-Qasim (or Abu ʾl-Tayyib) (d. ca 340/951)   235, 308, 338
al-Farisi *see* Abu ʿAbdallah al-Farisi or Abu ʿAli al-Farisi or Abu ʾl-Husayn al-Farisi or al-Tamastani, Abu Bakr al-Farisi
al-Farraʾ *see* Muhammad b. Ahmad b. Hamdun
Fars   71, 261, 374
Fath b. Saʿid al-Mawsili, Abu Nasr (d. 220/835)   225, 382, 411
Fath b. Shakhraf b. Dawud b. Muzahim al-Kissi, Abu Nasr (d. 273/887)   41
Fatima, daughter (bint) of Muhammad (d. 11/632-2)   92, 157, 191, 228
Fatima, sister (ukht) of Abu ʿAli al-Rudhabari   284, 314, 385
Fatima, Umm ʿAli *see* Umm ʿAli Fatima
Fayruz/Firuz   332
al-Fazari *see* Abu Ishaq Ibrahim b. Muhammad
Fear (khawf and taqwa)   93, 103, 112, 125–30, 142–50, 156, 157, 164, 170, 192–4, 204, 227, 233, 270, 273, 286, 359, 361–2, 402
al-Firyabi *see* Jaʿfar b. Muhammad al-Firyabi or Muhammad b. Yusuf b. Waqid
Fish   132, 159, 196, 369, 370, 373, 378, 382–3
Fixity *see* Stability (tamkin)
Flashes (lawamiʿ)   99–100, 242–3, 330, 355
Freedom (hurriya)   229–31
Friend(s) of God (wali, pl., awliyaʾ)   124, 142, 151, 168, 182, 186, 238, 267–73, 281, 283, 341, 347, 357–63, 372–7, 383–7, 392
Friendship with God (wilaya)   268–70, 322, 341, 358
al-Fudayl b. ʿIyad b. Masʿud b. Bishr al-Tamimi al-Yarbuʿi al-Khurasani, Abu ʿAli (d. 187/803)   18, 20–1, 138, 142, 144, 157, 162–3, 165, 209, 221, 229, 237, 253, 256, 259, 376

Fustat 20, 388–90
al-Fuwati *see* Abu ᵓl-Hasan b. ᶜAbdallah al-Fuwati

G
Gabriel (angel) 12, 36, 147, 149, 150, 180, 203, 220, 235, 275–6, 325–6
Gallant ones *see* Chivalrious ones
Garment(s), *see* Clothing
Gehenna, *see* Hell
Generosity/Munificence (sakhaᵓ; jud) 227–8, 253, 257–64, 286, 290
al-Ghallabi 226
Ghassan b. ᶜUbayd b. Abi ᶜAtika Tarif b. Salman 111
Ghaylan b. ᶜAbd al-Samad 179
Ghaylan b. Jarir al-Miᶜwali al-Azdi al-Basri (d. 129/746–7) 252
al-Ghitrifi, Abu Muhammad (probably a mistaken rendition of the name of Abu Ahmad Muhammad b. Ahmad b. al-Husayn b. al-Qasim b. al-Ghitrif al-Ribati al-Jurjani al-ᶜAbdi, d. 377/987) 392
Ghulam Khalil = Ahmad b. Muhammad b. Ghalib b. Khalid b. Mirdas al-Bahili al-Basri, better known as Ghulam Khalil (d. 275/888–9) 258
Glimmers (lawaᶜih) 78, 99–100
[Divine] Gnosis (maᶜrifa) 5–6, 108, 275, 319–25, 333, 413
[Divine] Gnostic (ᶜarif) 106, 123, 135, 136–40, 142, 218, 236, 294–5, 309, 320–5, 331, 338, 361, 413
Good manners/Proper behavior (adab) 2–3, 138, 141, 183, 198, 274, 292–6, 303, 404, 413
Gratitude/Gratefulness (shukr) 188–93, 286

H
Habib al-ᶜAjami, Abu Muhammad b. Muhammad (d. 156/772) 186, 375, 380, 396–7
Habib al-Maghribi 72
al-Habir 55
al-Haddad *see* Abu Hafs al-Naysaburi or ᶜAli b. Ibrahim al-Haddad or Abu Jaᶜfar al-Haddad or al-Hasan al-Haddad
Hadith 24–5, 156, 201, 215, 278
Hadramawt 262
Hafs b. ᶜAsim b. ᶜUmar b. al-Khattab 210
Hafs b. ᶜUmar al-ᶜUmari 356
al-Hajabi, *see* ᶜAbdallah b. ᶜAbd al-Wahhab al-Hajabi
al-Hajari, Ibrahim, *see* Ibrahim b. Muslim al-ᶜAbdi
al-Hajjaj b. Furafisa 158
Hajjaj b. Muhammad al-Missisi al-Aᶜwar, Abu Muhammad (d. 206/821–2) 297
al-Hajjaj b. Yusuf al-Thaqafi (d. 95/714) 173, 376
al-Hajjaji, Abu ᵓl-Husayn (or Abu ᵓl-Hasan) Muhammad b. Muhammad b. Yaᶜqub b. al-Hajjaj al-Naysaburi (d. 368/978–9) 26

al-Hakam b. ᶜAbd al-Muttalib 258
al-Hakam b. Aslam 213
al-Hakam b. Hisham (b. al-Hakam) b. ᶜAbd al-Rahman al-Thaqafi al-Kufi, Abu Muhammad 134
al-Hakam b. Musa (b. Abi Zuhayr Shirzad al-Baghdadi; d. ca 232/847) 111
al-Hakam b. Nafiᶜ al-Bahrani *see* Abu ᵓl-Yaman al-Hakam b. Nafiᶜ
al-Hakim al-Tirmidhi *see* al-Tirmidhi, Abu ᶜAbdallah Muhammad b. ᶜAli or al-Warraq, Abu Bakr Muhammad
al-Hallaj, al-Husayn b. Mansur (killed in 309/922) 6–8, 14, 56, 128, 146, 158, 231, 247, 253, 289–90, 329–30, 341
Hamdun al-Qassar, Abu Salih b. Ahmad b. ᶜUmara (d. 271/884–5) 63, 166, 179, 180, 183, 189, 282, 290, 313
Hamid al-Aswad 235, 378–9, 384
Hamid al-Laffaf *see* Hamid b. Mahmud b. Harb
Hamid b. Mahmud b. Harb al-Naysaburi al-Laffaf, Abu ᶜAli (d. 266/976–7) 36
Hammad al-Khayyat 269
Hammad b. Salama b. Dinar al-Basri, Abu Salama (d. 167/784) 178
Hammad b. Zayd b. Dirham al-Jahdami al-Basri al-Azraq, Abu Ismaᶜil (d. 179/795–6) 306, 335, 377
Hammam b. Munabbih 325
Hamza b. al-ᶜAbbas al-Bazzaz, Abu Ahmad 264, 280–1, 392–3
Hamza b. ᶜAbdallah al-ᶜAbbadani, Abu Habib: Sahl al-Tustari bei 34
Hamza b. ᶜAbdallah al-ᶜAlawi al-Husayni, Abu ᵓl-Qasim 367–8
Hamza b. Yusuf b. Ibrahim b. Musa b. Ibrahim al-Sahmi al-Jurjani, Abu ᵓl-Qasim (d. 428/1036–7 or 427/1035–6) 134, 174, 222, 268–9, 274, 279, 306, 334, 389–91
Hanbalite(s) 9–10, 308–9
Haniᵓ b. ᶜAbd al-Rahman b. Abi ᶜAbla al-ᶜUqayli 220
Harb b. Shaddad al-Yashkuri al-Basri, Abu ᵓl-Khattab (d. 161/777–8) 264
al-Harbi *see* Abu Bakr al-Harbi or Ibrahim b. Ishaq b. Bashir or Mansur b. Ahmad al-Harbi
Harim b. Hayyan b. Malik alᵓAbdi al-Azdi (d. ca 26/646) 366
al-Harith b. Abi Usama *see* al-Harith b. Muhammad b. Abi Usama
al-Harith b. Muhammad b. Abi Usama al-Tamimi (d. 282/896) 343
al-Harith al-Muhasibi *see* al-Muhasibi, Abu ᶜAbdallah al-Harith
Harith b. Shihab 171
Haritha b. Suraqa b. al-Harith b. ᶜAdi b. Malik al-Ansari (killed at Badr in 2/624) 230

Harun, Abu Hamza b. al-Mughira b. Hakim al-Bajali al-Razi 356
Harun b. Maʿruf al-Marwazi al-Khazzaz al-Darir, Abu ʿAli (d. 231/845–6) 232
Harun b. Muhammad al-Daqqaq 158
Harun al-Rashid, caliph (r. 170–193/786–809) 133, 401
al-Hasan b. al-ʿAbbas 257
al-Hasan b. ʿAbdallah b. Saʿid al-ʿAskari, Abu Ahmad (d. 382/993) 21
al-Hasan b. ʿAlawayh (ʿAlluya) *see* al-Hasan b. ʿAli b. Muhammad b. Sulayman
al-Hasan b. ʿAli 32, 167, 285, 287
al-Hasan b. ʿAli b. Abi Talib, Abu Muhammad (d. 49/669–70, possibly later) 262, 313
al-Hasan b. ʿAli b. Muhammad b. Sulayman al-Qattan, better known as Ibn ʿal-Alawayh (ʿAlluya), Abu Muhammad (d. 298/911) 130, 209
al-Hasan b. ʿAmr b. al-Jahm al-Sabiʿi (or al-Shiʿi), Abu ʾl-Husayn (d. 288/901) 161, 384
al-Hasan b. ʿArafa b. Yazid al-ʿAbdi al-Baghdadi al-Muʿaddib, Abu ʿAli (d. 257/870–1) 390
al-Hasan al-Basri, Abu Saʿid b. Abi ʾl-Hasan Yasar (d. 110/728) 132–3, 136, 157, 161, 174, 220, 235, 254, 275, 294, 397, 401
al-Hasan al-Haddad 227, 244, 248
al-Hasan b. Hammad b. Fadala 334–5
al-Hasan (or al-Husayn) b. al-Harith al-Ahwazi 340, 344
al-Hasan b. ʿIsam al-Shaybani 396
al-Hasan b. Khalid 148
al-Hasan al-Khayyat 185
al-Hasan b. Musa 325
al-Hasan al-Qazzaz al-Dinawari 119, 354
al-Hasan b. Rashiq al-ʿAskari, Abu Muhammad (d. 370/980) 20
al-Hasan b. Safwan 150
al-Hasan al-Sawi 164
al-Hasan (al-Husayn), brother (akhu) of Sinan 183
Hashim b. Khalid 145
Hashim b. al-Qasim b. Muslim, *see* Abu ʾl-Nadr Hashim b. al-Qasim
al-Hasnuyi, *see* Ahmad b. ʿAli b. al-Hasan
Hassan b. Abu Sinan b. Abi Awfa al-Tanukhi (d. probably 180/796–7) 133
Hatim al-Asamm, Abu ʿAbd al-Rahman b. ʿUnwan (d. 237/851–2) 30–1, 36–7, 40, 137, 145, 147, 170, 179, 215, 254
Haytham b. Kharija al-Khurasani al-Marwazi, Abu Muhammad (d. 227/842) 233, 325
Heart (qalb) 97–8, 106–10, 112–18, 121, 123–5, 135–7, 139–42, 144–5, 149–50, 156, 161–6, 168, 171–2, 175, 189–90, 214–16, 218, 220–3, 225–9, 231–4, 236, 244–6, 248–9, 257, 266–7, 270, 274–6, 279, 282–3, 285–7, 294–5, 297–8, 310–12, 315–18, 320–2, 327–8, 330–1, 334–6, 347–8, 354–6, 367–9, 393, 402, 406–13, 416

Hell 38, 77, 92, 155, 160–1, 173, 179, 191, 208, 256–7, 332, 339, 398, 402
Hellfire *see* Hell
Hereafter ([al-]akhira) 135, 143, 144, 150, 155, 156–8, 166–7, 175, 184, 193, 194, 201, 222, 226–30, 238, 270, 282, 288, 294, 308–9, 312, 323–5, 343, 359, 362, 398, 406, 416
[al-]Hijaz 173, 317, 343, 385, 391
Hilal b. Ahmad 10
Hilal b. Muhammad 284
al-Hilali *see* ʿAli b. al-Hasan b. Musa
al-Hira 62, 271, 387
al-Hiri, Abu ʿUthman Saʿid b. Ismaʿil b. Saʿid b. Mansur al-Razi (d. 298/910) 45–6, 49, 62, 67, 69, 78–9, 113, 117, 121, 130, 132, 135–6, 143, 145, 157, 181, 189–90, 193, 198, 209, 216, 221, 227, 233, 236, 244, 256, 296–8, 318–19, 335–6, 338, 341, 349
Hisham b. ʿAbd al-Malik al-Bahili al-Tayalisi al-Basri, Abu ʾl-Walid (d. 227/841) 157, 213
Hisham al-Kattani 325
Hisham b. ʿUrwa b. al-Zubayr b. al-ʿAwwam al-Asadi, Abu ʾl-Mundhir (d. 145–7/762–5) 344
Holy war (jihad) 118, 125, 173, 381, 399
Hope (rajaʾ) 19, 93, 112, 146, 148–50, 179, 204, 273, 312, 412
al-Hubab b. Muhammad al-Tustari 344
Hud (prophet) 218
Hudhayfa b. Qatada al-Marʿashi (d. 207/822–3) 129, 161, 187, 220–1
Hudhayfa b. al-Yaman (d. 36/656) 220
Humayd b. Abi Humayd al-Khuzaʿi al-Basri al-Tawil, Abu ʿUbayda (d. 143–1 or 142/759–60) 213, 232, 342–3
Humayd al-Tusi (d. 210/825–6) and Dawud al-Taʾi 29
Humayyim b. Humam/Hammam 334
Humility (khushuʿ) *see* Modesty (tawaduʿ)
Hunger (juʿ) 157–9, 211
al-Husayn b. ʿAbdallah b. Saʿid, Abu ʿAbdallah 155
al-Husayn (al-Husayn) b. Ahmad al-Farisi 383, 391–2
al-Husayn b. Ahmad b. Jaʿfar al-Razi better known as Ibn al-Baghdadi, Abu ʿAbdallah (d. 404/1014) 49, 57, 130, 219, 253, 284, 292, 347, 369
al-Husayn b. ʿAli 117
Husayn b. ʿAli al-Qirmisini 169
al-Husayn b. ʿAlluya 38, 118
al-Husayn al-Ansari 337
al-Husayn b. Hurayth *see* Abu ʿAmmar Al-Husayn b. Hurayth
al-Husayn b. Ismaʿil *see* al-Mahamili, Abu ʿAbdallah
al-Husayn b. Jaʿfar 288

al-Husayn al-Maghazili *see* al-Maghazili, al-Husayn
al-Husayn b. Mansur *see* al-Hallaj
al-Husayn b. Muhammad b. Bahram al-Tamimi al-Muruwadhi, Abu Muhammad (d. 213/828–9)   364
al-Husayn b. Muhammad b. Musa b. Khalid b. Salim al-Azdi (d. 348/959–60)   321
al-Husayn b. Muhammad b. Zayd, Abu ʿAli   392
al-Husayn b. Safwan b. Ishaq b. Ibrahim al-Bardhaʿi, Abu ʿAli (d. 340/952)   232
al-Husayn b. Shujaʿ b. al-Hasan b. Musa al-Sufi al-Mawsili al-Bazzaz, Abu ʿAbdallah (d. 423/1032)   280
al-Husayn b. Yahya al-Shafiʿi   28, 169, 191, 196, 197, 236, 325
al-Husayn b. Yusuf al-Qazwini, Abu ʿAli   285, 287
al-Husri, Abu ʿAbdallah   287, 411
al-Husri, Abu ʾl-Hasan ʿAli b. Ibrahim al-Basri (d. 371/981)   73, 291, 298, 308, 348, 406

I

Iblis (Devil; Satan)   13, 36, 43, 53, 56, 64, 70, 106, 138, 144, 147, 160, 161, 171, 190, 221, 236, 282, 305, 344, 356, 370, 388, 393–5, 397, 401, 406
Ibn ʿAbbas *see* ʿAbdallah b. ʿAbbas
Ibn Abi ʾl-Dunya, Abu Bakr ʿAbdallah b. Muhammad b. ʿUbayd b. Sufyan al-Qurashi (d. 281/894)   27, 150, 233
Ibn Abi Hassan al-Anmati *see* Ishaq b. Ibrahim b. Abi Hassan
Ibn Abi ʾl-Hawari, Abu ʾl-Hasan Ahmad b. Maymun (d. 230/844–5)   35, 39, 46, 129, 145, 159, 165, 175, 184, 193, 207, 209, 212, 215, 222, 227, 294, 303, 321, 348, 355, 386, 401
Ibn Abi Hazim *see* ʿAbd al-ʿAziz b. Ali Hazim
Ibn Abi Qammash   229, 335
Ibn Abi Sadaqa   306
Ibn Abi Shaykh *see* Ahmad b. Muhammad b. Ahmad b. Zakariya
Ibn ʿAlawayh (ʿAlluya) *see* al-Hasan b. ʿAli b. Muhammad b. Sulayman
Ibn al-Anbari, Abu Bakr Muhammad b. al-Qasim b. Muhammad b. Bashshar (d. 328/940)   246
Ibn al-Aʿrabi, Abu Saʿid Ahmad b. Muhammad b. Ziyad b. Bishr al-ʿAnazi (d. 341/952)   66–7, 164, 310, 402
Ibn ʿAtaʾ *see* Ahmad b. ʿAtaʾ, Abu ʾl-ʿAbbas b. Muhammad b. Sahl b. ʿAtaʾ or Ahmad b. ʿAtaʾ, Abu ʿAbdallah al-Rudhabari
Ibn al-ʿAttar *see* ʿAli b. al-Hasan b. Jaʿfar al-ʿAttar
Ibn ʿAwn *see* ʿAbdallah b. ʿAwn
Ibn Bakawayh (Bakuya), Abu ʿAbdallah Muhammad b. ʿAbdallah al-Shirazi al-Sufi (d. 428/1037)   70, 160

Ibn al-Barqi (not to be confused with the better known Abu Bakr b. al-Barqi, Ahmad b. Abdallah b. ʿAbd al-Rahim al-Zuhri al-Misri, d. 270/884)   249
Ibn Batta *see* ʿUbaydallah b. Muhammad
Ibn Bunan *see* Abu ʾl-Husayn b. Bunan
Ibn Faris *see* Abu ʾl-Husayn b. Faris
Ibn Fatik, *see* Ibrahim b. Fatik
Ibn Furak *see* Abu Bakr Muhammad b. al-Hasan b. Furak
Ibn al-Fuwati   353
Ibn Jahdam *see* ʿAli b. ʿAbdallah b. al-Hasan b. Jahdam
Ibn al-Jallaʾ, Abu ʿAbdallah Ahmad b. Yahya al-Baghdadi al-Shami (d. 306/918)   40, 41, 47, 51–2, 59, 62, 68, 130, 135, 144, 284, 286, 291, 351, 371, 381, 398
Ibn Jurayj *see* ʿAbd al-Malik b. ʿAbd al-ʿAziz b. Jurayj
Ibn al-Karnabi, Abu Jaʿfar   317
Ibn Kasib   118
Ibn al-Katib, Abu ʿAli al-Hasan b. Ahmad (d. ca 340/951–2)   65, 72, 249
Ibn Khadrawayh *see* Ahmad b. Khadrawayh (Khidruya) al-Balkhi
Ibn Khafif, Abu ʿAbdallah Muhammad b. Khafif al-Dabbi al-Shirazi (d. around 371/981)   28, 48, 55–6, 70, 107, 135, 156, 208, 286, 337
Ibn al-Khashshab *see* Abu ʾl-ʿAbbas b. al-Khashshab
Ibn Khubayq *see* ʿAbdallah b. Khubayq
Ibn Kullab, Abu Muhammad ʿAbdallah b. Saʿid al-Qattan (d. 240/854 or later)   405
Ibn Lahiʿa, *see* ʿAbdallah b. Lahiʿa
Ibn Makhlad, *see* Muhammad b. Makhlad b. Hafs
Ibn al-Maliki   186
Ibn Masruq *see* Abu ʾl-ʿAbbas Ahmad b. Muhammad b. Masruq or Muhammad b. Masruq
Ibn Masʿud, Abu ʿAbd al-Rahman ʿAbdallah b. Masʿud b. Ghafil al-Hudhali (d. 32/653)   140, 171, 226
Ibn Milhan, ʿAbdallah b. Qatada   345
Ibn Miqsam *see* Abu ʾl-Hasan Ahmad b. Muhammad b. al-Hasan b. Yaʿqub
Ibn al-Mubarak *see* ʿAbdallah b. al-Mubarak
Ibn al-Muʿtazz, Abu ʾl-ʿAbbas ʿAbdallah b. Muhammad (d. 296/909)   172
Ibn Nujayd *see* Ismaʿil b. Nujayd
Ibn al-Qattan *see* ʿAbdallah b. ʿAdi b. ʿAbdallah
Ibn Rashiq *see* al-Hasan b. Rashiq
Ibn al-Saʾigh *see* Abu ʾl-Hasan b. al-Saʾigh
Ibn Salim *see* Ahmad b. Muhammad b. Ahmad b. Salim or ʿAli b. Salim or Muhammad b. Ahmad b. Salim.
Ibn al-Sammak   141
Ibn al-Sammak, Abu ʾl-ʿAbbas Muhammad b. Sabih (d. 183/799–800)   22–3, 387

Ibn al-Sammak, Abu ʿAmr ʿUthman b. Ahmad b. ʿAbdallah b. Yazid al-Daqqaq (d. 344/955) 275
Ibn Sayyar *see* al-Sayyari, Abu ʾl-ʿAbbas
Ibn Shadhan *see* Muhammad b. ʿAbdallah b. Muhammad b. ʿAbd al-ʿAziz b. Shadhan
Ibn Shahin 12
Ibn Shihab *see* al-Zuhri, Muhammad b. Muslim b. ʿUbaydallah
Ibn Shubruma *see* ʿAbdallah b. Shubruma.
Ibn Sirin, Abu Bakr Muhammad (d. 110/728) 127, 148, 173, 226, 294, 306
Ibn Surayj, Abu ʾl-ʿAbbas *see* Abu ʾl-ʿAbbas Ahmad b. ʿUmar b. Surayj
Ibn Tahir *see* Abu Bakr ʿAbdallah b. Tahir al-Abhari
Ibn Tulun *see* Ahmad b. Tulun
Ibn ʿUmar *see* ʿAbdallah b. ʿUmar b. al-Khattab
Ibn ʿUyayna *see* Sufyan b. ʿUyayna
Ibn Wahb *see* ʿAbdallah b. Wahb b. Muslim
Ibn al-Wasiti *see* Abu ʿAbdallah al-Ramli
Ibn Yazdaniyar *see* Abu Bakr al-Husayn b. ʿAli b. Yazdaniyar
Ibn Ziyad, Abu Ismaʿil 238
Ibn Zizi, Abu Yaʿqub 114, 348
Ibrahim b. ʿAbdallah (b. Hatim al-Harawi, Abu Ishaq, d. 244/858–9?) 162
Ibrahim b. Adham b. Mansur, Abu Ishaq (d. ca 162/778–9) 18–19, 119, 127–9, 131, 141, 152, 166, 173, 188, 232, 254–6, 271, 281, 283, 297, 303–5, 373–4, 377–80, 384
Ibrahim b. Ahmad al-Maristani, Abu Ishaq 56, 176, 351
Ibrahim b. Ahmad b. Muhammad b. Rajaʾ al-Fazari 281
Ibrahim b. Ahmad b. Muhammad al-Tabari, Abu Ishaq 384
Ibrahim b. Ahmad b. al-Muwallad al-Raqqi, Abu Ishaq (d. 342/953–4) 284–5, 301, 367
Ibrahim b. Ahmad al-Tabari *see* Ibrahim b. Ahmad b. Muhammad al-Tabari
Ibrahim al-Ajurri al-Saghir al-Baghdadi, Abu Ishaq 375
Ibrahim b. al-Ashʿath 229
Ibrahim b. Bashshar b. Muhammad al-Khurasani, Abu Ishaq (d. ca 240/854–5) 18
Ibrahim al-Dabbagh al-Shirazi 71
Ibrahim b. Dawha al-Ribati al-Harawi, Abu Ishaq 225
Ibrahim b. Fatik b. Saʿid al-Baghdadi, Abu ʾl-Fatik 11, 136, 163, 195, 330–1
Ibrahim b. Firas 34
Ibrahim al-Hajari *see* Ibrahim b. Muslim al-ʿAbdi
Ibrahim al-Harbi *see* Ibrahim b. Ishaq b. Bashir
Ibrahim b. al-Harith 334
Ibrahim b. Ishaq b. Ibrahim b. Bashir b. ʿAbdallah al-Baghdadi al-Harbi, Abu Ishaq (d. 285/898) 63

Ibrahim b. al-Junayd, Abu Ishaq (d. ca 260/873–4) 263
Ibrahim b. Khalid b. Abi ʾl-Yaman *see* Abu ʾl-Thawr Ibrahim b. Khalid
Ibrahim al-Khawwas, Abu Ishaq b. Ahmad b. Ismaʿil (d. 291/904) 56, 182, 350, 373, 378
Ibrahim al-Maristani *see* Ibrahim b. Ahmad al-Maristani
Ibrahim b. Miqsam 168
Ibrahim b. Muhammad b. al-Harith 160
Ibrahim b. Muhammad b. al-Haytham 226
Ibrahim b. Muhammad al-Maliki 386
Ibrahim b. Muhammad b. Yahya al-Muzakki al-Naysaburi, Abu Ishaq (d. 362/973) 30
Ibrahim b. Muslim al-ʿAbdi al-Kufi, Abu Ishaq al-maʿruf bi-ʾl-Hajari 182
Ibrahim b. al-Muwallad *see* Ibrahim b. Ahmad b. al-Muwallad
Ibrahim al-Nakhaʿi *see* Ibrahim b. Yazid (b. Qays) b. al-Aswad
Ibrahim al-Qassar *see* al-Raqqi, Abu Ishaq Ibrahim
Ibrahim al-Raqqi *see* Ibrahim b. Ahmad b. al-Muwallad or al-Raqqi, Abu Ishaq Ibrahim
Ibrahim al-Ribati *see* Ibrahim b. Dawha
Ibrahim (b.) Shayba (Sitanba) al-Harawi, Abu Ishaq 225, 387
Ibrahim b. Shayban al-Qirmisini, Abu Ishaq (d. ca 300/912) 54, 66–7, 145, 164, 169, 266, 304, 383
Ibrahim al-Utrush 155
Ibrahim b. Yahya 384
Ibrahim b. Yazid b. Qays b. al-Aswad b. ʿAmr al-Nakhaʿi, Abu ʿImran (d. 96/814) 132, 161
Idris 390
ʿImran b. Musa al-Isfanji 134
Inconstancy (talwin) 100–2
India 200, 333
Innermost self/Innermost secret (sirr) 106, 110, 123–4, 142–3, 150, 162, 179–80, 184–5, 188, 194, 199, 203, 205, 214–15, 218, 223–5, 234–5, 243, 310–11, 313, 322, 372, 407
Insight (basira) 359
Intimacy (uns) 81–3, 104, 122–4, 146, 167, 227, 236, 271, 285, 323, 327
Intoxication (sukr) 93–4, 332
   see also Drunkenness
Inward *see* Outward
Iram 85
Iran 7, 11, 21, 34, 37, 51–2, 54, 61, 71, 127, 239, 247, 261, 277, 315, 367, 382
Iraq(is) 22–3, 29, 43, 57, 60, 206–8, 237, 248, 262, 271, 302, 387, 389, 391
ʿIsa b. Aban b. Sadaqa, Abu Musa (d. 221/836) 57
ʿIsa b. Adam *see* Abu Musa ʿIsa b. Adam
ʿIsa b. Maryam *see* Jesus
ʿIsa al-Qassar al-Dinawari 299

ʿIsa b. Talha b. ʿUbaydallah al-Tamimi al-Madani, Abu Muhammad (d. 100/718–9) 142
ʿIsa b. Yunus b. Abi Ishaq ʿAmr al-Sabiʿi al-Hamdani al-Kufi, Abu ʿAmr (d. 188/803 or 191/806–7) 135
Isaac 168
ʿIsam b. Yusuf al-Balkhi (d. probably 215/830–31) 170
Isfahan/Isbahan 399
al-Isfanjani (or perhaps Isfijabi?), Abu Nasr Ahmad b. Saʿid 6
al-Isfanji *see* ʿImran b. Musa
al-Isfaraini *see* ʿAbd al-Malik b. al-Hasan al-Isfaraini, Abu Nuʿaym or Abu Tahir al-Isfaraini or al-Isfaraini, Abu Ishaq
al-Isfaraini, Abu ʾl-Ishaq Ibrahim b. Muhammad b. Ibrahim b. Mihran (d. 418/1027) 11, 358
Ishaq b. Ahmad 370
Ishaq b. Ibrahim 339
Ishaq b. Ibrahim b. ʿAbbad *see* al-Dabari, Abu Yaʿqub
Ishaq b. Ibrahim b. Abi Hassan al-Anmati, Abu Yaʿqub (d. 302/914) 35, 175
Ishaq b. Ibrahim al-Munqari 392
Ishaq b. ʿIsa b. Bint Dawud b. Abi Hind al-Qushayri 173
Ishaq b. Khalaf al-maʿruf bi-Ibn al-Tabib (d. ca 230/844–5) 129
Ishmael (prophet) 266, 394
Islam *see* Faith
Ismaʿil *see* Ishmael
Ismaʿil b. Abi Khalid al-Ahmasi (d. 146/763–4) 203, 222, 390
Ismaʿil b. ʿAmr b. Kamil 390
Ismaʿil b. ʿAyyash b. Sulaym al-ʿAnsi al-Himsi, Abu ʿUtba (d. 181/797–8 or 182/798–9) 233
Ismaʿil b. al-Fadl 171, 237, 356
Ismaʿil b. Jaʿfar b. Abi Kathir al-Ansari al-Zarqi, Abu Ishaq (d. 180/796–7) 213
Ismaʿil al-Makki *see* Ismaʿil b. Muslim al-Makki
Ismaʿil b. Masʿud al-Jahdari al-Basri, Abu Masʿud (d. 248/862–3) 179
Ismaʿil b. Muhammad b. Ismaʿil b. Salih b. ʿAbd al-Rahman al-Saffar al-Nahwi, Abu ʿAli (d. 341/952) 208, 390
Ismaʿil b. Muslim al-Makki al-Basri, Abu Ishaq 229
Ismaʿil b. Nujayd b. Ahmad b. Yusuf b. Khalid, Abu ʿAmr al-Sulami al-Naysaburi (d. 366/976–7) 40, 46, 67, 69, 113, 119, 211, 245, 356
Ismaʿil b. ʿUlayya, Abu Bishr (d. 193/809) 345
Ismaʿil b. Zakariya b. Murra al-Khulqani, Abu Ziyad (d. 173/789–90, possibly 174/790–91) 175
Ismaʿil b. Ziyad al-Taʾi (al-Sakuni?, d. 247/861–2) 30
Ismaʿil b. Zurara 335

Israel 133, 147, 338, 351, 364, 371, 374
Israfil (angel) 228
Istakhr 374
al-Istakhri *see* ʿAbdallah b. Ahmad al-Istakhri or Abu ʿAmr (or ʿUmar or ʿImran) al-Istakhri *or* Yahya al-Istakhri
Iyas b. Muʿawiya b. Qurra al-Basri al-Muzani, Abu Wathila (d. 121/739 or 122/740) 173
ʿIzraʾil (the angel of death) 60

J

Jabala b. Suhaym al-Taymi al-Kufi (d. 125 or 126/742–4) 259, 351
Jabir b. ʿAbdallah b. ʿAmr b. Haram b. Thaʿlaba al-Khazraji al-Salami (d. probably 78/697–8) 167, 175, 233
Jabir al-Rahbi 374
Jacob 156, 168, 202, 352
Jaʿfar b. Ahmad b. Muhammad al-Muqriʾ al-Razi, Abu ʾl-Qasim (d. 378/988–9) 159, 216
Jaʿfar al-Daybuli 389
Jaʿfar al-Hadhdhaʿ, Abu Muhammad (d. 341/952–3) 374
Jaʿfar b. Hanzala al-Bahrani 256
Jaʿfar al-Khawwas *see* Jaʿfar b. al Qasim al-Khawwas or Jaʿfar b. Muhammad al-Khawwas
Jaʿfar al-Khuldi *see* Jaʿfar b. Muhammad b. Nusayr
Jaʿfar b. Muhammad b. Nusayr, Abu Muhammad al-Khuldi (d. 348/959–60) 12–14, 24, 28, 35–7, 51, 68, 81, 170, 174, 181–2, 196–7, 211, 216, 246, 251, 289, 298, 303, 308, 340, 368, 370
Jaʿfar b. Muhammad al-Sadiq (d. 148/765) 12, 241, 277
Jaʿfar b. Muhammad b. Shakir al-Baghdadi, Abu Muhammad al-Saʿigh (d. 279/893) 280
Jaʿfar b. Mujashiʿ 134
Jaʿfar b. Nusayr *see* Jaʿfar b. Muhammad b. Nusayr
Jaʿfar b. al-Qasim al-Khawwas 224, 378
Jaʿfar al-Sadiq *see* Jaʿfar b. Muhammad al-Sadiq
Jaʿfar b. Sulayman 160
al-Jahiz, Abu ʿUthman ʿAmr b. Bahr b. Mahbub al-Kinaʿi (255/868–9) 397
Jahm al-Raqqi 86
al-Jalajili al-Basri 293
al-Janbi, Abu Zurʿa *see* Abu Zurʿa al-Janbi
al-Jannabi, Abu Tahir Sulayman b. Abi Saʿid (d. 332/943–4) 55
Jarir b. ʿAbdallah b. Jabir al-Bajali, Abu ʿAmr (d. 51/671 or later) 203
Jarir b. Hazim (b. Zayd) b. ʿAbdallah b. Shujaʿ al-Azdi al-ʿAtaki al-Basri, Abu ʾl-Nadr (d. 175/791–2) 364
al-Jawhari, Abu ʾl-Qasim *see* Abu ʾl-Qasim al-Jawhari
al-Jawhari, Muhammad b. al-Husayn 10
Jealousy (*ghayra*) 264–8
Jerusalem 127–8, 195, 208, 373

Jesus (ʿIsa) 133, 147, 228, 296, 364, 396
Jew(s) 148, 165, 250–2, 319, 375, 389
(al-)Jibal (province) 52
Jinn (spirits) 5, 82–3, 138, 141, 182, 231, 346
Job 202, 296
Joseph (Yusuf) 90–1, 101, 168, 202, 227, 337
Joy 108
al-Judi (mountain) 162
al-Junayd, Abu ʾl-Qasim b. Muhammad b. al-Junayd (d. 297/910) 4–7, 9, 11–14, 22–4, 28, 35, 39, 43–7, 49, 51–2, 54–65, 67–8, 79, 81–4, 89, 92, 98, 107, 114–15, 118, 124, 128–9, 135–7, 145, 161, 164, 168, 170–1, 174–5, 178, 184, 189–91, 194–5, 197, 204, 208–9, 215–16, 219–21, 223–4, 229, 231, 236–8, 248–9, 251–2, 255, 258, 274, 282, 285, 289–90, 294–7, 303–5, 308–10, 312–14, 316–18, 322–4, 328–33, 338–40, 347–8, 350–2, 361, 369–71, 373–4, 376–8, 385, 389, 404–5
Junayd al-Hajjam (the Cupper) 29
Jurayj (Gregorius) 363–4
al-Jurayri, Abu Muhammad Muhammad b. al-Husayn (d. 311/923–4) 4, 25, 43, 55, 69–72, 84, 123, 128, 199, 203–5, 209–11, 213, 223, 227, 236, 241, 250–3, 255, 283, 289, 291, 294, 308, 312, 319, 324, 355, 398
al-Juzi see Muhammad b. ʿAli al-Juzi
al-Juzjani, Abu ʿAli al-Hasan b. ʿAli 213, 218, 271

K
[al-]Kaʿba 19, 49, 64, 132, 152–4, 165, 196, 200, 278, 318–19, 353, 372, 378, 380–4, 410
Kahmas, Abu Muhammad b. al-Husayn al-Hamadhani 132
Kamil b. Talha al-Jahdari al-Basri, Abu Yahya (d. 231/845–6) 273
al-Karini/al-Karnabi 283, 317
al-Karnabi see al-Karini
Karramiyya 9–10
Kathir b. Hisham al-Kilabi al-Raqqi, Abu Sahl (d. probably 207/911) 134
al-Kattani, Abu Bakr Muhammad b. ʿAli b. Jaʿfar (d. 322/934) 49–50, 64, 126, 137, 176, 180, 212, 215, 234, 243, 253, 279, 287, 290, 298–301, 304, 325, 329, 333, 381–2, 387, 395, 400, 402
Kerbela 208
Khadija 157
al-Khadir/al-Khidr 18, 26, 124, 177, 181, 340, 363, 385–9, 391
al-Khadir, Abu ʾl-ʿAbbas 374
Khalaf b. Tamim, Abu ʾl-Ahwas 306
Khalaf b. al-Walid 149
Khalid b. ʿAbdallah b. Safwan 233
Khalid b. Yahya 179
Khalid b. Yazid al-Jumahi al-Basri, Abu ʿAbd al-Rahman (d. 139/ 756–7) 203, 273

Khalid b. Zayd b. Kulayb see Abu Ayyub al-Ansari
Kharija b. Musʿab b. Kharija al-Khurasani al-Sarakhsi (d. 168/785) 151
al-Kharraz, Abu Muhammad ʿAbdallah b. Muhammad al-Razi (d. before 310/922–3) 57
al-Kharraz, Abu Saʿid Ahmad b. ʿIsa al-Baghdadi (d. 277/890–1) 13, 18, 52–3, 56, 60, 64–6, 82, 133, 181, 186, 196, 205, 221, 243, 249, 253, 272, 282, 290, 292, 311, 313, 319, 325, 334, 349, 354, 371, 377, 402
al-Kharraz, Ahmad b. ʿAli 196–7
Kharw 247
al-Khashshab see Abu Sahl al-Khashshab al-Kabir
al-Khassaf see Abu Jaʿfar al-Khassaf
al-Khattabi see Abu ʾl-Harith al-Khattabi
al-Khawwas see Abu Sulayman al Khawwas or Bilal al-Khawwas or Jaʿfar b. Muhammad al-Khawwas or Jaʿfar b. al-Qasim al Khawwas or Ibrahim al-Khawwas
Khayr al-Nassaj, Muhammad b. Ismaʿil al-Samarri (d. 322/934) 60–1, 183, 251, 355, 371, 385
Khaythama b. ʿAbd al-Rahman b. Abi Sabra al-Juʿfi al-Kufi (d. ca 80/699–700) 193
Khazraj 344
al-Khidr 124, 177, 181
Khubayb b. ʿAbd-al-Rahman b. Khubayb b. Yasaf al-Ansari al-Khazraji al-Madani, Abu ʾl-Harith (d. 132/749–50) 210
al-Khudri, Abu Saʿid Saʿd b. Malik b. Sinan al-Khazraji (d. ca 74/693) 118, 125, 155, 163, 210, 242
al-Khuldi, Jaʿfar see Jaʿfar b. Muhammad b. Nusayr
Khurasan(ians) 5, 11, 20–1, 30, 36–9, 44–5, 58, 69–70, 72, 160, 173, 206, 237, 240, 256, 391
Khuzistan 381–2
al-Kudaymi see Muhammad b. Yunus b. Musa
Kufa 22, 41, 60, 63, 91–2, 124, 187–8, 201, 262, 296, 310–12, 387
Kuradabadh 39
Kurdistan 162
Kurz b. Wabra, Abu ʿAbdallah (d. 110/728–9) 399

L
Laughter 151, 175, 402
[Divine] Law (Shariʿa) 3, 17, 20, 293–5, 371, 405, 414–15
Layla 139, 329
al-Layth 278
al-Layth b. Saʿd b. ʿAbd al-Rahman al-Fahmi al-Misri, Abu ʾl-Harith (d. 175/791) 262, 346
Lebanon 73, 267, 301, 377
Lights (lawaʾih) 78, 99, 245, 252, 271–2, 276, 323, 334, 407

Lion(s)   57, 186, 205–6, 236, 366–8, 374, 378–9, 384, 387–9
Listening to music (*samaʿ*)   342–56, 408
Longing *see* Passionate longing and Desire
Love (*mahabba; hubb*)   7, 313–17, 325–38
Lover/Beloved (*muhibb/habib*)   106, 142–3, 150, 187, 199, 200, 208–9, 279, 286–7, 290, 302–3, 313–14, 317–19, 327–33, 334–5, 350
al-Lukam (or Lukkam)   169, 243
Luqman   255
Lust *see* Passion and Desire

M

Maʿbad (probably Maʿbad b. ʿAbdallah b. Ukaym al-Juhani, murdered in 83/702–3)   171
al-Madaʾin   51
al-Maghazili, ʿAbdallah   26, 47, 51
al-Maghazili, Abu ʿAli al-Asamm al-Baghdadi   351, 384
Maghrib(i)   64, 351
al-Maghribi *see* Abu ʿAbdallah al-Maghribi *or* Abu ʿUthman al-Maghribi *or* Habib al-Maghribi
Magian(s)   151, 238, 257
al-Mahamili, Abu ʿAbadallah al-Husayn b. Ismaʿil b. Muhammad b. Ismaʿil b. Saʿid b. Aban al-Dabbi (d. 330/941)   26
Mahfuz b. Mahmud al-Naysaburi (d. 303/915–6 or 304/916–7)   143, 284
Maidens of Paradise (*houries*)   206, 349, 355, 381, 398
Majnun   329
Makhlad b. al-Husayn al-Azdi al-Muhallabi al-Basri (d. 191/806–7)   158, 285
Makhul b. Abi Muslim Shuhrab al-Shami al-Hudhali, Abu ʿAbdallah (d. 112–119/730–737)   175, 222, 313
al-Makhzumi, Muhammad b. al-Hasan   185–6
al-Malamati *see* Muhammad b. Ahmad al-Malamati
Malamatiyya   38, 39, 42, 44–5, 63
Malik (angel)   397
Malik b. Anas b. Malik b. Abi ʿAmir al-Asbahi al-Himyari, Abu ʿAbdallah (d. 179/795)   150, 210, 262–3, 280–1, 325–6, 342–3, 397
Malik b. Dinar, Abu Yahya (d. 131/748–9 or earlier)   131, 148, 152, 160, 255, 275, 286, 298–9, 339, 395, 399
Malik b. Masʿud   124
Malik b. Mighwal b. ʿAsim b. Ghaziya b. Haritha al-Kufi, Abu ʿAbdallah (d. 159/776, possibly earlier)   145
Maʿmar b. Rashid al-Azdi al-Basri, Abu ʿUrwa (d. 152/769 or 153/770)   138, 232, 325
Manbij   258
Manliness (*muruwa*)   176–7, 237–8
Mansur b. ʿAbdallah (al-Dhuhli or al-Isbahani; possibly the same as Mansur b. ʿAbdallah b. Khalid)   31–2, 38, 44, 62, 63–4, 66, 71, 85, 114, 119–21 123–4, 150, 178, 223, 224, 246, 271–3, 282, 285–7, 309–10, 329, 331–2, 357, 379
Mansur b. ʿAbdallah al-Dimarti al-Isbahani, Abu ʾl-Hasan   357
Mansur b. ʿAbdallah b. Khalid b. Ahmad al-Khalidi al-Dhuhli, Abu ʿAli (d. ca 400/1009–10)   8, 14, 19, 62, 63–4, 85, 114, 119–21, 123, 150, 168, 187
Mansur b. Abi Muzahim Bashir al-Turki al-Baghdadi, Abu Nasr (d. 235/850)   392
al-Mansur, Abu Jaʿfar (caliph; r. 136–158/754–775)   133, 308
Mansur b. Ahmad al-Harbi   181–2
Mansur b. ʿAmmar al-Dandanaqani, Abu ʾl-Sari (d. 225/839–40)   42, 153–4
Mansur al-Faqih *see* Mansur b. Muhammad b. Ibrahim al-Faqih
Mansur b. Khalaf al-Maghribi   96–7, 146–7, 240, 285, 295, 303, 308, 315, 368, 374, 398–9
Mansur al-Maghribi *see* Mansur b. Khalaf al-Maghribi
Mansur b. Muhammad b. Ibrahim al-Faqih, Abu Nasr   37, 231
Mansur b. al-Muʿtamir b. ʿAbdallah b. Rabiʿa al-Kufi, Abu ʿAttab (d. 132/749–50)   222–4
al-Maraghi *see* Abu Muhammad al-Maraghi
Mardawayh al-Saʿigh *see* ʿAbd al-Samad b. Yazid al-Saʿigh
Marhum b. ʿAbd al-ʿAziz b. Mihran al-ʿAttar al-Umawi, Abu Muhammad (d. 188/803–4)   334, 339
al-Maristani *see* Ibrahim b. Ahmad al-Maristani
Market-place *see* Bazaar
Maʿruf b. Fayruz al-Karkhi, Abu Mahfuz (d. 200/815–6)   21–3, 130, 155, 255, 277, 289–90, 305–6, 338, 378, 380–1, 392
Marw/Merv   8, 20, 25, 42, 58, 68, 141, 298
Marwan b. Muʿawiya b. al-Harith b. Asmaʾ b. Kharija al-Fazari al-Kufi, Abu ʿAbdallah (d. 193/808–9)   149, 257
al-Marwazi, Abu Zayd *see* Muhammad b. Ahmad b. ʿAbdallah b. Muhammad al-Marwazi
Mary   133, 363–4, 396
al-Masʿudi *see* ʿAbd al-Rahman b. ʿAbdallah b. ʿUtba
Maymun al-Ghazzal, Abu ʿAbdallah   30
al-Mayyafariqini *see* Abu ʾl-Azhar al-Mayyafariqini
al-Mazabili *see* Abu Yaʿqub al-Mazabili
Mecca   9, 17–18, 20–1, 33, 35, 41, 49, 57, 60–1, 67–9, 72, 86, 117–18, 130, 132, 154, 158, 182–8, 191, 195–6, 200, 212, 243, 249–50, 255, 262, 284, 287, 298, 301–2, 313, 316–19, 333, 343, 369–70, 376, 378, 381–3, 389, 391, 397, 401
Medina   17, 71, 164–5, 188, 241, 249, 258, 275–6, 302, 316, 342, 360, 372–4, 385, 389, 398
Meditation (*tafakkur; fikr; fikra*) *see* Contemplation/Self-scrutiny

Meshhed 54, 247
Mesopotamia 162
Michael (angel) 147
al-Mihrijani *see* Ahmad b. Muhammad b. Ibrahim
Mimshadh al-Dinawari (d. 299/911–2) 59, 140, 185, 214, 314, 317, 347, 354
Mimshadh b. Saʿid al-ʿUkbari, Abu ʿAli 335
Mina 376
Minjab b. al-Harith b. ʿAbd al-Rahman al-Tamimi al-Kufi, Abu Muhammad (d. 231/845–6) 188
al-Miqdad b. ʿAmr b. Thaʿlaba b. Malik al-Kindi, Abu Maʿbad yuʿrafu bi-Ibn al-Aswad (d. 33/653–4) 228
Miracle [of a friend of God]/Divine grace (*karama*) 218, 270, 357–8
Modesty (*tawaduʿ*)/Humility (*khushuʿ*) 19, 161–6, 170, 215, 270, 277, 279, 286, 322–3, 349, 410
[Mystical] Moment (*waqt*) 75–7, 96, 100–1, 106, 141, 205–6, 265, 267, 274–5, 286, 289–90, 295–6, 320, 324, 349, 356, 370, 412, 415
Money 27, 37–8, 74, 132, 154, 165, 176, 182, 183, 185, 196, 241, 244, 257, 258–62, 277, 284, 287, 302, 304, 376, 380, 382, 401, 416
Monk(s) 122, 142, 236, 280, 373, 376, 415
Moral character (*khuluq*) 252–7, 289, 300, 370, 401
Moral character *see also* Character Traits
Moses (Musa) 18, 26, 94, 97, 101, 131, 163, 164, 172–3, 177, 190, 207, 217, 228, 235, 256, 276, 277, 283, 291, 299, 306, 337, 339, 351, 355–6, 363
Mosul 248
Muʿadh b. Jabal b. ʿAmr b. Aws b. ʿAʾid al-Ansari al-Khazraji, Abu ʿAbd al-Rahman (d. 18/639) 140–1, 144, 167, 232, 346
Muʿadh b. al-Muthanna 257
Muʿadh al-Nasafi 281
Muʿafa b. ʿImran b. Nufayl al-Azdi al-Mawsili, Abu Masʿud (d. 184–6/800–2) 26, 171
Muʿalla b. Mahdi 252
Muʿawiyya b. Abi Sufyan Sakhr b. Harb b. Umayya (ruled 41–60/661–680) 173, 208–9, 254, 263
al-Mubarrad *see* Muhammad b. Yazid b. ʿAbd al-Akbar
Mughira b. Abi Qurra ʿUbayd b. Qays al-Sadusi al-Basri 179
Muhammad/Prophet 4, 5, 12, 15–17, 20, 25, 28, 35, 39, 42–3, 44, 46, 52, 56, 59, 70–1, 73, 79, 85, 91–2, 97, 101, 103, 111, 125, 127–30, 132–4, 148–9, 152, 161, 164–5, 167, 171, 174, 178–83, 188, 190–3, 195, 197, 201–3, 206, 208–10, 212–13, 217–18, 220, 222–3, 226, 228, 230–2, 237, 246, 249, 252–5, 257, 265, 269, 270, 274–6, 280–1, 283–5, 292–3, 295–6, 302–3, 312–13, 325–6, 329–30, 334, 338–9, 343–4, 356–7, 360, 364, 367, 392, 395–6, 398, 401–2
Muhammad b. al-ʿAbbas 27
Muhammad b. al-ʿAbbas b. al-Dirafsh al-Dimashqi 165
Muhammad b. ʿAbd al-ʿAziz al-Marwazi, Abu Bakr 58
Muhammad b. ʿAbd al-ʿAziz the Muezzin (*al-muʿadhdhin*), Abu ʾl-Husayn 38
Muhammad b. ʿAbd al-Malik 226
Muhammad b. ʿAbd Rabbihi (al-Hadrami) 221, 275
Muhammad b. ʿAbd al-Rahman b. ʿUbayd al-Qurashi al-Tamimi, a client of the Al Talha tribe 142
Muhammad b. ʿAbd al-Wahhab al-ʿAsqalani *see* Abu Qirsafa Muhammad
Muhammad b. ʿAbd al-Wahhab b. Habib b. Mihran al-ʿAbdi al-Naysaburi al-Farraʿ, Abu Ahmad (d. 272/885–6) 226
Muhammad b. ʿAbdallah 9, 138, 157–8, 205, 232, 234, 243
Muhammad b. ʿAbdallah b. ʿAbd al-ʿAziz al-Tabari, Abu Bakr 49, 55, 288
Muhammad b. ʿAbdallah al-Farghani *see* al-Farghani, Abu Jaʿfar
Muhammad b. ʿAbdallah al-Khuzaʿi 337
Muhammad b. ʿAbdallah b. Muhammad b. ʿAbd al-ʿAziz b. Shadhan al-Waʿiz al-Razi, Abu Bakr (d. 376/986) 5–6, 9, 20, 22–5, 37, 43, 49, 68, 120, 138, 140, 155, 164, 169, 183, 199, 213–15, 222, 226–7, 232, 234, 243, 253, 264, 271–2, 308, 323, 325, 346, 356
Muhammad b. ʿAbdallah b. Mutarrif (or Matraf) 387
Muhammad b. ʿAbdallah al-Razi *see* Muhammad b. ʿAbdallah b. Muhammad b. ʿAbd al-ʿAziz
Muhammad b. ʿAbdallah b. Shadhan *see* Muhammad b. ʿAbdallah b. Muhammad b. ʿAbd al-ʿAziz b. Shadhan
Muhammad b. ʿAbdallah al-Shirazi *see* Ibn Bakuya
Muhammad b. ʿAbdallah al-Sufi *see* Ibn Bakawayh/Bakuya
Muhammad b. ʿAbdallah al-Tabari *see* Muhammad b. ʿAbdallah b. ʿAbd al-ʿAziz
Muhammad b. ʿAbdallah b. ʿUbaydallah 158–61
Muhammad b. ʿAbdallah al-Waʿiz *see* Muhammad b. ʿAbdallah b. Muhammad b. ʿAbd al-ʿAziz b. Shadhan
Muhammad b. ʿAbdun b. ʿIsa al-Qattan, Abu Bakr 185, 227
Muhammad b. Abi Bakr b. ʿAli b. ʿAtaʾ b. Muqaddam al-Muqaddami al-Thaqafi al-Basri, Abu ʿAbdallah (d. 234/848–9) 225–6
Muhammad b. Abi ʾl-Furat *see* Muhammad b. al-Furat
Muhammad b. Abi Humayd Ibrahim al-Ansari al-Zuraqi, Abu Ibrahim 173

Muhammad b. Ahmad   117
Muhammad b. Ahmad, Abu Bakr al-Qindili *see* Abu Bakr Muhammad b. Ahmad
Muhammad b. Ahmad b. ʿAbdallah b. Muhammad al-Marwazi *see* Abu Zayd Muhammad b. Ahmad b. ʿAbdallah
Muhammad b. Ahmad al-ʿAbdi   306
Muhammad b. Ahmad b. ʿAbdus al-Hiri al-Muzakki al-ʿAdl, Abu Bakr   142–3, 226, 264, 393
Muhammad b. Ahmad al-Balkhi *see* Abu Bakr Muhammad b. Ahmad al-Balkhi
Muhammad b. Ahmad b. Dalawayh (Dalluya) al-Daqqaq, Abu Bakr   142, 215, 221
Muhammad b. Ahmad al-Farisi *see* Abu ʾl-Husayn al-Farisi
Muhammad b. Ahmad b. Hamdan b. ʿAli b. ʿAbdallah b. Sinan al-Hiri al-Naysaburi, Abu ʿAmr (d. 376/987, possibly later)   45, 209
Muhammad b. Ahmad b. Hamdun, Abu Bakr al-Farraʾ (d. 370/980–1)   11, 49–50, 121, 126, 166–7, 233
Muhammad b. Ahmad b. Harun (al-ʿUdi?)   165
Muhammad b. Ahmad b. Harun al-ʿUdi   273
Muhammad b. Ahmad al-Isbahani   310
Muhammad b. Ahmad al-Juzjani   229
Muhammad b. Ahmad al-Malamati   46
Muhammad b. Ahmad al-Marwazi *see* Abu Zayd Muhammad b. Ahmad b. ʿAbdallah
Muhammad b. Ahmad b. Muhammad b. Jaʿfar *see* Ibn al-Haddad
Muhammad b. Ahmad b. Muhammad b. Sahl al-Sayrafi, Abu ʾl-Fadl (d. 347/958)   20, 180, 208, 322
Muhammad b. Ahmad b. Muhammad al-Tamimi *see* Abu Hatim al-Sijistani
Muhammad b. Ahmad b. Muhammad b. Yahya al-Sufi *see* Abu Hatim al-Sijistani al-Sufi
Muhammad b. Ahmad al-Najjar   298, 371, 411
Muhammad b. Ahmad b. al-Qasim   334
Muhammad b. Ahmad b. Sahl *see* Muhammad b. Ahmad b. Muhammad b. Sahl
Muhammad b. Ahmad b. Saʿid al Razi al-Mukattib, Abu Jaʿfar   159, 193, 294, 321, 322
Muhammad b. Ahmad b. al-Sakan   242
Muhammad b. Ahmad al-Sufi *see* Abu Hatim al-Sijistani al-Sufi
Muhammad b. Ahmad b. Tahir al Sufi   201
Muhammad b. Ahmad al-Tamimi *see* Abu Hatim al-Sijistani
Muhammad b. Ahmad al-ʿUdi *see* Muhammad b. Ahmad b. Harun al-ʿUdi
Muhammad b. Ahmad b. Yahya *see* Abu Hatim al-Sijistani al-Sufi
Muhammad b. Ahmad b. Yaʿqub al-Tusi, Abu Nasr   226

Muhammad b. ʿAli b. ʿAbdallah b. Yaʿqub b. Ismaʿil al-Sulami, Abu ʾl-Hasan, yuʿrafu biʾl-Hibri   143
Muhammad b. ʿAli al-ʿAlawi   159, 298, 329
Muhammad b. ʿAli al-Hafiz   13
Muhammad b. ʿAli al-Hibri *see* Muhammad b. ʿAli b. ʿAbdallah b. Yaʿqub
Muhammad b. ʿAli b. al-Husayn   179
Muhammad b. ʿAli b. al-Husayn al-Muqriʿ   381–2
Muhammad b. ʿAli al-Juzi (al-Jawzi), Abu ʿAbdallah   382
Muhammad b. ʿAli al-Kattani *see* al-Kattani, Abu Bakr Muhammad b. ʿAli
Muhammad b. ʿAli al-Marwazi *see* Muhammad b. ʿAli b. Shaqiq
Muhammad b. ʿAli b. Muhammad al-Mukharrimi   405
Muhammad b. ʿAli al-Nahawandi, Abu Mansur   144
Muhammad b. ʿAli al-Qassab *see* al-Qassab, Abu Jaʿfar
Muhammad b. ʿAli al-Takriti, Abu Bakr   387
Muhammad b. ʿAli al-Tirmidhi *see* al-Tirmidhi, Abu ʿAbdallah
Muhammad b. ʿAmmar al-Hamadani, Abu ʿAbdallah   289
Muhammad b. ʿAmr b. ʿAlqama b. Waqqas al-Laythi al-Madani, Abu ʿAbdallah (d. 144–5/761–3)   280
Muhammad b. ʿAmr b. ʿAtaʾ b. ʿAbbas b. ʿAlqama al-ʿAmiri al-Qurashi al-Madani, Abu ʿAbdallah   155, 181
Muhammad b. Ashras   320
Muhammad b. ʿAtiya   369
Muhammad b. ʿAwf b. Sufyan al-Taʿi al-Himsi, Abu Jaʿfar (d. 272–3/885–7)   365
Muhammad b. Ayyub   334
Muhammad b. Bakr b. ʿUthman al-Bursani al-Basri, Abu ʿAbdallah (d. ca 203/819)   344
Muhammad al-Baqir *see* Muhammad b. ʿAli b. al-Husayn b. ʿAli b. Abi Talib
Muhammad b. Bishr   158
Muhammad b. Dawud al-Dinawari *see* al-Duqqi, Abu Bakr Muhammad b. Dawud
Muhammad b. Dawud b. Sulayman al-Zahid al-Naysaburi (d. 342/953)   129
Muhammad b. al-Fadl b. al-ʿAbbas b. Hafs, Abu ʿAbdallah al-Balkhi (d. 319/931)   49, 120, 136, 290, 325, 330, 341–2, 382–3
Muhammad b. (al-)Fadl b. Jabir   111, 125, 161, 330
Muhammad b. al-Faraj b. ʿAbd al-Warith al-Baghdadi-al-Qurashi al-Azraq, Abu ʿAbdallah (d. 236/850–1)   297
Muhammad b. Farhan   177, 339, 374
Muhammad b. Faris al-Farisi   385

Muhammad al-Farraʾ *see* Muhammad b. Ahmad b. Hamdun
Muhammad b. al-Furat al-Tamimi al-Kufi, Abu ʿAli 264
Muhammad b. Ghalib *see* Tamtam, Abu Jaʿfar
Muhammad b. Hamid b. Muhammad b. Ibrahim b. Ismaʿil al-Sulami al-Khurasani, Abu Ahmad 19, 38, 119, 123, 179
Muhammad b. Harun b. Humayd, Abu Bakr 269
Muhammad b. Harun al-Muqri 269
Muhammad b. al-Hasan *see* al-Shaybani, Abu ʿAbdallah
Muhammad b. al-Hasan 138, 145
Muhammad b. al-Hasan al-ʿAlawi 305
Muhammad b. al-Hasan al-ʿAsqalani 387
Muhammad b. al-Hasan al-Baghdadi *see* Abu ʾl-ʿAbbas al-Khashshab
Muhammad b. al-Hasan b. Khalid al-Baghdadi 216
Muhammad b. al-Hasan b. al-Khashshab *see* Abu ʾl-ʿAbbas al-Khashshab
Muhammad b. al-Hasan al-Mukharrimi *see* Abu ʾl-ʿAbbas al-Khahshsab
Muhammad b. al-Hasan b. Qutayba al-ʿAsqalani (d. 310/922–3) 129
Muhammad b. al-Hassan *see* Abu ʿUbayd al-Busri
Muhammad b. Hassan 266
Muhammad b. al-Husayn *see* al-Jawhari *or* Muhammad b. al-Husayn al-Baghdadi *or* Muhammad b. al-Husayn al-Bastami *or* Muhammad b. al-Husayn b. al-Hasan b. Khalil *or* Muhammad b. al-Husayn b. Muhammad *or* Muhammad b. al-Husayn al-Qattan *or* al-Sulami, Abu ʿAbd al-Rahman
Muhammad b. al-Husayn al-ʿAlawi *see* Abu ʾl-Hasan al-Hamadhani al-ʿAlawi
Muhammad b. al-Husayn al-Baghdadi 43–4, 52–3, 251–2, 383–4
Muhammad b. al-Husayn al-Bistami 251
Muhammad b. al-Husayn b. al-Hasan b. al-Khalil, Abu Bakr 173
Muhammad b. al-Husayn b. Muhammad b. al-Fadl al-Azraq al-Qattan, Abu ʾl-Husayn (d. 415/1024) 114–17, 136, 191, 205, 211–12, 215–16, 223–4, 227–33, 235–7, 243, 246, 249, 283–6, 294, 299, 301, 305, 308, 329–31, 338, 390
Muhammad b. al-Husayn al-Qattan, Abu Bakr (possibly, the same as above) 138, 390
Muhammad b. Ibrahim b. al-Fadl al-Hashimi 115, 231
Muhammad b. Ibrahim b. al-Harith b. Khalid al-Qurashi al-Taymi, Abu ʿAbdallah (d. 119/737–8) 209
Muhammad b. Ibrahim al-Ismaʿili, Abu Saʿid 173, 226

Muhammad b. ʿIsa 196
Muhammad b. Ismaʿil 36, 60
Muhammad b. Ismaʿil al-Farghani, Abu Bakr 298
Muhammad b. Ismaʿil b. Ibrahim b. Mughira al-Bukhari al-Juʿfi (d. 256/870) 201
Muhammad b. Jaʿfar 138
Muhammad b. Jaʿfar al-Baghdadi *see* Abu Bakr Muhammad b. Jaʿfar
Muhammad b. Jaʿfar al-Imam 339
Muhammad b. Jaʿfar al-Khassaf 220
Muhammad b. Jaʿfar b. Muhammad 180
Muhammad b. Jaʿfar b. Muhammad b. al-Haytham b. ʿImran b. Burayd al-Anbari, Abu Bakr al-Bundar (d. 360/970) 280
Muhammad b. Jaʿfar b. Muhammad b. Matar 344
Muhammad b. Jaʿfar al-Naysaburi *see* Abu ʿAmr b. Matar
Muhammad b. Kathir b. Abi ʿAtaʾ al-Thaqafi al-Sanʿani al-Massisi (d. 216/831–2 or later) 162
Muhammad b. Kathir al-Qurashi al-Kufi, Abu Ishaq 242
Muhammad b. Khalid *see* Muhammad b. al-Hasan b. Khalid
Muhammad b. Khuzayma 278
Muhammad b. al-Layth b. Muhammad b. Yazid al-Jawhari, Abu Bakr (d. 297/910 or 299/912) 36
Muhammad b. al-Mahbub 8
Muhammad b. Makhlad b. Hafs al-Duri al-ʿAttar, Abu ʿAbdallah (d. 331/943) 160, 226
Muhammad b. Mansur b. Dawud b. Ibrahim al-Tusi, Abu Jaʿfar (d. 254/868) 378
Muhammad b. Mardawayh 237
Muhammad b. Masruq 28
Muhammad b. Mirdas al-Ansari al Basri, Abu ʿAbdallah (d. 249/863–4) 197
Muhammad b. Muʿammar, Abu Bakr 51, 390–1
Muhammad b. Muʿawiyya b. Aʿyan al-Naysaburi, Abu ʿAli (d. 229/843–4) 167
Muhammad b. al-Mubarak b. Yaʿla al-Qurasi al-Suri al-Qalanisi, Abu ʿAbdallah (d. 215/830) 373
Muhammad b. Muhammad b. ʿAbd al-Rahim 222
Muhammad b. Muhammad b. ʿAbd al-Wahhab 320
Muhammad b. Muhammad b. Ahmad b. Ishaq al-Hakim al-Kabir al-Naysaburi, al-Karabisi, Abu Ahmad (d. 378/988) 288
Muhammad b. Muhammad b. Ahyad b. Mujahid al-Qattan al-Balkhi, Abu Bakr (d. probably 347/958–9) 53
Muhammad b. Muhammad b. Ghalib, Abu Bakr 6, 181
Muhammad b. Muhammad al-Jurjani 38

Muhammad b. al-Munkadir b. ʿAbdallah b.
   al-Hudayr al-Taymi (d. possibly 130/747–8)
   167, 206
Muhammad b. Musa *see* al-Wasiti, Abu Bakr
   Muhammad b. Musa
Muhammad b. Musa al-Hulwani   175
Muhammad b. al-Musayyib b. Ishaq al-Naysaburi
   al-Arghiyani al-Isfanji (d. 315/927–8)   145
Muhammad b. Muslim *see* Abu ʾl Zubayr
   Muhammad b. Muslim *or* al-Zuhri,
   Muhammad b. Muslim
Muhammad b. al-Nadr al-Harithi, Abu ʿAbd
   al-Rahman   306
Muhammad b. Nasr b. Mansur b. ʿAbd al-Rahman
   b. Hisham al-Saʿigh, Abu Jaʿfar (d. 297/910)
   142, 163, 237
Muhammad b. al-Qasim al-ʿAtaki   320
Muhammad b. al-Rumi   115, 231
Muhammad b. Saʿid *see* Abu Bakr al-Harbi
Muhammad b. Saʿid al-Basri   389
Muhammad b. Saʿid b. Sulayman b. ʿAbdallah al-Kufi,
   Abu Jaʿfar b. al-Isbahani (d. 220/835)   138
Muhammad b. Salih b. Mihran al-maʿruf bi-Ibn
   al-Nattah, Abu ʿAbdallah or Abu Jaʿfar
   (d. 252/866)   229
Muhammad b. Sawwar al-Basri   33
Muhammad b. Sirin *see* Ibn Sirin, Abu Bakr
   Muhammad
Muhammad b. Tahir b. Muhammad *see* Abu Nasr
   al-Waziri
Muhammad al-Tusi al-Muaʿllim (possibly the same
   as Muhammad b. Mansur b. Dawud)   399
Muhammad b. ʿUmar b. al-Fadl b. Ghalib b. Salama
   al-Juʿfi, Abu ʿAbdallah (d. 361/972)   23
Muhammad b. ʿUmar al-Ramli   339
Muhammad b. Usayd al-Raqqi, Abu Tahir   174
Muhammad b. ʿUthman   145
Muhammad b. Wasiʿ b. Jabir b. al-Akhnas al-Azdi,
   Abu ʿAbdallah (or Abu Bakr) (d. 120/737)
   286
Muhammad b. Yazid b. ʿAbd al-Akbar al-Thumali
   al-Azdi al-Mubarrad, Abu ʾl-ʿAbbas
   (d. 285/898)   208
Muhammad b. Yazid al-Qaratisi   222
Muhammad b. Yunus b. Musa b. Sulayman
   al-Kudaymi al-Sami al-Basri, Abu ʾl-ʿAbbas
   (d. 286/899–900)   205, 345
Muhammad b. Yusuf   30
Muhammad b. Yusuf al-Bannaʿ   370
Muhammad b. Yusuf b. Waqid b. ʿUthman
   al-Firyabi (d. 212/827)   129
Muhammad b. Zakariya al-Muqaddasi (al-Maqdisi),
   Abu Talib   222
al-Muhasibi, Abu ʿAbdallah al-Harith b. Asad
   (d. 243/857)   28, 41–3, 54, 114, 131, 184,
   209, 225, 238, 253, 330, 347
Muhriz b. ʿAbdallah al-Jazari, Abu ʾl-Rajaʿ   175

Mujahid b. Jabr al-Makki, Abu ʾl-Hajjaj (d. 104/772)
   125, 162, 349
al-Mukharrimi *see* Abu ʾl-ʿAbbas al-Khashshab *or*
   Muhammad b. ʿAli b. Muhammad
Mulqabadh   60, 62
al-Munadi *see* Abu ʾl-Qasim al-Munadi
al-Munkadir b. Muhammad b. al-Munkadir
   al-Qurashi al-Taymi al-Madani (d. 180/796-7)
   175
al-Muqaddami *see* Muhammad b. Abi Bakr b. ʿAli b.
   ʿAtaʿ
Muriq *see* Muwarriq b. Mushamrij
Murra b. Sharahil al-Hamdani al-Saksaki al-Kufi
   al-maʿruf bi-Murra al-Tayyib wa-Murra
   al-Khayr, Abu Ismaʿil (d. 76/695–6)   226
al-Murtaʿish, Abu Muhammad ʿAbdallah b.
   Muhammad (d. 328/939–40)   46, 62, 72,
   120, 190, 205, 242, 251, 284–5, 371
Musa b. Dawud al-Dabbi al-Tarsusi al-Khulqani
   (d. 217/832–3)   242
Musa b. al-Hajjaj   275
Musa b. Hayyan   226
Musa b. ʿIsa al-Bastami *see* ʿAmmi al-Bastami/
   al-Bistami
Musa b. Ismaʿil al-Minqari al-Tabudhaki al-Basri,
   Abu Salama (d. 223/837–8)   201
Musa b. Wardan al-Qurashi al-ʿAmiri al-Basri, Abu
   ʿUmar (d. 117/735–6)   173
Musʿab b. Shayba b. Jubayr b. Shayba b. ʿUthman
   b. Abi Talha b. ʿAbd al-ʿUzza al-ʿAbdari
   al-Makki al-Hujjabi   292
Musabbih b. Hatim al-ʿUqli   306
Muslim al-Aʿwar *see* Muslim b. Kaysan
Muslim b. Kaysan al-Dabbi al-Mulaʿi al-Barrad
   al-Aʿwar, Abu ʿAbdallah   161
Muslim b. Salim   151
al-Musuhi, Abu ʿAli al-Hasan b. ʿAli   57
al-Musuhi, Muhammad   286
al-Mutanabbi, Abu ʾl-Tayyib Ahmad b. al-Husayn
   b. al-Hasan b. ʿAbd al-Samad al-Juʿfi al-Kufi
   (killed 354/965)   263
Mutarrif b. ʿAbdallah b. al-Shikhkhir al-ʿAmiri
   al-Harashi, Abu ʿAbdallah (d. probably
   87/706)   261
al-Mutarriz   244
al-Mutawakkil, Jaʿfar b. Muhammad (ruled
   232-247/847–861)   19
Muʿtazilite(s)   9–10, 14, 65, 309, 397
Muwarriq (or Muriq) b. Mushamrij al-ʿIjli al-Basri,
   Abu Muʿtamir (d. ca 100/718)   258
al-Muzaffar al-Jassas   385
al-Muzaffar al-Qirmisini   65, 286
al-Muzakki *see* ʿAbd al-Rahman b. Ibrahim b.
   Muhammad b. Yahya al-Muzakki *or* Ibrahim
   b. Muhammad b. Yahya al-Muzakki
al-Muzani, Ismaʿil b. Yahya b. Ismaʿil al-Misri, Abu
   Ibrahim (d. 264/877–8)   212

al-Muzayyin al-Kabir (the Elder), Abu Jaʿfar (sometimes difficult to distinguish from the one below)   285, 291, 300, 316–18
al-Muzayyin al-Saghir (the Junior), Abu ʾl-Hasan ʿAli b. Muhammad (d. 328/939–40)   65, 285, 291, 318

N
al-Nadir   161
al-Nadr b. Shumayl b. Kharasha b. Yazid al-Mazini al-Tamimi (d. 203/818–9)   388
Nafiʿ mawla ʿAbdallah b. ʿUmar al-Madani, Abu ʿAbdallah (d. 117/735 or later)   226, 281
Nafiʿ b. Hurmuz, Abu Hurmuz   125
al-Nahrajuri, Abu Yaʿqub Ishaq b. Muhammad b. Ayyub (d. 330/941–2)   59, 64–5, 180, 196, 318, 322, 331, 347
al-Nakhaʿi see Ibrahim b. Yazid b. al-Aswad
al-Naqqash   284
Nasa (city)   240, 244
al-Nasibini see Abu ʿAbdallah al-Nasibini
Nasr b. Abi Nasr see Nasr b. Muhammad b. Ahmad
Nasr b. Ahmad   34
Nasr b. Ahmad b. ʿAbd al-Malik, Abu ʾl-Fath   279
Nasr b. al-Faraj, Abu Hamza   380
Nasr al-Kharrat   385
Nasr b. Muhammad b. Ahmad b. Yaʿqub b. Abi Nasr al-ʿAttar al-Tusi, Abu ʾl-Fadl   26, 176
al-Nasrabadhi, Abu ʾl-Qasim Ibrahim b. Muhammad (d. 366/976–7)   10–11, 72–3, 87–8, 121, 126, 135, 137, 150, 204, 212–13, 222, 237–8, 242, 267, 271, 300–1, 305, 329, 336, 356
Naysabur/Nishapur   8, 11, 37–9, 42, 44–5, 60–3, 69, 71–2, 77–8, 92, 143, 240, 244, 246, 251, 261, 270, 278, 297, 399
Nibaj   41, 158
al-Nibaji, Abu ʿAbdallah Saʿid b. Yazzid   53, 212, 398, 401
Nihawand   43, 360
Nishapur see Naysabur
Noah   142, 162
[Sufi] Novice see Aspirant
Nuʿaym b. Muwarriʿ b. Tawba b. Abi ʾl-Asad Kaysan b. Rashid al-Basri   229
Nuʿaym b. Salim al-Qurashi   303
Nuba   19
Nuh al-ʿAyyar al-Naysaburi (al-Nishapuri)   240
al-Nuri, Abu ʾl-Husayn Ahmad   64, 67–8, 84, 98, 105, 115, 144, 184, 195, 209, 245, 258–9, 268, 285, 287, 290, 315, 330–1, 348, 369, 385, 389
al-Nuri, Abu ʾl-Husayn Ahmad b. Muhammad (d. 295/907–8)   8, 10, 46–7, 56, 58

O
Occurrence/Divine visitation (*warid*)   108, 246, 347, 354, 412

Oman   301
Oneness of God/Declaration of oneness of God (*tawhid*)   13, 122, 180, 218–19, 266, 293–4, 306–12, 405
Outward/Inward (*zahir/batin*)   145, 205, 223, 245, 256, 264, 271–2, 294, 408–10, 415

P
Palestine   47, 374
Paradise   8, 10, 24, 27, 38, 72, 133, 144, 147, 161, 162, 167, 173, 179, 186, 192, 206–8, 227, 233, 235, 256–7, 267, 270, 278, 281, 296, 315, 317, 337–9, 355, 359, 393–4, 398–9, 401
Passion (*hawaʾ*)   85–6, 119, 143, 161, 167, 170, 187, 221, 316–17, 330–3, 334–7
see also Desire
Passionate longing (*ʿishq, shawq*)   78, 93–4, 264–5, 279, 317, 327, 332, 335–9
see also Desire
Patience (*sabr*)   197–202, 213, 215, 274, 286
Perspicacity see Spiritual Insight
Pharaoh   10, 42, 337
Pilgrimage (*hajj*)   92, 111–12, 120, 154, 165, 170, 178, 183–4, 186, 203, 212, 219, 224, 251, 255, 297–8, 333, 373, 375–8, 389, 410
Potiphar (al-ʿAziz)   334
Poverty (*faqr*)   19, 136, 159, 211, 229, 257, 280–8, 402, 407
Prayer/Supplication (*wird*; pl. *awrad*)   84, 300
see also Supplicatory Prayer and Canonical Prayer
Presence [with God] (*hudur, muhadara*)   3, 91–3, 97–8, 145–6, 194–5, 295, 349, 408
Pride/Hubris (*kibr; takabbur*)   106–7, 161, 170–1
Prophet (Muhammad) see Muhammad
Prophetic custom see Sunna
Proximity to God (*qurb*)   103–5, 115, 150, 207, 232–3, 268, 272–3, 295, 308–9, 409

Q
Qabisa b. ʿUqba b. Muhammad b. Sufyan b. ʿUqba b. Rabiʿa al-Suwaʿi al-Kufi, Abu ʿAmir (d. 215/830–1)   280
al-Qahtabi, Abu Bakr   80
al-Qalanisi, Abu Ahmad Musʿab b. Ahmad Musʿab (d. 270/884 or later)   50, 304
al-Qaʿnabi, Abu ʿAbd al-Rahman ʿAbdallah b. Maslama b. Qaʿnab al-Harithi (d. 221/835–6)   122
al-Qannad, Abu ʾl-Hasan ʿAli b. ʿAbd al-Rahman al-Wasiti (d. probably 330/941)   223, 311
al-Qarafi see Abu ʾl-Husayn al-Qarafi
al-Qaratisi see Muhammad b. Yazid al-Qaratisi *or* ʿUmar b. Saʿid b. ʿAbd al-Rahman
Qarmatis/Carmathians   55, 249
Qasim b. Ahmad   30
al-Qasim b. Muhammad   145

al-Qasim b. Muhammad b. Abi Bakr al-Siddiq,
    Abu Muhammad (d. 106/724–5, or somewhat
    earlier)   320
al-Qasim b. Munabbih b. Yasin al-Harbi, Abu
    Muhammad   305
al-Qasim b. al-Qasim *see* al-Sayyari, Abu ʾl-ʿAbbas
    al-Qasim b. al-Qasim
al-Qassab, Abu Jaʿfar Muhammad b. ʿAli al-Sufi
    (d. 275/888–9)   43, 50, 289
al-Qassar *see* Hamdun al-Qassar *or* al-Raqqi, Abu
    Ishaq
Qasyun (mount)   65
Qatada b. Diʿama b. Qatada b. ʿAziz b. ʿAmr b.
    Rabiʿa b. ʿAmr b. al Harith al-Sadusi, Abu
    ʾl-Khattab (d. ca 117/735)   143, 345
al-Qattan *see* al-Hasan b. ʿAli b. Muhammad b.
    Sulayman al-Qattan *or* Muhammad al-Husayn
    al-Qattan
Qays b. Abi Hazim Husayn b. ʿAwf al-Baghali
    al-Kufi, Abu ʿAbdallah (d. 84/703 or later)
    203
Qays b. ʿAsim b. Sinan b. Khalid al-Minqari
    al-Saʿdi al-Tamimi (d.47/667)   253–4
Qays b. Saʿd b. ʿUbada b. Dulaym b. Haritha
    al-Ansari al-Khazrji (d. a 60/679–80)
    259–60
al-Qazwini *see* ʿAli b. Muhammad b. Mihruya *or*
    al-Husayn b. Yusuf al-Qazwini
al-Qazzaz *see* Abu Salm Muhammad b. Yahya *or*
    Ahmad b. Ali b. Jaʿfar al-Qazzaz *or* al-asan
    al-Qazzaz
al-Qirmisini *see* Ahmad b. Muhammad al-Qirmisini
    or Ibrahim b. Shayban *or* Muzaffar al-Qirmisini
al-Qurashi *see* Abu ʿAbdallah al-Qurashi *or* Abu
    Saʿid al-Qurashi
Quraysh   265–6, 382
Qurayza   161

R
al-Rabbani   158
al-Rabiʿ b. Badr b. ʿAmr b. Jarad al-Tamimi al-Saʿdi
    al-Basri, Abu ʾl-ʿAlaʾ (d. 178/794–5)   174
al-Rabiʿ b. Khuthaym b. ʿAʾidh al-Thawri al-Kufi,
    Abu Yazid (d. 61/680 or later)   91, 283, 395
Rabiʿa al-ʿAdawiyya (d. 185/801)   116–17, 133,
    156, 208, 267, 277, 334–5, 402–3
Rajaʾ b. Haya b. Jarwal al-Kindi, Abu ʾl-Miqdam
    (d. 112/730–1)   166
al-Rahba   374
Ramadan   62, 158, 203, 225, 351, 371
Ramla   47
al-Ramli *see* Abu ʿAbdallah al-Ramli *or* Muhammad
    b. ʿUmasr al-Ramli
Raphael *see* Angels
al-Raqashi *see* al-Fadl b. ʿIsa b. Aban *or* Yazid b.
    Aban
al-Raqqam   258

al-Raqqi, Abu Ishaq Ibrahim b. Dawud al-Qassar
    (d. 326/937–8)   59, 367
al-Raqqi, Abu Tahir   391
al-Rashidi, Abu Bakr al-Faqih   399
Rayy   7, 45, 52, 56, 57, 352
Remembrance/recollection (*dhikr*)   123, 232–6,
    272–3, 285, 290, 323, 351–2, 384–5, 407–9,
    416
Renunciation *see* Abstention
Repentance (*tawba*), (*inaba*)   77, 90, 111–17, 153,
    244, 249
[Solitary] Retreat (*khalwa*)   113, 122–4, 215, 294,
    409
al-Ribati *see* Abu ʿAli al-Ribati
Ridwan *see* Angels
Riyah b. ʿAmr al-Qaysi, Abu Muhasir   154
al-Rudhbari *see* Ahmad b. ʿAtaʿ, Abu ʿAbdallah
    al-Rudhbari *or* al Rudhbari, Abu ʿAli
al-Rudhbari, Abu ʿAli Ahmad b. Muhammad (or
    Abu ʿAli Muhammad b. Ahmad) b. al-Qasim
    (d. 322/934)   44, 57, 62, 65, 73–4, 119–20,
    150, 160, 178, 184, 221, 273, 284, 287, 290,
    300, 314–18, 323, 328, 347–50, 357, 381, 385
Rules of trvel *see* Travel
Ruse (*makr*)   270, 358, 362, 409
Rustam al-Shirazi al-Sufi   159
Ruwaym b. Ahmad b. Yazid b. Ruwaym, Abu
    Muhammad (d. 303/915–6)   5, 28, 48,
    67–70, 115, 128, 136, 189, 198, 208–9, 221,
    282, 290–1, 299, 311, 313, 322–3, 348, 354

S
al-Sabbah b. Muhammad b. Abi Hazim al-Baghali
    al-Ahmasi al-Kufi   226
Sadaqa bt. Abi ʿImran   344–5
Sadaqa al-Dimashqi (Abu ʾl-ʿAbbas Sadaqa b.
    Khalid al-Umawi or Abu Muʿawiya b.
    ʿAbdallah al-Samin)   325
Sadness (*huzn*)   108, 155–7
al-Saffar *see* Abu ʾl-Hasan al-Saffar al-Basri *or* Abu
    Saʿid al-Saffar *or* Ismaʿil b. Muhammad b.
    Ismaʿil
Sahl b. ʿAbdallah *see* Sahl al-Tustari
Sahl b. Ibrahim   19
Sahl al-Suʿluki, Abu ʾl-Tayyib (d. 402/1011 or
    404/1014)   399
Sahl al-Tustari, Abu Muhammad b. ʿAbdallah b.
    Yunus b. ʿIsa (d. 283/896)   8, 13, 27, 33–4,
    55, 65, 114–15, 123–6, 131–2, 140, 158–9,
    161, 168, 178, 181–2, 190–1, 193–4, 211,
    221–3, 225, 235–6, 238, 246, 257, 271, 273,
    283, 286, 290, 294–5, 297, 304–5, 309, 319,
    322, 341, 350, 354, 367, 370, 384, 386
Sahl b. ʿUthman b. Faris al-Kindi al-ʿAskari, Abu
    Masʿud (d. 235/849–50)   174
Saʿid b. ʿAbd al-ʿAziz al-Halabi al-Zahid
    (d. 318/930–1)   39

Saʿid b. ʿAbdallah 111
Saʿid b. Abi Hilal al-Laythi al-Misri, Abu ʾl-ʿAlaʾ (d. 135/752–3 or 133/750–1 or 149/766–7) 273
Saʿid b. Ahmad al-Balkhi *see* Abu ʿAli Saʿid b. Ahmad
Saʿid b. Ahmad b. Muhammad b. Jaʿfar al-Naysaburi, Abu ʿUthman (d. 369/979) 20, 124, 135, 180
Saʿid b. ʿAmr 30
Saʿid b. Jubayr b. Hisham al-Asadi al-Walibi, Abu ʿAbdallah (killed 95/714) 162, 356, 395
Saʿid b. al-Musayyib b. Hazn b. Abi Wahb al-Makhzumi al-Qurashi, Abu Muhammad (d. 94/713) 293
Saʿid b. Muslim 257
Saʿid b. Sallam *see* Abu ʿUthman al-Maghribi
Saʿid b. ʿUthman b. ʿAyyash al-Khayyat, Abu ʿUthman (d. 294/906–7) 19–20, 180, 208, 322
Saʿid b. Yahya al-Basri 382–3
Saʿid b. Zayd b. ʿAmr b. Nuqayl b. ʿAbd al-ʿUzza al-ʿAdawi, Abu ʾl-Aʿwar (d. 51/671) al-Saʿigh *see* ʿAbd al-Samad b. Yazid *or* Muhammad b. Nasr b. Mansur
al-Saʿih *see* Abu Bakr al-Saʿih *or* ʿAli al-Saʿih
Sainthood *see* Friendship with God
Salama b. Dinar *see* Abu Hazim Salama b. Dinar
Salama b. Saʿid b. ʿAtiya al-Basri al-Salami *see* ʿAbdallah b. Musa b. al-Husayn al-Salami
Salih b. Bashir al-Murri, Abu Bishr (d. 172/778–9 or 176/792–3) 277
Salim b. ʿAbdallah b. ʿUmar b. al-Khattab al-ʿAdawi, Abu ʿUmar (d. probably 106/725) 365
Salim b. al-Jaʿd al-Gharafani al-Ashjaʿi al-Kufi (d. 97/715–16 or 98/716–17) 217, 364
Salim al-Maghribi 20, 388
Salm al-Barusi *see* al-Barusi, Abu ʾl-Hasan
Salman al-Farisi (d. 35–36/655–7) 339, 366
al-Samadani 158
Samarqand/Samarkand 20, 48, 71, 185
Samarra 60, 177
Sammak b. Harb *see* Simak b. Harb
Samnun b. Hamza or b. ʿAbdallah al-Khawwas al-Muhibb, Abuʾ l-Hasan (d. ca 300/912) 50–1, 68–9, 290, 329, 331–3
Sanaa 262
Sarakhs 21
al-Sari b. Mughallis al-Saqati, Abu ʾl-Hasan (d. 251/865 or later) 23–5, 41–3, 46, 50, 53–4, 57, 60, 114–15, 118, 121, 129, 135–6, 156–7, 170, 190, 195–6, 201, 221, 227, 236, 252, 263–4, 267, 305, 331, 338–40, 352, 362, 370, 378, 382, 384
Sariya b. Zunaym al-Duʿli (d. ca 30/650) 360
al-Sarraj, Abu ʾl-ʿAbbas Muhammad b. Ishaq *see* Muhammad b. Ishaq
al-Sarraj, Abu Nasr ʿAbdallah b. ʿAli b. Muhammad b. Yahya al-Tamimi al-Tusi (d. 378/988) 5, 7, 24–6, 32, 57, 61, 115, 140, 159, 164, 178–80, 255, 290–1, 293–5, 304, 310–11, 323, 346, 348, 351–3, 367–70, 391–2
Satan *see* Iblis
Satisfaction (*rida*) 176, 205–10, 212–13, 273–4, 285, 327, 337, 412–15
see also Contentment
Sawwar 312
Saydaʿ 377
al-Saydalani, Abu Bakr 271
al-Saydalani, Abu Jaʿfar 9, 205
al-Sayrafi *see* Abu ʾl-Hasan ʿAli b. Muhammad al-Sirafi (al-Sayrafi) *or* Abu ʾl-Qasim al-Sirafi (al-Say-rafi)
al-Sayyad *see* Abu ʾl-ʿAbbas al-Sayyad
al-Sayyari, ʿAbd al-Wahid b. ʿAli al-Naysaburi (d. 375/985–6) 10
al-Sayyari, Abu ʾl-ʿAbbas al-Qasim b. al-Qasim b. Mahdi b. Bint Ahmad b. Sayyar al-Marwazi (d. 342/953–4) 7–8, 68
Scrupulousness (*waraʿ*) 129–33, 227
Seclusion (*ʿuzla*) *see* Retreat
Secret thought(s) (*khatir*; pl. *khawatir*) 106, 223, 259, 295, 414
Seeker (*murid*) *see* Aspirant/ Novice
Self-annihilation in God (*fanaʾ*) 3, 85–6, 89–91, 120, 180, 198, 311, 322, 333
Self-exertion (*jihad*)/spiritual struggle (*mujahada*) 19, 106–7, 109, 118, 140, 214, 231, 343, 347
Self-manifestation/Self-revelation of God (*tajalli*) 96, 349
Self-scrutiny/self-examination (*muhasaba*) 203–5, 245
Separation/Detachment [from God] (*farq*; *tafriqa*) 87–9, 98, 105–13, 245, 397
Servanthood (*ʿubudiyya*) 197, 210, 230, 274
al-Shabbuwi *see* Abu ʿAli al-Shabbuwi
al-Shafiʿi, Muhammad b. Idris (d. 204/820) 26, 243, 258, 262, 343–5, 404
Shah b. Shujaʿ al-Kirmani, Abu ʾl-Fawaris (d. 270/883–4) 45, 52, 141, 144, 149, 245–6, 254, 395
al-Shahham (possibly the same as below) 258
al-Shahham, Abu Saʿid 399
Shahr b. Hawshab 148
Shame (*hayaʾ*) 226–9, 279
Shaqiq al-Balkhi, Abu ʿAli b. Ibrahim al-Azdi (d. 194/810) 30, 136, 241, 341
Shaqiq b. Salama *see* Abu Waʿil
Sharik b. ʿAbdallah b. Abi Namir al-Qurashi al-Madani, Abu ʿAbdallah (d. ca 140/757–8) 193
Shayban al-Raʿi, Muhammad b. ʿAbdallah (d. 158/774–5) 378, 404
Shibl al-Marwazi 390

al-Shibli, Abu Bakr Dulaf b. Jahdar (d. 334/946) 5, 10, 12, 60–2, 66, 71–3, 82, 85, 92, 96, 108, 124, 129, 136, 148, 165, 182, 190, 198–200, 208, 219, 230, 233, 246, 265–6, 268, 283–5, 290–1, 295, 297, 305, 310–12, 314, 316, 320, 323, 328–9, 331, 347, 351, 355–7, 389, 394, 398, 402–6

Ship 372, 380, 386

Shiraz 7, 28, 107, 239, 374, 383

Shuʿayb (prophet) 339, 365

Shuʿayb b. Harb al-Madaʾini al-Baghdadi, Abu Salih (d. 197/812–13) 124, 165

Shuʿba b. al-Hajjaj b. al-Ward al-ʿAtaki al-Azdi al-Wasiti al-Basri, Abu ʾl-Bistam (d. 160/776–7) 143, 161, 217, 223, 343–4

al-Shuniziyya (mosque) 62, 174, 183, 377–8, 397

al-Siddiq see Abu Bakr al-Siddiq

Sign (shahid) see Witness

al-Sijzi see Abu ʿAbdallah al-Sijzi

Silence (samt) 138–42, 275

Simak (Sammak) b. Harb b. Aws b. Khalid al-Dhuhli al-Bakri al-Kufi, Abu ʾl-Mughira (d. ca 121/739) 403

Sin 111–12, 115, 117, 121, 132, 156, 171–3, 200, 204, 236, 322, 361, 399, 411

Sinai 26, 49, 163

Sincerity (ikhlas) 194, 219–23, 362

al-Sirawani, Abu ʾl-Hasan ʿAli b. Jaʿfar b. Dawud 292

Sobriety (sahw) 85, 88, 93–4, 321, 348, 354, 362

Solomon 114, 171–2, 177, 323, 335, 360

Soul (nafs) 106–7, 109–10, 118–21, 123, 137, 140, 142–4, 146, 160, 167–73, 184, 186, 194, 199, 205–8, 210, 215, 221–2, 243, 275–6, 285, 295, 323, 347, 393, 401, 408, 414

Spirit (ruh) 11, 110, 210, 234–5, 245, 269, 313–17, 330, 334, 394–5, 411

Spiritual advice (wasiyya) 403–16

Spiritual insight/Perspicacity (firasa) 242, 388

Stability/Fixity (tamkin) 100–2

[Mystical]/[Spiritual] State (hal) 3, 19, 78–9, 83, 87–92, 95, 100–2, 106, 108, 116, 120, 141, 200, 206–8, 217–19, 223, 265, 273–5, 291, 303, 308–11, 316, 324–5, 348–50, 353–4, 356, 358, 362–8, 370, 379, 388, 397–400, 405, 408, 412–13

[Mystical] Station (maqam) 77–8, 81, 111, 194, 206, 218, 310–11, 325, 414

Striving (mujahada) see Self-exertion

Subsistence/survival in God (baqaʾ) 89–91

Sufism (tasawwuf) 17, 288–92

Sufyan b. (al-)Husayn b. al-Hasan al-Wasiti 173

Sufyan b. Muhammad al-Jawhari, Abu ʾl-Fadl 161

Sufyan b. Saʿid b. Masruq al-Thawri, Abu ʿAbdallah (d. 161/777–8) 18, 129–30, 133, 135, 148–9, 164, 174, 193, 236, 278, 280–1, 286, 313, 335, 378, 392, 396, 401

Sufyan al-Thawri see Sufyan b. Saʿid al-Thawri

Sufyan b. ʿUyayna b. Abi ʿImran Maymun al-Hilali al-Kufi, Abu Muhammad (d. 198/814) 118, 156, 193, 201

Suhayl b. Abi Salih Dakwan al-Samman al-Madani, Abu Yazid (d. during a reign of al-Mansur, 136–158/754–775) 326

al-Sulami, Abu ʿAbd al-Rahman Muhammad b. al-Husayn b. Muhammad b. Musa (d. 412/1021) 6–10, 13, 18–29, 31–42, 43–53, 57, 60–70, 72–3, 81, 85–8, 114–20, 123–6, 129, 134–8, 140, 143–5, 150, 157, 159–63, 164–70, 174–8, 179–82, 185–6, 190–1, 193–8, 201, 203–9, 211–13, 216, 218, 220–4, 226–38, 241–2, 245–7, 249–55, 260–2, 264, 266, 271–3, 281–2, 284–6, 289, 292, 298, 306–9, 312, 314, 319–23, 325, 329–31, 335–6, 339–41, 344, 346–9, 354, 356, 369, 379, 382–8, 391, 405

al-Sulami, Ahmad b. Yusuf see Ahmad b. Yusuf b. Khalid

Sulayman b. Abi Sulayman 176

Sulayman b. Dawud see Solomon

Sulayman b. Dawud al-ʿAtaki al-Zahrani al-Basri, Abu ʾl-Rabiʿ (d. 234/848–9) 160, 345

Sulayman b. Dawud b. Jarud see Abu Dawud al-Tayalisi

Sulayman d. ʿIsa b. Najih al-Sijzi (or al-Shajari) 320

Sulayman al-Khawwas 129

Sulayman b. Mihran al-Asadi al-Kahili al-Aʿmash, Abu Muhammad (d. 148/765–6) 218, 335

Sulayman b. Tarkhan al-Taymi al-Basri, Abu ʾl-Muʿtamir (d. 143/760–1) 193

Sulayman al-Taymi see Sulayman b. Tarkhan

al-Suʿluki, Abu Sahl Muhammad b. Sulayman b. Muhammad b. Harun (d. 369/980) 87, 151, 190, 261, 292, 340, 349, 397

Sunna [of the Prophet] 4, 8, 17, 258

Supplicatory prayer (duʿaʾ) 273–80

al-Susi see Abu Yaʿqub al-Susi

Suwayd b. Ibrahim al-Jahdari al-Hannat al-Basri, Abu Hatim (d. 167/783–4) 201

Sweet basil 272

Syria 18, 45, 47, 59, 63–4, 68–9, 73–4, 166–7, 169, 173, 183–5, 237, 258, 275, 301, 313, 374, 398–401

T

al-Tabari see Muhammad b. ʿAbdallah b. ʿAbd al-ʿAziz al-Tabari

al-Taharti see ʿAli b. Musa al-Taharti

Tahir b. Ismaʿil al-Razi 11

al-Takriti see Muhammad b. ʿAli al-Takriti

Talha al-Ghadaʾiri al-Basri 371

al-Talhi see ʿAbdallah b. Yahya al-Talhi

Talq b. Habib al-ʿAnazi al-Basri (d. ca 90/708) 126

al-Tamastani, Abu Bakr al-Farisi (d. ca 340/951–2) 71, 140, 271, 306, 311
al-Tamimi *see* Abu Hatim al-Sij-istani *or* Abu Muʿawiya al-Darir *or* ʿAli b. Abi Muhammad *or* al-Fudayl b. ʿIyad *or* al-Sarraj, Abu Nasr ʿAbdallah b. ʿAli *or* Talha b. ʿUbaydallah
Tammam 167
Tamtam, Abu Jaʿfar Muhammad b. Ghalib b. Harb al-Dabbi al-Basri (d. 283/896) 264, 281
Tarif b. Shihab, Abu Sufyan *see* Abu Sufyan Tarif
Tarsus 284, 301, 382
Tasting (*dhawq*) and Drinking (*shurb*) 95, 242, 334
Tawus b. Kaysan al-Yamani al-Himyari al-Janadi, Abu ʿAbd al-Rahman (d. ca 100–106/718–725 or possibly later) 229
al-Tayalisi *see* Abu Dawud al-Tayalisi *or* Hisham b. ʿAbd al-Malik al-Bahili
Tayfur al-Bastami/al-Bistami 32
Tayfur b. ʿIsa b. Adam b. ʿIsa b. ʿAli al-Bastami/al-Bistami, Abu Yazid al-Saghir (or al-Asghar) 32
Taynat 64
Tehran 315
Thabit b. Aslam al-Bunani al-Basri, Abu Muhammad (d. 127/744–5 or 123/740–1) 232, 312
al-Thaghri *see* Ahmad b. Muhammad al-Thaghri
Thaʿlabiyya 391
al-Thaqafi, Abu ʿAli Muhammad b. ʿAbd al-Wahhab (d. 328/940) 39, 63, 223, 336
Thawban b. Bughdud, Abu ʿAbdallah (d. 54/673–4) 218
al-Thawri, Sufyan *see* Sufyan b. Saʿid al-Thawri
Thoughts/Promptings (*khawatir*) 9, 106–8, 184, 202–4, 221, 223, 295, 322, 393, 401, 408
Tigris (river) 60, 155, 255, 353, 368–70, 380
al-Tinati *see* Abu ʾl-Khayr al-Aqtaʿ
al-Tirmidhi *see* al-Tirmidhi, Abu ʿAbdallah Muhammad *or* al-Warraq, Abu Bakr
al-Tirmidhi, Abu ʿAbdallah Muhammad b. ʿAli al-Hakim (d. ca 300/912) 52–3, 161, 176, 237–8
Torah 156, 338, 339
Transoxiana 61
Travel (*safar*) 117, 182, 297–300, 407–8, 413–15
Trial *see* Affliction
Tripoli (city) 301
True Reality/Truth (*haqiqa*) 81, 85, 87, 97, 101, 104–5, 162–3, 167–8, 193–4, 208, 210, 245–6, 282, 288, 295, 309, 311, 328, 338, 348, 358, 371, 405, 414, 416
Trust in God/Reliance on God (*tawakkul*) 30, 77, 178–86, 206–7, 250, 276
Truth *see* True Reality
Truth of certainty (*haqq al-yaqin*) *see* Certainty
Truthfulness (*sidq*) 203, 206, 219, 221, 222–5, 231, 237, 246, 358, 401–2

Truthfulness *see also* Sincerity (*ikhlas*)
Turkey 284, 301, 381
Turkmenistan 20, 25
Turks 31, 166, 173
al-Turughbadhi, Abu ʿAbdallah Muhammad b. Muhammad b. al-Hasan (d. ca 350/961) 247
Tus (city) 54, 247
Tustar (city) 34, 367
Tyre (city) 73

U

ʿUbayd b. Sharik 210, 326
ʿUbayd b. ʿUmar b. Qatada b. Saʿid b. ʿAmir al-Laythi al-Jundaʿi al-Makki, Abu ʿAsim (d. 68/687–8) 188
ʿUbaydallah b. Abi Bakra al-Thaqafi, Abu Hatim (d. 79/698–9) 259
ʿUbaydallah b. Ahmad b. Yaʿqub al-Muqriʿ 134
ʿUbaydallah b. Luʾluʾ b. Jaʿfar b. Hammuya al-Sulami al-Saji, Abu ʾl-Qasim 34
ʿUbaydallah b. Muhammad b. Ahmad (or b. Muhammad) b. Hamdan al-ʿUkbari al-maʿruf bi-Ibn Batta, Abu ʿAbdallah (d. 387/997) 37
ʿUbaydallah b. ʿUmar b. Hafs b. ʿAsim b. ʿUmar b. al-Khattab al-ʿAdawi al-ʿUmari, Abu ʿUthman (d. 147/764) 226
ʿUbaydallah b. ʿUthman b. Yahya al-Daqqaq better known as Janiqa, Abu ʾl-Qasim (d. 390/1000) 27
ʿUbaydallah b. Zuhr al-Damri 128, 138
Ubulla 353
al-ʿUdhafir 356
al-ʿUkbari *see* Abu ʾl-Faraj al-Ukbari *or* ʿAli b. Ibrahim *or* imshadh b. Saʿid *or* ʿUbaydallah b. Muhammad
ʿUkkasha b. Muhsin b. Hurthan al-Asadi (d. 12/633) 178
ʿUlaym al-Majnun 148
ʿUmar b. ʿAbd al-ʿAziz (r. 99–101/717–720) 132, 140, 162–6, 171–2, 192
ʿUmar b. ʿAbdallah 233
ʿUmar al-Hammal 400
ʿUmar b. al-Khattab (killed in 23/644) 164, 167, 201, 204, 209–10, 218, 253, 281, 295, 344, 360, 366
ʿUmar b. Muhammad b. Ahmad 86
ʿUmar b. Muhammad b. Ahmad al-Shirazi 374
ʿUmar b. Muslim al-Thaqafi 148
ʿUmar b. Rashid al-Madani al-Jari, Abu Hafs 281
ʿUmar b. Saʿid b. ʿAbd al-Rahman al-Qaratisi, Abu Bakr 27
ʿUmar b. Sinan 181
ʿUmar b. Wasil al-Basri al-ʿAnbari, Abu ʾl-Husayn (d. probably 312/924) 8, 34, 309
ʿUmar b. Yahya al-Ardabili 371
ʿUmayy al-Bastami *see* ʿAmmi al-Bastami

Umm ʿAli, Fatima   238
Umm al-Dardaʾ, Hujayma bint.Hayy al-Awsabiya al-Dimashqiya (d. 81/700)   148
Unification (*jamʿ*)   87–9, 105, 311–12, 397–8
Unification of Unification (*jamʿ al-jamʿ*)   88, 245
Unseen/Realm of divine mystery (*ghayb*)   105, 144, 183, 187, 193–5, 205, 207, 242–4, 324, 335, 405
Unveiling (*kashf/mukashafa*)   94, 97–100, 139, 193–5, 203–4, 243, 331, 350
Uprightness (*istiqama*)   217–19
ʿUqayl b. Khalid b. ʿAqil al-Ayli al-Umawi, Abu Khalid (d. 144/761–2, possibly earlier)   346
ʿUqba b. ʿAmir b. ʿAbs b. ʿAmr b. ʿAdi al-Juhani (d. ca 58/678)   138
ʿUqba b. Nafiʿ b. ʿAbd al-Qays al-Umawi al-Qurashi al-Fihri (killed in 63/683)   278
Urmiya   67
ʿUrwa b. al-Zubayr b. al-ʿAwwam al-Asadi, Abu ʿAbdallah (d. 94/712–13)   164, 269
Usama b. Zayd al-Laythi al-Madani, Abu Zayd (d. 153/770)   155
Usayd b. (al-)Hudayr b. Simak b. ʿAtik b. Imruʾal-Qays, Abu Yahya (d. 20/640–1 or 21/641–2)   366
Usayd b. Zayd   197
Usrushana   61
ʿUtba b. Aban b. Samʿa al-Ghulam   127, 209, 353, 378, 398
ʿUthman b. ʿAbdallah b. Suraqa b. al-Muʿtamir al-Qurashi al-ʿAdawi al-Madani, Abu ʿAbdallah (d. 118/736–7)   303
ʿUthman b. Abi ʾl-ʿAtika Sulayman al-Azdi al-Dimashqi al-Qadi, Abu Hafs (d. 155/771–2)   379
ʿUthman b. ʿAffan (caliph, killed in 35/655)   249, 263–4, 295, 397
ʿUthman b. Ahmad b. ʿAbdallah *see* Ibn al-Sammak, Abu ʿAmr ʿUthman
ʿUthman b. Badr, Abu ʿAmr   356
ʿUthman b. Maʿbad b. Nuh al-Muqriʾ (d. 261/874)   281
ʿUthman b. ʿUmar al-Dabbi   344
Uways b. ʿAmir b. Jazʾ b. Malik al-Qarani (d. ca 37/657)   254, 366
Uzbekistan   58, 251

V
Vision (*ruʾya*)   350, 362, 392–3
Vizier (*wazir*)   203, 278, 316

W
Wahb b. Jarir b. Hazim b. Zayd b. ʿAbdallah b. Shujaʿ al-Azdi al-Basri, Abu ʾl-ʿAbbas (d. 207/822)   164, 176, 363
Wahb b. Kaysan al-Qurashi al-Madani al-Makki, Abu Nuʿaym (d. 127/744–5)   367

Wahb b. Munabbih al-Anbari al-Sanʿani al-Dhimari, Abu ʿAbdallah (d. 114/733)   254
al-Wajihi, Ahmad b. ʿAli al-Karaji (or al-Karkhi), Abu Bakr   178, 221, 255, 317, 323, 347, 355, 370
Wakiʿ b. al-Jarrah b. Malih al-Ruʿasi al-Kufi, Abu Sufyan (d. 196/812 or 197/812)   135, 157
al-Walid b. Bukayr *see* Abu Khabab
al-Walid b. ʿUtba al-Ashjaʿi al-Dimashqi, Abu ʾl-ʿAbbas (d. 240/854)   294
al-Warathani *see* ʿAbd al-Wahid b. Bakr
al-Warraq, Abu ʿAli   289
al-Warraq, Abu Bakr Muhammad b. ʿUmar al-Balkhi al-Tirmidhi al-Hakim (d. ca 280/893 or later)   53, 123, 189, 195, 196, 215, 229, 237
al-Warraq, Abu ʾl-Husayn Muhammad b. Saʿid (d. 320/932)   46, 121, 157
Wasil al-Ahdab *see* Wasil b. Hayyan
Wasil b. Hayyan al-Ahdab al-Asadi al-Kufi (d. 120/738 or 129/746–7)   376
al-Wasiti, Abu Bakr Muhammad b. Musa (d. 320/932)   9–10, 14, 58, 68, 78, 115–16, 126, 144–6, 205–8, 212, 215–16, 219, 224, 229, 233, 242, 253, 272, 274, 279, 291, 321, 411
Wathila b. al-Asqaʿ (d. 83/702–3)   175
Weeping (*bukaʾ*)   261–3, 313, 322–3, 325, 339, 352, 401
[Satanʾs/Devilish] Whisperings (*waswas*; pl. *wasawis*)   106, 122, 222, 251, 320, 407
Witness (*shahid*)   108–9, 411
Witness *see also* Sign
Witnessing (*mushahada; muʿayana*)   5–6, 97–8, 107–8, 193–6, 203, 213, 233, 244–5, 251, 321, 333, 407
Woman/women   2, 210, 244, 249, 250, 254–5, 259, 262, 274, 279–80, 313–14, 376, 378, 385, 390–1, 402, 413, 415
Works *see* Deeds/Actions
Worship of God (*ʿibada; ʿubudiyya*)   67, 119, 124, 145, 197, 210, 230, 274, 295

Y
Yahya b. ʿAbdallah b. Bukayr al-Qurashi al-Makhzumi al-Misri, Abu Zakariya (d. 231/845)   346
Yahya b. Abi Kathir al-Taʾi, Abu Nasr (d. 129/746–7)   124, 264
Yahya b. Aktham b. Muhammad b. Qatan al-Tamimi, Abu Muhammad (d. 242/857, probably later)   155
Yahya b. Ayyub al-Ghafiqi al-Misri, Abu ʾl-ʿAbbas (d. 168/784–5)   128, 138, 151
Yahya b. al-ʿAyzar   129
Yahya b. Bukayr *see* Yahya b. ʿAbdallah b. Bukayr
Yahya b. Habib b. ʿArabi al-Harithi al-Basri, Abu Zakariya (d. 248/862)   334

Yahya b. Hammad b. Abi Ziyad al-Shaybani al-Basri, Abu Bakr (d. 215/830–1)   161
Yahya al-Istakhri   314
Yahya al-Jallaʿ   47, 51
Yahya b. Makhlad al-Miqsami al-Baghdadi, Abu Zakariya   171
Yahya b. Maʿna b. ʿAwn b. Ziyad b. Bistam al-Murri al-Ghatafani al-Baghdadi, Abu Zakariya (d. 233/847–8)   257
Yahya b. Muʿadh b. Jaʿfar al-Razi al-Waʿiz, Abu Zakariya (d. 258/872)   11, 37–8, 45, 95, 113, 115, 117, 123, 130, 135–7, 141, 144, 150, 158–9, 165, 174, 179–81, 198, 216, 228–9, 231, 271–2, 276, 282–3, 286, 294, 323–5, 329, 331–3, 336
Yahya b. Muhammad al-Adib, Abu Zakariya   155
Yahya b. Muhammad al-Jayyani   303
Yahya b. al-Rida al-ʿAlawi   353
Yahya b. Saʿid (possibly the same as one of those below)   134, 257, 392
Yahya b. Saʿid b. Farrukh al-Qattan al-Tamimi al-Basri, Abu Saʿid (d. 198/813–14)   143, 275, 392–6
Yahya b. Saʿid b. Qays b. ʿAmr b. Sahl b. Thaʿlaba al-Ansari al-Najjari al-Madani, Abu Saʿid (d. 143/760 or later)   392
Yahya b. Yaʿla b. Razi   188, 356
Yahya b. Yaman al-ʿAjali al-Kufi, Abu Zakariya (d. 188/803–4 or 189/804–5)   145
Yahya b. Ziyad b. ʿUbaydallah al-Harithi, Abu ʾl-Fadl (d. ca 160/776–7)   256
Yaʿla b. ʿUbayd b. Abi Umayya al-Iyadi al-Tanafisi al-Kufi, Abu Yusuf (d. 209/825 or 207/823)   226
Yaʿqub al-ʿAmmi   125
Yaʿqub b. Humayd b. Kasib al-Makani (d. 240–1/854–6)   237
Yaʿqub b. Ishaq b. Ibrahim   152, 232
Yaʿqub b. Ismaʿil al-Sallal (or al-Sallak?)   205
Yaʿqub b. al-Layth al-Saffar (d. 265/879)   277
Yazid b. Aban al-Raqashi al-Basri, Abu ʿAmr (d. 129/746–7)   401
Yazid b. ʿAbd al-Samad al-Dimashqi   365
Yazid b. ʿAbdallah b. Usama b. al-Hadi al-Laythi al-Madani, Abu ʿAbdallah (d. 139/756–7)   209
Yazid b. al-Hadi see Yazid b. ʿAbdallah b. Usama b. al-Hadi
Yazid b. Kaysan al-Yashkuri al-Kufi, Abu Ismaʿil   257
Yazid al-Raqashi see Yazid b. Aban
Yazid b. Sinan see Abu Farwa
Yemen(i)   262, 300, 380, 390
Yunus b. ʿAbd al-Aʿla b. Musa b. Maysara b. Hafs al-Sadafi al-Misri, Abu Musa (d. 264/877)   366
Yunus b. Habib b. ʿAbd al-Qahir al-ʿIjli al-Isbahani, Abu Bishr (d. 267/880–1)   178, 217, 222

Yunus b. ʿUbayd b. Dinar al-ʿAbdi (d. 139/756–7)   130
Yunus b. Yazid b. Abi ʾl-Najjad al-Ayli, Abu Yazid (d. 159/775–6)   366
Yusuf b. Ahmad b. ʿAbdallah al-Sufi al-Baghdadi, Abu Yaʿqub   386
Yusuf b. ʿAli   323
Yusuf b. Asbat b. Wasil al-Shaybani (d. 195/810–11 or 196/811–12 or 199/814–15)   41, 129, 136, 170–1, 225, 284, 286
Yusuf b. ʿAtiya b. Thabit al-Saffar al-Ansari al-Saʿdi (d. 187/803)   197
Yusuf b. al-Husayn al-Razi, Abu Yaʿqub (d. 304/916–7)   7, 20, 40, 52, 66, 69, 71, 120, 160, 215–16, 222, 305, 308, 310, 315–16, 323, 352, 372, 388, 399
Yusuf b. Musa (Muslim)   231
Yusuf b. Saʿid b. Musallam al-Missisi al-Antaki, Abu Yaʿqub (d. 271/884–5)   203
Yusuf b. ʿUmar b. Masrur al-Qawwas al-Baghdadi al-Zahid, Abu ʾl-Fath (d. 385/995)   34, 369
Yusuf b. Yaʿqub b. Ishaq see Joseph

Z

Zachariah (prophet)   363
Zadhan al-Kindi al-Kufi al-Darir al-Bazzaz, Abu ʿAbdallah (d. 82/701–2)   344
al-Zahirabadhi, Abu Bakr   6
Zahra   212
al-Zajjaji, Abu ʿAmr see Abu ʿAmr al-Zajjaji
al-Zajjaji, Abu Sahl   151, 396
Zakariya b. Nafiʿ   222
Zakariya al-Shakhtani   244
Zamzam   130–1, 183, 378
Al-Zanjawayh (Zanjuya) b. Muhammad b. al-Hasan b. ʿUmar al-Labbad, Abu Muhammad (d. 318/930–1)   228
al-Zaqqaq, Abu Bakr Ahmad b. Nasr al-Kabir or Muhammad b. ʿAbdallah al-Saghir (the Junior)   286, 298, 316
al-Zaqqaq al-Kabir (the Elder), Abu Bakr Ahmad b. Nasr al-Misri (d. 290–1/902–4)   49, 67, 133
al-Zarrad, Abu ʿAbdallah Muhammad b. ʿAli al-Basri   399
al-Zawzani see al-ʿAbbas al-Zawzani
Zayd b. Aslam al-ʿAdawi, Abu Usama (d. probably 130/747)   151
Zayd b. Ismaʿil   134
Zayd b. Thabit b. al-Dahhak al-Ansari al-Furdi al-Katib, Abu Kharija (d. 45/665–6 or later)   164–5, 237
Zaytuna   385
al-Zayyat, Abu Sahih Dakwan al-Samman al-Madani (d. 101/719–20)   197
Zirr b. Hubaysh b. Hubasha b. Aw al-Asadi, Abu Maryam (d. 81–83/700–702)   178

Ziyad b. Abi Ziyad Maysara al-Makhzumi al-Madani, client of ʿAbdallah b. ʿAyyash b. Abi Rabiʿa (d. 135/752–3)   232, 288
Zoroastri(an)(ism)   32–3, 78, 190
  see also Magian(s)
Zubala   389
Zubayda bint Jaʿfar b. al-Mansur al-Hashimiya, Umm Jaʿfar (d. 216/831)   133, 401
al-Zubayri   246
al-Zuhri, Muhammad b. Muslim b. ʿUbaydallah b. ʿAbdallah b. Shihab al-Madani (= Ibn Shihab), Abu Bakr (d. 124/742)   138, 232, 365

Zulaykha *see* Joseph
Zurayq   351
Zuzan   282

CENTER FOR MUSLIM CONTRIBUTION TO CIVILIZATION

The Center for Muslim Contribution to Civilization, a non-government, non-profit making cultural organization, strives to lead Muslims and non-Muslims alike to a better understanding of the Muslim contribution to civilization and to a better knowledge of Islam.

Located in Doha, State of Qatar, the Center has the warm support of its patron, the Emir of Qatar, H.H. Sheikh Hamad Bin Khalifa Al-Thani. Presenting accurate translations of some of the best known works of the most eminent Muslim savants, spanning the 800 years of the classical period of Islamic civilization (*c.* 620 AD to *c.* 1500 AD), since its establishment in 1983 the Center has produced nine volumes covering five major works in different fields of knowledge.

For further information on the work of the Center, all correspondence should be directed to

The General Supervisor
Center for Muslim Contribution to Civilization
P.O. Box 13006
Doha
State of Qatar
Arabian Gulf